MASS COMMUNICATION
An Introductory Survey

James D. Harless
Ohio State University

ᴡᴄᴃ Wm. C. Brown Publishers, Dubuque, Iowa

Book Team
Judith A. Clayton *Senior Developmental Editor*
Vickie Blosch *Production Editor*
Anne Magno *Designer*
Mavis M. Oeth *Permissions Editor*
Faye M. Schilling *Photo Research Editor*

wcb group

Wm. C. Brown *Chairman of the Board*
Mark C. Falb *President and Chief Executive Officer*

wcb

Wm. C. Brown Publishers, College Division
Lawrence E. Cremer *President*
James L. Romig *Vice-President, Product Development*
David A. Corona *Vice-President, Production and Design*
E. F. Jogerst *Vice-President, Cost Analyst*
Bob McLaughlin *National Sales Manager*
Marcia H. Stout *Marketing Manager*
Craig S. Marty *Director of Marketing Research*
Eugenia M. Collins *Production Editorial Manager*
Marilyn A. Phelps *Manager of Design*
Mary M. Heller *Photo Research Manager*

Library of Congress Catalog Card Number: 84–71585

ISBN 0–697–00124–5

Printed in the United States of America
10 9 8 7 6 5 4 3 2

Contents

List of Boxes

Preface

As the title of this book indicates, this text is an introductory survey of the field of mass communication. With DeFleur, it takes the theoretical position that mass communication is a social system that includes not only the mass media, but government, financial backers, advertising and public relations, several types of audiences, and the media professions. The text, therefore, considers not only the functions, structure, and performance of the individual mass media (newspapers, recording, movies, television, etc.) but also auxiliaries within the system (press associations, advertising, and public relations, etc.) and relationships between the media and government, the mass audience, and interest groups within the audience. It presents the subject at the introductory level and gives both the would-be professional and the general-interest or consumer student a realistic and comprehensive overview of the media, their problems, and their performance.

Wherever possible, provocative examples and case materials have been used, while complex writing has been avoided. The aim is not to be simple but to be clear, interesting, and instructive. To these ends, every effort has been made to keep a long list of names and concepts—the encyclopedic sentences that cover everyone and everything—from the text. Where advanced technical terminology is used, the technical name is given and defined immediately.

Another primary goal was to make the text as objective as possible to avoid blunting its teaching effectiveness with personal opinion or an ideological stance. In the author's view, the best perspective on the media paraphrases Winston Churchill: Our mass communication system is probably the worst in the world—except for all others. The attempt here is to deal with them fairly and to impartially describe how they operate, survive, and succeed.

Organization

The text is divided into six parts: (1) communication and mass communication theory; (2) historical development; (3) the modern media; (4) media auxiliaries; (5) freedom, the government, and the citizen; and (6) audience concerns and hope for the future. **Part one** takes a building-block approach to communication and mass communication theory, putting each in the proper perspective. It develops intrapersonal and interpersonal communication as founding and foundation processes, introduces communication media and communication in primitive and traditional societies, then concludes with a discussion of the rise of industrial society and the development of the mass communication system. Throughout, the student is reminded that mass communication is human communication. It should not be viewed as merely related to, or separate from, human communication. It is, in fact, a process that at one time or another incorporates all other types of human communication. Media technology, at the same time, is not presented as the cause of mass communication but only as the intermediary that allows such a complex extension of and addition to our means of communication.

Part two traces the historical development of the individual mass media in two chapters. They follow Robert Park's suggestion that the media have a "natural history" and were not shaped by a few "willful men," stressing events and decisions that contributed to the structure, practices, and content of the modern media and advertising, and public relations. The text moves from one medium to the next, as historical trends dictate, so that the development of a given medium can be read by "skipping" from one section to another within a chapter. Furthermore, the history of any medium can be easily related to its respective media chapter. The more recent and significant developments are included in the respective media chapters.

Part three is composed of seven chapters, each of which covers one medium: newspapers, magazines, books, recordings, movies, radio, and television/cable. A discussion of the operations and problems, as well as a table of a typical media organization, is presented for each medium. In general, the media are presented as businesses—cultural businesses, as Dessauer has put it. While they do deal in cultural materials—information, entertainment, etc.—they must profit from the sale of those messages in order to survive and continue to offer their services. (The few noncommercial media, of course, survive by producing a message-product that attracts funds from philanthropic sources in business, the government, and the public.) Each chapter strives for an objective view of the media as business, assuming profit (or fund collecting) as an obvious fact and avoiding both the "profit-comes-from-trash" and the "quality-abhors-profits" fables that are common in popular media criticism. For the would-be media professional who plans to earn a living in media work, each media chapter ends with a section on career information that includes current salary scales.

Part four discusses media auxiliaries—system organizations that do not produce messages directly for the mass audience but operate in support of or through the various media. This section covers press associations, syndicates, satellite auxiliaries, the increasingly important VCR, advertising, and public relations, reflecting the importance of these areas within the media professional sequences. Historical development, current operations, and professional performance are also presented in this section for the ad, PR, and press association auxiliaries. Again, career information is presented where applicable.

For many, the vital part of any introduction to mass communication text is the chapter, or chapters, on freedom of speech and the press. **Part five** devotes three chapters to media freedoms and responsibilities. There is one full chapter on prior restraint and the First Amendment freedoms of speech and press. It includes a discussion of freedom and the student press and contrasts American definitions of freedom with those from other countries, including the Soviet Union. The second chapter in part five reviews the rights in conflict in media vs. government, media vs. courts, and media vs. the citizen relationships. Detailed attention is given to the adversary and symbiotic relationships and the conflict of rights over access and secrecy with government; the conflict over fair trial and the right of access for reporters and cameras; the demands of the courts for confidential news media information; and the demands of the news media for the right to withhold confidential information. A review of libel, privacy, and copyright laws and the citizen's right of access to media publication summarizes media-citizen conflicts. The third chapter reviews problems of regulation and self-regulation in the media system, including the recent broadcast and advertising deregulation movement, and active, ongoing self-regulatory attempts in the codes and regulatory councils of the media professions themselves. The chapter concludes with a discussion of audience interest groups and their efforts to regulate aspects of media content.

Finally, **Part six** reviews long-standing hopes and fears about the media, as well as the behavioral-science methodology that has been adopted to obtain reliable information and evaluation of media processes and effects. A review of the concern about media effects traces the development of the "power of the press" concept from the Spanish-American War and World War I to the recent reports of research scientists and the National Institute of Mental Health in relation to the effects of media on media audiences. The review also points out recurring concerns of media performance: proper socialization and violence in the case of the entertainment media; concerns about inaccuracy, callousness, bias; and charges that the news media fabricate stories.

The section concludes with a preview of the rapidly developing "information network" system, which is predicted to make every home an "electronic cottage"—complete with a cable TV home entertainment center and a home computer connected to special information banks, libraries, grocery stores, and financial institutions.

Special Features

Mass Communication: An Introductory Survey includes a variety of pedagogical devices intended to involve the students in the learning process and to stimulate interest in the subject matter. The six major parts open with a combination of photos and narrative. These pictorial essays are designed to stimulate reader interest in the coming chapters and to encourage thoughtful consideration of their content.

Each chapter begins with an outline of its contents and closes with a summary, questions for discussion, and references. Boxed information includes cases, examples, and comments that relate to chapter material but may be considered independently.

The text's visual program includes photographs, art, and graphics that heighten reader interest, illustrate the narrative, and contribute to a complete learning experience.

Back matter includes a bibliography and an index.

Instructor's Manual

An instructor's manual, written by the author, is available to adopters of *Mass Communication: An Introductory Survey.* It is designed to help instructors plan classwork and includes a variety of resource materials and an extensive file of classroom-validated test items.

wcb TestPak®, a computerized program, is also available to adopters. More information on **wcb** TestPak® may be obtained by contacting the publisher.

Acknowledgments

Mass Communication: An Introductory Survey, of course, was written not in the future, but in the past. The author could not rely on instantaneous information networks for data for the text, but he was able to call on those in his own personal communication networks for help. Many contributed to this effort. In Columbus and at Ohio State, colleagues and friends Lee Becker, Eleanor Block, Warwick Blood, Bill Hall, Thom McCain, Jim McDonald, Paul Peterson, Henry Shulte, Tom Schwartz, Walt Seifert, Bill Toran, and Paul Underwood gave guidance, advice, and information or contributed bibliographic material. Several graduate students provided assistance, also. John Bryczkowski researched fiber optics;

Russell Carey contributed information about radio in his native England; Steve Curcio analyzed FCC technicalities; Rick Hatem provided examples from Church public relations; Jim Heimerich collected the records of FCC deregulation; David Patton investigated courtrooms and cameras, and professional PR in the court of public opinion. I owe much to friends Dave and Peg Carrigan for reading the material and for their timely demonstrations of the joys of the VCR. The contributions of all these people have become part of this book, but any errors should reflect on the author.

The insights and recommendations of colleagues who reviewed the text are deeply appreciated. The reviewers were Carol Burnett, California State University, Sacramento; Raymond L. Carroll, The University of Alabama; Donna Roman Downes, California State University, Fullerton; Michael Emery, California State University, Northridge; Dimitri M. Gemelos, Brooklyn College of The City University of New York; Felix F. Gutierrez, University of Southern California; Val E. Limburg, Washington State University; Mark Popovich, Ball State University; Barbara Straus Reed, Rutgers, The State University of New Jersey; George Rodman, Brooklyn College of The City University of New York; Harold A. Servis, New Mexico State University.

James D. Harless
E. Tulane Road
Columbus, Ohio

MASS COMMUNICATION

Part One

Understanding Mass Communication

They have been called the best of things.

They have been called the worst of things.

In one form or another they have been called the best teachers in the world, the great preservers of art, the instruments that can place the world at the feet of every American plowboy. But they also have been decried as utterly devoid of social and cultural value, for leading the young into crime and vice—for making mental oysters of us all.

They are the media of mass communication: newspapers, books, magazines, records, the movies, radio, and television. And whether we love them or hate them, trust or fear them, they are a part of our lives every hour of the day, every day of the week. More than 70 percent of the American adult population reads a newspaper every weekday, 68 percent listen to a radio station, and 83 percent watch some television. Ninety-eight percent or more of all American homes have one television set. And studies during the past few years indicate the average set is in use six to seven hours every day.

This is not to say we do not read. The U.S. Department of Commerce reports Americans spend about $3 billion for books each year. Annual book sales have topped $6 billion in recent years, and the number of books sold annually is about 1.7 billion. The American book publishing industry produces thirty to forty thousand titles each year.

Our appetite for magazines is even more voracious. The American magazine industry publishes eleven thousand periodicals that range in subject matter from the general interest *Reader's Digest* to the trade-oriented *Scrap Age*. Some magazine circulation figures are so large they seem more

like populations of cities than numbers of readers. The three million people who buy *Cosmopolitan* are enough to populate both Dallas and Fort Worth. *Playboy* has had as many as five million readers per issue, or an audience that is almost as large as the 7.3 million population of the city of Chicago, the place of its birth. During the past few years the magazine with the largest circulation was *TV Guide*. At one point its circulation reached twenty million—or the equivalent of the populations of New York City and Shanghai combined.

Motion picture industry surveys indicate about thirty million Americans see a movie every week. With sixteen thousand theatres—including 3,800 drive-ins—showing films every day, box office receipts on a feature film can reach tens of millions of dollars within a matter of days. In 1978 *Grease* collected $10 million in its first three days of showing. Thus far, the all-time short-term money winner is *Star Trek II: The Wrath of Kahn,* which earned $24 million in the first three days of its showing in 1982. At last report, *Star Wars* had collected some $300 million in theatre,

video tape, disc, and second-run revenues. The third film in the *Star Wars* series, *Return of the Jedi,* collected more than $68 million in its first six months in 1983. One of the greatest box office successes to date has been *E.T., The Extra-Terrestrial. E.T.* earned $100 million in its first month of exhibition and went on to pass *Jaws* ($134 million) and *Star Wars* in total receipts. Observers predict the story of the small alien trying to return home will gross $400 million before its exhibition value is exhausted.

The time and money we spend on the mass media are good indications of the importance we assign them. But considering their importance, it is at least disturbing to see how uninformed, even misinformed, many Americans are about the media and their operations. In a recent survey in the Midwest, media researchers Lee Becker, Charles Whitney, and Erik Collins found, in part, that:

1. Twenty-seven percent in the survey sample did not know if the television networks owned the local stations that show network programs. (Some are owned by the networks and some are not. An individual or corporation is allowed to own only a few television stations and not enough to form a large television network.)

2. Fifty percent of those interviewed could not say if an American citizen is required to obtain a government license in order to operate a newspaper. (Absolutely not. Under the First Amendment, the government can not regulate newspapers to that extent. Historically, the government license has been a method of controlling the press, and still is in some countries.)

3. Eighty-five percent could not give a clear explanation of how news reporters obtain the information they report in newspapers and on newscasts. (More often than not, the news is gathered by beat or story assignment. What is reported depends a great deal on where reporters look for news, when they look for it, and what their editors think of their ideas and work.)

In one sense, our ignorance of our mass communication system is understandable. The media tell us about many things, but more often than not they do not find time or space to tell us about themselves. At the same time, the study of the mass media is a relatively new discipline. Most of the serious research and writing on the subject has been done since World War II. Most of the scientists who have done the work, as mass media theoretician Wilbur Schramm has pointed out, are still alive and writing today. The situation is such that we probably know more about the Civil War, the Roman Empire, and the solar system than we know about mass communication.

At this writing, most of the progress we have made in understanding communication and mass communication have come from applying the theories and methods of the behavioral sciences to communication studies. That is, instead of beginning with the assumption the media function through some preordained ideal, that they are threats to life, or that they are a boon and

salvation for human life, mass communication scientists have made progress by studying the media with scientific objectivity—and as *human behavior.*

It is not an easy task. Even in our daily lives—in our most casual conversations—we tend to ignore the fact that mass communication, with its ink and machinery, its words, pictures, noise, and technology, is actually *human* communication. The press and television are not the moving forces of mass communication. Human beings are. Humans created it, humans run it, and without human beings there would be no point in having it—not on this planet anyway. And since mass communication is based on human behavior and human communication, it is with human beings and human communication processes that our understanding of mass communication must begin.

References

Becker, Lee B., D. Charles Whitney, and Erik L. Collins. "Public Understanding of How the News Media Operate." *Journalism Quarterly* 57, no. 4 (1980): 571–78.

Davis, Robert Edward. "Response to Innovation: A Study of Popular Argument About Mass Media." Ph.D. diss. University of Iowa, 1965.

Facts About Newspapers, A Statistical Summary of the Newspaper Business. Washington, D.C.: The American Newspapers Publishers Association, 1982.

Schramm, Wilbur, and William E. Porter. *Men, Women, Messages, and Media.* New York: Harper & Row, 1982.

Chapter
1

Understanding Human Communication

Intrapersonal Communication

Interpersonal Communication

The Process

Important Interpersonal Communications Concepts

Channel Noise and Semantic Noise

Feedback

Extending Communication: Public Communication

Role Taking

Human Communications Networks

Media

The Five Communication Situations

The definitive nature, the defining mark of the human race: communication.

Since the first half of the twentieth century, social scientists and philosophers have come to realize that communication, like tool making, is one of humankind's most important abilities. In 1921, for example, Alfred Korzybski, the founder of the general semantics movement, wrote that the "peculiar power, the characteristic energy, the definitive nature, the defining mark of man is the capacity to accumulate experience, enlarge on it, and transmit it for future expansion." That is to say, the peculiar power, the definitive nature, the defining mark of the human race is the ability to communicate.

Those who have studied human communication since Korzybski's time have come to recognize that communication is not only a vital process but a complicated one as well. Early attempts to chart the field with linguistic definitions proved troublesome at best since even skillfull writers found the process difficult to capture in words. In time, some of the best written definitions even proved to be misleading. We still suffer, for example, from one popular suggestion that communication is an "exchange of ideas," although, as we shall see, it is not.

As a result of these shortcomings, and following the lead of science in general, communication science turned from writing comprehensive definitions to constructing graphic and mathematical models instead, in hopes of gaining a more accurate picture of the communication process. Rather than ask "what" human communication "is," scientists learned to subdivide the field into areas of study and make careful observations of specific parts. Most of what we know about human communication today has been acquired this way.

As communication theorist Wilbur Schramm has observed, all human communication includes the processes of sending and receiving messages. At the heart of the sending and receiving is the human being and intrapersonal communication, the study of communication that takes place *within* the individual. Since most of the sending and receiving process takes place within us, intrapersonal communication is vital to all kinds of human communication. It is, for example, the foundation for interpersonal communication, the study of communication between two or more people. At the same time, both within-person and between-person communication processes are basic to, and reflected in, more complicated group, public, and mediated communication. We could have intrapersonal and interpersonal communication without mass communication, as many tribes and societies do today, but we could not have mass communication without personal communication.

To understand mass communication, then, we will first consider intrapersonal (within) and interpersonal (between person) communication. In this chapter we will review these two generic processes, then go on to discuss how we extend them—with role playing, human communications networks, public communication and communications media—into wider reaching mass communication. Mass communication, with its complicated sending organizations, its technological media, and its masses of human receivers, is the most complicated type of human communication. It consists of all other types of communication. We will discuss mass communication, the social factors required for its development, and sketch out its place in modern society in the following chapter.

Intrapersonal Communication

Intrapersonal communication, or within-person communication, includes thinking, dreaming, listening, the process of message creation, and the "inner dialogue," the talking to ourselves we do every day. At the heart of intrapersonal communication are three processes by which we accumulate and enlarge upon knowledge: duplication, or perception of the environment, memory, and consciousness.

Duplication, as psychologist Sylvan Tomkins observed, is essential to human mobility. We could hardly cross an open field without some ability to sense its slope, its holes and rocks, or what might be charging over it and at us. To survive we must be able to survey the opportunities and dangers of the environment. To do that we "duplicate" it, by seeing, hearing, feeling, smelling and even tasting it. Our duplicating senses are so much a part of us we usually overlook them. Our view of an object—a tree, for example—consists of at least two objects: the actual object "out there" and the duplicate we "see" in our minds. We all know how trees and other objects change in appearance or detail as we approach or view them from a different angle. The details are there all along, of course; it is our duplication of them that changes.

Memory allows us to store duplications and recall them later. Without it, we would not and could not recall anything. We would live in a world of constant surprise with every glimpse of the world about us—including the sight of our own toes or fingers—a startling new experience. Without memory we could not remember language and symbols, our own names, or that we had a name.

Consciousness gives us the ability to be aware of ourselves and what we are doing, and to reflect on what we have duplicated and stored in memory. The most important object of consciousness is the self, the complex of stored values and attitudes we build up and think of as ourselves. As sociologist Herbert Blumer has maintained, anything we are conscious of—the ticking of a clock, a knock at the door, a remark, or any piece of thought we consider—is something we are indicating to the self. Much of what we call intrapersonal communication is contained in this flow of self-indications—this on-going, active interpretation of things, events, and people about us.

Our duplicating, remembering, storing, and interpretation processes hardly are objective. We tend to recognize the limitations our particular angle of duplication imposes on our perception of a situation. Less recognized is our pronounced tendency to look for, pay attention to, and recall those pictures, ideas, and data that are sympathetic to our personal goals. (Who notices ads for automobiles, the person who wants to buy a car or the person who does not?) Through selective exposure we tend to avoid material in conflict with what we believe. Through selective perception we tend to collect facts and opinions that support our predispositions. Through selective retention we tend to remember what we agree with, while forgetting what we disagree with. Selective exposure, attention, and retention are not inevitable problems, but they are persistent ones. They challenge us to make conscious efforts to control them.

The on-going inner dialogue of intrapersonal communication is essential to all human communication. When two humans meet, for example, even in a brief encounter, each automatically makes some interpretation of the other. No word need be spoken. As the two ap-

The passing encounter includes sending and receiving in dress, demeanor, and movement, and the rudiments of between-person communication.

proach each other they send and receive signals, even though the messages sent may be only the ones each prepared when he or she dressed that morning. The interpretations made—the messages received—depend on the intrapersonal self-indication interests of the two involved. Any of the following interpretations might result:

"A salesman?"
"Nice beard!"
"Cock-a-doodle-do. The Martians have landed."
"There's a person who's going somewhere."

Sending signals by their very presence, and receiving them by nature, the two passing strangers step from intrapersonal into interpersonal communication.

Interpersonal Communication

The Process

The passing encounter is at the threshold of interpersonal communication. At the same time the long-term relationships among friends and lovers—those with recurring and extended face-to-face encounters—might be considered the most developed type of interpersonal communication. Somewhere in between we can place the brief conversations we have with sales clerks, traffic cops, and customer service representatives, and the longer discussions we have with attorneys, ministers, casual friends, old school chums, college teachers, and counselors. On a given day, any of these face-to-face encounters might be agreeable or disagreeable, cheering or depressing, nice or downright nasty. As communications theorists Mark Steinberg and Gerald R. Miller have suggested, interpersonal communication gives us the opportunity to share with others the knowledge, sights, and experiences we have acquired in our private, intrapersonal experience. But it is important to remember that face-to-face communication also can include verbal attacks, attempts at manipulation, and heated conflict—as any separating couple readily can testify.

For any interpersonal relationship to extend itself through time the communicators involved must adopt two kinds of interrelated rules for their sending and receiving: rules about structure (how and when communication shall take place) and rules about content (what messages and subjects are acceptable to both parties). Some of the rules are provided by society, but many must be created as the relationship develops. Society or the situation usually determine whether or not communication is symmetrical or asymmetrical. In symmetrical communication we signal back and forth equally, sending and receiving for about the same amount of time. In the asymmetrical relationship one person dominates the sending while the other, or others, receive. In an office, for example, two salespeople can talk with each other in a symmetrical conversation, with each speaking and listening about the same amount of time. But neither would expect "equal time" in a face-to-face briefing session with the company president, who would be expected to do most of the talking. (Of no little concern are the people who strive to control the conversation in every interaction—attempting to establish an asymmetrical relationship even when they do not have the status or the expertise, and even when the partner does not want to be on the receiving end of so much communication activity.)

Rule-making between two communicating partners begins with the testing of message topics. Each communicating partner offers message topics to see how the other reacts. The raucous joke that draws a frown is ruled not acceptable while the one that draws a laugh is ruled acceptable—under the conditions at hand. In time both parties will have sensed how much they may talk about women's liberation or baseball as

Figure 1.1 We often forget that we duplicate the world about us, making high quality copies of it for our safety and for exploitation. The world we see, hear, and smell is actually our own world, but it does reflect the real world in the way a map reflects a territory.

well as who may talk where and when and how much—including who may assert dominance over whom and where. In long-standing relationships, typical rules for men include indulging in ribald humor at cocktail parties, large social gatherings and in private but not during romantic moments.

Women may assert dominance in some groups but not in others. And with some men or partners she may never dominate.

The rules of what may be said, and when, are integral parts of all public communication, as any public speaker knows. The continuing public debate over whether violence, obscenity, "race horse" news coverage of political campaigns, and sexist language should be allowed in the mass media indicates we still are making rules and testing topics for mass communication.

However brief or long-lived interpersonal communication is, and whatever the rules regarding its structure and content, we need to ask how between-person communication (and, therefore, much of human communication) works. Semanticist Wendell Johnson has suggested the following steps make up the process (see figures 1.1 and 1.2):

1. Person A encounters an event—say a sudden shower of rain, an automobile whose horn is stuck, or a large feathery tree. She . . .
2. duplicates the event through her senses of sight, smell, sound, etc. . . . .

Figure 1.2 The process of two people speaking to each other is the process of encoding and decoding signals and symbols that we associate with our own personal fields of experience and learning. External noise or internal problems of decoding can complicate the process. "Tree," for example, can mean many things—a large wooded plant, a refuge or trap for a hunted animal, or, through error, a number. We cannot send meaningless art symbols, or inject meaning into listeners with them. To reach understanding, we often must rely on feedback, our skill, and our knowledge of the other's experience and background.

3. through nervous impulses that travel to her brain, memory, muscles, glands, producing tensions and preverbal feelings . . .
4. which A begins to encode into words, according to her accustomed verbal patterns . . .
5. selecting certain ones and then . . .
6. by means of sound and light waves speaks to person B . . .
7. whose ears and eyes duplicate or pick up the sounds and the motions A makes as she speaks . . .
8. so that B can decode the sounds of the words, producing his own tensions and feelings . . .
9. which B then encodes into words according to his accustomed verbal patterns . . .
10. and then speaks to B or acts accordingly. . . .

And so the process goes—duplicating and encoding, duplicating and decoding, and on and on—all with complications.

Important Interpersonal Communications Concepts

To help describe the communications process, theoreticians have adopted several phrases from the mathematical theory of communication. These include encoding, decoding, noise, and feedback.

Encoding is the selection of words or symbols to express feelings and ideas. Decoding is the selection of ideas and feelings to match words and symbols. Senders encode. Receivers decode. Communication theorists also have borrowed the word *channel* to indicate the path chosen for the transmission of signals. We speak, for example, in the verbal channel while we give visual signals (facial expressions, attire, perfume, hand movements) in nonverbal channels. We use both verbal and nonverbal channels to communicate in face-to-face communication, sometimes emphasizing the verbal, other times the nonverbal, often blending the two. A raised eyebrow can make a point with or without a word being spoken. And more than one college graduate has found a businesslike appearance—including a businesslike hair length—as valuable in getting a first job as a college diploma or a "Phi Beta Kappa" vocabulary.

Channel Noise and Semantic Noise

Not all messages move from sender to receiver as intended. Noise competes with the message for channel space. Channel noise is anything that interferes with the signal as it passes along the communications channel between the two communicators. It comes, literally, from everywhere. A roaring wind or a passing car horn can smash any signal in the verbal channel. And anyone who has attempted to converse face-to-face with someone while facing the sun knows how painfully disruptive visual noise can be. (Mass communication noise includes static on the set, and mud on a newspaper.) The signal that survives channel noise still may be defeated by *semantic noise*. Semantic noise occurs within the communicator as, or after, the message is received. The sender may be distracted and "misspeak," suggesting *snake* for supper rather than *steak*. Or the receiver may be distracted so that he or she misconstrues what is said. For example:

"I'm going to mow the lawn while you're so busy there."
"I can't, I've got to finish this work."

We also encounter semantic noise in regional variations in vocabulary. More than one traveler has encountered the *soda* and *charged water* problem. In some parts of the country soda means an ice cream fizz; in others, a soft drink, a Coke or Pepsi, or club soda (from the bar). A request for charged water brings club soda in parts of the North and Midwest, but puzzled looks in the South. By the same token, people in one part of the United States call the bathroom "Mrs. Murphy's." Others know it as "the john." Any sailor will assure you it is "the head."

Feedback

Feedback consists of the signals the receiver sends back to the sender—intended or not—in response to the message. It offers the sender one of the best available means for checking to see if his or her message is being received as intended. The term originated in the railroad practice of connecting control booth lights to rail switches in the yard. If a lever in the booth was thrown and the switch in the yard closed, the feedback light would come on and all was fine. But if the yard switch did not close, the feedback light would not come on, and the yard crew took steps to correct the situation to avoid an accident. When we speak to others we look for a smile or a nod of approval to confirm that our messages are understood. If the receiver smiles we continue. If he or she frowns, or yawns, we consider corrections. Like the train yard crew we use feedback to avoid communication accidents.

Feedback is more than a communication luxury. We would not communicate as well without it. If we review step 6 of person A talking to person B (p. 13) we realize that sound and light waves are the *only* things sent from A to B, and from B to A. Until the message-waves are duplicated and interpreted by someone, they remain only waves. It is the human sender and the human receiver who provide the meaning for the message. The sender frames the message with its meaning in mind. But that meaning stays behind as the message is transmitted. The human communication message of light and sound waves does not carry meaning. As the receiver duplicates and decodes it, he or she gives it meaning again—not the sender's meaning, the receiver's.

The ever-present problem and challenge of human communication is that we can not exchange meaning or ideas with each other. We can never "get" each other's meaning, we can only guess at it. And circumstance does not always allow us to speak the same language and share social and cultural backgrounds with the people we need to understand. There are several ways we can improve our chances of understanding each other. One is by improving our communication skills. By sharpening our powers of duplication—of observation—we can combat channel noise. By improving our encoding and decoding—our language skills—we combat semantic noise. To combat our inability to transmit meaning, we can strive to be more empathetic, and with our imagination put ourselves in the place of others to try and understand how they encode and interpret words and symbols. As Schramm has suggested, in human communication we need to listen with our "third ear."

Extending Communication: Public Communication

We readily extend personal, face-to-face communication into group and public communication by adding to the number of people involved. In asymmetrical public communication one sender projects a message—face-to-face—to a group of receivers, perhaps to a very large audience. Symmetrical public communication includes face-to-face group discussion as in the town hall meeting. As a civilized people we have dedicated much of our social and political energy to public discussion and public address, and to building conversation pits, classrooms, auditoriums, and cathedrals as centers for these types of public communication.

Moving from personal to public communication presents both old and new *disadvantages.* Channel noise—aural and visual—is much more of a problem. ("Quiet! Down in front!"). Public communication is still face-to-face communication, but it is face-to-face at long distance. As the audience grows larger and spreads out, the opportunities for feedback are greatly reduced. The public speaker must speak out, and read the mood of the audience—its restlessness, the volume of its laughter or applause—as feedback of his or her message's success. Also, the increase in the number of receivers means more differences in receiver backgrounds and fields of experience, and greater possibilities for semantic noise and misunderstanding.

Public communication also offers important advantages. It allows the speaker to present a message to many receivers at one time, removing the necessity of using the time-consuming, noise-filled communication chain in which A tells B who tells C who tells D and so forth until the message finally arrives at Z, more than a bit distorted. Public communication also offers its participants the excitement of being a member of the audience and of associating with others.

Much of our history testifies to the effectiveness of the public communication situation. The Christian disciples spread their beliefs around the world, in large part, by public address, speaking to large audiences. Some of the watchwords of our nation were first delivered in public speeches—Patrick Henry's "Give me liberty, or give me death," is only one of many good examples.

Role Taking

Consciousness, our ability to be aware of the group, of ourselves, and our relationships to the group makes role taking possible. A sudden sound and the animal herd reacts as one. It stampedes. Any human group, on the other hand, is capable of giving several responses—at once—to a sudden sound or event. The various members of a baseball team, for example, will not react as one person to the crack of the bat. Each player will assume a role in support of the team effort, with the player closest to the ball moving for it: the first baseman moving toward the first base bag, the catcher running to back him up, and the pitcher probably staying out of the way. Humans assume roles to support a communications effort as well. We could not have one of the basic requirements of mass communication, the media organization, without role taking.

Our primitive ancestors used role playing to great success in the hunt, signaling back and forth in a team effort to effectively corner and kill game. The Reindeer people who lived in northern Europe twenty thousand to forty thousand years ago probably knew the role of chief.

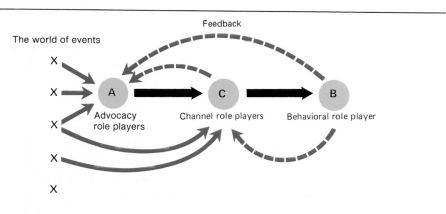

Figure 1.3 In the Westley and Maclean conceptual model of communication, A's are advocates, while C's are channel role players. Both convey information to human behavioral role players (B's). A and C compete with events (x's) for B's attention, and pay close attention to the feedback (f) they get to insure they give the information B wants. If they fail, B will turn to other A's or C's for messages. Note that A's and C's also take feedback (f) from each other for use in their service to B's. The model includes basic relationships involved in mass communication.

The wise man, the messenger, and the scout are other roles known to primitive societies. The shaman or wise man gave cohesion and direction to the tribe by convincing everyone that his visionary field of experience was significant for the group. The scout, searching for and finding the distant herd, could return with the news or send it back through another role player, a messenger, so all could have food more quickly.

We know these tribal roles in more generalized forms today. The sentry, the messenger, and the scout are special cases of channel roles, as communications theorists Bruce Westley and Malcolm S. MacLean, Jr., have called them. Channel roles include all those role takers who report information. News reporters, bank examiners, intelligence agents, and meteorologists are modern examples. Their function is to gather information and channel it to receivers and audiences.

The leader, the wise man, and the witch doctor, are special cases of the advocacy role assumed by any communicator whose intent is to persuade receivers and audiences. Advocates wish to change the behavior of receivers. Our nation has known many powerful advocates: Franklin Roosevelt, the Reverend Martin Luther King, Jr., and Germaine Greer.

Westley and MacLean have constructed an A, B, C of communication roles, using A for advocacy roles, C for channel or reporting roles, and B for behavioral or receiver roles. (See figure 1.3.) Individuals, groups, and corporations all play communication roles, and each may assume any of the three roles at a point in time. For example, one group may collect and report (C role) data on the effects of pesticides while another listens to the data (B role) then uses it to argue against (A role) further use of pesticides. Those in B roles look to As and Cs, respectively, for advice and information. They adopt the role of receiver in their own self-interest, in order to improve their knowledge of a situation, some part of their lives, or their living conditions. If the advice and information prove inaccurate or unworkable, B quite likely will abandon these current As and Cs and seek other experts.

Human Communications Networks

Clearly, role taking represents a great victory over time and space for humans. By turning to advocates and channel role players, we time- and land-locked humans extend our ability to acquire more information than we could have otherwise. At the same time, by assuming channel and advocacy roles, we add to the information of our friends and those about us. Sociologists have shown we all maintain personal communications networks: networks of people around the areas where we live and work and social networks of friends and relatives. We rely on these networks for information and advice, and we pass on to them the information and advice we feel qualified to give. The neighbor who calls you at work to say your house is on fire is a channel role player from your spatial network. The friend who calls and advises you on ways of making insurance claims from the fire is playing an advocacy role in your social network.

Media

As our primitive ancestors discovered centuries ago, success in oral, face-to-face communication is highly dependent on human memory. While memory is capable of remarkable feats of recall, it also fades. And it can play tricks. Often, too, there is much to be stored that simply can not be memorized—long lists of numbers and important records, for example.

The earliest communications media were mnemonic devices—memory aids—used to count kills of the hunt and keep records of the harvest. The Reindeer tribesmen of Europe kept tallies of their hunting kills by making scratches on bones. Other bone records from the period include calendars of the cycle of the moon. Every known society has used some kind of media to keep records. These memory aids have ranged from the sophisticated quipis of the Incas—a set of cords with a code of knots to record complicated tax and historical information—to the wampum beads of the North American Indians, and the clay cuneiform writing tablets of the Sumarians. Our own media—especially those we call the print media—are descendants of the handwritten books and scrolls of the Romans and the Egyptians.

We use the word *media* because the media function as intermediaries. They act as go-betweens and carry messages from senders to receivers separated in time and/or space. For these reasons, the most useful media have been those that are permanent enough to withstand the passage of time and portable enough to make passage through space.

Our society has advanced in great part because of the efficacy of our print media—phonetic writing, paper, and printing. Our newer media—photography, sound recording, radio, and television—really are duplicating media. They enable us to copy images and sounds directly from the world and send the images and sounds across time and space. Today it is not unusual for members of families to record and send audio and video tape messages to each other. (Even without recordings, radio and television literally leap across space and allow us to share aural and visual information with others.) All together, our media give us the ability to store great amounts of information and distribute it around the world.

The Five Communication Situations

As communication theorist Paul Deutschmann observed, our everyday communication processes and skills are reflected in five communication situations. (See figure 1.4.) As already noted, the first is the face-to-face, personal communication situation that includes usually only two people and ranges from the brief encounter of passing strangers to the communication in relationships that last for years.

The second is the face-to-face public situation that involves larger numbers of people and includes group discussion, church services, the theatrical presentation, and meetings such as the school graduation.

The addition of media to these two face-to-face situations gives us three more valuable communication situations. The use of writing, the telephone, and the telegram creates private, mediated communication. The invention of instruments to mediate public communication—sound recording, motion pictures, and broadcasting—gives us two public mediated situations. In one, the media audience is assembled—at a movie or television theatre, for example. In the other, the audience is not assembled—the audiences that read magazines or watch television, for example.

The personal and public media communication situations offer both advantages and disadvantages, so many in fact we can not review all of them here. But the letter writer soon learns how limited are the opportunities for feedback as he or she writes. The telephone allows instant personal conversation at long distance, but the sender's problems include a complete loss of nonverbal (visual) feedback. The telegram is quick but little more than a brief message. Media may carry messages farther or longer, and even record data that are not available to human perception (with slow or stop motion photography, for example), but they usually are more limited in their ability to carry verbal and nonverbal information than face-to-face communication. Even motion pictures and television cannot do an accurate job of portraying people the way they actually look in person.

Figure 1.4 The five communication situations: (Top left) Personal, face-to-face communication with its advantages of using oral, visual, and other sense channels to send and receive messages. (Top right) Public, face-to-face communication offers less opportunity for feedback and two-way communication but gives many receivers the message at one time. (Bottom left) Personal mediated communication—by telephone, letter, telegraph, etc.—reduces the number of channels available but enables the sending and receiving of private messages through time and space. (Bottom center and right) Public mediated communication has two conditions: it allows a mediated message to be sent to an assembled group or to large numbers of individuals not assembled in the same place. Teleconferences and movies are in the former type, television and newspapers are in the latter.

Mediated public communication also suffers great limitations in feedback. And the sender's knowledge of the backgrounds of the large, distant audience is more difficult still. But mediated public communication can send information farther and faster, to more people, than any other type of communication. And since the media messages aimed at the public audience are accurate copies of the original, the public media can deliver more information to more people more accurately than any other form of communication.

We begin to understand the complexity of mass communication when we realize that all the intrapersonal communications processes, all three communications roles—advocate, behavioral, and channel—the communications networks, and all five communication situations are vital to the mass communications process. At one time or another, all come into play to support the process of mass communication. Media managers and writers, for example, discuss their work face-to-face, by phone, and by letter. The mass media corporations present conferences and teleconferences for groups of their distributors and sales personnel. The local media organization that does not have a face-to-face Christmas party or a Fourth of July group shindig probably is not much of a local media organization. Private and public communication are used by the media organization to attack company problems, just as they are used by politicians and social critics to attack the mass media. The audiences of the mass media engage in face-to-face and mediated communication as well. With their friends from their communication networks they react to media content by letter and telephone—protesting or praising as they see fit.

With all this there is still one more important component to consider in the makeup of mass communication. Mass communication requires a system of beliefs and values, a society with an economy that can support it.

Summary

Communication is the peculiar power, the definitive mark of the human race. At its foundations are the processes of intrapersonal, within-person, communication, and interpersonal, or between-person, communication. Group, public, mediated, and mass communication are founded in the same process, and would not be possible without them. Mass communication is the most complicated type of human communication, as it requires all other types to maintain its operations.

Intrapersonal communication includes duplicating or perception, memory, and consciousness. Duplication allows us to gather information about the world, memory to store and recall it, consciousness to reflect on it and ourselves. Interpersonal communication can be symmetrical or asymmetrical. In symmetrical communication relationships senders and receivers transmit messages in a more or less equal exchange of messages. In asymmetrical communication one communicator dominates. People communicate with messages encoded and decoded from their intrapersonal experience. Messages may be encoded verbally or nonverbally—in spoken or written words, or in facial, hand, and body movements. Only signals, not meaning, are transmitted in human communication. Communications scientists use the term *noise* to indicate disruptions in the message. Channel noise affects the signal as it passes from sender to receiver. Semantic noise can occur within the sender or receiver when either is distracted or if coding malfunctions. Feedback is used to determine the effectiveness of the message. The sender observes the responses of the receiver for positive or negative signs as the message is delivered.

In small group, public, and mediated communication, noise is more of a problem and feedback more difficult to obtain. More receivers mean more individual backgrounds and experience, making understanding more difficult. But public communication allows more rapid dissemination of information. Role taking is another important means of amplifying communication. There are three basic communications roles: A (advocacy) roles, B (behavioral) roles, and C (channel) roles. Communication networks rapidly relay messages through space, and store information and advice.

Early media systems developed from mnemonic devices (memory aids). The best communications media are both permanent and portable. The adoption of media into communication adds three media communication situations to the two basic face-to-face situations: (1) personal or private media (letters, telephone), (2) public media, audience assembled (movie theatres, television conferences), and (3) public media audience not assembled (newspapers, magazines, radio, television).

We begin to understand the complexity of mass communication when we understand that the process of mass communication includes all other types of communication. Mass communication also involves more than the sum of these other types of communication. To be understood it must be viewed in a social context.

Questions for Discussion

1. Communication theorists now maintain human communicators can not transmit meaning in messages when they attempt to communicate. They insist there is no transfer of meaning, no exchange of ideas, in human communication. Do we exchange ideas when we talk? How can your idea get into the head of someone else? Reverse the situation: What would our free society be like? What would your life be like?

2. We say that communications media bolster memory. How would colleges and universities operate if there were no media, if (1) there were no notepads and pencils, (2) no textbooks, no library, and (3) no chalkboards, microphones, films or overhead projectors? How would their absence affect your approach to class work? How would it affect the kind of education you would get?

3. How much time do you spend in interpersonal communication? It might prove useful if for one week you kept a diary of your communications with others, noting how long you spend in conversation each day, what topics you discussed, and what conflicts you encountered. Try to pay special attention to nonverbal cues—yours and others, where possible. How much talking is not really talking?

4. Write a good definition of human communication.

References

Berlo, David. *The Process of Communication.* New York: Holt, Rinehart and Winston, 1960.

Blumer, Herbert. "Society as Symbolic Interaction." In *Symbolic Interaction.* 2nd ed., edited by Jerome G. Manis and Bernard N. Meltzer. Boston: Allyn and Bacon, 1972.

Cartier, Francis A. "Three Misconceptions of Communication." In *Messages,* edited by Jean M. Civikly. New York: Random House, 1974.

Dance, Frank E. X. "The 'Concept' of Communication." *The Journal of Communication* 20 (June 1970): 201–210.

Deutschmann, Paul J. "The Sign-Situation Classification of Human Communication." *Journal of Communication* 7 (1967): 54–63.

Dobelhofer, Ernst. *Voices in Stone.* New York: The Viking Press, 1961.

Gordon, George N. *The Language of Communication.* New York: Hastings House, 1969.

Johnson, Wendell. "The Communication Process and General Semantic Principles." In *Mass Communications.* 2nd ed., edited by Wilbur Schramm. Urbana: University of Illinois Press, 1960.

Klapper, Joseph T. *The Effects of Mass Communication.* Glencoe: The Free Press, 1960.

Korzyski, Alfred. *Manhood of Humanity.* 2nd ed. Lakeville, Conn.: The International Non-Aristotelian Library Publishing Company, 1921.

Lin, Nan. "Analysis of Communication Relations." In *Communication and Behavior,* edited by Gerhard J. Hanneman and William J. McEwen. Reading, Mass.: Addison-Wesley, 1975.

Schramm, Wilbur. "The Nature of Communication Between Humans." In *The Process and Effects of Mass Communication,* edited by Wilbur Schramm and Donald F. Roberts. Urbana: University of Illinois Press, 1971.

Schramm, Wilbur, and William E. Porter. *Men, Women, Messages, and Media.* New York: Harper & Row, 1982.

Steinberg, Mark, and Gerald R. Miller. "Interpersonal Communication: A Sharing Process." In *Communication and Behavior,* edited by Gerhard J. Hanneman and William J. McEwen. Reading, Mass.: Addison-Wesley, 1975.

Tomkins, Sylvan. *Affect, Imagery, Consciousness.* New York: Springer Publishing Company, 1962.

Westley, Bruce H., and Malcolm S. MacLean, Jr. "A Conceptual Model for Communications Research." *Journalism Quarterly* 34, no. 1 (1975): 31–38.

Chapter
2

Making and Maintaining Mass Communication

Communication and Social Systems

A mnemonic device of the late fourteenth century. As taxes were collected, the tax collector notched the tally stick of the tax payer. When the two sticks matched, the taxes were paid.

As sociologist Daniel Lerner has written, people who live together in a social and political group—a common "polity"—develop distinctive patterns and ways of distributing information, just as they develop distinct ways of distributing other commodities. The communications systems they create are products of their social systems, and reflect the social values, actions, and needs of that society. Anthropologist Margaret Mead studied three small societies of the Pacific some years ago, for example, and found each had developed distinct communications systems that reflected the needs of their societies. One group studied, the Arapesh, lived in the hilly country of New Guinea, farming isolated patches in the mountainous terrain. Their principal communication system consisted of shouting and beating slit gong alarms to call the isolated tribe members together to receive further, more detailed reports about an event. The Manus of the Admiralty Islands, in contrast, were a society of tenacious traders, with an elaborate numbering system. Their drum-beat messages contained very detailed information about feasts—addressed to individuals and signed with a distinctive signature. The third society, the Balinese, lived in tightly knit villages. Their lives centered around an elaborate calendar on which was recorded the society's religious ceremonies and feast days. The Balinese used a town crier—a C role messenger—to carry instructions concerning upcoming religious festivals about the village, from hut to hut, presenting each hut's prescribed contributions in specific detail. Even though every society shapes its communication system to suit its needs, there remains the question of how any society can move from a rudimentary slit gong, oral system, with little or no writing, into the literate and highly technical mass communication systems found today in developed countries in Western Europe or North America. We do not beg the question when we reply, "very slowly."

Mass Communication and Primitive Society

In modern society there seems to be a surprising number of people who believe that all that is necessary to build a mass communication system in any backward country is to provide the country with media technology: printing presses, radio stations, television sets, and movie projectors. The truth is, no society has ever become a mediated society simply by acquiring media technology. Mass communication is beside the point for the primitive society because, by definition, it has no written language and, therefore, little need for printing. It lacks electricity to power presses, transmitters, or projectors. It spends much of its time hunting and foraging for food. What is more, there is evidence that media technology introduced into small, illiterate, and isolated groups would not

Without a written language or electricity, the close, primitive society has little need for mass communication, and might not understand it if it were given to them.

encourage or enhearten so much as astonish, even panic them, and produce far-reaching religious and social changes. (Press reports indicate one isolated tribe did adopt a World War II airplane as an object of worship several years ago.) Whatever the reaction, it is more reasonable to expect the primitive tribe to adapt media technology to its own needs—to convert a printing press and type into clubs, religious charms, or slingshot, for example—rather than for it to restructure its social patterns to accommodate mass communication media.

Mass Communication and Traditional Society

Even larger, more modern, traditional societies find difficulty supporting the complicated and expensive business of mass communication. The traditional society, as sociologist David Riesman has suggested, is a very stable society of family and kinship ties that finds its meaning for life in the adoption of age-old patterns and traditions, and following the traditional religion and wisdom of its forefathers. Status and livelihood are derived in the family's time-honored trade. What is produced is, generally speaking, what is consumed. And there is little discretionary capital or leisure time for such frivolities as books or reading. Riesman has cited the countries of Western Europe in the eighteenth and early nineteenth centuries as good examples of traditional societies. Modern examples can be found among the many countries of the Far East, Africa, and Latin America.

Even the traditional society, though far more advanced than the primitive society, does not have the basic resources required for mass communication. There is a written language, but mass illiteracy prevents most of the society from reading. There also are few means for creating or supporting a school system to teach reading. With few readers there is little demand or need for *mass* media messages. At best, there also is a limited capacity for media production. There is a limited supply of even the smaller pieces of media production technology—typewriters, linotype machines, photoengraving equipment, hand presses, cameras. There are no buildings, offices, or studios in which to work, and utilities are limited. Electricity may be rationed and unavailable at certain times of the day. With few production and technical facilities, it follows that there can be no ready supply of skilled personnel to operate media equipment, a fact that is compounded further by, again, the lack of educational facilities to train them.

Mass Communication and Industrialization

If a society is to develop mass communication, it must develop the social values, consumer attitudes and consumer audiences, and the general economic capabilities of an industrialized society. The reason for this is not difficult to understand. Mass media messages, whether messages of information, entertainment, or advertising, are a *commodity*. They are produced, distributed, and consumed in the same manner as other commodities, and are, therefore, under the domain of the marketplace. If a society is to have mass communication it must have the economic capacity to produce media technology, train skilled media practitioners, and develop media audiences who have the time, education, inclination, and money to consume both the media messages and the products the media advertise. These basic requirements clearly are not available in the living-off-nature primitive societies, or in the tight-pursed, no frivolities economies of traditional societies.

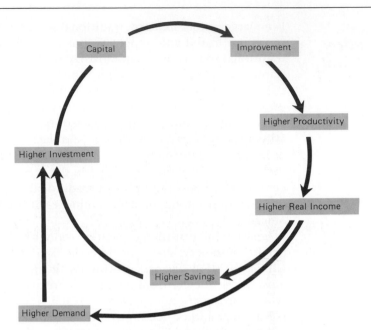

Figure 2.1 Lerner's diagram of the upward cycle of economic growth. Industrialization develops through savings and investment which make possible factories, educational facilities, and the consumer audience with its demand for goods. From the same savings-investment sequence comes the buildings, equipment, and training that makes mass media possible. Primitive and traditional societies find it difficult to save and catch the upward cycle.

Emerging Mass Media Societies

The construction of mass communication facilities in emerging industrial societies is usually a function of the political needs and values of the society. The media of developing countries often are assigned the role of faithful follower. Their function is to publish the views and policies the government wishes published, without change or contradiction. As we shall see in later chapters, the Tudors, who ruled in England before and during Shakespeare's time, and the Stuarts, who followed beginning in the seventeenth century, assigned such a function to the English press, and attempted to enforce their wishes with censorship and restraint. The current Nationalist Chinese government on Taiwan gives special instructions to editors on what the government considers to be important stories, that is, ones involving government and national security. On Taiwan, Chinese language newspapers are managed only by editors who have been able to obtain a government license to print. The licenses are given to those who demonstrate firm support of the regime. Still, observers feel the Nationalist Chinese media enjoy more freedom than the media in most developing countries.

In sharp contrast to the Nationalist Chinese system is the one developed by the Communist Chinese. The Communist Chinese have created an extensive media bureaucracy, the Department of Propaganda, to supervise and distribute public information. Centralization of their propaganda effort allows the Red Chinese government to deliver the same official message to all citizens, from all media, whether the information

Part of the public communication system in China. The papers fixed to the walls report an attempted coup in Shanghai in 1976, the year the picture was taken.

is delivered from the New China News Agency, the large newspaper the *People's Daily,* or the famous wall newspapers. The Chinese Communist media have several important functions. They often are used in internal battles within the Communist party. They see service, too, in the indoctrination of the public in Communist ideology. A major goal of the mainland Chinese media is to support the modernization of the nation, and bring the tasks and methods of work to the masses in the quickest, most extensive way. In this they follow a proclamation of Chairman Mao who once wrote, "Once the masses know the truth and have a common aim, they will work together with one heart."

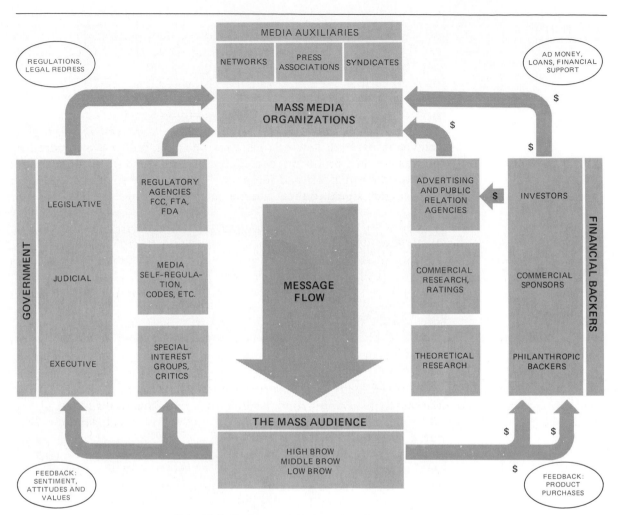

Figure 2.2 Mass communication as a social system.

Mass Communication in the United States

Our own mass communication system offers a sharp contrast to those in developing countries. Our great number of industrial, political, and social interest groups, along with numerous media corporations, produce so many media messages that diversity of media content is more the rule than the exception. In our earliest years as a nation we rejected central control of our media. Rather than have them speak as one voice with one heart we established them as individual social institutions in their own right, separate from each other and independent from government. (A diagram of our mass communication system is presented in figure 2.2.)

Sources

Mass communication, like all human communication, includes the sending and receiving of messages, but in mass communication sending is performed by a complex organization of many people rather than by one individual. The media organization includes a sizable production staff that is maintained at considerable expense. The American newspaper, for example, spends almost half of every dollar—forty-two cents—on employees and employee benefits. Production of one nightly television network newscast requires one hundred to two hundred reporters, writers, producers, and studio workers—and that figure does not include the engineers and telephone company personnel who deliver the program signal to local stations for broadcasting.

Audience

The messages of the mass media are public. They are distributed regularly, rapidly, and with the intention of reaching a mass audience in a short time. The audiences or receivers are large, heterogeneous, and anonymous to both the media organizations that send the messages as well as to other receivers. We usually underestimate the size of the media audience. A large, modern football stadium will seat 100,000 people, for example, but each of the top thirty daily newspapers in this country is circulated to at least two times that number, or 200,000 papers to 200,000 people every day. The final episode of the television series "M*A*S*H" attracted an audience of approximately 125 million men, women, and children of all ages, interests, and tastes. To accommodate the audience for that one "M*A*S*H" episode, the modern football stadium would have to be filled 1,250 times, or every Saturday afternoon for twenty-four years and two weeks.

Messages

Producing messages for audiences with a wide variety of interests and tastes is a difficult task for media organizations. Our social backgrounds and personalities give us all slightly different experiences to bring to media content. Journalist Douglas Cater has argued, for example, that thinking people find less to interest them on television than do most television consumers. The thinkers like news documentaries, news programs, and serious drama, Cater has pointed out, rather than the game shows, soap operas, and action dramas the majority seem to prefer.

Media researcher Phillip Anast has found that college students who regularly attend movies have a continuing interest in violence and scenic disaster—content that many other media viewers feel is the worst the media can offer. Other college students—those who show interest in personal achievement and adventure—prefer to be out and active rather than passively watch the excitement at the movie theatre.

Organization of mass communication.

The amount of education, level of income, size of the city we live in, and even the regional location of that city help determine whether or not we read a newspaper every day. For example, only 50 percent of adults with low incomes and educations, and who live in rural areas, read a daily newspaper. Yet 80 percent of those with higher incomes, more than a high school education, and living in larger cities read a daily newspaper.

Organization of mass communication *continued*

Regulators

Figure 2.2 lists organizations and institutions usually ignored in popular definitions of mass communication. On the left are the organizations and groups which have influence in regulating the media: the government and its controlling agencies, and voluntary control groups from the public and the media professions. The public groups—community, family, and special interest organizations—can influence media performance by asking the government for controls. Professional media groups, on the other hand, rarely attempt to bring government pressure on their co-workers, limiting their actions to the public and critical reviews of media performance in hopes the unfavorable publicity will encourage the improvement they desire.

Financial Backers   The media financial backers, on the right of figure 2.2 and their auxiliaries—advertising, public relations and media research agencies—provide the media with money, advertising messages, information, and research. Most of the financial backers are businesses that use the media to advertise their products and services. With the help of ad agencies they create advertising messages that are placed within media content to give the product the best exposure to its potential buyers. If the product sells well, the company profits and reinvests in further advertising. If sales are disappointing, adjustments are made. Financial backers, ad agencies, and media corporations flourish or fail by this financial flow from advertising. The media that do not advertise—the movies, book publishing—may call on financial backers for loans to produce a media message, and repay the loans with profits from sales. Both movie producers and book publishers spend vast amounts of money to advertise their products in the other media.

Still another type of financial backer does not advertise or lend money to the media, but instead donates funds, philanthropically, for media support. The Ford Foundation, for example, contributed millions of dollars to educational radio and television in the years following World War II. Mobil Oil has led in the development and support of programs for public television, in exchange for being identified as a Public Broadcasting Service sponsor—or for the goodwill it wins. The federally supported National Endowment for the Humanities and the National Endowment for the Arts have provided funds for cultural productions advertisers would not sponsor. Less affluent backers also contribute to media support. During the 1960s, many FM radio stations survived on small contributions from listeners. And most local public television stations and many ethnic newspapers can operate today only because their audiences contribute money to keep them alive.

Researchers   In general, there are two types of mass communications research: academic research and commercial research.

Academic research is theoretical and descriptive. It investigates the nature of the mass media, their impact on society, and collects information useful in building scientific theories about mass communication. Most academic and theoretical research is performed by researchers at colleges and universities.

Commercially sponsored research looks for solutions to specific commercial problems. It usually is performed by advertising and public relations agencies, independent agencies, and research departments in media organizations. One type of commercial research project might be undertaken to determine the public image of a product or corporation. Much commercial research is undertaken to obtain information about media audiences. Studies of readership, circulation, and ratings are so important to media operations that an important audience research industry has grown up to service the industry's needs. Commercial media research is performed by advertising, commercial research and public relations agencies, and research departments of the various media.

Societal Functions

The most important questions we ask about the mass media is why they exist, and what it is society expects of its mass communication system. We already have touched on the answer in our discussion of human beings and human communication. The media serve society in the same way communication serves the individual human. Media extend, improve, and enrich our lives with information and entertainment. Specifically:

1. They survey the environment, and publish news of the opportunities and dangers around us. Like our senses, they inform us of good things and warn us of approaching beasts, whether political, economic, or meteorological. In our society, the news media also pride themselves on watchdogging government for signs of corruption and incompetence.
2. They correlate the parts of the society to help audiences respond to the environment. Even radio's brief morning traffic report helps us map our driving to avoid unnecessary delays. Reports from the Middle East, from the site of a devastating tornado, or views of management and labor in an unsettled strike help us understand problems near and far and deal with them more intelligently.
3. They transmit the social heritage from one generation to the next. Not only books, but also motion pictures and music recordings serve us in this way. The media celebrate Easter, the Fourth of July, Christmas, and support our social customs. That our modern morality still centers around the Judeo-Christian tradition is due in large part to the fact that millions have read the Bible since its first printing five hundred years ago.
4. They entertain with games, adventure, drama, and variety shows, giving us a chance to cry, laugh, express emotion, or just relax and take our minds off things for a while.

5. They publish advertisements, bringing buyer and seller together, promoting commercial enterprise and the economic system.

In performing these functions our media organizations have one overriding need. They must make money. They must show a profit. It is not popular to suggest the first and foremost goal of American newspapers, magazines, and films, and all American mass media is to make money, but it is true. Making money is not their only goal, but of necessity it is the first.

A Cultural Business

The mass media are cultural businesses. They must show a profit *and* offer quality communications for audience consumption. Good media practice is often good media business. In 1976, for example, many cheered when ABC–TV announced it had hired newswoman Barbara Walters from NBC's "Today" show, with a five-year contract for $1 million. The move seemed an exceptionally responsible one for ABC, since it meant Walters would become the first network evening news anchorwoman, helping other women gain equal status in their own professions. At the same time, however, it was an astute business move. The contract for $1 million won ABC–TV more free publicity than it could have bought with the same amount of money. And by "stealing" Walters from NBC, ABC was able to reduce "Today's" ratings and bolster ratings of its own "Good Morning, America." ABC then was able to raise the advertising rates on "Good Morning, America," and more than replace its $1 million investment within a few months.

With only a few exceptions—cases where media with small audiences must be supported by private or government philanthropy—our mass media are special, cultural businesses. Their ability to provide important communications services, withstand undue pressures from the government, the public, and financial backers, as well as make a profit, is important to us all.

In the following chapters, we discuss the components of our mass communication system, beginning with two chapters on the historical development of the media, followed by individual chapters (5 through 11) on mass media organizations. Special attention also is given the media auxiliary organizations—"wire" services, syndicates, advertising, and public relations (chapters 12 through 14). Chapters 15 and 16 review the legal relationships between media and government, and media and the individual; chapter 17 explores several methods of media regulation—from the government, the media professions themselves, and special interest groups within the audience. Chapter 18 summarizes our concern regarding the media's effect on society, and the attempts of media researchers to find scientific evidence to substantiate or disprove these concerns. In chapter 19, we will estimate what the future holds for the media and our mediated society. By then we should be much better informed—and much less misinformed—about what mass communications is and how it operates in America today.

Summary

Every social and political group develops its own way of distributing information. And while all societies develop communication systems, not all societies develop mass communication systems. No society has ever moved from an oral communication system to mass communication simply by acquiring mass media technology. Instead, the society must develop the needs and values of a modern, industrial society, with a literate population that can afford to buy media messages and the projects the media advertise.

Unlike personal and public communication, sending in mass communication is performed by complex organizations maintained at considerable expense. Messages are public and rapid while receivers are found in large heterogeneous audiences—anonymous to the media organizations and each other.

Media organizations face potential regulation, directly or indirectly, from government, the community, and professional media groups.

Most financial backing for the media comes from businesses that use the media to advertise products. Ad and public relations agencies prepare advertising and publicity for their business clients. Media that do not advertise either derive their backing from the sale of their media products, or look to philanthropic sources to sustain their efforts.

The system includes two kinds of research: academic and commercial. Academic research attempts to understand mass communication scientifically. Commercial research probes specific problems for the media and media-associated organizations.

Mass communication serves the society by:

1. surveying the environment,
2. correlating the responses of the society,
3. transmitting the social heritage,
4. entertaining,
5. supporting the economy.

To survive, the media are obliged to make money. But the media are cultural businesses, too, and also must provide quality communication for social consumption. Their ability to meet this dual obligation is important to us all.

Questions for Discussion

1. The mass media are said to be the best and the worst things that have happened to the human race. Why is mass communication so controversial? What have you heard or read, read in this book, that would help account for this controversy?

2. How much time do you spend with mass communication? For a week keep a record of your use of the mass media. What do you read? Did you go to the movies? What do you watch on television? How long do you spend doing this? How much of the knowledge you use and rely on comes from the media? Compare your media record with your interpersonal communication record. Do you pay attention to the same subjects in the media you like to listen to and talk about in person?

3. The evidence is that only societies that become industrialized can become mediated societies, with mass communications systems. Why isn't it possible for governments in emerging nations to accelerate the modernization process by buying media technology, transmitters, receivers, and then speeding up the industrialization process by using the mass media to instruct the population?

4. What is mass communication? Write a comprehensive definition of it.

References

Anast, Phillip. "Differential Movie Appeals as Correlates of Attendance." *Journalism Quarterly* 44, no. 1 (1967): 86–90.

Bishop, Robert I., and Judy Hansen. "Content of Taiwan's English and Chinese Press." *Journalism Quarterly* 58, no. 3 (1981): 456–60.

Bogard, Leo. "Negro and White Media Exposure: New Evidence." *Journalism Quarterly* 49, no. 1 (1972): 15–21.

Chu, Godwin, C. "The Current Structure and Functions of China's Mass Media." In *Mass Communication Review Yearbook 2, edited by G. Clevel and Wilhoit. Beverly Hills: Sage, 1981.*

Cowan, Geoffrey. See No Evil. New York: Simon and Schuster, 1978.

DeFleur, Melvin, and Sandra Ball-Rokeach. *Theories of Mass Communication.* 3d ed. New York: David McKay Co., Inc., 1975.

Hansen, Judy P., and Robert L. Bishop. "Press Freedom on Taiwan: The Mini Hundred Flowers Period." *Journalism Quarterly* 58, no. 1 (1981): 38–42.

Lasswell, Harold D. "Attention Structure and Social Structure." In *The Process and Effects of Mass Communication,* edited by Wilbur Schramm and Donald F. Roberts. Urbana: University of Illinois Press, 1971.

Lerner, Daniel. "Communication Systems and Social Systems: A Statistical Exploration in History and Policy." *Behavioral Science* 2 (1957): 266–75.

Riesman, David. *The Lonely Crowd: A Study of the Changing American Character.* New Haven: Yale University Press, 1961.

Wright, Charles R. *Mass Communication, A Sociological Perspective,* 2d ed. New York: Random House, 1975.

Part Two

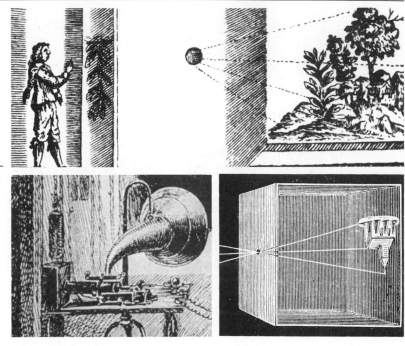

The Development of the Mass Media

As sociologist Robert E. Park has suggested, the mass media have a history, but it is a natural history. The media are not products of any group of willful people. Instead, they have developed from the work of many hands and many factors. They have grown the way islands or cities grow: gradually, and in many directions at one time.

The media are among the most recent developments in human communication. They have been in existence for only some five hundred years, less than .002 percent of the thirty million years of human development. (See the accompa-

nying table.) We get an even clearer understanding of how recent they are if we compress those thirty million years of growing and evolving by a ratio of five million to one, or into six years. On our new six-year scale, the printing press has a history of only fifty-five minutes. The first successful American newspaper was founded less than thirty minutes ago; radio and the movies have been around for about nine minutes; and the first television station went on the air only five and one-half minutes ago. All of mass communication has been in operation for less than an hour of humankind's six years of existence.

The media were late in developing because human communication—spoken and written language—were necessary first. The media and all human communication were shaped by sources buried deep in prehistoric time, so deep we may never know how it all began. One theory places the development of the facial structure that made lip control and human speech possible as far back as nineteen million years ago. A more conservative estimate would place the beginning at a half million years ago when our primitive ances-

40

tors lived in caves and signaled to each other across the hunt.

The dawn of both art and writing can be traced back at least forty thousand years ago, when reindeer hunting tribes made drawings on cave walls in France and Spain. These early pictures of bison and mammoths, fighting reindeer, the hunt, and ritual dancing are remarkably clear even today, and still give viewers a vivid impression of the animals and events they depict. The written alphabets of modern languages are direct descendants of these drawings, and represent the result of a long,

wearing down process of the older sign languages. In early picture writing, for example, a scene told the whole story to be communicated. Later, several pictures would recount a story, with a picture of a man or woman and a picture of a fish indicating someone fishing, or the catch of the day. Still later stages saw pictures representing ideas rather than objects, with the sun drawn to represent happiness and a picture of a man to represent all people. These stages of writing were independent of spoken language, just as the sign languages of early North Americans were independent of the spoken word.

The idea-picture languages were very cumbersome. When we consider that in 2900 B.C. the Sumarians had a written language of five hundred ideograms (graphic symbols that represent ideas but have no verbal name), we can appreciate the efficiency of the twenty-six letters we use to represent spoken English.

Speech was linked to writing when the picture of an object was understood to mean both the object and the sound of the word for that object. For example, the picture of a tree came to represent the sound "tree" while the picture of the sun represented the sound

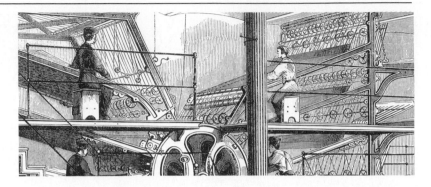

"sun." To write *treason,* then, one put a tree beside a sun. In time, the pictures of tree and sun became letters of the language.

A grand variety of materials was used to record writing as it developed. Prehistoric tribes made moon calendars on bone. In Babylon, messages were recorded in clay through the use of wedge-shaped reed pens. By 3000 B.C. Egyptian scribes had produced the famous *Book of the Dead,* the story of the soul's progress after death. The writing surface was made from papyrus, reeds that grew in the Nile; they were lapped over each other and compressed into serviceable sheets. Papyrus texts survive today and still are readable.

As students of Roman history know, the Romans produced great volumes of books at low cost (twenty-four cents each). They were handwritten on parchment, or treated sheepskin, by slave-scribes. The Romans also produced and distributed the *Acta Diurna,* the daily report from the Roman Senate. Both the Greeks and the Romans did much to spread literacy throughout Western civilization.

When interest in reading waned during the Dark Ages, the church, with its priest-scribes, assumed responsibility for the books of the world to perpetuate the Christian heritage. The tone of the Dark Ages seems best described by the acts of the Christian Crusaders who conquered Constantinople in 1204 and derided and destroyed the public pen and ink stands of the city as "weapons" of a race of "students." It was two hundred years before interest in reading revived, and when it did the demand was so great it sent the monks to work early and late to meet the clamor for copies of texts. The demand also raised interest in an invention that could make large numbers of accurate and inexpensive copies of texts.

That invention, printing with movable type, also was the work of many hands, but more important it was the first communications machinery in history able to produce multiple copies of a message in a short time. The invention of printing with movable type marks the beginning of mass communication.

References

Braidwood, Robert. *Prehistoric Men.* Glenview, Ill.: Scott, Foresman, 1975.

Deringer, David. *Writing.* New York: Frederick A. Praeger, 1962.

DeVinne, Theo. L. *The Invention of Printing.* New York: Francis Hart, 1876; Gale Research, 1969.

Leakey, L. S. B. *Olduvai Gorge.* Cambridge: Cambridge University, 1969.

Ogg, Oscar. *The 26 Letters.* New York: Crowell, 1971.

Park, Robert E. "The Natural History of the Newspaper." In *Mass Communications,* edited by Wilbur Schramm. Urbana: University of Illinois Press, 1970.

Schramm, Wilbur and William E. Porter. *Men, Women, Messages, and Media.* 2d ed. New York: Harper & Row, 1982.

A BRIEF CALENDAR OF THE DEVELOPMENT OF HUMAN COMMUNICATION

800,000 to 500,000 years ago

Peking man develops rudimentary language and story telling ability

Two months ago

10,000 years ago

Humans become food producers instead of food gatherers and move from rock shelters to villages

Thirty-two hours ago

1878

Edison invents phonograph

Eleven minutes ago

30 to 20 million years ago

Humanoid life appears on earth

Six years ago

19 to 14 million years ago

Canine fossa has evolved in humanoid types, a preview of lip control for human speech

Three years, nine months ago

40,000 to 20,000 years ago

Modern humans make artful pictures and mnemonic tally bones

Two and one-half weeks ago

3500 B.C.

The Sumarians write on clay tablets with wedge tipped pens: cuniform

Nine and one-half hours ago

1928

First television station established

Five and one-half minutes ago

| 6 yrs. | 5 yrs. | 4 yrs. | 3 yrs. | 2 yrs. | 1 yr. |

(Relative Scale: 5 million years = 1 year)

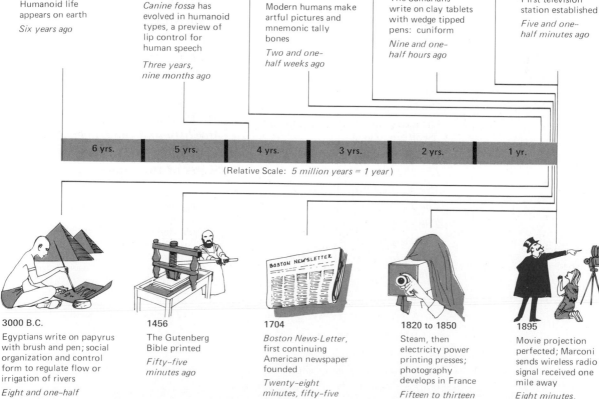

3000 B.C.

Egyptians write on papyrus with brush and pen; social organization and control form to regulate flow or irrigation of rivers

Eight and one-half hours ago

1456

The Gutenberg Bible printed

Fifty-five minutes ago

1704

Boston News-Letter, first continuing American newspaper founded

Twenty-eight minutes, fifty-five seconds ago

1820 to 1850

Steam, then electricity power printing presses; photography develops in France

Fifteen to thirteen minutes ago

1895

Movie projection perfected; Marconi sends wireless radio signal received one mile away

Eight minutes, fifty-five seconds ago

Chapter
3

Paper making circa 1500. The vat was used to cook wood pulp, rags, and water into a mush which then was dipped, drained, and dried to form individual sheets.

An early "wine" press.

The Beginning in Europe

Those who study the history and development of the mass media long since have agreed that the history of mass communication began in Germany in the middle fifteenth century with the invention and use of movable type in printing. As is usually the case with inventions, the "breakthrough" in textual printing did not come overnight. As several inventors began working to create a serviceable type to capitalize on the public demand for texts, the rudiments of a textual printing system were already at hand. Already in existence were:

1. a printing press, derived from presses used to make wine and press linen. It had been used to print playing cards, and books of religious picture stories.

2. paper, invented in China in A.D. 105 and introduced into Europe by the Moors. Parchment, the writing surface created by treating sheepskins, had been used by the Greeks for handwritten scrolls. But it did not absorb ink well and was an inadequate surface for printing. Just as important, printing, with its ability to print multiple copies of texts soon created such a demand for printing surfaces there would not have been enough sheep in Europe to provide parchment needed for the number of books published by 1600.

3. an oil base ink, derived from artist paints, which would produce a readable imprint of the small letters of type without running.

The Gutenberg Contribution

The fourth ingredient was invented by a goldsmith, Johann Gutenberg, who worked on the problem for several years. To print textual material—pages of words—an inexpensive, uniform, sturdy type was needed, one that would not crack in the press as did wooden plates and letters. Gutenberg solved the problem by casting individual letters in molten lead. The lead, when cool, made uniform-sized type that gave clear impressions, imprint after imprint. By 1459 Gutenberg had produced enough type and gained the skill necessary to print two versions of the Bible.

And then it was as if a dam had burst. William Caxton printed the first book in English in 1475, his translation of the *Illiad* from French. He established the first press in England the next year and was able to print some one hundred books before his death in 1491. By 1500 twelve countries had print shops with movable type, and nearly forty thousand books had been published.

Broadsheets, News Books, and Journals

Printers soon developed other uses for their presses. In Europe, news was carried by gossips and town criers, and in hand written newsletters read aloud for a price. (In Italy, the price was less than a penny, a gazeta, the source for the modern newspaper title "Gazette.") In 1513 Richard Fowles published a single issue news sheet—a broadsheet—entitled "The Treu Encountre," a report of the defeat of the Scot, James IV, who was killed in his attempt to invade England. Many broadsheets followed. All were accounts of one significant event, printed on one side of a sheet the size of modern notebook paper, and hawked about the streets for public sale.

In the early seventeenth century, another type of news publication emerged from the turmoil of the Thirty Years War. Dutch printers, recognizing the English would be interested in war news from the continent, began publishing news books, or corantos, in English in 1620. The corantos, unlike modern news magazines, were published irregularly, but they quickly became so popular in England that Nathaniel Butter, who was distributing them, joined Thomas Archer and Nicholas Bourne to publish a domestic version filled with foreign news for English readers. The books were eight to forty-two pages in length, composed of news items collected from various sources. Their series ended in 1641, the same year the first English newspaper of regular issue, the *Diurnal Occurrence,* began publication, offering readers accounts of domestic news events.

Writers found the political pamphlet useful during the same period. The pamphlets of William Carter, an English Catholic, so angered Anglican Queen Elizabeth that Carter was executed in 1584. The poet

John Milton published his famous pamphlet *Areopagitica* in 1644, with its strong argument against censorship and for the free and open encounter of ideas.

In the eighteenth century, the essay newspaper, or editorial journal, became a vehicle for some of the prominent names in English letters: Daniel DeFoe, Jonathan Swift, Richard Steele, and Joseph Addison. Steele's *Tatler,* then the Addison and Steele *Spectator,* were greatly admired for their wit and satire by an estimated sixty thousand readers in the Old and the New World.

The Authoritarian Factor

Printing was introduced in Europe at a time when religious and secular authoritarianism pervaded most of European thinking. Philosopher Thomas Hobbes argued during the seventeenth century, for example, that the proper role of the individual was to submit to the ruling monarch, whose government was established to protect against anarchy and a society where people lived in small families and robbed and despoiled one another. Criticism, even personal criticism of the monarch, lowered the crown's esteem in the eyes of subjects, and as a result was a threat to both civic peace and reason. Citizens, and the press, therefore, were to support, and not criticize, the actions of the monarch and state. Why should an uninformed printer be allowed to criticize the policies which the better-informed monarch had determined as the best course for all?

Authoritarianism and the Press in the Colonies

Authoritarian philosophy was dying slowly as the American colonies formed their societies, but it still was strong enough to cause concern in the early 1700s. The first printing press in the colonies was established at Harvard University in 1638. Under watchful church authority, it produced an almanac, sermons, a catechism, a psalter, and in 1640 a fast-selling *Whole Book of Psalmes.*

The first attempt to publish a newspaper met with stiff opposition. In 1690 in Boston, Benjamin Harris published a small, saucy newspaper entitled *Public Occurrences Both Foreign and Domestick.* Harris criticized the colony's Indian allies for their barbarous treatment of prisoners, and also reported that the French King had taken sexual liberties with his own daughter-in-law. Massachusetts needed its Indian allies in the war with the French, and the Boston clergy were outraged over the story about the French King's adultery. Since Harris had not submitted the newspaper for government approval, it was readily suppressed after its first edition.

In contrast, the first successful colonial newspaper, founded twelve years later, was dull, filled with reports of meetings, legal notices, ship arrivals, and reprints of stories from Europe. But Boston Postmaster John

A seventeenth-century pillory. One form of punishment for errant printers.

Campbell kept the Boston *News-Letter,* with its circulation of two hundred to three hundred readers, alive by submitting his material to the governor's office for approval before printing. He published the *News-Letter* from 1702 until he relinquished control of it in 1723. It became one of the longest-lived American papers of the eighteenth century and, ironically enough, a center of anti-authoritarian, or patriot, journalism during the years that led to the Revolution.

Despite the *News-Letter's* early bow to censorship, the ideological tide was turning more and more toward libertarianism. Increasingly, journalists and printers were able to defy colonial authority and continue to print. James Franklin was the first to do so. In 1721 he and his Hell Fire Club group of friends openly attacked members of Boston's Puritan clergy, the Mather family, in the pages of the *New England Courant.* (One of Franklin's taunts suggested the government would send a ship to deal with some dangerous pirates "some time this month, if wind and weather permit.") Franklin was thrown into jail for a month, then released. When he took up the attack again, the General Court of Massachusetts called for absolute censorship of his newspaper. But in May 1723 a grand jury found the charges distasteful, and refused to indict him.

Popular support helped release printer John Peter Zenger from jail in 1735. Zenger was the printer of the New York *Journal*, which was published in opposition to high-handed Governor William Cosby and his party. Cosby had begun his service to the colony by arriving a year late from England to assume his appointment. He then made claims on administrative fees collected before he took office, became involved in some illegal real estate transactions, and rigged council elections and removed judges in his own interests. As the newspaper attacks from Zenger and his merchant supporters mounted, the governor grew more and more vexed until finally he arranged to have Zenger charged and imprisoned for "raising sedition."

After months in jail, Zenger was brought to trial in 1735. His attorney, octagenarian Andrew Hamilton of Philadelphia, immediately admitted his client had printed the newspapers in question. The prosecution was elated. Under authoritarian law, any criticism of the government—true or false—defamed the government, and was "seditious libel," an attempt to overthrow the government by lowering its esteem in the eyes of the public. The prosecution called for a verdict of guilty.

Hamilton objected. It is the falsehood, not the publication, that creates the scandal and the libel, he argued. When the judge replied that according to the law of the day there was no precedent for such an argument, Hamilton turned and pleaded his case to the jury. It was, he said, the right of everyone to expose and oppose arbitrary power by speaking and writing the truth. Moved by Hamilton's pleas, the jury returned a verdict of not guilty. It was years before truth as a defense for libel became a part of American law, but the Zenger case did have immediate effects. After 1735 no other attempt was made to prosecute a colonial printer for what he printed about the government.

The Printer Entrepreneurs

With little commerce and advertising, with illiteracy high, and with colonial life attuned, of necessity, to hard work, hunting and fishing, printing spread slowly through the colonies. Half of all colonial newspapers failed. Delaware and New Jersey were still without newspapers in 1765. The newspapers and print shops that did succeed were those run by imaginative entrepreneurs who survived by printing handbills, newspapers, and lottery tickets, and engaging in that most profitable of colonial printing sidelines: the pirating of English fiction.

Undoubtedly, the best journalist of the colonial period was Benjamin Franklin. Franklin sold coffee, soap, wine, patent medicines, spectacles, and cheese in his *Pennsylvania Gazette* shop in Philadelphia. His almanac, like others on the market, was a money-maker. It sold ten thousand copies a year between 1725 and 1764. Franklin was also in the business of providing financial backing to talented printers. For example, he financed Lewis and Elizabeth Timothy in their management of the South Carolina *Gazette* in 1733, giving America its first woman editor in the bargain. When Lewis died as the result of an "unhappy accident" in 1738, Elizabeth, the mother of six and pregnant with her seventh, took charge of the paper, editing it with competence. (It has been estimated that as many as a dozen colonial women also became newspaper publishers under similar conditions.) Elizabeth Timothy remained in charge of the *Gazette* until 1740, when she relinquished control to her eldest son when he came of age.

Colonial Newspapers and Magazines

Like the coranto publishers before them, colonial newspaper publishers were much more likely to collect stories from other newspapers and sources at hand rather than go into the field and gather news firsthand. Fast-breaking news as we know it was not the province of the colonial newspaper. The local news—of a fire, or accident—flashed around the small colonial towns by word of mouth. The printed news was from afar. It came in newspapers from Europe, or in a letter which the receiver shared with the newspaper publisher. Highly important to colonial editors were the exchanges, the newspapers the publisher received in exchange for subscriptions to his own newspaper. Every editor borrowed freely from these exchanges, which served as a rudimentary press association. Items picked up at the coffeehouse, or gleaned from a chat with a sea captain, also helped fill out the paper. Franklin, like other publishers, printed such items as recipes and "proven" formulas for the cure of rabies. Most publishers also developed a close circle of friends who contributed articles and commentaries much the same way James Franklin's Hell Fire Club wrote political essays for his New England *Courant*.

Printer/publisher Andrew Bradford stole the idea for printing a magazine from Benjamin Franklin, then published the first colonial magazine in 1741, beating Franklin into print by three days. His *American Magazine* or *Monthly View of the Political States of the British Colonies* lasted only three months, however. Franklin's *General Magazine and Historical Chronical for All the British Plantations in America* lasted six. Of the one hundred magazines attempted before 1800, 60 percent did not complete their first year of publication. A poor and expensive postal service and a lack of cross-colony or national advertising made publishing an all-colony magazine difficult. What is more, collecting delinquent subscriptions was next to impossible. At the same time, the magazines themselves had little popular appeal. Most were "museums," or collections of poems, sermons, medical advice, and political essays. They were published for the few colonials who could keep a private library, and also with the hope of impressing readers in England with the high degree of culture and sophistication that had developed in the raw New World.

Advocating Separation and Revolution

With the end of the French and Indian war, the Mother country began to levy special taxes to reduce the war debt. The taxes were collected in addition to those assessed by colonial legislatures, adding resentment to that already felt for other represssive British bureaucratic blunders. Also important to the unrest was an emerging struggle between middle class elements who believed aristocrats in colonial society were too much in control, and the Tories, who remained loyal to the Crown. (They did so, historian Edwin Emery has suggested, in hopes of continuing to govern by right of property, heredity, position, and tradition, or through the attributes of nobility.) The middle class opponents were lawyers, printers, business people, and ministers who pressed for a more democratic order. One of them, patriot Sam Adams of Massachusetts, raised the cry of "no taxation without representation" in 1764, before the first special tax was passed.

The first of the taxes, the Stamp Act, came in 1765. It required that all legal documents, official papers, books, and newspapers, be printed on stamped paper—with the stamp signifying the tax had been paid with the price of the paper. Newspapers were taxed one penny per four pages, with a separate tax of two shillings on each advertisement. It was a high tax, adding as much as 50 percent to the price of a newspaper. And it hit directly at lawyers and journalists, two of the more vociferous advocates in colonial life. Both came quickly to the forefront of the opposition. Printers filled their papers with accounts of all colonial government proceedings that protested the new tax. They also published the names of stamp tax collectors, along with stories of mobs hanging them in effigy. The act was passed in March, but by November, the time it was to go into effect, public opinion was so inflamed no one dared distribute the stamped paper. The act was repealed in 1767.

The British continued to press the colonies with other taxes on commodities, however, and unhappy dissidents continued to put their case before the colonies with pamphlet and newspaper. Beginning in 1767 the Pennsylvania *Chronicle* published John Dickinson's famous plea to the Mother country for redress of grievances: "Letters From A Farmer in Pennsylvania to the Inhabitants of the British Colonies." The total of twelve articles were reprinted in every newspaper in the colonies in 1767 and 1768. Meanwhile, the more radical Sam Adams was rapidly becoming the leading advocate for separation from England. He organized his Committees of Correspondence to collect and distribute to patriots in every state information and arguments useful to the patriot cause. As journalism–historian Emery has written, Adams realized separation depended on arousing the masses to revolution, and he set about instilling hatred of the enemy, neutralizing logical and reasonable arguments from the opposition, and reducing all issues to black and white. He attacked

A colonial newspaper. Isaiah
Thomas's *Massachusetts Spy.*

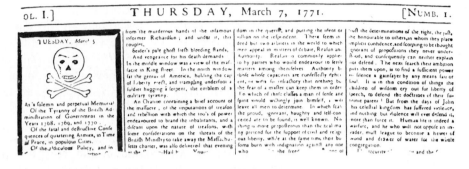

the British elite in devastating style and was rewarded with the title "assassin of reputations." His ability to organize patriot propaganda activities won him the label "master of puppets" from the Tories. His propagandistic masterpiece was the Boston Tea Party in 1773, which Adams contrived with careful political manipulation, and staged so that a large group of spectators was on hand to follow the "Indians" and watch as the tea was dumped dramatically into the harbor. Even Tory governor Thomas Hutchinson of Massachusetts called the Tea Party the "boldest stroke which had yet been struck in America."

The best-selling publication of the period was another proseparation masterpiece. In 1776 Thomas Paine's pamphlet *Common Sense* sold 100,000 copies within the first ten days after it was published.

As the Revolution began, news coverage of the war was at best haphazard. Some eye-witness accounts of battles did appear in patriot newspapers. Most were of battles that took place near the reporting newspaper's hometown. But when the war ended, there was no reporter standing by to record the moment, and the announcement of final victory took weeks to reach most newspapers. One announcement carried the title "Be It Remembered," and stated only that British general Cornwallis and his troops had surrendered to His Excellency General George Washington on the 17th of October, 1781. Washington had written and dispatched the "story" himself.

The Mercantile Press

As the Revolution developed, a new type of newspaper appeared in colonial seaports. Published for the merchant, it contained news of ship arrivals, cargoes, imports for sale, and pirate activity. The first of the mercantile papers was the *Pennsylvania Packet and Advertiser,* founded in 1771. It became a daily in 1784. Its financial success brought wide imitation. By 1800 there were eleven mercantile dailies in New York and Philadelphia and two in Charleston. The mercantile papers are the forerunners of the modern business press and the *Wall Street Journal.* They were more aggressive in gathering news than had been their colonial counterparts. Mercantile news reporters sailed out to board incoming ocean ships, to gather news and exchange newspapers at sea, so they could then rush their news into print as soon as the ship docked. These boat reporters are the first beat reporters of American journalism.

Left and Right: The Partisans

With the British in defeat and driven from the land, the citizens of the new republic discovered an old internal problem. The class conflict that had helped separate them from England appeared again in a new domestic form. On the Left were those who farmed, worked in the cities—the "mechanics" as they were called—along with intellectuals dedicated to social change and experiment. Led by Thomas Jefferson, the Left feared that the establishment of a strong central government would return tyranny and authoritarian monarchy to the country. To the Right were those with property and capital, business people who feared anarchy, mob rule, and the destruction of property rights. The Right looked to George Washington and Alexander Hamilton for leadership.

The two factions came into conflict almost at once regarding the new Constitution, with its proposal for a strong central government. Alexander Hamilton, James Madison, and others of the Right produced a series of eighty-five articles, the *Federalist Papers,* arguing for ratification. The articles were printed and reprinted in newspapers, in pamphlets, and books. Written in plain language under deadline pressure, each developed one basic idea. They are considered the forerunners of the modern American newspaper editorial. They did not win many votes from the Left, however. Jefferson's followers agreed to the Constitution only after the Bill of Rights was added to protect the rights of individuals under the strong central government.

The Partisan Press Period

As the new government formed, both parties established political newspapers to serve their parties and promulgate their two political points of view. Both arranged government jobs for their respective editors. Alexander Hamilton arranged for a government printing job for John Fenno at $2,500 a year so Fenno could edit the *Gazette of the United*

States for the Federalist party. Among other papers that joined the Federalist camp were Noah Webster's *American Minerva* in New York and William Cobbett's *Porcupine's Gazette* in Philadelphia.

Anti-Federalist Thomas Jefferson, meanwhile, obtained a $250-a-year job for poet Phillip Freneau, as government translator. Freneau became the editor of the anti-Federalist *National Gazette.* Other anti-Federalist publishers included brash Benjamin Franklin Bache (old Ben's grandson), publisher of the *Aurora* in Philadelphia.

The debate between the two groups of political newspapers was moderate at first but it soon heated up. What is more, the mercantile papers, and some magazines, began to take sides by assuming partisan affiliations and printing partisan comment and editorials. The attacks became sharp, then bitter, then worse. Federalist Cobbett, writing under the pen name Peter Porcupine, attacked farmers and mechanics as the "swinish multitude." Anti-Federalist Bache, who had a sheer hatred for aristocracy, struck out at George Washington as the epitome of all aristocrats. Bache called him the "debaucher" of the American nation, and found and printed reports Washington had taken advance pay from the national treasury.

The Extremists and the Alien and Sedition Acts

Finally, extremists in the Federalist Congress struck back, passing the Alien and Sedition Acts of 1798. The former was aimed at the flood of immigrants in the country. The latter made it a crime to write, print, utter, or publish false, scandalous, or malicious writings against the government.

A New Jersey man who wished aloud President John Adams was dead was arrested on the spot. Anti-Federalist U.S. Representative Matthew Lyon was arrested and sentenced to four months in jail, with a $1,000 fine, for calling President Adams pompous and selfish in a personal *letter.* An editor who started a lottery to help pay Lyon's fine was hustled off to jail for aiding a criminal. The Federalists won fourteen indictments and ten convictions under the act, but the public became so alarmed over their power it voted the Federalists out of office in 1800. The acts themselves lapsed in 1801, and were not revived. With them died the worst of the partisan newspapers, and the idea of financial support from government for maintaining political newspapers. The papers that did survive were still political papers—including those mercantile papers that had taken on political affiliations before the mudslinging began—but they were not the scurrilous and vindicative publications young Bache and Peter Porcupine had published. In 1801 Alexander Hamilton founded the *New York Evening Post,* and filled it with high-quality editorials to provide his party with a reputable political newspaper. It became, and still is, the oldest newspaper in the country—although it long ago gave up its political character. Perhaps the most important political newspaper during the first half of the nineteenth century was the *National Intelligencer.* Thomas Jefferson encouraged Samuel Harrison Smith to establish the paper in the nation's new capital in 1800. Smith made it the semiofficial reporter of Congress, and a paper that clearly was politically noncombative. For more than fifty years it continued as such, under Smith and the editors/publishers who succeeded him.

The Growing Nation

The first half of the nineteenth century saw striking developments in the new nation. A new wave of immigrants joined the move westward and into the cities. As important, the illiteracy rate also was declining, and by 1850 was down to about 9 percent of all whites aged twenty years and older. The rise of industry and a growing economy brought money for advertising and the buying of newspapers, magazines, and books.

Congress encouraged the growth of the media with a postal act in 1792. Between 1820 and 1860 the number of post offices increased from 4,500 to 28,000. Pursuing an extensive program in canal and road building, Congress extended post road mileage from 72,000 to 140,000 miles during the same period. That these improvements contributed to media growth is seen in the fact that by 1830 90 percent of all U.S. mail was subscriber and exchange newspapers.

The Printing Revolution

Important changes in print technology encouraged media growth, too. Printing presses during the American Revolution were basically the same presses Johann Gutenberg knew. Improved hand presses, such as the Washington Hand Press of 1827, were taken West into the small towns.

In Europe in 1811 Friedrich Koenig constructed a steam-powered flat-bed press. David Napier, following the same design, constructed a steam press for the New York *Advertiser* in 1825. By 1847 Richard Hoe had introduced a press that would make twenty thousand impressions an hour. It used two opposing cylinders, the type fixed to the cylinder to make the imprint. It was so fast it was called the "lightning" press. Unfortunately, to keep the type on the cylinder, it was necessary to lock it in place in one-column widths. Thus, the press produced a newspaper of dull, vertical columns with tombstone-like headlines at the top. (See figure 3.1.) To meet the need for paper for the steam presses, Thomas Gilpin and James Ames developed a machine that would dip fiber from the pulp and then place it on rollers to dry. By 1830 they could produce twenty-four miles of paper a day.

Figure 3.1 (a) The makeup of newspapers printed by early rotary presses took on a tombstone look; (b) full-page stereotyping, on the other hand, opened page makeup to banner headlines and large pictures.

One of Hoe's "lightning" presses in the New York *Tribune*, 1861.

Magazines and Magazinists

With the social and technological changes came a new range of magazines for the American reader. Between 1801 and 1827 Joseph Dennie published *The Port Folio* a witty, bohemian magazine that satirized the crudities of American life. One example: How do you preserve an empty bench in a crowded coffeehouse? Plop your feet on the bench and pick your teeth.

In 1815 *The North American Review* reached out to the serious intellectual. Henry W. Longfellow, Ralph W. Emerson, and Mark Twain contributed to it over the years. It was published into the World War II era.

In 1821 Samuel C. Atkinson and Charles Alexander founded the *Saturday Evening Post* as a literary miscellany or anthology. The *Post* featured stories by Edgar Allan Poe, Harriet Beecher Stowe, and Nathaniel Hawthorne, among others. One year's subscription cost two and a half dollars. There were ninety thousand *Post* subscribers before the Civil War.

In 1830 Louis A. Godey founded one of the most famous of nineteenth century women's magazines: *Godey's Lady's Book*. His gifted copublisher was feminist Sarah Josepha Hale, the author of the poem "Mary's Lamb." Godey's magazine was not the best of the women's magazines, but it was the most popular. It featured hand-colored engravings, articles on manners and morals, and sentimental stories that won it a circulation of 100,000 by 1861.

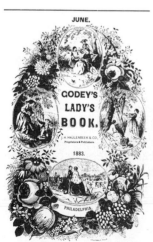

In 1850 Harper Brothers book publishers introduced *Harper's Monthly* as a low-cost collection of pirated stories by Charles Dickens, William Thackery, and Wilkie Collins; it also featured large, woodcut illustrations. It won fifty thousand readers its first year.

The new magazines were written by a new professional: the "magazinist," as Edgar Allan Poe called him. For the first time in American history, men and women found they could earn their living by working or writing for magazines. Poe received five dollars a page for his stories. Nathaniel Parker Willis, the "star" writer of the period, commanded eleven dollars a page.

The Publisher Pirates

American book publishers, on the other hand, were still without capital to finance unknown American writers. Books had small readerships, and any investment in the publication of an unknown writer was a large gamble for a slight profit. It was much safer to pirate known English writers. The most pirated author of the day, Sir Walter Scott, lost an estimated $500,000 in royalties from American editions that sold for one-fourth the price of the regular British copies. Two pirated editions of Scott's *Waverly* were published in the United States. As cutthroat competition between pirating publishers grew, the major publishers moved to end it by agreeing to award printing "rights" to the publisher who paid for the advance sheets of a foreign book. The agreement favored the well-to-do publishers, such as Harper Brothers, since they could outbid the competition for advance sheets. Still, the agreement did bring some degree of respectability to an otherwise disreputable profession. The practice of sharing publication costs with authors continued in America until the 1850s.

The "Cheap" Novel

The pirated fiction market was so attractive some newspaper printers also began offering pirated novels in "story newspapers" for six cents a copy. Distribution of the story papers was dealt a crippling blow in 1845 when the post office began charging book rates for their mailing. The low-cost novel finally came to America when the sentimental novel, written by women, for women, was introduced in the 1850s. The genre soon set sales records, outstripping such competition as the pirated editions of Dickens and Thackery and established American writers like Herman Melville and Henry David Thoreau. We seldom hear of Fanny Fern, Maria Susanna Cummins, or Mrs. E. D. E. N. Southworth today. They were the best-selling writers of their time, helping establish the popular, "cheap" novel as a staple of American publishing.

The Penny Press

The 1828 Presidential election of Andrew Jackson—the "darling of the masses"—and the appearance of low-cost magazines and books reflected the growing importance of the common person in the nation's cultural and political life. The first mass newspaper was issued in 1833. Its publisher was Benjamin Day, and it was named the New York *Sun* ("It Shines for All"). It was filled with local, sometimes violent, human interest stories, tearjerkers—one about a young man trapped in a cave-in the day before his wedding—and guffaws about night court riff-raff. One series of stories in the *Sun* on a marvelous new telescope reported that man-bat inhabitants had been sighted on the moon. Circulation leaped to nineteen thousand readers. After writer Richard Adams Locke admitted it all was a hoax, *Sun* readers laughed and circulation jumped to thirty thousand.

The *Sun* was fresh and breezy in comparison with the abstract political newspapers, and it was much less expensive, too. The political papers were distributed to subscribers for about six cents a copy—the price of a pint of whisky—and would have cost, in today's terms, about three and a half dollars an issue. Day recognized that working people seldom had enough money at one time to buy a subscription, and so had the *Sun* hawked about the streets for one cent a copy.

Thirty-five "penny" newspapers were started in New York alone in the 1830s. Most failed, but some of the ones that survived became important names in American newspaper journalism.

One of them was the New York *Herald,* founded by James Gordon Bennett in 1835. Bennett had been both a boat reporter for the mercantile press and a political correspondent in Washington. He imitated the *Sun's* breezy style, but he filled the *Herald* with hard, if sensational, news reports. He reported news from the police beat, from Washington, and even developed society news and a letters column. He was proud of his Wall Street "money page," and was offering sports news long before others saw the need. The *Herald,* one journalism historian has written, "led the pack" in hounding news from all areas. When the newspaper came under fire from a group of clergymen as blasphemous, Bennett answered the charge by sending his best reporters out to cover the church beats. He had found another neglected public he could cultivate. Students of journalism history consider him the father of American reporting.

Another was the New York *Tribune,* founded by Horace Greeley in 1841. Greeley became the master advocate of his day. If his editorials were bombastic, even irrational, he fostered and supported the important issues: western expansion ("Go West, young man"), feminism, equal distribution of wealth, and abolition. He introduced the interview story to journalism when he traveled to Salt Lake City to question Brigham Young about Mormonism, slavery, and polygamy.

The third important paper was the New York *Daily Times,* founded by Henry J. Raymond in 1851. Raymond, at one time head of the Republican Party, strived to present the news dispassionately and with "decensy," as he put it. Bennett's poor taste and Greeley's pomposity were repugnant to the *Times,* which quickly gained the reputation as reasonable and objective, with excellent foreign news coverage.

Advertisers soon recognized that one ad in the *Sun, Herald, Tribune,* or *Times* produced better advertising results and cost less than a dozen ads in as many political papers. Such was the wide audience appeal of the penny papers. And since apolitical news coverage appeared to be the most popular content with Penny Press readers, the publishers began to experiment with new methods of gathering news to please them. Bennett used steamships, railroads, and even pigeons to bring stories to the *Herald.* More important, the reporter became a regular member of the Penny Press newspaper staff.

The Telegraph and Instant News

When Samuel Morse put his telegraph into operation in 1844, newspapers were quick to adapt it to news reporting. In 1846 a group of New York papers formed a cooperative to share costs of telegraphing state news reports. In 1848 the high cost of pony express and telegraph dispatches from the Mexican War led six New York, Philadelphia, and Baltimore papers to form the New York Associated Press. The new association shared costs of telegraphing news and maintaining boats to meet incoming steamers. It also agreed to sell association news to other papers. The agreement marked the beginning of the press association.

By the 1860s one newspaper story in ten was a telegraphed story. When the Atlantic cable was successfully completed in 1866, the Associated Press and the nation were linked to London, and a service that delivered "instant" news across the North Atlantic.

The Media and the Civil War

One of the most significant groups of publishers to date in the United States was the abolitionist publishers, the early, determined advocates of the abolition of slavery before the Civil War. All were radicals for their time. And although they did not reach vast audiences with their publications, they managed to keep their cause alive with the faithful who read their low-circulation publications. Later, others with larger-circulation publications were able to popularize the ideas with the general public. As has been pointed out, the American Civil War was not caused by slavery, but it was the cause for which the war was fought.

The Atlantic Cable comes ashore on American soil in Newfoundland, July 27, 1866.

The Abolitionist Press

One of the earliest abolitionist papers was published by two black freemen, John Russwurm and Samuel Cornish, to tell "our" story, as they put it. Between 1827 and 1829, their *Freedom's Journal* made ruthless attacks on slavery, then ceased publication, probably for lack of funds. Frederick Douglass was the leading black journalist of the nineteenth century. Douglass escaped from slavery in Maryland, managed to gain a formal education, then wrote a moving autobiography of his life in slavery. He edited *The Ram's Horn* and *The North Star* in 1847, with the latter becoming a part of *Frederick Douglass' Paper* in 1851.

William Lloyd Garrison founded *The Liberator* in 1831, often living on little more than bread and water to keep it going. Although *The Liberator's* readership never rose beyond three hundred, the state of Massachusetts was so concerned about its sharp, anti-slavery attacks that it almost refused to export it on one occasion.

Elijah Lovejoy paid the highest price of all the abolitionists. In 1835 in western Illinois near St. Louis, an angry mob killed him as he prepared again to print his anti-slavery newspaper.

Horace Greeley adopted the abolitionist issue into the editorial policies of his New York *Tribune* in 1849; other newspapers followed suit. Probably one of the most effective of all the abolitionist advocates was Harriet Beecher Stowe. Her novel, *Uncle Tom's Cabin,* published in 1852, sold 305,000 copies in twelve months in the United States alone.

Reporting the Civil War

A flood of reporters joined the Northern army soldiers as they went into the field to fight the war. Bennett's *Herald* alone spent one million dollars on war coverage. If many of the Union army regulars were green and unproved, many of the reporters—called "specials" by the army—were hardly the professional correspondents of modern times. There was at least one incident of faked news in field reports. What troubled the Northern generals, however, was that the specials telegraphed news reports about the army directly to their newspapers and, the generals felt, indirectly to the Confederates. As the conflict mounted, reporters, fearful the army might retaliate against them for the stories they wrote, began using pen names (Agate, for example). Finally, General Sherman arrested one New York *Herald* reporter and threatened to hang him as a spy. President Lincoln, accepting the point, intervened and established the policy that reporters, to be accredited, had to be acceptable to the general in the field. The practice still is adhered to today.

In the South, reporting the war took a different slant. J. S. Thrasher, superintendent of the PA, or Press Association of the Confederate states, was able to arrange a voluntary censorship plan with Confederate generals that worked almost until the end of the war. In an effort to maintain good relations with the generals, Thrasher ordered his reporters to withhold all opinions from their reports. PA's coverage, therefore, was more objective, a step toward the growing trend in objective reporting.

Some Wartime Reading

Understandably, the Civil War soldier looked for escape from his daily exposure to the war. He could find it in magazines—the *Saturday Evening Post* or the more erudite *Harper's Monthly*—but cheaper fare also was available. There were the story papers such as the New York *Ledger,* which gave its readers collections of short stories in newspaper form. The *Ledger,* published by inventive Robert Bonner, had been a mercantile paper. By converting the paper into a short story paper, Bonner had attracted 400,000 story-reading clients even before the war began. For a few pennies more, the soldier could buy a dime novel published by Erastus Beadle. Beadle's formula was to promote the spirit of individualism while lauding the worth of the common people—in seventy-five thousand words. He printed sixty-five thousand copies of each dime novel—to achieve what was considered wide distribution at that time.

Toward a Modern Media System: Some Trends and Technology

Immigration, the westward movement, the growth of the cities, a growing economy, and improving technology continued to spur print media growth and print media audiences after the Civil War. Educational facilities were increasing and illiteracy was slipping lower. Between 1870 and 1890 illiteracy fell from 20 percent of all Americans ten years of age and older to about 13 percent. A huge reading audience was developing,

The half-tone process: dots that print pictures.

with the money to buy media and media-advertised products. And media management found new, improved technology was required to reach it.

New, high-speed electric presses came into use. The web-fed, perfecting press, that printed on both sides of a continuous roll or web of paper, had an attachment at the end of the press to cut and fold the printed papers. In use before the Civil War, it became the standard of the newspaper industry in the 1870s and 1880s. The electric presses could print first six, then eight newspaper pages in one continuous run.

Stereotyping, the casting of a curved lead plate from which to print, had been used in book publishing before the Civil War. R. Hoe & Company produced a newspaper press that used stereotypes in 1861. The process was widely adopted by printers after the war. It added speed to newspaper printing but, more important, it also improved newspaper makeup. As noted earlier, before stereotyping, it was necessary to lock type and illustrations on the rotating press drums (see figure 3.1). The solid stereotype plate locked the type and pictures firmly together before they were put on the press, and allowed headlines across columns and illustrations of virtually any width. With stereotyping, the modern "banner," or full-page headline, and large, two- and three-column illustrations came into daily use.

The Fourdrinier paper-making process, imported from Germany in 1867, greatly reduced the cost of paper made from wood pulp, and lowered the price of newspapers and other publications.

The quality of illustrations improved greatly, too. Zincograph etching and then photoengraving were introduced to newspapers and magazines. It was not possible to print pictures—including those taken by Matthew Brady during the Civil War—until Frederick E. Ives perfected his halftone process in 1886. Ives discovered he could break the dark and light areas in the photographs into masses of dots, which could be engraved in a plate to imprint ink.

The Lovell–Bredenberg automatic periodical covering machine was introduced in the 1890s. It could stitch magazines at a rate of fifteen hundred magazines an hour. With improvements, it soon reached twenty-four hundred an hour.

The typewriter and the telephone both were adopted by the newspaper and magazine office in the 1870s. The typewriter produced copy more clearly and more quickly than handwriting. The telephone proved to be an invaluable tool in gathering news. Before its adoption the best way for a reporter to get news was with the horse-drawn trolley. With the telephone, a "leg man" (some were women, of course) who went out to cover news could call back to a newspaper rewrite "man" (who also might be a woman) who could turn facts into a press-ready story before the "leg man" could get back to the office. The roles were only two of many that were developing in the newspapers of the day. They are still important in news work today.

The Development of Advertising: The Ad Agency

The growth in production of goods—the industrial growth of the nation—and the rapid spread and development of the newspaper and magazine media began to create growing pains for the media even before the Civil War. The nation and the media were expanding so rapidly it often was difficult for advertisers to know where they could best place their advertising. The shoe factory in New England could manufacture more than enough shoes and boots to sell close to home. To expand production it needed to find newspapers and magazines that reached customers in, say, the South and West. Newspaper publishers at the same time had little way of finding advertisers. Advertising was important to newspapers—by the 1850s 45 percent of Bennett's New York *Herald* was comprised of advertising—but publishers were obliged to settle for the advertising that came to them "through the door." (See chapter 5.) Into the gap between merchant and advertiser stepped the advertising agent, a sales representative for ad space in several newspapers. The first of these was Volney B. Palmer, who became the ad representative for a group of newspapers in 1841. Palmer, like other ad agents, sought out merchants and sold them ad space in the newspapers he represented for the sales commissions the newspapers paid.

The agents soon found, however, that ad rates were highly unstable, and that they could sell ads at the going rate or below to merchants; they then could bargain for even lower rates from newspapers, and keep the change. After the Civil War, the more enterprising agents discovered they could buy large blocks of ad space at wholesale prices, then sell smaller sections to merchants, at rates below those the merchants would pay if they bought directly from the newspapers. Ad space wholesaling had advantages for newspapers, advertisers, and the ad agents as well. It helped newspaper publishers by giving them needed cash, with little effort on their part, for advertising space. It benefited merchant advertisers because they saved a great deal of money in ad costs. The ad space wholesalers, of course, were left with handsome profits.

But when the ad wholesalers tried to go one step further and establish themselves as agents for both the media and the advertising customer, they encountered sharp conflicts of interest. The agent who assumed responsibility for selling all of a paper's ad space, and who also agreed to take charge of ad placement, often felt the displeasure of both the paper and the advertiser. Publishers grew angry if they did not get advertising from all the merchant clients the agent represented. On the other hand, merchant advertisers felt cheated if their ads turned up in an agent's newspaper that seemed an improper vehicle for their product. Possibilities for cheating on all sides made the situation even worse. Between 1875 and 1890 responsible ad agents, such as George P. Rowell, N. W. Ayer and Son, and J. Walter Thompson, adopted the policy of first serving, or representing, their advertising clients. To do so, they began to develop services related to the planning, producing, and placing of advertising, all major functions of the modern ad agency. One holdover from the old ad agent days remains in agency practice today. The ad agency prepares and places advertising for its client, but it still takes its pay in the commissions paid by the ad medium in which the ads are placed.

Some Notes on Style

From the days of the colonial newspaper until well after the Civil War, American advertisements were small and often dull. Colonial printers did try to brighten their ads with illustrations, but the Penny Press publishers, in order to discourage the ridiculous and bombastic claims of the patent medicine manufacturers, limited their ads to one column in width, to small, agate type, and no artwork. The result was an ad very much like the modern want ad. (See p. 66.)

The break with the dull gray ad began with resourceful story paper publisher Robert Bonner, who advertised the features of his paper, the New York *Ledger,* in Bennett's *Herald.* Bonner found he could stay within the one-column width, keep the type small, and still produce a lively ad message by repeating sentences, or phrases, over and over again. For example, one of Bonner's ads read:

Read Mrs. Southwold's new story in the *Ledger.*
Read Mrs. Southwold's new story in the *Ledger.*
Read Mrs. Southwold's new story in the *Ledger.*

Bonner filled columns, then pages, with first one, then another simple announcement, repeated again and again.

There can be no doubt that stereotype plate printing also contributed greatly to display advertising as we know it, with its pictures and varied type. But probably the man who contributed most to the style of advertising in the nineteenth century was the great press agent, Phineas T. (P. T.) Barnum. Barnum's genius was his ability not only to know what the American public wanted, but also his ability to advertise or publicize it so as to attract the public to it. His was an expansive style. His motto, "The Greatest Show on Earth," is reflected in such slogans as Goodyear's "The Greatest Name in Rubber" and the Chicago *Tribune's* slogan "The World's Greatest Newspaper."

Barnum's promotional talent is illustrated by a scheme he used to promote a museum he had gained control of—the American Museum of

New York. He paid a man to go into the street and lay five bricks on the sidewalk, one at a time, march around them, pick them up, and move on, then lay the bricks again—all without speaking. He was told to make sure he worked the military routine so he was back at the museum door every hour. The curious, silent drama always drew a crowd, some of whom entered the museum after the performance reached the front door. Barnum had gained customers as well as much free newspaper advertising before police called a halt to the stunt in the interest of public safety.

Many who attempted to imitate Barnum made the mistake of attributing his success to the hoopla in his style, and seemed to take too seriously Barnum's suggestion there was a "sucker born every minute." Barnum's own warnings about publicity included the belief it was not possible to fool the buyer with advertising more than one time. The product should always be satisfactory, he believed, since the customer who was tricked into buying a shoddy product would not be easily tricked again. Whatever negative is said about him, Barnum's main contribution was that he, with his own striking successes, encouraged reluctant merchants to accept advertising as an important tool of business.

In the 1880s and 1890s as advertising appeared with more space and a brighter style, slogans and trade characters became part of advertising parcels. With the growth of industry and the availability of more and more products, there was a trend away from merely announcing products and toward persuading customers to buy. (See chapter 13.) Thomas J. Barrat of the English Pears' Soap firm was able to convince Henry Ward Beecher, the famous American religious leader, to testify for Pears', although Beecher had never used the soap. Beecher contributed the phrase "Cleanliness is next to Godliness" to Pears' advertising and to American folklore. Other Pears' ads included the memorable exchange, "How do you spell soap?" and the reply, "Why P–E–A–R–S, of course." (The version heard more recently begins by asking how to spell *relief.*) Aunt Jemima, the Prudential rock, the Quaker Oats Quaker, the Cracker Jack sailor, and the slogan "The Beer that Made Milwaukee Famous" all came into being during this period.

The Developing Newspaper: Pulitzer and the New Journalism

Newspaper publishers who had worked hard to cover the Civil War found the second half of the nineteenth century an era of equally great challenges in reporting and investigation. In the West, there was the bungling and dishonesty that created the Indian wars, while the East discovered it was inundated by corruption in government—especially city government. In New York City alone the now infamous Boss Tweed ring casually milked $200 million from public funds before news exposés in the New York *Times* and *Harper's Magazine* alerted the public

Joseph Pulitzer.

to the problem. The newspapers of the second half of the nineteenth century became, more than ever, newspapers that reported and investigated government and industry—especially the robber barons, who exploited opportunities to steal from government and American business enterprises.

The newspaperman of the post–Civil War period who set the standards for accurate, investigative journalism, and newspaper crusades in the public interest, and who did more than any other to shape the modern American newspaper was Joseph Pulitzer. Pulitzer was born in Europe of a Magyar–Jewish father and an Austro–German mother. He was raised in a home of wealth and refinement and given a private school education. Interested in a military career, he volunteered to fight with the Union army near the end of the Civil War. But poor eyesight and disillusionment with military life caused him to leave the service at the end of the war. He worked his way across country to St. Louis, where he took a job as a newspaper reporter. With hard work and a shrewd business sense he was able, in 1878, to combine two newspapers into the St. Louis *Post-Dispatch*. His success in St. Louis, and unfortunate publicity from a shooting, which saw an editor kill an irate reader in self-defense in the newspaper office, encouraged him to expand his operations to New York. With profits from the *Post-Dispatch,* he made a down payment on the all-but-failing New York *World* in 1883. He quickly paid the balance with profits from the improved *World.*

Pulitzer's journalism has been called the new journalism. His formula married Barnum-like promotion with extensive news coverage. He filled his papers with coupons, contests, self-promotions, and stunts, but also with vital news of the city, and a well-developed editorial section. As journalism historian Frank Luther Mott has written, Pulitzer's policies put a "hula girl in front of a cathedral." The contests, and stunts of the hula girl, were designed to attract the reader into the cathedral-like editorial section of the paper. The stunts included sending female reporter Nellie Bly (Elizabeth Cochran) around the world, a la Jules Verne, writing comments as she went. World promotions included holding strawberry festivals for children each year. It was the *World* that led the successful campaign to raise the $100,000 needed to pay for the pedestal of the Statute of Liberty. On the more serious side were such revealing, inside stories as the one Nellie Bly obtained by committing herself to an insane asylum to report on conditions inside. Standard Oil, the errant railroads, Bell Telephone, and other giant corporations also came under *World* scrutiny in the 1880s and 1890s. Pulitzer's journalism was called the "new journalism" for its impartiality in gathering and reporting news, its independence from partisan pressures in editorials, and its crusading in the public interest—all done in an interesting, entertaining style.

Elizabeth Cochran Seaman, or "Nellie Bly," who often put herself in the middle of a news story to write about it.

Hearst and Yellow Journalism

Chief among Pulitzer's admirers was William Randolph Hearst. The son of a wealthy mining family, young Hearst convinced his father to give him control of one of the family holdings, the San Francisco *Examiner.* He was only twenty-four years old when he became publisher/editor in 1887. Using Pulitzer's methods, with embellishments, Hearst made the *Examiner* into a brilliant, enterprising, highly sensational paper. Within five years, it was the second most profitable newspaper in the country. His dream was to own a newspaper in every major American city. In 1895 he bought the struggling New York *Journal,* and moved into direct competition with Joseph Pulitzer. To make the *Journal* competitive with Pulitzer's *World,* Hearst set about hiring a staff—Joseph Pulitzer's staff. When Hearst hired R. F. Outcault, creator of the *World's* popular cartoon series, "The Yellow Kid of Hogan's Alley," Pulitzer replaced the cartoonist with another artist. The result was that both the *World* and the *Journal* carried "Yellow Kid" strips that featured a grinning, moon-faced boy who wore a one-piece yellow night shirt. In time, the popular night-shirted kid was used to promote the circulation of both newspapers, and his presence around town gave New Yorkers their symbol for the journalism Hearst had created: yellow journalism. The term denoted scare headlines, superficial writing, faked pictures and interviews, along with Hearst's great support for the underdog. To give one example, in its agitation for war with Spain the *Journal* published sensational stories of Spanish atrocities, reporting on one occasion that a young American lady was stripped and searched on the open deck of the USS *Olivette* by brutal Spanish officials. The story was illustrated with suggestive line drawings. The reporter later admitted, however, despite the written descriptions and artist's sketches, the lady actually was searched in a private state room by a police matron.

An even darker side of Hearst's journalism is shown in his attitude toward Spain in its war with Cuba. The cause of the explosion that destroyed the battleship *Maine* is still uncertain, but the *Journal* attributed the blast first to "an enemy" and then to Spain. As the *Journal's* circulation increased, Pulitzer's *World* joined in; both fanned the flames of war, reporting that a war frenzy was sweeping the country and urging the president and Congress to act. The daily circulation of each paper passed the one million mark, then hit one and a half million during the war itself.

By 1900 one-third or more of the daily newspapers in major American cities had adopted Hearst's yellow journalism methods. The approach also had a strong impact on newspapers that did not adopt it. The New York *Times,* for example, had had an exemplary history in public

William Randolph Hearst.

R. F. Outcault's barefooted
and night-shirted "Yellow Kid."

service and investigative reporting in the 1870s. But after the 1880s, the
paper's management had become old fashioned and failed to compete
with the more flamboyant Pulitzer and Hearst. The *Times* had a circulation of only nine thousand and was losing a thousand dollars a day when
Tennessee publisher Adolph S. Ochs arrived to take charge of it in 1896.
He saved the paper by avoiding the yellow journalism approach. He first
lowered the price from three cents to a penny, then began to build the
paper's reputation for reliable news information in finance, government,
and politics—printing complete texts of important speeches and documents. While Hearst ran flashy, scare headlines, the *Times* used smaller,
accurate ones, along with careful editing and good printing, to foster the
impression of dependability. Within a year, circulation increased to
75,000, and advertising by one-half. Within ten years it had risen to
150,000; in ten more, to three hundred thousand.

The Mass Magazine: Munsey, Bok, and Curtis

THE
LADIES' HOME JOURNAL

APRIL 1895   TEN CENTS
The · Curtis Publishing · Company · Philadelphia

Imaginative promotion and covers helped the *Ladies' Home Journal* to success. This cover by Charles Dana Gibson who created the "Gibson Girl" appeared as an ad in *Harper's Monthly*.

McClure and the Muckrakers

As magazine historian Theodore Peterson has put it, Frank Munsey, Edward Bok, and S. S. McClure "pretty much invented the modern magazine." Munsey struggled for years to make his *Munsey's* and *Golden Argosy* magazines profitable. At one point he was so short of funds he couldn't afford to buy fiction for the two publications so he wrote it all himself to keep them going. Finally, in 1893, he took a calculated gamble. He dropped the price of his magazines below cost, theorizing the lower price would attract more readers and therefore greater circulation, which would in turn allow him to more than make up losses at the newsstands with higher advertising rates. It worked. His circulations and advertising began to rise dramatically, and so did his profits. Others soon followed his example.

Cyrus H. K. Curtis also took his *Ladies' Home Journal* into mass circulation with lower newsstand costs, and a combination of child care, cooking and fashion articles, sentimental fiction, and imaginative promotion. In 1889 Curtis hired dashing male editor Edward Bok to direct the woman's magazine, gaining not only an excellent editor but the promotional value of Bok's gender. (A man editing a woman's magazine!) He paid Bok a high salary, which he used for promotional value as well—in the same way modern professional football teams promote the high salaries they pay recruits. Bok meanwhile proved to be a great editor. He introduced the magazine convention of changing the cover each issue, and of "jumping" stories to the back of the magazine to improve the value of ad space there. He even wrote a successful advice column for young women readers under the pen name Ruth Ashmore. Bok's *Journal,* by putting the American woman on a pedestal, was pushing for a circulation of one million by 1900.

Many of the new mass magazines were more than new covers and advice columns, however. As he traveled in the West and Midwest selling syndicated fiction to newspapers in the 1880s and 1890s, S. S. McClure discovered a huge audience had developed for a magazine of public affairs. The country wanted to know more about its government and its leaders, and about the huge corporations that had come into such prominence in the nation's affairs. In 1893 McClure and partner John Sanborn Phillips founded *McClure's Magazine.* They filled it with excellent fiction, pictures of the prominent, and thoroughly researched reports on government and corporate affairs. Reporter Ida Tarbell's "History of the Standard Oil Company" depicted that huge company as having risen by graft and corruption. Lincoln Steffen's "Shame of the Cities" focused on corruption in city government, reporting, for example, that Philadelphia's voting lists were padded with the names of dead dogs and patriots

Ida Tarbell, a premiere reporter of the muckraking period.

(Thomas Jefferson, etc.) to allow politicians to stuff ballot boxes. The impact of *McClure's* was great. In the 1900s other magazines and writers joined the trend toward attacking corrupt government and business. The leading magazine muckrakers—*Collier's, Cosmopolitan,* and *Everybody's*—explored subjects from corruption in the Senate to drugs in patent medicine. In 1906 novelist Upton Sinclair's *The Jungle* shocked the nation with its depiction of gross conditions in the meat-packing industry. Congress passed the Pure Food and Drug Act the same year.

Meanwhile, President Theodore Roosevelt, disgusted by the sensational, sometimes sleazy attacks gave the muckrakers their name. He took the title from a character in *Pilgrim's Progress,* the one who seemed to prefer raking through the muck at his feet rather than looking up at the stars. The public, too, soon sickened of the excesses of many of the investigations, and muckraking passed from public favor.

The Public Be Damned

The attacks of the press, and especially their excesses, put American business—innocent and guilty alike—on the defensive. Business had put faith in a "silence is golden" policy for sometime, believing in an absolute right to do business. Some had come to view reporters as manifest evil, and their right to ignore the public as God-given. The phrase that seemed to cap the attitude of business was attributed to railroad magnate William Vanderbilt. When asked about plans to drop a train from his company's schedule despite the public interest in it, Vanderbilt was said to reply, "The public be damned." He added the company would act in its own rather than in the public's interests. Paired with the thievery and deceit of big business reported by the muckrakers the phrase took on an aura of arrogance.

To defend themselves against more and more frequent attacks in the press, many business giants turned to press agents. No doubt some saw the agents' role as one of covering up problems. And some press agents soon were involved in whitewashing operations designed to thwart the public will rather than correct any false impressions distributed by the press. The first independent press agency, the Publicity Agency, was founded in 1900, and ended its career in 1905 after it joined the railroad interests in an unethical campaign to stop much-needed regulation of the roads.

Standing clear of both the secrecy of the business world and the whitewashing of the unethical press agents was the remarkable Ivy Ledbetter Lee. Lee was a newspaperman who turned to publicity because he found he had trouble keeping body and soul together on newspaper pay. Lee believed that good performance, truth, and honesty were the best means of winning public approval. As a publicist he followed an "open bureau" policy. When an accident on the Pennsylvania Railroad brought a call from company officials to restrict information on the disaster, Lee, as publicist for the railroad, reversed the order. Instead he called for a special car to carry news reporters to the scene, where he helped reporters with details and picture coverage. When the New York Central hushed up another accident soon after, newspaper editorials condemned the Central but praised the Pennsylvania, giving it good press for the first time in years.

Signs of the Times

The departmentalized newspapers, magazines, and book publishing companies at the turn of the century were, for the most part, the media organizations we know today. The colonial printer, with his presses and apprentices, had disappeared with the past. The major printing firms had grown so large it was no longer possible for publishers—especially newspaper publishers—to maintain personal contact with their staffs the way Greeley and Bennett had at mid-century. City editors had been added to newspapers in the 1850s, night and telegraph editors in the 1870s, literary editorial, sports, and fashion editors about 1900. Pulitzer's *World* had thirteen hundred full-time employees, and an operating budget of $2 million by the end of the century. The organized labor movement had created four highly specialized back shop or printers' unions. Those in charge of the large print media organizations were no longer poets or

Ivy Ledbetter Lee, for many, the father of modern public relations.

reporters or writers; they were corporate managers, tuned to labor problems, mail rates, distribution, advertising sales, and profits. The management function was institutionalized in 1887 with the formation of the American Newspaper Publishers' Association which became—and remains a leading speaker for the newspaper industry.

The division of labor within the media organization had also reached modern standards. The newspaper that began in colonial times as a sideline in a print shop had developed into an institution in its own right, with the ability to cover its home city with a web of reporters. Police, city hall, and fire departments were covered regularly, as were other vital government agencies. Muckraking died, but a more serious type of investigative reporting eventually took its place. In time, the troubles of the Great Depression and the social-economic revolution of the New Deal years continued the demand for more reporting and news interpretation, bringing the political columnist—foreign and domestic—the investigative reporter, and the specialist (agricultural, financial, environmental, economic reporter, etc.) into newspaper columns.

The scene also was set for dramatic change and expansion in book and magazine publishing. The United States signed its first international copyright bill in 1891, setting the stage for renovations. The inexpensive, pirated novel or fiction piece was gone, and fiction editors were forced more than ever to search for outside talent and new material to print. The editor who encouraged authors while critiquing his or her work was added to magazine and book publishing staffs. Another new addition was the outside literary agent who acted as go-between for publisher and writer, screening literary work for the publisher, while serving the author as friend, protector, and helpful critic.

A hint of a major upcoming problem began at *McClure's* magazine in 1906, when muckraking publisher McClure began to feel uneasy about the formula of his magazine. It had grossed one million dollars that year, but McClure feared the readership had grown tired of it, and the magazine would fail unless it was changed quickly. He and his partner disagreed on what changes should be made, and so the partner left to join the *American Magazine,* taking a good selection of *McClure's* best investigative writers with him. Unfortunately, McClure was wrong. The change in the magazine—his new formula—brought it to ruin. He had lost contact with his audience. The problem of knowing what the vast, unseen audience wants, stills plagues media management today and is the genesis of a large audience research establishment within the media system.

As important as any of these signs of the times was the idea of newspaper "chains." William Randolph Hearst's dream of a newspaper in every major city never was achieved, but Hearst was able to establish a large group of newspapers in important cities around the country. And Edward Wyllis Scripps, founder of the Scripps-Howard chain of newspapers, was busy building his own group of papers—all tightly edited and dedicated to serving workers in industrial cities. And so even though the large, newspaper companies that dominate daily newspaper publishing today— Knight Rider, Newhouse, Times Mirror,—had not yet been born, they had been conceived.

There were other ideas and media innovations, too. Print dominated much of American life until the 1920s, but by then it felt the impact of the newer, audiovisual media. First the phonograph, then motion pictures, then radio, then television, then all four challenged the print media's hold on audience attention and the advertising dollar. By the 1960s print had become part of the media mix of music, sight and sound, radio news, and television entertainment—something else to choose from among a growing variety of media offerings.

But that is another story.

Summary

The development of communication is buried in our prehistorical past, but we date the beginning of mass communication with the invention of movable type in the fifteenth century. The first printed works were religious texts, followed by newsheets, news books, pamphlets, and editorial journals. Printing was slowed by authoritarian attitudes of government.

The colonial printer survived not only by printing newspapers and magazines but also by pirating books and making lottery tickets. And although the press made important contributions to the Revolutionary War, coverage was haphazard at best.

A second type of newspaper, the mercantile press, the forerunner of the modern business press, evolved in the seacoast cities in the 1770s to serve the merchant class. Following the war, the division of political interests created the partisan press, in which two political parties supported partisan newspapers.

Attitudes toward the importance of the common citizen in social and political life created the first mass newspaper, the Penny Press, and popular, inexpensive novels in the 1830s and 1840s. The Penny Press gave good coverage to the Civil War.

Following the war, newspapers and magazines found corruption in government and corporate business a source of continuing interest for their reading publics. With improved printing technology, typesetting machines, photographs, the telegraph and the telephone, the newspaper began to take on the appearance of the modern newspaper organization.

Advertising evolved from a want ad format. Much of the advertising style of the period was that of P. T. Barnum. The modern ad agency was created out of a need for an intermediary between media and advertiser.

Joseph Pulitzer's nonpartisan new journalism married excellent news coverage and distinguished editorial page direction with dazzling promotions and crusades. William Randolph Hearst copied Pulitzer to create yellow journalism, with scare headlines, fake pictures, and appeals to the underdog. Continuing concern with deceit in government and business produced the muckrakers, and caused many business people to turn to press agents in self-defense. While some were unethical, Ivy Lee called for responsibility, arguing that openness, honesty, good public behavior and policies were the best means of winning public support.

Magazine publishers, meanwhile, learned they could set their price below cost and more than make the loss back through increased advertising produced by large circulations. At the same time, media audiences became so large that publishers had trouble knowing their wants and needs.

Questions for Discussion

1. It has been suggested by several scholars that the media affect the way we think. What might happen if American society suddenly had to revert to the hand press as its principal method of printing? How would the American life-style, government, or business be affected? What would happen to the daily newspaper? The magazine? The book publishing business?

2. The Penny Press was filled with tearjerking stories, even a faked moon telescope story. Have we done away with tearjerkers today? If not, where might we find them? What place in life and human communication do these types of stories have? Are they always more popular than news? For whom?

3. The abolitionists were able to keep their cause alive until the media with more popular appeal adopted it for discussion. What "hot" issues have been kept alive in our society recently? What seems necessary to get vital issues before the public, especially unpopular ones? How do we currently view such topics as tobacco subsidies, licensing of fire arms, or legalization of marijuana?

4. How do you account for the fact that women were editors and reporters of newspapers and magazines in the mid 1800s but relegated to society pages and women's magazines after the turn of the nineteenth century? Did the feminist movement bring this about? The women's magazines? The male-dominated society?

5. Is there any evidence at all that the mass media were invented by a group of successful, heroic figures? If you feel so, describe what the following willful people might have done if they lived in different times:

William Randolph Hearst in the colonial period.
Ivy Lee during the American Revolution.
P. T. Barnum in authoritarian England.
Benjamin Franklin in World War II.

References

Baker, Ira L. "Elizabeth Timothy: America's First Woman Editor." *Journalism Quarterly* 54, no. 2 (1977): 280–85.

Bird, Harry Lewis. *This Fascinating Advertising Business.* Indianapolis: Bobbs-Merrill, 1947.

Comporato, Frank E. *Books for the Millions.* Harrisburg: Stackpole Company, 1971.

Derry, T. K., and Trevor I. Williams. *A Short History of Technology.* New York: Oxford University Press, 1961.

DeVinne, Theo. L. *The Invention of Printing.* New York: Francis Hart, 1876; Gale Research Company, 1969.

Emery, Edwin. *The Press and America.* 3rd ed., Englewood Cliffs, N.J.: Prentice-Hall, 1972.

Hiebert, Ray Eldon. *Courtier to the Crowd.* Ames: Iowa State University Press, 1966.

Hobbes, Thomas. *Leviathan.* New York: Collier Books, 1962.

Kobre, Sidney. *Development of American Journalism.* Dubuque, Iowa: Wm. C. Brown, 1969.

Leder, Lawrence H. *The Meaning of the American Revolution.* Chicago: Quadrangle Books, 1969.

Madison, Charles A. *Book Publishing in America.* New York: McGraw-Hill, 1966.

Mott, Frank Luther. *A History of American Magazines* 4, Cambridge: Harvard University Press, 1956.

———. *American Journalism.* 3rd ed., New York: Macmillan, 1962.

Peterson, R. D. "The Evolution of Advertising Agency Services." *Akron Business and Economic Review,* Summer, 1979, 18–21.

Peterson, Theodore. "Magazines in the Seventies: Whatever Happened to that Nice Old Edward Bok?" In *Mass Media Issues,* edited by Leonard L. Sellers and William L. Rivers. Englewood Cliffs, N.J.: Prentice-Hall, 1977.

Pickett, Calder. *Voices of the Past.* Columbus, Ohio: Grid, Inc., 1977.

Raucher, Alan R. *Public Relations and Business 1900–1929.* Baltimore: Johns Hopkins Press, 1968.

Schwarzlose, Richard A. "The Nation's First Wire Service: Evidence Supporting a Footnote." *Journalism Quarterly* 57, no. 4 (1980): 555–62.

Shaw, Donald L. "News Bias and the Telegraph: A Study of Historical Change." *Journalism Quarterly* 44, no. 1 (1967): 3–12.

———. "At the Crossroads: Change and Continuity in American Press News, 1820–1860" (Paper presented to the History Division, Association for Education in Journalism, annual convention, Michigan State University, East Lansing, August, 1981).

Siebert, Fred S., Theodore Peterson, and Wilbur Schramm. *Four Theories of the Press.* Chicago: University of Illinois Press, 1956.

Smith, Jeffrey A. "James Franklin and Freedom of the Press in Massachusetts and Rhode Island, 1717–1735." (Paper presented to the History Division, Association for Education in Journalism, annual convention, Michigan State University, East Lansing, August, 1981.)

Stewart, Donald H. *The Opposition Press of the Federalist Period.* Albany: State University of New York Press, 1969.

Turner, E. S. *The Shocking History of Advertising.* New York: E. P. Dutton, 1953.

Wood, James Playsted. *Magazines in the United States.* 3rd ed., New York: Ronald Press, 1971.

Chapter
4

Duplicating the Real World: The Audio/Visual Media

Duplicating the real world in sight and sound.

Until the nineteenth century, our only means of capturing and communicating sights and sounds from the world about us were music, art, and mimicry. But in that century a regiment of inventive tinkerers and scientists, spurred by the industrial revolution and the knowledge accumulated in print, grappled with chemicals, wax, and electromagnetic waves to create communication machinery that could duplicate and store sights and sounds the way humans do—and even transmit them across great reaches of space.

First came photography. Close behind it, sound recording. Motion pictures, radio, then television searched for a place with audiences and found it, in competition with the others. All were the work of many hands. With the possible exception of television, which was developed by those who intended from the beginning to use it as a mass medium, each underwent considerable trial and experimentation before its place as a mass medium was recognized. In its early years each struggled to find its niche as a communication medium, and, as it grew, each was shaped into a social institution in its own right.

From Invention to Mass Medium
Camera and Film

Still photography developed from two separate roots. The camera came first, then film evolved to fit it. The camera can be dated to the tenth century, when Arabian scholars reported the fascinating *camera obscura:* the fact that a dark chamber in a tent could show an upside down image on one wall of the tent if a pinhole were made to let the light stream in from the opposite wall. In the sixteenth century, Giovanni Battista della Porta improved on this natural phenomenon by adding a lens, mirrors, and a white screen to sharpen the image and turn it upright. He

Antecedents of the photographic camera: the chambre obscura and the camera obscura.

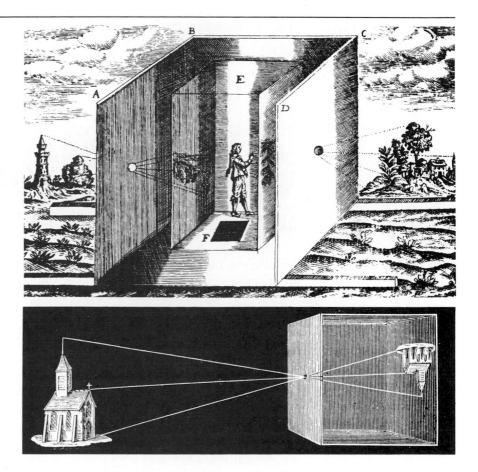

then could copy outdoor scenes to make sets for theatrical productions. By 1575 other artists had constructed portable *camera obscuras* to take into the field to sketch images of landscapes.

The German chemist Johann Henrich Schulze discovered in 1727 that silver nitrate and silver carbonate were sensitive to light. About 1800, using that discovery, Thomas Wedgwood, son of the famous potter, placed chemically treated paper in his *camera obscura* and caught impressions of lace. But there was a problem. The chemical process would "start" alright, or give an image when exposed to light. But there seemed to be no way to "stop" the process so it did not continue to change. And there was no way to "fix" the image so that it did not fade away.

The first to master all three steps was Joseph Niepce. His famous associate, Louis Daguerre, produced a method of making permanent, positive photographs in silver plate in 1835. The silver daguerreotypes

Matthew Brady, Civil War photographer, with his wagon "dark room."

became the rage of Europe, even though adults had to sit breathlessly, their necks in a clamp for thirty seconds to record their image. William Henry Fox Talbot introduced a dry, negative picture process in 1835, but the process adopted by most by mid-century was the wet-plate process of Frederick Scott Archer. Archer's chemically coated glass plates provided a sharp image, but they had to be developed while the plates still were moist. The wet-plate photographer, like the famous Civil War photographer Matthew Brady, for example, had to carry his darkroom with him to process his plates before they dried out. Brady's covered wagon became famous on Civil War battlefields.

In 1878 Charles Harper Bennett discovered he could speed up the dry, gelatin film (like Talbot's) by storing it at ninety degrees Fahrenheit for several days. The film then could be carried for days, in or outside the camera, and developed later—by anyone. George Eastman made the final step into modern photographic film when he introduced nitrocellulose roll film in 1889.

That same year the New York *Herald* adopted the printing of news pictures as a way to compete with the *World*. More than one newspaper had printed news pictures by that time, using Frederick Ives' halftone process, but the two New York papers were soon competing with six to eight small pictures a day in each of their twelve-page newspapers. Reporter-photographers covered the Spanish-American War, and after the war photography syndicates sprang up to serve newspapers with news photographs. Beginning in 1919 Captain Joseph Medill Patterson of the Chicago *Tribune* family helped establish photography as a journalistic device in his new tabloid the New York *Illustrated Daily News*. The *Daily*

News, and its sensational "jazz journalism" competitors in the 1920s, often put pictures before words in splashy news coverage. One of the famous front-page pictures of the period is of murderess Ruth Snyder sitting in the electric chair at Sing Sing as the lethal voltage shoots through her body.

From Stills to Motion Pictures

Meanwhile, motion pictures were developing from a penny arcade peep show into a full-screen extravaganza. The invention of the motion picture was delayed somewhat because those pursuing it did not realize that motion could be captured in a series of still pictures shown one after another. As Peter Mark Roget, author of the thesaurus, demonstrated, the human eye retains an image for a split second after an object has moved from sight. In 1877 photographer Eadweard Muybridge took a series of pictures of a galloping horse to help Leland Stanford win a bet. Muybridge's pictures, taken as the horse passed each of twelve cameras along the track, proved the horse actually left the ground at one point in its stride. Stanford won the bet, and Muybridge won an avocation. He learned to project the series of pictures from a wheel onto a screen so that they gave a clear, if brief, illusion of motion.

The Edison Motion Picture Production System

Edison and his assistant W. K. L. Dickson produced the first motion pictures in 1889, using George Eastman's roll film. Fred Ott, a worker at the Edison factory, performed his popular sneeze routine for the occasion. Edison named his new, large, movie camera the kinetograph, and took out a patent on it in 1891. He also took out a patent on his kinetoscope— a penny arcade viewing machine—but he did not patent a movie projector. Unfortunately, he decided a "screen machine," which could show films to large groups at one time, would quickly use up all films available, and put an end to the motion picture business before it was established. He also decided not to take out foreign patents on the new machines. Experience told him they would not be worth the money ($150).

The films for the peep show machines were produced in the studio Edison built at his factory. It was covered with tar paper, and set on a revolving platform so it could be turned to catch the light anytime of the day. The Edison workers dubbed it the "Black Maria," after the black, covered, horse-drawn police wagons of the day. Vaudevillians and Edison workers trooped before the camera day after day: jugglers, dog acts, a silent violin performance, and two factory workers dancing with each other. The fare was poor, but the lifelike motion was amazing.

Eadweard Muybridge's still picture sequence of a running race horse conveyed motion when projected on a screen and suggested that motion pictures could be created with a series of still pictures. In 1889 Edison's kinetograph movie camera shot the first motion picture sequence of Edison worker Fred Ott "sneezing" for the camera.

The Edison motion picture "system": Short novelty films were photographed in the Black Maria studio for distribution at penny arcade "peep shows."

Some found it even more amazing there was no patent on the invention. In London, instrument-maker Robert W. Paul repaired the imported Edison machines at first, then manufactured his own camera and began to shoot his own films. In Paris, Louis and August Lumiere developed their own cinematograph, a portable machine that could shoot, develop, and project film virtually anywhere. It was only a matter of time until the Paul and Lumiere equipment—and all like it—made its way back to the United States to compete with the Edison equipment that had fostered it.

The Screen Machine and the Movie Theater

By 1895 Edison had realized his mistake about the movie projector. He was working hard to produce one when one of his distributors told him Thomas Armat had developed a machine and was willing to share profits with Edison to gain the benefits the wizard's name would give the product in the marketplace. Edison balked, but a deal was struck. The Edison-Armat Vitascope, the prototype of the modern movie projector, was introduced at a gala demonstration in 1896; and the screen machine began to transfer movies from penny arcades into vaudeville houses and stores converted into theaters. As Edison had feared, however, the movie projector rapidly exhausted the supply of films. Exhibitors found they either had to trade with each other to get fresh films, go on the road to find fresh audiences, or do both. The vaudeville houses soon found their films of pillow fights and approaching trains were more effective in chasing the audience from the house than drawing them in.

Tell Me a Story

Fortunately, a new type of film was on the way. In France, magician George Melies was experimenting with film effects, discovering many of the basic techniques used in film and television today, including the fade, the dissolve, and making film characters disappear. Rather than just copy the real world, Melies attempted to entertain and charm the audience the way a magician entertains and charms. His *Trip to the Moon* (1902) is a fantasy sequence that shows something of a chorus line cheering as a manned rocket blasts off to hit the man in the moon. The struck moon man grimaces in comic pain as the film ends.

In 1903 Edwin S. Porter of Edison's staff produced the first narrative film, *The Great Train Robbery*. It dramatized the slugging of a station master, the blowing of a strong box, a chase, and a shootout with the crooks—all in eight minutes. Its suspense and action attracted audiences for years. Its success sent a swarm of would-be moviemakers into the field to shoot film stories.

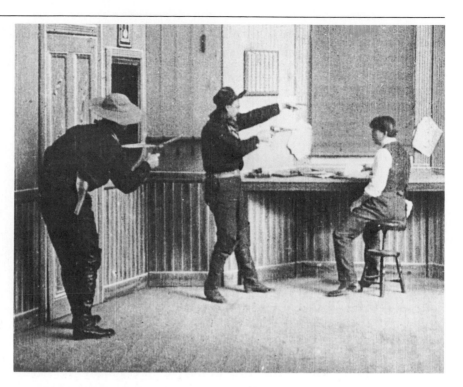

A scene from the first narrative film, *The Great Train Robbery.* Note the stagelike frame of the camera.

Nickelodeons and the New Jersey Indians

New York had little open space for moviemaking, so nearby New Jersey became America's first movie lot. In the 1900s, knights, Confederate soldiers, and Indians all fought and died again and again near Hoboken and Fort Lee. The audiences for these one-reel cliff-hangers (from real New Jersey cliffs) sat in converted stores in big cities—usually in working class neighborhoods. The first of these new theaters to use the name *nickelodeon* opened in Pittsburgh in 1905. By 1907 there were three thousand; by 1910, ten thousand. Most nickelodeons presented an hour's worth of action and entertainment—for a nickel.

Edison was far from pleased about the growing popularity of the movies, however. He had not sold one single camera, but film companies were shooting movies all around his West Orange, New Jersey factory. And so he went to court to press his patent claims, arguing that all movie cameras, of whatever country and inventor, were taken from his kinetograph. In 1907 the court upheld his claim against one movie company and other patent holders, rather than fight, decided to join the inventor in an effort to control the new industry. They formed the Motion Picture Patents Company in 1908.

A scene from D. W. Griffith's *Birth of a Nation*. Rather than use a head-to-toe, stagelike framing in his picture, Griffith moved his camera into close-ups, pans, and other modern camera techniques to bring the audience into the story.

The Stars Come Out

The trust, as the patent company was called, attempted to control the industry in at least two ways. First, it leased cameras and projectors only to those moviemakers and exhibitors who agreed to abide by its rules. Among other things, moviemakers were to hold all films to one reel in length (ten to twelve minutes), and use only a "stage" perspective with their camera: the top of the picture frame was at the top of the actors' heads, the bottom just below their feet. Second, the trust used some strong arm tactics. It sent private "dicks" into the field to harass film companies that were shooting without trust-leased equipment.

In the end, it all failed. The independents were too imaginative. Adolph Zukor, for example, ignored the trust monopoly in 1912, and distributed the art film *Queen Elizabeth,* five reels long, using major theaters not under trust control. The film that did the most to change movies from the trust's one reelers to modern feature films was D. W. Griffith's *Birth of a Nation* in 1915. The film, a bigoted story of the reconstruction South, was the first to use modern cinema techniques. Rather than head-to-toe shots, Griffith employed closeups and long, sweeping landscape shots. He crosscut from one action sequence to another. He and cameraman G. W. "Billy" Bitzer even placed a camera in an automobile so they could speed along with the action and shoot breathtaking shots of galloping horses.

By the 1920s the first-run, major motion picture theaters were plush "up town" establishments, while the old nickelodeon store-theaters had developed into "second run" houses.

The trust films did not identify their actors, but the independents found audiences came to film after film to see players they liked. And so billing and "stars" were born. Fox publicity man John Goldfarb actually created Theda Bara, the "vamp" (for vampire), who ruined men with kisses. (Theda was really Theodosia Goodman, a nice Jewish girl from the Midwest.) The first stars were Mary Pickford and Charlie Chaplin. Both had annual contracts for $1 million in 1917.

The trust fell in 1917, the result of an antitrust suit in federal court. It was the independents who survived to build the dream factory in Hollywood.

Moving West and Moving On

The move from New Jersey to Hollywood began as early as 1910. Trust and independent companies alike soon were moving West to take advantage of year-round sunshine, a wider variety of land- and seascapes, inexpensive real estate, and tax inducements. The demand for feature length films also brought other changes. The expensive feature film had to be aimed at the middle-class audience—those who could pay a dollar or more for admission. The first downtown movie palace, The Strand, opened on Broadway in New York in 1914, and grand movie houses with crystal chandeliers began to appear in every part of the country. Distributors soon discovered that the glamor and publicity of these "first-run" palaces made a movie more valuable for the old nickelodeon, or "second-run" theaters. (In fact, the second-run houses did not want a film that was not profitable in its first run.)

To reach their new audience, the production companies set about building their own glittering chains of first-run movie houses. And fearing they would be unable to obtain films, some theater owners decided to protect themselves by plunging into the movie production business.

Theater owner Marcus Loew, for example, bought the Metro studio in 1920, eventually turning it into Metro-Goldwyn-Mayer. Ironically, less than five years after seeing the trust dissolve in an antitrust suit, the movie independents had laid the foundation for their own antitrust downfall by locking themselves into production-distribution companies.

Sound Recording

In the nineteenth century, the dream of recording the human speaking voice was held by more than one inventive thinker. In 1857 Edourd-Leon Scott de Martinville designed a machine to chart the speaking voice. Twenty years later, Charles Gros outlined a method of photoengraving those charts in discs so they might be played back. Both men registered their ideas with the French Academy of Science.

The man who actually invented the first working phonograph, however, was following an idea of his own. Thomas Edison drew a sketch of a machine with a cylinder, a needle, and a speaking horn for one of his assistants to build. In 1877, he spoke into the finished machine, then adjusted it, and listened as he cranked the handle again. ''Mary had a little lamb. . . .'' It was muffled but understandable. He exploited the invention as a vaudeville attraction for two years—until audiences tired of its recorded sneezes, dog barks, and off-speed giggling—then put it away and turned to other work.

But two men, Chichester Bell and Charles Sumner Tainter of Alexander Graham Bell's laboratories remained intrigued by the new machine. They improved it, adding a wax cylinder, better needle action, and more consistent speed control. They called their machine the graphophone, and in 1885 they approached Edison, offering to let him share in their improvements. Angry, he dealt with them as trespassers, and refused. They went off to sell their patented machine to a group of Washington, D.C. businessmen, while Edison quickly reworked his own.

Stenography and Music

Within months, Edison and the Washington group were in business together. They joined in a venture to lease the two talking machines to offices as stenographic equipment. The Washington group did well with its District of Columbia territory and government offices. But elsewhere the stenographic venture was a disaster. The two machines were unreliable and the male stenographers, whose jobs were threatened, saw to it they were even more unreliable. To save his investment, Louis Glass of the Pacific Phonograph Company placed a coin-operated machine with a music recording in a saloon in San Francisco. It proved to be a bonanza. Leasing a machine for dictation paid only twenty dollars a year. But in 1891 the average coin machine returned more than one hundred times that: forty dollars a week! Suddenly, the rush was to music.

Edison (r) and his first
phonograph. An ad for the
disk-playing gram-o-phone,
with smaller horn, is at the
upper left.

Unfortunately, due to contractual arrangements, Edison was unable to extricate himself from the stenographic company. The Washington group, however, had informal ties with the company; so they plunged into the music business, retaining their stenographic name, Columbia Phonograph. Edison was never to lead the industry again.

Berliner's Disc Recordings

Columbia's competition came from Emile Berliner, a brilliant German-American. Berliner read the papers of Scott and Gross and perfected a way to etch grooves in zinc discs so they could be photoengraved for an endless number of high-quality copies. In 1894 he incorporated his United States Gramophone Company and set out to establish disc recordings as a mass medium of music. He had two partners: Frank Seaman, in charge of sales and promotion, and Eldredge Johnson, in charge of manufacturing.

Without a patent in disc recordings, Columbia found the competition stiff. Almost in desperation, they filed a patent infringement suit, charging the gramophone's stylus and "floating action" were stolen from their graphophone. The charge was unfounded, at best, but they made the charges stick for awhile, since Seaman, angry over his share of the gramophone business, testified against Berliner and Johnson. The judge put both under court order to refrain from selling their own merchandise, pending a full hearing. Johnson, however, had little choice but to defy the order. He had borrowed money to finance the record players he had manufactured and had to sell the mechandise to meet his debts. In time he was called into court again. This time, however, he was prepared. He defended his own equipment, brilliantly, removing all doubt of authenticity. The court freed him to sell the recording equipment he had manufactured, but it did place one restraint on him. The title *Gramophone* was Berliner's patented label, and the court ordered Johnson to refrain from infringing on the trademark. He returned to his New Jersey factory elated; his only problem was to choose a new name for his company. Fresh from his success in court, he chose the name *Victor*. When Berliner also was free of the bogus patent suit, he and Johnson formed the Victor Talking Machine Company in 1901. (*Gramophone* remained an important title in England, of course.)

In time Columbia, by sheer luck, captured a patent that gave it an entrée into disc recording. Rather than continue their court battles, however, the two companies agreed to pool their patents—or share what phonograph patents they had—making it possible for the two to dominate the industry until the patents ran out fifteen years later.

The First Rise of the Phonograph Industry

The new industry enjoyed tremendous growth between 1900 and 1920. Victor alone rose from a company with assets of three million to one of thirty-three million dollars by 1917. Player and record production for the industry reached $158 million by 1919. Better records and record players accounted for much of the growth. In 1906 Victor introduced its lavish, piano-finished Victrola, with the horn inside the cabinet. Victor's Johnson also created a new line of recordings, the "red seal" recordings, which featured the young tenor Enrico Caruso.

Both Victor and Columbia capitalized on the dance mania that swept the country in 1913. The recording repertoire also grew with the recording of original cast albums of London musical reviews, songs of World War I ("My Buddy," "Poor Butterfly"), Dixieland, and "le jazz hot" (or improvised jazz), and the "race" records of Louis Armstrong and Kid Ory. Symphonic music did not record well, however. The acoustic recording methods did not do justice to strings, and the eight-minute (two sides) recording time was too short for any symphony.

The crash came in 1920. The war boom was over. There was a growing banking depression. Columbia, in debt for cabinets that would not sell, was bankrupt by 1923. Even Victor suffered a 20 percent drop in sales in 1924, due mostly to a new competitor in the music business: the radio.

Enter Radio, Clicking

The natural history of broadcasting began with the experimental work of physicist Heinrich Hertz in 1888. Expanding on the theories of Scot physicist James Clerk Maxwell, Hertz demonstrated the existence of electromagnetic waves, detecting, bending, and reflecting them. His published research set a multitude of engineers to work applying his findings to communication: to making a wireless telegraph.

The first to succeed was Guglielmo Marconi, who produced a complete dots and dashes wireless sending and receiving system in 1894. The invention so amazed both the British Navy and many wealthy Americans that young Marconi was able to form two corporations, one in Britain and the other in the United States; he was just twenty-five years old. His dream was to build a world monopoly, a communication empire like Western Union or Bell Telephone. He decided he would build shore stations and lease his equipment to ships at sea—including the British and the American navies—and provide trained operators to handle and maintain the wireless equipment.

Life and Death at Sea

Wireless was of great benefit at sea. In 1909 alone, the new communications systems saved lives in some twenty-two sea mishaps.

In 1912 a great tragedy brought regulations that tightened the system. The Titanic, on its maiden voyage across the North Atlantic, struck an iceberg and sank. The Marconi operator signaled for help until he lost power, but help did not arrive until the early morning hours. Fifteen hundred lives were lost. The power of wireless was demonstrated by the fact that many of the messages transmitted from the Titanic during the crisis were received by a young wireless operator in a New York department store. Young David Sarnoff stayed at his key for seventy-two hours, passing news of the tragedy to the world.

As the rescue ships returned home with their survivors, however, communication with shore stations was hampered by interference from amateurs and other wireless operators on shore. In reaction to the problems, Congress passed the Radio Act of 1912, tightening requirements

Guglielmo Marconi.

for wireless and wireless operators on sea-going ships. To reduce interference it decided to cut down on the number of wireless transmitters by requiring all operators to obtain a license from the secretary of commerce. The act made no provision for denying licenses.

The Wireless Patents and the First Patent Pool

Marconi's dream to build a world monopoly, meanwhile, received a fatal blow when the U.S. Navy decided that leasing Marconi equipment was not politically acceptable and moved to build its own wireless system. The Navy's search for an alternative wireless system introduced new, competing equipment into the United States; at the same time, refinement of the wireless was bringing more and more patents into the complicated field. Soon, there was a major obstacle to progress. Many of the wireless patents issued protected improvements on equipment already protected. As a result, it became difficult for any one patent holder to control an invention. For example, the three-stage vacuum tube, very important in voice and music transmission, had three separate patents on it. There was a patent on the first two stages of the tube, a separate one on the third stage, and still another on a feedback circuit that made the tube highly efficient. Not one of three patent holders could control the use of the tube.

In the interests of the war effort, the American government ended the patent deadlock in 1917 by placing all wireless patents in a patent pool under control of the Navy. And because so much progress was made in wireless during World War I, there was strong sentiment to continue the pool after the war was over. But more than one organization—the

Army especially—did not relish the idea of having the Navy in control. Others disliked the idea of having government involved in controlling patents. There also was fear that wireless still might develop under the control of a foreign element (i.e., British Marconi). And so the nation accepted the suggestion of Owen D. Young, an attorney for General Electric, who proposed, patriotically enough, a private American corporation be formed to manage the patent pool. In 1919, with General Electric, Westinghouse, and American Telephone and Telegraph as principal patent holders, the Radio Corporation of America was formed. American Marconi also was invited to join, and did so immediately. Not joining would have meant losing access to the wealth of patents in the pool while facing the awesome competition the pool would create. (Joining RCA with the Marconi company was David Sarnoff, of Titanic disaster fame, whose name was to become synonymous with RCA in the years ahead.)

From Wireless to Radio

Reginald Fessenden and Ernest F. W. Alexanderson made the first broadcast of voice and music radio on Christmas Eve 1906. Lee De Forest broadcast music from the stage of the Metropolitan Opera in 1910. The broadcast that caught the imagination of the American public came on November 2, 1920. Dr. Frank Conrad, and other Westinghouse officials, noting the warm reception Conrad's experimental station was receiving from crystal set listeners, obtained a station license from the secretary of commerce. They placed a tent studio for the new station, KDKA, on top of the Westinghouse building in Pittsburgh. The broadcast was advertised as a home and club activity, and aired returns from the Harding-Cox presidential election.

As they hoped, the public soon was standing in line to buy radio receiver sets. By 1925 one out of five hundred American homes had a radio. By 1926 one out of twenty had one.

What neither Conrad and Westinghouse nor anyone else had anticipated was the rapid increase in the number of broadcasting stations. By 1923 there were six hundred stations on the air. Chicago alone had forty stations by 1925. Very quickly there were so many signals and so much interference that some stations simply could not get their broadcast signals to the radio audience.

Licensing and Freedom from Interference

The man whose job it was to solve the problem was Secretary of Commerce Herbert Hoover. With limited authority Hoover moved to create new wavelengths, refused to issue new licenses and to seal up stations that would not stay on frequency. He inaugurated a series of conferences to gain advice from leaders in the field on what course of action to take. Finally, in 1926 the courts put an end to his attempts to deal with the situation. Eugene F. McDonald of the Zenith Corporation applied for a

Westinghouse's Dr. Frank Conrad.

license for a station, got it, and then without authorization, began broadcasting on a Canadian frequency with little interference. Hoover took him to court to force him to return to the assigned frequency. The court, however, reviewing the secretary's authority, ruled the Radio Act of 1912 gave him absolutely no power to regulate radio—and no power to deny licenses. He returned to his office to approve two hundred more stations in the seven remaining months of that year.

By then reception was so poor, and the outcry so loud, Congress was willing to act. In 1927 it passed the Federal Radio Act, creating a five person Federal Radio Commission to regulate broadcasting in the "public interest, convenience and necessity," without compromising First Amendment freedoms. As Senator Wallace White of Maine put it, the right of the public to receive radio service was greater than the right of any individual to broadcast them. The new commission quickly reduced the number of stations on the air and executed a plan to equalize reception. In the Communications Act of 1934, Congress expanded the commission to seven members; it also placed wire communication under its control. The 1934 act remains the basic broadcast regulation act today.

The Networks Arrive   Meanwhile, members of the radio patent pool were chafing in their agreements. RCA, GE, and Westinghouse—the radio group—and AT&T with subsidiary Western Electric—the telephone group—had set out to manufacture wireless equipment, but broadcast radio suddenly appeared instead. Both groups had developed chains of radio stations, but they were in conflict regarding their rights under the 1919 agreement.

Could the radio group rent voice lines to present sports and news reports on their radio networks? Was the telephone group limited to the manufacture of transmitters as it had been when wireless was the dominant system? After some tough confrontations, the two groups decided to separate. RCA, now under the imaginative leadership of David Sarnoff, formed a new radio company subsidiary, the National Broadcasting Company. For one million dollars, NBC took control of all AT&T radio properties, including its high-quality radio network. AT&T returned to the telephone business, with the prospect of making a great deal of money by leasing telephone lines to the radio group for its networks. Thus, in 1926 NBC began operation of two radio networks: the one purchased from AT&T, with WEAF as its flagship station, and the other founded by the radio group, with WJZ as its flagship. When the two networks were sketched out on a map, the WEAF network was in red, and the WJZ network in blue. And so they became the NBC Red and the NBC Blue networks respectively.

AT&T's retirement from broadcasting also resolved another dilemma. AT&T had supported its radio network with much the same operating philosophy it used in the telephone business. If someone wished to make a telephone call, he or she could rent the AT&T phone system for a short while for a nickel. In radio, AT&T's toll broadcasting philosophy allowed those who wished to speak to the radio audience to use AT&T's radio system for a short while for a fee. The first radio commercial was a ten-minute talk about a cooperative apartment development in Jackson Heights, New York. It was given over AT&T's flagship station WEAF in New York. The radio group, meanwhile, had called for the taxation of the sale of radio sets to support programming costs. Those in the radio group gave program time to any organization that would bear the cost of the program—whether it was a stock market report or a banjo recital. This created indirect advertising, or presentations by groups clearly identified with their sponsor—but with no direct advertising sales message. For publicity, hotels sponsored band broadcasts from their ballrooms. Oil companies presented bands named after the company (Magnolia Petroleum, etc.). With AT&T no longer in the field, however, the radio group adopted the toll broadcasting philosophy and turned to direct advertising sales, charging advertisers for time and allowing sales announcements as their principal method of supporting programs. (See p. 365.) Most of American broadcasting has been commercial broadcasting since that time.

Artist's agent Arthur Judson and his colleague George A. Coates founded the United Independent Broadcasters Network in 1927. They struggled at first, watching a series of financial backers come and go. One,

Columbia Phonograph, departed leaving its name on the organization that in time became the Columbia Broadcasting System. In 1928 young William Paley of Philadelphia assumed control, using family money from its successful, advertising-conscious La Palina cigar business. He quickly sold 49 percent of CBS stock to Adolph Zukor of Paramount Studios, gaining credit and a reputation for leadership. CBS rose to the forefront of American broadcasting in a few short years. Paley continued in active leadership of the network until 1983.

The third major network, the American Broadcasting Company, evolved from a complaint of unfair competition against NBC's Red and Blue network operations. About 35 percent of all radio stations on the air were affiliated with NBC through one or the other of the two networks. (CBS could claim only 16 percent.) In 1941 the Federal Communications Commission (FCC) forced NBC to sell the Blue network, with the famous chain broadcasting rule, which limited networks to the operation of only one radio network. Edward J. Noble, the Lifesaver candy manufacturer, bought the Blue network from NBC for $8 million in 1943. The FCC, meanwhile, had authorized commercial FM in 1940, and a group of fifteen FM station owners established the American Network of FM stations. The advent of World War II stopped FM station construction; Noble bought the title *American* from the disappointed FM group in 1944.

In Business in Mass Communication

Radio and Records

The problems of the recording companies in the early 1920s grew more profound as America learned to listen to radio. There not only was music—often high-quality music—there was vaudeville, games, dramas, melodramas, sports, and news commentary. True, the music listener had to be patient to hear the songs he or she wanted to hear, but that was a relatively small price to pay for good, free music.

The record companies struggled against the onslaught of radio and lost, consistently, until 1925, when Joseph Maxfield of the Bell Laboratories produced a new electrical recording technique that greatly improved the old acoustic method. Maxfield replaced the sound horn and diaphragm introduced by Edison with a microphone, a vacuum tube amplifier, and electromagnetic speakers, to give recordings a fuller, richer sound. For the first time, too, there was true, positive control over the volume. With appropriate publicity, the new recordings put Columbia in the black again. Eldredge Johnson took the opportunity to sell Victor, and retire.

Radio was still the dominant medium, however. RCA bought Victor in 1928, and used the Victrola plant at Camden to manufacture radio sets. In time Columbia Phonograph also succumbed to radio. In 1938 CBS bought its namesake as a music recording subsidiary to diversify its operations.

In the 1930s the Great Depression proved as formidable an opponent for the recording industry as radio. Sales dropped from 104 million records in the late 1920s to 6 million by 1932. The successful strategy for the period came from Decca records, an English import, and Decca manager Joe Kapp. Decca offered a new line of low-priced, high-quality recordings at thirty-five cents instead of the usual seventy-five cents a record. He also was able to sign such popular performers as Jimmy and Tommy Dorsey, Guy Lombardo, and Bing Crosby. Crosby alone accounted for 10 percent of Decca's sales during the period.

Technology came to the rescue again; this time in the form of the jukebox, a coin-in-the-slot machine named after the juke joints where they were found. Although times were bad, most Americans could afford to pay a nickel to hear a tune. In 1939 jukeboxes were the top distributors of records, using thirteen million, as jukebox music filled cafes, malt shops, and bars across the country.

But radio was playing more records, too. In 1942 Glenn Wallich of Capital Records decided to gamble on what many people had believed all along, that radio was a good way of promoting new recording and record sales. He began sending all new Capital releases to fifty influential disc jockeys across the country, with the hope they would play and therefore promote the records to radio listeners. They did. The disc jockeys needed the music to fill their programs. By 1944 Capital sales were doubling every year, and a new and important relationship between radio and recordings was being established.

The Hollywood Empire

Movie attendance, like record sales, began to decline in the 1920s—until moviemakers, who had been overly proud of their silent films, switched to talkies. In 1927 Fox Studios distributed sound newsreels for the first time. The same year Warner Brothers presented Al Jolson in *The Jazz Singer,* using disc recordings synchronized to some of the singing and talking in the film. Jolson's singing and his famous "You ain't heard nothin' yet . . ." caught the imagination of the movie audience. The change to sound was on. Ironically, the system adopted was not the disc method used by Warner Brothers, but the RCA-Western Electric sound-on-film strip also introduced in 1927 by Fox newsreels. Only the smallest theaters were without sound after 1930.

The Jazz Singer did not have a complete sound track, but it had enough recorded songs and spoken lines for Al Jolson's personality to enthrall the public's imagination and lead to the conversion of the industry to sound production in three years.

The talkies brought the "golden years" to the Hollywood studio/factories in the 1930s and 1940s. Five major studios dominated movie production: Paramount, Loew's (MGM), RKO, Twentieth Century Fox, and Warner Brothers. The five majors were the studios that had collected or constructed their own first-run theater chains in cities across the country. Second in movie production were the three minor studios: Columbia, Universal, and United Artists. Independent filmmakers, such as Sam Goldwyn and David Selznick, and the smaller studios—Disney and Republic (the home of the cheap western), among others—rounded out the picture.

In effect, the five major and three minor studios were the ruling group—the oligarchy—of the Hollywood of the 1930s. The oligarchy controlled film traffic and film production through trading and cooperating among themselves. An important function of the minor studios was to produce low-cost B movies to fill out double bills with films from the major studios. In the 1930s movie bills changed once a week in some first-run houses, and three or more times a week in neighborhood theaters, and so the B movie was a valuable filler on the industry's menu. The majors, of course, provided an equally valuable service for the minor studios: first-run distribution in major movie theaters.

Independent producers paid dearly to get first-run distribution. David Selznick gave up 35 percent of his box office receipts from *Gone With The Wind* for distribution. Independent theater owners had problems with the system, too. To get films from the movie industry, they had to agree to show several poor ones in order to book one or two good ones. Also, they often had to agree to show films not yet in production and for which title or cast was not determined. The former was called "block booking"; the latter, "blind booking." Still, there was little the independent producers or exhibitors could do. Only the Hollywood oligarchy could provide the theaters and the movies needed to stay in business.

In 1938 the Justice Department brought an antitrust suit against Adolph Zukor's Paramount Studios in particular and the motion picture industry in general. The case struggled through the courts, was slowed by World War II, then revived in 1945. In 1948, the Supreme Court ordered the studios to divest themselves of their distribution companies and theaters. No longer were the studios to own or control all three phases of the motion picture process. Production, distribution, and exhibition of films were to be under separate control, and independent of each other.

The decision could not have come at a worse time for Hollywood. The end of the war had revived some old labor unrest and raised labor costs. In Europe, war-weary Europeans, in search of revenue, were taxing movie receipts. What was worse, the American electronics industry was ready to plunge into business with a picture product of its own: television.

Talking Pictures at Home

Television had been in preparation as early as the 1880s, with mechanical picture scanner experiments in Europe. In 1920 H. E. Ives of AT&T transmitted pictures by wire and perfected the coaxial cable, making modern network and cable television possible. Vladimir Zworykin patented the first television picture tube in 1923. The brilliant, twenty-one-year-old Philo T. Farnsworth produced his own complete television scanning system in 1927. Allen Dumont produced his cathode ray tube in 1931, and marketed the first home television receiver in 1939.

At RCA, Sarnoff pushed the development of television from the 1930s on, with an all-out research effort at the old Victor plant in Camden, New Jersey. While research was underway, one important distraction arose. The brilliant engineer Edwin Armstrong produced and patented a new, static-free, frequency modulation (FM) radio system. Armstrong's demonstrations of the system impressed everyone, including Sarnoff. But Sarnoff realized that backing FM would mean the complete renovation of the AM radio system as it then existed. For him, such a change meant spending a lot of money to gain only minor improvement in an already workable system. On the other hand, perfecting television meant a new medium which the public was highly interested in and which had great profit-making potential. And so, while Armstrong continued to demonstrate his invention in hopes of gaining support, RCA and Sarnoff struggled to perfect television. NBC began sustained telecasting from the New York World's Fair in 1939. By 1941 there was a total of twenty-three stations on the air. Six broadcast through World War II.

FM, meanwhile, continued to struggle to establish itself. After the war the FCC changed the location of the FM band, making all prewar receivers obsolete. Then it went on to allow stations to simulcast (duplicate) their AM programs on their FM stations. As a result, FM did not develop a distinct personality—an audience of its own—until the 1970s when the simulcasting policy was revoked. (See p. 267.)

As it entered the postwar era, the industry faced some indecision. RCA wanted to continue the work it had started with television—without further delay. The giant corporation had black and white television production equipment and receiving sets ready for marketing and wanted to press ahead, facing any problems as they arose. However, since CBS had a color television system ready for production, it wanted to delay marketing black and white television until FCC consideration of color television was complete. Most in the industry tended to favor the RCA position, since the public seemed more eager for new gadgets than refined older ones.

After considerable testimony and debate, the FCC issued a report in 1945 which, among other things, authorized the exploitation of thirteen channels (1 through 13) of black and white television in VHF, or very high frequency band (30,000 kilocycles to 3,000 megacycles). As a result, the number of stations jumped from seventeen to forty-one in 1948 as television networks began regular programming. Within three years, however, it was obvious that a major error had been made. Reports of interference in television signals raised ghosts of the chaotic days of 1920s radio. Stations in Detroit and Cleveland, for example, although ninety miles apart, were interfering with each other. To gather testimony and evaluate the situation, the commission placed a temporary freeze on new television licenses in 1948.

The freeze lasted four years. When the hearings were finally over, the commission announced in its Sixth Report and Order of 1952 the revised tables that established American television broadcasting as we know it. Rather than maintain the thirteen channel allocation system of 1945, the commission expanded the system to accommodate a larger number of stations. There were to be two television bands in the electromagnetic spectrum. There would be twelve channels (2 through 13) in the VHF band, and seventy in the UHF, or ultra high frequency band (300 megacycles to 3,000 megacycles). Besides increasing the number of frequencies available, the commission also issued a new table of frequency allocations that established 2,053 television stations for 1,291 towns; this was an attempt to make television available to "all parts of the United States." Commissioner Frieda B. Hennock, the first female commissioner, led the move to designate 242 of the available television channels (both VHF and UHF) for educational use. These stations later became the basis for the public broadcasting system.

The question of which color system to use, CBS's or RCA's, was debated until 1953. The CBS system had two definite weaknesses. To provide color, it depended on a mechanical wheel, and mechanical devices are considered a weakness in electronic gear. The CBS system also was not compatible with existing black and white sets. All sets sold and in use at the time would have to be modified—at the owner's expense— if they were to catch any picture at all from the CBS system. The RCA all-electronic color system, on the other hand, was compatible with existing black and white television broadcasting, but the color quality was inferior. (In one test the RCA system produced purple monkeys.)

In 1950 the FCC decided to accept the CBS system as the industry standard. But before CBS could get into production, RCA began delaying tactics. It filed suit against the FCC rules, and pushed the case to the Supreme Court. By delaying, RCA won time to improve its own color system, and time for more and more black and white sets to go into American homes. With every passing day, it became more difficult for the FCC to rationalize forcing people to modify their sets to receive a black and white picture they already received. The government helped, inadvertently, when it halted the manufacture of color television equipment during the Korean War. Finally, with the support of RCA and major television manufacturers, a National Television System Committee created an alternative proposal for a compatible, all-electronic color system and presented it to the FCC. In 1953 the FCC reversed its color decision and accepted the new RCA-NTSC standards.

The Television Networks

The first coast-to-coast television broadcast was the signing of the Japanese Peace Treaty from San Francisco in 1951. As the coaxial cable and microwave relay system began to interconnect the country, four television networks came into existence: ABC, CBS, and NBC, all extensions of the radio networks, and Dumont, the child of inventor Allen Dumont. Although high in technical quality, the Dumont network dropped from the competition after 1954, unable to collect the affiliates, program talent, and financial backing needed to compete with the established networks. (One of Dumont's "finds" was comedian Jackie Gleason, however.)

The first star of television was vaudeville-radio trooper Milton Berle of NBC's "Texaco Star Theatre." Berle's slapstick comedy was a contrast to the more sophisticated "Your Show of Shows," also at NBC, which featured such now-famous comedians as Sid Caesar, Imogene Coca, Carl Reiner, and Howard Morris, and writer Mel Brooks. CBS led in talk-variety shows with Arthur Godfrey and his "Talent Scouts" and "Friends" shows, and Ed Sullivan's Sunday night variety show, "Toast of the Town." "Studio One," "Goodyear Television Playhouse," and "U.S. Steel Hour" presented original dramas written for television by such talented newcomers as Paddy Chayefsky and Rod Serling.

One truly innovative program format was introduced at NBC by Sylvester "Pat" Weaver. He concocted the "Today" show magazine format in 1951. The late-evening "Tonight" followed a few months later. Most of the new television shows, however, were converted radio programs: game shows, detective dramas, situation comedies. From the early 1950s one of the most popular shows was "I Love Lucy," a situation comedy filmed in Hollywood. But the television programmers who looked to radio for inspiration and guidance preferred live programs to filmed, or "canned," shows.

In the early years of television, slapstick was the first king of comedy and Milton Berle was its Prince.

The Hollywood Connection

As television developed its program formats in the 1950s, Hollywood was making every attempt to regain its former glory. The film community could see that "dishwater gray" television did not have the polish and verve of the movie product. Still, the movie audiences were gone, as were many of the old neighborhood, second-run theaters which had attracted them. The movie industry had two basic problems. First, box office receipts and therefore revenue were down due to the loss of theaters and the impact of television. Second, the industry had grown unsure as to how to reach the movie-going audience that remained.

The studios met the first problem by cutting back on expenses—especially their payrolls—putting many talented moviemakers out of work. Film budgets also were cut, with many productions going overseas to find cheap labor. There seemed to be one answer for the second problem: the way to regain audiences was to offer them something big, something spectacular. To compete with the small, gray television screen, the industry turned to sweeping stories on new, wide screens, and to movies in color and 3D. One of the largest of the new movie offerings was Cinerama, a process that used three screens and three projectors to capture the viewer's full range of vision—including peripheral vision. When Cinerama projected pictures taken from a moving roller coaster, the audience was so involved in the scene it felt motion sickness. Cinerama was popular, but small theater owners found the $75,000 required to adapt their theaters unaffordable. The widescreen Todd A. O. and VistaVision productions were more successful, but the 3D films of the 1950s (*Bwana Devil* and *The House of Wax*) were little more than thrill exploitation films, just as 3D films are today (Warhol's *Frankenstein,* for example).

With the studios no longer in complete control of production and distribution, and with many talented people available for film work, the independent production company began to gain greater importance in the Hollywood scheme of things. The movement had been growing from the end of World War II. Arthur Krim and Robert Benjamin gave it a big boost in 1951 when they bought United Artists and sold its studio facilities to make UA a financing and distributing company for independent productions. Between 1954 and 1962 seven of the best pictures of the year were produced by independent producers. Film scholar Thomas Bohn has pointed out that by the middle 1960s about 80 percent of all American films were produced by independent companies.

One of the first successful deals struck between Hollywood and television was between ABC-TV and Walt Disney Studios. ABC, still struggling to survive following its separation from NBC a few years before, was the poor relation in the industry and in need of funds and programming. In 1953 Leonard Goldenson of United Paramount Theatres bought ABC, and began looking among his Hollywood contacts for programs. Goldenson went to Walt Disney with a proposal. He would give Disney ten minutes of time to promote Disney studio films on ABC television if Disney would put entertainment in the remaining fifty minutes. While the offer came at a time when many in Hollywood still felt superior to television, Disney saw it as a marvelous opportunity to advertise his movies at a time when box office receipts were declining. He accepted the offer. Goldenson found Warner Brothers Studios interested in the arrangement, too. Warner Brothers filled their entertainment program time with tried-and-true adventure stories—remakes of successful Warner movies. The Warner series introduced a new list of television stars to the home audience: huge Clint Walker as Cheyenne, and James Garner as the more sophisticated Maverick. The ratings success of the Warner western series brought a stampede of Hollywood cowboy programs to the home screen: "The Life and Legend of Wyatt Earp," "Broken Arrow," "Rawhide," as well as "Gunsmoke," the longest-running telefilm series to date.

The Quiz Show Scandals

Even with westerns available, the most popular shows on television in the late 1950s were quiz shows. Suspenseful, with astronomical money prizes, and a see-through isolation booth, they attracted audiences and droves of would-be contestants. The "$64,000 Question" had twenty thousand applicants each week. (One, a Dr. Joyce Brothers, won the $64,000 by recalling boxing records and statistics.) Rumors persisted

The big quiz shows: Host Hal March questions contestants in the isolation booth of the highly popular "$64,000 Question." The lady in the booth, one of several successful contestants, is Dr. Joyce Brothers.

that some of the big prize shows were fixed, however. In 1958 twenty of the shows left the air as Charles Van Doran, a popular contestant on the program "Twenty One," admitted he was coached before the weekly competition. Following the practice established in radio, the quiz programs had been produced by advertising agencies, who created them as advertising vehicles for their clients. The agency producers had fixed the shows, helping popular contestants win, and arranging for them to lose when their popularity waned. The quiz shows scandals brought an incensed cry from the public, and demands from government, including the FCC, for the networks to take tighter control of their programming.

With the ad agencies no longer an acceptable source of network programs, television turned more and more to independent film packagers in Hollywood. The Hollywood product continued to be popular with the television audience. Desilu Studios, operating in the old RKO facilities, had created television's most popular show, "I Love Lucy." The movie industry not only had the talent but the facilities and experience to factory produce the quantity of shows the three networks needed. The telefilm producers also offered another advantage: they had no "outside" clients to represent. And since television was the only market available for the telefilm product, the Hollywood producers had to meet television's demands in order to sell their product. Few could complain that the networks, by going to the West Coast for programs, had again relinquished control of their broadcast time.

By 1960, 40 percent of Warner Brother's income was from telefilm program packages. By the 1980s almost 80 percent of all network programs came from Hollywood, and the advertising agencies had all but faded from television production.

The New Hollywood

The film studios of the 1930s and 1940s had maintained a strict code of conduct, producing films acceptable to the family audience and portraying middle class values as prescribed by such religious groups as the Catholic Legion of Decency. But with family drama on television, film producers and theater owners found they needed different content to maintain their businesses. For some time, there had been growing evidence of varying degrees of taste and intelligence in the movie audience. In the 1950s one group of theaters, the art houses, had discovered a steady clientele for imported films. The themes of these films varied considerably from those developed in Hollywood. European films, for example, dared to include nudity and portray sexual themes more explicitly than any American film.

As the 1950s progressed, the American movie industry and the movie-going public became more and more willing to abandon the self-imposed production code of the 1930s and deliver a more sophisticated film product to the theatres. Otto Preminger and United Artists challenged the code in 1953 and again in 1956 with *The Moon Is Blue* and *The Man with the Golden Arm.* The former was an adaptation from a Broadway play and included such ''sexual'' words as *virgin.* The latter was a powerful drama dealing with narcotics addiction—a topic the code specifically forbade. The Motion Picture Association of America (MPAA) denied a seal of approval to *The Moon Is Blue,* but that did not prevent it from becoming a box office success. Rather than see another film succeed without its approval, the MPAA in 1956 altered its code concerning narcotics addiction.

Pressures for increased freedom continued to mount until 1968 when the MPAA, under the leadership of President Jack Valenti, adopted a system of film ratings to supplant the code. By labeling films as appropriate for one of four types of audiences (G, PG, R, or X), the industry was free to attract viewers with varying tastes, without offending the sensibilities of others. Suddenly, a new range of films appeared, some with highly imaginative themes and mature treatment: *The Graduate* (1967), *Bonnie and Clyde* (1967), *Easy Rider* (1969), and *Cool Hand Luke* (1972). There was a disadvantage to the rating system, though. It also allowed a steady stream of blatantly pornographic films to be shown. Most successful to date have been *The Devil in Miss Jones* and *Deep Throat* (in the early 1970s).

To accommodate the new range of films and the smaller, more diverse audiences, theaters converted from single screen operations to ones of two, three or even more screens. Theaters constructed in the 1980s are designed to show six or more films simultaneously, allowing diversified film distribution to diversified audiences.

Stage Three: From Development to Specialization

In recent years it has become increasingly clear that the media are no longer expanding as they did in the nineteenth and the first half of this century. They seem to have entered a new stage in their development.

As sociologist Richard Maisel has suggested, traditional theory has held that the development of the mass media has occurred in only two distinct stages, with the first coming in the preindustrial economy and society, serviced by face-to-face communication. The introduction of the printing press in the fifteenth century economy of Europe is the best example of this first stage. In the second stage the mass media grew and expanded rapidly as the society begins to industrialize. Industrialization supports the growth of the media, with technology, products to advertise, and consumers capable of buying the media and the advertised products.

As Maisel has suggested, we tend to assume the second stage continues indefinitely. But the evidence now seems clear that our own industrialization is leading us along a new path to a postindustrial society, as Maisel has called it. In recent years the media are not developing and/or growing as much as they are beginning to specialize, or looking for the relatively small, special interest audience rather than the more general, larger, mass audience. Media history gives us more than enough evidence to document the trend.

For example, the mass circulation magazines of the first half of this century—*Life, Look, The Saturday Evening Post, Collier's, American*—no longer are printed, or they are printed only as small, special interest publications. In place of the general interest or mass magazines are *Golf, Ms., Motor Trend, Working Mother,* and *Hustler,* which appeal to readers with more specific interests.

Network radio, the mass medium of the 1930s and 1940s, said goodbye to the last of its mass entertainment programs, the radio soap opera, in 1960. Radio programming now is much more specialized. To survive stations reach out to special interest audiences with any one of several highly tailored radio formats. A popular one, for example, is urban contemporary, which appeals to the ethnically mixed urban audience. Other stations have found success broadcasting big band or oldies music. Still popular with one type of audience is the country music format. Some stations program only news, while others rely on specialized interviews, audience call-ins, and public discussion, or talk shows.

It is predicted that the newest, "most mass" of the mass media, television, will lose as much as 30 percent of its audience by the end of the 1980s as other media, especially cable television, begin to take away parts of the mass audience with more specialized fare. (See chapter 11.)

The trend is far from ominous. In fact, it promises Americans, who now enjoy the widest range of media known to any society, an even wider, more diverse range of choices.

There is so much available from the modern media now, as Maisel has observed, we already have found it necessary to enhance our ability to receive messages—through speed reading, and recording and copying machines that hold messages for use at our convenience. Rather than think of the media audience as receiving standardized mass media messages we will be forced to think of the audience as individuals with access to many powerful media tools, all providing a wide range of enriched communications for his or her personal selection and use.

The current situation provides two challenges: the media organizations must: (1) not only discover and produce the special interest message that a medium's particular audience wants, (2) but also do it in an attractive way to keep the audience from switching to competing media which offer similar messages. In a growing and changing society, the growing mass medium both must serve the needs of the audience and meet considerable marketplace competition—if it is to survive.

The problems that individual media organizations have with their audiences and competitors, and how they meet those problems, will be discussed in the next section.

Summary

The duplicating media—taking, storing, and transmitting images and sounds directly from the real world—have a long history of development, but the inventions themselves can be traced to the nineteenth century.

Sound recording was invented by Thomas Edison in 1877, but Emile Berliner's disc recording became the dominant way to distribute music. The recorded music industry grew dramatically between 1900 and 1920. The large, elegant Victrola became the central attraction in the family parlor.

Because it was free and had richer tones than mechanical recordings, radio brought unexpected disaster to the infant recording industry. Record sales slumped while radio set sales leaped higher in the 1920s.

Photography traces its history to the *camera obscura,* and Johann Heinrich Schulze's experiments with light sensitive chemicals. The first true picture was made in silver by Louis Daguerre in the 1800s. Edison and his assistant W. L. K. Dickson used Eastman's roll film to create the first motion pictures.

Edison patented a kinetoscope camera and a kinetograph peep show machine in 1891. In 1908 he and other patent holders formed the Motion Picture Patents Company (the trust) in an attempt to control the nickleodeon movie industry. But the independents continued to attract audiences with their productions; the patent company died in 1917 in an antitrust case. Feature films such as *Birth of a Nation* (1915) pushed movie exhibition into more expensive theaters, with patrons who could afford higher admissions, thus supporting more expensive feature films.

Movie production moved to Southern California to gain year-round sunshine and a better variety of scenic conditions. In Hollywood, the industry formed five major and three minor companies—an oligarchy that controlled production and distribution of films.

The history of broadcasting began when Guglielmo Marconi created the first workable wireless radio system in 1894, and then created a wireless monopoly. But fearing Marconi's foreign connections, the American Navy decided to build its own system. During World War I, the Navy put all wireless patents into a patent pool, and after the war all parties agreed to the formation of a private pool: the Radio Corporation of America.

In 1920 Westinghouse's KDKA broadcast the Harding-Cox presidential election returns, catching the popular imagination and selling many receiver sets. So many radio stations were created that reception became almost impossible. To correct the problem, Congress passed the Radio Act of 1927, which created a new commission to regulate radio in the "public interest, convenience and necessity." The act was expanded into the Communications Act of 1934, the basis for regulation today.

Meanwhile, the two groups that had formed the RCA patent pool found themselves at odds with each other. The telephone group (AT&T and Western Electric) decided to leave broadcasting to the radio group (RCA, Westinghouse, and General Electric). In 1926, RCA formed NBC to manage the two radio networks the two sides had constructed. NBC adopted the AT&T toll, or commercial broadcasting philosophy, to support the venture. CBS was founded the following year, taking its name from Columbia Phonograph. In 1945, the Federal Communications Commission required NBC to divest itself of one of its networks, and the American Broadcasting Company was born.

Radio technology helped revive the recording industry in the 1920s. It survived the Depression with low-priced, high-quality recordings of popular music distributed by the jukebox. Electrical amplification and recording also allowed movies to talk.

Television's arrival was slowed by World War II and an FCC-imposed freeze between 1948 and 1952 to study station allocations. The first coast-to-coast television program showed the signing of the Japanese peace treaty in San Francisco in 1951. In 1953, ABC turned to Hollywood for programs. Movie studios were suffering from television competition and an antitrust ruling separating them from control of their theater chains. ABC's Leonard Goldenson arranged for programs from Walt Disney and Warner Brothers. Under pressure from the quiz show scandals, all the networks soon turned to the movie producers to gain better control over their program packages.

As television became a major distribution system for Hollywood's movies and telefilms, the movie industry was free to find other audiences for its first-run features.

Today all the media show signs of becoming more specialized in audience appeal. Radio already appeals to specialized audiences, and shows signs of diversifying, too. Just as general interest magazines *Life* and *Look* gave way to special interest *Golf* and *Working Mother,* the major networks now see competition from more specialized cable and pay-television channels.

Questions for Discussion

1. Several historians have identified common patterns of development for all of the mass media. Can you find a pattern (or two) in the development of (1) the print media, (2) sound recording, and (3) radio? What stages did they go through in their development?

2. The three stage development theory reported in this chapter remains somewhat controversial. What might indicate that Professor Maisel is in error? Are the mass media still the mass media? Will mass television split into specialized media messages? What is the evidence?

3. We noted in our discussion of the development of television that David Sarnoff of RCA slowed the development of FM radio in favor of developing television. Was his decision correct? Was it ethical? Much has been written on the fight to win approval for color television by RCA and CBS. Some say CBS had the better color system, but lost out to RCA because RCA dragged its feet. What were the facts in that case? (You might check the references for a source.)

4. How important is radio to the recording business? How important are recordings to radio?

References

Balio, Tino, ed. *The American Film Industry*. Madison: University of Wisconsin Press, 1976.

Barnouw, Eric. *The Golden Web*. New York: Oxford University Press, 1968.

————. *The Image Empire*. New York: Oxford University Press, 1970.

————. *A Tower in Babel*. New York: Oxford University Press, 1966.

Bohn, Thomas, and Stromgren, Richard. *Light and Shadows: A History of Motion Pictures*. 2d ed., Sherman Oaks, Calif.: Alfred Publishing, 1978.

Gelatt, Roland. *The Fabulous Phonograph*. New York: Lippincott, 1955.

Gordon, George N. *The Communications Revolution*. New York: Hastings House, 1977.

Head, Sydney W. *Broadcasting in America*. Boston: Houghton Mifflin, 1956.

Hughbanks, Leroy. *Talking Wax*. New York: Hobson Book Press, 1945.

Kahn, Frank J. *Documents of American Broadcasting*. 3d ed., Englewood Cliffs, N.J.: Prentice-Hall, 1978.

Macgowan, Kenneth. *Behind the Screen*. New York: Delacorte, 1965.

Maisel, Richard. "The Decline of Mass Media." *The Public Opinion Quarterly* 37, no. 2 (1973): 160–70.

Mast, Gerald. *A Short History of the Movies*. New York: Bobbs-Merrill, 1971.

Metz, Robert. *CBS, Reflections in a Bloodshot Eye*. New York: New American Library, 1975.

Mitchell, Curtis. *Cavalcade of Broadcasting*. Chicago: Follett, 1966.

North, Joseph H. *The Early Development of the Motion Picture*. New York: Arno Press, 1973.

Schicke, C. A. *Revolution in Sound*. Boston: Little, Brown, 1974.

Spehr, Paul C. *The Movies Begin*. Newark: The Newark Museum, 1977.

Sklar, Robert. "Hollywood's Collapse." In *American Mass Media*, edited by Robert Atwan, Barry Orton, and William Vesterman, New York: Random House, 1978.

Sterling, Christopher H., John M. Kittross. *Stay Tuned, A Concise History of American Broadcasting*. Belmont, Calif.: Wadsworth, 1981.

Taylor, Deems. *A Pictorial History of the Movies*. 2d ed., New York: Simon and Schuster, 1949.

White, Llewellyn. *The American Radio*. New York: Arno Press, 1971.

Part Three

The Mass Media: Cultural Businesses

The heart of the mass communications system is the media production and distribution organization. In our society, the media are, first and foremost, businesses. But as several observers have pointed out, they are special kinds of businesses. They are cultural businesses. To paraphrase author John Dessauer, the media produce cultural products—ideas, instruments of education, literature, facts, and stories—that are promoted and sold to the public through commercial means. The media create and deliver messages that people want—and are willing to pay for.

Profit in a cultural business, like profit in other businesses, is the measure of success. It results from the media organization's creative ability to reach the unseen and unknown public. Profit is the key to all the media organization's goals. "In all cases survival, and therefore the opportunity to realize nonmonetary objectives, presupposes financial competency," Dessauer has said. That is, if the media business does not make money, it goes out of business, losing all chance of performing well.

As a business, the media organization must deal with three basic challenges if it is to survive in the marketplace. First, it must control the resources that are vital to its operation—the paper, telefilms, or music required to continue its operation. Second, it must meet its competition with its cultural products, producing messages the public will pay money to have, or use. Third, it must find ways to diversify its media products so that a loss of one does not mean the failure of the company. RCA, for example, has owned Random

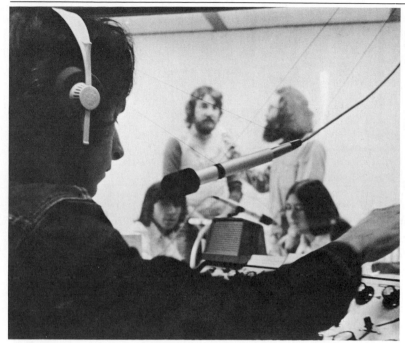

House book publishers, Ballantine Books, Alfred Knopf, Pantheon, Vintage, and Modern Library as well as a line of frozen foods. The Chicago *Tribune* has invested in baseball, with the widely publicized purchase of the Chicago Cubs.

In the next seven chapters we will discuss the media organizations themselves, reviewing their individual functions and purposes, their organizational structure, their operations, their problems, their successes and failures, and career opportunities. And we will discuss and review them as cultural businesses—organizations that promote and sell cultural products with commercial means.

References

Dessauer, John. "Profit." *Publisher's Weekly,* January 28, 1982, 35–37.

Tillinghast, Diana. "The Los Angeles Times: Insuring Organizational Survival by Controlling, Adapting to, or Containing the External Environment" (Paper presented to the Newspaper Division, Association for Education in Journalism, annual convention, Michigan State University, East Lansing, August, 1981.)

Chapter
5

The American Newspaper

Words, to computers, to paper. Making the modern newspaper.

The progress made in motion pictures, radio, and television in recent years has not diminished the fact the American newspaper remains one of the most important of the mass media in our social and political life. No other medium charts our ways and means of getting from day to day with the same depth and detail. As industry spokesmen are proud of pointing out, the newspaper enlightens, informs, and entertains while also acting as watchdog of government and society and as guardian of the people's right to know. In a very real way, too, the newspaper marks the daily pattern of our lives, recording our births, deaths, marriages, and prejudices—even if, as often happens, it records the prejudices unknowingly and unintentionally.

The importance of the newspaper is reflected in the growth of the industry. Since World War II, newspapers have become one of the largest employers in the country, surpassing both the steel and automobile industries. In 1980 newspaper employees—reporters, editors, press personnel—numbered more than 432,000, and the newspaper work force was growing at an annual rate of 3.9 percent, faster than the American work force as a whole.

The economic strength of the industry is indicated by the fact newspapers lead all other media in attracting advertising revenue. More than 27 percent of all advertising dollars goes to the daily newspaper, while television wins only 21 percent and radio, 7 percent. Newspapers are a $15 billion industry in annual advertising revenues alone.

A Profile of the Newspaper Industry

There are approximately 1,700 daily newspapers in the United States. They circulate more than sixty-two million copies every day. The 770 Sunday newspapers distribute more than fifty-six million copies, while the 7,547 nondaily or weekly papers distribute forty-three million copies each edition.

Overall, the industry seems quite stable. While dailies have suffered from inflation, then recession, as well as problems of competition, the number of daily newspapers has not changed dramatically since World War II. There has been a noticeable decline in the number and circulation of evening dailies, but those losses have been accompanied by circulation gains in morning dailies, growth in the number of suburban papers, and the appearance of new entries into the field—the national daily *USA Today,* for example.

The average nondaily newspaper has an estimated circulation of only 5,700 papers. Still, nondailies have an important impact on their audiences. For the total forty-three million copies they publish with each edition, there are 172 million readers—or about four readers for every copy of the nondaily paper. The "pass-along" rate for daily newspapers is 2.2 readers per copy.

Types of Newspapers

The newspaper industry categorizes its papers by frequency of publication, dividing its products into dailies and nondailies, with the latter including weekly papers as well as those that publish two and three times a week. Within the industry, there are devotees of both types of papers. To review the two types, we will begin with the less familiar nondailies and then move on to the better known metropolitan dailies and the national newspapers.

The NonDailies or Weeklies

Small Community Papers

The weeklies, semiweeklies, biweeklies, and triweekly papers are published, more often than not, in rural-agricultural communities, and resemble in several ways the newspapers of the American colonial period. By providing detailed community information, they render a unique service to their small communities.

In 1981, for example, Edon, Ohio (population 950) was shocked to learn the out-of-town owners of the town's only paper, the Edon *Commercial* (circulation 750), were about to close down the 100–year-old publication and deprive the community of its only source of local news.

Pulitzer Prize winners David and Catherine Mitchell of the Point Reyes, California, *Light.*

The death of the *Commercial,* as one villager pointed out, meant the town would lose an important part of its community life. If a local kid hit a home run, there would be no newspaper to report it. The realization prompted one Edon couple to buy the *Commercial* to try to keep it alive to serve the community.

The image of the quiet town weekly reporting Little League ball scores is not the only correct one of course. More than one small newspaper has excelled in hard-hitting investigative reporting. The Point Reyes, California, *Light* won a Pulitzer Prize in 1979 when a dedicated young couple, David and Catherine Mitchell, beat all city dailies and news syndicates in reporting irregularities in the Synanon drug-rehabilitation center located in their area. The Mitchells had sold their house to buy the 2,700-circulation paper. They won their Pulitzer with a reporting staff of three—themselves and one other reporter.

The Alternative Press

The alternative press is an advocate of social and political values often in sharp contrast to mainstream American values expressed by the general interest newspaper. Alternative newspaper editors have taken their cues from the polemicists in American history—Thomas Paine, Sam Adams, the more aggressive muckrakers, and the radical labor press of the early twentieth century. As polemicists, the alternative papers have made aggressive, polarized arguments against traditional American institutions—marriage, work, money, property, and styles of dress. During the 1960s alternative writers filled their columns with attacks on the presence of the American military in Vietnam, the immorality of racial inequality, and what they considered to be a two-faced attitude on sex and morality—a combination of public Puritanism and private greed and cheating. Their intense interest in illegal drugs, especially LSD and marijuana, offended many, and probably encouraged the label *underground press.* Their use of four-letter words, in headlines and story copy, contributed to the title as well. One alternative paper used the headline "Shit Hits Fan" to describe the shooting of students at Kent State University in 1970.

The alternative press found a home in every part of the country. Norman Mailer, Don Wolfe, John Wilcock, Ed Fancher, and others founded the *Village Voice* in New York City in 1955 to promote liberal and cultural views from Greenwich Village. Art Kunkin founded the Los Angeles *Free Press* in 1964. The "Freep," as it came to be called, consisted of forty-eight pages and a paid circulation of 95,000 in 1970, a success due in no small part to its sexual want ads paid for by straight or gay advertisers who proclaimed their willingness to "swing" with others. There were underground papers in the heartland as well. Milwaukee's *Kaleidoscope,* Atlanta's *Great Speckled Bird,* Detroit's *Fifth Estate,* and the Jackson, Mississippi *Kudzu* also took up alternative advocation on culture, politics, drugs, and sex. Although there were some five hundred alternative papers subscribing to the Underground Press Syndicate or its competitor, the Liberation News Service in the early 1970s, the movement faded appreciably in the late 1970s. The Los Angeles *Free Press* and the *Berkeley Barb,* two of the more radical alternative papers, were both gone by the early 1980s. With the Vietnam war over, and popular culture and sexual mores changing, the radical voice no longer seemed the one that could most effectively challenge the establishment.

Former *Berkeley Barb* editor-turned-book-writer David Armstrong has suggested the 1980s will see "peaceful but militant" advocacy by the alternative papers, with more attention to excellence in local political reporting, a more vital consumer approach to the arts and humanities, and such features as critical reviews of neighborhood dining and entertainment opportunities. The alternative press of the 1990s, he has insisted, will not be the alternative press of the 1970s.

The Ethnic Press

The ethnic press is another type of newspaper—usually a weekly paper—whose purpose is to serve an ethnic audience, perhaps in a foreign language. Newspaper scholar Ernest Hynds reports there are some four hundred foreign language papers in the United States, printed in thirty-eight languages, and with a total circulation of two million.

A prominent part of the ethnic press—if a recent addition—is the Chicano press. It differs from other Spanish-language newspapers because it is usually bilingual and more radical. One of the first Chicano papers, *El Malcriado* (the precocious, ill-bred child), began as a union newspaper during the Cesar Chavez-led strikes in California in 1964. Chicano editors are advocates rather than reporters, focusing their editorial attention on the needs and interests of the Mexican-American community. Few Chicano papers carry advertising and most lose money, surviving on contributions from readers. Still, the rapid rise in numbers of Chicano papers indicates wide acceptance in the Chicano community.

The black press had its beginning in the abolitionist press movement of nineteenth century America. The first nonabolitionist black paper, the *Weekly Advocate,* was founded in 1842. Later renamed the *Colored American,* it became an excellent family newspaper under editor Charles Bennett Ray. In recent years research in the black community has shown black Americans continue to feel they should tell their own story, from their own point of view, and with their own newspapers.

The plight of the ethnic press:
a plea for financial support.

פֿאָרווערטס

GIVE US A MAZEL TOV!

The Jewish Daily Forward today reaches its 85th Birthday. This would be an achievement for any daily newspaper; few have lasted longer. But for a Yiddish-language daily, the durability of the Forward is surely remarkable.

The need for its services continues, not only for the many thousands for whom Yiddish is still "Mame Loshen," the mother tongue, but also for what the Forward represents as a voice of authentic Jewish expression and an instrument for Yiddish cultural survival.

The Forward was brought into being in 1897 by contributions from immigrant working people who wanted to give expression to their hopes and strivings in a free America. It has been published by a body of volunteers, the Forward Association, and never has a penny of its income been distributed as profit or dividend. It has no shareholders and no stock.

WHAT OTHERS HAVE SAID ABOUT THE FORWARD

. . . When Louis Marshall spoke about the great achievement of the Forward as a teacher, an interpretor of the American principles, he underscored the responsibility of a free press in our country . . .
. . . My best wishes that you should continue to serve your readers in the brilliant tradition of American journalism.
    President Dwight D. Eisenhower, May 1957

. . . From its earliest days the Forward has played a vital and important role in the lives of its readers . . .
. . . The dedication of the Jewish Daily Forward to the causes of justice and social, economic and political freedom for all our citizens merits the special commendation and gratitude of us all . . .
    President John F. Kennedy, Dec. 1962

. . . Since its first days, under its two prominent editors, Ab Cahan and then Hillel Rogoff, the newspaper played a central role in reporting the spiritual and cultural life of the Jewish community in the United States and also throughout the entire world . . .
    Premier Golda Meir, State of Israel, May 1972

. . . There must be hundreds of thousands of New Yorkers like me, who have warm everlasting memories of the Forward . . . As an editor, and particularly of an American paper, the Forward seems to me more important than ever . . .
    A. M. Rosenthal
    Executive Editor, N.Y. Times.

The 60th Jubilee of the Forward, the largest Yiddish paper in the world, is not only a holiday for the Jewish workers nor only a Jubilee for the Jewish press but also a great happening in the new era of the Jewish people . . .
    Premier Ben Gurion, State of Israel, May 1957

. . . I have called the Forward "indispensable" and I believe that to be so. The loss of this splendid newspaper would be a loss to us all and a severe set back in the fight to make America what it ought to be . . .
    AFL-CIO President George Meany, May 1977

. . . The Jewish Daily Forward has been for a number of talented writers not only an organ where they could publish their works, but also a kind of literary laboratory. This was certainly the case of my brother I. J. Singer and myself. While I publish there my stories and my novels I am in contact with my readers who came from lands and knew more or less what I knew. You could not cheat them with ornate phrases . . .
    Isaac Bashevis Singer
    Nobel Laureate In Literature

. . . I am writing in behalf of the Rabbinical Council of America to state categorically that the Forward serves an indispensable function in Jewish Life . . .
. . . Of equal importance is the fact that it preserves in living and dynamic form a language that has in effect become a universal language among Jews around the world.
    Rabbi Sol Roth
    President

We at the Forward are proud of these remarks and appreciate the good wishes expressed on those occasions. These have been embellished many times over by our devoted readers and the various Jewish organizations who still need and want the Forward.

But good wishes and kind remarks are not enough to sustain this newspaper. Our objective is to assure the continuity of the Forward as a daily paper. Towards this end we launched a fund raising campaign which will culminate at our 85th Anniversary celebration on Sunday, May 23, 1982. On that day we will be publishing an enlarged and enriched edition which we are sure will be of historic character. We have been encouraged by the campaign results to date, but still have a long way to go.

We are grateful for the support so far, but we know that out there in the cities and suburbs from coast to coast, there are many whom our appeal has not yet reached. We know that there is a great reservoir of appreciation for what the Forward has been and what it has meant to many generations of Americans and for its special role in American Jewish life.

BECOME A PARTNER IN THE SURVIVAL OF YIDDISH AND THE YIDDISH PRESS

We reach out to you wherever you are; the time has come when you are crucial to our continuation. PLEASE RESPOND — PLEASE HELP!! Do your share to keep the Forward alive.

Your contribution, no matter what amount, will be a Mitzvah and you will share our Mazel Tov with us. Contributions should be made out and mailed to:
    The Forward Association
    45 East 33rd Street
    New York, New York 10016
    Paid for by Friends of The Forward

Since the 1940s, however, the number of black newspapers has dropped from three hundred to 165. Black newspaper circulation had dropped from four million to three million by the late 1970s. The black newspaper suffers from several recurring problems. The black community remains undecided as to whether it wants white advertising in its newspapers. The result has been a loss of advertising revenue for the newspapers. At the same time, ad agencies attempting to reach the black consumer often find these smaller papers inefficient as advertising media. It may be more economical to reach the black consumer through the mass media. Another problem is the difficulty a potential advertiser has in determining whether advertising in a black newspaper really is a good buy. Advertising rates and verified circulation figures for many black newspapers simply are not available. The ad agent is forced to estimate audience size and the cost of reaching the appropriate segment of the audience. Still, as Hynds has suggested, as long as there is a black community there will be a need for black newspapers. And those that survive, like the New York City *Amsterdam News,* the largest black newspaper in the United States, will do so by focusing their content on what is relevant to the black community.

The Suburban Press
A cross between the weekly community newspaper and the daily is the suburban newspaper. A survey of weekly newspapers a few years ago indicated that 35 percent of all weeklies are published in a suburban area, with more than 50 percent published in big city suburbs. America began moving to the suburbs following World War II. More than 62 percent of the population had settled there by 1980. The suburban papers followed. The family that had moved "out" wanted to read about its new community, and have ads with which to shop that community, even if the head of the household did travel back to the city to work every week day. Suburban papers, born in the shadows of large city dailies, were created from an interest in local news and local advertising. The growth potential for the suburban paper today lies in its ability to expand its news coverage. Many suburban papers began as little more than a community bulletin board and want ad service. Some are still "shoppers," or all-advertising papers. To grow, the suburban paper must provide state, regional, and national news coverage. For, that is the format needed to attract both national and regional advertisers as well as the family currently subscribing to the metropolitan daily.

To improve their product, the suburban papers formed a corporation in 1970—U.S. Suburban Press Inc.—and a trade association in 1971—Suburban Newspapers of America. The corporation (USSPI) acts as a sales representative to attract national advertising accounts while the trade association (SNA) fosters improvement throughout the industry.

The quality of suburban papers is likely to become critical to their survival. Several major metropolitan newspapers already have entered into direct competition with the suburbanites by creating special suburban editions and special-insert sections for suburban audiences. The large dailies eventually must find a way to makeup the losses in circulation they suffered when the population began its move from the city to the suburbs.

The Dailies

The great majority of all daily newspapers—80 percent—are small dailies with circulations less than 50,000. Only 16 percent of all dailies, or 263, have circulations between 50,000 and 250,000. But only 3 percent, or fifty-two, have circulations larger than 250,000.

Small- and Medium-Sized Dailies

These papers, of course, serve small- and medium-sized towns and cities. An important factor in determining the news content of either, however, is the presence or absence of a metropolitan paper nearby. With a large city and a large newspaper nearby, the smaller daily survives just as a suburban paper does, by giving its readers news and advertising from its own community, and with the depth and detail the larger newspaper can not produce. The potholes in the public streets, the lack of funds to sustain the local high school glee club tour, the winner of the weekend nine-hole golf course tournament may be inconsequential to the nearby metropolitan paper, but it's the crux of the hometown daily.

The larger the paper the more likely it is to give extensive coverage of local news. The middle-sized St. Petersburg (Fla.) *Times,* for example, with a circulation of only 222,000 won a Pulitzer Prize in 1980 with its investigation into the clandestine Church of Scientology. Many feel the *Times,* despite its size, is one of the best newspapers in the nation. (It even has its own Washington reporter.) But the paper did not become involved with the nationally known scientology movement until scientology introduced itself into the St. Petersburg community with a questionable real estate purchase. The *Times'* "digging" into other local stories has resulted in an investigation of individual condominium associations, and extensive coverage of petty local crimes and accidents.

Metropolitan Dailies

Many consider metropolitan dailies to be in the forefront of American journalism. While most dailies are small, the metropolitan dailies account for most of American newspaper circulation: 60 percent. Metropolitan dailies also have more facilities and larger staffs than their smaller counterparts. While small dailies might have as many as ten reporters, and a medium-sized paper fifty, reporters on metropolitan dailies number in the hundreds. (If the Washington *Post*—circulation 618,000—had not had the reportorial staff to allow reporters Bob Woodward and Carl Bernstein to work full-time on the perplexing Watergate burglary during the Nixon administration, the story might never had been written.)

The big city dailies have the money to offer a wide range of wire, feature, and syndicated material. More important they have the staff to engage in extensive, firsthand investigative reporting. The Chicago *Sun-Times* (circulation 655,000) spent more than $20,000 in association with the Better Government Association in Chicago, in the operation of a bar—"The Mirage Bar, Watering Hole and Pub"—for a period of four months. As a result, reporters and photographers uncovered and recorded extensive corruption, estimated at $16 million, on the part of Chicago's health, safety, and liquor inspectors. A smaller paper might have had difficulty supporting an investigation half as ambitious.

The National Newspaper

Considering the importance of local news to almost all types of newspapers, it is easy to understand the old journalistic maxim that all news is local. American newspapers developed as newspapers of places, and most still retain a locale-place orientation. The Memphis *Commercial-Appeal,* the Minneapolis *Tribune,* and the Long Beach *Press-Telegram* all include their cities' names in their titles, as do most American newspapers.

The hope has persisted for years that the U.S. would be able to establish, in addition to a local press, a national press with national distribution. One regrettable failure in the pursuit of that goal came in 1977 when the *National Observer,* a national weekly published by Dow Jones & Company, folded. Although the *Observer* was recognized as a publication of high quality, it evidently failed to clearly establish its identity in the minds of readers.

More successful as a national newspaper has been the *Christian Science Monitor.* Founded in 1908 by religious leader Mary Baker Eddy, the *Monitor* long since has transcended its religious heritage to become, many critics feel, one of the truly excellent daily newspapers in the country. It emphasizes national and international news while ignoring the local or sensational stories other newspapers carry. Unfortunately, its circulation has not kept up with its high quality and cosmopolitan character. While America has grown into a nation of more than two hundred million people, *Monitor* circulation has reached only 175,000.

Ironically, the nation's largest-circulation newspaper is distributed nationally, but it does not qualify as a general interest daily newspaper because of its specialized content. The *Wall Street Journal,* without comics, sports, or even photographs, attained a daily circulation just less than two million in 1980, outstripping the New York *Daily News* as the nation's largest circulation daily. The *Journal* is vital to the commercial community, with its accurate reports of stocks, earnings, and business futures. It is written for readers between thirty-five and fifty-five years of age, with above-average incomes, and who are in business, government, and the professions. Its daily, national distribution is achieved through a system of regional printing plants that make up and print the paper from images of pages received by space satellite.

No doubt the larger national audience also will be reached through a similar satellite-to-plant arrangement. The newspaper with the necessary technology, and also general interest news content, is *USA Today,* the daily national newspaper inaugurated by the Gannett Corporation in 1982. Gannett, parent company of the largest newspaper chain in the country, made a two-year feasibility study before it decided to market the paper. A circulation of three million is *USA Today's* distribution goal, or approximately the total circulation of Gannett's chain of more than eighty newspapers.

Another group of national publications also has enjoyed national distribution, but they are best described as newspapers in format only. Celebrity papers such as the *National Enquirer, Globe,* and *Star* have attained high circulations of three or even four million. But their preference for sensational reporting of "psychic events" of Hollywood and other celebrities, and their lack of attention to significant political and social issues, makes them consumer magazines, not newspapers.

The Organization of the Newspaper Company

Needless to say, the establishments that print and distribute the modern American newspaper do not resemble the cheese, wine, and print shops that published the newspapers of colonial days. The modern establishments have become multifaceted and computer-oriented printing and news-gathering organizations. And the trend toward a pronounced division of labor that began in print shops of the 1770s has resulted in a newspaper organization with two general divisions: editorial and business. Business includes production. A diagram of a typical organization is provided in Figure 5.1.

Editorial

The editorial, or "front shop," staff of the paper does the gathering and processing of the news. The modern newpaper attempts to cast a net over its home territory by sending reporters out on "beats," to cover places, areas, or topics of continuing interest and significance to readers. The police and city hall beats (patrols) are important to every newspaper. Newspapers with large universities in their area almost always have education beats, just as newspapers in state capitals have state government beats and newspapers with large factories in their towns devise beats to cover those factories.

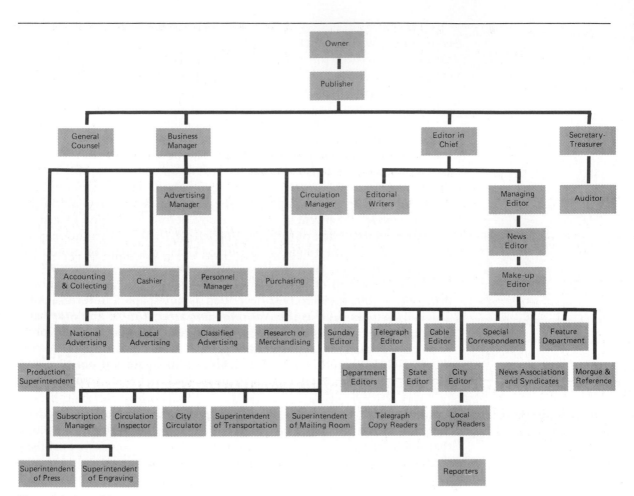

Figure 5.1 A modern newspaper organization.

The reporter can count on support from his or her editor—the city, or state, or sports editor—depending on the beat. City, state, and sports editor positions are common to almost all newspapers. The larger the paper, the more diverse the editorial roles, of course. With their years of experience, editors can question and advise reporters, and they can guide a reporter's work with information drawn from considerable in-house reference material, including the newspaper's "morgue," the well-maintained files of news stories from past editions, and the wealth of information the editor can call up from computer information services. The story that goes into the newspaper is shaped in good part by the give-and-take between reporter and editor.

Wall Street experts estimate the Gannett Corporation invested $40 to $50 million to launch the national daily *USA Today,* putting as much as $1 million
into prepublication research alone. The paper has been designed to reach the
upscale reader; in other words, the highly educated, professional or mana-
gerial person with money to spend. Research indicated these readers wanted
short, tightly written stories, colorful charts and graphs, and no "thumbsuck-
ingly" long stories.

Few would disagree that *USA Today* is an attractive paper. It makes lavish
use of color and attractive graphics—including a splashy, colorful weather
map—but the paper has not won the admiration of the newspaper fraternity.
The *Wall Street Journal* has called it the "Rodney Dangerfield of the newspaper business" since it received little respect for its news content. Many
complain that the stories in *USA Today* are too short. Journalist Katherine
Seelye has found, for example, *USA Today* gave one Congressional story nine
paragraphs, while the Washington *Post* gave it forty-seven. Because of its "fast
food" approach to news, the new paper is, *Newsweek* declared, the "Big Mac"
of newspapers.

Still, *USA Today* has managed to find a large reading audience, building a
circulation of 1.3 million by the end of its second year (in 1984), making it
reasonable to believe, as public opinion and marketing expert Louis Harris
has suggested, that the paper could well "change the face" of print journalist
for generations to come—for better or worse.

Business and Production

The business of the American newspaper is to stay in business. In the
simplest terms, the newspaper, like other businesses—media or otherwise—must gain enough revenue to pay its *fixed* and *varying costs* and
win enough profit to survive and expand. Fixed costs include paper, ink,
reporters, printers, even typewriter maintenance. Varying costs are those
that cannot be anticipated exactly: for example, a sudden eruption of a
volcano that must be covered whatever the cost, including helicopter
transportation and extensive reporter overtime.

The paper sets its prices and advertising rates to meet these demands. Fortunately, newspapers do not have as many variable costs as,
say, book publishers. A rule of thumb in weekly newspaper publishing
has been to estimate fixed and variable costs then double them to set ad
and sales prices. But the problem of setting prices also is a problem of
knowing what the market will allow. In the 1970s inflation forced some
publishers of dailies to raise prices from ten to twenty-five cents a copy.
The increase cost the industry 4 percent of its daily circulation but raised
revenues almost 16 percent, making it a profitable move.

While subscriptions and advertising sales make up the largest part
of newspaper revenue, newspapers, especially smaller ones, also earn
some 5 percent of income through their production facilities. Wedding

announcements, club pamphlets, or school yearbooks may help keep expensive presses busy during slack time. And newspaper-composing facilities often provide business clients with professional advertising layouts.

Whatever its means of income, the modern newspaper, if it is to survive in the modern media mix, must do more than make a profit. The managing editor must be able to pay debts and then show retained earnings. The paper must acquire enough capital to make the company grow—to buy new equipment, hire new reporters, and explore new subject matter for readers. If not, the paper slips into obsolesence, and begins to die.

Production or the back shop prints the newspaper—words, ads, and pictures. As the decade began, 15 percent of the metropolitan daily work force was in editorial work, 37 percent in business, advertising, and circulation, and 48 percent was in production and maintenance. The most striking changes in the modern newspaper in recent years have come in new technology in production facilities, with improved printing, typesetting, and news story processing technology.

The Newspaper Business
The New Technology

Certainly, the best business investment the industry has made in many years began in the 1970s with the adoption of a new, revolutionary production system. Even twenty years after the end of World War II, most newspapers were dependent on the same, basic printing methodology used by Gutenberg. While technology was more advanced, Gutenburg's "letterpress" printing still depended on casting type in molten lead which, when cooled and inked, made the impressions for reading.

"Hot type" printing methods were improved considerably in the nineteenth century. As noted in chapter 3, the linotype machine, invented by Ottmar Mergenthaler, speeded up typesetting by making it possible to cast rows, or "slugs," of type at once. The presses were "web" fed, printing on continuous rolls of paper; they printed whole pages from lead stereotypes, allowing a much more interesting page layout than was possible before. (See chapter 3.) Still, letterpress printing was expensive, cumbersome, and time consuming.

Photocomposition and offset printing were the first improvements on the hot type system. The hot lead and the linotype machine were replaced by "cold type" and photocomposition machines. These machines contained "pictures" of typefaces that were exposed on light-sensitive paper. With darkroom development, photocomposition could produce type of any size—and on paper instead of in expensive lead. Phototype was cheap, clean, fast, and as easy to handle as a typewriter and darkroom

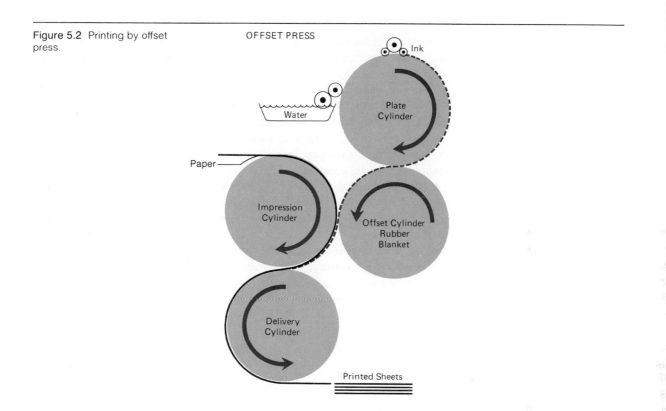

Figure 5.2 Printing by offset press.

OFFSET PRESS

Ink

Plate Cylinder

Water

Paper

Impression Cylinder

Offset Cylinder Rubber Blanket

Delivery Cylinder

Printed Sheets

negatives. When developed it could be waxed into place on a page—and easily removed and placed a second, or third time, if necessary, before the page was finally engraved for the press.

Offset printing was derived from lithography, a duplicating method used for many years by artists who made prints by forming pictures on flat stones and pressing paper directly onto the paints. As they lifted the paper they "caught up" the picture, or one layer of the *paint*. The offset presses developed for newspaper work place ink on a thin, moist, lightly engraved, chemically treated plate. The oil-base ink does not mix with the water on the plate. It forms instead in the treated, photoengraved depressions of the plate where it "puddles" to be caught up by a rubber roller. The roller (or "blanket") then rolls the formed ink onto the paper. No type touches the paper, only the formed ink. (See figure 5.2) The result is an especially clear imprint that cannot be duplicated with the lead type of letterpress, since the type always leaves noticeable surface marks as it makes its imprint.

In the 1960s weekly newspapers found they could replace their wornout hot type equipment with photocomposition and offset equipment and save money. Those who made the change found cost and ease of production more than worth the problems of changing old habits. Some weekly publishers decided to join with others in their area and share the cost of buying the new photocomposition and offset equipment. With the equipment at a central location they not only were able to set and print their own newspapers but also offer a high-quality printing service to others—ethnic, counterculture and school publications, for example—at a reasonable price. The costs of operating offset presses for long runs were not attractive to larger circulation papers at first, but according to the American Newspaper Publishers Association Research Institute 97 percent of all daily newspapers were using photocomposition and offset printing methods by the later 1970s.

Even more important to the industry has been the adoption of computer based news copy processing. Using video display terminals (VDTs) and computer terminal keyboards in conjunction with phototype setting equipment, a reporter in the new computerized newsroom can type a story into the computer, edit it, then send it onto the editor who, with his or her own word processing computer terminal, can read and edit it and, by striking a key, have it set in type. Even the phototype copy can be corrected or added to before it finally is sent along to page composition for insertion in the newspaper.

With optical character recognition (OCR) equipment, copy can be fed directly into the computer and then into phototype composition, if the copy is prepared on white paper using the proper style of electric typewriter face. A mayor's speech, a late-breaking announcement, or even a last-minute want ad can go directly into the paper without being retyped.

Computer based copy processing has saved money and significantly reduced both processing time and news story error in modern newspapers. It is little wonder the use of computers in newspaper work has not stopped with VDTs and OCRs. Already in use is a system to handle classified advertising. It classifies then alphabetizes ads, and prints them out in order, ready for waxing to the final newspaper page. Programs and systems with the ability to do regular newspaper page layout are on the horizon, and may be available before 1990.

Experimentation continues, too, with computer controlled plateless presses—ones that spray ink directly onto the paper. Such a press could give incredible savings to the metropolitan daily newspaper. In the late 1970s, for example, the Los Angeles *Times* was cutting between five and ten thousand stereotype plates a day. The *Times* paid $1 million for a new laser system to cut the plates, but it was so efficient it saved

The dying afternoon daily: the last edition of the *Washington Star.*

$500,000 a year, paying for itself in two years, and saving the company half-a-million dollars a year after that. A press that performed well without the cost of plates or a plate cutting system could gain wide industry adoption—quickly.

Death in the Afternoon

The overall success of the newspaper industry has not hidden one troublesome, even ominous problem. Since World War II, first one, then another stellar afternoon metropolitan daily has lost circulation, then money, then been forced to cease publication. Recent notable departures have included the Chicago *Daily News* in 1978, the Washington *Star* in 1981, and both the Philadelphia *Bulletin* and the Cleveland *Press* in 1982.

The *Daily News* had a distinguished journalistic history, winning a total of fifteen Pulitzer prizes. It was the sixth largest newspaper in the country, but it was losing $11 million a year when it died. The *Star* won two Pulitzer prizes between 1978 and 1981, while losing $85 million—so much money that owner-publisher Time, Inc., decided to abandon it. The Philadelphia *Bulletin,* losing $20 million a year, avoided folding in 1981 by gaining union concessions worth $4.9 million. Still, the Bulletin died in 1982, as losses mounted and a new "blue-collar" news policy did little to improve readership and circulation in a city that already had two blue-collar papers. Meanwhile, in 1980 the Cleveland *Press,* under

The sudden eruption of a volcano, like other unexpected events, challenges the news budget for coverage expenses.

Joseph E. Cole, launched a bright new Sunday edition to attract subscribers and Sunday advertisers and compete with the grayer but more popular Sunday edition of the Cleveland *Plain-Dealer.* The hope was to attract advertising and circulation for the afternoon edition of the *Press.* But the innovative strategy did not work. In the summer of 1982, the *Press* ceased publication with annual losses of $6 million.

Some afternoon dailies have found other ways to solve their circulation dilemma. The Minneapolis *Star,* a stalwart performer for many years in the Upper Midwest, merged with its morning sibling, the *Tribune,* in 1982, after experimenting with changes in format and content. A similar fate befell the Lexington (Kentucky) *Leader* the same year. As journalists Dennis Holder and Elizabeth Franklin discovered, ten of the 114 cities where separate dailies were published in 1982 lost one of their newspapers to mergers, including Tampa, Des Moines, Portland (Oregon), Oakland, and Spartanburg, South Carolina.

The merger of a morning and an afternoon daily, both of which are owned by the same company, has created a new kind of newspaper, the all-day paper. Newspaper analyst John Morton has predicted the trend will continue, largely due to the stagnant economy of recent years, but also because of increased media competition for advertising dollars from the other mass media. The two newspaper company will find it more and more difficult to abide the ad competition between its own two newspapers and also fight off competition from radio, television, magazines, and the national media, Morton has warned. A principal concern is that two merged papers will not be able to maintain high quality news coverage, including the thorough watchdogging of government two papers can provide by operating separately.

The Newspaper Preservation Act

Newspapers not owned by the same company have had to be more careful in their attempts to merge. In 1940 two Tucson, Arizona, newspapers, the *Citizen* and the *Star* combined their operations to set advertising prices, protect each other's operations within the county, and even pool profits. In 1965 the Supreme Court ruled the Tucson agreement was illegal, a violation of the antitrust laws. The decision shook the industry. Many joint-operating agreements were in existence—although not all had been made for profit. Some had been reached when one of the two newspaper companies was on the verge of financial collapse. By combining printing plants or business offices with their former competitor the failing paper reduced costs and managed to survive.

With the support of the newspaper industry, Congress passed the Newspaper Preservation Act in 1970 to allow failing newspapers to merge with other newspaper companies without incurring antitrust action. If one paper is failing in a newspaper market, two companies in the market can merge, set joint-advertising rates, pool profits, and protect each other in their area of operation. But the two newspapers may not merge their editorial and reporting staffs. They must continue to have distinct editorial voices if they are to avoid antitrust action. At last report, there were almost two dozen cities in the country where two companies were publishing newspapers under joint-operating agreements. Birmingham, Alabama; Bristol, Tennessee; Cincinnati and Columbus, Ohio; El Paso; Tulsa; San Francisco; and Pittsburgh were among them.

Newspaper Content and the Changing Reader

It would be easy, as journalist and critic Dan Rottenberg has observed, to blame the failure of afternoon dailies on the "twin devils" of "television and suburbanization." But the record is far from clear that such is the case. Suburban newspapers have provided aggressive competition for many afternoon big city dailies. But, as Newspaper Advertising Bureau researcher Leo Bogart has pointed out, television news does not steal newspaper readers. As a matter of fact, television news ratings have been found to be higher in cities where afternoon papers also are able to make circulation gains. And in bigger cities, television news audiences and newspaper readership often shrink simultaneously. "The reason why individual newspapers prosper or falter are many and complex," Bogart has concluded, "but TV news competition cannot be numbered among them."

Other research has confirmed Bogart's conclusion. In 1978, Jack McLeod and Sun Yuel Choe, in research for the American Newspaper Publishers Association (ANPA), found that marital status, time of residence in a city, party affiliation, and political participation are more strongly related to newspaper reading than television viewing. The following year, John P. Robinson and Leo W. Jeffers, in a study of more than fifteen hundred newspaper readers, found people who watch television news more likely to read newspapers than those who do not.

These findings and others lead newspaper publishers to conclude that the type and quality of newspaper coverage is the key to holding or regaining circulation within the community.

New Directions in Newspaper Coverage

Studies of newspaper content by the ANPA indicate 60 to 70 percent of the total content of the average daily newspaper is advertising. Of the remaining news and entertainment content, general interest news of state political and social significance make up 15 to 20 percent, with business, sports, women's news, and crossword puzzles contributing the remaining 10 to 15 percent. And so the daily newspaper must do much of its news reporting with less than 30 percent of its total content.

One general theme heard in the industry for several years is that newspapers will win out in modern media competition if they fill their news "holes" with news that complements information found in other media. Allen Neuharth, president of the Gannett newspaper chain, has argued newspapers must take advantage of appetites whetted by the other media, or by elaborating on themes and events presented on television and cable television.

As already noted, some dailies—especially the afternoon metropolitan dailies—are trying to reach news and audiences with new appeals. More than one has turned its attention to the up-scale reader, the professional with interests in business, the arts, and the city's lifestyle, and little interest in gossipy crime coverage and bleeding heart features. At the same time, other editors are looking to the inner-city blue-collar reader. Editor Dan Forst of the afternoon daily the Boston *Herald-American* has said he wants to "grab" his reader "by the throat" on his front page. When the Boston subway ground to a halt, the *Herald-American's* headline on the story growled, "Start Walking."

There are other news coverage innovations too; here are a few of the most significant.

Precision Journalism

The use of social and behavioral science tools to gather information and news has become known as precision journalism. Polls, sampling, and data analysis are featured regularly in newspapers that wish to present scientifically reliable news. This information is based on more than one or two interviewee's observations or interviews that only tap one of many issues in a story.

Business News

In the past, business news has more often been ignored than reported by many newspapers. Dailies have expanded their business news coverage in recent years and now devote more of their news "holes" to business matters. A 1978 survey by *Editor & Publisher* found more than 60 percent of all dailies give at least 5 percent of their news content to business coverage.

Entertainment and the Arts

Dailies have come to provide important coverage for entertainment and the arts. The television/cable logs, with program notes, has grown so important many dailies now have a television TV/entertainment editor. Film and entertainment critiques also have become a regular feature in most metropolitan dailies, while the Sunday edition of the paper may well carry a complete arts/entertainment section as well as a separate book review section.

People, Fashion, and Food

Pages covering these topics have been part of the newspaper since the nineteenth century. Recent changes, as Hynds has suggested, include a de-emphasis on society news (weddings and club news, etc.) and increased coverage of issues of interest to women. The woman's page now includes news of women's rights, consumer issues, and social issues such as alcoholism and abortion. At the same time, newspapers have not abandoned the career homemaker. Eighty-five percent of all papers surveyed in 1983 ran food sections (usually on Wednesday). And the trend in food page coverage is away from the "payola" story. In 1974 the Newspaper Food Editors and Writers Association officially endorsed a policy of objectivity in food page news reporting, denouncing the practice of carrying stories or recipes that promoted products that appeared in the newspaper's advertising columns, "by coincidence."

The New New Journalism

A reporting style that developed in the 1960s and 1970s has found its way into many newspapers. Unrelated to the new journalism of Joseph Pulitzer, the new journalism of this century is a reporting style that uses fiction techniques—extended dialogue, characters, even composite characters—to tell a factual news story. As Hynds has pointed out, the trend offers newspaper reporting an additional dimension, but one major drawback is that the fictional style might attract incompetent reporters who will not completely immerse themselves in the subject before writing. As a result, the story will not be accurate and the newspaper's credibility will suffer.

The important question to ask of newspaper coverage is whether newspapers offer what readers want to read. Recent research gives an unsettling answer to this question. In 1983, research by the National Advertising Bureau concluded that readers want a variety of content in their papers, but they read the paper more for news than for entertainment. They want national and international news first, local news second—but they also want to be entertained. Meanwhile, there has been a noticeable trend away from hard news to "soft," or feature news, probably in the interest of competing with and offering an alternative to harder television news reporting. For the last decade, newspaper content has been in direct contrast to what readers say they like to read, a trend more than one newspaper president has called "alarming." As National Advertising Bureau general manager Leo Bogart has observed, newspapers could lose much if they continue "chicken dinner" news as competition to television. If the trend continues, he has argued, newspapers will lose touch with the real concerns of readers, and fail to bring them what they need most: vivid interpretation of the bewildering news that comes to them daily.

The Leading Dailies

Naming the leading newspaper, or the leading newspapers, has become an increasingly difficult task. Professional critics and observers who have attempted to do so have had a difficult time choosing from among many good newspapers in the field. Still, those who recently have undertaken the task seem to be remarkably consistent. There seems to be about fifteen daily newspapers that are ranked again and again at the top of the list. They are:

The Atlanta *Constitution*
The Baltimore *Sun*
The Boston *Globe*
The Chicago *Tribune*
The *Christian Science Monitor*
The Kansas City *Star*
The Los Angeles *Times*
The Louisville *Courier-Journal*
The Miami *Herald*
The Milwaukee *Journal*
Newsday (Long Island, New York)
The New York *Times*
The St. Louis *Post-Dispatch*
The Wall Street *Journal*
The Washington *Post*

If we had to choose the top five newspapers in the country, the vote would probably include the *Christian Science Monitor,* the New York *Times*, the Washington *Post,* and the *Wall Street Journal*. All excel in foreign and national news coverage, in interpretative reporting, and in offering readers a wide range of high-quality editorial opinion.

Success Story

One of the true success stories of newspapering since World War II is the Los Angeles *Times,* and its parent company, the Times Mirror Company. The *Times* is frequently mentioned as one of the top five papers in the country, although as recently as 1960 it was considered little more than a regional, mediocre, Republican mouthpiece. That year, Otis Chandler became the publisher of the family paper (following his father) and began to make it both an excellent newspaper and a business success; it now is the third largest daily in the country. (See figure 5.3.) Since 1960 the paper's editorial budget has increased ten times—from $3.6 million to more than $36 million a year. Its editorial staff has increased to 787 positions—as opposed to 261 on the respectable St. Louis *Post-Dispatch*. As Professor Diana Tillinghast has pointed out, the Times Mirror Company has grown as a business organization by using the three

Figure 5.3

U.S. Daily Newspaper Circulation—1983's 20 Largest[1]

Daily Circulation

The Wall Street Journal	2,020,132 (m)
New York Daily News	1,395,504 (m)
Los Angeles Times	1,038,499 (m)
New York Post	962,078 (all day)
The New York Times	910,538 (m)
Chicago Tribune	751,024 (all day)
The Washington Post	718,842 (m)
The Detroit News	650,683 (all day)
Chicago Sun-Times	639,134 (m)
Detroit Free Press	635,114 (m)
The Philadelphia Inquirer	533,176 (m)
San Francisco Chronicle	530,954 (m)
Newsday	525,216 (e)
The Boston Globe	514,817 (all day)
The Cleveland Plain Dealer	493,329 (m)
Houston Chronicle	459,225 (all day)
The Newark Star-Ledger	432,110 (m)
The Miami Herald	406,656 (m)
The Houston Post	402,181 (m)
Minneapolis Star and Tribune	361,747 (m)

[1]ABC FAS-FAX figures as of Sept. 30, 1983

(USA Today circulation, not audited by ABC, estimated at 1,041,667 as of Sept. 30, 1983.)

Source: *"Facts About Newspapers '84,"* American Newspaper Publishers Association

vital strategies: (1) it has extended its control over resources needed in its operation; (2) it has met its competition without losing control of it; and (3) it has diversified its own media products and decreased its dependence on individual audiences.

The Times Mirror Company has gained control over its needed resources in several ways. It owns more than 200,000 acres of timberland in Oregon and Washington. The timber, along with two paper mills, allows the company to withstand better than many of its competitors abrupt rises in newsprint prices. In 1976 the company also formed its own newspaper delivery system. By eliminating outside delivery middlemen (their contracts were bought up) the *Times* was able to realize more profit from the paper without raising prices. In 1981 Times Mirror built its own power plant to stabilize rising energy costs. The company now sells its surplus electricity to the city of Los Angeles.

The *Times'* local competition includes twenty suburban dailies, almost all well-financed by other newspaper chains. To meet this tough competition, it has continually improved its news coverage, making the

Otis Chandler has made the Los Angeles *Times* one of the most respected and influential newspapers in America since becoming publisher in 1960.

newspaper as indispensable as possible to its readers. It has inaugurated extensive coverage of the suburban areas and in 1978 even moved into the San Diego area with a daily and a Sunday publication.

Hopes are high that a huge new printing plant will provide the ability to print a more diverse newspaper product—needed to reach the many different suburbs in Los Angeles with special runs and special editions.

To diversify its profits, Times Mirror has moved into broadcasting and cable television, and into newspaper publishing in other cities. In 1984 it owned seven television stations and ranked sixth in cable television ownership. Some 27 percent of the homes in Southern California subscribe to the *Times*. If readers abandon the paper, Times Mirror can fall back on profits from such out-of-town papers as *Newsday* in Long Island, New York, the *Times-Herald* in Dallas, and the Hartford *Courant* in Connecticut. Perhaps one of the company's most successful ventures has been the founding of, in cooperation with the Washington *Post,* the Times-Post news service, which also has given the *Times* prestige and visibility on the East Coast.

The Newspaper Group

The success of the Times Mirror Company is echoed in the successes of other newspaper groups across the country.

The modern newspaper group can be traced in the U.S. to William Randolph Hearst and Edward Wyllis Scripps, who in the late 1800s pursued the goal of publishing their own string of newspapers in cities across the country. There were at least sixty newspaper chains involving three hundred newspapers by the late 1920s. Frank E. Gannett acquired sixteen newspapers in New York State in the 1930s. John S. Knight added the Miami *Herald* and the Detroit *Free Press* to his Akron *Beacon-Journal* by the 1940s. S. I. Newhouse was acquiring his group in the East during the same period. All are major newspaper chains today. (See figure 5.4.)

They vary greatly in size and composition. Some are made up of large, high circulation metropolitan dailies (Hearst, Scripps-Howard, and Newhouse). Others are primarily small papers or medium-sized dailies (Thomson and Gannett). Most have acquired broadcast and cable operations along with newspapers.

There has been much concern over their growth. The top twenty newspaper groups now control more than half the total daily U.S. newspaper circulation. Such a concentration of control seems a threat in itself—firsthand proof of an evolving dictatorship of policies in the marketplace of ideas. There are even stronger fears about the entrance of nonnewspaper corporations or conglomerates into the publishing field.

U.S. Newspaper Companies—1983's 20 Largest
Ranked by Daily Circulation

	Daily Circulation[1]	Number of Dailies	Sunday Circulation[1]	Number of Sunday Editions
Gannett Co. Inc.[2]	4,483,483	85	3,472,915	56
Knight-Ridder Newspapers Inc.	3,651,369	29	4,347,439	22
Newhouse Newspapers	3,202,759	27	3,551,315	21
Tribune Co.	2,756,062	8	3,702,702	7
Dow Jones & Company Inc.	2,558,341	21	388,884	10
Times Mirror Co.	2,340,844	7	2,934,891	7
News America Publishing Inc.	2,087,681	5	1,120,243	3
Scripps-Howard Newspapers	1,459,880	16	1,576,782	7
The New York Times Co.	1,367,338	21	1,911,659	10
Thomson Newspapers Inc. (U.S.)	1,294,711	84	804,802	38
Cox Enterprises Inc.	1,196,448	18	1,363,987	13
Hearst Newspapers	969,193	14	1,927,760	8
Capital Cities Communication Inc.	965,063	9	824,015	5
Freedom Newspapers Inc.	849,413	29	802,983	19
Central Newspapers Inc.	804,641	7	842,223	4
The Washington Post Co.	774,167	2	1,052,185	2
Cowles Newspapers	713,398	6	1,081,659	6
The Copley Press Inc.	708,071	11	641,976	6
Evening News Association	690,289	5	788,203	1
Donrey Media Group	617,690	49	588,257	42

[1]Average for six months ended Sept. 30, 1983
[2]Includes estimated average of 1,041,667 for USA Today
Source: *"Facts About Newspapers '84,"* American Newspaper Publishers Association

Figure 5.4

Can these huge businesses, steeped in traditions of secrecy and profits, live up to the responsibilities that newspapers inherit along with their First Amendment freedoms?

A case in point developed in the late 1970s when the Panax Corporation, a business concern that had purchased several small daily newspapers, sent a news release to its editors asking for front page placement as soon as possible. The two "stories" indicated then-President Carter encouraged male members of his staff to engage in sexual promiscuity, and also that the president was grooming his wife Rosalynn to become vice-president. Six of the editors ran the two stories as requested. Two others did not. One resigned in protest, insisting the material was not front page, but, at best, editorial page material. The other was fired. In the confusion that followed, Panax president John P. McGoff issued a statement arguing he had the right to "distribute whatever news copy

Death, Taxes, and the Rise of the Groups

Young publisher Charles M. Young paid $1,500 for the Helena *World* in 1910, then competed successfully with fourteen other newspapers to survive as the single paper in his small, east Arkansas town. When Young died in 1979, at the age of ninety-seven, his son Porter was forced to sell the *World* to Park Newspapers of New York. Keeping the paper meant Porter would have had to pay 70 percent of the appraised value of the newspaper in estate tax. A newspaper earning only $250,000 each year might have a value of $12 million in today's newspaper market, making the estate tax $8.5 million. If the heir sought to borrow that money to pay the taxes, the annual interest cost would be as much as three times what the newspaper could earn.

Economist James Dertouzos of the Rand Corporation has said estate taxes are the major factor causing independents to sell their newspapers to a newspaper group. Buying newspapers can be profitable for the groups, too, Dertouzos has argued. He has estimated a major group, such as Gannett, or Copley, can afford to pay good prices for a good newspaper, because as much as forty-five cents of every dollar paid comes back in the form of income tax writeoffs. (Group officials argue it is more like twenty cents.)

Whatever advantages there are for the group buyer and the indpendent seller, most observers agree the rising market in independent newspapers has contributed mightily to the rising sales prices of independent newspapers. The group interest in buying good newspapers raises the potential value of newspapers, which in turn inflates the appraised values and consequently the taxes the estate must pay on an inherited newspaper. This consequently raises the probability that the family inheriting a newspaper will sell it to a newspaper group. Whether or not this vicious cycle will continue under the estate tax changes passed by Congress is not yet clear. The 1981 Economic Tax Recovery Act increases the amount of an estate that is exempt from taxation (up to $600,000 by 1987), and reduces the amount paid from 70 to 50 percent. Property left a spouse is not taxed.

he deems appropriate and to demand, if necessary, that such copy be printed . . . ." Most journalists would not agree. Few experienced publishers would attempt to bypass the democratic publisher-editor-reporter debate most papers encourage as a check on errors and falsehoods. But Panax, with its corporationlike approach to publishing, did.

Charges that a chain will milk a newspaper for profits—even if it does not use it for political propaganda—are supported by other cases. In 1976 Australian Rupert Murdoch bought the staid but respectable New York *Post,* and turned it into a sex and scandal sheet, similar to his supermarket tabloid *Star,* published in Canada. Murdoch's purchase of the Chicago *Sun Times* in 1984, saw that investigative newspaper turn to using such headlines as "Men Bear Children?"

Writers Janet Higbie, Mary Farrell, and Robert Potter made a detailed study of the small Connellsville, Pennsylvania, *Daily Courier* in 1975, after it was purchased by the Thomson USA chain. At first, Thomson brought strict business management to the paper, an advantage of chain operation. But then, strict cost-cutting followed: (1) a raise in advertising rates, and (2) a substitution of cheaper wire service news for more expensive local news reports. The writers charge the changes meant profits for Thomson and greatly reduced local news coverage for Connellsville readers.

Whatever the charges, it is difficult to prove chain ownership by newspaper or nonnewspaper corporations is inherently bad. Group purchase, like newspaper mergers, has helped some papers by giving them improved management with realistic business practices. It also has been argued that group support can keep an individual paper going in the face of an advertising rebellion against, say, an unpopular but worthy editorial policy. And not all chains attempt to dictate editorial policy to their papers. During the 1950s and 1960s some Newshouse papers were determinedly liberal on civil liberties issues; others decidedly conservative. Gannett now publicly advertises its policy of keeping individual Gannett papers free to serve their own communities as local Gannett professional managers see fit.

For better or worse, chain growth seems likely to continue. Inflation, especially the rising costs of newsprint, makes independent newspaper operation difficult and unfavorable inheritance taxes are eliminating the large, family newspaper just as they are the large family farm. Chain ownership, with good professional management, however, can improve its profits, as well as the news service for the community it serves. Knight-Ridder, Times Mirror, and the New York *Times* groups, among others, all have proved such can be the case.

Careers in Newspapers

If you choose to pursue a newspaper career, you can look forward to being a part of a well-supported, growing industry—but one with keen competition for the better positions. Research by the Newspaper Fund indicates editors now are forced to give close scrutiny to the educational backgrounds and training of those who apply for work as reporters, editors, or photographers. Eighty-three percent of all entry level jobs on dailies go to college journalism graduates. The same survey indicates 76 percent of the editors in key editorial positions (executive editor to business editor) are also journalism graduates. While it is possible to enter newspaper work without professional journalism training, those who do and those who get promoted are in the minority. One editor estimates that college journalism training gives its graduates a five year advantage over nonjournalism college graduates, or that the latter must work five years to catch up with journalism grads.

The best advice for the beginning media applicant is to be prepared to move. One of the best ways to enter the profession is to gain a good range of experience in one, two, or even three small papers before moving to the big city. Large newspapers can pay for experience. And they now hire few people directly from college. But the better the would-be journalist can become at witnessing events, at capturing them in words or on film, the more marketable he or she becomes for the job competition that exists with metropolitan dailies. (Some journalists will be satisfied to stay with the smaller papers, of course, and with the *many* advantages of living in a smaller town.)

Beginning weekly newspaper salaries in the early 1980s were reported to range from $161 to $170 per week, with dailies paying beginners $181 to $190. Newspaper labor writer Clark Newsom has reported surveys that indicate daily newspapers with circulations of over 50,000 paid beginning reporters an average of $301 per week as of January 1, 1984. At the same time, starting reporters' average salaries in the 120 papers holding contracts with the American Newspaper Guild was $330.50. Smaller and nonunion papers paid much less. Newsom reported that one survey found Illinois papers with circulations under 15,000 paid beginning reporters $185 per week in 1984.

After a trial period, most newspapers raise reporters' salaries appreciably. Even small daily papers give a $10 raise after probation, and usually give some compensation for experience and years of service—a "top minimum" pay scale as it is often called. A review of beginning, top minimum, and night shift pay schedules reported in contracts filed with the American Newspaper Publisher's Association is presented in figure 5.5.

Among the highest paid newspaper professionals are metropolitan daily editors on papers with circulations of 100,000 or more. They earn about $50,000 a year, while small town daily editors (c. 25,000) earn $28,000. Newsom also reported that, as a rule of thumb, a large metropolitan daily will pay twice or more the salary for a top position, such as director of advertising or circulation, than a paper with only 50,000 circulation.

A very few exceptional reporters may free-lance—writing their own books and articles for the national audience. Luck, persistence, and a great deal of talent can bring them an annual income in six figures. Most

Selected Examples of Reporter's Weekly Salaries in ANPA Newspapers Beginning and Top Minimum Salaries

From Contracts on file July, 1984
Average Weekly Starting Salary: $318.07
With 2 to 6 Years Service: (Average Top Minimum): $503.37

	Begin. Salary	Top Min. Year Paid	Night Shift	Contract Effective
New York *Times* (total c. 908,585)	$814.26	$843.26 (3rd)	+$34.30	3/84
Detroit *News* (total c. 623,763)	$376.84	$574.14 (5th)	+$25	6/83
Seattle *Post-Intelligencer* (c.186,628) *Times* (c. 260,675)	$426.50	$625.35 (6th)	+$5.00	7/83
Richmond (Va.) *Times-Dispatch, News-Leader* (total c. 249,318)	$307.69	$500.00 (5th)	+$7.50/$10.00	5/83
San Antonio *Light* (total c. 115,556)	$218.69	$409.76 (6th)	+$10.00	3/83
Lexington (Ky.) *Herald, Leader* (total c. 105,249)	$260.00	$385.00 (5th)	+$10.00	9/83
Gary (Ind.) *Post-Tribune* (total c. 81,543)	$309.76	$562.00 (6th)	+$20.00	10/83
Birmingham (Ala.) *Post-Herald* (total c. 66,643)	$221.00	$420.00 (7th)	+$10.00	3/83
Pueblo (Colo.) *Chieftain, Star-Journal* (total c. 51,866)	$213.00	$425.00 (6th)	+$11.50	12/83
Yakima (Wash.) *Herald-Republic* (total c. 39,661)	$310.75	$413.25 (5th)	+$10.00	5/83
Bristol (Conn.) *Press* (total c. 21,851)	$208.55	$352.26 (5th)	+$10.00	9/81
Burlington (Iowa) *Hawk Eye* (total c. 19,807)	$180.00	$240.00 (5th)	(+$2.00 Saturday Night)	9/83

Source: *Presstime,* journal of the American Newspaper Publishers Association, August 1984.

Figure 5.5

journalists, however, look forward to a career of involvement in local or metropolitan newspaper work, and a profession that, research suggests, is very high in job satisfaction.

The newspaper industry also has job opportunities in news production, circulation, graphic design, computer technology, and advertising and promotion. Advertising salaries are comparable to reporting and editing salaries. Figures for the other positions vary widely and are more difficult to obtain. Check the want ads in the trade publication *Editor & Publisher* for estimates for those positions, or write the ANPA, Box 17407, Washington, D.C., 20041.

The Newspaper Guild   Generally, the highest salaries in the newspaper profession are paid by newspapers and news organizations that have contracts with the Newspaper Guild. The guild, the union for the working newspaperperson, was born in 1933. It survived a troubled childhood in the 1930s and 1940s, when guild members were jailed for handing out strike bills and attacked by "goon squads" with clubs. The roughhouse tactics are long gone, and the guild now holds more than two hundred contracts with newspapers in Canada and the United States. Some newspapers have contracts with independent newspaper unions. Most newspapers do not have labor contracts with their editorial staffs. More than one third of all guild membership is under contract with five big locals in New York, Washington-Baltimore, Toronto, San Francisco-Oakland, and the Wire Service Guild. Shop contracts require those who join the staffs of guild newspapers to join the guild.

Summary

The American newspaper industry is one of the largest employers in the country. It also leads all media in advertising revenue.

Professionals in the field usually refer to newspapers according to their frequency of distribution and their purpose. Most nondailies are published in rural-agricultural communities. There are, however, several other types of nondailies:

1. Alternative or underground papers lead the attack on American popular culture in the 1960s and 1970s, but now apparently are turning their attention to local political and cultural reporting.
2. Ethnic newspapers serve foreign language communities, or the black or Chicano reader.
3. The suburban press has established itself in suburban areas around larger cities.

Small- and medium-sized dailies survey local problems—with significant support from local advertisers. The medium-sized daily is capable of a wider range of news coverage and syndicated feature material than the small daily. Metropolitan papers have the revenue and the staff size to present wire service news, news services, syndicated columnists, political cartoonists, comic strips and extensive investigative reporting.

A serious attempt to establish a general interest, nationally distributed newspaper began in 1982 with the Gannett Corporation's *USA Today*. It joined the *Christian Science Monitor* and the *Wall Street Journal* in reaching a national audience.

Newspapers are divided into two departments: editorial and business. Business includes production. The editorial staff collects and edits the news. The business division keeps the books and solicits advertising. Production puts the news and advertising into print. Production of the newspaper has gone through a major technological revolution since World War II. "Hot-type" has been replaced by "cold," or phototype. Letterpress printing has given way to offset. Today, computer-based word processing has been installed in many news rooms.

Most revenue comes from advertising; other revenue is from newspaper sales. About 5 percent comes from production facility services, such as printing and layout.

The newspaper with the most difficult time at present is the afternoon metropolitan daily. Loss of circulation and/or advertising dollars has plagued it since the 1960s. Several have changed their editorial content to attract new readers, including more business news, objective food page reporting, precision journalism, and new, new journalism.

The successful newspaper survives by controlling resources vital to its operation (wood pulp/newsprint, etc.), meeting the competition, and diversifying its own media products. Failing newspapers now are allowed to control competition somewhat by forming joint-operating agreements with other area newspapers.

The growth of newspaper groups—and the purchase of newspapers by nonnewspaper corporations—has raised concern over the loss of voices in the market place. Despite some striking individual cases, it is difficult to prove chain ownership is necessarily good or bad. Inflation and unfavorable inheritance taxes, among other things, have led many independent publishers to sell their papers. The trend toward group growth seems likely to continue.

Experience suggests job seekers should first find a job with a small daily. Metropolitan dailies do not usually hire personnel directly from college.

Questions for Discussion

1. We have said the newspaper industry is one of the largest in the country, even larger in some years than the steel and automobile industries. Are these statistics biased? In what ways, for example, might the steel industry be said to be larger than the newspaper industry? How do salaries in other industries compare with newspaper salaries? How do you account for these differences?

2. It is believed by some that the afternoon daily is dying due to losses in circulation. How important is circulation to the newspaper? Why? Are there other ways of measuring a newspaper's health? What are they and how do they relate to circulation?

3. Try to understand the problems of the afternoon daily from the readers' viewpoint. Does your own afternoon and evening usually include reading a daily newspaper? What media do you use during that period? Under what conditions might you read an afternoon paper?

4. Newspaper content is changing. As a reader would you prefer to have (1) a thorough business section, (2) more entertainment/arts criticism, (3) more surveys and polls on public opinion, or (4) more sports news? What type of information do you usually look for in the newspaper? How do your news interests differ from (1) your closest friend, (2) your parents?

5. Careful consideration suggests all newspapers have one kind of ethnic bias or another. Compare three issues of a regular weekly newspaper from a small town with three issues of an ethnic, black, or Chicano paper. How does the content in the two newspapers differ? Are they more different than alike? More alike than different? Be sure to compare pictures, too.

References

"The Afternoon Syndrome." *Newsweek,* August 17, 1981, 64.

"Are Readers Getting What They Want?" *Editor & Publisher.* December 3, 1983, 16–17.

"The Best Selling U.S. Daily." *Newsweek,* April 21, 1980, 64.

"The Big Mac of Newspapers." *Newsweek,* January 17, 1983, 48.

Bogart, Leo. "How the Challenge of Television News Affects the Prosperity of Daily Newspapers," *Journalism Quarterly* 52 (1975):430–10.

"Death in the Afternoon." *Washington Journalism Review,* October 1981, 41–45.

Facts About Newspapers 1984. Washington: American Newspaper Publishers Association, 1984.

"Fat Times in Los Angeles." *Newsweek,* September 22, 1980, 46.

Galloways, Paul. "The Mirage, Story of a Chicago Newspaper's Bar & Grill." *The Quill.* February, 1978, 12–16.

Good, Jeffrey. "Fugitives from a Chain Gang." *Washington Journalism Review,* May, 1981, 34–37.

Hulting, John L. "The Performance or the Power?" *The Quill,* October, 1977, 23 et seq.

Hynds, Ernest C. *American Newspapers in the 1980's.* New York: Hastings House, 1980.

Holder, Dennis. "What's a Zippy Newspaper Like the *Times* Doing in a Town Like St. Petersburg?" *Washington Journalism Review.* October 1981, 16–20.

———, and Elizabeth Franklin. "Mergers." *Washington Journalism Review.* April, 83, 28–33.

Journalism Career and Scholarship Guide. Princeton: Newspaper Fund, 1982.

McLeod, Jack M. and Sun Yuel Choe. "An Analysis of Five Factors Affecting Newspaper Circulation." *ANPA News Research Report.* no. 10 (March 14, 1978).

Merrill, John C. *The Elite Press.* New York: Pitman, 1968.

"A New National Daily?" *Newsweek,* December 29, 1980, 59.

News and Editorial Content and Readership of the Daily Newspaper Washington: American Newspaper Publishers Association, 1973.

Newson, Clark. "Wages." *Presstime.* August, 1984. 6–9.

The Newspaper Business. Reprints from the Washington *Post,* 1977.

Reston, James. "Small-Time Paper Outshines 'Em All," Columbus (Ohio) *Citizen-Journal,* New York *Times* Service, April 18, 1979, 4.

Robinson, John P. and Jeffers, Leo W., "The Changing Role of Newspapers in the Age of Television," *Journalism Monographs,* no. 63. (September, 1979).

Seelye, Katharine, "Al Newharth's Technicolor Baby," *Columbia Journalism Review.* March/April, 1983, 27–35.

Tillinghast, Diana, "The Los Angeles *Times:* Ensuring Organizational Survival by Controlling, Adapting to, or Containing the External Environment" (Paper presented to the Newspaper Division, Association for Education in Journalism, annual convention, Michigan State University, East Lansing, August, 1981).

Trayes, Edward J. "Newsroom Manning Levels of Daily Newspapers Over 10,000 Circulation." *Journalism Quarterly* 49 (1972).579–81.

"*USA Today* Gains Commercially," The *Wall Street Journal,* January 28, 1983, 29.

Chapter 6

The American Magazine: A Range of Reading

The
Specialization
Specialist

Of all the mass media none seems more vibrant, growing, or alive than the modern magazine. There are magazines to read news from, magazines to cook gourmet meals by, magazines to help build and rehabilitate houses, and even magazines from which to review and order pornographic video. No matter what the profession or trade, there is at least one magazine to serve its interests. And more than one company or corporation has found the magazine to be a valuable medium for keeping in contact with employees and helping them to keep up-to-date with company plans and problems. The magazine can and does serve the widest range of needs and interests, and the widest range of interest groups. The newspaper may be tied to its daily or weekly schedule and its geographic location, but magazines rise and fall, soar or crash, on the interests and needs of a reading audience—wherever it is located. Given a subject or cause, a magazine is there to encourage and confirm, to edify and extend, to offer advice and techniques to win the goal.

The Trend
Toward
Specialization

Only recently have we learned to think of the magazine as a special interest medium. Of course special interest magazines have been around for some time. There was, for example, *Outdoor Life* in 1889, and *Model Railroader* in 1934. But, for the most part, during the first half of the twentieth century the magazine was seen as an instructor, entertainer, and advertiser to the American family—a general interest mass medium in the fullest sense of the phrase. The arrival of network television in the 1950s and the 1960s gave the American family more entertainment more cheaply and more dynamically than magazines could. At the same time, television also provided advertisers with a less expensive means of reaching the general audience. The general interest family magazines such as *Collier's, Saturday Evening Post, American, Look,* and *Life*—the magazines competing directly with television for audiences and advertising dollars—began to wither and die.

Mourning the death of the magazine proved to be premature, however. In time it became clear that while some general interest magazines were passing away, total magazine circulation was not dropping. Also, for every magazine that failed in the 1970s four new ones were created. The magazine was not dying; it was beginning to specialize. Rather than having a large group of large circulation magazines, the industry was evolving into one characterized by a much wider range of magazines with healthy, if not massive, subscription lists. In the 1980s it became clear, too, that bigness in circulation, if no longer a staple in the industry, was not impossible. As Magazine Publisher's Association head Kent Rhodes has observed, specialization did not rule out bigness for such widely circulated magazines as *Family Circle* and *Woman's Day.* They have grown as large or larger than the mass circulation magazines of the 1950s and

1960s—despite strong competition for audiences and ad dollars from television. *Reader's Digest*—the "little wonder," with its easy-to-read summaries of articles from other magazines and books—also continued to grow to a circulation of about eighteen million.

Time also proved the dual trends of bigness and specialization were compatible. Special interest magazines—ones that served hobby groups or any one of a large number of professions—grew in number without hampering the growth of larger circulation magazines serving more general interests. The prime example is *TV Guide,* which reached a circulation of twenty million copies in the early 1980s by providing details of local television program information in each weekly edition. Even some old mass-circulation family magazines found they could survive by reaching their own special interest audience. The *Saturday Evening Post* and *Life* both disappeared in competition with television, only to return to newstands by 1980. Today they have tighter budgets and smaller staffs, and are aimed at smaller, more nostalgic, and photographically interested audiences of their own.

Some Factors Affecting Specialization

Harvard University Professor Benjamin M. Compaine has suggested there are two important factors that have shaped magazines into the specialized media they are today. The first has to do with recent trends and changes in American culture and society. The other reflects the way we use magazines in daily life. There are, he has suggested, five social and cultural factors that have affected the magazine:

First, strong trends toward job specialization have created a society of work specializations: doctors, lawyers, insurance agents, realtors, and carpenters, among others that provide a basis for an extensive number of trade, professional, and business magazines.

Second, our society has experienced significant change, including changes in social attitudes. Even the social changes inherent in the arrival of the mass media, for example, have helped expand the magazine. The motion picture created fan magazines. Televised sports stimulated sports magazine sales. And television, seen first as an enemy, inspired one of the largest circulation magazines to date: *TV Guide.* Changes in social attitudes toward sex have fostered an extensive array of sex-oriented magazines, including *Playboy, Penthouse, Oui,* and *Playgirl.* Changing attitudes toward the environment have encouraged such publications as *Mother Earth News.* The love for rock music, and an all-too-apparent generation gap, found expression in *Rolling Stone.*

Third, the magazine has found support, as have all the print media, in our nation's continued dedication to education and the creation of a large, highly literate audience.

Fourth, we continue to enjoy a consumer base of great strength and depth. There seems to be enough discretionary income at almost every level of our society to purchase magazines and the products they advertise.

Fifth, there has been an increase in leisure time—beginning as far back as 1900—making it possible for audiences to pursue a variety of activities in their waking hours and creating a need for magazines to support those activities, whether they are *Personal Computing, Yachting,* or exploration of the *Self.*

Compaine has suggested magazines also can offer two types of information. Some offer "passive" information for the edification of the reader. Others offer "active" information more in the nature of instruction and advice. The sports enthusiast who reads a long account of how Hank Aaron hit his 715th home run is receiving passive information. On the other hand, the golf enthusiast who reads a magazine article on how to play from a sand trap is seeking active information—information to use to improve his or her game. Passive magazine articles are read by observers. Active magazine articles are read by practitioners.

Passive and active information can attract mass or limited audiences. *Reader's Digest* is a mass audience magazine with passive content, while the intellectual *Kenyon Review* offers passive content to a much smaller audience. *Outdoor Life* is an active, mass audience magazine. *Shooting Times* also is active, but has a more limited audience. Further examples of Compaine's passive/active and mass/limited categories are given in figure 6.1. They do much to explain the variety of magazines available at the present time, since almost any cause or interest can create both participants and observers and double the number of magazines published for a special interest audience.

Types of Magazines

Professionals in the field divide magazines into three basic categories:

1. consumer magazines, or those sold to the public with the support of consumer advertising. Most people mean consumer magazines when they use the word *magazine;*
2. trade, professional, or business magazines, intended for members of a trade or profession, and usually supported by trade advertising. In trade publications, advertising agencies advertise to advertisers, drug and medical equipment companies advertise to physicians, and farm product companies advertise to farmers. Confusingly enough, all these publications are referred to as business magazines by some authorities;

Figure 6.1

Sample Magazines by Editorial Content and Type of Audience

	Passive Editorial Content (Median Circulation = 668,000)	**Active Editorial Content (Median Circulation = 406,000)**
Mass audience	Reader's Digest TV Guide People Ladies' Home Journal Sports Illustrated Newsweek Playboy Ebony Esquire National Geographic Psychology Today	Family Circle Better Homes and Gardens Outdoor Life Glamour Popular Mechanics Sports Afield Popular Science
Limited audience	Saturday Evening Post Harper's New Yorker Ms. New Republic Ellery Queen Mystery Magazine Philadelphia Forbes Rolling Stone Commentary Modern Romance Gourmet	Golf Digest Trains Popular Photography Flying Yachting Ski Modern Bride Camping Journal Antiques Dirt Bike Car & Driver High Fidelity Shooting Times Trailer Life

Source: Reprinted from "The Magazine Industry: Developing the Special Interest Audience" by Benjamin M. Compaine, Volume 30, Number 2. © 1980 *Journal of Communication.*

3. the industrial, company, or *sponsored magazine* published by a corporation or interest group to maintain contact with employees or promote the group's cause with the public. Internal publication magazines usually carry little outside advertising.

Consumer Magazines

The consumer magazine is the most important to the industry, if for no other reason than that it accounts for three-fifths of all industry revenue. *Time, Cosmopolitan, Hot Rod Magazine, The Atlantic Monthly,* and *Family Computing* are all consumer magazines, as are all antique, teen, occult, children's, and women's magazines. Contributing to the great range of consumer magazine content is the fact that publishers can aim their publications at various levels of the social ladder—to "upscale" or "down-scale" readers (or to high-, middle- and low-brow readers)—in the same way that newspaper publishers do.

News Magazines

The news publications of Time, Inc., for example, clearly demonstrate the variety of appeals possible even with factual publications. Henry Luce and Briton Hadden founded *Time* in 1923 to appeal to middle-to-upper-middle-class readers who wished to keep informed about world conditions. It was laid out in subject compartments (books, business, law, etc.) and written as if by one writer. *Newsweek* and *U.S. News and World Report* adopted the approach with a good degree of success.

In 1930 Luce started *Fortune,* another news magazine, aiming it at a more upscale reader, one at the highest level of the executive world. Luce felt that American business was supposed to act responsibly and in the public interest. One major purpose of *Fortune* was to hold the business community, including executives, up to scrutiny. As such, the magazine regularly investigates business while also exploring nonbusiness topics as well—topics of interest to the corporate investor, for example. *Fortune* has studied the development, or lack of development, in the cable industry, the reasons behind the extensive numbers of arsons in the Bronx in New York City, and the problems of short water supply in the Southwestern states.

Time, Inc.'s original "low-brow" magazine was the original *Life* magazine. From the 1930s through the 1950s, its big pictures of disasters, movie stars, and gangsters made easy reading at the barber or beauty shop, but copies of *Life* were seldom found in the club or boardroom. Its modern successor is *People Weekly,* or *People,* as it is usually called. *People* first was issued in 1974 with the hope it would make enough money through newsstand and supermarket checkout sales to keep it going. Thus its appeal had to be instant and clearly displayed on the cover. The magazine leans heavily on interviews and personality sketches with television stars, movie stars, athletes and other celebrities, and on the ability of the cover pictures of these celebrities to draw readers into the "book." Its stories are true, although light, chatty—and even gossipy.

Still, if *People* is downscale or low brow, it is in sharp contrast to several non–Time, Inc., publications sold through news and supermarket counters. The ultra low-brow *National Enquirer,* for example, also reports news of celebrities, but the *Enquirer's* stories ignore *People's* everyday life coverage in favor of scandal. *Enquirer* pages often carry explorations of the occult, "reports" of UFO's (over Moscow?), weight loss diets, and advice to young women who discover they have married homosexuals.

News Magazines:
Number Two Tries
Harder

One of the toughest competitions for the reading audience has been fought by the news magazines during the past several years. *Time* (circulation 4.5 million), the first news magazine, leads the field. *Newsweek* (circulation 3 million) is second and *U.S. News & World Report* (circulation 2.2 million) is third. *U.S. News & World Report* seems to have found a niche reporting political news and informative service news from its base in Washington, D.C. *Time* and *Newsweek* are the contestants in the race to be the nation's number one news magazine. Although *Time* draws $44 million more advertising revenue a year, the two are much the same in weekly news coverage.

In 1982 publisher Katherine Graham of *Newsweek's* parent Washington *Post* company, known for changing *Newsweek* editors with little notice, named Bill Broyles the new editor-in-chief. Broyles, educated at Rice University, and with a master's degree from Oxford, had performed a minor miracle as editor of the *Texas Monthly,* converting the obscure state publication into one of national reputation. He followed that with success as editor of *California,* another state magazine. His appointment seemed to underscore Graham's determination to change and improve *Newsweek,* but it shocked news magazine professionals. *Newsweek* editors-in-chief traditionally had come from the ranks. And Broyles not only was an "outsider" to *Newsweek,* he was an outsider to "hard" news as well.

In 1982 the business office launched *Newsweek on Campus,* an innovative thirty-two page magazine distributed as inserts in college newspapers. And with Graham's support, Broyles set about reshaping *Newsweek* itself, telling his editors to "beef up" the "back of the book" with more life-style coverage. The magazine began running more original cover stories ("A Secret War in Nicaragua"), articles by big name writers (Henry Kissinger on "How to Deal with Moscow"), and less news recaps.

But from the first, Broyles's "outside" status and his decision not to discuss his policies with reporters contributed grist for the office rumor mill. One rumor charged Broyles was abandoning hard news for magazine-like articles about gay America and gifted children, others complained he handled internal affairs badly—especially hirings and firings. Others persisted: Broyles had resigned; another portrayed the editor as relieved he was on vacation when one big story broke, keeping him from having to go through the grind of getting it into the magazine. Writer Hillary Johnson has suggested all the rumors characterized Broyles as an interloper, and as one who lacked the right stuff to work in the news magazine business.

As it turned out, Broyles did resign, professing dislike for the confinement of weekly news magazine work and a desire to pursue new ventures. In January, 1984 he was replaced by Richard M. Smith, a thirteen-year veteran of *Newsweek* and its sixth editor-in-chief in twelve years. One former *Newsweek* editor observed, *Time* is like the old Green Bay Packers. They just make touchdown after touchdown. *Newsweek* keeps getting a new quarterback every season. It's not a recipe for sustained success.

Women's Magazines   As noted in chapter 3, women's magazines were among the first and most successful of the mass magazines. Those like *Godey's Lady's Book* served hundreds of thousands of readers, while the *Ladies' Home Journal* was the first American magazine to reach a circulation of one million. Magazine scholar Theodore Peterson has suggested that these early, home-oriented woman's magazines were "trade papers" for the women of their day. They succeeded with a general formula of fashion, foods, family, and fiction.

The home-oriented format continues to be popular with women today. Expanded to meet the needs of modern homemakers, this format attracts audiences numbered in the millions in each of several magazines of its type. Current circulation leaders are *Family Circle* (circulation 7.2 million), *Woman's Day* (circulation 7 million), *McCall's* (circulation 6.4 million), and *Good Housekeeping,* (circulation 5.4 million). Their expanded formats include recipes ("Colossal Cookies"), articles on consumer information, nutrition, entertaining ("When a Whole Community Comes to Dinner, It's Superparty!"), marriage relations ("Stuff and Nonsense Women Still Believe about Men and Sex"), home and money management, health ("How to Cure Your Aching Back"), raising children ("Understanding Underachievers"), beauty and fashion, how-to articles ("Breathtaking Sweaters to Knit"), as well as articles on politics and job opportunities. Titles given here are from a recent edition of *Woman's Day.* Rather than trade papers, the modern general-interest woman's magazines are more of a cornucopia of pertinent information for the woman who is managing her life with a family and a home.

The homemaker format no longer dominates the woman's magazine. Competition thinned many magazines from the crowded field in the 1930s, and cultural changes have since created new types of women consumers and women audiences. One is the single working woman; another is the married career woman—who is not raising a family. Still another is the single or divorced parent who is working. Furthermore, the economy remains strong enough to support magazines for special interests or hobbies, for selected age groups, and even a few for women who live in specific locales.

One of the new entries, now in its second decade of publication, is the intellectual *Ms.* (circulation 480,000). Founded by Patricia Carbine and Gloria Steinem and associates in 1972, its self-professed goal has been to portray women accurately and to depict what women really need and want, without hiding them in the usual stereotypes of clotheshorses, wives, mothers, or hostesses. The policy is reflected in an early decision by the *Ms.* advertising staff on an ad contract with Virginia Slims cigarettes. The staff felt that the ads' message that women had "arrived" because they had won the right to vote and could now smoke in public was uncomplimentary to feminine achievements, and unrealistic regarding women's goals. Although the magazine needed the $80,000 in revenue that the contract offered, they turned it down. *Ms.* appeals to the intellectual side of women with such erudite topics as "What Lies Beyond 'The Woman as Victim' Construct?" and such socially oriented topics as "Anti-Abortion Violence on the Rise—How Far Will It Go?" Even lighter articles reflect a dedication to the problems of the modern woman. An article on stand-up comics asked, "Can You Be a Funny Woman Without Making Fun of Women?" A personality profile of pop singer Cyndi Lauper discovered "The Surprising Mind Behind 'The Girl Who Just Wants to Have Fun.' " Similar in appeal to *Ms.* is *New Woman.*

More middle-brow in content are the women's magazines that lead in circulation: *Mademoiselle, Glamour, and Cosmopolitan. Mademoiselle* was one of the first magazines created for the single working woman. It entered the field in 1935 as a guide to fashion and beauty, often presenting fashions designed specifically for the publication. Over the years it has also featured columns on careers, and articles on working women professionals.

Peterson reports that Conde Nast Publishing launched *Glamour* in 1939, "for the young woman with a job," and as a little sister to Nast's high fashion and upscale *Vogue.* In 1959, Nast merged *Glamour* with a second woman's magazine, *Charm,* boosting circulation to over a million in the early 1960s. *Glamour* has featured columns on books, movies, health, and sex, as well as "how-to" articles. There have been articles such as "How to Put Up With or Put Down a Difficult Man" (written by a younger Gloria Steinem), articles on women in prisons, safety tips for women travelling alone, and tips on investing in the stock market.

Perhaps the most controversial woman's magazine is *Cosmopolitan.* First issued as a family monthly in 1866, it became a muckraking magazine—the one that prompted Theodore Roosevelt to coin the term "muckraking"—a literary magazine, and then an entertainment magazine for men and women before bestselling author Helen Gurley Brown (*Sex and the Single Girl, Sex and the Office,* etc.) was named editor in 1965.

Editor Brown turned "Cosmo" into a companion for the working woman, and a counselor on career and sexual matters. She published such ones as "How I Chose My Career," as well as more controversial articles such as "Why I Wear My False Eyelashes to Bed," and "Petite? Big Boned? Average? Tricks for Looking Sexy at Any Size." *Cosmopolitan* was the first woman's magazine to adopt a nude male centerfold (Burt Reynolds in 1972). While Brown has drawn much criticism for her frank approach to sex, she has also been applauded for her leadership in declaring women's legitimate interests in the subject. And some critics feel the Cosmo articles telling young women how to cope in the world present a more realistic perspective than the overly glamorous approach taken by other magazines. Whatever its faults or values, the Brown formula has pushed *Cosmopolitan's* circulation from 800,000 to 3 million and a comfortable lead over second placed *Glamour* (circulation 2.3 million) and third place *Mademoiselle* (circulation 1.3 million).

More frankly sexual is *Playgirl* (circulation 641,000), a female reflection of *Playboy,* which features career information, discussions of political issues, the arts, and fashion and fitness. Its centerfolds picture nude males, with nude or seminude females.

In contrast to *Ms., Cosmopolitan,* and *Playgirl* is the downscale *True Story* (circulation 1.6 million). Written for the young working-class woman, its confession articles tell an emotional, firsthand account of a moral or social error on the part of the heroine, who, by recanting her "sin," sees her error and mends her ways. There is often more guilt than scandal in the true-confession heroine's sad but sweet tale.

A sizable group of magazines serves the working woman who has the second role of homemaker. *Redbook* (circulation 4 million) is published, according to its editors, for the young woman who is juggling the demands and rewards of husband, child, and job. *Self* (circulation 1 million) is publication firm Conde Nast's offering for the woman in two worlds—business and home. McCall publishes *Working Mother,* (circulation 485,000) with job and career information, child rearing, family health, beauty, and money management articles. *Working Woman* and *Woman* are aimed at the same audience.

Some magazines offer general interest content to women of a specific locale: *Alaskan Woman, Dawn for the Orange County Woman,* in California, and *Hartford Woman,* in Connecticut. Others offer specific content to women across the nation. For those interested in sewing, there is *Workbasket* (circulation 1.9 million). There is *Beauty Digest* (circulation 175,000) and *Shape* (circulation 4.4 million) for feminine beauty and fitness. *Bride's* advises on all steps of the wedding from planning to the honeymoon. Still popular are magazines for young women with the special interests of the teen years, for example: *Seventeen* (circulation 1.7 million), and *Young Miss* (circulation 800,000).

These lists, of course, are not exhaustive.

Men's Magazines

As Peterson has pointed out, most of the men's magazines that appeared in the nineteenth century and in the first half of the twentieth century were written for men with areas of specific interests: hunting, fishing, hobbies, or sports. There was *Field & Stream* and *Hunting and Fishing, Popular Mechanics* and *Mechanix Illustrated,* and the boxing magazine *Ring.* The few with general interest content included the *Police Gazette,* with its articles on crime and sports and pictures of buxom ladies, fraternal magazines such as the *American Legion* and *Elks Magazine,* and the smaller circulation *Gentry* and *Esquire,* which catered to elite, fashion-conscious audiences.

A large group of general magazines for men did emerge during World War II but, as Peterson has suggested, a more appropriate title for the group would have been "true adventure" magazines since their stock in trade was the factual article about crime, hunting, science, sports, or sex. Titles from some of the articles are indicative: "My Life as a Headhunter," "I Was Hitler's Master Spy," and "Virginity Complex" ("are YOU afraid to love?"). Between 1940 and 1949, men's adventure-magazine sales pushed all men's magazine sales up 134 percent.

The first of the type was *True,* published in 1931. It led the field in circulation from the 1940s into the 1960s (circulation 2.4 million in 1961). One of *True's* editors has suggested that the format was a success because it provided male readers with a refuge from women, and with escapist (if true) adventure articles that ignored doom-is-just-around-the-corner angles. *True's* articles were written by well-known authors and were supported by many color illustrations. Other successful magazines in this field included *Argosy,* the adult fiction magazine from the 1890s which was converted to the true-adventure format, *Adventure, Man's Adventure, Cavalier, Escape, Saga,* and *Real.*

Throughout the period, the contrast to the man's outdoor adventure magazine was *Esquire* with its dedication to men who enjoyed such inside activities as literary fiction, sophisticated articles and cartoons on sex, articles on social issues, and men's fashion. *Esquire* rather than *True* proved to be the forerunner of the contemporary man's magazine.

Esquire itself grew out of trade publications designed to serve men's clothing stores. In 1927 advertising men David and Alfred Smart and William H. Weintraub issued the *National Men's Wear Salesman,* a sophisticated catalog for men's clothing stores. Its success, and the acceptance of their syndicated style guide publications, which also were distributed through clothing stores, led to the creation of *Apparel Arts* in 1931. *Apparel Arts* copied the new *Fortune* magazine in artwork and design. In 1933 it was enlarged into a consumer magazine. The publishers considered such titles as *Trend, Stag, Beau,* and *Trim,* until informed by the U.S. Patent Office that all already were taken. They settled on *Esquire,* after noticing the title *Esq.* on the letter from the patent attorney. The founders gambled that men would pay the then-exorbitant price of fifty cents a copy for the elegant publication. And they were right. The first edition sold so well, in fact, all but a few of the copies distributed to men's stores had to be recaptured and placed in newsstands to meet public demand. In the years that followed, Arnold Gingrich, editor from the trade magazine days, turned *Esquire* into a magazine of literary distinction, attracting stories by Ernest Hemingway, John Dos Passos, Erskine Caldwell, and Dashiell Hammett. An important part of the formula, too, was the magazine's "smoking car" humor of jokes and full-page cartoons, as well as the hand-drawn, nymphlike Petty Girl pinups. The sexy, long-limbed, scantily clad Petty Girls were the forerunners of today's magazine centerfolds.

The *Esquire* of pre–World War II years became the model for *Playboy*. In 1953, Hugh Hefner, *Playboy's* founder, was working for *Esquire* in Chicago when the magazine's management asked him to move to New York. But when *Esquire* refused to give him the $5 increase in salary that he felt he should have ($25 instead of $20 a week), he resigned and remained in Chicago to create his own magazine. In a letter to a friend, Hefner indicated that he planned to establish an entertainment magazine for the "city-bred guy—breezy and sophisticated," using quality "girlie features" to guarantee initial sales, but removing the features and increasing the quality of the rest as the magazine became established. Borrowing money from banks and friends and selling stock in the proposed publication, he raised $7,000 and published the first edition of *Playboy* in December 1953. The magazine was an immediate success, due in part to its now-famous nude centerfold photograph of Marilyn Monroe. Within ten years, Hefner had constructed a $20 million publishing and entertainment empire on the *Playboy* foundation.

Needless to say, the "girlie features" have proved to be too important to drop from the format. As the magazine has grown in popularity, the nude photo essays have increased in number and have become more sexually explicit. But, as Hefner planned, quality writing in articles and fiction has become an important part of the magazine. Over the years, *Playboy* has published the work of some of the best-known names in modern letters—Evelyn Waugh, Nelson Algren, Alberto Moravio, and Norman Mailer among them. It has also given its readers a long series of provocative interviews with significant and otherwise unaccessible personalities of our time. The *Playboy* formula includes "party jokes," and life-style service features on clothing and food—all presented with highly attractive graphics and layout—done, as Peterson has observed, with a "somewhat undergraduate air of sophistication mingled with naivete." At last report, the magazine's circulation was 4.2 million.

A steady challenger for men's field circulation leadership has been *Penthouse* (circulation 3.5 million). Using much the same format as *Playboy,* American Bob Guccione published *Penthouse* in England for four years before importing it to the United States in the late 1960s. *Penthouse* has a history of being more sexually explicit and of offering less fiction but more articles—especially articles on provocative sexual matters—with more earthy nude-photo essays.

Gallery (circulation 500,000), *Genesis* (circulation 285,000), and *Hustler* offer similar male entertainment formats, with variations for particular interest groups in the audience. *Players* (circulation 205,000) appeals to the black male.

Meanwhile, the *Playboy* "middle-brow" format has not driven the elite men's magazines from the field. *Esquire* continues with a circulation of 764,000 and *Gentlemen's Quarterly,* published "for the active urban male," has 573,000 subscribers.

The special-interest magazine remains important in the men's field also. *Auto Week, Cycle World, Motor Trend, and Road and Track* (circulation 770,000) serve the speed and motor enthusiast. *Mechanix Illustrated* (circulation 1.6 million), *Popular Mechanics,* and *Handyman* serve the mechanical and do-it-yourself minded. *Field & Stream* (circulation 2 million) *Sports Afield, Southern Outdoors,* and *Texas Fisherman* continue outdoor formats that are still popular. *The Elks Magazine* (circulation 1.6 million) and *Kiwanis* continue as fraternal magazines.

Some special interest men's publications deal with home and national security. *Soldier of Fortune* (circulation 188,000) offers military articles and stands as an advocate for the right to bear arms. *Gung-Ho* (circulation 90,000) covers military operations and programs, survival techniques, and tests of assault weapons. *S.W.A.T.* (circulation 76,500) also reviews survival techniques, weapons, and tactics. *Survive* (circulation 49,400) focuses on home security, self-defense, and nuclear survival skills.

Ethnic Magazines

Most ethnic magazines are foreign language publications, or publications that present only portions of their content in English. At the same time, some ethnic magazines—usually the ones with larger circulations—are printed entirely in English, for larger minority audiences—such as the black American or Spanish American audience.

Like the ethnic newspaper, the ethnic magazine functions to maintain the ethnic community's identity and cohesiveness by expressing its hopes and aspirations and by presenting its common concerns and purposes. As ethnic-press scholars Lubomyr and Anna Wynar have noted, the ethnic press helped newly arrived immigrant groups adjust to and survive in the New World. It then helped maintain group cohesiveness, while pointing to ways in which the immigrants could gain participation in the general society. The place of the ethnic press seems assured so long as the needs of the ethnic community go unnoticed by the mass media of the dominant society.

Wynar and Wynar suggest there are at least twelve kinds of ethnic periodicals: (1) political and ideological, (2) fraternal, (3) religious, (4) scholarly and academic, (5) educational, (6) professional and trade,

John H. Johnson with *Ebony* magazine.

(7) cultural, (8) youth, (9) women's, (10) sports and recreational, (11) veterans' publications, and (12) bibliographic periodicals. The bibliographic periodicals list, discuss, and review new books and other materials published by their respective ethnic group. The other categories seem self-explanatory.

Ayer's Directory of Publications reports an extensive list of ethnic magazines that are printed in foreign languages from Arabic to Yugoslavic. (But it does not always make clear which publications are printed entirely in foreign languages, and which have portions in English.) For example, the political *Viet Nam Hai Ngoai* (circulation 5,500) of San Diego, still supports the cause of Viet Nam nationalism in Vietnamese. Fraternal magazines include the monthly *American Sokol* (circulation 5,800), printed in Czech in Berwyn, Illinois, and the Lithuanian *Vytis* (Knight) of Centerville, New York. In Minneapolis, the Sons of Norway fraternal group publishes *The Viking* in Norwegian (circulation 75,000). Among the current ethnic religious magazines are the *U.R.O.B.A. Messenger,* of the United Russian Orthodox Brotherhood of America; *Nasa Nada* (Our Hope, circulation 5,000), published in Croatian for Catholic men, and the Lithuanian *Kristaus Karaliaus Laivas* (Ship of Christ the King, circulation 9,000), published in Chicago. Armenian cultural interests are discussed in *Hoosharar—The Prompter* (circulation 6,000), *La Follia di New York* and *Il Pensiero* of St. Louis review Italian culture. There is *Voice of Youth* (circulation 7,000) in Yugoslavic and *Pioneer Woman* (circulation 30,000) in Yiddish (and English?). *Hispanic Times* discusses business and careers in Spanish and in English for its 25,000 Anglo-Spanish readers. Perhaps the largest group of ethnic magazines in North America is comprised of those printed in French, with many of them originating in the sizable sphere of French culture centered in Canada.

While some of the larger circulation foreign-language publications may have subscribers in the tens of thousands, subscribers of *Ebony,* the leading black magazine, number 1.5 million. The rise of black magazines has been both recent and phenomenal. In less than fifty years, the black magazine industry has grown from one without a successful commercial publication, to an industry with several commercially successful publications.

A leader in the rise of the black magazine has been John H. Johnson, of Chicago, who was the first to enjoy commercial success with black publications—*Ebony, Negro Digest, Jet,* and *Ebony, Jr.* His success as a publisher did much to free the black magazine from its dependence on interest groups and fraternal organizations for financial support. His first publication, *Negro Digest,* issued in 1942, became a commercial success as a black *Reader's Digest,* reaching the black audience with such

Digest-like articles as ''My Most Humiliating Jim Crow Experience.'' It lasted until 1951 when Johnson decided to abandon it and give his attention to his second successful publication, *Ebony*. With reader demand he returned the *Digest* to publication in 1961, giving it a more original and creative format that included revolutionary editorials, fiction, poetry, and discussion of black issues and causes. In 1970, with the term ''Negro'' in disfavor, it was renamed *Black World*. But *Black World's* appeal proved too limited and the magazine soon passed from the scene. (Johnson's entry into the popular romance field, *Tan Confessions,* issued in 1950, also failed to find an audience and was withdrawn from the market.)

Observers feel Johnson's major commercial success, *Ebony,* has done much to generate self-respect in the black community. Founded in 1945 as a black copy of *Life,* it attracted newsstand buyers with sensation and sex, while editorializing on mistreatment of black soldiers and discrimination in war industries. With the war over, it took the bright view of Negro life in America, and a positive approach to race relations, advocating the work ethic as the way to win the better life. It printed ''rags to riches'' stories about black celebrities (Lena Horne and Sammy Davis, Jr., etc.) and held up the ideal of the self-made man and woman as the model for the black community. *Ebony* was not a leader in the early years of the civil rights movement; it took the position that blacks should work within the status quo and prove themselves before the general public to win equality. But, following the march on Washington in 1963 it took a stronger stance with the movement, turning its editorial emphasis from fostering white values to reviewing the black American's social frustrations and the needs of the black family. All the while it continued to call for blacks to rely on work and education to improve their situation.

In 1973 Johnson issued *Ebony, Jr.,* for children from kindergarten to the sixth grade. It features stories, articles, games, puzzles, songs, contests, and personalities which help young blacks prepare for making decisions in their lives. *Jet,* Johnson's weekly pocket-sized newsmagazine, has been in publication since 1951.

The most successful black woman's magazine at the present time is *Essence*—sometimes referred to as the black woman's *Cosmopolitan*. *Essence* was created by a partnership of four men (Jonathan Blount, Clarence Smith, Cyril Hill, and Ed Lewis) who acquired backing from Wall Street interests and set out to establish a magazine ''more woman and less black'' in content. It stresses beauty and fashion, public affairs, education, consumer advice, entertainment, fiction, poetry, and articles on topics that range from travel to labor news.

Black Enterprise, first published in 1970, also came into being as a result of the efforts of a large group of supporters. It was created to encourage the black youngster to seek a career in business or the professions, and with the hope of establishing a class of black merchants. Its content was aimed first at "Mom and Pop" businesses, but it has since been adjusted to interest the many blacks who have risen to positions in business corporations.

City Magazines

City magazines now are among the more successful consumer magazines. New York had a city magazine, *Town Topics,* before 1900. But the prototype of the more than one hundred modern city magazines is the *New Yorker,* founded in 1925. The *New Yorker's* success both in and outside New York brought emulators in Chicago, Cleveland, and Washington, D.C., as well as within the New York city itself. Some city magazines developed out of television or dining guides. Others came from Sunday magazines (as did the famous *New York*). Most have featured personality interviews, investigative journalism, and an editorial approach that paints the magazine's home area as chic and exciting. Above all, city magazines function as survival kits for their hometowns, and are more colorful than their more objective competitors, the city newspapers.

Regional Magazines

Like city magazines, regional magazines are "class" publications. In both editorial and advertising content, they aim for the affluent middle class. One of the more successful, *Sunset,* began as a railroad publication designed to lure tourists to the West on the Sunset Limited. Larry Lane turned it into a life-style magazine in the 1930s, by featuring articles on food, home, travel, and gardening—with a *Better Homes and Gardens* influence. *Sunset* continues today with a circulation of one and a half million readers west of the Mississippi. *Yankee* serves New England. In 1963, the Progressive Farmer Company adopted the *Sunset* formula to *Southern Living,* a publication for the Southeast. Both *Sunset* and *Southern Living* devote about 60 percent of their content to the charm and the excitement of their region. The remainder of the magazines consists of general fare on house remodeling and gourmet cooking.

Sunday Supplements

The Sunday supplements that come with the comics in the Sunday newspaper may be the endangered species of the magazine field. The Sunday magazines, such as *Sunday* and *Parade,* or their local versions, have a very low pass-along rate. *Newsweek* and *Glamour* are found in airplanes and waiting rooms. Movie magazines feature famous people. *Business Week* is topical. But the Sunday magazine has little to get it passed around from reader to reader. It is read, then usually discarded with Sunday's newspaper. The hope for the Sunday supplement is in its immediate, family impact. Advertisers who need a mass audience on Sunday may find the thoroughly read Sunday magazine an excellent advertising medium, as may those who need a high impact ad that can be tied to other timely promotion ads in radio and television.

Cultural Minority Magazines

Another important type of consumer magazine is the one Peterson has called the magazine for cultural minorities. They are the cultural, literary, and political magazines aimed at the intellectual, or the highbrow reader. The *Atlantic Monthly* and *Harper's* are two of the most recognizable. The category also includes the *Saturday Review* and "little" literary magazines such as the *Kenyon Review* and the *Antioch Review*. Modern political magazines include the left-wing *Progressive* and the right-wing *National Review*.

Cultural minority magazines are consumer publications without many consumers, and therefore, with little advertising. Their circulations are so limited they are unable to attract advertising. As a result, they are forced to rely on philanthropy to survive; raising their cover prices to meet the cost of publication would only drive readers away. William F. Buckley's *National Review* lost at least $100,000 a year in each of its first three years of publication. The thirty-year-old *Kenyon Review,* although highly respected, was forced to cease publication in 1970. It was revived in 1980, the same year *Atlantic, Harper's* and *Saturday Review*—all on the verge of folding—were rescued by philanthropic buyers. (*Newsweek* had even written *Harper's* obituary: "*Harper's* 1850–1980.") Despite a debt of $1.5 million, in 1979, *Harper's* was picked up by the MacArthur Foundation, a $750 million insurance fund, with help from Atlantic Richfield (ARCO). The foundation paid $250,000 for the magazine and ARCO contributed $3 million in operating expenses. The contributors promised to stay clear of any editorial control of the magazine and only act in maintaining its independence.

Trade and Professional Magazines

Of the almost 11,000 periodicals listed in the *Ayer Directory of Periodicals,* some 70 percent are business, trade, or professional magazines. They run the range from *Advertising Age* (circulation 75,000) to *Scrap Age* (circulation 2,900). There are magazines for air conditioning trades people, and farm mechanics and thirteen periodicals for the baking trade alone.

Business Publications

Among the most important of the group are business magazines. Best known to the general public are McGraw-Hill's *Business Week, Forbes,* and *Fortune.* All have circulations of 600,000 or more, and report news of business and the business community in general. A large number of business magazines serve a narrower public in the various business trades

Twenty Leading Business Magazines by Circulation and by Revenue

Rank	Magazine	Circulation	Rank	Magazine	Advertising Revenue
1	Real Estate Today	608,440	1	Computerworld	28,531
2	Nursing '82	545,712	2	Women's Wear Daily	25,220
3	RN Magazine	374,830	3	Oil & Gas Journal	19,894
4	ABA Journal	350,000	4	Electronic Design	19,147
5	American Jrnl. of Nursing	345,329	5	Medical Economics	18,189
6	American Medical News	329,352	6	Advertising Age	18,040
7	Industry Week	300,664	7	Restaurants & Institutions	17,805
8	JAMA	290,836	8	Electronic News	16,873
9	Instructor	263,933	9	Machine Design	16,500
10	AOPA Pilot	258,898	10	EDN	15,278
11	Journal of Accountancy	255,569	11	Industry Week	13,798
12	Spectrum	213,902	12	Design News	13,143
13	New England Jrnl. of Med.	204,313	13	Plant Engineering	12,714
14	New Equipment Digest	197,965	14	Electronics	12,426
15	Hospital Practice	195,729	15	JAMA	12,289
16	Industrial Equip. News	195,686	16	Datamation	12,175
17	Medical Economics	182,693	17	Engineering News Record	12,068
18	Diversion	176,215	18	Chemical Engineering	11,133
19	Machine Design	165,416	19	Restaurant Business	10,987
20	Science	157,658	20	Purchasing Magazine	10,567

Source: Courtesy The Folio: 400, Folio Publishing Corporation, New Canaan, Connecticut.

Figure 6.2

and professions. For the garment industry, there is *Women's Wear Daily.* For the steel industry there is *Iron Age. Restaurants & Institutions* speaks, as a title, for itself.

Professional Magazines

These are published for the nonbusiness professional. The professional magazine with the largest number of subscriptions is *Nursing,* followed closely by the *New England Journal of Medicine.* The professional journal—business or otherwise—with the largest circulation—is *Today's Education,* with 1.7 million subscribers.

The media professions support an extensive list of their own professional periodicals. Newspaper people look to *Editor and Publisher* (circulation 26,000) and *Presstime* for news of the newspaper business. Reporters and editors in all the news media turn to *Columbia Journalism Review* (circulation 34,000) and *Washington Journalism Review,* a more recent publication. Sigma Delta Chi, the professional journalism society, publishes *Quill* for its members.

Folio: The Magazine for Magazine Management (circulation 8,900) reviews the magazine industry each quarter with management-oriented reports. Providing important information to the many free-lance writers is *Writer's Digest* (circulation 163,000).

Broadcasting (circulation 34,000), now more than fifty years old, serves radio, television, and cable management professionals. Broadcast journalists follow *Communicator,* published by the Radio and Television News Director's Association. *Billboard* (circulation 46,600) covers the music and recording industry, and is important reading for radio management and disc jockeys. *Advertising Age* and *Public Relations Journal* are vital to the advertising and public relations professions respectively.

The film industry relies heavily on *Box Office* for reports on film ticket sales. *American Film* lends a supportive voice to film industry endeavors, along with evaluation of trends and problems; *Film Quarterly* offers a more scholarly approach. The tabloid *Variety* is important to all of the entertainment industry. The *Hollywood Reporter* reports Hollywood.

The several professions that study mass communication from within the academic world also have a large number of research journals for their edification:

Human Communication Research
Journal of Broadcasting
Journal of Communication
Journalism Quarterly
Journal of Speech
Public Opinion Quarterly

All have circulations of less than 10,000, and are supported primarily by academic associations rather than advertisers.

Farm Publications

Farm publications make up about 6 percent of the listings in the *Ayer Directory.* The "ag" magazines include 4-H and college farm periodicals, farm bureau, and cooperative publications. Some are dedicated to agricultural trades (*Fur Farming, Bovine Practice,* and *The National Cranberry,* etc.). The two leaders in the field, *Farm Journal* and *The Progressive Farmer,* both have circulations of more than one million, and attract readers and advertisers with a general farm interest formula. Agricultural journals, or agriculture research journals, are two of the most numerous of all academic research journals.

Company and Sponsored Magazines

Still another form of magazine publishing exists in the corporate world—the company magazine published to communicate with employees. One estimate puts their number at 11,000 or more. *The Working Press of the Nation* reports there are 4,000 companies, clubs, or government agencies that now publish their own magazines. As a rule, these are distributed to employees, outside influentials, stockholders, and the general public. Many are distributed only to current and retired employees. The broader the distribution, the broader the magazine's subject matter.

The Wynn Oil Company publishes the *Wynner's Circle* for all its employees and company retirees. *Zenith News* goes to 6,500. *Ford World* reaches more than 300,000 employees. An excellent example of a company magazine is *Gannetteer,* the monthly publication of the Gannett newspaper chain. The *Gannetteer* serves as a cheering squad for Gannett employees, as well as a way for the corporation to explain itself to the rank and file. A recent edition, for example, reported how one Gannett reporter refused to reveal in court the contents of a confidential interview she conducted—and how she spent seven and one-half hours in jail. (Reporter-court conflict on this issue has been growing for years. See chapter 15.) Ten pages of one *Gannetteer* compared how several Gannett newspapers covered the attempted assassination of President Reagan. The first six pages of the same magazine, meanwhile, carried an explanation of GANSAT, the Gannett Satellite Information Network, giving employees definitions for such terms as *transponder, downlink,* and *geostationary.*

The company magazine can be a cheering squad for company efforts as well as a channel for reporting to employees what the company is up to.

Some companies publish magazines for influential readers outside their organizations, giving them company viewpoints on important issues. *Exxon USA,* for example, carries stories of the oil industry, relating the problems of oil exploration with high-quality writing and color photography. A continuing theme seems to be Exxon's good citizenship, and the corporation's belief in producing and selling petroleum in a responsible manner. General Motor's *The Changing Challenge* is also well produced, and gives an extremely tasteful presentation of that company's views.

The Magazine Business

A delicate editorial balance exists in company publications: giving employees what they want to read while also relaying the company message.

Like all the other commercial mass media, consumer and trade magazines must attract enough revenue to meet fixed and variable costs and then show a profit. The good news about magazines is that there are only a few "diseases" that can afflict their profits. The bad news is that some of the diseases may be fatal, before they are diagnosed. Magazine analyst James B. Kobak has pointed to a few internal and external "diseases." Some internal ones include:

1. Circulation efforts can be weak or too strong. Less than adequate circulation means lost ad revenue, but more than one magazine has shot beyond its natural circulation to hold readers the magazine's advertisers do not want. The biggest circulation is not always the best. The best circulation is the best.
2. Advertising efforts can be weak. If the ad department can not sell, or does not know the magazine's market well enough to sell, even the brightest magazine will not survive.
3. Pricing policies may be too aggressive, or they may not be aggressive enough. Raising prices and ad rates too quickly can price the publication out of the market. More common, however, is the failure to advance prices rapidly enough to continue good profits and revenue.
4. Planning and research often are poor when the publisher is trained in editorial work and not in planning and business. Kobak has found that the number of publishers who do not hire accountants is astonishing. Too often a publisher believes good writing, good layout, and good photography will solve problems of distribution or promotion; they can not.
5. Ineffective buying can eat up profits. Most magazines "hire" not only their printing and production work, but also buy many of their articles and stories from free-lance writers. Successful editors negotiate their printing contracts with great care, and are equally careful not to put too much money into their article and story "bank."

Several external situations can kill:

1. The need can disappear, leaving an extinct magazine. Magazines in the trailer and recreational vehicle businesses suffered greatly following the sharp rise of gasoline prices in the 1970s.
2. The formula can cease to interest the public. Both *Life* and the *Saturday Review* have had a touch of this disease. S. S. McClure *thought* he did.
3. The magazine may have an identity crisis. If the editorial staff and the advertising department do not agree on the identity of the magazine, or if the editorial formula is not clear to the

Twenty Leading Consumer Magazines by Circulation and by Revenue

Ad Revenue

1982 Rank	1981 Rank	Magazine	Advertising Revenue
1	1	Time	256,410
2	2	TV Guide	241,473
3	3	Newsweek	195,359
4	4	Sports Illustrated	162,887
5	6	People	159,319
6	5	Parade	157,256
7	7	Business Week	133,947
8	9	Good Housekeeping	110,465
9	11	Family Circle	106,197
10	8	Reader's Digest	104,860
11	10	Family Weekly	101,420
12	ni	Better Homes & Gardens	100,289
13	12	Woman's Day	88,909
14	13	U.S. News & World Rep.	83,821
15	15	Fortune	76,150
16	14	Playboy	76,018
17	16	N.Y. Times Magazine	76,000
18	18	Cosmopolitan	67,615
19	20	Forbes	64,172
20	17	McCall's Magazine	62,001

Circulation

1982 Rank	1981 Rank	Magazine	Circulation
1	1	Parade	21,781,708
2	2	Reader's Digest	18,035,959
3	3	TV Guide	17,260,297
4	4	Family Weekly	12,472,075
5	5	National Geographic	10,543,815
6	8	Modern Maturity	8,222,225
7	6	Better Homes & Gardens	8,070,843
8	7	Family Circle	7,217,081
9	9	Woman's Day	6,967,614
10	10	McCall's Magazine	6,234,623
11	12	Good Housekeeping	5,421,181
12	11	Ladies' Home Journal	5,170,031
13	14	National Enquirer	5,094,303
14	13	Playboy	4,676,344
15	15	Time	4,509,918
16	16	Redbook	4,078,522
17	18	The Star	3,905,382
18	17	Penthouse	3,898,525
19	19	Guideposts	3,670,490
20	20	Consumer Reports	3,102,000

Source: Courtesy The Folio: 400, Folio Publishing Corporation, New Canaan, Connecticut.

Figure 6.3

reader, the magazine suffers from an identity crisis—a split personality—as the *Saturday Evening Post* once did.

4. The reader is given too little, or too much. Thin magazines with cheap graphics and little substance have little appeal. As Magazines must have heft, or convey at first glance that it is worth the cover price. Again, the happy medium is important. Needless length in articles can raise production costs drastically.

In short, to keep the magazine healthy, the magazine publisher must keep business, circulation and advertising tuned, and editorial content targeted to the best audience.

Fighting Inflation

As an industry, magazines have done well in recent years. Some important external forces have brought important pricing changes, however. The rising costs of paper, printing, and postage began to pinch publishers during the 1970s; a slowdown in ad purchases hurt the industry starting in the early 1980s. Some profits proved to be losses when revenues were corrected for inflation.

To meet increased costs, most publishers chose to raise cover prices. The average price of a consumer magazine more than doubled between 1972 and 1979, then rose another 10 percent the following year. In 1972, 48 percent of magazine receipts came from sales and 52 percent from advertising. By 1978 the figures had all but reversed, and readers who once paid a quarter, or fifty cents, for their favorite magazine were paying almost a dollar and a half on the average.

Publishers can not continue to raise cover prices indefinitely without losing circulation. Fortunately, predictions for the immediate future are for a leveling off in the cost of paper. Paper has risen as much as 12 percent per year since the 1970s, but demand brought an increase in production from several American mills in the early 1980s. At the same time, ink prices have been going up 20 percent and more. Since printer's ink is oil based, its prices reflect changes in petroleum prices.

Meanwhile, the industry has been experimenting for some time with alternative distribution methods. Large circulation weeklies, such as *Time* and *Newsweek,* have followed other print media in using satellites and telephone land lines to forward prepress material to regional printing plants. Regional printing means faster, cheaper mail delivery since the magazine is created closer to its destination.

More than a million copies of magazines are delivered each month by "alternative carrier" methods. Two new methods have met with success: detached labels and piggybacking. Rather than send magazines to carriers with names and addresses attached, publishers now send magazines with detached labels; distribution is made from a card list. This greatly reduces sorting and handling time. Piggybacking consists of selling local merchants the right to "stuff" local ad circulars into carrier-delivered magazines, adding revenue while reducing delivery costs.

At present, the best hope for the magazine seems to be tighter, more judicious business control—aided by computerized operations. Improvements in printing technology will help, as will wider use of automated bindery equipment. Most helpful, perhaps, may be the long-term upward trend apparent in U.S. advertising expenditures. Publishers raised advertising rates only moderately during the 1970s, but the magazine industry's share of the advertising dollar still rose at a rate higher than the average of all other media. Magazines are recognized as a good advertising medium. And, only magazines and cable television can produce the special audiences many advertisers seem to want.

Some magazines of the
communications professions.

The Modern
Magazine
Organization

Since most magazines do not print their own publication, the magazine company has no "back shop." It usually is divided into an editorial department, and an advertising and a circulation department. (See figure 6.4.)

A confusing aspect of the magazine business is that staff titles do not always carry the same value or meaning from one publication to the next. In 1983, Time, Inc. listed Henry Anatole Grunwald as "Editor-in-Chief," and placed his name and position above that of "President J. Richard Munro" in the *Time* masthead. At *Woman's Day* on the other hand, the traditional title "Publisher" is printed above that of "Editor," which in turn is ranked higher than "Executive Editor," evidently the way military commanding officers are "above" executive officers. Some magazine titles, too, denote positions that are tailor-made for their specific magazine. *Woman's Day* has editorial staff positions in needlework, and fashions and patterns.

As in newspaper work, however, editors edit, reporters report, and writers write and rewrite, and ad people sell ads. And the art director is usually the person who adds charts, graphs, and sketches and lays out the magazine for the printer. It is unusual to find a magazine without a picture editor or department within the editorial staff. Sometimes art and picture people are referred to as the graphics staff.

People has perhaps the most modern of all major consumer magazine organizations. Second only to *TV Guide* in newsstand sales, it has a full-time staff of 100 people, including:

10 associate editors	10 senior writers	1 art director
12 assistant editors	4 in editorial production	4 in art department
11 on copy desk		1 picture editor
3 in copy processing	5 in editorial services	9 in picture department
17 researchers	45 or more special correspondents in cities around the country— and overseas.	8 in office administration

Outside Help: Free Lancers

Both large and small magazines acquire a good deal of their content from outside, or free-lance, contributors. Larger magazines such as *People* give free-lance writers story assignments. Smaller ones look to unsolicited contributions from writers who are moonlighting on other writing jobs. Writer Alex Haley spent off-hours during his Coast Guard years submitting manuscripts to magazines. Eventually he became known for his writing and won writing and reporting assignments from magazines. His best-selling novel *Roots* developed from this experience.

The hopefuls who submit manuscripts for publication create a necessary chore for magazine editors who search through a mountain of mail in hopes of finding a manuscript they can use. In a year's time, *Harper's* has received as many as twenty thousand manuscripts and eight thousand letters with suggestions for articles. Only some two hundred of the total manuscripts submitted and only a few of the ideas are usable.

Free-lance writers can be a valuable magazine commodity since they can add breadth and range to the writing of the in-house staff. But the problem with most free-lance manuscripts—even the ones written by experienced and talented writers—is they do not reflect the editorial formula of the magazine. The story or article may not be tuned to the social level of the audience, or it may hit an editorial taboo in precisely the wrong way. (Which men's and women's magazines deal with pregnancy, for example, and in what ways do they handle it?) Timing also can be a problem. Consumer magazines (except for the weekly news magazines) usually work three to four months ahead of their publication date. Christmas comes in August for some magazines. Because of the problems of formula and timing, veteran free lancers and staff reporters

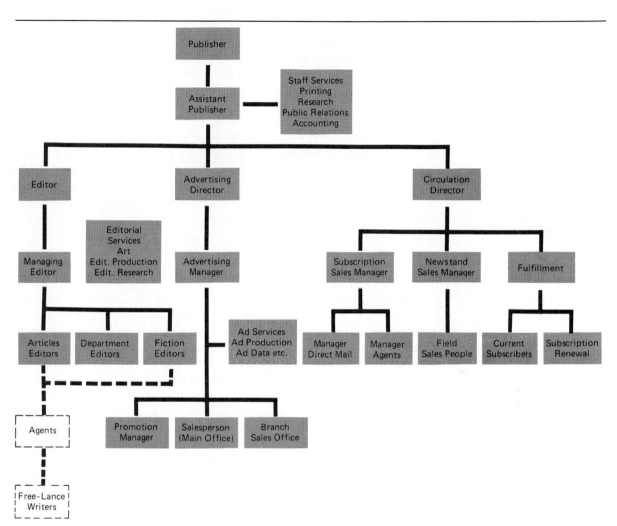

Figure 6.4 A modern
magazine organization.

alike usually submit fact and perspective sheets rather than written
stories. Staff writers then prepare the material to meet the edition's requirements, when the time comes.

Outside Help:
Agents

The literary agent has become the industry's go-between for free lancers.
Through contract with editors, agents develop an understanding of what
editors want, both in general and for a given edition. Since the agent is
in contact with several editors during a period of time, he or she can

supply several potential markets for a free-lance manuscript. As a matter of fact, agents have become so well established in the industry that editors often contact them in search of stories and articles.

The agent can do more than market though; he or she also can give a detailed, faster, more efficient, and more humane feedback on manuscripts than an editor, or on the editor's printed rejection slip.

Literary agencies now come in three sizes: up to sixty clients, sixty to 100, and more than 100 clients. For years agents have charged 10 percent of any sales they make for the writer, but *Writer's Market* reports inflation pushed the figure to 15 percent in the early 1980s. Agents usually will not accept a new client who does not have a record of manuscript sales. They also will not handle clients who are writing genre fiction: detective, romance, and western stories, for example. There are some eighty literary agencies listed in *Writer's Market* at the present time.

Careers in Magazines

The skills of magazine journalism are in great part the skills of newspaper journalism. For this reason, one pathway into a magazine career is through college journalism training. Along with courses in newspaper skills, most journalism departments offer at least one magazine course, usually feature writing. Many offer more.

Since so many magazines are published by corporations, some students have entered the magazine field through public relations work. The company magazine is an important channel of communication between administration and employee. Reaching that employee public can be valuable training experience for anyone wishing to move into consumer magazine editing. At the same time, it is important to remember that many company publications are published by one editor, or by staffs of two or three, and finding a place on such a publication may be a matter of luck or timing.

Recent college graduates have found their college journalism training acceptable to city magazine publishers. The city magazine often must depend on local talent. A knowledge of the town, and an even greater enthusiasm for it, serves beginners well in this job market. A move "up" from the local newspaper is often possible here, too.

One school of thought suggests that, rather than start at the bottom with a small industrial or trade magazine, it is better to strike for the top as soon as possible. Research has shown the person who gets ahead is quite often the person who is available when advancement is possible. A talented editor or writer working in the backwoods will not land a job with a consumer magazine as quickly as one who is known and available when the big chance opens up. The best road to a successful magazine career is to go to New York, Philadelphia, or Chicago, where the major magazine companies operate, the argument continues. All magazines need researchers ("How many trees are there in the Vienna Woods?"), secretaries, and "gofers" ("Gofer a ham and cheese on rye, will you?"). At the top, then, the candidate becomes *very good,* submitting his or her article suggestions and manuscripts to the boss, working hard, and progressing through the organization. More than one person has done it that way. But only the self-confident and the adventuresome need apply.

Some believe it also is possible to stay at the bottom of the magazine ladder—as a free lancer—and rise to the top from outside. A few years ago, some feature writing textbooks encouraged this notion. A few writers do support themselves by free-lance writing. But, generally speaking, the glamour and rewards in free lancing have been greatly exaggerated. Selling half-a-dozen stories or articles a year is not likely to bring what a staff newspaper or magazine reporter can make, even if the stories go to the best-paying markets such as *Playboy* or *Reader's Digest.* Few free-lance writers can sell five major articles a year. Free-lance work also can be a very lonely profession. As one reformed, successful writer once remarked, "I got tired of spending all my time doing research in county libraries, with no one to talk to all day."

The beginning free lancer should try to sell articles to any magazine that accepts manuscripts (Sunday supplements and city magazines, for example), and then turn to a literary agent for help. A two-paged, personalized resume, with a report of sales made, is the best introduction to an agent. Most important, be prepared to spend many years thinking of free-lance work as an avocation rather than as a career.

Summary

Despite some recent competition for the advertising dollar from television, magazines still are a vibrant medium in modern mass communications. With the disappearance of the large circulation family, or general interest, magazine the industry has turned toward specialized publications.

Some magazines offer information and entertainment (passive information); some offer how to articles (active information). Either can be used to attract limited or mass audiences.

There are three general types of magazines: (1) consumer, (2) trade or business, and (3) company- or club-sponsored magazines.

Consumer magazines are sold to the public and use various appeals. News, women's, men's, ethnic, and city magazines are all consumer publications, as are Sunday supplements.

Trade and Professional magazines are published for various trades, businesses and professions—from advertising to medicine to junkyards.

Company magazines are published to encourage employees and channel communication between company management and staff. Some are distributed only to employees and retirees, others also go to outside influentials.

Magazines are susceptible to only a few business diseases, but some can be fatal. Poor circulation, advertising, pricing, and buying policies devour profits quickly. At the same time, the need for the magazine can disappear, or the magazine can lose sight of its identity. The magazine may lose readers by giving them too little. It loses money by giving too much.

The major costs of magazine publishing—paper, printing, and postage—have been rising since the 1970s. To cover these costs publishers doubled cover and subscription prices between 1972 and 1979.

The best hope for the future of magazines is the long-term trend in U.S. advertising expenditures. Recently, magazines have attracted a much larger share of the advertising dollar, and with only moderate efforts. Only cable television has the potential to compete for the special interest audience that magazines now hold.

Magazine production and printing usually are provided through outside contracts. The magazine organization has two basic departments: editorial and business. Outside help also comes from free-lance contributors and literary agents. Free-lance writers and photographers may be assigned to a story while others may contribute material unsolicited. The literary agent acts as a go-between for the free lancer.

Beginners in the field should consider a college degree in journalism or a related field—taking all the magazine courses available. Since so many industrial magazines are published, some magazine students find public relations a good major. The industrial publication offers invaluable beginning experience for a magazine career.

City magazines and Sunday supplements also offer a place to start. City magazines accept college journalism graduates and those who have worked with newspapers. Sunday supplements are a good market for the beginning free-lance writer.

Only a very few free lancers are able to support themselves with their writing. The person determined to free lance should think of it as a long-term *avocation*.

Questions for Discussion

1. Benjamin Compaine believes magazines publish active and passive information. Go through a copy of (1) your favorite consumer magazine, and (2) a copy of a professional magazine that interests you. Are these magazines active or passive? Is it

possible for a technical or trade publication to be passive? Is some of the content active while other parts are passive? Which parts? How can you tell?

2. Consider for a moment the factors that Compaine lists as affecting magazine growth. Assume you have friends with money who want to start a magazine for students. What would be the formula for the magazine? Which of the factors would push sales? Which would hinder them?

3. Is James Kobak correct when he argues that a magazine must have identity and the proper heft? Check through the magazines you are interested in, then check through some of the magazines you dislike (men's or women's, etc.). Are they light and cheap at first glance? Are you rejecting them because they offer a formula you do not understand, or do not like? If you can find copies, compare *The Press* with *Washington Journalism Review*.

4. If you have often dreamed of becoming a free-lance writer, why not see if your dream will work? Study several issues of your favorite magazine—the one for which you really would like to write. What is the formula? (For *Playboy*? For *Ms.*?) What will the magazine be publishing four months from now? Try to figure out what you might write for that edition. Are you confident enough to query the editor about the prospective article? (A query is a letter outlining the idea and asking the editor if he or she would like to read the proposed article.) How much time would it take to write the article? Could you do *two* articles for the same magazine?

References

"Angels Rescind Obit for Harper's." *Newsweek,* July 21, 1980, 84.

Canape, Charlene. "The Race Among the Newsweeklies," *Washington Journalism Review,* January/February, 1983, 14–25.

Compaine, Benjamin M. "The Magazine Industry: Developing the Special Interest Audience." *Journal of Communication* 30 (1980): 98–103.

Daniel, Walter C. *Black Journals of the United States.* Westport: Greenwood Press, 1982.

Dennis, Everette E. "The New Journalism: How It Came to Be." In *Readings in Mass Communication.* 2nd ed. edited by Michael C. Emery and Ted Curtis Smythe. Dubuque, Iowa: Wm. C. Brown Publishers, 1977.

Fletcher, Alan D. "City Magazines Find a Niche in the Media Marketplace." *Journalism Quarterly* 54 (1977): 740–43.

———. "Metropolitan Magazine Boom Continues, But Problems Remain." (Paper presented to the Advertising Division, Association for Education in Journalism, annual convention, Michigan State University, East Lansing, August, 1981.)

"Harpers: 1850–1980." *Newsweek,* June 30, 1980, 71.

"The Hot Magazines Aim at Special Targets." *Business Week,* May 2, 1970, 64–65 et seq.

Johnson, Hillary. "Deep in the Heart of *Newsweek.*" *Columbia Journalism Review,* January/February, 1984, 37–41.

Kobak, James B. "Curing the Sick Magazine." *Folio,* September, 1981.

The Media Book. New York: Media Book, Inc., 1977.

Miller, Gwen. "Career-Oriented Women's Magazines." *Magazine Profiles.* Evanston: Medill School of Journalism, 1974.

Moon, Ben. "City Magazines Past and Present." *Journalism Quarterly* 47 (1970): 711–18.

Peterson, Theodore. "Magazines in the Seventies: Whatever Happened to that Nice Old Edward Bok?" In *Mass Media Issues,* edited by Leonard L. Sellers and William L. Rivers. Englewood Cliffs: Prentice-Hall, 1977.

———. *Magazines in the Twentieth Century.* 2nd ed., Urbana: University of Illinois Press, 1964.

"Talking Business with Rhodes of Magazine Publishers Group." New York *Times,* November 18, 1980.

U.S. Department of Commerce. *U.S. Industrial Outlook For 200 Industries with Projections For 1985.* Washington, D.C.: Government Printing Office, 1981.

Whitehurst, Susan Allen. "Regional Lifestyles." *Magazine Profiles.* Evanston: Medill School of Journalism, 1974.

Wolesley, Roland E. *Understanding Magazines.* 2nd ed., Ames: Iowa State University Press, 1969.

Wood, James Playsted. *Magazines in the United States.* 3rd ed., New York: Ronald Press, 1971.

The Working Press of the Nation, Vol. 5. Burlington, Iowa: The National Research Bureau, 1979.

Writer's Market. Cincinnati: Writer's Digest Books, Inc., 1980.

Chapter
7

Book Publishing

The Time-Honored Book

The oldest and most prestigious of all the mass media is the book. Even if we discount ancient Mesopotamian clay tablets and Egyptian papyrus scrolls, we still can date the book's beginning to the fifth century and the codex, the first volume of parchment bound on one side. Well before the advent of printing, the book had gained prestige as a servant of art, culture, and religion by transporting pictures, words and "the word" from generation to generation.

Even the introduction of printing did not make the book generally available, however. For many years, books and reading were the province of the wealthy. In America during the colonial years only the wealthy had access to libraries—their own or those of wealthy friends and acquaintances. The personal libraries of some colonial Americans were impressive in their size and scope. In 1643 the estate of one New England gentleman included a library of 323 books in English, and sixty-four others in Latin. (The collecting of Latin volumes, of course, was retained from the earliest days of printing when the Latin classic, preserved for centuries by the church, became the staple of learning in the Western world.) The library of religious leader Cotton Mather probably was one of the finest in the world. It had three thousand volumes at his death in 1728. In the South, the plantation owner's library often was a technical necessity as well as a cultural comfort for the isolated plantation family.

As noted in chapter 3, book publishing and book reading took a more democratic turn in America in the nineteenth century, with the pirating of novels and other books from England. Novels in newspaper format, and distributed as weekly serials, were the first cheap American paperback reprints of quality books. The romance novel and the dime adventure novel soon followed. By 1900 schools were commonplace and literacy was widespread even among working people. A best-seller meant at least 600,000 copies distributed in the English-speaking world.

By that time, too, such publishing houses as J. B. Lippincott, John Wiley & Sons, G. & C. Merriam, Houghton, Mifflin, E. P. Dutton, and Doubleday had been established. Some, such as Harper Brothers, had grown through shrewd business judgment and tastefully pirated books; others began by publishing educational, professional, and/or religious texts. In 1910 the Macmillan company named its first children's book editor, leading the way to the time when there would be sixty-five or more book departments in American publishing houses specializing in junior or juvenile books.

Some Types of Publishing Houses

The publishing industry divides itself by its markets and by the methods it uses to reach those markets. For example, there are general interest, or trade markets, children's trade markets, adult trade markets, and educational, professional, and religious book markets. One of the more profitable types of publishing in the 1970s was the paperback or mass market publishing house. Mail-order publishers usually print and distribute expensive books for a more selective audience. Some publishing houses incorporate several types of publishing departments in one house, while others specialize in one area exclusively.

Trade Publishers

Trade publishers reach the general consumer through bookstores and libraries. Hobby, sports, fiction, biography, art, and travel books are trade publications, as are the recent "how to get rich during economic bad times" books. Novels and classics used in classrooms are considered trade, not textbooks, unless they are published specifically for the educational market. The wide range of books aimed at children and adolescents (from Dr. Seuss to Nancy Drew) also are trade books.

Professional Book Publishers

The segment of the industry that caters to the trades, professions, and sciences is comprised of the professional book publishers. The Association of American Publishers recognizes three general areas within professional publishing: (1) technical and scientific books, (2) medical books, and (3) business and other professional books.

Religious Book Publishers

Bibles, testaments, hymnals, theological tracts, and personal devotion literature constitute one of the most consistently successful areas of book publishing. A recent trend is for religious publishers to issue nonreligious books on social topics. However, the industry does not consider the newer books religious, despite their publication source.

Mass Market or Paperback Publishers

The modern soft- or paperback book offers the reader everything from adventure to romance to reprints of classic literature.

Soft-bound books distributed through the mass channels of newsstands, drugstores, and supermarkets are produced by mass market or paperback publishers. The twentieth-century paperback began with Robert De Graff's Pocket Books in the 1930s. De Graff used the roll-fed printing press and reprint rights to sell quality trade novels for a quarter. His list included *Lost Horizon, Topper,* and *Bridge of San Luis Rey,* under the imprint of "Gertrude the Kangeroo."

His use of magazine wholesale distributors introduced one of modern publishing's most important innovations. In the 1970s paperback sales reached 3.5 million copies a year. Both reprint and original paperbacks are distributed through the same mass distribution system. Some are intended for the trade market, others for the mass market. About the only way to distinguish between the two is by the quality of their paper—or the artwork on the covers.

An offshoot of these various types of publishers is the book club. The first was started in the 1920s when Harry Scherman and Max Sackheim founded the Book of the Month Club to market trade books through the mail. Their plan was to offer readers convenience and guidance in book purchases. A panel of judges recommended a new book for purchase each month. The industry disliked the idea at first, until publishers saw the club experts' monthly selection was also being purchased by nonclub members.

There are now some three to five hundred book clubs, ranging from consumer to professional to special interest books. General interest, detective, history, cooking, military, and outdoor hobbyists all have book clubs to serve their needs. Book clubs are considered a part of publishing since most prepare special editions of their books for distribution. A few clubs now originate their own books.

Mail-Order Publishers

Mail-order publications are aimed at the general consumer and offered by direct mail. Book clubs collect books from other publishers, but mail-order publishers are in the business of printing and distributing their own books, usually multivolume sets. They often offer one volume of the set for inspection, then send other volumes if the customer agrees to take them. For example, Grolier Enterprises recently offered by mail *The Harvard Classics,* which includes works of Plato, Shakespeare, and others, in a twenty-seven volume, leather-bound set. The first volume was free. Subsequent volumes, if ordered, cost $24.95, plus postage, delivered each month.

For Love and Money: The Romance Novel

The romance novel: a $300 million-a-year industry.

In many ways romance novel publishing is an industry in its own right, with $300 million dollars in annual sales (40 percent of all paperback book sales) and, according to bibliographist Mary June Kay, 3,700 authors who published 19,000 romance novels between the late 1960s and early 1980s.

The acknowledged Queen of Romance is Britain's Barbara Cartland, who has published more than 350 "sweet and spicy" novels and earned a total of $300 million with her novels. Cartland, now in her 80s, wears pink and pearls and precious jewels, and attracts devoted listeners to her speeches on writing romance fiction for money. As *Newsweek* reported in 1983, the romance novelists themselves are not frustrated housewives, as is often thought. One romance author once owned a hang glider company; another has a master's degree in history; still a third was a policewoman before turning to writing full time. The formula for success? It is not clear, but there are ground rules. "High writing standards," advises one. "Silk sheets, music and French kissing," says another. Sensuous but not graphic love scenes, suggests another. Most believe hard-core porn will not sell in this genre.

In 1982 the top romance novel was *Surrender to Love* by Rosemary Rogers, with sales of 2.5 million copies. The eighth, ninth and tenth best-sellers were *Bold Breathless Love, Rash Reckless Love,* and *Wild Willful Love,* all by Valerie Sherwood. Each sold more than one million copies. Harlequin, the largest publisher of romances, reported only that it sold 200 million in 1982.

University Presses

Many large universities run a subsidized press for the purpose of printing significant books that otherwise would go unpublished. Colleges, museums, research institutions as well as universities publish these scholarly books; they often find their way into the classroom or into trade bookstores. One University of Alabama Press publication became the theme for a motion picture set in turn-of-the-century New Orleans: *Pretty Baby,* with Brooke Shields.

Educational Publishers

There are a large number of publishers that create textbooks, workbooks, and manuals for elementary and secondary schools as well as for colleges and universities. They also produce filmstrips, slides, audio visuals, and multimedia packages (slides with sound). College textbook publishers serve higher education at all levels. Some college books, like mass paperback books, are difficult to distinguish from trade books. Often the only difference is the presence of a dust jacket on the trade book. Chapter summaries, references or footnotes, and discussion questions at the end of chapters are typical of the college text.

Estimated U.S. Consumer Expenditures on Books, 1982 and 1981
(Millions of Dollars and Units)

	1982		1981		% Change		Dollars Per Unit		
	Dollars	Units	Dollars	Units	Dollars	Units	1982	1981	% Change
Trade	2,278.1	408.64	22.185	396.15	3.1	2.7	5.57	5.60	.5
Adult Hardbound	1,225.6	139.27	1,333.2	166.74	8.1	16.5	8.80	7.99	10.1
Adult Paperbound	648.3	106.95	531.8	104.11	21.9	2.7	6.06	5.10	18.8
Children's Hardbound	286.9	76.98	263.3	70.18	9.0	9.7	3.72	3.75	− .8
Children's Paperbound	117.3	85.44	101.1	55.12	16.0	55.0	1.37	1.83	−25.1
Religious	632.6	98.40	574.6	96.29	10.1	2.2	6.42	5.96	7.7
Hardbound	442.5	39.66	403.6	39.23	9.6	1.1	11.15	10.28	8.5
Paperbound	190.1	58.74	171.0	57.06	11.2	2.9	3.23	2.99	8.0
Professional	1,223.7	55.13	1,099.4	51.94	11.3	6.1	22.19	21.16	4.9
Hardbound	958.1	29.21	869.9	28.95	10.1	.9	32.80	30.04	9.2
Paperbound	265.6	25.92	229.5	22.99	15.7	12.7	10.24	9.98	2.6
Book Club	564.5	180.40	555.1	210.49	1.7	14.3	3.12	2.63	18.6
Hardbound	438.3	56.94	431.4	65.07	1.6	12.5	7.69	6.62	16.2
Paperbound	126.2	123.46	123.7	145.42	2.0	15.1	1.02	.85	20.0
Mail Order Publications	617.4	54.53	675.2	59.85	−8.6	8.9	11.32	11.28	.4
Mass Market Publications	1,549.5	582.57	1,397.8	563.68	10.9	3.4	2.65	2.47	7.3
University Presses	94.0	9.80	86.6	9.64	8.5	1.7	9.59	8.98	6.8
Hardbound	65.8	4.12	60.5	3.94	8.8	4.6	15.97	15.35	4.0
Paperbound	28.2	5.86	26.1	5.70	8.0	.4	4.96	4.57	8.5
Elhi Text	1,075.0	247.25	996.0	252.75	7.9	−2.2	4.34	3.94	10.2
Hardbound	595.5	101.71	558.5	102.13	6.6	− .4	5.85	5.46	7.1
Paperbound	479.5	145.54	437.5	150.62	9.6	3.4	3.29	2.90	13.4
College Text	1,338.5	97.88	1,209.7	98.04	10.6	.1	13.67	12.33	10.9
Hardbound	997.6	62.66	908.9	63.50	9.8	1.3	15.92	14.31	11.3
Paperbound	340.9	35.32	300.8	34.54	13.3	2.3	9.65	8.79	9.8
Subscription Reference	333.4	1.00	328.5	1.00	1.5	.0	333.40	328.50	1.5
TOTAL	9,706.7	1,735.70	9,141.2	1,741.85	6.2	− .4	5.59	5.24	6.7

Reprinted from the November 4, 1983 issue of *Publishers Weekly,* published by R. R. Bowker Company, a Xerox company. Copyright © 1983 by Xerox Corporation.

Figure 7.1

Subscription Reference Publishers

The publishing and marketing of reference works door to door is the domain of subscription reference publishers. Dictionaries, atlases, encyclopedias, and similar publications also are published and distributed in the same manner, with schools and libraries an important second market.

Preparing to print a
promotional poster at the
Logan Elm Press.

A breakdown of consumer book purchases for 1981 and 1982 is presented in figure 7.1. The industry attracted $8.2 billion dollars in purchases as the decade began, a 12.9 percent increase over dollars spent in 1979. Trade publishers won the highest percentage of the total, more than 24 percent, and lead all others in percentage of revenue gained, almost 40 percent.

It is difficult to find reliable figures on the exact number of publishers active in the market, and in the various types of publishing. The *Literary Market Place* (*LMP*) for 1982 lists 1,450 publishers who produced five or more titles during that year. The *LMP*'s publisher, R. R. Bowker, reported there are at least five thousand others who publish fewer than five titles each year.

The Small Press

Fortunately it is still possible for interested individuals to form their own publishing houses or presses with little more than desire and the price of some antique printing equipment. These small presses usually publish works of interest to cultural minorities. Bootlegger Press, for example, a feminist press, is dedicated to publishing novels and books that reach beyond the "housewife in revolt" and "how to get ahead as a female executive" themes. The Logan Elm Press, founded in 1979 by art professor Robert Tauber of Ohio State University, works in an educational setting as an artist's support system. Tauber has stressed that the small presses be "socially minded" and serve the community. He has

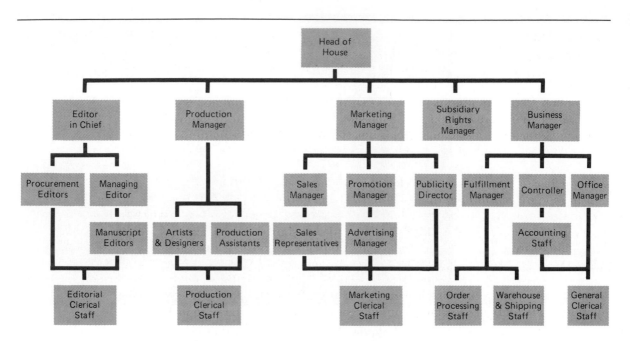

printed poems by e. e. cummings, an interview with a Jamaican religious leader, and a poem in Bliss symbolics, a system of writing that can be learned by moderately retarded people. "Before, all retarded people had to read was first-grade readers," Tauber has said. It has been his hope to brighten the lives of these once ignored readers. Logan Elm books are handbound, limited editions.

The Organization of the Publishing House

Job titles in book publishing, like titles in magazine publishing, often are confusing and contradictory from one publishing house to another. A general outline of publishing house organization is given in figure 7.2.

Business and Subsidiary Rights

As in other media organizations, the business department supervises financial goals and policies, analyzes financial returns, handles computer and bookkeeping services, and manages the firm's personnel—hiring, firing, and promoting. Since publishing is not supported by advertising revenue, the advertising function is under the control of the marketing manager, along with book promotion and other marketing activities.

The subsidiary rights manager is often the forgotten manager in the publishing house. He or she is responsible for arranging the sale of foreign, paperback, reprint, television, magazine serial, and/or movie rights.

Sales and Marketing

The department that has grown the most since World War II is the sales and marketing department. Publicity and sales both are vital to publishing, since most books and book ideas are new to the public. Books by unknown authors require a good deal of publicity, and a lot of luck, to attract enough customers to gain revenues. Promotion means lunches with critics, asking critics for reviews, and sending press releases and free copies of books to newspapers and broadcasting stations in hopes of winning more reviews. Persistence and ingenuity are required. Julia Knickerbocker, the publicity director at William Morrow, once sent a racy novel about a rabbi's wife to a group of rabbis. The religious men were shocked at the book's contents, and denounced it as a "terrible book" to their flocks, who then hurried out to buy the book to see what the fuss was all about.

Sales personnel work on national, regional, and local levels. The national salespeople prepare brochures and material for the department. The regional sales manager oversees regional territories and local salespeople. The sales staff contacts the bookstores and bookstore chains. Local paperback salespeople work with wholesale magazine distributors. Educational salespeople contact university and college professors. There are approximately 13,000 to 14,000 independent bookstores, a growing number of book chains, and more than 2,200 magazine and book wholesale distributors.

The industry underestimated the importance of its distribution system for many years. Many cities were completely without bookstores in the 1930s, a situation that encouraged the expansion of the buy-by-mail book clubs, and drugstore and dime store paperback distribution. One of several attempts to improve distribution has been the formation of special distribution departments.

Viking, Harper & Row, and Doubleday, among others, now make direct contact with shops and other outlets that cater to special interest customers in hobbies, trades, or professions. Horse books and fishing books are promoted to tack shops and fishing or tackle shops. Gourmet, balloon, and even casket companies have bought books directly from publishers. The casket company buys two hundred books on death and dying each year for reference, and to give to employees. One children's nutrition book sold well from a children's clothing shop. Camera books do well in camera shops. Simon & Schuster and Bantam Books have good success selling books as premiums, or to be given away to clients and friends as favors. Recently, Warner published *Confessions of a Medical Heretic,* a sharp attack on the American medical profession. Several chiropractors put in bulk orders for the book to give as gifts to patients.

Editorial and Production

Editorial and production departments oversee the acquisition, preparation, and production of the book. The editor and editorial personnel scout out authors, then prepare the text of the book. Art and production personnel select type and design the cover, trying at all times to keep costs down.

Making Books: A Success Story

Finding a manuscript worth printing is much more difficult than most people realize. Some 30,000 unsolicited novels are sent to trade publishers each year. Most cannot be considered for publication. Most are replays of recent best-sellers—painful divorces, galactic federations in conflict, assassination plots, or deaths from cancer. Most publishing houses now refuse to read unsolicited manuscripts. Some will not return them if postage is not enclosed. As in magazine publishing, the agent remains an important go-between for both writer and editor. If the publishing firm does accept unsolicited manuscripts, it assigns a junior editorial staff member to read them. He or she forwards any potentially acceptable ones, together with a thorough analysis, to a senior editor.

Some books are developed from queries, others from editorial staff ideas. Peter Benchley's first novel, *Jaws,* for example, was worked out with the active participation of editors at Doubleday. The development of the smash hit gives a definitive example of the publication process.

Benchley, the son of Nathaniel and the grandson of Robert Benchley, published his first magazine article in *Vogue* when he was a teenager. He worked for the Washington *Post* and the *National Geographic* before he met Doubleday editor Tom Congdon to discuss an idea for a book in June, 1971. Over lunch, Benchley told Congdon he wanted to write a book about pirates—the way they "really were," without Errol Flynn. Congdon, who was only mildly interested, then asked Benchley if he had ever thought about writing a novel. Benchley was an avid skin diver, and had been diving for sunken treasure off Bermuda in recent weeks. He said he had, as a matter of fact, been thinking about a novel about a great white shark that suddenly appeared off a Long Island resort town. The second idea was much more interesting to Congdon, and he asked Benchley to send him a one-page proposal for a book.

The summary arrived at Doubleday two days later. It outlined a story of a community suddenly attacked by a natural disaster. One young woman is killed and the community reaction develops along with the plot. To Congdon the idea still seemed good, but Benchley had asked for advance payment. Advances are rare today, even for proven writers. After considerable debate, Doubleday advanced Benchley $1,000, which he could keep if he wrote four chapters by April 15, 1972, just six months away.

The four chapters arrived from Roberta Pryor, Benchley's agent. Congdon read the manuscript and asked for rewriting. The shark scenes were realistic, but the editor did not like Benchley's chief of police, who cracked corny jokes throughout the book. He found other parts of the story "mild." Benchley took the position that the editors at Doubleday knew more about book writing than he did, and went to work on the corrections.

By April 28, the four chapters were rewritten, and Doubleday offered Benchley another $6,500 to finish the book. He agreed, and Congdon sent a stream of suggestions. The editor did not like a sex scene between the police chief and his wife, suggesting it was out of place in such a violent novel. Benchley rewrote the scene as an adulterous affair between the wife and the marine specialist—presenting it as an exchange of fantasies during lunch, without specific bedroom descriptions.

When the final manuscript was delivered on January 2, 1973, Congdon showed it first to several Doubleday editors. Then the search for a title began. Benchley suggested *A Stillness in the Water.* Congdon's first suggestion was *The Summer of the Shark.* They tried a total of 237 others, including the suggestion of another Doubleday editor, *The Jaws of the Leviathan.* But *leviathan* seemed flat, as did *The Year They Closed the Beaches.* Finally, at lunch again, Congdon scribbled *Why Us?* Benchley replied, "Why not just *Jaws?*" Despite the possible dental study interpretation, they decided to go with that.

With a title to work with, Congdon turned to the sales staff in the company, sending them the first five pages of the manuscript for reaction. They reacted positively, as did Doubleday's subsidiary rights manager Bob Banker. Bantam Books editor Oscar Dystel read the book and also was excited. He made a first offer of $200,000 for the paperback reprint rights. Banker decided to wait and set up an auction among seven interested paperback publishers for the reprint rights. He also sent manuscript copies to the book clubs for their consideration.

On April 8, a sales conference brought salespeople and the art director together to confer on the cover. The art department had drawn up a prospective cover depicting a peaceful town seen through the jaws of a shark. Salespeople in publishing typically have about an hour to sell a buyer some sixty or seventy titles. They need a "handle"—a summary-slogan—with which to pitch each title to bookstore buyers. The handle for *Jaws* is "The exciting tale of a resort town fighting for its life against a great white shark."

The regional sales managers worried about the cover design. They feared the shark's jaws and teeth were too threatening—in a Freudian way. They asked for changes. They also decided the book might sell twenty-five thousand copies. The advertising department proposed a $25,000 ad budget, or one dollar per book for advertising. Following the sales conference, three book clubs announced they had decided to distribute the book. Their advances, before publication, totaled $85,000.

On April 23, subsidiary rights manager Bob Banker set up an auction for the paperback reprint rights. Auctions also were held for the right to publish the original manuscript. (Publishers often are willing to bid into the hundreds of thousands of dollars for the right to a book by a name novelist.) The bidding for the reprint rights of *Jaws* rose to $500,000. Then, New American Library editor Elaine Geiger withdrew from the bidding. She decided she would not bid higher for a book with that name. Bantam still had a bid, however, and Bantam's Dystel thought *Jaws* could sell a million paperback copies. Movie rights were pending, and they would stimulate paperback sales. Besides, Bantam needed a big book to attract buyers to other Bantam books already on magazine racks across the country. Dystel bid $575,000, and won the reprint rights for *Jaws*.

The problem with the artwork for the cover continued. After considerable debate the shark teeth motif was rejected and replaced with an underwater scene and a shark rising from the deep toward a swimming woman. Publicity head Julie Coryn began promoting the book as suspenseful, a "page turner," a book "you can't put down." Congdon investigated the possibility of giving actual shark's teeth to book reviewers, but the idea was dropped as too expensive. (Shark's teeth cost $5 to $40 each.) The promotional letters to the media paid off. On January 12, 1974, Benchley appeared on the NBC *Today* show.

Meanwhile, Benchley's agent, Roberta Pryor, announced she sold the movie rights of *Jaws* to Brown-Zanuck Productions for $150,000, with an added $25,000 for Benchley to write the screenplay.

By mid-March, the book sold 40,000 hardback copies and was third on the best-seller list. Television spot advertising was scheduled to push the book to buyers who usually did not frequent bookstores. The new ad budget was expected to reach $50,000 or $60,000.

Now Doubleday's distribution staff had to estimate the potential sales of the book. Too many copies would jam the warehouse. Too few, and the demand could die off before the printer could catch up. Either would mean a loss of revenue.

Peter Benchley, meanwhile, prepared to write the screenplay for the movie. (He wrote, then rewrote it three times.) According to one estimate he earned about $600,000 from *Jaws,* his first novel. His agent, Roberta Pryor, received 10 percent of his share. All this occurred before work began on *Jaws 2* and *3*. Doubleday earned $330,000 from paperback and book club advances, and about $65,000 on the first 100,000 copies of *Jaws*. And Tom Congdon? He was named editor-in-chief of adult trade books at E. P. Dutton & Co.

Making It as a Cultural Business

Of all the media industries, none seems less interested in being a business than book publishing. Prior to World War II, book publishers, especially trade book publishers, eked out a marginal existence, often depending on their educational textbook departments to keep them going. Profits and salaries were low; the industry had little growth and attracted little investment. A book could make the best-seller list by selling less than 50,000 copies. The trade publishing houses were trapped in their expensive downtown locations with few outlets for their books.

Following World War II the industry was saved by a reading revolution. The G.I. bill, the Soviet success at placing its first Sputnik satellite into orbit, and the wartime "baby boom" combined to create a rapidly expanding educational book market, and, consequently, an expanding, affluent, and literate audience. With more leisure time and money, the public pushed annual book sales from $1.7 to $2.7 billion between 1962 and 1969, an increase of 59 percent.

The prospects for these better returns brought new investors, and better management. Some houses sold stock to the public to gain capital to finance their growth. And outside corporations began to buy into publishing as a means of diversifying their own operations (CBS and Warner Brothers were among them).

Surviving in publishing today, John Dessauer has suggested, means being aware that publishing is a cultural business. It produces cultural products—ideas, instruments of education, and literature—that are promoted and sold to the public by commercial means. Profit, Dessauer has written, is an inadequate motive for devoting one's life to books and publishing. There are much more profitable ventures elsewhere. But profit normally is the best measure of the public's acceptance of a book, and responsible management can not ignore it. "If a book doesn't sell, it is usually because a manuscript was ill chosen, or poorly written, or poorly edited and marketed . . . lost in over production . . . or unable to survive the pitfalls of a chaotic distribution system," he has argued.

Profits and Publishing

Dessauer has argued that publishing profits depend on four basic factors: (1) price, (2) gross margin, (3) turnover, and (4) operating expense.

Pricing is even more critical in book publishing than in newspaper or magazine publishing, since books do not have advertising revenue to depend on, and since the sale of a book's subsidiary rights may or may not develop. If the price is too low, the book may sell but lose money. Priced too high, it may meet customer resistance. Paperback publishers already have found resistance to the $3 paperback, while readers still seem willing to pay much more ($15? $25?) for hardcovers they feel are indispensable to their profession, avocation, or recreation. Even trade novels now sell steadily at $14 or $15, twice the price of the original hardcover edition of *Jaws*.

The book warehouse.

The lower prices of paperbacks mean, of course, that there is relatively less profit in fast-selling paperbacks than in slower-selling, higher-priced hardcover books. In 1980 the industry sold 762 million softcovers and 290 million hardcovers, but paperbacks brought almost $1.8 billion in retail, while hardcover books sold for $3 billion. That is, 472 million *fewer* hardcover books sold for $1.2 billion *more* than the softcover books. Today a publisher must sell six $3 paperbacks to realize the profit he can earn from one $25 hardcover.

Gross margin is the proportion of the sales price left after all production and distribution costs are subtracted—including editing, printing, royalty, and bookstore costs. One important cost in publishing is the cost of book returns. If a grocer buys cabbage, and it doesn't sell, he throws it out and writes off the cost. If bookstores order books and they do not sell, the bookstore returns them to the publisher where they acquire new warehouse storage costs, or costs of redistributing them to markets where they will sell, greatly reducing gross margins.

Since approximately 60 percent of all books printed lose money, publishers are eager to maintain as high a gross margin as possible to help defray the costs of poor selling books. Publishers often attempt to keep gross margins high by cutting manufacturing costs and reducing royalty payments.

The solution to the problem, Dessauer has argued, usually is better turnover—better selection of books for the public and better distribution.

Turnover is to publishing what circulation is to newspapers and magazines. The faster books turn over, the fewer the returns, the more rapid the sales, the greater the publishing profit. A serious problem in the industry for many years has been its chaotic distribution system. The fulfillment departments in publishing houses are responsible for the filling and delivery of book orders. Too often they have not been capable of delivering book orders with promptness or accuracy. (One horror story from a few years ago had one buyer order fifty copies of a paperback novel three times without ever getting the correct novel.)

The largest share of books are distributed by companies and organizations outside the publishing company. More than 35 percent of all book sales are made by bookstores. (See figure 7.3.) The bookstores, therefore, can affect turnover significantly—by failing to stock popular books, by merchandising books in uninviting stores, or by driving away potential customers in any one of a dozen ways. Many bookstore owners, for example, exhibit a decidedly snobbish attitude, putting a definite chill on their own store traffic and on book sales.

Channels of U.S. Book Distribution—Estimated Consumer Expenditures
(Millions of Dollars and Units)

	1982		1981		% Change	
	Dollars	Units	Dollars	Units	Dollars	Units
General Retailers	3,754.1	814.48	3,497.8	785.41	7.3	3.7
College Stores	1,791.9	204.32	1,624.5	201.47	10.3	1.4
Libraries & Institutions	751.2	62.42	683.2	66.16	10.0	− 5.7
Schools	1,329.6	282.61	1,267.9	293.45	4.9	− 3.7
Direct to Consumer	1,938.5	293.15	1,949.8	25.80	− .6	−10.0
Other	141.4	78.79	118.0	69.54	19.8	13.3
TOTAL	9,706.7	1,735.70	9,141.2	1,741.83	6.2	− .4

Reprinted from the November 4, 1983 issue of *Publishers Weekly,* published by R. R. Bowker Company, a Xerox company. Copyright © 1983 by Xerox Corporation.

Figure 7.3

Operating expenses are the other side of gross margin, but they must be considered investments in book publishing rather than liabilities, Dessauer has suggested. The salaries paid editors must result in books the public wants and needs. Salespeople, advertisers, and publicists— all of whom are paid regular salaries—must get the book into the marketplace. If operating expenses are well spent, profit will follow, he has argued.

One highly controversial operating expense is the increasingly high amounts paid authors for the rights to publish their manuscripts. Payments before publication have gone into six figures. One first novel drew a prepublication payment of $850,000 in 1981. St. Martin's Press negotiated a $3.6 million package for the memoirs of English veterinarian James Herriot's fourth book, *The Lord God Made Them All.* A concern is that such high figures produce operating costs that can not be recaptured in book sales and subsidiary rights. Others, agents and writers included, argue that large advances reduce what can be paid other authors, especially those who write mid-range books that sell from 10,000 to 20,000 copies. The fear is the ''big book'' will greatly reduce the total number of books published.

Those who support paying big advances, however, argue they are a wise operational investment. (Veterinarian Herriot's books all have sold well, and continue to do so.) They argue publishers should gamble on such good properties. Robert G. Diforio, president of the New American Library, admitted his prepublication payment of more than $800,000 to ad executive Anne Tolstoi Wallach for her first novel *Women's Work* was a gamble, but also said he was sure the novel would be a winner and sell 75,000 hardcover copies and a million paperbacks.

Stuart Applebaum, the publicity director of Bantam Books, has aruged that out of necessity paperback publishers will continue to "bid up" potential best-sellers. A book publisher has to have one or two extraordinary books every month, he has pointed out, to keep drugstore and supermarket customers clamoring for them. Otherwise, there is not enough paperback distribution space to hold enough moderately selling books to meet costs and return a profit for both distributors and publishing houses.

Maintaining Quality

If there is a decline in the numbers of novels and trade books that sell 10,000 to 20,000 copies, it will be a lamentable situation for the industry. Books in that range are frequently quality books of the adult trade—the literature of our modern day. Good fiction—fiction with satire, parody, and scintillating word play—is difficult to sell. Serious books require serious readers, and a very good book by a beginning writer may attract only 5,000 or 6,000 of them the first time out.

To build a following for a good writer, Irving Goodman, president of Viking Press, has said his strategy is to improve sales a notch at a time. If the author sells 10,000 copies of one book, Viking tries to get 15,000 or 20,000 with the next book—to keep the morale of the author up, if for no other reason. Viking has a cliche, Goodman has said. "We say the thing we like best is a good book that sells; the thing we like next best is a good book that doesn't sell." He has described Viking as a "moderately profitable" publishing house, and has said the strength of publishing is working with authors who try to get better with each book.

Trade publishing in general continues to be a moderately profitable business. The industry has relied more and more on the sale of reprint, book club, and film rights for profits. In 1979 and 1980 subsidiary rights accounted for almost 150 percent of their total profits. In short, trade publishers would have been deeply in debt without them. Meanwhile, paperback publishers are feeling their own inflationary pressures, and are in less and less of a position to bid high figures for reprint rights. Between 1975 and 1980 they contributed diminishing percentages (from 60 to 37 percent) of the total subsidiary rights paid to trade publishers.

Then, too, while paperback publishers still look for the highly promoted blockbuster book, the shift in paperbacks is away from the individual author and the recognized title toward the genre book: the woman's romance, the western, man's action, or science fiction. Genre books do not depend on prior publication by trade publishers. They are, instead, magazine-books, books with a more-of-the-same quality. The trend has not been strong enough to salvage the mass market paperback industry from its problems, however. To gain more profits, it has moved into the trade field, buying first publication rights and introducing hard-cover books of its own.

Trade publishers now find that reprint revenues not only have fallen off, but that they are competing with paperback publishers for first publication rights and even hardcover shelf space in general interest bookstores. Publishing consultant Leonard Shatzkin has said the competition will result in the loss of both trade and mass market publishing houses. The trade houses that survive will be the ones that learn to make money in original publishing—through retrenchment and with innovative mail-order sales, special sales, and improved distribution. In Cleveland, for example, one bookstore chain, Under Cover Books, is experimenting with a slight change in distribution that could double hardcover sales. Under Cover has decided to allow publishing company salespeople to order books for its stores, in the belief that salespeople know more about books and how well they are likely to sell. Under Cover's own staff, meanwhile, can spend its valuable time working with customers rather than listening to all-too-brief book summaries from salespeople. Shatzkin has stated that book sales could double under such an arrangement.

Outlook for the Industry

If trade publishers are looking to a time when they must tighten controls to keep their businesses, the outlook for the publishing industry in general is more promising. Rising transportation costs led to a decline in bookstore profits near the end of the 1970s, but promises of tax cuts and, therefore, consumers with more discretionary funds, has led the U.S. Department of Commerce to predict brighter days for the 1980s.

The outlook for educational publishers also has been predicted to be bright with any decline in school enrollment outweighed by increasing per capita expenditures for instructional texts. Growth in adult college courses was expected to offset any drop in enrollment in other college classes.

Religious books, aided by an increase in religious bookstores, enjoyed an annual rate of growth of more than 10 percent between 1972 and 1982.

Professional book sales also advanced between 1972 and 1982, at a rate of more than 11 percent a year. Professional books remain one of the fastest-growing segments of the publishing industry. Medical, legal, business, and other professional books accounted for as much as 15 percent of all U.S. book shipments in the early 1980s. The continuing national trend toward job specialization probably will encourage growth in professional book publishing in the years immediately ahead.

Also "hot" in recent years have been sales in children's or juvenile books. Even after deducting a 6.9 percent average increase in cost between 1979 and 1980, juvenile book sales still rose 23 percent, and increased another 9 percent between 1981 and 1982.

Reference books—dictionaries, encyclopedias, atlases—have not maintained pace with other types of publishing, however. The main cause was the slowdown in funding for library and institutional buying that accompanied the inflation/recession cutbacks of the early 1980s. Reference publishers also are beginning to feel the competition from computer data banks.

Publishing has begun its conversion to computer and data processing. Some of the equipment adopted is for in-house word processing and manuscript composition. Some is used for inventory control, to fill orders, and some to improve weak distribution systems. With the development of a more readable text for television tubes, cable television is ready to provide an even speedier delivery of books to the home television—almost the instant the manuscript is set in type and delivered into computer memory.

The brightest prospect for the industry, however, seems to be the growing number of college students who graduate each year to become book customers. In 1982 CBS publishing vice-president George Allen predicted the country could look forward to ten years of "super growth" in book publishing based on the demands of well-educated, relatively affluent graduates. The growth rate of this prime, college graduate audience will outstrip the entire population in the years before 1990. It will be as if a whole new nation of book buyers has been added to the American population, Allen has pointed out.

Careers in Book Publishing

In 1983 the United States Department of Commerce indicated there were about 100,000 employees in the publishing industry in the early 1980s, with 51,000 or more being production workers. The industry remains one of small companies. Eighty percent of all publishing houses have less than twenty persons. Fewer than ten publishing houses have 1,000 or more employees. While employment slowed in the industry in the late 1970s, the long-term trend promises to be one of growth. Richard Morgan, president of Macmillan's school division, has said his division always seems to be looking for people.

Editor-writer Roberta Morgan, in her book *How To Break into Publishing,* has written that the industry's hiring practices are haphazard and completely without standardized tests and guidelines. Education, job experience, self-presentation, and "being at the right place" all can be important factors in getting a publishing house position. Educational requirements at one time included a college degree in English or classical literature. But some editors now avoid graduates with those backgrounds, since they find them too scholarly and academically oriented. Degree preferences now range from English to journalism, to the liberal arts and even mathematics and chemistry. Special interest degrees have great value for houses that publish special interest texts, of course, just as knowledge of a given profession is invaluable to a professional publishing house. A good degree, with good grades, is basic to the industry.

Job experience also is highly useful. Part-time work in a bookstore, writing and editing for the college newspaper, magazine, or yearbook, internships, summer jobs with book distributors, ad agencies, or a readership research project give excellent experience and add to the beginner's résumé. They also can help make important contacts in the publishing business.

Self-presentation is very important, editor Morgan has suggested. Excellent self-presentation includes being "pleasant, humble, and eager," and is necessary in personal contacts, personal interviews, the résumé, and at work. Detailed information on résumé preparation is available in Morgan's book.

Being at the right place at the right time may be easier than it first seems, since the publishing industry has representatives scattered across the country—even if a large percentage is located in the metropolitan East. A good place for the beginner to start is *Literary Market Place,* a comprehensive directory of U.S. book publishers and publishing services. From it collect names of editors in your field of interest, then write a letter to each, explaining your background and career interests and asking for an interview. Polite telephone callbacks to see if the editor received the letter are in order. Persistence is valued in book publishing. College placement offices and help-wanted ads in *Publisher's Weekly* are other potential contacts.

There is little doubt the talented, dedicated person who wishes a career in publishing can find one. Competition for positions open in publishing are keen, but as one publishing executive has put it, there's a "woeful lack of good talent" coming into the industry.

According to one survey conducted in the early 1980s, entry level salaries for editorial assistants in publishing ranged from $10,000 to $15,000, production assistants $12,000 to $18,000, and trade salespeople from $13,500 to $18,000.

Summary

Books are the oldest and probably the most prestigious of the mass media. A rising literacy rate helped democratize the book in America in the nineteenth century.

Modern publishing divides itself according to its markets, and the way it reaches those markets.

Trade publishers appeal to the general audience through bookstores and libraries with books of interest to adults, children, and juveniles.

Professional publishers print technical and scientific books, medical, or business books.

Religious publishers feature Bibles, theological and devotional books.

Many books aimed at the popular taste are the work of mass market and/or paperback publishers who distribute their books at popular prices through drugstores, supermarkets and newsstands.

Book clubs and mail-order publishers distribute through the mails. Book clubs distribute both their own publications and those of other publishers. Mail-order publishers print special interest books. Subscription reference publishers market reference books door to door.

University press publishers print scholarly works, while college publishers print textbooks for the college level student. Elementary and secondary publishers (ElHi) serve the lower grades with texts and teaching aids.

The publishing industry is an $8.2 billion industry, and growing. The largest part of industry is made up of trade publishers who contribute 24 percent of the total sales. Small presses, like small newspapers and magazines, often service cultural minorities and special interest audiences.

The large publishing houses are organized into departments with department managers. Business keeps the books, maintains financial goals and policies, and the hiring, firing, and promoting. Subsidiary rights managers oversee reprint, foreign, television, magazine serial, movie and/or paperback rights. Sales and marketing advertises, promotes, and distributes the book product.

Distribution remains a major problem for the industry. Most publishers rely on distribution from independently owned bookstores or chains. The industry also actively promotes special sales to special outlets—tack shops, sports stores, and camera stores.

The editorial division is responsible for acquiring and editing manuscripts, and making them into books in conjunction with the production department.

Although the quality of what is printed is important, profits are normally the best measure of a book's success. Profits are controlled by pricing, gross margin, turnover, and operating expenses.

Many in the industry are concerned with the sharp increase in one operational expense: the trend toward bigger and bigger prepublication payments for manuscripts. Some feel the trend will reduce profits and the number of quality books produced by the industry. Others contend, however, that paperback publishers regularly need "big books" to attract buyers.

The industry can look to the future with hope. Educational and professional publishing seems likely to prosper and grow during the 1980s. The industry is adapting to the coming computer age, and is likely to accommodate itself well to cable television distribution.

The brightest prospect, however, may be in the growing number of college students who are graduating and going into the working world. Well-educated and relatively affluent, this potential audience will grow faster than the rest of the population, and present publishing with a whole new group of potential readers.

Questions for Discussion

1. The codex is said to be the first book. Were bound pages a significant breakthrough? How much trouble would it be, for example, if this textbook came in scroll form? At the same time, reference works (in book form) now are being put in computer data banks. What advantages does the electronic book have over the printed one? Would a computer book make a good textbook? Why not?

2. One view expressed in this chapter was that expensive books important to people in their profession or daily life sell better than light, inexpensive novels. Compare this idea to the discussion of active and passive magazine content in the last chapter. Is it possible to understand magazine and book sales from this viewpoint? Would this new format change the types of books categorized in modern publishing as religious, professional, reference, and trade?

3. Again and again publishing industry observers complain about the book distribution system. How difficult is it for you to buy (1) a trade book—a novel or other general interest book, (2) a professional book of your chosen field, (3) a textbook? In your experience, are bookstores as comfortable to be in as department stores, for example? What is the range of books offered at the largest drugstores or supermarkets near you? Do you think you might read more, or buy more books, if you had better access to them?

4. One small press publisher has printed a book for the moderately retarded reader. How do you explain the fact that larger publishers have not published this type of literature? Should the government enact a quota system for publishers, requiring them to print a few public service books for every five or six novels they produce?

References

"All Aboard For Love and Money." *Newsweek,* May 2, 1983, 64.

Benjamin, Curtis G. "Book Publishing's Hidden Bonanza." In *Readings in Mass Communication,* edited by Michael C. Emery and Ted Curtis Smythe, 2nd ed. Dubuque, Iowa: Wm. C. Brown Publishers, 1974.

Constable, Lesley. "Community Printer." *The Columbus Dispatch,* February 7, 1982, F1.

Dahlin, Robert. "The Job Market: How Bad Is It?" *Publishers Weekly,* January 29, 1982.

Dessauer, John P. *Book Publishing, What It Is, What It Does.* New York and London: R. R. Bowker, 1981.

———. "Profit, What It Is—and Some Suggestions on Achieving It." *Publishers Weekly,* January 29, 1982.

———. "Book Sales in 1980." *Publishers Weekly,* November 20, 1981.

———. "1982 Book Purchases: A Hard Year." *Publishers Weekly,* November 4, 1983.

Evans, Nancy. "Publicists, Ingenuity Lights the Fire; Perseverance Fans the Flames." *Publishers Weekly,* March 14, 1980.

Grannis, Chandler, ed. *What Happens in Publishing.* New York: Columbia University Press, 1967.

Heilbrun, Carolyn G. "Hers." The New York *Times,* February 26, 1981, C2.

Hogan, Randolph. "A Book Fair for Small Presses Opens in the 'Village.'" The New York *Times,* March 27, 1981, C24.

Kleinfield, N. R. "Special Strategies for Special Books." The New York *Times,* September 7, 1981, D1.

Madison, Charles. *Book Publishing in America.* New York: McGraw-Hill, 1966.

Maryles, Daisy. "Wholesalers and Publishers Offer Optimistic Forecasts for the '80's." *Publishers Weekly,* November 20, 1981, 40–41.

McDowell, Edwin. "First Novels Garner Top Prices, But Average Advances Decline." The New York *Times,* February 26, 1981, C16.

Menaker, Daniel. "Unsolicited, Unloved MSS." *The New York Times Book Review,* March 1, 1981, 3, 22.

Morgan, Roberta. *How To Break into Publishing.* New York: Barnes and Noble, 1980.

Morgan, Ted. "Sharks: The Making of a Best Seller." *The New York Times Magazine,* April 21, 1974, 10 et seq.

Petersen, Clarence. *The Bantam Story.* New York: Bantam Books, 1970.

Shatzkin, Leonard. "The Developing Crisis in Trade Books." *Publishers Weekly,* January 22, 1982, 24–25.

Small, Bertrice W. "What Is Romance Fiction?" *Publishers Weekly,* November 13, 1981, 26 et seq.

U.S. Department of Commerce. *U.S. Industrial Outlook, 1981.* Washington, D.C.: Government Printing Office.

———. *Statistical Abstracts of the United States, 1982–83.* Washington, D.C.: Government Printing Office.

Walters, Ray. "Paperback Talk." *The New York Times Book Review,* March 8, 1981, 35.

Chapter
8

Music, Music, Music: The Recording Industry

199

It touches almost every corner of our lives—anywhere we can hear, any hour of the day or night. It plays in the Styrofoam earphones of the neighborhood paperboy as he skates along his route. It reaches the businessman or businesswoman as their elevator rises to the office. It cheers the commuter as he or she drives to work, and the proud mechanic joyriding in his or her rebuilt Mustang. The housewife listens to it as she completes her shopping list, and then again as she navigates the aisles of the supermarket. For many, it is a quiet evening at the symphony or a jazz session in one's own apartment.

It, of course, is music—recorded music—pop and classical, country and rock, jazz and bluegrass. We use it to fill out our day, to perk up the humdrum routine, to dance and romance by, to congregate with, to feel majestic and stirred—to slip off to sleep by. To have tunes, as the expression goes, is one of the more enjoyable aspects of modern living.

Inventing the Modern Music Industry

If necessity is the mother of invention, invention has to be the mother of the modern music industry. At more than one stage in its development, recorded music has been helped, perhaps saved, by the timely intervention by a much-needed innovation. The coin-in-the-slot machine converted the talking machine into a profitable music player in San Francisco in the 1890s. In 1925 Joseph Maxfield replaced Edison's speaking horn, diaphragm and stylus with a microphone, a vacuum tube amplifier, and electromagnetic speakers, enabling recorded music to survive the competition of radio music. Since World War II, a series of miraculous inventions has greatly improved the quality of musical recordings and the richness of the listening experience as well as the methods for listening to records. When World War II ended, the 78 rpm shellac recording was the staple of the industry. A recording lasted for three and a half minutes, was mostly composed of bass sound, and played on a small phonograph of modest price. RCA Victor had promoted the Duo, Jr. for $16.50, to encourage record collecting during the Depression. There were few symphonic recordings, since concert music did not divide well by three and a half.

The Speed Trap and Help from Sonar

In 1947, a major breakthrough occurred at the Columbia record company. Dr. Peter Goldmark perfected a workable long-playing (LP) record by constructing a cutting head that made consistent, hair-width grooves in vinylite plastic, and a new phono pickup and equalization system that could track the narrow grooves and pick up high-quality, undistorted music for a full twenty-three minutes. To promote the new 33 1/3 rpm LP, Columbia invited all other recording companies to make use of the new method without charge. RCA Victor and David Sarnoff were given a

Recording music.

The RCA forty-five, with changer.

Steel Wire, Paper, and Plastic Tape

personal demonstration that stunned the RCA experts. But RCA, nevertheless, declined the offer, and the following year surprised the industry by announcing its own new record and record player: the microgroove 45 rpm. The RCA 45 played for the same length of time as the old 78 rpm, and its unique donut-shaped record required a special changer. Rather than give in to the Columbia LP, and throw away the money spent on the development of the 45, RCA decided to slug it out in the marketplace. The "battle of the speeds" was on. The industry suffered as a confused public slowed its record buying. Sales fell by $45 million. The majority of the record companies accepted Columbia's offer to use the LP without charge, but RCA continued to promote the 45, especially for popular music.

Finally, in 1950, things fell into place. RCA capitulated, announcing it too would use the LP for its great artists and classical (Red Seal) recordings. To smooth the way for peace, Columbia reciprocated by adopting the 45 for its popular records. The battle was over.

About the same time, one of the most important recording innovations came with the creation in England of "ffrr," or full frequency range recording. The ffrr recording method was developed by London records—a subsidiary of Decca—from sonar technology designed during World War II to detect differences between British and German submarines. The improved sound quality quickly acquired the nickname "high fidelity." Its amazing fidelity and a back-from-the-war boom brought the return of the record collector, who had all but disappeared during the Depression. American phonograph units, counted at 16.8 million in 1950, rose to 34 million in 1960, and to 58.7 million in 1970. The new "hi-fi" recordings also created a new type of record collector, one interested in precise and authentic sound reproduction. To serve that new collector, an entirely new industry arose to engineer turntables without rumbles, amplifiers without noise, and speakers with a fuller, more realistic sound range. The hi-fi collector preferred good recordings of boat whistles, passing trains, or even geese in flight to the muddy music of the old 78s.

Meanwhile, World War II also had produced successes in one long-forgotten method of sound recording: magnetic recording. Valdemar Poulsen had succeeded in recording sound on steel wire in 1889 by using telephone and electromagnetic equipment. But since the quality was poor and the volume low, the method was abandoned until radio technology and especially vacuum tube amplification revived interest in the method. In the late 1930s Bell Laboratories operated a magnetic recording system with high-grade steel tape as the recording medium. Similar systems were employed in Germany and England, but the steel tape was expensive ($1.50 per foot in America), and the fidelity still was low.

The inventor of the magnetic wire recorder, Valdemar Poulson, and "Der Bingle," Bing Crosby, whose support of magnetic tape recording did much to bring out its development and adoption in radio.

The Armour Research Foundation developed a wire recorder which it put on the market in 1943 with Webster of Chicago. But the thin wire—1/100 of an inch—was susceptible to breaking, and the breaks created monumental whiplash tangles. Although the broken wire could be repaired with a square knot, the resulting lump could damage the head of the machine as the wire played.

The modern plastic tape recording machine evolved from those that recorded on magnetic oxides affixed to paper tape. The Germans programmed Radio Luxembourg with high-quality recorded tapes in 1941. The American armed forces in Europe at the end of the war were surprised to find radio stations operating with reels of recordings rather than live performers—such was the quality of the German Magnetophone tape machines. A number of the captured machines were brought back to the United States, where American technology refined the invention further. Minnesota Mining and Manufacturing (3M) perfected a high-quality recording tape with a plastic backing (and put the famous *Scotch* name on it). The Ampex Corporation created a high-quality recording machine that in the 1950s became the standard of the industry. (Both 3M and Ampex later would prove to be leaders in video tape recording, too.) It would be remiss to ignore the contribution of popular singer Bing Crosby, also. Crosby's love of golf, and his desire to record his radio programs in his own good time (rather than be forced to give two live radio performances each week to meet time zone demands) encouraged him to contribute much money and personal support to tape recording.

Magnetic tape now is not only of high quality, and long playing, it can be edited, something that was impossible with both wire and disc recordings. One recent use of tape editing, for example, has been to copy (dub) old 78 rpm recordings, with the tape running at very high speed. Then, slowing the tape down, it is possible to edit out the pops and clicks created by years of grime and use—without disturbing the music. The result is a fresh, clear piece of music from the past.

Stereo and Beyond

Magnetic tape was used to produce stereo music in 1956. The stereo effect had been demonstrated in 1931 by A. D. Blumlein of the English Columbia company. But engineers had trouble producing two, side-by-side channels of sound from a disc without cutting playback time in half. With tape recording, stereo was only a matter of using half the tape and half a recording head for one track and the other half of the tape and head for the other track. Soon after stereo tape was introduced, the modern stereo disc came onto the market (in 1958). The problem of playback time was solved by cutting the two stereo tracks *inside* the same

Figure 8.1

Record Sales by Repertoire (1980)

Types of Music	Percentages
Contemporary (pop, rock)	51.2%
Country	14.3
Soul	10.5
Children's	5.7
Jazz	4.2
MOR	4.0
Classical	4.0
Comedy	1.3
Others	1.6

Source: National Association of Recording Manufacturers, Cherry Hill, New Jersey.

LP groove, one on top of the other. The industry began its effort to convert to stereo beginning in 1967. All monaural, or single track, recording prices were raised to the stereo level.

The introduction of quadraphonic, eight-track, and cassette tapes complicated the picture in the 1970s but did little to drive the LP and disc singles from the market. (See figure 8.1.) Instead, reel-to-reel tape recordings, quadraphonic tapes, and four-track tapes have decreased while the smaller, self-contained, and easy-to-store and handle cassette has increased in sales year by year. The stereo cassette can be played through a cassette tape deck in the home stereo, or car, or in portable machines. The availability of recorded music on cassette tape, and the simplicity of dubbing one cassette to another to copy a recording, not only has made the blank cassette important in sales, it also has created a threat to record company products. (See p. 213.)

The Sony Corporation introduced the first of the personal stereo tape players, the Sony Walkman, in 1979. Estimates are that Sony shipped two million Walkman units to the U.S. in 1980 and 1981; numerous copies also poured from the assembly lines of some twenty other manufacturers. Use of the machines quickly spread from joggers and bikers to assembly-line workers and even dental patients.

The New Dream Sound: Digital

The newest and most sensational of all the inventions that have kept the record industry alive was announced in the early 1980s. It is "digital" recording. Since Edison's original phonograph, all recording had been analogue recording. That is, for every note of music, there was a bump, groove turn, or electromagnetic "thing" on the cylinder, disc, or tape. Digital recording, on the other hand, translates the signals of the music into a mathematical code, breaking it into small bits of information that are stored numerically. This system greatly reduces the effect of noise in the recording process. And since digital recording is actually a string of numbers that are placed on a disc and read back by a laser beam, the life of the recording is extended indefinitely; dust and grime have little effect on the number of playbacks.

Digital recording is expected to dominate the industry in the 1990s. There are many hybrid digital/analogue recordings on the market now. They are recordings made on digital equipment, and then produced for analogue playback with traditional analogue record masters. The great improvement the digital/analogue hybrids offer in the fidelity of sound recording is expected to make them important to high-fidelity enthusiasts in the years just ahead.

The major recording corporations also have entered the video recording field and are exploring home video markets and cable television. (See chapter 11.)

The State of the Art

Whatever support inventions give the music business, it is the recorded music itself and its acceptance by the public that determines the industry's success.

Most recorded music, of course, is popular music: pop, rock, soul, disco, or MOR (middle-of-the-road). Pop and rock account for more than 51 percent of all record sales each year. (See figure 8.1.) (The two types are placed together because it is now difficult to tell the difference.) Since the 1970s country music has been one of the fastest-growing musical types. Special smaller audiences buy lesser numbers of classical, children's jazz, and comedy recordings.

The Mass Sound

Rock, or one of its variations, dominated record sales for the twenty years between the late 1950s and the late 1970s. Beginning with the Crew Cuts' rock and roll "Sh-Boom" and Bill Haley and the Comets' "Rock Around the Clock," rock rose to popularity with such performers as Buddy Holly and Elvis Presley; teenage audiences loved it as dance music. The rock of The Beatles, Rolling Stones, and others created a strong sense of community among rock followers, and eventually made it a mass sound, with fifty rock recording artists or groups making three to seven times more money than the highest-paid executive in America, the president of AT&T. Rod Stewart charged $40,000 for a personal appearance. England's Deep Purple had a reported annual income of 5 million pounds, or about $9.2 million, during the period.

The first signs that America's ardor had cooled for rock came in the mid-1970s when disco suddenly became an important challenger in the race for record sales. By 1979 disco and "beautiful music" radio formats each attracted more listeners than rock. Three rock counterattacks—punk, new wave, and the new music (really a throwback to rock and

Sha Na Na, like many popular music groups, enact a kind of childish escapism in their performances and songs.

roll)—all gained audience support in the 1970s and 1980s, but all three failed to regain dominance as the mass sound. Blondi's Debbie Harry, for example, did not achieve the superstar status of Elton John, Bob Dylan, or Mick Jagger.

Toy Music

New York *Times* music critic Stephen Holden has said there is one clear strain in most contemporary popular music. He argues that since most recordings are produced for teenagers and young adults, a theme required for acceptance is one of "pure, childish escapism" which he calls "toy music."

Examples abound. There was Little Richard's "Tutti Frutti," and the angelic-sounding Bee Gees in the *Saturday Night Fever* movie sound track. Add Sha Na Na, much of the Beatles, the Electric Light Orchestra, the Village People, Donna Summer—even Donna Fargo, and more. The Swedish group Abba, one of the best-selling musical groups in modern recording, often sounds like a child's choir, Holden has written, with its two female lead singers.

The undisputed leader in toy music, however, is the charming Australian Olivia Newton-John. Holden has suggested that even when she tries to sound sexually aggressive (as in her hit "Physical") her tone suggests a child pretending to be an adult—an incongruity that may account for the appeal, and the limitations, of her artistry.

At heart, Holden has written, toy music thrives because of its child-ish art and ideas, its gibberish and nonsense—even with a synthesizer in the background—that appeals to all age groups, not just the young set.

The Classics and Jazz

There remains a continuing market for both classical and jazz recordings. A recent trend in classical recording is the live performance recording. One estimate in 1982 suggested as much as one-fourth of available classical music is of this type, much of it from small labels—and of dubious quality. Established classical musicians still find, even as Caruso did, that recording some popular records can be rewarding. One of today's leading tenors, Placido Domingo, recorded an album with pop singer John Denver that sold more than one million copies. Domingo also has recorded an album of Argentine tangos.

Jazz musicians, meanwhile, complain that the large recording companies are ignoring pure jazz for the more profitable rock-jazz and commercial jazz blends of music. Much of the best jazz still comes from smaller, independent labels. But these labels do not have the money to place records before the public, or promote and advertise the relatively unknown groups who record them.

Meanwhile, MOR, comedy, and children's records all seem to have a self-regenerating audience. MOR seems made for office Muzak and supermarket FM. Comedy recordings can provide a channel for the sophisticated comedian that only the night club—certainly not family radio or television—can equal.

The Record Industry

The Record Industry Association of America (RIAA) has reported there are now 1,310 recording and tape production companies in the United States. With 125 record pressing plants, and some 250 tape duplicating plants, the industry currently ships approximately 157 million single disc recordings, 308 million LP recordings, 99 million cassettes, and 85 million eight-track tapes each year—or enough to give every living American two recordings of some kind every twelve months.

The production facilities of the industry are supported by an extensive wholesale distribution system that places recordings in jukeboxes and retail outlet stores. The RIAA has estimated there are 14,000 outlet stores, and these are the principal sources of recordings for the buying audience.

The creation of vinyl plastic LPs and 45s made the mailing of recordings possible. Columbia formed the first record club in 1955, and today both Columbia and RCA distribute disc and tape recordings to club members by mail. Other record producers also find the mail useful for sales and distribution. Just as mail-order book publishers prepare special volumes for sale, some record producers collect recordings and old masters into albums to offer the public. They may be Big Band era rereleases, a collection of Slim Whitman's country pop hits, or an anthology of arias from major operas.

F & G Marketing, Inc., for example, compiles albums of well-known gospel singers from prerecorded masters. The company's first album cost $15,000 to produce. With television promotion on three hundred stations, it sold one million copies in four months and "went platinum." (Sales of more than 500,000 records result in a gold record, sales of more than one million a platinum.) All the orders came in by telephone and all were filled by mail. The company did find one problem: COD rejections. By the time the album arrived, people had forgotten they ordered it. But the success of the $6.98, twenty-song album put the company in business and lead to twenty other reissue albums—including one by Elvis Presley.

This Ole House: The Record Production Company

Administration

Record company administration staff sets company goals, deciding, for example, what percentage of rock, how much jazz, or how much disco will be published. It coordinates the internal workings of the organization, including the troublesome business of settling differences among recording artists, production, and sales staffs. Administration also has final control of the business, accounting, and legal staffs. The accounting and legal departments are part of the company because of an old and still potentially explosive problem. Recording artists usually have contracts that call for the payment of royalties from recording profits. Just what is and is not profit is not always easy to decide. For example, the recording industry, like the publishing industry, struggles with the problem of returns. Recordings that are not sold at record distributors are returned, under certain conditions, to the record company. The accounting department must tally sales while subtracting records not sold by retail stores. The recording artists' royalties rise and fall with that tally. The complexity of record industry bookkeeping, and its importance to good relations with recording artists, encouraged the industry to be among the first to adopt computerized bookkeeping some years ago.

Operations

Operations includes the personnel who work in the recording studios: sound technicians, musicians, music arrangers, and the producer, as well as those who duplicate discs and tapes, and manage the warehouse. New York, Nashville, and Los Angeles are the three principal recording centers in the United States. (But there are recording studios open to the public in virtually every major city in the country.) The recording companies that maintain warehouses have storage facilities in major cities across the country for easy regional distribution.

Artist and Repertoire   The artist and repertoire division is the heart of the recording company. The "A & R people," like many editors in book publishing, are the talent scouts of the business. Their job is to find and develop recording talent. One of the great A&R men of early recording years was Frank Walker of Columbia, who discovered not only the country genius Hank Williams but also the great blues singer Bessie Smith. (He found Bessie singing barefooted in a night spot in Selma, Alabama.) More recently, the almost legendary Sam Phillips, founder of Sun Records, discovered and signed Jerry Lee Lewis, Carl Perkins, Roy Orbison, Charlie Rich, Elvis Presley, and Johnny Cash.

From Recording Session to Record

The Producer

Once the decision is made to record, the producer takes charge of the project. There are three types of producers: executive, staff, and independent. The executive producer is instrumental in deciding to produce the recording and in determining its sales potential. The staff producer works for the record company as a salaried member of the A&R division. Independent producers free-lance among record companies for advance payment and royalties, with a $50,000 advance and 5 percent a reasonable estimate of their rates.

   The staff or independent producer brings together the music, the arrangement, the artists and engineers involved in production, and the technology to produce a marketable record at reasonable cost. Knowledge of each aspect of the recording process is essential. Producers must know the popular taste and how to cater to it. They must also have the technical skill to mix the output of as many as thirty microphones with as many voices and musical instruments. Those who produce, and produce well, have become valuable to both the industry and its recording stars. Independent producer Richard Perry, for example, has earned $500,000 a year producing records with Carly Simon, Barbra Streisand, and Ringo Starr. John Farrar is the long-standing producer of Olivia Newton-John's recordings.

The Master

The recorded session can be on tape or disc. Tape helps keep recording costs down, since it can be edited. An error or a poor performance in one part of a tape can be replaced with good performance from another tape. Since the master stamp for the record can only be made from a disc recording, the finished tape is used to make the disc. Recording on tape, then "dubbing" to disc, introduces more noise than recording directly on disc. To get a cleaner disc, therefore, some producers recently have dropped the use of tape in recording sessions, although it means more careful work in the recording sessions since editing a disc is not possible. The disc that comes from the session, either directly or as a dub from a tape, is sprayed with silver dust and put through electrolysis to form a negative master plate. The negative master then is used to form the mother or positive plate, which, in turn, forms the mold that stamps the record.

Making tape cassette duplications is more costly and time consuming. A master tape machine feeds the record signal to several "slave" machines. To save time, the recordings are made using machines that run at thirty-two times the normal playback speed. A great deal of labor and time is required to handle the tapes—for both the master and the slave machines—although now the only requirement is the insertion of cassette tapes. Sealing, labeling, and boxing tape also is time consuming.

Marketing and Promotion

Once issued, the success of the record is in the hands of the marketing and promotion departments. Packaging, sleeve (cover) design, and copy all help make the recording visible and attractive. Also important are the courting of music critics and retailers with giveaways and ad cutouts (artwork or pictures to stand on the counter in the store), and advertising through the trade press (*Billboard* and *Downbeat*) or *Rolling Stone*.

King of the Road

One of the most successful promotional gambits is the personal appearance tour. Road tours bring both promotional and monetary rewards to an artist or group. And the more outrageous the act the greater the potential for both. Alice Cooper killed "babies." KISS vomited "blood." Even less successful groups were as outrageous as possible. The Plasmatics used chain saws to chomp through electric guitars; and at one time the female member of the act performed in a shaving cream bra—until it became clear the police would not let the performance continue.

As Angus Young of AC/DC has put it, the act does not really mean anything. Rather it is expressive. It should be wild and exciting, providing a chance for teenagers to use up energy at the concert rather than on the street.

Indispensable Radio Land

While television appearances can help promote new recordings, the most effective form of promotion still is the continuing play a recording can get on a radio station. In fact, radio is so important that a new recording may not become financially successful if it does not get radio play. A classic example: Simon and Garfunkel made an album in 1964, but it was on sale a full year before a Boston disc jockey began to play "Sound of Silence." Then the entire album started to sell. The sharp rise of country music during the 1970s can be traced to the growth in the number of country format radio stations. (See chapter 10.)

With radio play so important, it should not be surprising that the courting of disc jockeys with favors and "freebies" has from time to time bordered not only on the unethical but the illegal. Paying for radio play

The personal appearance tour is one of the most valuable ways of promoting records and making money. There are those who feel it succeeds on raw, expressive energy.

became all too common in the 1950s. A major scandal rocked the industry in 1959 when a disc jockey convention in Miami turned into a "booze, broads, and payola orgy." The resulting Congressional legislation created an antipayola law, making any undercover payment for record promotion or announcements a crime punishable by a $10,000 fine and a year in prison. Still, in the late 1970s the industry heard rumors and charges of "drugola" or pay-for-play-with-drugs.

Distribution: Indies and Branches

Recordings are distributed to retail outlets by two types of organizations: (1) independent companies, or "indies," not connected with the entertainment conglomerates that own the major labels; and (2) branches, or distributors directly linked to the conglomerates, especially the six leading ones: CBS, Warner, Polygram, Capitol/EMI, RCA, and MCA.

There has been growing concern that the indie distributor is disappearing from the industry, and that more control of the recording business is passing into the hands of the branches and the Big Six. Historically, the independent companies have been producers and distributors of musical specialties, testing musical trends for the more conservative majors. The early "race records" of pre-World War II days, which featured black artists in jazz and rhythm and blues numbers, came from such indie labels as Okeh and Vocalion. More recently, Herb Alpert founded his own indie label, A&M, to produce and distribute artists the majors would not touch. Alpert made a fortune producing records with such "unrecordable" talent as the Tijuana Brass and the Carpenters. The loss of the independent recording companies, many feel, would mean the loss of much creativity in the field, and a move toward homogenization in popular music.

The use of the indies for distribution is considered by many to be "doing your own thing." As smaller companies, indies can give more personal service to their albums, and to the albums of those who distribute with them, than do branch distributors. What is more, the indies offer slightly more profit per album than do the branches, and they can act without having to check policy at corporate headquarters.

Still, the branch distributors have been winning more and more labels, and for important reasons. The branches have more clout with the outlet retailers. If a dealer wants ten thousand new copies of a hot album, the branch can provide them—as long as the dealer is willing to take with the same order a hundred or so of ten other new acts. The branch, too, with its corporate backing, can offer dealers albums at wholesale prices lower than the indie's, giving the retailer more leeway to gamble on new, unknown recording talent. Corporate backing also means national merchandising and promotional organizations, with marketing research and national feedback. In sum, the branch is set up to sell records, and that is what recording companies need to do.

Critic Ira Mayer estimates inflation pushed the cost of producing and marketing an album to between $75,000 and $125,000 as the 1980s began. A company now has trouble breaking even, let alone showing a profit, on an LP that sells only fifty thousand copies. Branch distribution, with its corporate backing, is more able to risk money to push lots of recordings, which explains why the Big Six major recording companies already control 85 percent of all record distribution in the country.

Nobody Knows the Trouble . . .

The growing control of the industry's distribution system by the Big Six companies is a reflection of a trend toward consolidation that has been going on for several years. Figures collected in the early 1980s by media researchers Eric Rothenbuhler and John Dimmick indicate that more and more of the industry's hits are being produced by the leading recording firms. (See figure 8.2.) In 1974, for example, the eight firms that led in hit production (those that made the top ten on *Billboard's* Hot 100) produced 79 percent of the hits that year, 81 percent in 1977, 86 percent in 1978, 94 percent in 1979, and 98 percent in 1980. Similar changes occurred in relation to producer and record hits. During the period, hit recordings also came more under the control of top record producers. In 1974, at the beginning of the period, 26 percent of the hits were created by the industry's top producers, while in 1980, 33 percent had come from them. It also is important to note that there were fewer hits from the industry during the same period.

Rothenbuhler and Dimmick conclude that fewer record companies and producers are controlling more and more of a recording industry

Relationship Among Number of Firms, Market Concentration, and Number of Hits

Year	No. of Firms with Hits	No. of Firms with Only One Hit	% of Hits by Top Four Firms	% of Hits by Top Eight Firms	No. of Hits	No. of Number One Hits
1974	19	4	55	79	113	36
1975	21	7	51	75	111	37
1976	18	4	56	77	90	27
1977	16	3	60	81	82	29
1978	16	6	67	86	78	20
1979	10	1	71	94	72	24
1980	9	0	76	98	82	17

Reprinted from "Popular Music: Concentration and Diversity in the Industry, 1974–1980" by Eric W. Rothenbuhler and John W. Dimmick, Volume 32, Number 1. © 1983 *Journal of Communication.*

Figure 8.2

that has become less and less diversified. In other words, as they put it, the popular music business shows signs of homogenizing. The trend seems to have been well underway before inflation and a recession dropped record sales from $4.13 billion in 1979 to $3 billion in the early 1980s.

Recent sales problems did give the industry an opportunity to abandon some of its more wasteful habits. Ad and promotion budgets, bloated from the free spending days of the 1970s, were cut. The free clothing promos—T-shirts, hats, and jackets with logos of artists and companies on them—disappeared, as did the large limos that transported musical talents and their friends to concerts. At recent launchings of new recordings, observers have noted, there is less champagne and less "coke" (perhaps more Coca-Cola but less cocaine).

Meanwhile, buying trends have been leaning toward recordings from the known stars of the field—and in any one of several musical fields. In popular music such standbys as Barbra Streisand and Frank Sinatra continue to sell large numbers of records. In rock music large sales have been registered by the Rolling Stones, and by the final John Lennon albums produced by Yoko Ono. The best-selling records still total three to four million copies, but middle-range ones by new, unknown artists have dropped from 250,000 copies to 50,000.

Some blamed the drop on the economy, while others say it was the failure of the record companies to promote new artists and new albums properly. Still others accused a more spooky villain: Pac-Man and the time and money spent on playing the "alien" video games. Some industry experts attributed industry losses of $1 billion a year to the video toys.

Tape by Configuration for 1970s

	1979 $	% Change	% Dist.	1978 $	% Change	% Dist.	1977 $	% Change	% Dist.	1976 $	% Change	% Dist.
8–Track	684.3	−28.0	54	948.0	17.0	68	81.1	19.6	76.5	678.0	16.3	81.8
Cassettes	580.6	+29.0	46	449.8	80.0	32	249.6	71.3	23.5	145.7	47.5	17.8
Reel to Reel	—	—	—	—	—	—	—	—	—	—	—	—
4–tr. & Others	—	—	—	—	—	—	—	—	—	—	—	—
Quad 8T & Reel	—	—	—	—	—	—	—	—	—	5.1	37.0	.6
Total Sales	1,264.9	−10.0	100	1,397.8	32.0	100	1,060.6	15.9	100	828.8	19.8	100.0

All figures in millions	Courtesy of *Billboard Magazine* and the Recording Industry Association of America, Inc.

	1975 $	% Change	% Dist.	1974 $	% Change	% Dist.	1973 $	% Change	% Dist.
8–Track	583.0	6.2	84.2	549.2	12.3	84.5	489	15.1	84.1
Cassettes	98.8	13.3	14.3	87.2	14.7	13.4	76	25.5	13.1
Reel to Reel	2.0	23.4	.3	2.6	35.8	.4	.4	50.0	.7
4–tr. & Others	—	—	—	—	—	—	—	—	—
Quad 8T & Reel	8.2	−27.4	1.2	11.3	5.8	1.7	12	100.0	2.1
Total Sales	692.8	6.4	100.0	850.3	11.9	100.0	581	7.4	100.0

	1972 $	% Change	% Dist.	1971 $	% Change	% Dist.	1970 $	% Change	% Dist.
8–Track	425	10.4	76.6	385	1.8	70.4	378	26.0	79.1
Cassettes	102	6.3	18.9	96	24.7	19.5	77	2.7	16.1
Reel to Reel	0	33.3	1.5	12	33.3	2.4	18	10.0	3.8
4–tr. & Others	—	—	—	—	—	—	5	−76.2	1.0
Quad 8T & Reel	6	—	1.0	—	—	—	—	—	—
Total Sales	541	9.7	100.0	493	9.7	100.0	478	14.9	100.0

Figure 8.3

The cruelest cut in revenue came from the cassette tape itself—unrecorded or blank cassette tape. It did not take long for many record fans to discover that a $3 cassette tape can record the music from two $8 albums. Cassette tape sales have been rising steadily since 1973, while records have had their ups and downs. And the dubbing of recorded music onto blank tape for auto stereo, personal Walkman stereos, or even home stereo has become common. Many in the industry support legislation adopted by several European countries that places taxes on blank cassettes, and gives the proceeds to royalty funds for artists.

The pirating of music with the home cassette recorder is a serious industry problem, but more serious is the professional pirate who copies prerecorded tapes and albums for volume sales. Pirates have gained control of 10 percent of the world recording market, and 18 percent of all tape and album sales in the United States. In Turkey, pirates were so efficient they pirated recordings of the films *Grease* and *Saturday Night Fever* on the market ahead of the authorized versions. Counterfeit cassettes have been distributed through some discount houses in this country. The tape quality is poor, but the quality of the labels, and the price of the counterfeits, has been high. Pirating is all too easy. Tape technology is so readily available and inexpensive that the machinery can be paid for in only forty hours of running time. The result has been a $1.5 billion a year loss in royalties for American recording companies and musicians.

The Future—Near and Here

Whatever problems the industry faces, a new group of inventions is standing by to help increase sales and attract new audiences. Warner is now offering its Music Television (MTV) cable service, or music with audio and video. New microcassettes could reduce tape prices to a dollar in the near future, and bring price-shy music buyers back into the market. Even more startling, Robert Lester, an inventor, patented a digital music player in 1981 that stores music on plastic discs the size of half dollars. The Sonadisc, as he calls it, has no moving parts and could last forever. The discs are placed in receptacles on top of the machine where they can be played, one after another, without interruption. It may well be that invention will become the mother of the next era of music recording—again.

Careers in the Recording Industry

There are three general areas of employment in the industry: (1) administration and business, (2) record production, and (3) sales and promotion.

Beginners can train for administration jobs through traditional college and university business courses. (More than one recording company president has come from a business rather than a recording background.)

Those interested in record production—the actual arranging, recording, and editing of recordings—will have a long, hard road to follow, according to one former producer and record company president, John Culshaw. Very few people are employed in the industry in this way. There is little free-lance work even for successful producers, and the pay is poor for the most part. A college degree helps, as does the ability to read musical scores and handle highly charged people. A producer has to have a sense of records, nerve, tact, and a talent for making the right decisions under pressure. (Most decisions on a recording session come in the last fifteen minutes before the session starts.) And usually the only way to get such a job is to latch on somewhere as a gofer.

Jobs in sales and record promotion, like all such jobs, have their roots in college business courses and public relations. Since there are many small indies throughout the country, getting a start in this area of recording may depend primarily on persistence.

Summary

Inventions and technological innovations in music recording have improved the quality of recorded music and brought it into every aspect of our daily lives. Post–World War II improvements of the recording methods of the 1930s have been dramatic. Hi-fi developed from World War II sonar technology. RCA's introduction of the 45 rpm record precipitated a ''battle of speeds'' between the 45 and 33 1/3, which ended with RCA accepting the LP as the medium for classical music, and Columbia reciprocating by issuing its popular recordings as 45s.

Tape recording was introduced in post-war years, a result of improvements made on magnetic recording equipment produced by the Germans. The 3M Company and Ampex created high-quality magnetic-backed tape, and tape recording and playing equipment.

Digital recordings and equipment now have been introduced to the market and are expected to dominate record industry sales in the 1990s. Digital recording translates sound to a mathematic base, greatly improving fidelity and reducing noise.

About 51 percent of modern recorded music is pop and rock, while country accounts for as much as 14 percent of total sales. Classical and jazz have respectable, steady sales, as do MOR, or middle-of-the-road, comedy, and children's records. A ''pure, childish escapism'' pervades many pop records, however. Critic Stephen Holden has called it ''toy music.''

Record company administration coordinates the divisions of the company and sets the recording agenda. Past conflict over royalties have made legal services and computer-based accounting an important part of company operations. Operations includes those who record, make, and store the records for distribution. The artists and repertoire division is the heart of the recording company—the talent scouts and talent relations people of the business.

Once the decision to record is made, a producer takes charge. It is his job to produce, at a reasonable cost, a record that will attract an audience. Some producers are company employees; others are free-lancers.

Promotion is vital to all record sales. Personal appearance tours offer many promotional advantages, as do television appearances. But the most important kind of publicity is the continued play a record receives from a radio station.

Of concern to industry observers is the concentration of power within the Big Six major record companies, as more hit records fall under their control. Much of the industry's record distribution also is controlled by branch distributors of the major companies.

Since the 1980s the record buying public seems to have shown a preference for known artists while sales of new unknowns have dropped appreciably. Record sales have felt the effect, too, of new competition from video games, and home copying of music onto blank tapes. (Professional pirating of recordings is now a $1.5 billion industry.)

As troubles mount, however, a new set of inventions is standing by to help pull the industry through: video musical tapes, a one dollar microcassette recording has the potential for offering even lower-cost music, and a new digital recording system, with no working parts that will play half-dollar-sized records virtually forever.

Questions for Discussion

1. The text suggests that invention is the mother of the recording industry, but also that people buy music when they pay for recordings. Are these statements in conflict? Will good music, interesting music, fail as a result of inferior technology? Will poor music succeed as a result of bright and innovative technology? Can you support your position with examples?

2. Toy music, one critic has said, is the childish, nonsense quality that takes a recording beyond its primary audience to a more general audience. Is toy music the basic ingredient in record hits? Is there a toy theme in the acts of most popular recording groups? Does the toy theme separate the top musical hits from the less successful ones? Is there toy music in country? In disco? In Cole Porter's music?

3. What is wrong, ethically, with payola? Why should it be a crime for a record promotion representative to give a disc jockey money to play a recording? If a poor record gains radio time can it become a hit? Or would the disc jockey who is playing the poor recording suffer in the long run? Is making payola illegal the same as making tips for waiters, waitresses, or taxi drivers illegal? Why not?

4. Some record industry spokespeople have advocated taxing blank cassette tapes and giving the returns to musicians and sheet music companies. The industry complains that blank tapes are used to pirate commercial recordings and, therefore, cost the industry much needed revenue. Would such a tax be fair? Try to name five regular users of blank tape who would pay the music tax although they do not use tape to pirate music. What other solution to the home pirating of music can you see for the music industry?

References

Barnouw, Erik. *A Tower in Babel.* New York: Oxford University Press, 1966.

Davis, Peter G. "Will Technology Be the Death of 'Golden-Age' Legends?" The New York *Times,* July 19, 1981, D19.

Fantel, Hans. "Putting Quality in Disks." The New York *Times* (guide), April 5, 1981, 22.

———. "Counterfeit Cassettes—A Bad Bargain." The New York *Times,* May 3, 1981, B19.

"40 Countries Meet on Piracy in Recording Industry." The New York *Times,* April 5, 1981, 21.

Gelatt, Roland. *The Fabulous Phonograph.* Philadelphia and New York: J. B. Lippincott, 1955.

Greenberg, Jonathan. "Fast Forward." *Forbes,* May 25, 1981, 75 et seq.

Hirsch, Paul. *The Structure of the Popular Music Industry.* Ann Arbor, Mich.: Survey Research Center, 1973.

Holden, Stephen. "A Childlike Spirit Buoys 'Toy Music.' " The New York *Times,* January 17, 1982, B21.

Jones, Stacy V. "Tiny Disks For Music Player." The New York *Times,* September 5, 1981, 28.

Mayer, Ira. "Record Distribution: The Big 6 Take Over." *Backbeat,* October 1979, 132 et seq.

Metz, Robert. "Gentle Revolution." *American Mass Media.* New York: Random House, 1982.

Nicholson, Tom, Janet Huck, and Frank Givney, Jr. "Record Companies Turn for the Better." *Newsweek,* October 12, 1981, 78.

Palmer, Robert. "New Bands on Small Labels Are the Innovators of the 80's." The New York *Times,* September 6, 1981, D17.

———. "A Nervousness About Future of Jazz Recording." The New York *Times,* July 3, 1981, 14.

Pollack, Andrew. "Personal Stereo Market Swells." The New York *Times,* June 5, 1981, D1.

Rothenbuhler, Eric W., and John W. Dimmick. "Popular Music: Concentration and Diversity in the Industry, 1974–1980." *Journal of Communication,* Winter, 1982, 143–49.

Schicke, C. A. *Revolution in Sound.* Boston: Little, Brown, 1974.

Sterling, Christopher H., and John M. Kittross. *Stay Tuned.* Belmont, Calif.: Wadsworth, 1978.

Chapter
9

**Son of Hollywood:
The Motion Picture
Industry**

A movie myth unfolding: the working crew of the space cargo ship Nostromo begin their encounter with strange and unusual forces in the sci-fi film *Alien*.

The movies.

Even in this age of television the phrase still has a magical quality. It still connotes adventure, romance, something-else-again thrills, danger—glory!

There is reason to believe the movies mean even more than that to us. As psychologist Bruno Bettelheim has written, the movies bring literature, acting, stage design, music, dance, and the beauty of nature together to portray major American myths. The movies not only enlighten and entertain with stories and visions of the world around us, the stories themselves often serve to bind the country together by exhibiting common values and goals. Bettelheim believes the original American myth was the western, which taught us such important American values as cooperation, patience, endurance, and the need to accept the constraints of law and the civil world. These values were portrayed as desirable and useful in westerns, with long wagon train journeys, and taut frontier conflicts between gunfighters and sheriffs.

The Greeks used drama and public sculpture to tell their story. Early European civilization raised cathedrals to tell its story. Americans have used the motion picture, and it has become the most popular and democratic form of myth making to date—or so Bettelheim would argue.

It may be difficult to think of Cheech and Chong movies, and such horror films as *Halloween* and *Happy Birthday to Me* as the cohesive force in American life, but Bettelheim is not alone in his arguments. Movies, many critics agree, are the new literature. For most Americans, what is fine and good comes from them. And the American family goes to the movies on the weekend the way some used to go, and still go, to church on Sunday.

The Dream Machine

The source of the nation's moving pictures is virtually a mythical community itself—Hollywood—scattered about in the sunshine, smog, and urban sprawl of Los Angeles, California. There are really two Hollywoods. The first is the corporate suburb of Los Angeles; the second, the generic concept for the industry itself. This generic, or mythic, Hollywood includes the motion picture studios in Burbank, Universal City, and Culver City—as well as in Hollywood the city. Warner Brothers, Columbia, and Disney are in Burbank. MGM is in Culver City. Hollywood, the city, is the home of Paramount.

Ancilliary production companies are also scattered about the Los Angeles area. Republic Studios, the B factory of the 1940s, no longer makes "Gabby" Hayes, Gene Autry, Roy Rodgers, or John Wayne westerns. Instead, as Consolidated Film Industries, it now specializes in developing and printing films, and creating optical effects. Eastman Kodak maintains an office and warehouse in Hollywood, as does Western Costume, owner of one of the largest collections of rentable costumes in the world. Screening and sound service companies are plentiful in the area also.

The center of the Hollywood production system is the studio. Established in the early days of filmmaking to control costs and improve profits, the studio remains a dominant force in the industry. It is the best means of financing, producing, and distributing the film product. Today there are three basic types of movie studios: the majors, the mini-majors, and the independents.

The Major Studios

The major studios include Warner Brothers, Paramount, Columbia, Twentieth Century-Fox, Universal, and MGM/UA from the golden days of the medium. (MGM bought United Artists in 1981, forming MGM/UA.) Important newcomers include Embassy, Filmways, and Disney, which have grown to major status in the last twenty years. The majors not only produce films but also obtain financing and handle film distribution. Both the mini-major studios and the independents look to the majors for one or both of these services from time to time.

Finances

The money for films comes from financiers who specialize in entertainment speculation, from reinvestment of a studio's profits from other films, and from large bank loans. The Bank of America rose to prominence, as some say, on the back of Hollywood films. Since some of the major studios also are owned by large conglomerates, they have access to funds from parent companies that may wish to invest corporate profits in films as a means of diversifying. MCA, for example, might invest some of its profits from the recording business in its own Universal Studio productions. On the other hand, outside financing usually is sought when the studio feels a film may be a high risk. The studio then trades off a portion of the potential profits in exchange for a share of the risk.

Smaller studios cannot command the financial backing needed to produce a large number of films. They have no conglomerate parent, and they generally are without real collateral for bank loans. Their best source of financial backing is the major studios themselves. (United Artists provided much of the production money for *Apocalypse Now* and *Heaven's Gate,* for example.) And since the major studios must show discretion in choosing films other than their own to fund, their control of the industry also extends to the independents.

Distribution

The majors control much of the industry's theatre distribution, too. In the 1970s they were spending $10 million a year in North America alone to maintain record sales, and distribution contacts with theatre owners. Again, these are expenses in time and staff that smaller studios can not afford. As a result, the major studios remain the acknowledged masters of the distribution art, even though studio distribution of a given film may cost the producer 35 percent or more of the film's rental returns.

The Mini-Majors

The mini-majors are similar to the major studios in everything but size, distribution facilities, and real estate. The staffs of the mini-majors are smaller, and their offices and sound stages are rented—usually from the major studios. Lorimar, Orion, Polygram, the Ladd Company, and Tri-Star are a few of the prominent mini-majors. Lorimar's credits include *Being There, The Big Red One,* and *The Postman Always Rings Twice.* Orion produced *10, Sharkey's Machine, Gorky Park, Amadeus,* and *The Woman in Red.* Polygram gave movie goers *The Deep, Midnight Express, Endless Love,* and *An American Werewolf in London.* Among the Ladd Company's productions are *Blade Runner, Divine Madness, Outland,* and *Body Heat,* while Tri-Star, a relatively new studio created by Columbia, CBS, and HBO, has produced *The Natural, The Evil Men Do, Places in the Heart,* and *The Muppets Take Manhattan.*

Finances   The mini-major's vice-president for fund-raising is probably the most important person in the studio. Although often looking to banks for financial banking, he or she also searches out more volatile lenders, including foreign distributors, tax-shelter groups, outside groups, and major studios.

Distribution   The major/mini-major relationship is beneficial for both parties. The mini-major specializes in the creative aspects of movie production. The major studio distributes the product for a percentage of the profits. Fortunately for the mini-major, competition among the major studios for good films to distribute is keen, and a good film with a good star can attract financial backing from a major studio even before the film is shot, if the major studio is given the right to distribute the film. The major studios often are willing to take big gambles on talented people. When Alan Ladd, Jr., and two of his colleagues grew weary of running Twentieth Century-Fox and formed their own mini-major, the Ladd Company, they found Warner Brothers willing to advance considerable money to help the new firm. The reason: exclusive rights to distribute films the promising new company would produce.

It is easy to understand why mini-majors often are called "boutique" studios. They have one primary function—making movies. They depend on their talent and reputation as creative movie producers to attract financing for their films, and they distribute them through facilities of the major studios.

The Independents   The independent movie producer is one of the last American entrepreneurs. To succeed, the independent must (1) write, produce, and direct the film using rented equipment and locations; (2) operate with financial backing probably collected on his or her own; and (3) personally distribute the film to an indifferent, even antagonistic, group of theatre owners without benefit of publicity, advertising, or name actors.

Even so, some independents have been very successful. Russ Meyer's string of money-making "nudie" films include *The Immoral Mr. Teas* and *The Vixens*. Roger Corman found success with several low-budget, motorcycle pictures. Corman's *Attack of the Crab Monsters* and *The Little Shop of Horrors* helped win him the title "king of the B movies," and push his independent studio toward mini-major status.

Finances   The independents find their financial backers outside the movie industry. Since the banks and the studios usually ignore their productions, independents turn instead to friends and acquaintances anxious to make money or back a film with a message they like. Nurses, restaurant owners, ranchers, and even the idle rich have been among the backers of independent films at one time or another. Russ Meyer, at last report, was still paying back a nurse who lost $5,000 in savings on the ill-fated *Blacksnake,* his picture about slaves that failed at the box office.

Distribution

Distribution also is a major problem for the independent. No-name, inadequately advertised films are just as expensive to show as first-run features from major and mini-major studios, but the returns are seldom as high. To win distribution, the independents often must give up 75 to 85 percent of box office profits, while the majors, with their ability to deliver more films with known actors and known directors, usually book a theatre for 90 percent of profits. Observers fear the problems of distribution have driven many independents away from theatrical films and into cable and television work. If so, the loss has been a great one for the movie industry. The independent studio has been a starting place of many of Hollywood's leading talents, including Francis Ford Coppola, Peter Bogdonovich, and Jack Nicholson.

The Theatre Distribution System

The Paramount arch, a time-honored symbol of the major movie studio. While the big studios no longer dominate the industry, they are vital to it as film producers, sources of financing, production facilities, and theatre distribution services.

Most studio film productions reach the American public through local movie theatres. There are now more than 17,000 of them in the country. About 76 percent are indoor theatres, and the rest are drive-ins. Eight of ten indoor houses have two screens while one in ten has more than two. Indoor theatres seat an average of 500 persons while the drive-ins handle an average of 550 automobiles. Together, the theatres attract 20 million people each week and more than one billion each year.

The theatres themselves come in various sizes, from large national and regional chains to mom-and-pop neighborhood indoor and drive-in theatres. Acceptance of a film by one of the large chains, such as Loews, can mean exhibition in 850 theatres across the country. Knowing where a particular film is likely to earn the most money is the business of the major studio distributors, however, and they earn their money—or their percentage of box office profits—with informed timing and placement. Swedish producer/director Ingmar Bergman's films usually do not do well in small American towns, for example. And the old Ma and Pa Kettle series of the factory studio years did not play well in Southern areas. Woody Allen films do well on college campuses. Theatre owners and distributors must know timing, too. The life span of a film is only from six months to two years. After that, it will die at the box office—regardless of admission price.

The Television Networks and Cable

Since the 1950s television networks have become, with movie theatres, an important part of Hollywood's distribution system. Feature films from Republic and RKO made up a significant part of television programming in the early years. By the 1960s most major studios had opened their film vaults to the new home medium. The continuing popularity of movies on television has encouraged networks to give financial backing to original film productions in exchange for early access to the films after their first theatre run. Films made primarily for television and Hollywood's production of television series, the new B movie, are discussed in chapter 11.

All studios look to television and cable as a source of needed revenue. Experience has taught producers, however, that a $2 million network rental deal can disappear if the film in question does not draw at the theatre box office. At the same time, the number of cable television movie channels in operation has created considerable demand for Hollywood's products. Cable channel operations, such as Home Box Office (HBO), Showtime/The Movie Channel, and Cinemax, depend on motion picture feature films for most if not all of their around-the-clock program time. Elliot Minsker, president of Knowledge Industry Publications, Inc., has estimated that cable channels need 550 different movie titles each year. Most cable-television channels still do not make a profit (see chapter 11). High demand for films and the limited ability of the movie channels to pay has brought more than one box office failure to cable viewers. The struggling *Swamp Thing,* the unusual *Pennies From Heaven,* with Steve Martin, *The Seduction,* with Morgan Fairchild, the vampire thriller *The Hunger,* and *Airplane II: The Sequel,* all stumbled rather quickly from theatres into pay cable in the early 1980s.

Television, including cable, rentals often are thought of as insurance the film will at least break even. A cable rental fee of $1 million is usual, but there have been notable exceptions. The award-winning family film, *Breaking Away,* was offered $4.5 million by pay cable management, enough to convince the film's owners to cut its theatre run short and agree to pay television exhibition early. In late 1983 Paramount and Showtime/The Movie Channel signed an agreement that gave Showtime/TMC exclusive rights to seventy-five films, including such box office hits as *Flashdance, Trading Places,* and *Terms of Endearment.* The price was reported at $500 million, or about $6.7 million per film.

Some media observers believe television and cable television soon will be the dominant means of movie distribution. Minsker, for example, has argued the new arrangement began when HBO signed a deal with Twentieth Century-Fox for three made-for-cable-television features. The first, *The Terry Fox Story,* the film of the young marathon runner who contracted cancer, was shown on HBO in 1983. *The Far Pavilions,* set in British India, and *Sakharov,* the acclaimed story of the Soviet dissident, were among the HBO films that followed in 1984.

A growing market is the home video movie, recorded and offered to the public as a sales or rental item. Between 1980 and 1982 Paramount's home video business jumped from zero to $30 million a year. MGM and CBS have joined forces to offer first-run home video films fresh from the movie houses. One impediment to the home video market has been the confusion of formats. The variety of video tape and video disc recordings and playbacks available proved as troublesome to the buying public as 33 1/3s and 45s were during recorded music's "war of the speeds" after World War II (see chapter 8).

The Movie Studio

Movie studios, like publishing houses and recording companies, vary in how they are organized, but the general functions common to all are the executive production, publicity, merchandising, and distribution functions. The larger the studio, the more likely all functions are internal. The smaller the studio, the more likely they are rented or farmed out.

The movie studio of the 1930s and 1940s was a factory-like operation with workers (actors and artisans) on contract and an assembly line that seemed to send pictures out to the movie theatres on the hour. With the arrival of television, the cost of maintaining such large payrolls in the face of greatly reduced theatre attendance proved too high. So as studios trimmed their budgets, they signed producers, actors, and production team workers for one film, or a series of films, releasing them to other studios and films afterwards.

The studios of the 1930s and 1940s finished one picture after another. Today a sound stage may be empty one week, jump with actors and production workers the next, then empty the third week. Hollywood has become an ad hoc industry of free-lance professionals. Except for the relatively few continuing executives, a studio seems to die and come to life again with each new picture. The change has cost the studio its previous ability to pool many contracted talents to make a film, but now it can use the best specialists available in Hollywood on every film project. It all seems for the better. Few would argue that Hollywood's last decade has not been one of its best.

The Inscrutable Budget

The primary function of the executive division of the studio is to determine and then watch over the budget and the financial expenditures of the film. Setting the budget can be an exasperating exercise. Every motion picture is unique. Costs must be estimated for new actors, new scenery, and new locations. Movie production proves Murphy's Law— that nothing planned will go well. The weather alone usually makes the point.

**New Movies,
New Stars**

John Wayne once told a national television audience that he was always careful to present the same recognizable character in each movie he played, to be sure he satisfied the people who came to see his movies. Many of the stars of the 1930s and 1940s were skillful thespians who acted their parts from the vantage point of a recognizable personality. Cary Grant, Jimmy Stewart, Bette Davis, and Katharine Hepburn were among them.

The rise of independent production companies and the widening of the range of motion picture content and themes has fostered a change in actors and acting, however. Rather than play similar characters in familiar situations, the actor likely is called on to play a diverse range of different characters in highly different situations. There are exceptions—the characters in the *Star Wars* series and the *Rocky* sequels, for example—but the rule is variety.

In five of his films, Dustin Hoffman has played a young grad, an old Indian fighter, a dying homosexual, a single father, and a young woman. Meryl Streep has played the title role in *The French Lieutenant's Woman* and a Polish Jew who survived a Nazi concentration camp.

The new actors reject traditional stardom, *Newsweek* has written, and the trappings that go with it. For many of them the proper tone for acting was set by Faye Dunaway's uncompromising yet understanding portrayal of Golden Age star Joan Crawford in *Mommie Dearest*.

And there is another important problem to consider. Only two of ten movies make a profit, and only two others break even. Six of ten movies lose money. Good, profit-making movies, like books, must carry the losers. The situation has resulted in some hot and angry debates—to say the least.

One interesting aspect of Hollywood business practice is the openness with which studios, producers, and directors discuss a film's budget. Most businesses try to conceal their expenditures, but Hollywood believes in open budget talks. A big budget film will attract more news coverage and more public discussion, and may even signal to the public the birth of a big picture—or so Hollywood feels.

The budget usually is divided into two categories. The first is for the creative aspects of the film: money for screen rights of a book or an original screenplay, and costs of hiring actors and a director. These "above the line" costs then are matched with "below the line" costs of scenery, film, plumbers, carpenters, and other production workers. If the studio and the director can reasonably estimate a price, the picture goes into preproduction.

Preproduction

When the money becomes available, casting, set design, costume creation or rental, and the search for locations begin. The major studios do much of this work themselves while independents find these services in the Hollywood community. Most of the studios are union shops and casting is from the Screen Actors Guild, with minimum salaries about $900 a week. The leading actors have higher-asking prices, of course, trading on the star system approach that has been useful to actors and studios alike. Paul Newman asks $3 million, Burt Reynolds $5 million a film, and Barbra Streisand has gotten $3.5 million or more—plus a percentage of profits. One of the important ground rules between executive producer and studio is which name actors may or may not be used in the film. This limitation is one way the studio has of controlling the budget and keeping costs down.

On the Set

Once actual production of the film begins, the lights, cameras, and sound are handled by union workers who honor a tight division of labor. Sound people do not touch lights; camera people do not touch sound equipment.

Lights and cameras are the responsibility of the camera crew, which includes (1) the director of photography (or D.P.), who lights the scene, (2) the camera operator, who takes the scenes the director orders, (3) the gaffer, and his assistant the "best boy," who rigs the lights as the D.P. instructs, and (4) the electrician, who keeps the electricity running, from gasoline-powered generators if necessary.

The sound crew does most of its work in the sound studio after the film is shot. The sound recordist, or mixer, and the assistant, the boom operator, record sound on the scene primarily for reference. After the film is shot, the actors cut the sound track by matching their lines to the lip movements shot on location. The sound tracks from location almost always are of poor quality.

Others in the production crew may include a greens worker, a wrangler, and/or an animal trainer. The greens worker keeps plants on the set; the wrangler handles animals. The animal trainer is in charge of special or trick performers such as the cobra and the horses in *The Black Stallion* and the horses in *The Black Stallion Returns*. The make-up people, hairdressers, stunt men and women, and stunt coordinators have become well-known specialists from Hollywood movies and television series. Special effects people construct roofs that fall in on cue, or they make the earth split open to swallow people.

Each production crew also has a publicist to draw attention to the production while it is under way. Usually the publicist attracts the print or electronic media by offering interviews with the stars on the set. Jane

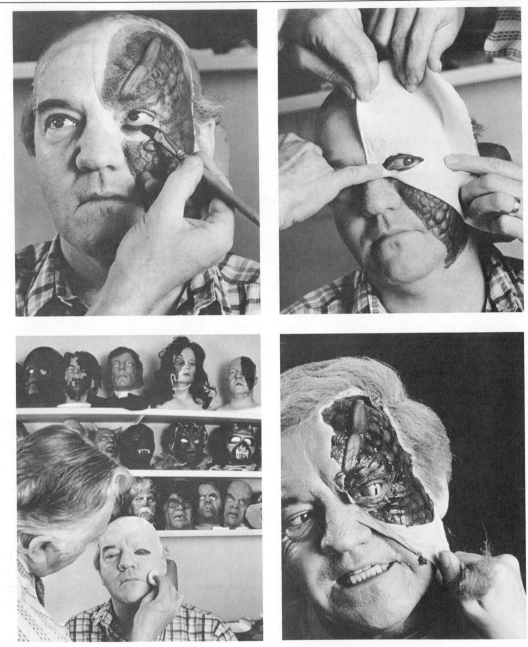

Below the line movie costs may include costs of extravagant makeup. So that actor Richard Herd could play a lizardlike villain in the television production "V," makeup director Leo Lotito coated his face (1) with a reptilelike latex skin topped (2) with a second layer to again make him appear human (3). During the melodrama, rebelling earthlings rip off the "human" layer (4) and reveal the snake-like being lurking underneath.

On location in the desert with camera and sound crews, actors, and animals. The film footage became part of the highly lauded *Lawrence of Arabia*.

Fonda and Robert Redford rarely give interviews at any other time or place. Picture and press releases of the film in production are aimed more at theatre owners than movie audiences. Later a more succinct advertising campaign is created for the public.

The one who puts it all together, who defines the action, the camera shots, the performance of the actors, is the director. The director sets the pace, and highlights the nuances that make the photoplay. The director's assistant, the script supervisor, keeps a detailed record of what is filmed. The dialogue coach feeds lines and also cues actors. The assistant director keeps production on time by knowing where people are and making sure everything is where it is needed. The assistant director usually graduates to the position of producer, not director.

The producer deals with the problems and logistics of getting the film made. The producer's assistant, the company accountant, keeps up with production expenditures while the production secretary acts as secretary for the whole production unit, relaying phone calls, typing letters, and acting as gofer. The producer's private gofers are personal production assistants, who forage, as need be, for equipment and materials.

Coordinating a large production crew through several weeks or months of shooting can be a frustrating and astonishingly expensive process. Executive producer Michael Gruskoff's *Quest For Fire,* a story about prehistorical beings, was funded, despite some serious doubts, by studio executives. Understandably, they worried that audiences would laugh at actors who wore skins and grunted at each other without speaking English. But the real trouble began in production. An actors' strike forced the production crew to abandon Iceland as a shooting location and switch to Scotland. Four weeks of shooting there, and then five more in Kenya led to another four-month delay due to bad weather; then there was five weeks of shooting in Canada. Each location shift meant a move not only for the "prehistorical" actors but for the troupe's large cast of animals: elephants, lions, wolves, and bears. *Quest For Fire* still came in within its $12 million budget and a fighting chance of making its money back at the box office.

From Postproduction to Hollywood Roulette

When the film has been edited, the sound track mixed and completed, and titles and credits prepared and added, the negative is printed. A positive print for exhibition costs about $1,000. A film that opens in major cities around the country on one day could require nine hundred prints for exhibition.

As the film moves from postproduction to exhibition, it moves into one of the most troublesome phases in the motion picture industry. Film distribution requires most theatre owners to agree to film contracts—even guarantee the studios large amounts of money—without ever having seen the films. The process is called "blind bidding." Six months before a picture is to be released, and while it is still in production, the distributing studios send bid letters to theatre owners. The letter describes the film's story, cast, and director, pointing out the appeal of each to the public. It also suggests a minimum cash guarantee ($20,000?) the exhibitor might offer for a suggested playing time (12 weeks?), and the percentage of the returns the studio expects from box office profits (90 percent). The theatre owners always subtract their expenses from the box office receipts before paying the studio's 90 percent rental fee, but the blind bid guarantee is paid whether the film shows a profit or not. The system has existed for many years, and the owners have grown more and more bitter about it. It is too much like gambling, they have argued. You can win at it, but you can also lose, and lose badly.

Several years ago, for example, a buyer for a string of Denver theatres saw only a six-minute clip of a sci-fi flick before he bid $35,000 for the right to show the finished film in his area theatres. The movie was *Star Wars,* and it grossed more than $2 million in the fifty-three weeks it ran in Denver. A few years later, however, the same buyer was looking for a comedy for the Christmas season—one of the industry's most important seasons. Unable to view even a clip, he settled on a film called

Director James Brooks, Shirley MacLaine, and Jack Nicholson with 1983 Oscars for *Terms of Endearment.* The annual academy awards are one of the most important of all of Hollywood's promotional activities.

Pennies From Heaven, with comedian Steve Martin. *Pennies* was not intended as a comedy, as its later ads testified. It proved to be very unpopular with moviegoers, although it was well made and won considerable critical acclaim; it was withdrawn from the market.

Morris Goldschlager of United Artists Theatre Circuit has charged, "Without being given the opportunity to make a judgment about the product, we're being asked to share the loss on a bad one. And we're blamed, fined, and called on the carpet by the city fathers if it's morally objectionable."

The studios, on the other hand, continue to insist blind bidding is a necessary part of the business. The average movie costs $10 million or more to produce, and $6 to $8 million to advertise. Much of the money for production is borrowed, with interest. Delays in exhibition, especially delays in extended screenings of the film for many exhibitors, would be expensive in interest costs alone. Most films are introduced in the summer or during the Christmas season, when the motion picture's major interest group is out of school. Jack Valenti, president of the Motion Picture Association of America (MPAA), argues that delays in peak season releases for theatre owner screenings could cost the industry as much as 30 percent of its revenue. Films costing $25 million to produce would be left $8 million in debt, excluding loan interest and advertising costs. Such a loss of revenue could put a mini-major out of business.

Twenty-one state legislatures have sided with local theatre owners and passed antiblind-bidding laws. The studios have retaliated with threats to cease all shooting on locations within those states. And the threat has teeth. New York State, for example, could lose as much as $1 billion a year under a film company boycott—depending on the year. Cases contesting the legality of the blind-bidding laws, meanwhile, have reached the federal courts. The question has become, as one Paramount executive has pointed out, whether the industry can settle its differences over the issue before it becomes moot, since television, home video tape, cassettes, and pay television may soon put an end to the controversy—or transport it to new settings.

The Hucksters

Almost everyone in Hollywood today knows that it is almost impossible for a film to succeed without advertising. A budget of at least $5 million is considered essential—although there are marketing variations that might reduce that figure.

The most visible movie ads, the "trailers," are not a part of the studio's ad campaign. Specialty companies make the short preview clips of coming attractions with scenes provided by the studios. The theatre owners rent them for about $50 a week—to use as a part of their own advertising effort.

At the studio, the marketing, advertising, and distribution divisions all help develop ad strategy. The primary rule is to maximize the film's potential publicity: the big budget, the stars, themes, action, setting. A general appeal works better than a special appeal—or at least so some advertising executives believe. The musical *All That Jazz,* for example, was advertised not as an intimate look at the life of a specific Broadway director, but as "all that music," "all that excitement," "all that glitter," and "all that jazz."

Tie-ins and Toys

Some films lend themselves to the merchandising of toys, clothing, or other products. *Star Wars* watches sold for $12 even before the *Empire Strikes Back* continued the trend, and sales of space clothing and toys raised profits to $20 million. The studios always refuse to underwrite the cost of product merchandising, but they usually are quick to offer free advertising assistance with clothing or product tie-ins. A studio ad department might suggest the sale of a national company's boots and jeans with the release of a western film. It also might promote the company's clothing as worn by life-sized cardboard cutouts of the film's star. The Walt Disney Studio is the exception. It promotes products through a corp of active sales personnel, obviously viewing toy merchandising as more than advertising for its pictures.

Four Walling

The 1970s saw the rebirth of an old advertising/marketing technique. Its new name is "four walling." The film distributor, stuck perhaps with a questionable movie product, rents a theatre—all four walls—for a flat fee. Then with a well-designed saturation ad campaign in radio, television, and newspapers the distributor pushes the film for a limited run—not long enough for local word-of-mouth advertising to get around. The ad campaign is sensational, provocative, and compelling. The unknown film, with no bad reviews, fills the theatre for the run, and then disappears to another market and another four-wall campaign. The hit-and-run approach helped Tom Laughlin revive his $1 million film *Billy Jack* from a loser to a winner, with profits in excess of $65 million. The method is not foolproof, however. Some other attempts have met with disappointing results.

The Academy Awards

Clearly the most important promotional activity for motion pictures is the annual awards activities of the Academy of Motion Pictures Arts and Sciences. The academy awards, and especially the televising of the awards ceremony, give the industry status and promote individual films and actors as well.

They are financial dynamite for the individual films. Woody Allen's *Annie Hall* came out briefly in 1977, submerged until Oscar time, then as best picture of the year returned to theaters for two times the box office business it had done before. A best picture Oscar can add $10 million to a film's gross receipts. A best or supporting actor award can raise an actor's asking price $250,000 per film or more.

With so much at stake it is not surprising that the studios with nominated films usually mount an active campaign for votes of the 4,400 members of the academy. They fill the trade papers with advertising (face-to-face solicitation of votes is not permitted) and provide academy members with free screenings. Theoretically, those academy members who do not view films nominated do not vote for them. Universal's campaign to have the *Deer Hunter* named best picture of the year cost $250,000, much of which went for trade advertising the public never saw.

Too often, studios use the awards to promote a film or an actor rather than honor excellence. In 1981, for example, Paramount backed the nomination of Howard E. Rollins, one of the leading actors from *Ragtime,* for best supporting actor. Paramount hoped Rollins, an excellent actor, would win an Oscar, but doubted he could do so in competition with Henry Fonda, Burt Lancaster, and Paul Newman, who also were nominated that year. As it turned out, Fonda won the best actor award, and John Gielgud won the best supporting actor award. But Rollins did have the honor of being nominated; he also received valuable publicity from a string of television interviews and news and magazine stories.

Top Twenty-Five Revenue Producing Films (as of Jan. 1984)
(Of U.S.-Canada Market)

Title	Director-Producer-Distributor	Total Rentals
E. T. The Extra-Terrestrial	(S. Spielberg; S. Spielberg/K. Kennedy; U; 1982)	$ 209,587,000
Star Wars	(G. Lucas; G. Kurtz; Fox; 1977)	193,500,000
Return Of The Jedi	(R. Marquand; H. Kazanjian/G. Lucas/Lucasfilm Ltd.; Fox; 1983)	165,500,000
The Empire Strikes Back	(I. Kershner; G. Lucas/G. Kurtz; Fox; 1980)	146,600,000
Jaws	(S. Spielberg; R. Zanuck/D. Brown; U; 1975)	133,435,000
Raiders of the Lost Ark	(S. Spielberg; F. Marshall/H. Kazanjian/G. Lucas; Par; 1981)	115,596,000
Grease	(R. Kleiser; R. Stigwood/A. Carr; Par; 1978)	96,300,000
Tootsie	(S. Pollack; S. Pollack/D. Richards; Col; 1982)	94,571,613
The Exorcist	(W. Friedkin; W. P. Blatty; WB; 1973)	89,000,000
The Godfather	(F. F. Coppola; A. Ruddy; Par; 1972)	86,275,000
Close Encounters of the Third Kind	(S. Spielberg; J. & M. Phillips; Col; 1977/1980)	83,452,000
Superman	(R. Donner; P. Spengler; WB; 1978)	82,800,000
The Sound of Music	(R. Wise; Fox; 1965)	79,748,000
The Sting	(G. R. Hill; T. Bill/M. & J. Phillips; U; 1973)	79,419,900
Gone With The Wind	(V. Fleming; D. Selznick; MGM/UA; 1939)	76,700,000
Saturday Night Fever	(J. Badham; R. Stigwood; Par; 1977)	74,100,000
National Lampoon's Animal House	(J. Landis; M. Simmons/I. Reitman; U; 1978)	74,000,000
Nine To Five	(C. Higgins; B. Gilbert; Fox; 1980)	66,200,000
Rocky III	(S. Stallone; I. Winkler/R. Chartoff; MGM/UA; 1982)	65,763,177
Superman II	(R. Lester; P. Spengler; WB; 1981)	65,100,000
On Golden Pond	(M. Rydell; B. Gilbert/TTC/IPC; U/AFD; 1981)	63,000,000
Kramer Vs. Kramer	(R. Benton; S. Jaffe; Col; 1979)	61,734,000
Smokey and the Bandit	(H. Needham; M. Engelberg; U; 1977)	61,055,000
One Flew Over the Cuckoo's Nest	(M. Forman; S. Zaentz/M. Douglas; UA; 1975)	59,205,000
Stir Crazy	(S. Poitier; H. Weinstein; Col; 1980)	58,408,000

Courtesy: *Variety.*

Figure 9.1

Troubles with the Product

As Hollywood goes to market with its advertised product it faces a continuing paradox from the public itself: complaints about sex, violence, and strong language used in many motion pictures, and a continuing demand at the box office for such content. Some of Hollywood's most profitable pictures have been crammed with brutal violence, as a current list of leading money-makers indicates. (See figure 9.1.) *Jaws, Jaws II, The Godfather, Godfather II, Rocky, Rocky II, Rocky III, The Shining* are good examples. Other leaders have featured frank sexual themes *(The Graduate, Body Heat)* or shocking portrayals of sexual acts *(The Exorcist)*.

Since the film-rating system was inaugurated in 1968, 38 percent of all films distributed have been rated PG, and 40 percent have been R. Thus, 78 percent of all industry films tend to have strong language, nudity and/or sexual portrayals, or violence to such an extent that they are questionable for youngsters. X-rated films make up 6 percent of the ratings, leaving only 16 percent of Hollywood's films with a G rating—suitable for general audiences and small children.

The ratings have been under persistent, if not heated, discussion for some years now. Of concern to many is that they are not enforceable, that theatre managers are either lax or money hungry when it comes to selling tickets to moviegoers obviously not old and mature enough to see PG, R, and X films. Some theatre managers counter the charge by arguing it is the parents' responsibility to see that youngsters do not attend films clearly advertised as unsuitable for them.

Critics and parents alike argue, however, that PG and R ratings are far from definitive. The two categories now include so many films and such a range of activity it is difficult for the movieviewer to know just what might or might not be acceptable for youngsters. Compare, for example, two recent films: *Conan The Destroyer* with Arnold Schwarzenegger and *Cannonball Run II* with Burt Reynolds. The *Conan* film included sexual overtones and incidents of extreme violence and brutality—a dramatized beheading and an attempt at roasting a man alive. *Cannonball* was pale by comparison, mostly offering sexual innuendo and drag strip humor. Yet both films were rated PG. In 1984, following complaints about the surprisingly violent adventure film *Indiana Jones and the Temple of Doom,* the MPAA announced a new rating, PG-13, to warn that a film required parental guidance for children thirteen years old and under. Some critics feel that PG and R should be divided into even more ratings—as many as six or more—to function properly.

Meanwhile, the many thrills and delights of PG, R, and X films—of "mature films"—have given the old G or family film a new stigma—that of being bland and dull. Many producers add strong language and sex to films just to avoid the G rating. There are many in the industry, however, who believe that G-rated films of significance would find a large audience. As MPAA president Jack Valenti has observed, his own favorite film, *A Man for All Seasons,* would qualify for a G rating. It was named best picture of the year in 1966.

Trouble Within: Creative Bookkeeping

Every media profession knows conflict, and one conflict all the media experience from time to time is the clash between those who create the messages and those who run the business. In short, the creative people versus the money people.

In recent years the chief creative people in Hollywood have been the directors. With a long string of successful, profitable films, directors Francis Ford Coppola (*Godfather I* and *II*), Robert Altman (*M*A*S*H, Nashville*) and others became the wunderkind (boy wonders) of filmmaking. They were in demand, and growing in power. Then problems began. Coppola's *Apocalypse Now* ran into budget troubles and struggled at the box office. Altman's *Health* and *Popeye* also had box office difficulties. The loudest crash heard, however, was in November, 1980 with the opening and closing of director Michael Cimino's *Heaven's Gate.* Reviews were so bad the film was withdrawn from its New York exhibition before the end of its first week. Cimino, who won an Oscar for *The Deer Hunter,* had been given a free hand to make *Heaven's Gate,* a sweeping western epic about a range war. To make it he spent $35 to $40 million of United Artist's money. At last report, recut and reissued, *Heaven's Gate* still had not returned a fraction of its investment, and the recut version, although an improvement, was not likely to either. (According to news reports MGM added the cost of the film to the purchase price when it bought UA in 1981.)

The series of box office disasters by known producer/directors brought a strong reaction from studio executives. They began to withdraw their unlimited support from directors and take tighter control of the purse strings. MGM executive Freddie Fields seemed to sum up the new studio attitude when he told New York *Times* reporter Robert Lindsey, "You can't let the inmates run the asylum."

The creative people, on the other hand, were quick to point out that few movie executives know how to make a movie. What is more, they have said, budget problems begin with the studios, and the inflated prices they charge, allegedly to cover overhead and distribution costs. One popular Hollywood label for the financial department is "the bottomless pit," so-called for its insatiable appetite for billing and swallowing up money.

Here's one brief version of how creative bookkeeping works:

A $10 million teleseries is sold to a network for $8 million. The cost of the series is likely to be padded, critics charge, since props and services given by the studios are billed at full price, again and again, as if the props were new each time. And so the series begins its first year with a loss of $2 million.

The series runs for five years (at $8 million per year), which is recorded as a $10 million loss ($2 million times five years).

There is a 10 percent sales commission, or $800,000, for five years (total $4 million), which the studio pays itself; the studio also charges interest on its loss (say, $2.2 million), putting the production $16.2 million in debt after a successful five-year run in prime time.

Hollywood's billing policies indicate there is a problem. In the 1960s, for example, Fess Parker became a national hero playing Daniel Boone for Twentieth Century-Fox. The show stayed on NBC for seven seasons, then went on to runs overseas. Parker decided not to take a large salary for his work, but agreed instead to take less pay and two-thirds of the profits from the series. Although it has now grossed more than $40 million, he has yet to receive any money from the profits. The book-keepers at Twentieth Century-Fox claim there have been none. Not yet, anyway. James Garner's series "The Rockford Files" has reportedly earned $52 million in sales here and abroad, yet Universal Studio tells Garner the series is still millions of dollars in the red. Sean Connery and Michael Caine have sued Allied Artists, claiming they both were denied profits from *The Man Who Would Be King.*

There seems to be no way to beat the system—or so Parker might argue. But former Fox and Universal executive Robert Leeper, Jr., has suggested those who prefer to be paid with a percentage rather than a high salary should try for a different percentage—a percentage of gross receipts rather than of profits. As Leeper has pointed out, gross receipts are public knowledge, and they also are not subject to depletion from hidden costs, sales fees, or 40 percent distribution fees.

Success Story

The movie business itself tends to be feast or famine, with ups and downs common. One remarkable success, however, was fashioned in the 1970s at Paramount. Under the direction of chairman Barry Diller and president Michael D. Eisner, Paramount made a sudden and sharp rise from sixth in the industry to first in box office revenues. Within eighteen months the studio produced twenty hits, including *Saturday Night Fever, Grease,* and *Heaven Can Wait.* The studio owned so many profitable films that at one point half of them were on the top ten list. The turnaround was attributed by industry analyst A. D. Murphy of *Variety* to "something to do with management."

Both Eisner and Diller came to Paramount from ABC-TV where they had built reputations as the youngest vice-presidents in network history. Diller had given audiences the movies of the week in the 1960s; Eisner had brought many of ABC's big hits to the air: "Happy Days," "Laverne & Shirley," and "Charlie's Angels," among others. At Paramount, Diller spent two years replacing all but the top twenty-five officers and reorganizing the studio so the chain of command could face the demands of television production as well as make its own movies. To encourage his staff to think about movies, he moved company offices back into the studio buildings and quadrupled Paramount's spending for acquisition of scripts and movie rights. Diller and Eisner remained careful about spending money for big budget films and allowing prior attachments to producers or stars affect their judgment of a script. It paid off. One of their financial successes of the 1970s was *Up in Smoke* with Cheech and Chong. The $2 million investment returned $15 million only months after its release. "It isn't necessary to risk the entire store on one movie," Diller told *Business Week.*

Their television backgrounds encouraged Diller and Eisner to reconsider Hollywood's traditional distribution strategies also. Paramount for years had followed the industry distribution formula of beginning with a lavish promotion for a New York or Hollywood film premier, and then establishing the film in key markets. A new strategy seemed in order. The job of promoting films was given to forty local advertising agencies to work with the national agencies used by Paramount. This allowed ads to be tailored to the local market. *Saturday Night Fever* was promoted through music and sound track albums sent to radio stations with brochures about the film. Music from the film was on the air and known before the film arrived at local theatres. The studio also exploited its major Hollywood premiers by taping and then making them into hour-long specials given free to television stations. Finally, the old Hollywood practice of distributing films from an opening base of one hundred theatres was dropped. Rather than hope for a "filter down," word of mouth advertising to build, Diller decided to open *King Kong* in one thousand theatres in 1976—and doubling the number of theatres used in the past. Meanwhile, Diller and Eisner did not forget television, recruiting top executives from successful MTM Enterprises and introducing such television hits as "Mork and Mindy" and "Taxi" to prime-time viewers.

Paramount's revenues climbed 66 percent in fiscal 1978 to $384 million. In time, both men found even more rewarding positions in the admiring movie industry.

Off to See the Wizard: Hope for the Future

The future now looks bright for the motion picture industry. It has survived its conflict with television, and theatre revenues once again are increasing. (See figure 9.2.) Box office receipts climbed at a rate of 11 percent between 1972 and 1981, and motion picture facilities are in great demand.

MGM gets all of its studio overhead from one tenant, Lorimar, the producer of television series "Dallas," and other shows. Leasing of sound stages and offices is so profitable that major studios—with one exception—no longer sell their valuable real estate holdings in the Los Angeles area. (More than one could sell huge back lots for $1 million an acre.) Only Fox, under owner and real estate magnate Marvin Davis, has decided to develop its studio property. Davis preferred to rent sound stages for moviemaking rather than shoot on choice real estate.

The major change facing the industry during the remainder of the decade is the shift of most movie distribution from theatres to cable, commercial television, and home video recording. Just how rapidly that change will occur, or to what extent cable and home video will affect the change, is not clear. The movie industry would prefer to keep the more profitable theatre distribution system, despite the conflict over blind bidding.

Motion Picture Theaters (SIC 783): Trends and Projections, 1972–82
(In Millions of Current Dollars Except as Noted)

	1972	1977	1978	1979	1980	1981[1]	Compound Annual Rate of Growth 1972–81	1982[1]	Percent Change 1981–82
Theater Receipts Gross (millions of dollars)	1,833	2,606	2,722	2,866	3,184	3,500	7.4	3,800	9.0
Theaters, Employment (000) ...	127.4	127.0	127.6	128.3	126.3	127.6	0.1	128.9	1.0

[1]Estimated by the Bureau of Industrial Economics.
Source: Bureau of the Census, Bureau of Industrial Economics, and Bureau of Labor Statistics.

Figure 9.2

But theatre attendance has softened recently. Admission prices jumped 15 percent between 1980 and 1981, to an average of $2.90 per person. Dinner and a movie has become an expensive evening—very expensive when one figures the cost of driving. As attendance falls off, theatre management also feels the drop in concession sales (soft drinks and popcorn), one of the most important sources of profit. One industry prediction is that as many as one-third of the theatres (about 5,800) will close by 1990. Drive-ins are expected to disappear first—especially in cold climates—as owners find it more profitable to develop their land rather than keep it as a movie showplace.

One of the industry's strongest allies in keeping the theaters in operation is its strongest audience: the twelve to twenty-four year olds. The movie theater is an important part of the maturation and dating patterns of America's young. Younger teenagers use the theater as an escape from home, while high school, college students, and young singles make the movies an important part of their social life. They use movies for dating and as a place to go with the gang. Losing theaters would mean the loss of an important American social institution.

Unfortunately, this age group is declining in size, and is predicted to lose 4 percent of its total number by the end of the 1980s. With fewer clientele, and with more moviegoers at their cable-supported home theatres, movie-house owners must find imaginative ways to market their entertainment services. One trend was evident in the Southeast and Northeast in the early 1980s, where two new chains of movie houses were offering films with bar and food service—or an evening of beer, wine, popcorn, pizza, sandwiches, and film entertainment—for $10 a couple.

Whatever the novelty, it will depend first on movies for survival. An old Hollywood adage insists there is nothing wrong with the motion picture business that a good movie can't cure. Good movies created theatres, beginning with *The Great Train Robbery* in 1903. If Hollywood can continue to make films its young audience likes, it can keep theatres alive for years—if only as a special interest, or special class, breaking away theatre system.

Careers in Motion Pictures

The paths to becoming a director, or working with the camera crew, are many and varied. Some have found their way into a career in motion pictures by beginning with the small, independent studios. Others have constructed a successful movie career on a foundation of television experience. Robert Altman (*M*A*S*H, Nashville, Popeye,* etc.) was a successful director of industrial films in St. Louis before moving to Hollywood and theatrical films. On the other hand, Blake Edwards (*10, S.O.B., Victor/Victoria, The Man Who Loved Women,* as well as the Pink Panther films) began his career in television.

One avenue to a Hollywood career is script writing. Francis Ford Coppola helped write the screenplay for *Patton,* then used that success to advance in a career that has included directing and/or producing the Godfather pictures, the Black Stallion pictures, and *Apocalypse Now.* Policeman Joseph Wambaugh gained entry to Hollywood with his police novels. His credits include the acclaimed television movie "The Blue Knight," and the striking feature film *The Onion Field,* which he produced through his own independent company, Black Marble productions. It should be remembered, however, that the selling of screenplays is very much like selling stories to national magazines—or like attempting to sell manuscripts to book publishers. It is a very demanding business. Many try. Few succeed.

The person who is dedicated to the pursuit of an acting career has a difficult challenge. Years ago, Lana Turner was discovered in a drugstore in Hollywood, and began a long career as a sex symbol. Turner's career came at a time, however, when the factory movie studios developed actors over a period of years, first giving them small then larger parts until moviegoers recognized the actor. The studios could also exploit the star in showcase feature films. The free-lance Hollywood of today no longer discovers and develops stars. It exploits actors already known to the public or the trade. Burt Reynolds and Morgan Fairchild were television actors who worked their way into movies. Meryl Streep came to Hollywood with impressive legitimate acting credits. For would-be movie stars today, Hollywood begins in summer stock.

A staple of the movie industry: movies for audiences in the age range of twelve to twenty-four years old.

Here are current salaries for beginners, according to union contracts or studio reports:

Directors:	$ 29,359	(eleven week minimum with a budget under $500,000)
Producers:	25,000	(for picture with budget of $1.5 or less)
Writers:	14,175	(for picture with budget under $1 million, screenplay and treatment)
Agents:	10	percent
Studio head of production:	350,000	(annually)
Director of photography:	282	(daily)
Sound mixer:	375	(weekly)

Summary

There is reason to believe the moving picture is our principal myth-making medium. The film gives us social myths the way medieval cathedrals gave Europeans their myths.

The major studios, many of whom survived the Hollywood of the 1930s and 1940s act as sources of funding for pictures, as production facilities, and as principal distributors of films.

The mini-major studios specialize in movie production, but frequently turn to majors for funding and distribution.

The independents are smaller still. They fund their films from sources outside the industry. The independents also distribute films on their own.

Commercial television and pay cable television add to film revenue. The television networks, like major film studios, now back films financially in order to get early bookings for films. Television remains more interested in films that do well at the box office, however.

Modern film studios now operate on an ad hoc basis rather than the old factory method of picture making. Talent is hired for a specific picture, or a series of pictures, then it moves on to another contract with another studio.

The important job of setting a movie budget is difficult, since every film is unique and all costs must be estimated anew. The picture goes into production after the studio and the director estimate the cost of the film.

On the set, the production crew, all union personnel, follow a strict division of labor. The camera crew, sound crew, director's crew and producer's staff work together to complete the film.

While the film is in production theatre owners can make a firm bid for the right to exhibit the film for a given period of time. They usually do not have the opportunity to view the film before it is booked. The studios say the system is necessary to get films to market before interest rates bite into profits. Twenty-one states have passed legislation against this blind bidding.

Advertising a film is essential to its success. Theatre owners can rent "trailers" for in-theatre advertising. The primary rule for movie ads is to maximize the film's potential publicity in the ad campaign. Stars, budget, themes, and action shots from the story all are put into advertising service. General appeals rather than specific ones seem to work best.

All movie studios, with the exception of Disney, tend to view movie-related toy and clothing merchandising as pure advertising. Yet most refuse to underwrite the costs of merchandising, preferring instead to sell rights to manufacture and market them. The Disney studios, however, view movie-associated toys and clothing as a potential source of revenue. Returns can be high.

The annual Academy Award ceremonies are one of the most important industry advertising and promotion activities. In an attempt to increase box office revenues, the studios maneuver and campaign carefully to win academy votes and Oscars.

One type of ad campaign is "four walling." The distributor rents a theatre then launches a saturation ad campaign for the film. After a short run, the film is moved to another town and another rented theatre; that way critical media and word-of-mouth reviews are avoided.

Hollywood's films continually are derided for sex, violence and profanity, yet box office receipts prove these films are successful. If studios would produce them, there is reason to believe there is a large audience who would pay to see G films, such as the impressive *Man for All Seasons*.

The future looks bright for the industry. Box office receipts have been increasing. The years ahead promise to bring a shift from theatrical distribution to pay television and home video. It is predicted one-third of the nation's theatres will be closed by 1990.

Questions for Discussion

1. The observers of Hollywood film distribution insist that theatrical distribution is a demanding art. What evidence can you find that movie distributors have been selective in the placement of films in theatres in your area? Is placement reflected in newspaper ads? What type films usually show in the theatres that you frequent? What type film would never show up at the same houses?

2. There is some concern that independent movie producers can not readily get their films to the public as they could a few years ago. Have you seen an independently made movie this year? What was its rating (PG, G, X)? Are any independent films playing in your area at the present time? What are the names of the leading players?

3. In the next few years, theatres are predicted to lose and home screens are expected to win more and more of the industry's film distribution. How will the shift affect college students who now are among the theatre owner's most important clientele? Will dating patterns change? Can cable television be incorporated into dating patterns? Or will movies and theatres be replaced by (1) square dancing? (2) Pac-Man, or (3) an evening at the library? Or is there a new kind of business— some sort of movie-theatre distribution to serve daters that we have not discovered yet?

4. It could be argued that the reason the studios do not make G pictures of significance is because the people who run Hollywood are money people insensitive to the artistic need of many in their audience. See if you can do better. Pick a G story from one you have read in literature classes. Cast it with contemporary movie stars. Imagine you have produced it (with an unlimited budget). Now how will you advertise the new film? In what theatres in your town will you distribute it? Which of your friends or acquaintances will go to see it? Would your profit picture change if you added what is required to get a PG, R, or X rating?

References

Bettelheim, Bruno. "The Art of Moving Pictures." *Harper's,* October, 1981, 80–83.

Gordon, David. "Why the Movie Majors Are Major." In *The American Film Industry,* edited by Tino Balio. Madison: University of Wisconsin Press, 1978, 464–65.

Grant, Lee. "Coppola Faces Survival Test with 'Heart.' " Los Angeles *Times.* Published in *Columbus Dispatch,* February 21, 1982, D6.

Greer, Philip and Myron Kandel. "Pay TV Revenues to Top Those of Theaters Soon, Analyst [Elliot Minsker] Says." *Chicago Tribune.* Reported in the *Columbus Dispatch,* December 21, 1981, A11.

Harris, William. "Someday They'll Build a Town Here, Kate." *Forbes,* October 26, 1981, 135–59.

Jeffries, Georgia. "Movies: The Problem With G." *American Film,* June 1978.

Lees, David and Stan Berkowitz. *The Movie Business.* New York: Vintage Books, 1981.

Lindsey, Robert. "Who Wields the Power in Hollywood?" *The New York Times Magazine,* February 14, 1982, 1 et seq.

Litman, Barry Ro. "The Economics of the Television Market for Theatrical Movies." *Journal of Communication* 29, no. 4 (1949): 20–33.

Martin, Leonard, ed. *The Whole Film Sourcebook.* New York: New American Library, 1983.

Murphy, Mary. "Bending the Rules in Hollywood." *TV Guide,* January 16, 1982, 4 et seq.

"A New Breed of Actor." *Newsweek,* December 7, 1981, 90–95.

Nicholson, Tom, David T. Friendly, and Emily Newhall. "Hollywood Roulette." *Newsweek,* January 4, 1982, 57.

"Now Playing: Sipping Cinemas." *Time,* April 27, 1981, p. 55.

"Paramount Deal with Showtime Shakes Pay-TV." *TV Guide,* December 31, 1983, A1.

"Paramount Pictures: Applying a TV Formula for Success." *Business Week,* November 17, 1978, 94–100.

Rea, Steven X. "Evolution on the Big Screen." *Ampersand,* January/February, 1982, 6–7.

Sansweet, Stephen J. "New Summer Movies Draw Crowds to Box Offices, Reversing Trend." *The Wall Street Journal,* June 26, 1981, 21.

Swertlow, Frank. "How Hollywood Studios Flim Flam Their Stars." *TV Guide,* May 1, 1982, 6–14.

U.S. Department of Commerce. "Motion Pictures." *U.S. Industrial Outlook, 1982.* Washington, D.C.: U.S. Government Printing Office.

Wright, John W. *The American Almanac of Jobs and Salaries.* New York: Avon Books, 1982.

Chapter
10

The Musical Clock: Modern Radio

Tapes, discs, players, audio console, weather radar, and the ever-present DJ: the heart of a contemporary radio operation.

You can hear it morning, noon, or night. It might begin with an announcement of the time or the station's call letters, followed by a review of the weather (snow or sunshine, 20 percent chance of rain, partly sunny today, cooler tonight, etc.). Then there is a little music—fast or slow, loud or soft—followed almost certainly by a commercial and, quite likely, the news. All along there are jokes and community announcements, contests, and sometimes free prizes—all controlled and announced by "Chuck" or "Bob," "Spook" or "Jack and Amy," "Wolfman" or "Fox." They preside over events in a style acceptable to any one of several recognizable radio formats: for the young, the middle-aged, for jazz, rock or country lovers, the intellectually elite, or the beautiful music devotee.

It's called radio. It is a constant companion. It wakes people up, then informs and entertains them as they ride to and from work. It plays in the office and the factory, at the beach, or the backyard barbecue, in both bowling alleys and back alleys, at drag and restaurant strips, in horse and antique barns, discount and diamond stores.

Radio's ability to reach so many special audiences is the result of a real-life, modern day media miracle—a transformation that saw it develop from a general audience stay-at-home medium into the diversified, on-the-go, special audience medium it is today. For, as many can still recall, radio used to be television; that is, radio performed about the way television performs now—without pictures, of course—but strikingly like the television of today.

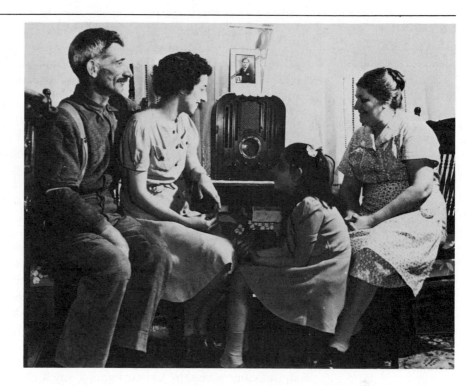

Radio was the principal medium for family entertainment in the 1930s and 1940s.

The Network Radio Formula

In the 1930s and 1940s the dominant form of radio was network radio—a medium of family entertainment and news—a kind of *Reader's Digest* of the airwaves. The huge mahogany AM radio set occupied a featured spot against the living room wall, and family members gathered around at various times during the day to study, read the newspaper, work or knit, and listen. There were homemaking features and soap operas for Mom during the day, adventure and comedy for the kids in the late afternoon (''Terry and the Pirates'' and ''Jack Armstrong,'' among others), and news and stock reports for Dad during the dinner hour. In the evening the entire family might gather to listen to dramas, melodramas, comedy programs, and quiz shows. In 1946, for example, a survey of radio stations found that radio stations were devoting:

1. Sixteen percent of their broadcast day to dramatic shows—mystery, comedy, and daytime serials;
2. Fourteen percent to homemaking, comedy and variety, and quiz and audience participation shows;
3. Eight percent to religious and religious music programs, and other programs;

4. Twenty-three percent to news, news commentators, sports, talks, and farm programs;

5. Forty percent or the remaining time, to music programs, including the classics, and popular dance music.

A few of the larger local stations found the local quiz or participation show to be profitable, and some local stations were able to produce dramatic shows on their own. WXYZ in Detroit, for example, had a loyal following for "The Lone Ranger," a program it initiated in 1933 and then syndicated. For the most part, however, the melodramas, comedies, game shows, and news and commentary originated in network studios. The networks accounted for 40 percent of the total programming offered by the average station and most of the programs that filled the evening prime time hours.

For drama and melodrama the networks offered the "Green Hornet" and "The Shadow" as well as Orson Welles' "Mercury Theatre," and the lighter "Lux Radio Theater," with its radio adaptations of Hollywood movies starring "name" Hollywood actors and actresses. Perhaps the epitome of radio melodrama was Arch Obler's hair-raising "Lights Out." One Obler program told the tale of a chicken heart that suddenly began growing and growing, thumping and thumping, until it covered the earth. Trying to kill the thumping mass proved futile. The last sound from the drama came when the last airplane, flying high to stay above the vibrating flesh, sputtered and fell in a whining dive into the thumping heart far below.

Radio comedians, like radio dramatists, learned to exploit their pictureless medium with sound. Among the more successful radio comedy programs was "Fibber McGee and Molly," a sitcom with one of radio's best recognized sound effects gags: McGee's closet. When lead character Fibber pulled open the closet door in search of some needed tool or trinket—despite the warning cries of his wife, Molly—a ton of crashing, sliding, tinkling, crunching sound effects followed. To the audience it was convincing aural evidence that Fibber again had been trapped in an uncontrollable mountain of trivia, a fact underscored with the sighing recognition he would have to "clean up that closet one of these days."

One master of radio comedy was Jack Benny. Benny's satirizations of stinginess included inventive use of the pregnant pause. In one memorable sound-only skit, tightwad Benny was confronted by a robber who growled, "Your money or your life."

There was no reply, then still no reply, until the audience, realizing the penny pincher's dilemma, began to laugh at the significance of the silence.

When the laughter peaked, the bandit asked, "Well?"

Benny replied, "I'm thinking! I'm thinking!" bringing even more laughter.

The leader in audience ratings was "Amos and Andy." The show was so popular historian Erik Barnouw has reported that during the Great Depression a minister who announced his next sermon would be from the Book of Amos found his church filled the following Sunday with a congregation expecting to hear about Andy as well.

Human interest programs and quiz shows became popular in the late 1930s as the radio audience tested itself against contestants on "Kay Kyser's Kollege of Musical Knowledge," "Dr. I.Q.," and "Truth or Consequences." As already noted in chapter 4, the radio quiz shows survived to become a heavy television liability in the 1950s.

The Rise of Network Radio News

News programs were among the first on the air. The election returns broadcast by KDKA in 1920 helped bring the medium to the attention of the American public. Presidential election campaign coverage in 1923 and 1924 included broadcasts of the national political party conventions as well as several campaign speeches to the nation. More than twenty million listeners heard President Coolidge speak on network radio the night before the election. Some stations interrupted programs with returns and political analyses during the night of the election, inaugurating a broadcasting practice that is an important part of broadcast journalism today.

The 1920s also saw the beginning of regular news commentary on radio. H. V. Kaltenborn and David Lawrence were two of the more notable commentators. Kaltenborn became a distinguished network commentator and reporter. Lawrence made his mark when he established the news magazine *U.S. News and World Report*.

The first regular hard news broadcasts, as Sterling and Kittross have written, began in 1930, with Lowell Thomas and his fifteen-minute, five-day-a-week newscasts on NBC-Blue. The popular program stayed on the air for almost fifty years, until 1976. Both Boake Carter and Edwin C. Hill began fifteen-minute evening newscasts in 1932. Network daytime news began with special coverage of the famous Lindbergh baby kidnapping in 1932. That, plus positive audience reaction to presidential campaign reporting the same year, convinced network officials there was an important radio audience for hard news during the day as well. But, as radio moved to expand news programs, the newspaper industry grew more and more uneasy. The loss of advertising revenue from the Depression had become a major concern for publishers; more than one disliked the idea of watching radio siphon off more newspaper revenue by attracting advertisers with what the publishers felt was their own product: hard news.

The Press–Radio War

The conflict that followed became known as the press–radio war. From the beginning, the newspapers seemed to have the advantage. The radio networks had little news-gathering experience, and less staff to gather the news. The publishers, on the other hand, controlled the three major wire services: Associated Press (AP), United Press (UP), and International News Service (INS). And the radio networks relied almost completely on the wire services for their news. When the publishers convinced the wire services to begin withholding news from the networks, CBS, disregarding copyright law, turned to the pages of the newspapers for stories, cutting and pasting what was needed to fill newscasts. In 1933 the conflict widened when the American Newspaper Publisher's Association decided to abandon the practice of printing radio station program logs without charge. Within weeks, the three major wire services joined the publishers and withdrew all but bulletin news services from stations affiliated with the radio networks. As broadcast historian Erik Barnouw has pointed out, this forced the radio networks to choose between gathering news on their own or giving up their regular newscasts.

The Network News Effort

Both NBC and CBS accepted the challenge and plunged into active news coverage. At NBC, A. A. "Abe" Schecter discovered almost anyone was willing to talk to NBC by telephone. He was soon "scooping" newspapers without leaving his desk. CBS, with former New York *Times* editor Ed Klauber, and former United Press reporter Paul White, mounted a more formidable effort. With financial support from General Mills, Klauber and White put together the Columbia News Service, establishing bureaus in major cities to furnish CBS with news reports from around the country.

NBC's news output was so great the newspaper publishers doubted Schecter alone was responsible for it. But they realized the CBS bureaus were a real threat to their dominance in the news business. They retaliated against Columbia News Service with a blackout of newspaper publicity for all CBS sponsors. To sponsor a CBS program meant losing all possibility of newspaper publicity—something no realistic national business concern could afford to do. CBS could not ignore the situation, either. Some sponsors were moving to NBC. And so when the newspaper publishers offered a compromise, CBS took it.

The Biltmore Agreement

In December 1933 representatives of the newspapers and wire services met with NBC, CBS, and the National Association of Broadcasters (NAB) at the Biltmore Hotel in New York to discuss a settlement. Their final agreement, referred to as the Biltmore agreement, limited the amount of news the networks could broadcast. The publishers were able to force CBS to dismantle its news bureaus and accept a new radio news service established by the press associations. It was called the Press–Radio Bureau, and it was to furnish them with bulletins of important, fast-breaking news as well as enough news for two—just two—five-minute newscasts a day. The newscasts were to be released between 9:30 A.M. and 9 P.M. to protect morning and afternoon newspaper distribution. And, the bulletins were to be presented on the air so as to "stimulate public interest in the newspaper report" of the event covered. In exchange for agreeing to accept these strict limitations on their news operations, the networks were released from the threat of a newspaper publicity blackout of sponsors. They also were free to continue broadcasting news commentary as they had since the 1920s.

The Victors and the Spoils

It appeared the networks had lost the war, but it was soon clear that was not quite the case. The Press–Radio Bureau opened on March 24, 1934, but its attempt to control news was ineffectual and short-lived. The day the bureau opened, three completely new radio news services opened, too. A fourth was in business in a matter of weeks. By August 1934 one of them, Transradio Press, formed in large part with the people and news bureaus CBS had been forced to abandon, had signed up 150 radio stations as news clients. Transradio quickly signed up a large number of clients—only ten fewer than the Press–Radio Bureau. There was a large number of local and independent stations eager to establish newscasts they could sell to sponsors. Transradio tapped this market, knowing there was no legitimate reason why they should not sell news—or sell the stations as much news as they wanted.

By 1935 the major independent stations were withdrawing from the Press–Radio Bureau. Watching the money flow from radio stations to new radio news services, UP and INS, the two commercial wire services, faced some inevitable conclusions. More in need of revenue than the larger Associated Press, which was a newspaper cooperative, United Press and International News Service decided on a new solution to the radio news problem: Rather than lose money, why not make money from it?

The two began selling their news services to radio on an unrestricted basis that year, offering stations fully prepared news stories and newscasts rather than short dispatches to be rewritten by the radio station news staff. AP finally offered its own radio news service for radio sponsorship in 1940. By then the Press–Radio Bureau was dead. NBC and CBS had dropped the service just before Christmas 1938. If the networks had lost the press–radio war, they had won the peace.

Hard News for Hard Times

The network victory over the restrictions of the Press–Radio Bureau came at a time when there was growing interest in news at home and abroad. At home the Depression was still dragging on. Radio brought not only news and commentary about the economic situation but delivered the voice of the chief executive himself into the American living room. Franklin Roosevelt's use of radio for his fireside chats is now legendary. Network radio carried a total of twenty-eight of the talks between 1932 and the president's death in 1945. Of these, sixteen were given between the Depression years of 1932 and 1940.

From overseas there was the growing threat of world war. In 1936 H. V. Kaltenborn found a vantage point on top of a haystack and broadcast an eyewitness account of a skirmish in the Spanish Civil War. By late 1939 CBS had fourteen full-time news employees in Europe under the direction of Edward R. Murrow in London. NBC established a comparable staff as the war heated up. Both networks were able to provide a continuous account, with commentary, of the rising inferno.

The man some have called the best journalist of the twentieth century: Edward R. Murrow.

The reporter/commentator who did the most to capture the imagination of the people, and enhance the stature of broadcast news reporting during the war, was Edward R. Murrow. Murrow's "This is London" broadcast between 1939 and 1941 and during the Blitz, gave Americans a firsthand account of what their English cousins endured during the bombings. The day following the Nazi takeover of Austria, Murrow broadcast:

> I'd like to forget the tired futile look of the Austrian army officers . . . and the pitiful uncertainty of those forced to lift the right hand and shout "Heil Hitler" for the first time. I'd like to forget the sound of smashing glass as the Jewish shop streets were raided; the hoots and jeers aimed at those forced to scrub the sidewalk . . . those are a few of the things that happened in Austria. . . .

Increase in News Broadcasting

As Sterling and Kittross have reported, the networks broadcast 850 hours of news and on-the-spot news specials in 1937, 1,250 hours in 1939, and 3,450 in 1941. Nearly all stations offered regular news programs by

1940 and 1941; some were providing news summaries every hour. By the time the war was over, network radio was established in the public's mind as a reliable source of hard news.

Except for the enterprise of the networks, radio, especially local radio, was not so much a news-gathering as a news-reporting medium. Many stations had decided to let the networks and the wire services gather and write their radio news and stuck to the decision.

End Run: Some Terminal Advertising Results

With its network formula of "something for everyone," radio was so popular in the 1930s and the 1940s that it appeared indestructible. Even the removal of restrictions on the tremendous growth of television following World War II hardly seemed a threat to old-line radio supporters. Radio's national advertising revenues dropped slightly from television competition in 1949—down $5 million to $129 million for that year. And radio's national ad revenues were down slightly again in 1950, by $4 million to $125 million. In 1952, however, with the television "freeze" lifting (See pp. 99–100), the total slipped to $103, down $22 million. Television was beginning to gain a reputation as a hot ad medium. Success stories such as the one told about the small Hazel Bishop Cosmetics firm helped. Hazel Bishop increased its annual income of $40,000 to $4.5 million a year between 1950 and 1952—using television advertising alone.

By the middle 1950s it was clear to many that network radio's loss of advertising was a part of a terminal disease: disappearing advertising and loss of vigor from an increasing lack of audience. The final complication was a loss of stars and programs. Some of the major stars and leading shows spotted the audience's move to television and jumped to stay with it. By 1954 the switch was pronounced. Historian Erik Barnouw has noted that one network executive described the exodus of the network radio staffs—administrative talent, actors, engineers—"like rats leaving sinking ships." It was over in 1960 when the last network programs, a few soap operas, finally left the air. Folksy soap opera heroine Ma Perkins signed off, in character, saying, "Goodbye, and may God bless you." The network news was still there, of course, but what had once been an all-day, seven-day-a-week schedule of national radio entertainment was gone. And it was far from certain that any new schedule would or could take its place.

The Rise from the Crash

Those who expected radio to turn belly-up and die under the death-ray-like glow of the television tube were soon disappointed. Radio was still a viable advertising medium. Between 1948 and 1952, while its national advertising revenue was dropping a total of $31 million, its local and regional ad revenue was rising $87 million. The local advertising potential alone was enough to make any rescue attempt worthwhile. The only question was, how could it be done?

The Independents

The beginning of an answer already was available. It came from the independent radio stations that had come on the air as radio expanded—especially after World War II—but had been unable to gain affiliation with any of the radio networks. The independents had learned to survive by programming recorded music. They had built large record libraries and had followed the example of the network programmers, scheduling different kinds of musical programs at different times of the day: mellow music for late evening, big bands during the day, dinner music at dinner time, and so forth. The heart of the independent operation was the disc jockey, who selected and presented the music.

The Disc Jockey

One of the first recorded music programs was Al Jarvis's "The World's Largest Make-Believe Ballroom" on station KFWB in Los Angeles in 1932. Martin Block, a salesman for KFWB, took the recorded music program idea with him to New York when he joined independent WNEW a few months later. In 1935 Block played records and talked to fill time between reports from the Bruno Hauptmann trial. Audience response soon made the temporary bridge a regular feature. By 1941 Block's "Make Believe Ballroom" was drawing twelve thousand letters a month and had a waiting list of sponsors eager to get on the show. Block's success was due in large part to his imaginative chitchat, his presentation of the records, and, like other successful disc jockeys who followed him, his attractive air personality. The same year, 1941, the show business newspaper *Variety* introduced the term *disc jockey* to describe the person who presented the records.

A Necessary Consistency

Most radio stations turned to the disc jockey and recorded music programming in the 1950s. In competition for the audience that followed, station managers became convinced they could not attract and hold listeners through the day with a variety of music program types. Programming dinner music in the evening, big band in the afternoon, be-bop, top 40, or swing at night attracted an audience—but several different ones. It dissipated audiences, too. Each particular music audience would tune into its particular type of program, then tune out. To hold listeners, and create a regular audience, the station would have to be consistent, and play the same type of music all day.

Early favorites for consistent music styles were top 40, the records listed as the best-sellers across the country by *Billboard*. Another favorite style was MOR, or middle-of-the-road music, standard tunes by established groups or singers—Tony Bennett, Rosemary Clooney, Perry Como, Doris Day, the Hi-Lo's, Frank Sinatra. Beyond maintaining a consistent musical stance, station management also established new programming rules: play so many recordings an hour, give so many time checks an hour, give so many station identifications an hour, and run commercials only at specific times. Stations also experimented with their newscast schedule; some gave news on the hour, some at five before the hour, some on the half hour. The new approach had many names. Music and news was a popular early label. One critic called it gypsy radio because of its "ludicrously cheap" operating costs. The policy of following music with time checks prompted the musical clock title. For many it was formula radio for its tightly defined musical programming, production rules, and policies. More recently, it had been called format radio, for its development of any one of several musical program styles.

Transformation
Localization and Specialization

As radio historians Fornatale and Mills have pointed out, there were at least two distinct steps in the transformation of network radio into format radio: localization and specialization. Stations began to localize programming when they realized they had a unique ability to serve their local audiences. Network radio and network television could bring drama, sophisticated comedy, and news from the national scene, but they could not consistently satisfy local tastes, or keep the local community informed on important local events and issues—whether or not the bridge was out between home and grocery store, for example, or whether the schools would be open after a big snowstorm.

As stations localized their programming, they began to discover something that had been indicated by audience research. The Federal Communications Commission (FCC) had suggested as early as 1947 that carefully selected segments of the listening audience could provide an attractive target audience for advertisers. The next year, NBC released a study reporting that 64 percent of all urban teenagers owned their own radios and had an annual buying power of $6 billion. As stations reached out to serve local tastes and needs, they discovered within the local community several segments of listeners, with distinct interests and considerable buying power. It was as if the more they tried to serve the local community, the more local communities they found to serve. And all of these new, distinct audiences were available to radio format programming with no increase in operating costs and with only minor changes in program policy. By the 1960s radio was becoming highly specialized, broadcasting to teenagers, blacks, farmers, jazz lovers, religious groups, and foreign language audiences, among others, with a distinct radio format for each.

Improvements in Technology

Improvements in radio technology also supported the trend toward specialization. The invention of the transistor during World War II led to the production of the transistor radio, with handy, quality, mobile radio reception almost anywhere above water. The first commercial transistor radios went on sale in 1953 for forty dollars. By the early 1960s they were selling at a rate of thirteen million sets a year. War technology produced improvements in the car radio, too. The sixty million car radios in service in the early 1960s grew at a rate of six to ten million each year as the car, rather than the living room, became the major center for radio listening. It was Gerald Bartell, owner of one group of music and news stations in the Midwest, who coined the term *drive time* to point out that radio's new prime advertising time was no longer at night but during the morning and late afternoon hours when listeners were driving to and from work.

Leaders in the Revolution

Developer and promoter of the contemporary radio format, the radio sportscast, and local radio news: Gordon McLendon.

Many contributed to the development of format radio. Bartell promoted the use of top 40 music with the philosophy that radio management should deal with radio programming "objectively," meaning it should build its audience and the radio business by giving listeners what they wanted. Another leader was Robert Todd Storz, who pursued the radio audience with popular music and giveaway games. Storz's most succesful game was "Lucky House Number." Throughout the day, a Storz station announced house numbers drawn at random. A listener could win five hundred dollars if he or she phoned the station within one minute after his or her house number was read over the air. If no one phoned in, another house number was drawn and read.

The title "father of modern radio" seems best assigned, however, to Gordon McLendon. McLendon did much to develop the idea of the radio format. He pioneered top 40 and beautiful music, and was the first to put a commercially successful all news station, XETRA, on the air. Beginning in 1961 XETRA broadcast one newscast after another from Tijuana, Mexico to the Los Angeles area. McLendon's development of his own radio news department at KLIF was fantastic. He gave great attention to localizing the news by having prominent local citizens speak on issues in their area of expertise. His station's news cars provided extensive local coverage as they traveled the city for reports.

McLendon's sense of promotion was close to that of P. T. Barnum's. To give his Dallas station a distinctive sound, he trained a parrot to shriek "K–L–I–F!" on command, over and over. McLendon also was the first to adopt musical station identification jingles. He promoted his disc jockey, Johnny Rabbitt, by lining a Dallas expressway with overturned automobiles, with the words "I just flipped for Johnny Rabbitt" written on each car bottom. He had another deejay give away ten and twenty dollar bills. When the news media showed interest, the "mystery millionaire" finally was identified as the new KLIF disc jockey.

McLendon's one failure came at radio station KADS Los Angeles in 1967, when he attempted to broadcast an all-classified, all-want ad program schedule—with no music or news. The format did not survive its first year. McLendon blamed the failure on improper promotion. When he left radio in 1979, it was clear his achievements had been considerable, but he, like other format radio pioneers, had not been able to make a major impact on the metropolitan markets of the East and West coasts. As McLendon himself once observed, he and those like him produced their formats for stations in the Midwest. But the format ideas were so workable they were quickly adopted by and became successful in stations in the major markets on the coasts. As a result, McLendon and his colleagues found they could not buy into the larger markets when they decided to do so. The stations had become too expensive. The radio pioneers were barred from the "big time" by the success of their own formulas.

The Modern Radio Format
Distinct and Competitive

Finding the right format—musical or nonmusical—is the most important thing a station can do today. The format attracts and holds the station's target audience, which in turn attracts the advertiser. Radio program directors constantly study the market in search of new ways to hold or reach radio audiences. Good program policy favors a format that not only is distinct but is also competitive with other formats in the market. The adoption of country and western or "country" formats over the past fifteen years illustrates the principle. When the first radio formats became popular, they were so similar that some had to fail. As first one station, then another, struggled with the competition, the Country Music Association of America, in Nashville, began an active campaign to promote country as a format that could compete with other formats even in large cities. Country was adopted by 20 percent of AM stations on the air by 1974, and by many stations in cities of 100,000 or more—competitive

Figure 10.1

Adult Contemporary Total Week Leaders

Top 20 Shares, Persons 12+

1. Bloomington-Normal	WJBC	34.1
2. Omaha	KFAB	27.4
3. Huntington-Ashind	WKEE-FM	25.2
4. Hartford-New Britn	WTIC	21.1
5. Minneapolis	WCCO	20.9
6. Fort Wayne	WOWO	20.2
7. Honolulu	KSSK	19.1
8. Bridgeport	WICC	17.9
9. Canton	WHBC	17.3
10. Pittsburgh (tie)	KDKA	15.9
10. Indianapolis (tie)	WIBC	15.9
12. Raleigh-Durham	WPTF	15.2
13. Richmond	WRVA	14.1
14. New Hvn-Wtbry-Mrdn	WELI	13.9
15. Syracuse	WYYY (F)	13.6
16. Milwaukee	WTMJ	12.5
17. Grand Rapids	WOOD	12.4
18. Harrisburg	WHP	12.3
19. Lubbock	KSEL-FM	12.2
20. Albany-Schenectady	WGY	12.1

Source: *Television/Radio Age.* March 19, 1984.

format cities. Its stability as a format has been proved. Country holds its own in Chicago, Cleveland, and Atlanta, and 34 percent of all radio stations now use it. Country offers something distinctive and appealing to a large segment of the listening audience. (See p. 261)

Looking for New Formats

The search for larger and larger audiences has led to an increasing number of new formats. Many of the new ones are variations on the original top 40, beautiful music, soul, or black, classical, oldies. Some of the variations include rock, top 30, rock and roll, album, mellow music, black oldies, black rock, concert, semiclassical, album rock, and contemporary, to name only a few. Nonmusical formats include all news, and news information, or simply, talk.

Adult Contemporary

Adult contemporary has been a leading musical format for the past several years. Audience surveys indicate it has won as much as 41 percent of the AM and 19 percent of the FM audience in the top one hundred radio markets. A list of the twenty leading stations using the adult contemporary format is given in figure 10.1. Rising in popularity in the early

1980s, "urban contemporary" based its appeal on the presence of multi-ethnic groups in the largest cities and a combination of disco, jazz, rhythm, and blues, *and* adult contemporary. The adult contemporary format includes music by John Denver, Olivia Newton-John, and Billy Joel, while urban contemporary blends the music of Change, George Benson, Luther, Herbie Hancock, and Diana Ross. Urban contemporary's average share of 5.5 percent of the audiences in top ten markets (New York, Chicago, Houston, etc.) attracted an average of 750,000 listeners every quarter hour in 1982, giving this "small" format an audience similar to that of the New York *Times*.

News Information or Talk

Meanwhile, a growing number of stations, especially AM stations, have dropped musical formats in favor of news information or talk. Talk includes interviews with celebrities and experts—frequently with audience participation through telephone call-ins—regular newscasts and news features. The attraction of the call-in show, and its presentation of an authority who can and will answer questions, creates a large, loyal and affluent audience. People get "hooked" on information, as one observer has put it. Estimates indicate the cost of talk is four times as great as the cost of a music format, but stations that make the change report audience gains as high as 48 percent after the first year. The format's secret of success is management's ability to keep the initial costs low.

All News

All news programming differs from talk in that all information in the former is presented through a bona fide newscast. Following the Gordon McLendon format, all news presents one newscast after another, in a cycle that varies in time from station to station, but usually runs about twenty minutes. The expense of producing one newscast after another, hour after hour, is great. The format requires an extensive staff of reporters and news production teams, along with the automobiles, radio, and tape recording equipment required for rapid audio coverage of a large metropolitan city. At the same time, the audience for all news is relatively small. The expense and audience size make all news a big city format, since only the larger metropolitan areas can offer the audience and advertising support required to maintain it. Audience research also indicates that all news attracts a larger share of the radio audience in big cities, suggesting it may be more useful to metropolitan listeners.

Unformat Radio

While most of American radio fiddles around with classical, rock, urban rock, country, or music for the eighteen to twenty-five-year-old audience, WMT in Cedar Rapids, Iowa, remains one of the most successful stations in the nation with what the *Wall Street Journal* has called a "programming hodgepodge" that should guarantee the station a spot at the bottom rather than the top of the charts. WMT's morning show, for example, features "Ol' Cherokee" Jerry Carr, who awakens his listeners with a few rousing patriotic tunes, mixed with a classical piece or two, and a little poetry. During the program day, WMT offers such regular features as "The Doggone Bulletin Board," a lost-and-found pet service, a recipe-swapping program, reruns of "Fibber McGee and Molly," and a three-hour call-in program. Topics on the latter have included everything from the validity of ground hog day to abortion. Discussions on the latter continue, in part, because of one female caller who has contributed something on the subject almost daily for the past fifteen years.

Station manager Larry Edwards says WMT is just poking along, trying to "identify with the people." Others note, however, that many in WMT's audience are fifty-four years or older, and that since American society itself is growing older, the station may well be in the vanguard of radio programming. The time may soon come when other stations will tailor their formats to suit the audience WMT now serves so well.

They could do worse.

Of all stations in the country, WMT was the station with the highest share of its audience in 1982, and it was one of the top five stations every year for five years before that. Its closest competitor, a rock station, has only 17 percent while WMT has 30 percent of the 600,000 Cedar Rapids listeners. Controlling the lion's share of the radio audience as it does, WMT is able to attract 86 percent of all national, and 48 percent of all local radio advertising in the Cedar Rapids market.

The Format Mix

We can gain an idea of how radio formats compete from a study of the Philadelphia market conducted just a few years ago. (See table 10.2.) The twenty-four AM and FM stations in the city at that time were using a total of twelve different formats in their attempt to win a profitable share of the Philadelphia audience. The most popular station in the market was an MOR station with an average of more than 96,000 listeners every quarter hour.

The least popular, a new talk format, had 5,500 listeners. As researcher Peter Hesbacher and his associates have pointed out, shifts in listening audience can be achieved not only by the format itself at one station but by format changes at another. The latter can produce ripples of audience shifts, and a chance for stations with similar formats to gain at the expense of others. (See figure 10.2.)

Figure 10.2

Distribution of the Philadelphia Audience According to Sound Format, 1974–75

(1) July/Aug. 1974[a]

	Total Listenership	Listenership per Station	Percent of Total Listenership	Percent of Popular Music Listenership
Non-music				
News-Information All Talk	168,950	84,475	28.00	
Non-popular music				
Classical	18,000	18,000	2.98	
Beautiful Music	119,300	39,767	19.77	
Popular music				
Jazz	5,900	5,900	.98	1.98
Progressive	28,600	14,300	4.74	9.62
Contemporary	11,800	11,800	1.95	3.97
Country	12,000	12,000	1.99	4.04
Soul	34,700	17,350	5.75	11.68
Top 40	76,050	25,350	12.60	25.59
MOR	103,600	51,800	17.17	34.86
Gold	24,550	24,550	4.07	8.26

(IV) April/May 1975[a]

	Total Listenership	Listenership per Station	Percent of Total Listenership	Percent of Popular Music Listenership
Non-music				
News-Information	172,300	86,150	27.50	
All Talk	5,450	5,450	.87	
Non-popular music				
Classical	16,450	16,450	2.63	
Beautiful Music	140,000	46,667	22.34	
Popular music				
Jazz				
Progressive	35,100	17,550	5.60	12.01
Contemporary	11,700	11,700	1.87	4.00
Country	10,650	10,650	1.70	3.64
Soul	31,150	15,575	4.97	10.65
Top 40	64,450	21,483	10.29	22.04
MOR	96,150	96,150	15.34	32.88
Gold	43,200	21,600	6.89	14.78

[a]Between the two rating periods two stations underwent complete changes in their sound formats: WWDB-FM shifted from Jazz to All Talk and WPEN-AM/FM switched from MOR to Gold.

Reprinted from "Radio Format Strategies" by Peter Hesbacher, Nancy Clasby, Bruce Anderson and David G. Berger, Volume 26, Number 1. © 1976 *Journal of Communication.*

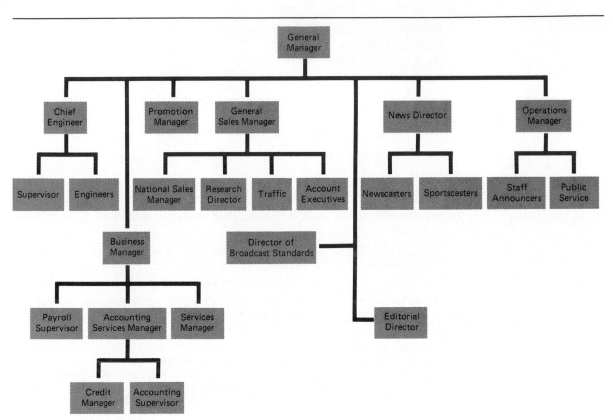

Figure 10.3 The broadcast organization.

The Broadcast Organization

Modern radio's organization is similar to that of other broadcast media operations. Like network radio, network television and local television, American radio stations are divided into five basic departments: management, programming, news, sales and business, and engineering. (See figure 10.3.) Local radio departments are not as complex as network radio or local television, but they function in much the same way as departments in the larger broadcast organization.

Radio Management

Management oversees the operation, sets the tone for station performance, is responsible for hiring and firing, maintaining relations with the community, and ascertaining the station's acceptance with listeners and advertisers. In smaller stations the manager may double as program director and/or chief time salesperson. More than one automated station has been run by little more than a manager with automated music tapes and commercials. The manager turns the station on each morning, then hits the street to sell commercials while the computer-programmed station plays. There is an engineer on call to maintain and repair the equipment when necessary.

Programming

Programming is responsible for production and scheduling of all on-air offerings, with the exception, usually, of news. A principal task for the program director is maintenance of the station's play list, the list of approved records the disc jockeys may use on their record shows. The play list is the program director's primary means of keeping tight control over the station's music format and format consistency. Any decision to add new records to the list, or take old ones off, is given careful consideration.

The production and traffic staff are both important to programming. Production includes recording engineers, announcers, disc jockeys, and program producers. The producers in music format stations are responsible for the tapes and records needed for music show production. The talk format producer might be responsible for contacting the show's guest expert or celebrity and managing in-coming telephone calls so the most interesting and significant questions get on the air. The traffic staff schedules commercials and public service announcements throughout the broadcast day. It makes sure commercial contracts are fulfilled and that the station's programming flows smoothly without loss of commercial time.

Business

The business department, and its sales staff, have the difficult task of selling enough commercial time to keep the station profitable and operating. The station's rate card specifies costs of the station's commercial time. Some cards are more flexible than others. Time periods when the station draws larger audiences—drive time, for example—command better prices than periods when audiences fall off—late at night, for example. A typical radio rate card is shown in figure 10.4. Since the station's format attracts a well-defined audience, the radio sales staff has the task of finding advertisers who want to advertise to the format's particular audience. Rock and roll format stations do not sell many lawn and garden implements, for example.

News

The news department of a small station may be little more than an AP or UPI wire service providing newscasts in a station's closet. "Rip and read" news is not as evident as it was in the early days of formula radio. Station managers have found that ripping the news off the wire and reading it over the air does not create a saleable newscast. A few special format and

Figure 10.4 A comparison of rates from two St. Louis stations. Note how grid prices decrease as more spots are purchased and as audience size decreases.

EZ 102
KEZK·FM
THE ADULT COMBO

KEZK (FM)
1968
ST. LOUIS

MAJOR MARKET RADIO SALES

RAB   **NRBA**

Media Code 4 226 6637 0.00   Mid 011780-000
Adams Radio of St. Louis, Inc.
7711 Carondelet Ave., St. Louis, MO 63105. Phone 314-727-2160.

PROGRAMMING DESCRIPTION
KEZK (FM): MUSIC: Easy Listening. NEWS: capsules at :58. COMMERCIAL POLICY: 4 commercial breaks an hour. Contact Representative for further details. Rec'd 7/1/83.

1. PERSONNEL
Pres. & Gen'l Mgr.—Matt Mills.
National Sales Manager—Cheryl Collins.

2. REPRESENTATIVES
Major Market Radio Sales.

3. FACILITIES
ERP 100,000 w. (horiz.), 100,000 w. (vert.); 102.5 mhz. Stereo.
Operating schedule: 24 hours daily. CST.
Antenna ht.: 500 ft. above average terrain.

4. AGENCY COMMISSION
15%.

5. GENERAL ADVERTISING See coded regulations
General: 2a, 2b, 3a, 3c, 3d, 4a, 4d, 5, 6b, 7b, 8.
Rate Protection: 10g, 11g, 12g.
Basic Rates: 20a, 20b, 21b, 21d, 22a, 23a, 28b, 28c, 29a, 33b.
Contracts: 40c, 41, 43, 44b, 45, 46, 48, 49.
Comb.; Cont. Discounts: 62d.
Cancellation: 70c, 71a, 73b.
Prod. Services: 80, 81.
AM facilities: WRTH.
Affiliated with Major Market Radio Network.
Sold in combination with WRTH. See that listing.

TIME RATES
KEZK (FM)/WRTH COMBINATION
Eff————Rec'd 11/23/83.
AM Drive—Mon thru Sat 5:30-10 am.
Midday—Mon thru Sat 10 am-3 pm.
PM Drive—Mon thru Sat 3-8 pm.
Evenings—Mon thru Sat 8 pm-1 am & Sun all day.

6. SPOT ANNOUNCEMENTS

GRID:	1	2	3	4	5	6	7
AMD	170	160	150	140	130	120	110
MD	180	170	160	150	140	130	120
PMD	170	160	150	140	130	120	110
Eve	120	110	100	90	80	70	60

30 sec: 80% of 1-min.
Sponsorship & fixed positions use next highest grid.

KEZK Only: 60% of KEZK (FM)/WRTH combination.

(A)

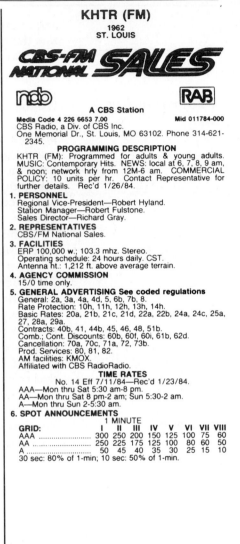

KHTR (FM)
1962
ST. LOUIS

CBS-FM NATIONAL SALES

ncb   **RAB**

A CBS Station
Media Code 4 226 6653 7.00   Mid 011784-000
CBS Radio, a Div. of CBS Inc.
One Memorial Dr., St. Louis, MO 63102. Phone 314-621-2345.

PROGRAMMING DESCRIPTION
KHTR (FM): Programmed for adults & young adults. MUSIC: Contemporary Hits. NEWS: local at 6, 7, 8, 9 am, & noon; network hrly from 12M-6 am. COMMERCIAL POLICY: 10 units per hr. Contact Representative for further details. Rec'd 1/26/84.

1. PERSONNEL
Regional Vice-President—Robert Hyland.
Station Manager—Robert Fulstone.
Sales Director—Richard Gray.

2. REPRESENTATIVES
CBS/FM National Sales.

3. FACILITIES
ERP 100,000 w.; 103.3 mhz. Stereo.
Operating schedule: 24 hours daily. CST.
Antenna ht.: 1,212 ft. above average terrain.

4. AGENCY COMMISSION
15/0 time only.

5. GENERAL ADVERTISING See coded regulations
General: 2a, 3a, 4a, 4d, 5, 6b, 7b, 8.
Rate Protection: 10h, 11h, 12h, 13h, 14h.
Basic Rates: 20a, 21b, 21c, 21d, 22a, 22b, 24a, 24c, 25a, 27, 28a, 29a.
Contracts: 40b, 41, 44b, 45, 46, 48, 51b.
Comb.; Cont. Discounts: 60b, 60f, 60i, 61b, 62d.
Cancellation: 70a, 70c, 71a, 72, 73b.
Prod. Services: 80, 81, 82.
AM facilities: KMOX.
Affiliated with CBS RadioRadio.

TIME RATES
No. 14 Eff 7/11/84—Rec'd 1/23/84.
AAA—Mon thru Sat 5:30 am-8 pm.
AA—Mon thru Sat 8 pm-2 am; Sun 5:30-2 am.
A—Mon thru Sun 2-5:30 am.

6. SPOT ANNOUNCEMENTS
1 MINUTE

GRID:	I	II	III	IV	V	VI	VII	VIII
AAA	300	250	200	150	125	100	75	60
AA	250	225	175	125	100	80	60	50
A	50	45	40	35	30	25	15	10

30 sec: 80% of 1-min; 10 sec: 50% of 1-min.

ethnic stations do not present news, but the strongest trend in radio news is toward the local newscast drawn from local news departments. Radio news departments range in size from one person who covers his or her market with a telephone and a good deal of shoe leather to the several reporters equipped with automobiles and two-way radios. News can be the most prestigious of a station's program offerings. And the radio audiences' interest in it is indicated by the fact that stations without newscasts and news departments often receive calls asking for information about the news—or a local news story.

Engineering

Engineering maintains the technical facilities of the station according to FCC standards, from studio equipment to the transmitter and the station's tower warning lights.

The Radio Industry Today

Radio today is stronger than ever before. Station revenues have risen steadily for more than a decade, with an average annual growth rate of 11.4 percent between 1972 and 1982. Radio's total income was $1.4 billion in 1972, and more than $4 billion in 1982. The forecast is for still more growth and an estimated $6.5 billion annual income by 1986.

Fears that radio's audience would be lost to television have all but vanished. While television has taken charge of the prime-time evening hours, a recent survey indicates the average American now listens to radio almost as much as he or she watches television: three and a half hours a day for radio and three and three-quarter hours a day for television. Radio's popularity and continued improvement in technology have given rise to a formidable array of radio stations. There are approximately 4,800 commercial AM stations, 3,600 commercial FM stations, and 1,200 noncommercial, public, or educational stations. By the end of the 1980s the industry will have shown decided growth. In 1983 the FCC approved plans to place one thousand more FM stations in service, with the first of these new stations to go on the air in 1986.

The industry has unique problems as it turns to the 1990s. Radio stations face sharp competition for the local advertising dollar, but the prospects for success are much brighter than they were in the 1950s, when television first siphoned off national advertising revenue. It seems likely the stations that identify with their listeners, and sharpen their programming accordingly, will survive. In the rising inflation of recent years the radio manager who has utilized effective cost controls has won radio profits. Surviving in public radio, of course, means fighting the same audience and cost control battle in a different arena, and with different backers.

Return of the Networks

One of the brightest aspects of radio's future remains its continued success as a local advertising medium. In 1981 local advertisers accounted for 74 percent, or $3 billion of all radio revenue. National and regional spot advertisers produced $900 million, or 21 percent of the total. The remaining money came from an old friend, network radio, which gave stations about $200 million, or about 5 percent of the total.

The local, regional, and network shares of advertising have remained stable during the past few years. But there are strong indications now that things have changed. Observers say that with local radio revenues rising more than 11 percent a year, network revenues will rise as much as 25 percent annually during the next few years. There are three reasons for the rise in radio network advertising. First, print and television advertising rates have continued to climb sharply during the past years, pushing advertisers toward radio. Second, the modern radio network offers an inexpensive way to narrowcast, or focus as the modern radio format does on specific listening groups (especially age groups). Third, communication satellites have made broadcast networks as much as 60 percent cheaper today than when they sent their signals about the country through wires in AT&T's old landline system. The satellite network also is of much better quality.

Contemporary radio's most popular newscaster/commentator: ABC's Paul Harvey.

Through satellite distribution, radio networks can now reach very large radio audiences at amazingly low costs. CBS' morning drive time "News on the Hour," with poetic Charles Osgood, reaches three million listeners. Mutual's nighttime talk host, Larry King, reaches three and a half million. The king of network radio, ABC's Paul Harvey, reads his . . . speaks his . . . shouts his *news*cast to eighteen million listeners . . . through 850 stations . . . every *day!* The costs of producing each of these radio shows is so low, and the audiences so large, that the networks are showing a 25 percent return on their investment.

Network shows are profitable for local stations, too. They gain money and saleable prestige from the arrangement. The programs pay well and national names and national advertising placed side-by-side with local deejays and local ads enhance both. Local stations are able to sell open spots in a network program to local merchants for premium prices. The potential for an advertising bonanza brought a rash of new networks into operation in the early 1980s. Network drama, sports, and symphonic music all returned to radio in search of the inexpensive-to-reach **target audience.** Estimates indicate there will be twenty or more networks active in radio program distribution before the mid–1980s. One potential threat to a successful return of the radio networks is and will be cable television, with its own celebrated ability to attract a variety of specialized audiences. But cable competition may be overrated. Radio is still the constant companion for an audience on the go. Forty percent of the radio audience listens in cars, at work, and at places where cable and its attention-grabbing television pictures are not likely to go or survive.

Success Story: The Rise of FM

People now spend more time listening to FM than AM radio. FM, after forty years of being like the unwanted child in a royal family, has finally come into its own, but not before its older, less-refined brother, AM, was able to intimidate it, and lock it into the closet two or three times.

AM produces its broadcast sound by modulating (varying) the volume or amplitude of the electromagnetic wave. FM, on the other hand, transmits its signal by modulating the frequency (pitch) of the wave. Early experimentation suggested that frequency modulation had too many problems for use in radio broadcasting, and so the adaptation of amplitude, or volume, modulation for radio seemed the proper course for the broadcast industry.

But with industry growth and development in the 1920s, the brilliant engineer, Edwin Armstrong, was able to overcome FM's problems and produce a workable FM system with all the advantages we know today: absence of background noise distortion and static, and a brilliant, more realistic sound range than AM broadcasting. As noted in chapter 4, Armstrong demonstrated his FM system for David Sarnoff and RCA engineers in 1935. The men were amazed, but Sarnoff realized that converting to the new system would make all existing radio equipment obsolete and slow the development of television. So he not only dismissed Armstrong's new invention but also opposed the inventor when he lobbied before the FCC for spectrum space for an experimental FM station. Armstrong did manage to get an experimental FM station on the air in 1939, however. With CBS support, thirty other FM stations were on the air before World War II began. But all broadcast expansion came to a halt in 1942, in the interest of the war effort.

Unfortunately, the end of the war brought new problems rather than renewed growth. First, the FCC decided it was necessary to move the FM broadcast band to the 88 to 108 MHZ (megaHertz) band, its present location. The change made all existing FM receivers obsolete, and forced FM stations to convince the audience to buy new FM receivers for a broadcast signal that had given only limited service before. Second, AM broadcasters were able, in 1944 and 1945, to convince the FCC that FM would develop faster if used to duplicate AM programs. About 80 percent of the FM stations going on the air were owned by AM stations, and they quickly became FM transmitters of AM programs. The practice was called "simulcasting," and the FCC made it absolute when it held that an FM station engaged in simulcasting had to carry *all* of the AM station's broadcast schedule or none of it. The purpose of the rule was to protect the AM advertisers who might not receive equal treatment if simulcasting were done only during part of the broadcast day. So while FM stations did go on the air, and in greater numbers than ever before, the simulcast programming policy gave listeners no reason to buy new, expensive FM receivers, since FM was little more than a colorless copy of AM.

Meanwhile, of the seven hundred FM stations on the air in the post-War period, ninety or so were independent stations who could not or would not duplicate AM programs. With little audience support, they struggled for a niche in the marketplace in competition not only with television, and the familiar sounds of AM radio, but with local newspapers as well. While the FM independents could offer high-quality music programming with little chatter or other interruptions, they found their small, select audiences less than appealing to most advertisers. Some stations hit on the idea of selling their listeners a program guide with detailed listings of the music to be played and notes on community events as well. (The same idea has since been used by both public and cable television organizations.) The FM program guides sometimes made more money for the station than did their over-the-air advertising.

Independent, "good music" FM stayed alive mainly through the efforts of those who believed in its superior quality and were willing to sacrifice to keep it. For example, one independent station manager in the Deep South kept his FM concert music station alive for years on a few ad sales, charity, and advertising "tradeouts." He took goods and services in exchange for station advertising, since he could not get money. It was a difficult life. He dressed in the best suits, ate at good restaurants—often entertaining friends—and drove a decent automobile (a classy Volkswagen van). But he could not tip the waiters, he had to watch his gasoline money, and more than once the electric company's representative appeared at the station's door to cut the power because the bill had not been paid.

FM's dual status as poor relation and ragamuffin radio began to change in the 1960s as technical improvements brought the medium into the mainstream of American life. The FCC authorized stereo for FM in 1961, enhancing FM's good music image and attracting a wider audience of high-fidelity buffs. The industry introduced FM car radios in 1963, and by 1965 transistor radios also had FM dials.

Even more significant was the FCC's decision to push for better use of FM by tightening restrictions on applications for licenses on the crowded AM band. By 1968 those who wanted a license to operate a radio station found they only could apply for an FM license. Finally, the FCC also began to phase out simulcasting by requiring FM stations in markets of 100,000 or more to program at least one half of their broadcast day with original programs.

The change brought new programming to FM from well-financed, professional broadcasters. Ironically, the FM format that made the first big impression was progressive radio, a mixture of counterculture ideology, album music, and Vietnam war protest. WOR-FM in New York led the way. One of WOR-FM's best-known deejays was "Murray the K" Kaufmann (the "fifth Beatle"). On the West Coast, Tom Donahue of KMPX San Francisco, decorated his studio with tapestries, candles, and a Viet Cong banner. A large number of progressive deejays also emerged at college FM stations. Progressive deejays played sets of music, or two or three cuts, without interruption, talked softly and did not give time and temperature checks. Progressive began to make money with advertising from sandal and head shops, rock concert promoters, and high-fi stores.

By the early 1970s other FM formats—especially beautiful music— were making an impression, too, and FM stations began to show up in audience surveys for the first time. By the middle 1970s, FM had taken as much as 40 percent of the total radio audience. By the late 1970s it had more than 50 percent. FM had arrived.

At last report, AM still was the leader in radio advertising revenue. Despite huge gains in audience shares, FM has been unable to top the older medium during the most lucrative time of the broadcast day: drive time. There are at least two reasons. First, the majority of FM stations do not broadcast formats compatible with drive time needs. Beautiful music does not always suit the bustle and hassle of life in the fast lane. A second reason, beyond FM's control, has been the practice of the American automobile industry, following its usual merchandising pattern, to sell the FM car radio as an extra. Through sales and industry promotion, AM frequently was presented as standard equipment. As a result, the FM-AM radio became the expensive option many buyers dropped when buying an automobile. Production and importation of FM-AM car radios rose steadily each year in the 1970s, but on the average, only 30 percent were FM-AM radios. As a result, the automobile and drive time audience remained, to use the statistical term, heavily skewed toward AM.

Even with their drive time advantage, AM managers have felt heavy pressure from FM's growth. In the 1970s they began searching for a way to compete with FM's quality stereo signal. They petitioned the FCC to revive an idea dropped years before to protect FM: AM stereo broadcasting. In 1980 the commission approved the use of AM stereo and the

AM stereo system manufactured by Magnavox. But the decision encountered a squall of protest. Broadcasters and manufacturers alike demanded that the commission withdraw adoption of the Magnavox system for the systems they favored or had placed in competition. The commission, showered with dissent, decided to leave selection of the technical system to open-market competition. Broadcasters were authorized to purchase and broadcast with any one of the five systems available. Observers now foresee a long period of trial and mistrial before AM radio can offer a reliable, consistent stereo service. Many fear consumers will pay for expensive AM stereo home and car receivers that will become obsolete when a different system is adapted.

Public Radio

Noncommercial or public radio, like FM, has had to fight to survive as a part of the radio industry. A large number of educational institutions put experimental stations on the air in the 1920s, but their hopes of providing educational (AM) radio courses for the public died in the chaos of signal interference before the 1927 radio act, or in the loss of economic support most educational institutions suffered in the Depression of the 1930s. Only thirty-eight of the two hundred licensed educational stations survived those early, troubled years. The others were converted into commercial stations by the late 1930s.

With commercial radio expanding rapidly in a limited spectrum, the educators had the problem of convincing the FCC to reserve space on the radio band until money could be found to rebuild the educational stations. The National Committee on Education by Radio (NCER, formed in 1929) and the National Association of Educational Broadcasters (NAEB, formed in 1934) led the fight. To promote educational radio, NAEB formed a center of exchange for radio programs, creating a rudimentary educational radio network. It was a "bicycle" network, however. The NAEB and its stations could not afford to distribute their programs over a telephone line network so the programs were "pedaled" from station to station—by mail—for broadcast when the individual stations could schedule them.

The educators won a few AM radio allocations in 1938. Then, after World War II, when the FCC moved the FM band to its present 88 to 108 MHZ location, the first twenty channels were given to noncommercial/educational use. And the FCC encouraged the building of educational stations by allowing them to go on the air with only 10 watt transmitters while commercial stations were required to have at least 250 watts. The 10 watt stations were both readily affordable and easy to maintain. Between 1949 and 1965 FM educational stations rose from forty-nine to almost three hundred in number.

In the 1950s the Ford Foundation helped educational broadcasting with large donations of money for program production and distribution. For example, it funded the Public Broadcasting Laboratory and the cost to interconnect stations for true network broadcasting. Then, in 1967, the Carnegie Foundation, in an extensive report (*Public Television: A Program For Action*), called for the establishment of a government corporation to receive and disburse funds in the public interest for public television programming. Congress took the cue and passed, the same year, the Public Broadcasting Act, which established the Corporation for Public Broadcasting (CPB) as a nonprofit educational corporation, with a board of directors of fifteen presidentially appointed members, to obtain grants from private, state, and federal sources.

In 1970, after a careful study of the eight hundred AM and FM educational stations on the air, CPB selected a total of seventy-three to become the foundation for the new National Public Radio (NPR) network. Since its inauguration, NPR has continued to upgrade its network program services, and has developed into an exceptional radio news service with such widely acclaimed programs as "All Things Considered," the evening drive time program on NPR stations. It also has continued to increase its number of affiliates—from the original seventy-three to more than two hundred by the early 1980s. Finally, with support of CPB, and to maintain control over network costs, NPR established satellite interconnection with its network in the 1970s, becoming an industry leader in satellite network interconnection. It now has the potential of broadcasting four separate program services over its own satellite system.

The problems of NPR and public radio, however, remain serious. In 1979 a second Carnegie Commission on Public Broadcasting, after considering the future of public broadcasting, reported that both public radio and public television had suffered from two recurring problems. First, they had not been properly funded. Second, they had not been properly isolated and protected from political pressures. Inflation and Reagan administration budget cutting did much to enhance the funding problem in the early 1980s. Historically, Congress has shown more interest in criticizing NPR's perceived political bias than in insulating the network from political pressure and criticism.

NPR is so visible one readily forgets that it and its more than two hundred affiliates do not comprise all of public radio. There are two other important public radio groups: community or alternative stations, and campus radio stations.

Community stations are dedicated to serving as outlets for individuals who wish to perform on radio—to play music, read their own poetry, or produce radio news documentaries. Lorenzo Milam, the founder of several of these stations, once said community radio is for "live people to talk their talk and walk their walk and know that they are not finally and irrevocably dead." Among the strongest of the community stations are the Pacifica stations, founded by Lewis Kimball Hill. A pacifist, Hill obtained a license for KPFA, a 1,000 watt station in San Francisco, in 1948. Since then Pacifica stations have gone on the air at Berkeley, Los Angeles, New York, Houston, and Washington, D.C. All depend on tax-deductible donations from their listeners for financial support. All broadcast an unusual alternative-culture mix of protest songs, classical music, and social advocacy.

The campus radio stations include educational FM stations of 100 watts or more, and carrier-current stations that send their signals to campus buildings through the campus electrical system. Many of the FM's were originally licensed as 10 watt educational stations in the post-War FCC program designed to encourage educational use of FM. The 10 watt stations now have been phased out, and the FCC no longer allows even educational FM stations on the air with fewer than 100 watts. Even the old 10 watt campus FM stations were hardly educational stations. While they and the carrier-current stations did prove to be good educational training grounds for would-be radio professionals, their programming was, like contemporary campus stations, aimed more at entertaining students with popular music and campus features than imparting information, knowledge, or fostering scholarly learning.

The scene is set for conflict among the three groups of public stations. On one side are the community/alternative stations under the leadership of the National Federation of Community Broadcasters. The NFCB is dedicated to the proposition that public radio should be a free service for the people without central, public control. In opposition is National Public Radio (NPR), and its affiliates, dedicated to building a centralized, network production system to provide a quality, cultural service it feels the public needs and deserves. The campus stations have already known the problem of being in the middle. They offer little in the way of potential expansion for either side. And some occupy spectrum space. It was a suggestion from the NFCB that led the FCC to freeze 10 watt licenses in 1980, and move all stations of 100 watts or less onto the commercial band. The change made room on the public band for more powerful community/alternative stations, and forced 10 watt campus stations to raise their power, or go off the air.

Careers in Radio

The current radio work force is estimated at 100,000 people. The average radio salary is $38,000 annually, or $730 a week. The average beginning salary for a college graduate entering the radio field is about the same as one entering television: $180 a week.

The radio job seeker is well advised to get his or her college degree before seeking full-time employment. A recent survey of radio station managers in the Midwest found that almost half felt the ideal job applicant should have a degree, while almost 60 percent said a person looking for a job in radio news should have a college degree in journalism. The managers also prefer the applicant who has collected some broadcasting experience while he or she earned the degree—through work at the college radio station or from a radio or radio news internship.

Needless to say, the student with the superior academic record is always in demand. Thirty-two percent of managers surveyed said they look for a grade point average of B or better to fill positions. But they also indicated a student's attitude is important. More than one survey has suggested the media manager places a high value on the applicant who shows enthusiasm for the job, and who seems willing to pitch in and "get the job done," as more than one manager has put it.

Radio is a very good medium in which to begin a career. The average station has only twelve employees, and chances are good the beginner will go to work in an organization small enough to get a good foundation in all aspects of the medium—a well-rounded picture of what broadcasting is all about.

Summary

Radio has become the constant companion to almost every American in almost every aspect of life. It wakes, entertains, informs, even rides with us to and from work. It has music and programs for most of us—whether poor or rich, intellectual or physical.

Modern radio is the result of a transformation that took place throughout several years. During the golden age of network radio in the 1930s and 1940s, it provided family entertainment.

With the introduction of television, however, radio's national advertising fell. The last dramatic network programs—soap operas—left the air in 1960. Radio survived as a local and regional ad medium while television was taking control of national advertising.

The disc jockey, recorded music, and local news provided the basis for the new radio. With the national radio network services gone, local management turned to serving local tastes and local information needs.

Stations now present formatted music or information throughout the day to hold their selected audiences. Technology also helped in radio's transformation, providing the transistor radio—for on the go listening—and an improved car radio for drive time listeners.

Several imaginative radio format pioneers led the change from old to new radio, but a good candidate for the title "father of modern radio" probably is Gordon McLendon. McLendon was instrumental in creating modern radio formats—top 40, beautiful music, all news—and developing the modern, radio news department with reporters, cars, and imaginative policies for localized news.

Careful study goes into creating a radio format that will compete with other formats in a station's market. The country music format, for example, has succeeded as a distinct musical format that seldom gives up listeners to top 40 or beautiful music formats.

Adult contemporary, though, has led musical formats in attracting audiences. An important newcomer is urban contemporary, a blend of disco, jazz, rhythm and blues, and adult contemporary. A large number of AM stations have gone to nonmusical talk formats recently to attract larger, more affluent audiences. Talk is much more expensive to produce than a music format, but the returns have been high. All-news differs from talk in that the former is usually a cycle of newscasts—one after another. All news has survived in large cities where larger audiences are available to support its higher operating costs.

The modern radio market is so tightly programmed that a change in format by one station can become an opportunity for other stations to pick up audience losses from the new format.

The radio station organization is basically the same as those of television and network broadcasting. Personnel include administration, programming, business and sales, news, and engineering.

The radio industry has enjoyed an annual growth rate in excess of 11 percent during the past few years. The forecast for the immediate future is for still more growth. Recent surveys indicate the average American spends almost as much time listening to radio as watching television. Meanwhile, rising costs of advertising in television and newspapers have brought a return of network radio programs and advertising to radio.

The new audience king of radio is FM, with more people spending more time listening to FM than AM. In the 1960s the FCC began to push the medium by tightening up on AM licenses and forcing AM stations with FMs to program original material on them or give them up. The introduction of FM stereo and FM car radios helped. AM still holds the advantage in share of advertising revenue, but tough competition with FM is ahead.

Educational, or public, radio has had to struggle to survive in the predominantly commercial American radio system. There still is considerable concern that public radio is underfunded and too often subjected to political pressure. Noncommercial radio has three major factions, the education/public stations often associated with National Public Radio, community/alternative stations which give time freely to performers and advocates from the community, and college campus radio stations.

Questions for Discussion

1. The radio stations that changed from network-type programming to formula radio came to believe that programming consistency was the most important factor in holding a radio audience. Does consistency work? Do most people stick with one station all day unless they are "turned away" by something inconsistent? Can you support the idea that people change from station to station throughout the day to escape being bored by a station's consistency? What are your own listening habits in this regard?

2. Gordon McLendon has been recognized and criticized for his sensational, even astonishing, radio promotions and stunts. What radio promotional stunts have you encountered lately? Are they going out of style? Have you encountered any that seem to be related to the two attributed in this chapter to McLendon? What can be said for radio promotions in general? Are they necessary? Are they ethical? Do they cheapen radio or just make it possible?

3. Name as many radio formats as you can from your personal knowledge. Name only the ones that you personally have heard. Which of these do you like? Which do you dislike? Which would you listen to if nothing else were on? Try to understand exactly what there is about the listening situation that leads you to prefer the format you do. Does the fact that your friends also listen to the format influence you? When you think of the music of the format do you think of people you know—or situations you were in? Do these people and those situations hold you to the format? What is the message of the format you like, what is the message of the one you dislike most?

4. The conflict in public radio seems to reflect arguments of central control versus arguments of grassroots control. The argument for central control by NPR is an argument for quality.

The argument for grassroots control by community stations is an argument for individual rights. Review the readings on libertarianism and authoritarianism in this text and try to relate them to this argument. What would be wrong with a centralized NPR radio? What would be wrong with decentralized, individualistic radio? What would be right? How might each side view the other as time passes?

References

Baker, Kenneth. "An Analysis of Radio's Programming" (1946). *Stay Tuned, A Concise History of American Broadcasting,* edited by Christopher Sterling and John Kittross. Belmont, Calif.: Wadsworth, 1981.

Barnouw, Erik. *A Tower in Bable.* New York: Oxford University Press, 1966.

————. *The Golden Web.* New York: Oxford University Press, 1968.

Blakely, Robert J. *Serve the Public Interest.* Syracuse: Syracuse University Press, 1979.

Byrne, John A. "Remember the Green Hornet? Lowell Thomas" *Forbes,* February 1, 1982, 72–76.

"FCC Issues 'Tenuous' AM Stereo Rankings." *Broadcasting,* March 22, 1982, 72–73.

Fornatale, Peter, and Joshua E. Mills. *Radio in the Television Age.* Woodstock: The Overlook Press, 1980.

Foster, Eugene S. *Understanding Broadcasting.* Reading, Mass.: Addison-Wesley, 1978.

Hesbacher, Peter, Nancy Clasby, Bruce Anderson, and David G. Berger. "Radio Format Strategies." *Journal of Communication* 26, no. 1 (1976): 110–19.

"Newscast Radio Contender: Urban Contemporary." *Television/Radio Age,* March 22, 1982, A1–A4.

"Public Radio's Capital City Roundup." *Broadcasting,* April 26, 1982, 66–68.

"Radio Broadcasting." *U.S. Industrial Outlook, 1982.* Washington, D.C.: U.S. Government Printing Office, 1982.

Sterling, Christopher H., and John M. Kittross. *Stay Tuned, A Concise History of American Broadcasting.* Belmont, Calif.: Wadsworth, 1981.

"Why AM Radio Stations Are Talking Up." *Business Week,* June 15, 1981, 99–100.

Chapter
11

The Magic Lantern: Television and Cable

The medium with mass appeal: Television.

Of all the media operating in America today, the one that appeals to the largest audience is television. While the magazine, the motion picture industry, and the radio have all attracted the mass audience at one time in their history, each now survives by appealing to special interest segments within their former audiences. Television has become the medium of big numbers—the one everybody watches.

When Neil Armstrong and Edward Aldrin landed on the moon in 1969, 125 million Americans watched on television. When Richard Nixon resigned as president of the United States in 1974, 110 million Americans—half of the population—saw and heard the resignation—on television. Today 98 percent of all American homes have at least one television set. And out of a total population of 230 million people, 85 to 105 million watch their sets every night—85 million on Friday, 105 million on Sunday night. Network suspense/mystery programs, such as "The A-Team" or "Magnum, P.I.," draw 25 million viewers on the average, while situation comedies such as "Cheers," "The Cosby Show," and "Diff'rent Strokes" attract 31 million viewers. Feature films have an average audience of 28 million, about the same as that for all programs in prime time, the period between 8 and 11 P.M. when the most recent programs are presented. Even the lowest-rated shows in prime time have audiences of 7 or 8 million households and more subscribers than such highly successful magazines as *Playboy* and *Cosmopolitan*. The evening network newscasts have audiences of at least 7 million homes each, more than two times the circulation of the largest daily newspaper, *The Wall Street Journal*.

Television audiences also tend to be the most varied audiences. While the *Penthouse* subscriber is usually a young man, and *Ms.* appeals to the "thinking" woman, the prime time television audience is made up of women (42 percent), men (35 percent), teenagers (10 percent), and children between the ages of two and eleven years old (12 percent). With only minimal literacy required for participation, television attracts young and old, rich and poor, the sick and the healthy, and people with widely different educational and occupational backgrounds.

The Television Delivery System

Television reaches its audience through a widely dispersed but carefully assigned array of television stations. From the early days of the medium the Federal Communications Commission attempted to assign stations so every set in America would be able to receive at least one station. This policy of establishing and preserving local service has resulted in the construction of 1,100 VHF and UHF stations across the country—many more than in Europe. In the United States there are approximately 525 commercial VHF stations, 275 commercial UHF stations, 100 non-commercial or public VHF stations, and 165 noncommercial or public UHF stations. VHF stations operate on channels 2 through 13, while UHF stations broadcast on channels 14 through 84. The FCC began adding new, low-powered stations to television in 1982 to serve neighborhoods and small communities with still more local television.

Networks

Television networks are a vital part of the commercial television system. ABC, CBS, and NBC each have about two hundred affiliates to carry their productions. The Public Broadcasting System (PBS) includes some 265 participating stations. There are about twenty-five "special events," or regional networks also. Hughes Television Network, for example, is a television sports network; the California Farm Network and the Wisconsin Educational Television Network serve functions explained in their titles.

Pay Television

An increasingly important part of the system is pay television. There are two types: over-the-air subscriber television (STV) and cable television. Since the 1950s STV has grown from one experimental station into an industry with over more than thirty stations and 1.5 million subscribers. STV sends signals over the air in scrambled form. The signals are un-scrambled by decoder boxes in subscriber homes. The cost of the service is borne by subscribers who also "pay per view" (PPV) for special alternative programs their STV station offers.

Cable also began in the early days of television, in the late 1940s. Originally it served towns in areas whose location or geography made television reception difficult. In the 1960s cable began to do more than relay existing television signals from near and far, and to evolve into a full-blown, multichannel service with in-house studio production of programs, and round-the-clock wire news, sports, weather, and movie channels. There now are more than 4,600 cable systems in operation with 2,500 more either waiting for approval or under construction.

In general, television is among the healthiest of the media industries. In recent years, television revenues have increased at an annual growth rate of 13 percent to more than $11 billion a year. And these figures do not include cable.

The industry's relative efficiency can be seen, too, in comparison with the newspaper industry. With fewer basic distribution units (1,100 television stations versus 1,700 daily newspapers), television reaches 20 million more homes (81.5 million television homes versus 62 million in newspaper circulation).

Television Organizations and Operations

The television organization is similar to the radio station and radio network organization. (See p. 262.) Local and network television stations have five departments: management, programming, business and sales, and news. The engineering department operates and maintains most of the technical broadcasting equipment.

Management

Management has the principal responsibility of setting the tone for the operation and the ascertainment of the needs and interests of the community. To retain its broadcast license, management must be able to demonstrate to the Federal Communications Commission that the television station's programming and public service has met community interest and needs.

Programming

Scheduling programs, advertisements, promotional and public service announcements, and all other material is the responsibility of the programming department. The program director is responsible for the station's studio productions, from children's shows to the television ads the station may produce for local ad agencies for a fee. The average station now programs about twenty hours a day (from sign on at 6 A.M. to sign off at 2 A.M., at the end of the late movie or late talk show), or 140 hours a week. If the station is affiliated with a national network, some 60 percent of that time goes to network programs. The rest is taken up with local programs, including local news, syndicated shows and reruns, and movies.

Business and Sales	The business and sales staff handles the station's business, including the time sales contracts with local and national accounts, and the network contract. About 40 percent of the local station's business comes from local accounts. The network contract usually yields close to 10 percent. The largest part of the station's revenue comes from national spot sales independent of the network contract. The station has a national representative (a "national rep") to help sell station time at the national and regional levels. National spots bring in most of the remaining 50 percent of station business.
News	News is now the most important and profitable of all local programs, and one of the more profitable program types for the national networks, too. The average local station has a staff of thirteen full-time news personnel and a news director. Depending on the size of the news staff, there also are news producers, who take charge of assembling individual newscasts; assignment editors, who assign reporters and video camera personnel to cover stories; and tape editors and news writers. In some large news departments, the roster of the news staff also may include a helicopter pilot.
Independent, Noncommercial, and Group Owned Stations	Station operation varies somewhat according to whether the station is independent, noncommercial, or group owned.

Independent stations, ones not affiliated with a national network, obviously must make more of an effort in programming and sales than stations with network affiliation. The over two hundred independents have at the least 10 percent more revenue to acquire, and 60 percent more programming to present to be on a par with network affiliates. Despite these handicaps, some independents have been highly successful.

Public stations, since they were established to broadcast noncommercially have made it their business to go to their audiences for financial support. Public television patrons sponsor or contribute to programming for little more than official, on-air recognition of their contribution, and help bear the cost of local public television offerings and 40 percent of the cost of Public Broadcasting Service (PBS) network broadcasts. Lately, however, rising costs have forced public stations, into ever greater efforts at gathering funds.

Group ownership also is an important factor in the station's operation. As of 1984, the FCC allowed an individual or company to own twelve AM, twelve FM, and seven television stations. Two of the televisions had to be UHF stations. (See chapter 17.) The three national networks own and operate a total of fifteen VHF stations. These "O & O's" have the major advantage of being able to attract highly influential national representation for spot advertising sales. Television groups, such as Westinghouse's Group W with seven AM, two FM, and five television stations, and Metromedia with six AM, seven FM, and seven television stations, also give their stations good sales representation on the national level. They serve, too, as a source of programming. Both the "Merv Griffin Show" and "Mike Douglas Show" began as group station projects. Group W started "PM Magazine," using the facilities of its stations. It has since expanded the production to include more than sixty other stations around the country.

The Program System

As economist Allen Parkman has pointed out, the purpose of television organization—station or network—is to produce viewers per minute of commercial time. Advertisers want numbers, large numbers of viewers before the television set when they present their advertising messages. Television programs are the bait that attracts and holds audiences.

Television has four principal sources of programs:

1. its own in-house program and news departments at the local and network levels;
2. the independent program packagers that work with the networks to produce the majority of network entertainment shows;
3. the program syndicators that distribute original and rerun programs to the local stations;
4. the movie studios, with their original movie productions, film libraries, and new, made-for-television films.

Most within-house programs at the local and network level are news and public affairs program productions. Local television attempted several types of entertainment programs in the 1950s. Following the programming example of network radio, they produced quiz shows, women's programs, and children's programs with some regularity. But locally produced entertainment shows, as indicated below, did little for the station's prestige or profit picture. With audience disinterest and rising production costs the hard-to-sell, amateurish productions were abandoned in the 1960s and news services were expanded. Nonnetwork entertainment shows that have survived usually are syndicated, ones produced by regional networks, or television groups. In time news and public affairs programs became the station's primary programming effort. News offered a distinct service, with less risk of alienating the audience and the advertiser.

As discussed in chapter 4, the development of television's Hollywood connection made Hollywood's independent program packagers the major source of the network prime time television series. The Hollywood product with a successful prime time run also a series becomes available as a local station program through syndication (see chapter 12). Meanwhile, Hollywood's movie studios are also a source of original and second-run material. With network financing and planning, the studios produce the network made-for-television films. In some cases, after prime time exhibition, Hollywood distributes these films in second-run or overseas theatres for added revenue. The studios' film libraries, of course, have been a source of programming since the earliest days of television. Hollywood's current productions now move from theatre to network exhibition with regularity.

In general, therefore, television programs develop from two production tracks: one within the organization that produces news and public affairs, and one outside, mostly in Hollywood, that produces entertainment.

Here Is the News

In the early years of television, historian James Baughman has written, both network and local television management tended to view broadcasting news as something of a "glorious burden." News did not make money; it cost money. But news programs were prestigious and in the public interest. Since they were programs that helped keep the wolves of Congress and government regulation from the door, stations and networks tried to carry them when they could. The local stations, in the early years of television, tended to think of news as a product of the networks and the wire services—possibly, one of many habits left over from network radio days. And since the networks were better funded than the local stations, they provided the leadership for the development of television news.

CBS and NBC began televising regular, fifteen-minute evening newscasts in 1947. To capture the visual aspects of the news, they hired camera personnel from the newsreel companies—companies that had supplied a weekly ration of news films to movie houses beginning in the 1920s. CBS-TV's "Douglas Edwards and the News" led NBC-TV's "Camel News Caravan," featuring snappy John Cameron Swayze. In the early years the newscasts reflected the influence of the newsreel camera people and a desire to present the visual: beauty contests, horse races, fires, and even ribbon cuttings. All had been "news" fare at movie houses for years. But in time the networks incorporated news film procedures into their news operations and their own radio news traditions and values. By 1952, as historians Sterling and Kittross have observed, television news had adopted from radio most of the program formats it would use for decades to come (including the news interview program and the eye-witness account). In time, newsreel filming was adapted to more timely, hard news reporting.

Testing their journalistic prowess, the television networks also covered some special events "live" with their electronic cameras. In 1950 and 1951 television cameras opened on the daytime sessions of Senator Estes Kefauver's probes of organized crime, with the evening newscasts rebroadcasting filmed highlights of the investigations. The first coast-to-coast news broadcast, the coverage of the signing of the Japanese peace treaty in San Francisco, came in 1951. Events of the first national presidential election campaign were broadcast the following year. Prominent in that campaign coverage was the now famous "Checkers" speech by Republican vice-presidential candidate Richard Nixon, in which Nixon successfully defended his financial situation and his candidacy. The 1952 campaign also gave an indication of the potential of television for political debate in a series broadcast in Massachusetts and won by Congressman John F. Kennedy over Henry Cabot Lodge. Among the big, nonpolitical stories of the era was the reporting of General Douglas MacArthur's homecoming, following removal from his Korean War command by President Truman.

The early 1950s more often are remembered for another type of television news program, however. In 1951 Edward R. Murrow brought his brilliant war reporting record to television with a new CBS weekly television series called "See It Now." Murrow and his producer/partner Fred W. Friendly created the show to provide more investigative reporting than the fifteen-minute daily newscasts. After experimenting for two years, the two men came head-to-head with the major public issue before the country: the question of the "enemy within" and its chief supporter, Senator Joseph McCarthy.

The encounter with the junior senator from Wisconsin proved to be more than dramatic. "See It Now" filmed the hearings being conducted by the senator and captured him and his tactics as he badgered and bullied witnesses with sneers, misleading insinuations, and an arrogant disregard for the truth. The "See It Now" broadcast gave many Americans a stunning, firsthand revelation of the man who had, for many months, seemed heroic while "speaking" from behind newspaper headlines. The morning after the show Murrow was applauded and cheered as he walked in the streets of New York. He and a friend had to take a cab to escape the crowd that gathered around to congratulate him.

In the early 1950s, the Murrow-Friendly "See It Now" program and, later, television coverage of the Senate's investigation of communist infiltration of the U.S. Army did much to negate Senator Joseph McCarthy's influence and his Red scare campaign by revealing his bullying and arrogant tactics. McCarthy is seated at the left, beside counselor Roy Cohen.

The new NBC-TV team of Chet Huntley (left) and David Brinkley at the Democratic National Convention in 1956.

Unfortunately, the Murrow–Friendly success was short-lived. Television production was growing more expensive by the year and "See It Now's" prime time ratings were low. Alcoa, the sponsor, withdrew support in 1955, fearful of being associated with so controversial a program. After two years of being shuffled around the CBS schedule, Madison Avenue shop talk decided "See It Now" would be better named "See It Now and Then." The show finally was cancelled during the recession of 1957–58, when CBS, in an economy drive, made deep cuts in its staff and programming. That "See It Now" was replaced by the game show "Beat the Clock" did little to quiet the outrage voiced by the program's supporters.

In 1959, as advertiser demand for television time picked up again, CBS presented a new "glorious burden" documentary program, "CBS Reports." It and other network news documentary programs, such as NBC's "White Paper," "David Brinkley's Journal," ABC's "Scope," ABC "Closeups," and ABC "News Reports" often were successful in winning awards. Yet they were always at the bottom of the network ratings and had to be sold to advertisers at rates below cost.

Perhaps the most important year of the 1950s for the development of television news was 1956. That year NBC decided to challenge the CBS lead in news and improve its coverage of the second Eisenhower-Stevenson presidential campaign. The move brought together a new reporting team, Chet Huntley ("old stone face") and David Brinkley ("impish"), to compete with the CBS team of Edward R. Murrow and Eric Sevareid. It worked. The NBC Huntley-Brinkley team proved to be more interesting—and less somber—than the competition, winning the ratings race for the convention broadcasts. Following that success, NBC moved Huntley and Brinkley into anchor positions to replace John Cameron Swayze in the evening newscast. (Swayze went on to do television commercials.) The popularity of the two helped establish the evening newscast in the public mind. Huntley was in New York and Brinkley in Washington, D.C., and the team's sign off, "Good night, David," "Good night, Chet," became a catch phrase around the country. The "Huntley-Brinkley Report" held the lead in ratings until 1970 when Huntley, by then a household name associated with a daily, household service, retired.

Walter Cronkite, meanwhile, had become the CBS evening news anchor in 1962, and had offered NBC serious competition for the largest share of the growing television news audience. With Huntley's retirement, CBS and Cronkite took the lead, holding it until 1980, when Cronkite retired. By then the evening network news ratings race was becoming more of a three-way ratings race. Under Roone Arledge, ABC challenged the CBS and NBC leaders by hiring top journalists from both of them (including NBC's David Brinkley and CBS's Hughes Rudd), dressing up the ABC evening news sets, and utilizing the electronic production techniques Arledge had mastered as ABC's director of sports programs. Arledge's attempts to hire Dan Rather forced CBS to make its own decision to retain Rather. To keep him CBS virtually guaranteed him the CBS evening news anchor following Cronkite's retirement.

The evening news is now among the most important and influential programs on network television. Having the leading evening newscast offers great rewards in prestige for the network. But since the evening newscast audiences now also are large enough to attract advertising accounts of considerable revenue, the networks are committed to winning the evening news ratings race for both prestige and the money that top ratings bring. The total revenue from network evening news commercials in 1983 was almost $350 million a year. The stakes are so high the networks are willing to pay the news anchors who can attract and hold the news audience millionaire salaries. Recent estimates put the annual salaries of CBS's Dan Rather at or near $2 million, NBC's Tom Brokaw at about $1.7 million a year, and ABC's Peter Jennings at $1 million. The anchors command such high salaries because of their financial importance to the networks. When the respected and popular Walter Cronkite retired in 1980, the CBS evening news ratings dropped, putting CBS behind ABC and the late anchorman Frank Reynolds. As a result, CBS had to cut its advertising rates for the evening news by $20,000 a minute. Such a cut, if continued, would cost a network $100,000 or more per news program, or $500,000 a week, and $260 million a year. The evening news, to say the least, has become big business.

In 1968 CBS introduced a new type of news program, "60 Minutes," which presented three to four stories from three or more correspondents rather than one long documentary exploring a single topic. The shorter investigative pieces explored a range of stories that included investigations of medical quacks, the used car business, the high salaries paid network evening news anchors, and the Soviet/Afghanistan war. (The latter included pictures of "Ghunga Dan" Rather in native disguise inside Afghanistan.) In the 1979–80 season, "60 Minutes" became the first regular network news program to earn the highest ratings of any program in prime time. In the early 1980s it was at or near the top of the ratings while ABC's similar "20/20" also had good success. While the news documentary failed with audiences, the bright, entertaining, investigative, news magazine program succeeded.

And Now, the Local News

The 1960s gave viewers television coverage of the assassination of President Kennedy in 1963 and the amazing "live" pictures of man's first landing on the moon in 1969. But probably the most important event of the decade for broadcast journalism came—also in 1963—when both NBC and CBS extended their fifteen-minute newscasts to half an hour. ABC made the change soon after. The change not only put more television network news into the American living room, it created more advertising spots for news at the network and the local levels, since the thirty-minute network newscasts allowed local stations to change from fifteen- to thirty-minute newscasts, too, or even to move to two thirty-minute newscasts "wrapped around" the network newscast: thirty minutes before the national news and thirty minutes after it.

The expansion of the evening news hour came at a time when local stations had confirmed it was difficult to produce local programs that could compete with slicker network and syndicated shows and be of interest to the local audience and local advertisers. Expanding the local evening newscast, and the station's local news service, proved to be a practical solution to the problem. A good news program could be produced more readily than the often embarrassing kiddie or ladies' shows that collected very little audience. News programs also were appealing to local and national advertisers. By 1969 local stations were doubling their news budgets. Viewers in larger cities (with six stations) found they could watch an average of five to six local newscasts per day per station. That the newscasts could still be counted as public service programs at license renewal time remained an added advantage. Today the newscast is usually the only program, or the most important program, the local television station produces. And it is a paying program.

Stations owned by newspapers, with their newswise management, led in the building of the local television news audience. In 1965 newspaper stations as a group had the highest newscast ratings in the top one hundred markets. But by 1975 television group-owned stations had caught up and passed them and led in local newscast ratings, probably as a result of being more adept at reporting the news on television.

The local newscast developed distinguishing characteristics: expensive sets, graphics, filmed reports, and smooth news delivery with appropriate sound tracks. The players on the set: an anchor, an enthusiastic sportscaster, a weather person (often a "weather girl") and, in time, a female anchor to talk in tandem with the male anchor. It seemed like an attractive family of four at times: the fatherly anchor, his sometimes seriously expert, sometimes crazily giddy weatherperson, a sporty son, and a fresh, female partner for father.

Figure 11.1 ENG or electronic news gathering equipment allows TV news to go into the field with portable cameras and video tape recorders, and to send "live" signals back to the studio by microwave (note studio monitors behind news anchors).

The New ENG Technology

One of the most important influences on television news came in the 1970s with the invention and adoption of modern ENG, or electronic news-gathering equipment. By teaming sophisticated portable electronic color cameras with high-quality microwave equipment and video tape recorders, the television news department was able to eliminate delays in developing and presenting motion picture news film. Stories on video tape could go on the air within minutes rather than hours. And the ENG crew needed little more than a clear shot back to the station for their microwave to "go live" with pictures and sound reports from the field, and two-way conversations with those at the scene. In time, finding line-of-sight locations became less of a handicap as ENG crews learned to bounce their signals off buildings and mountains or relay them by overhead helicopter to the evening newscast. The new technology, and skillful use of it, made the video tape news report, and the live news report from the field, a staple of the local television newscast. (See figure 11.1.)

Another important addition to news technology has been the communication satellite. When he addressed NBC listeners via Telstar from Europe in the 1960s, David Brinkley became the first to send news by satellite. Presidential visits to China, Olympic games—and reports of the Palestine Liberation Organization's kidnapping of Israeli athletes—speeches in England, and fighting in the Middle East all have come to America via the satellite "bird."

Direct reporting by ENG and satellite is not without its problems. The new technology has increased the mobility of the television reporter, but it has not given him or her increased story preparation time. The television reporter has only minutes to get ready for his or her "stand up" before it is delivered. As one television news producer has put it, the need for Renaissance men and women in broadcast journalism is now greater than ever. Television needs reporters who can go beyond covering the breaking elements of a story; ones who can think about the art and culture, the news reactors, and the news resources in the story area.

The News Doctors

Probably the most controversial factor in television news has been the work of the news consultants, or the "news doctors," as they have been called. The news consultants attempt to improve a newscast's ratings by suggesting changes in the broadcast, so it will attract a larger audience. They survey the audience to find out what is wanted from the program, then use the survey information to "package" the program for the viewer. As Frank Magid, a leading consultant, has written:

> Many journalists make the error of assuming that good factual reporting alone will involve typical "concerned" citizens. The truth is that there aren't too many "concerned" listeners out there. . . .

The consultants insist they do not interfere with the journalistic process or intrude in the news content of the newscast. Magid's recommendations to stations have included the following:

1. replacement of one or more news personnel with one or ones more acceptable to the audience;
2. use of the tandem format, where one anchor then the other delivers the news (like the old "Huntley-Brinkley Report," or the more recent Mudd-Brokaw "Nightly News" on NBC);
3. use of a certified meteorologist to deliver the weather report;
4. beginning a news or sports segment with an evocative opinion rather than a fact to attract attention ("The Angels lost the last shot they had at the World Series today and it's still only May!" versus "The Angels lost to Boston 5 to 4 this afternoon at Fenway Park.");

5. development of a team atmosphere among newscast personnel, including conversations between members of the news team and sets that show the news team sitting together;
6. use of promotional slogans that emphasize the friendliness and warmth of the station's news department;
7. use of evocative titles for the newscast ("The World Tonight," versus "The Six O'Clock News").

Those who criticize news consultants charge they have turned local television news into banal, happy talk news with more show business gimmicks than news and information. Those who applaud say they have made local stations aware of the importance of their news departments while showing them how to reach the news audience and talk to it "where it lives." The consultants ask, "Who wants to talk to an empty church?" The critics reply, "Who wants to cater to the mob?"

The $260 Million Question

Meanwhile, with both local and network news departments doing well, an inevitable conflict between the two finally came in 1982. When CBS and NBC moved to extend their thirty-minute evening newscasts to a full hour, the local stations rebelled. Since the networks made their first fifteen-minute extension in 1963, the FCC had decided to diversify the industry's television production capability. In the prime time access rule of 1972, the commission limited network programs to only three hours of station time, Monday through Saturday, to encourage stations to seek alternative program sources. But with local production expensive and chancey, the stations turned instead to syndicated game shows and reruns to fill the time (usually between 7 and 8 P.M.) and attract more local and national advertising. One estimate is that both CBS and NBC affiliates would have lost $260 million in advertising if they had given up the half hour and the ad time the networks wanted. The local stations' loss would have been the networks' gain. What is more, the $260 million in new ad revenue would have been gravy for the networks, since the advertising they already had in their first half hour of news would have paid for the new, hour-long newscast. The networks were spending about $240 million a year on their evening newscasts; the thirty-minute extension would have resulted in a profit of more than 100 percent.

With affiliate pressure rising, CBS and NBC decided to postpone any extension of their thirty-minute newscasts indefinitely. It probably is only a matter of time until the issue arises again, however. The hour-long evening newscast has audience and advertiser appeal the networks are not likely to ignore. Meanwhile, all three networks busied themselves with extending their news offerings to other hours of the broadcast schedule.

Here Is the News, Brought to You By a Pretty, Young Woman

Close to the charge that broadcast journalism is preoccupied with the cosmetic aspects of television—interested in reporters better trained to use a hair dryer than a typewriter—are the charges brought by women journalists who feel they are more often expected to be beauty queens than journalists. While television's women reporters are no longer asked, as the late Jessica Savitch once was, to tape their ankles together to be sure they sit primly before the cameras, there is good reason to believe women journalists are often hired to dress the set rather than address the camera.

In recent years nothing seems to illustrate the point better than the case of television newswoman Christine Craft. In 1982 thirty-seven-year-old news anchor Craft of KMBC-TV in Kansas City, Missouri, discovered the hard way how important "looks" are to female newscasters. Although her evening news had taken the lead in the ratings in the eight months she had been on the job, a news consultant market survey indicated the audience found her less than comely. "She's been ridden hard and put away wet [and looks] like 40 miles of bad road," reporter Jane Mayer quotes one survey response. The station decided to "spruce up" Craft's appearance with hair styling, cosmetics, and a coordinated wardrobe, but news doctor surveys indicated viewers still found her unattractive. When her news director offered her the choice of leaving the station or becoming a staff reporter, Craft decided she would leave—but also that she would sue. She returned to her former position as anchor at KEYT-TV in Santa Barbara, California. But she also filed a $1.2 million sex discrimination suit in Missouri courts, charging she was a journalist, not a beauty queen, and that she was not too old or unattractive to do her job.

In the legal battle that followed a jury awarded Craft $500,000 in damages in her first trial. And in 1984, after that trial was thrown out on appeal, she won $325,000 in damages in a second trial, on charges Metromedia, the defending corporation, had hired her under fraudulent conditions. Metromedia was considering an appeal at last report.

Craft's story has dramatized the frustration of many women who now serve as news anchors across the country. There seems to be an old, unspoken law that old anchorwomen never die; they just get replaced by younger faces. The Radio and Television News Director's Association reported recently as many as 36 percent of the estimated 1,400 anchor positions in U.S. newscasts are held by women. But, as still another survey has revealed, only 3 percent of those news anchors are women 40 or older.

Careful consideration of the situation suggests, however, that KMBC-TV was not a sexist tyrant in the Craft situation. The station was unable to present documented evidence that Craft, for all her journalistic skills, was not able to fill the role of anchor as needed, even after the station gave her support in the form of hair styling and wardrobe changes. More than one anchor*man,* with less support, has lost his job for not attracting a large enough audience. So if there is a villain in this piece, perhaps it is the audience. Viewers, with their socially established values, accept and reject news anchors. They should be blamed as much or more than some stereotypical "hard-hearted, chauvinistic station manager" who supposedly decides what faces deliver television news. It is the audience that should bear at least some of the responsibility for inequitable conditions women journalists now know in television.

Anchor-host Ted Koppel of ABC-TV's "Nightline," one of the first successful expansions of network news into late evening-hours programming.

ABC already had added "Nightline" to its late evening offerings. In the early 1980s CBS, NBC, and ABC all added overnight and early morning news programs to their schedules. There has been one "overnight" failure at NBC.

Fun and Games: The Entertainment Shows

The source for most entertainment programming for television networks and local stations alike—affiliate or independent—is Hollywood, the movie, television program, and syndication capital of the world. The independent program packagers produce the prime time television series. They include Stephen J. Cannel Productions ("Greatest American Hero," "The A-Team," "Hardcastle and McCormick," and "Hunter"), Lorimar ("Dallas," "Falcon Crest"), MTM Enterprises ("The Mary Tyler Moore Show," "Lou Grant," "Hill Street Blues," "Remington Steele," "St. Elsewhere"), Embassy TV ("Who's the Boss?" "Diff'rent Strokes") as well as Norman Lear ("All in the Family," "The Jeffersons") and Aaron Spelling Productions ("The Love Boat," "Hotel"). Some of the major movie studios are also active in television program production. Among Warner Brothers credits, for example, is "Alice." "Murder, She Wrote," and "Simon and Simon" belong to Universal, while Twentieth-Century Fox won prime network time with "AfterMASH."

To put it mildly, creating and establishing a successful television series is a difficult and expensive enterprise. For any two successes there are eight or more failures. In recent years, some new series have become instant flops, being jerked off the air before they completed their first season. Of the half dozen or so shows that do make it, however, the financial rewards can be astronomical by the time the first run is completed and syndication begins.

One hour of television entertainment costs $700,000. Therefore, every series, which has twenty-two to twenty-four original episodes to run and rerun through the 52 week year, costs $16,000,000. (Considering the costs, it is easy to understand how few companies other than the networks are willing to take a chance on financing a new series.)

The production of one network show takes about six months. The process begins when the producer decides on a story idea and assigns it to a writer.

The writer works on the story treatment for three weeks. The network standards department (the network "censor") then checks the treatment for "taste" and libel, and returns it to the writer who puts in another two weeks or so on it. With the producer, the writer then polishes the revised draft, for a week or two. After the script has received final approval—another two weeks—the preproduction process of budgeting, casting, and set construction begins.

The filming of the episode usually begins in the thirteenth or fourteenth week, and is completed in seven or eight days. Action/adventure episodes such as "The Fall Guy," "Knight Rider," and "Magnum, P.I." are shot on location. A sitcom such as "The Jeffersons," "Newhart," or "Three's Company" usually is filmed from beginning to end before a studio audience, as if it were a stage play. One practice is to perform the script for two different audiences. The producer can then choose the best parts (the best laughs, acting, etc.) from the two recordings and make one good version.

With the episode filmed, or on tape, postproduction work begins: the editing of the picture story and the recording of voice and musical tracks. Postproduction usually starts in the fifteenth week and takes about seven weeks to complete, so the episode is ready for delivery to the network by the end of the twenty-second week. If all goes well, it arrives one month before air time. *If all goes well.* Some shows have been delivered one day before air time. At least one was delivered just an hour before air time.

The investment in time and money required to make a television series is so great the independent packagers and the network producers do not like to gamble with untested story ideas. They prefer to go with a sure thing whenever possible. To do so, they often play follow the leader or ride on the coattails of other, successful productions. Like book and movie producers, they create new programs by imitating ones that have already met with success. The success of the melodrama "Dallas," for example, produced a string of imitators: "Dynasty," "Flamingo Road," and "Hotel." Obviously, not all were successful.

Carroll O'Connor as Archie Bunker and Rob Reiner as "Meathead" Mike Stivic of the innovative situation comedy "All in the Family." "Family" brought a new realism to television comedy; it also provided secondary characters that were "spun off" into lead characters in their own programs.

Another technique for creating new programs is the spinoff, or making a program by taking a popular, secondary character in a successful series and establishing him or her in another series of his or her own. Norman Lear lifted the principal characters for "Maude" and "The Jeffersons" from the highly successful "All in the Family" (which was itself adapted from a successful show on British television). Lou Grant was a bumbling, good-for-a-laugh television news editor on "The Mary Tyler Moore Show" before he was transformed into the tough city editor of the Los Angeles *Tribune* in "Lou Grant," a very successful series about newspapering.

Television producers also like a book title with a good reputation. The most successful program to date has been the television miniseries adapted from Alex Haley's novel *Roots. Shogun, East of Eden,* and *Rich Man, Poor Man* all were well-received novels before they were produced for television.

The majority of television programs, however, are derived from story types developed before the television era by network radio and the movie studios in Hollywood. In a study of the television shows produced during a twenty year period, Joseph R. Dominick and Millard C. Pearce delineated nine types of entertainment programs presented on television. They are, with some recent examples:

- quiz/game shows: "Family Feud," "Wheel of Fortune";
- interview/talk/demonstration: "Real People," "Hour Magazine";
- situation comedy (or sitcoms): "I Love Lucy," "Alice," "Mama's Family," "The Cosby Show";
- comedy/variety: "The Bob Hope Show," "Tonight," "Saturday Night Live";
- musical variety: "The Lawrence Welk Show," "Donny and Marie," "Solid Gold";
- general variety: "Toast of the Town," "Hollywood Palace";
- dramatic anthology: "The Twilight Zone," "Darkroom";
- action/adventure: "Chips," "Star Trek," "Hill Street Blues";
- general drama: "General Hospital," "M*A*S*H," "Masterpiece Theatre."

Dominick and Pearce have found that after production moved to Hollywood in the 1950s and 1960s, the networks began presenting more of Hollywood's private eyes, cowboys, and spys, or action/adventure, than anything else. ABC-TV, with its early association with Warner Brothers, led the way with action/adventure programs. NBC quickly jumped onto the coattails, as did CBS. (See figure 11.2.)

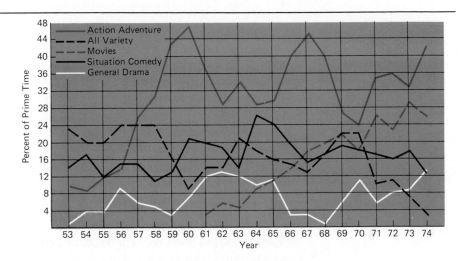

Figure 11.2 Dominick and Pearce's chart of prime time program types: 1953–74 Hollywood's action-adventure shows commanded the highest percentage of time during the period.

The popular action/adventure stories of the period were westerns. While sitcoms have remained popular for prime time viewers, game, quiz, and variety shows have all but disappeared from the prime time schedule. Quiz shows do appear regularly in the daytime network schedule, and they are likely to remain there for some time. No one wants a repeat of the quiz show scandals of the 1950s. Many feel the relatively low cost of producing the game show could bring it back into prime time as costs of Hollywood production continue to rise. For the time being, the networks seem satisfied to use the comedy and musical variety show as "specials" to break the boredom of two dozen or so reruns.

The Programming Game

Finding and producing a program that possibly will attract a large segment of the television audience is just the first step in programming at the network or the local station. To establish an audience for the program, the programmer must (1) consider its competition, (2) understand the audiences that are available at the proposed times, (3) know what programs come before and after the possible time slots for the new show, and (4) know if the potential audience will be large enough to attract enough revenue to return a profit.

Through the years, programmers have found that the hardest way to build an audience for a new show is to try to steal from an established one. It is wiser to offer a reasonable alternative to the established show, or counter program, rather than offer a similar program. It is more wise, also, to place a new program in competition with other shows where the audience is about equally divided. It's easier to take a little from two programs than a lot from one very successful one.

One of the easiest things to do, on the other hand, is to hold an audience that is left over from a show that has just signed off. New programs get a strong lead-in if they follow a successful show, even if the lead-in is the last show watched before the set is turned off at night. Sustaining an audience from hour to hour also is easier than creating a new audience.

Experience also has shown that it is better to bring the program to the audience rather than try to pull the audience to the program.

A good example of how the program game can be played came with the rise of "Dallas" from new program in 1978 to leading prime time program in the early 1980s. CBS entered "Dallas" in the Saturday evening offerings its first year in competition with two other new shows: "Fantasy Island" on ABC, and "Sword of Justice," a now-forgotten remake in modern dress of "The Mark of Zorro" on NBC. "Fantasy Island" had a popular lead-in with "Love Boat," which had been building an audience since 1977. "Dallas" did not fare as well. Its lead-in, "American Girls," was a coattail version of "Charlie's Angels" and was dropped within a month of its introduction. "Fantasy Island" finished the year as seventeenth in the ratings. "Dallas" survived the cut.

The next season, CBS moved the program to Friday night, in competition with ABC's "Friday Night Movie," and a police/adventure named "Eischied" on NBC. The great improvement was that "Dallas" had a new, solid lead-in program: "The Dukes of Hazzard." Together, the two climbed to the top of the ratings. "Dukes" was ninth and "Dallas" sixth by the end of the season. The following year, in the same time spots, with the same mutual support, "Dukes" rose to number two, and "Dallas" became number one. Both continued high in the ratings in the 1981–82 season as CBS added "Falcon Crest," another big family extravaganza to follow "Dallas." The intent, it seems safe to say, was to build another winner with the lead-in power from the successful show. Throughout the period, ABC and NBC followed counter-programming strategy, offering reasonable alternatives to the CBS lineup. ABC offered movies, including *The Deerslayer,* a thriller anthology named "Darkroom" featuring James Coburn as host, and NFL Football exhibition games. NBC competed with made-for-television movies, police drama "McLain's Law," and low-cost, low-audience, low-loss "NBC Magazine" from the NBC news department. Both ABC and NBC evidently found it prudent to ignore the CBS Friday night success and attack the schedule at other, weaker points.

Mighty Numbers: The Ratings

Success or failure in programming is measured by one important, controversial system: the ratings system. Broadcasting has had the problem of discovering the size and nature of its audience from the earliest days of radio—the first experimental radio broadcasts ended with a plea for

Linda Gray as Sue Ellen and Larry Hagman as the dastardly J. R. Ewing of "Dallas." Even the popular "Dallas" found that building a top television audience was not easy. It struggled for four seasons until it finally became the number-one-rated show on the air in 1980.

cards and letters from anyone who had heard the broadcast. The success of commercial radio in the 1920s and 1930s gave rise to systematic audience surveys with scientific sampling, personal, and telephone interviews, and a mnemonic device now called the media diary. Audience research is at heart interpersonal and intrapersonal communication. Audience members are asked to recall what they have viewed, or to keep a record of their own recollections of what they have viewed and report these data to survey teams. Television audience research also makes use of devices that record when the television set is turned on, what channels are watched, and when the set is off.

In general, there are three basic statistics that are used to describe the television audience:

1. HUT, or the percentage of Homes Using Television during any given period;
2. the share, as in radio, is the percentage of all sets turned on which are tuned to a particular program;
3. the rating, or the percentage of *all* the sets (on or off) that are tuned to a particular program.

HUT tells how large a viewing audience is at a particular time, a share indicates how well a program is doing in relation to its competition, and a rating indicates how well the program is doing with the television public. (See figure 11.3.) Ratings of thirty are unusual for network programs. "Dallas" had a 34.5 rating average to make it number one in 1980–81. There has not been a program with an average rating of forty since "Gunsmoke" in 1959. High ratings mean large audiences and a hot product for the television sales department. As ratings go up, sales rates go up, and as rapidly as the market will allow. Of course, if a program

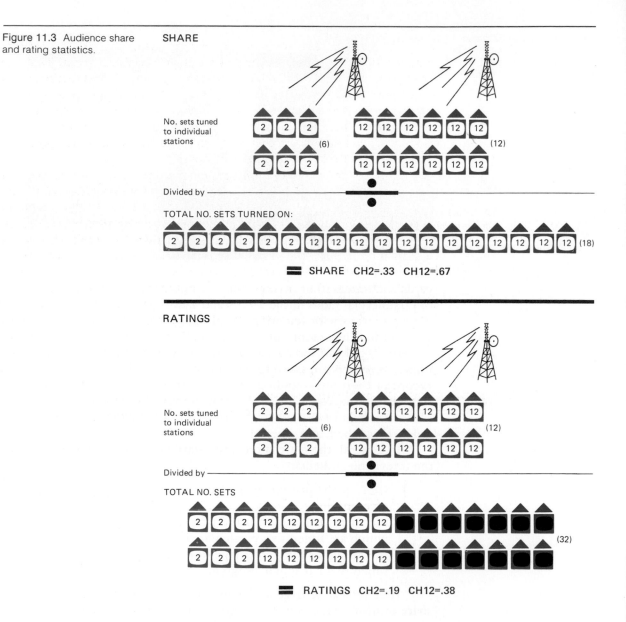

Figure 11.3 Audience share and rating statistics.

SHARE

No. sets tuned to individual stations

TOTAL NO. SETS TURNED ON:

SHARE CH2=.33 CH12=.67

RATINGS

No. sets tuned to individual stations

TOTAL NO. SETS

RATINGS CH2=.19 CH12=.38

is not doing well in the ratings, it still may not be time to "dump it" for something new. A rating of ten, with a share of forty, may indicate the program is doing well at a bad time and that a new program might do much worse. Network evening news usually draws a twelve rating or more on all three networks.

Since it is not practical to take a census of the viewing habits of 81.5 million television homes, all audience statistics are derived from samples of the audience. For the most part, viewing habits for the country are estimated by samples of about twelve hundred television homes—although samples of twenty-four hundred are used on a regular basis. For those with little knowledge of sampling theory, even a sample of twenty-four hundred seems unreasonably small as a basis for predicting the viewing habits of 81.5 million homes.

Those who defend sampling theory point out that a physician does not need all of a patient's blood to make an accurate blood test. There is good reason to believe that television audiences, like blood, are homogenous—consistent—enough to make accurate predictions from audiences samples. After all, most of us media users follow the same general life-style, eat about the same food, play the same games—don't we? It is true that a complete census of the television audience could give a more accurate description of viewing habits (although it would include more errors, too). But the question is, considering the cost of taking a complete census of 81.5 million homes, how much accuracy can we afford? The major research firms feel that with properly drawn samples they can predict audience viewing habits within 1.3 percentage points (plus or minus). That is, a national television program with a rating of thirty-five can be said with confidence to have a rating somewhere between 33.7 and 36.7, and an audience of between 27.5 and 29.9 million TV homes. For most in the television industry the present cost of more accurate estimates is too high.

To insure the integrity of broadcast audience ratings, the National Association of Broadcasters and the major television networks have formed the Broadcast Ratings Council (BRC) to audit and accredit companies engaged in continuous audience measurement. The BRC accredits two major television ratings firms: (1) The American Research Bureau, or Arbitron, which provides a rating service for local radio and TV; and (2) The A. C. Nielsen Company, which provides rating services for both local and national television. Nielsen is the only company performing television audience research at the national level.

Both Arbitron and Nielsen use diaries and television meters to keep records of programs watched. (See figure 11.4.) The Nielsen audimeter is attached directly to the television set and makes a record of the times and the channels the set is on and tuned to. Arbitron places twelve hundred of its recording meters in homes selected at random from telephone books, and uses samples of twenty-four hundred for its diary studies of viewing. Meter and diary results are compared as the audience statistics are formed.

Figure 11.4 (a) A page from the Arbitron Diary. (b) The Nielsen audimeter which, when attached to a television set, records the times the set is on and the channels to which it is tuned.

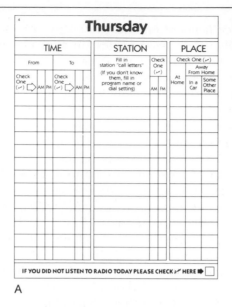

Thursday

TIME				STATION			PLACE		
From		To		Fill in station "call letters" (If you don't know them, fill in program name or dial setting)	Check One (✓)		Check One (✓)	Away From Home	
Check One (✓) ⇨	AM	PM	Check One (✓) ⇨	AM	PM		AM	FM	At Home	In a Car	Some Other Place

IF YOU DID NOT LISTEN TO RADIO TODAY PLEASE CHECK ✓ HERE ➡ ☐

A

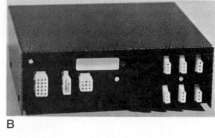

B

Both Nielsen and Arbitron "sweep" the local television audience for four weeks in February, May, and November, during "ratings week," as the periods are called. Nielsen also uses the audimeter to give weekly and overnight national audience viewing reports. The audimeters in sample homes are connected directly to Nielsen headquarters in central Florida, where their data is fed into computers. The daily audience reports are drawn from samples of television homes in large metropolitan areas.

Critics argue the audimeter does not report who is in front of the set when it is on, and that the diaries from sample homes may well be fabricated or at least filled with inaccurately recalled programs. Despite the criticism about audience samples, meters, and diaries, no one has yet proposed a more accurate or economical method for estimating the size and the viewing habits of the television audience.

Getting the Money

The rating system has helped commercial television stay a successful breadwinner in the advertising marketplace since the 1950s. Despite rising production costs and rising inflation, television advertising sales have either held their own or risen higher, even in recent years of inflation/depression.

In television, as in radio, the basic unit for sale is a piece of time: the second. The average network television commercial costs at least $1,000 a second, with six seconds of spot advertising on special productions such as the Super Bowl costing $60,000 and one thirty-second commercial, $300,000. The costs of commercial time are rising so rapidly it is wise to revise any estimate at least once a year.

The price of air time does not include the cost to produce the commercial. A cost of about $100,000 was reasonable for the average television commercial in the early 1980s. When Campbell Soup hired dancer Ann Miller and a large cast of Busby Berkeley-like Hollywood hoofers to create one of their commercials a few years ago, it cost a total of $250,000. About forty thousand commercials are produced for television each year.

That television commercial production is now an on-going business underscores an important fact. Television long ago gave up the old radio-created sponsor system in favor of a participating advertiser system. By the 1960s production costs had made it impossible for one sponsor to bear the cost of even a thirty-minute television program. By turning to spot, or participating, sponsorship, the networks were able to increase the number of sponsors and lower the cost of television advertising to the individual sponsor. They also could retain control of program content, since programs could be created without prior consultation with any one of the participating, or spot, advertisers.

As in radio, television rates vary by market, by time of day, or class of time. Large markets such as New York, Chicago, Los Angeles, and Philadelphia draw much higher rates than medium-sized and small markets. Prime time, of course, draws the highest rates; late and early hours the lowest. All broadcasting rates usually are negotiable, with the sharp bidder who can afford large amounts of time always winning much better prices than the timid customer who buys little.

Selling time is not the only way the station can make money. One widely used practice includes a sophisticated kind of bartering called the time bank. Stations sometimes trade advertising time for a program that will attract a good audience and advertisers. The agency that offers the program takes the station time (and that negotiated in other deals) and sells or uses it for revenue of its own. As much as 15 percent of all syndicated programs are bartered, including such popular programs as "Hee Haw" and "The Lawrence Welk Show." Barter gives the station a program it could not produce and a salable commodity for the time involved in the trade. Stations seldom lose advertising in the trade, since the agreement usually stipulates that all time the agency sells will be sold only to trade eligible sponsors or to those who have not advertised on the station within the past year.

The networks are also a source of station revenue. Networks *pay* local stations for carrying network programs with network commercials. The payment is made in accordance with a prenegotiated contract, and usually at a rate about 30 to 35 percent below what local stations would make if they sold the same time to local advertisers. Despite the loss in revenue, most stations maintain their network affiliation because, like barter, it has several advantages. In exchange for continuing as a part of the national network program and advertising distribution system, the station gets a large amount of quality, low-cost programming which contributes to the prestige of the station and its other programs. Occasionally, a network station will preempt a weak segment in the network's programming and run a movie instead, reaping higher revenues from the local advertising than it could possibly get from the network. But, as already noted, management has discovered that attempting to rely on weak, nonnetwork programming can alienate the audience and reduce the station's potential for both local and national spot business. So the stations generally accept the lower network revenue in exchange for the prestige and profit advantages that go with affiliation.

Whatever their contractual arrangements, the stations and the networks remain in competition for the national advertising dollar. In 1982 the two came into open conflict when ABC, under the pressure of inflation, announced it would increase its number of thirty-second, prime time spots by two every evening—or by fourteen a week. CBS immediately joined in for "competitive reasons." ABC affiliates did not view the new plan with favor, however. They feared it would drain as much as 5 percent, or $150 million, of their annual national and regional ad revenue, with it all going into the networks' pockets. They also raised an old, recurring concern in television: the fear that the new spots would bring back cries from the audience of advertising clutter—that there are too many commercials on television as it is, and that fewer not more commercials should be the goal.

The question of clutter, meanwhile, was complicated, unexpectedly, the same year. The National Association of Broadcasters (NAB) had attempted to address the problem of clutter by limiting the number of commercials and nonprogram announcements to nine minutes and thirty seconds of each hour in prime time and to twelve minutes of every hour in other program times. The NAB's code also limited the number of commercials that could be presented successively, the number of products a commercial could present, as well as the number of commercial interruptions within a program. In 1982 the U.S. Department of Justice startled the broadcast industry with charges that the NAB limitations were in violation of the Sherman Antitrust Act and that the rules forced the use of thirty-second commercials. The effect of the latter, the department argued, was to prevent innovative commercial formats and artificially limit the supply of commercial time, while also raising its costs.

The NAB was stunned. Rather than fight the charges it "threw in the towel," agreeing to change the code without being forced to do so. After some deliberation, however, the NAB and its attorneys decided in 1983 not to replace the ad regulations in the code. There seemed to be no way to do so without inviting another encounter with the Justice Department and another antitrust action.

The Fabled Cable

One of the greatest expenses of cable operation: laying the cable itself.

By the early 1980s, however, it was clear that television's greatest challenge was not network-station conflict or ironing out legal niceties for spot advertising but a new competitor: cable television. After struggling against the high costs of expansion and restrictions from FCC regulations, cable finally touched the 30 percent mark in its campaign to reach the national television audience; observers began predicting it would have 60 percent of the nation's television homes as subscribers, and 30 percent of the audiences loyal to over-the-air network broadcasting, by 1990. Cable's old promise, that every television home could have not just two, three or four television channels to watch but twenty, thirty, sixty, or even a hundred, seemed about to be fulfilled.

Cable got its start in isolated towns where over-the-air reception was difficult. It spread as a community antenna television service (CATV) throughout the 1950s until some television broadcasters began to complain that its signals from distant markets were destructive competition to local television service. By then, too, some of the larger operations of the 750 cable companies were producing their own programs, offering movie, talk show, and weather channels. In 1965 the FCC, backed by court decisions, moved to regulate cable in line with its policy of localism, of developing and encouraging local television service. To make sure local stations were not driven off the air by the new cable companies, it forced cable to carry all local signals, if requested, and to black out programs from afar if local television stations also were carrying them. An important decision came when the commission ruled that a cable operation could not import signals by microwave if the importation would destroy an existing local station.

The two principal effects of the ruling were to protect local television as well as restrict cable television to small- and medium-sized markets. Without the right to import signals from other markets, cable could not compete in larger markets since it could not offer the audiences there anything new. So between 1965 and 1972 the growth of cable, was put on hold.

In 1972 the FCC took a more systematic approach to the new industry, relaxing the signal importation rules and requiring cable systems to offer a "significant" amount of original programming. The commission did limit pay cable's ability to exhibit first-run movies and sporting events, however. The ruling was designed to insure that pay cable did not siphon off the best television program material for its own audiences, and, as a result, keep the programs from reaching the parts of the large commercial television audience that still could not receive cable.

The new, relaxed regulations gave cable new hope and new growth. All problems were not solved, however. For example, it cost $75,000 to $90,000 a mile to lay cable in a city, so even for a middle-sized metropolitan area with one million people a cable system was a sizable investment. Even after the cable was in place those who sold the new service met tough resistance, especially where several over-the-air stations were in operation and reception was good. It was not until cable was able to develop distinct, alternative programming that it was able to make inroads into the larger over-the-air television markets. In the 1970s three major innovations were symbolic of the program changes that contributed to cable's growth: (1) invention of the Home Box Office movie channel, (2) establishment of Warner Amex's two-way Qube cable system in Columbus, Ohio, and (3) introduction of the independent television station to cable, as well as creation of the Cable News Network cable channel—both by Ted Turner.

Levin and HBO

When Gerald Levin was named by Time, Inc., to take charge of its Home Box Office subsidiary, Levin decided that if cable had a future it was in offering the public unique fare not already available over the air. He also decided that a pay-by-the-month cable channel would be more acceptable to the home viewer than pay by the program, especially if the channel offered something the networks did not offer: high-quality movies. After consideration, he decided he could get the HBO movie service into homes more cheaply if he sent the signal by domestic communications satellite—or "the bird," as it is called—rather than by the overland, microwave system. Levin then convinced Time, Inc., to invest $7.5 million in leasing satellite space on Satcom I and take a chance that enough cable system operators would buy the new HBO service to pay the cost. The system worked so well, in fact, HBO became the first profitable pay cable service in the country—and, therefore, the first profitable pay-television service. By the beginning of 1984 HBO had more than eight million subscribers, or 60 percent of the pay cable television market. As noted earlier it had produced its first made-for-cable movie (*The Terry Fox Story*) and had two others shot and "in the can" (*Sakharov* and *The Blood of Others*). It was expanding into other cable investments and had established a second movie channel, Cinemax.

The Warner Amex Qube

In 1977, the Warner Qube cable experiment helped the cable industry attract attention and begin to build a respectable, more glamorous, and more marketable image. The Warner Amex corporation converted its existing cable operation in Columbus, Ohio, into an experimental cable operation named Qube. The new service included a two-way cable interaction between the audience and the cable studio. Qube's offerings included the usual relay of Columbus television signals (three commercial and one public), some free importation channels (Cleveland and Indianapolis), free information and entertainment channels (weather and local public affairs discussion programs) as well as pay-by-the-movie channels, including an adult, or pornography channel. Each subscriber was given a hand-sized terminal with buttons to select pay or nonpay channels and control the "talk back" or interaction feature. The latter was used to take audience feedback on programs and to play games—even allowing viewers to signal a change in the plot of an experimental dramatic show and "write" the story it wanted to see. On several occasions, Qube has taken instant public opinion polls of its viewers (including a question or two on the performance of then Ohio State head football coach Woody Hayes). But the polls were taken more to demonstrate new cable technology than as a serious attempt to measure public opinion. (The sample, for one thing, would be questionable.)

Many in the industry thought Warner Amex's early investment in Qube was ill-advised, but the detractors of the sophisticated system now have all but disappeared. Qube's publicity alone gave Warner Amex something to trade on, as dignitaries and celebrities (House Speaker Thomas "Tip" O'Neill, Phil Donahue, etc.) traveled to Columbus to experience firsthand the instant audience feedback operation. In 1981 *Newsweek* wrote, "Qube represents the most tangible evidence that the much-trumpeted 'cable revolution' is no longer beyond the blue horizon." In the early 1980s, with the reputation and experience gained from working with Qube, Warner took the system, with improvements, on the road, winning franchises in Cincinnati, Dallas, Houston, Pittsburg, and St. Louis. At last report, Warner and Qube had won the majority of the cable franchise competitions they had entered.

Turner, WTBS, and CNN

A third major contributor to the growth and progress of cable came from the flamboyant entrepreneur, "Captain Outrageous," "The Mouth of the South," Ted Turner. Turner had amassed a fortune in the billboard sign business, when in 1970 he paid $2.5 million for the license for UHF Channel 17 in Atlanta (WTBS). While the other UHF channels in the city failed, WTBS carried on for six years with reruns and movies. When he read of Gerald Levin's success in sending movies to cable systems via

Entrepreneur Ted Turner.

satellite, Turner began to envision more than survival for his station. He estimated that if he could send Channel 17's signal around the country to cable operators by satellite, he would have a low-cost television network with national advertising potential. His reasoning proved to be realistic. WTBS went "up on the bird" and became the first television "Superstation," attracting an advertising billing larger than that of major stations in major markets. The hope for network-like revenue came true. WTBS now is seen in more than twenty million cable homes and has returned a profit of $40 million a year. (In comparison, NBC, during the same period, and running last in network ratings, announced a profit of only $48 million a year.) WTBS's superstation approach has since been emulated by WGN-TV Chicago and WOR-TV New York.

Turner's greatest gamble came in 1980 with the launching of Cable News Network, a 24–hour news service. "A newspaper you can watch," as Turner called it. The CNN format is almost antithetical to regular network newscasts. Rather than one there are several anchors. CNN has no strict time limits to follow, and so rather than the short news stories the networks usually give, the news stories on CNN can run long and often do. While most television observers would agree CNN has not yet reached network quality with its news reporting, few doubt its ability to report. Before CNN went on the air, each of the three network news executives had three television sets in their offices to monitor both the "home team" and the competition. Now each has four.

Turner inaugurated a second cable news service in 1982, CNN2, since renamed CNN Headline News. By 1983 CNN had 21.7 million subscribers while CNN Headline News had 5.2 million. In the meanwhile, growth of the cable audience fostered competition. Westinghouse joined with ABC to launch the Satellite News Network in 1982. The challenge proved Turner's staying power. While SNN was losing $40 million with its seven million subscribers, CNN was losing an estimated $10 to $12 million in about the same time period—evidently paid for from the profits of WTBS. In October 1983 Turner was able to buy SNN for $25 million. Turner Broadcasting remains the principal source of news programming in the cable television industry.

More Narrowcasters

The HBO and CNN channels were only two of cable's new channels. A number of new cable channels—"narrowcasters," as they have been called by many—came into being in the late 1970s and early 1980s. Other than the SNN experiment, there have been several other prominent ventures.

One of them, ESPN (Entertainment and Sports Programming Network) covers sports all year, day in and day out. The channel offers some baseball, basketball, college and USFL football, golf, sports roundups and sportscasts, as well as such low-cost offerings as billiards tournaments, Australian rules football, and college lacrosse contests. Within FCC antisiphoning rules, ESPN can tape major sports events and play them back a day later.

Nickleodeon is a channel for children, teaching and entertaining them with cartoons, puppets, and stories. A regular feature has been "Black Beauty," adopted from the popular story about the magnificent horse. There are game shows by and for youngsters and programs that encourage participation in art, music, science, and athletics.

Several channel companies were established to attract the adult-viewing audience. Four cable operators formed the Rainbow Channel to offer a combination of adult films and cultural programming. The channel's format called for X and R movies (*The Happy Hooker,* etc.) on one evening and concerts and cultural programs on alternative evenings. The Playboy channel, fashioned after Hugh Hefner's *Playboy* magazine, became controversial with conservative groups almost immediately with strip poker-type games and features.

One of the most ambitious channel programming attempts was the performing arts channel offered by CBS Cable in 1982. The cultural effort offered serious dance, music, and drama (Shakespeare's *Macbeth,* for example). But it lost $20 to $30 million and was unable to sustain itself on available advertising revenue. Cable management at CBS blamed the failure on a depressed economy. RCA's attempt to establish a more middle-brow entertainment channel, featuring such fare as Broadway plays, also failed. On the other hand, one cultural channel, the ARTS channel (ABC/Hearst Corp.), which was created in 1981 to serve audiences interested in the performing arts, has survived. It narrowcasts two to four hours of music, dance, art films and drama every night.

Decidedly more successful has been the Music Television channel, or MTV, a channel which presents brief video dramatizations to accompany popular music recordings. As this book went to press, MTV was publishing Nielsen audience ratings which showed it as having the highest rating (1.1) of all basic cable channels—or Cable Network (CBN), the USA Network, ESPN, and the two cable news networks. To celebrate its success, MTV announced its first awards ceremony in September 1984. Among those who won awards for their "videos" were Cars for "You Might Think," male video performer David Bowie for "China Girl," and female video artist Cyndi Lauper for "Girls Just Want to Have Fun."

Cable and the Real World

Although cable television has come a long way, the industry still has several pressing problems to solve if it is to establish itself as the primary television delivery system in the country. There are problems of audience appeal for the cable product, political problems inherent in winning city franchises needed for expansion, and economic problems related to audience acceptance, and cable company administration.

First, cable's audience appeal has not been as strong as its supporters suggest. While an estimated 60 percent of all American homes were within reach of cable service by the mid-1980s, only half of those, or 30 percent of all U.S. homes, became cable subscribers. Of the homes that do subscribe to a cable service, 28 to 35 percent disconnect all or part of the service each year. While some move on to another cable service elsewhere, many say they disconnect because they don't watch enough to justify the monthly fees. Complaints continue, too, that cable's programming is not as good as promised. The local cable viewer often sees little more than syndicated reruns of banal, network television programs, which are no less banal when shown on cable for a monthly fee. Even the well-financed RCA entertainment channel, which promised entertainment with a broad appeal—broadway musicals, among other things—was so disappointing many of the 45,000 subscribers who signed up for the eight to twelve dollars a month service dropped it when they did not get the quality they expected. The channel folded in 1983 with losses of $50 million. Cable industry spokesmen admit there is much to learn about how to fill the channels they have created to reach the public.

Second, the politics of winning cable franchises has been a devastating problem. Many city governments seem to anticipate big revenues from cable's promise of a variety of colorful programs. As a result, they often demand "crazy" concessions for cable franchises, as one observer put it. For example, cable companies have been asked to provide the public with one hundred channels of cable television when it still is virtually impossible to collect good programs and sizable audiences for sixty channels. There have been demands that cable companies pay franchise fees to bail out city general funds, or contribute various non-cable-related gifts and services. The city of Boston demanded 8 percent of the cable operator's annual fees while holding the cable operator's monthly subscriber charge to two dollars. St. Louis demanded costly modern facilities for an inner-city market. Sacramento's cable company, to win its $90 million franchise, had to agree to provide the city with construction projects and job training programs. What is more, many of the franchise negotiations have been fraught with political opportunism and infighting, causing discussion and negotiations to drag on for years.

At least one attempt has been made to bring some relief from these problems. Senator Barry Goldwater introduced a bill in the U.S. Senate in 1983 to keep cities with four or more television stations from forcing cable systems to set their operating rates too low. The bill also would prevent cities from collecting annual cable franchise fees of more than 5 percent.

Third, high operating costs, less than ideal subscriber response and the troubled economy have not made cable a gold mine business. Those constructing cable systems in large cities have known they will have to wait many months before they can recapture their original investment. It seems obvious that cable must continue to increase its audiences to survive and grow. Rather than increase audiences by laying new cable in new cities and towns, one important group of cable companies has decided to take a different tact. They recently decided to expand by buying and merging existing cable companies. American Television & Communications Corporation (ATC), Tele-Communications, Inc., and Taft Cablevision Associates, Inc., already are operating under this strategy. They are buying relatively isolated cable companies that can be "clustered," or connected to one central office/production center with a computer, and studio equipment. The studio and facilities serve from seven to twenty-five clustered cable systems, greatly reducing costs in billing, staffing, marketing, and maintenance. By clustering many cable operations, ATC is able to create audiences comparable in size to those of newspapers and over-the-air television stations—increasing the possibility of advertising sales. Time will tell if a better cable service can follow.

The industry has much to learn about its own economic situation: How much advertising will cable subscribers tolerate? How many pay channels—or cable "tiers"—will home viewers buy? What combinations of tiers will he or she buy? Also vital: How can the small, splintered audiences of cable television be measured effectively and economically?

DBS, LPTV, and STV

The years ahead promise another problem for cable: competition from other television services. Two have been authorized recently; another already is in operation.

In 1982 the FCC authorized a new, direct broadcast satellite (DBS) service, designed to relay programs across the nation by way of domestic communication satellites. Using more powerful transmitters than earlier satellites and a dish-antenna small enough to mount on a rooftop, DBS bypasses local stations to go directly into homes. The service will offer both pay and commercial channels. As *Broadcasting* magazine has reported, the first DBS service, United Satellite Communication, Inc.

(USCI), went into operation serving northeastern states in November 1983. Its low-power, five-channel pay service was attracting a growing list of subscribers in the Baltimore-Washington, D.C. area in 1984. Other companies are scheduled to begin DBS programming in 1987 and 1988. (See pp. 351–52.) Of course, it cannot be clear just how much and what kind of competition DBS will offer cable until the new service has established itself. And that may take some time. DBS does not have to lay cable, but observers feel it must have twenty to thirty pay and advertising-supported channels in operation for the national audience before most families will go to the expense of mounting "earth station" dish-antennas on their roofs. Unless DBS becomes very attractive, the average family is likely to be satisfied with the network television, cable, or home video tape recordings already available.

The new DBS system promises to bring television directly to home viewers without a local TV station intermediary. Small towns and cities are expected to reap the largest benefits from it.

Another potential competitor for the television viewer's attention began developing in 1980, when the FCC inaugurated plans for low power television stations (LPTV). Low power television is something of the opposite of DBS's high-flying national service. LPTV is dedicated to the needs of the small community, with low power transmitters whose signal range is limited to only a dozen miles or so (with, of course, less risk of interference). Low power television was conceived as a commercial service for the neighborhood, the ethnic community, and the small town. Its success seems tied to its ability to provide not special interest programs—more or less in the way magazines or cable channels do—but programs of interest to a special locale—Little League sports, ethnic song festivals, news features, high school graduations, street festivals, garage sales, 4-H horse shows, city or school board meetings, or anything of interest to the small community within its signal range. The hope is programs will attract enough of an audience to make LPTV advertising rates attractive to the small businesses in the community.

Critics fear the LPTV's lower advertising costs will detract from the ad revenues of existing stations rather than create new television advertisers among small businesses. Others suggest the quality of LPTV programs will not be attractive to a significant share of the audience. Still, many are hopeful. One sign: LPTV licenses have been among the most sought after in the history of the FCC. When it began accepting applications, the commission received so many qualified ones it decided to issue construction permits by lottery (over 500 by 1985).

The final word, meanwhile, has not been written yet on another pay television system: STV, or subscriber TV. Subscriber television programs are sent as scrambled signals over the air to subscribers with decoding boxes to unscramble the signal. The system has much to offer. In large, relatively flat areas, such as metropolitan Los Angeles, STV has an economic advantage over cable. It can deliver a good signal to most parts of the earthly terrain without interference and the high cost required to lay cable in rural or metropolitan areas. Los Angeles is one STV showcase. Washington, D.C. could become another. There are about 500,000 subscribers in Los Angeles, with two over-the-air pay channels in operation. ON-TV and SelecTV broadcast a collection of sports programs, adult films, movies, and cartoons for charges comparable to monthly cable television.

As with cable television, the survival of STV seems to depend on the ability of the service to give customers something they want but cannot get on commercial television. But in programming, STV has a decided disadvantage. Instead of cable's thirty to sixty or more channels, the STV company only has one. All STV programs—movies, "adult" features, and cartoons—must wait their turn to get on the air. STV operators continue to search out uses for their medium. In 1984 ABC's video subsidiary, TeleFirst, offered broadcasts of scrambled movies (*Risky Business, Octopussy* and *War Games*) at 2 A.M. to subscribers in Chicago. The object was to attract subscribers with video cassette recorders, who would record the movies and play them back at their convenience. The monthly charge was $25.95, and the customer also had to install the scrambler (about $75) for playback. The experiment was ended the same year—for lack of an audience. Telefirst continues with plans to develop all ABC-TV affiliates as a source for STV programming, however.

One of STV's major problems has been program pirates. Once the black unscrambling boxes are given to the public, there is no way subscriber stations can keep them from being copied. As serious for the industry, recently, has been the steady decline in subscribers. STV households were down from a 1982 high of 1.4 million to 900,000 in 1984; cable households were counted at twenty to thirty times that figure in the same period. As *Wall Street Journal* reporter Jennifer Bingham Hull discovered, STV was going well in communities without cable; but when cable was introduced subscribers deserted STV for the new multiple channels. Pay television analyst Alan Cole-Ford found cable was able to steal one of every two STV customers when the two systems came into direct competition in Cincinnati. One reason seems related to what one gets for the money: one STV channel costs a household about the same as the thirty or more channels offered by cable.

Even with the loss in subscribers and the continuing invasion of their territory by cable, some STV executives believe their companies can survive and profit in the coming years—even if they do not dominate the pay television market. To compete with cable, they feel, STV must develop better marketing—including first of all, a more careful determination of audience members who are likely to stay with STV and then selling the service. Of great importance, too, is the need to develop better and more distinctive STV programming—programming television audiences want and cable television does not offer.

Any battle between cable and STV, if it comes, will probably be won on what the competitors give their audiences rather than how they give it. It may be, of course, that the battle will not come. With STV controlling flat areas and cable the mountains, each could find its own audience, and profits, without further problem.

PBS: The Poor Broadcasting Service

If STV and cable prove not to be the end of each other, many still will be convinced that pay television, especially cable, will be the end of public television. Since its formation by the Public Broadcasting Act of 1967, and the Public Broadcasting Financing Act of 1975, public television has lived a hand-to-mouth existence, gathering funds from public and philanthropic sources to match the revenue provided by Congress on a less-than-generous, short-term basis. In the 1970s about one dollar of federal money was matched with every $2.50 raised by the Corporation for Public Broadcasting.

The public system also has suffered from a clear definition of purpose. Since its days as "educational television" following World War II, it has retained a philosophy that it should be instructive—an instrument for teaching history and the manual arts to the public. Another point of view positions the system as the nation's distributor of culture and the arts—of Shakespeare, opera, ballet, and poetry. Still a third view holds it should function primarily as an alternative to the commercial networks, presenting what they (or the local stations) do not present are: education, culture, or just something different. The result is that viewers can watch opera, country music, Shakespeare, ballet, square dancing, instructions in automobile repair, philosophy, lowbrow British comedy, cowboy movies, reruns of the "Twilight Zone" and "Perry Mason" on public television stations.

To add to its problems, public television, like public radio, continues to be a political football. The Nixon administration, for example, saw public television as a potentially dangerous political machine and worked to see that PBS did not develop a strong centralized structure similar to the commercial networks. More than one congressional member publicly has declared he or she would not vote funds for public television when it actively promulgated political views and opinions contrary to his or her own.

With some of its support coming from federal funds, the system has been a ready target for critics upset by its presentations—especially its

A fund raising auction at a public television station. On the boards are listed goods and services donated as gifts, to obtain free advertising and as tax write offs. The auctioneer (center) solicits the highest bid to bring the station needed revenue.

news documentaries. The government of Saudi Arabia asked the American government that PBS not show a documentary on the execution of a Saudi Arabian princess and her lover, arguing the documentary was biased. No such request likely would be made of a commercial television network. In 1982 William J. Bennett, chairman of the National Endowment for the Humanities, one source of PBS funds, complained that the documentary "From the Ashes . . . Nicaragua," shown on PBS, was "unabashed socialist-realism propaganda" and not an appropriate project for federal funding.

Short of funds, and vulnerable to political attacks, public broadcasting can be called the weakest part of our television system, even though it has produced some of our best television moments.

Public television, like public radio, has three parts. The Corporation for Public Broadcasting (CPB), formed in 1967, receives funds from the federal government and private contributors to produce shows for public television stations. The Public Broadcasting Service (PBS) represents the independent stations and operates the interconnection service that sends programs across the nation by satellite. The local stations (whose FCC licenses are held by local and state governments, local civic groups, and/or educational institutions) are the grassroots of the system. Like local commercial stations, they can create their own programs (with the help of local patrons and their own budgets) but they must depend, like commercial stations, on their network for the bulk of their schedule.

CPB and PBS cooperate to create the PBS schedule, with the active participation by individual stations. A list of potential programs is compiled each year by CPB and distributed to the station managers by PBS. The local stations then go through several rounds of voting to decide which programs the network should carry the following season. Unlike commercial television, in which the networks pay the local stations to carry programs, the local stations in PBS contribute about 40 percent of the cost of PBS programs. While the commercial network producer may fear losing the cost of producing a show that does not succeed, the local PBS producer often is accused of choosing mediocre, long programs rather than interesting ones—just to be sure he covers his weekly schedule with the little money he has.

Few doubt PBS has accepted the challenge of its money problems. As funds disappeared with Reagan administration cutbacks in the early 1980s, some public stations, with congressional approval, experimented with selling advertising. The evidence suggested advertising could be an important source of funds. However, more than half of all public stations would have to change their local charters, or convince controlling boards to reverse policies, before they could engage in commercial operations. (It is significant that only ten of the 267 stations in the system decided to join the advertising experiment.) More workable has been the decision to use the PBS satellite interconnection technology ("dishes," etc.) to produce revenue. Thus far it has been leased to corporations who need a nonbroadcast satellite communications service, compatible with PBS uses (as public radio was able to do). The technology also has been matched with station studio facilities for revenue producing cross country, business teleconferences.

Meanwhile, CPB's and PBS's long-standing patrons (Ford, Mobil, Gulf, etc.) seem as willing as ever to support programming in exchange for an identifying credit. And, top leadership at PBS has scoffed at the idea that cable—or any other video technology—will drive PBS off the air. Former PBS president Larry Grossman has argued that cable has grown by presenting movies, sports, and pornography—middle-class rather than high culture—and that there is good reason to believe commercial broadcasting and cable may not be able to present large amounts of cultural programming. Cultural television audiences, like cultural magazine audiences, are small and, therefore, not attractive to advertisers. In fact, PBS was created to improve the cultural and educational fare in broadcasting because the highly profitable commercial broadcasting industry would not or could not provide it. The failure of CBS's effort to establish an advertising-supported cultural channel could be interpreted as a confirmation of Grossman's view. And, while the ABC/Hearst ARTS cable channel has survived, it has not yet been profitable and operates on a limited schedule of four hours a day.

If some research indicates public television suffers when cable comes into the home, there is reason to believe cable may help PBS. Since cable must carry all local stations on request, it will carry the local public station. Since two-thirds of these PBS outlets are UHF television stations, they will, more likely than not, gain in exposure by being on cable. On the average, Grossman has reported, 41 percent of all television homes watch PBS once a week, but 58 percent of all cable homes watch PBS once a week.

Careers in Television

The television industry has approximately 100,000 employees, with 14,000 of them employed by the networks. Only 40,000 of the total positions are related to on-air programs and production.

Competition is keen. Here are some average salaries for positions around the country:

Station Manager	$60,000	Top markets $100,000
Sales Manager	$80,000	Top markets $100,000
Program Director	$30,000	Top markets $80,000
Producers	$17,000	Top markets $100,000
Directors	$17,000	Top markets $30,000 and up
News Director	$32,000	Top markets $100,000
News Producer	$20,000	Top markets $60,000
Assignment Editor	not available	Top markets $30,000

News writers and reporters begin at the bottom, with salaries comparable to those of beginning newspaper reporters. The Writers' Guild of America holds $240 a week as base pay for news writers in some larger markets. The top pay for news people probably goes to the popular news anchors. Walter Cronkite and David Brinkley both are reported to have received $250,000 or more at CBS and NBC, respectively. In 1982 Tom Brokaw's seven year contract was for $18 million.

Traditionally, there have been two distinct ways to advance in television. Business, sales, and programming personnel move up to become administrators while, as a rule, news personnel become news editors and news directors. Rarely do they go into programming or management. Thus, if the goal is administration, it probably is better to stay out of news. If the goal is to be a network or metropolitan news anchor, or a news director, it is best to stay out or get out of programming.

The well-advised beginner also will be good as well as persistent. A thorough, accurate, neat vita, presented in a businesslike way, and presented often, is one of the best strategies for winning any position. Those who do the hiring seem to look first at the applicant's attitude: his or her willingness to do the work. The candidate's experience, education, and ability also rank high. Some would argue the college degree is now a requisite since so many candidates for television positions have that qualification. In short, television management respects a qualified, educated, experienced candidate who is dedicated to working in television.

A national survey of television news directors a few years ago, for example, revealed the great majority of TV reporters are hired either from other television stations, radio news departments, or college broadcast journalism sequences. The news directors said they preferred to hire candidates with broadcast news experience, background, and training (rather than newspaper training).

Just as important, those hired seemed not only to have convinced the news director that they were capable but also able to "get the job done." As one news director has put it, "We can't use prima donnas in this operation."

Summary

Television is the most mass of the mass media. Audiences of twenty-five million homes or more watch prime time programs on a regular basis.

There are 1,100 television stations, some 265 of which are non-commercial stations, and more than 400 of which are UHF stations. The remainder are commercial, VHF stations. The stations are serviced by three major commercial networks, one public television service, and more than twenty special function and regional networks. Viewers in many parts of the country have a choice of subscribing to one or more pay television services. The most popular is cable, which can give viewers sixty or more channels. Subscriber TV (STV) offers only one channel to subscribers. Its major advantage is that it can reach customers without the stringing of expensive cable. There were some 4,600 cable systems serving twenty-five million homes during the early 1980s. The thirty STV stations saw their audience drop from about 1.5 million homes to 900,000 during the same period.

The television organization has five basic departments: management, programming, business and sales, news and engineering. They function in much the same way as radio departments.

Television stations rely on local, syndicated and network programs for broadcasting. Movies and original television series usually are produced in Hollywood, specifically for network use. Once the shows run on network television they are syndicated and distributed to local stations as reruns to be sold to local advertisers. The principal production of the local television station is news and public affairs programming.

In its early years, television news was viewed as little more than a means to keep the station's license. As audience and advertiser support grew, the networks and the local stations worked to improve their news product. Stations were quick to adopt ENG, or electronic news gathering equipment to tape stories in the field or broadcast live by microwave. The networks have excelled in reporting news from around the world by communication satellite. Still, there is a need for reporters who have the knowledge to give depth and comprehension to the breaking story.

The most controversial person in television news is the news doctor, or consultant who surveys the local audience for its likes and dislikes. The consultants claim they do not interfere with the journalistic process; their critics claim they do, and that they also cater to the "mass" taste.

Network news also has expanded rapidly in recent years—to late night, overnight, and early morning time periods.

Creating a successful television series is difficult. With much time and money at stake, the networks often use tried-and-true formulas, such as spinoffs and novels adapted for television.

In programming a show, the competition and the programs before and after it are important. Programs rarely steal an audience. They usually build their own.

Television program audiences are measured in HUT's, shares, and ratings. Audience statistics are drawn from scientific samples, with viewing habits described by audience diaries and television set meters. The industry accredits two television ratings services: Arbitron and A. C. Nielsen.

Network time now costs at least $1,000 a second. A special program such as the Super Bowl can command $300,000 for thirty seconds. And these prices do not include the money the advertiser must spend to produce the commercial—an average of $100,000 in the early 1980s. Stations can profit from selling time and bartering it. Several agencies offer programs in exchange for station time, which the agencies then sell from the time bank. For the station, bartering is much cheaper. Local stations also collect revenue from the networks for showing network programs. The network contract determines the rate of pay.

The major challenge to over-the-air television is cable. Cable has had to fight expensive costs of expansion, and restrictive regulation, to reach the position it claims today, but observers feel it eventually will hold 60 percent of the nation's 81.5 million homes as subscribers and reduce network audiences by as much as 30 percent by 1990.

Cable's slow growth has been advanced by three major contributions since 1975: Home Box Office, Qube, and WTBS, the superstation.

The Corporation for Public Broadcasting was founded in 1967 to gather federal and corporation funds to produce programs for public television stations. The network facilities are operated by the Public Broadcasting Service with participation of local stations. The latter hold licenses from the FCC, under the control of local, state, and/or civic groups with educational or philanthropic interests. Each year, PBS distributes a list of programs prepared by CPB, suggesting programs for the network. After the stations vote, PBS programs are selected from the final list. Local stations contribute about 40 percent of the cost of producing and exhibiting PBS programs.

Questions for Discussion

1. Television, we have said, is the "most mass" of the mass media. But we have reason to believe that all the media are becoming specialized and dividing up to serve special interest audiences. What evidence is there that television is specializing? If cable is dividing the mass audience, how do you account for the fact that it seems to be doing so with programs and content (movies, sports) that have made television the mass medium it is? And if television is specializing, how do you account for the fact that the most likely television candidate to fail in the near future is public television, the most obviously specialized of the special audiences?

2. Television programmers believe it is next to impossible to steal an audience from an established program. Is this true? Name your two favorite television programs—ones that you watch more or less regularly. What shows are opposite them? Do you like the lead-in program that comes in front of your favorite show? Do you like what follows on the same channel? Are you a channel switcher or a channel follower?

3. A few years ago in congressional hearings on the television ratings system, one story revealed that a television set, connected to a Nielsen audimeter, was turned on each morning and "watched" by the family's dog—who used the time to sleep. How many sleeping dogs would there have to be in the sample before the sample statistics were off significantly? Can we consider that a number of sets are turned on for dogs all across the country every morning? How many, out of 81.5 million television homes, might there be?

References

"ABC to Telecast Recent Movies to CVR Owners." *TV Guide,* January 14–20, 1984, A1.

Barnouw, Erik. *The Golden Web.* New York: Oxford University Press, 1968.

———. *The Image Empire.* New York: Oxford University Press, 1970.

Baughman, James L. "The Strange Birth of 'CBS Reports' Revisited." (Presented to the annual convention of the Association for Education in Journalism, Michigan State University, East Lansing, 1981.)

"Cable TV: Coming of Age." *Newsweek,* August 24, 1981, 44–49.

"CBS drops out of running for DBS." *Broadcasting,* July 2, 1984, 38.

"Culture Shock on Cable." *Newsweek,* March 15, 1982, 85–87.

Dominick, Joseph R., and Millard C. Pearce. "Trends in Network Prime Time Programming, 1953–1974." *Journal of Communication* 26(1976): 70–80.

Facts on File. New York: Facts on File, Inc. 1982, 1983.

Foster, Eugene. *Understanding Broadcasting.* Reading, Mass.: Addison-Wesley, 1978.

Harless, James D., and Erik L. Collins. "TV News Directors Hire Many Staffers From Campuses." *Journalism Educator* 29, no. 3 (1974): 39–42.

Holder, Dennis. "Television News Enters the Redi-Whip Era." *Washington Journalism Review,* January/February, 1982, 20–24.

Hull, Jennifer Bingham. "Subscriber TV Market Seems To Be Fizzling." *Wall Street Journal,* November 23, 1983, 29.

Landro, Laura. "RCA Venture for Cable-TV Programs to End. *Wall Street Journal,* February 23, 1983, 12.

———. "Cable-TV Bidding War to Serve Large Cities Is Quickly Cooling Off." *The Wall Street Journal,* April 1, 1983, 1, 12.

Mann, James. "Is Cable Television Losing Its Luster?" *U.S. News & World Report,* November 22, 1982, 71–72.

Mayer, Jane. "TV Anchor Women Never Die, They Get Replaced by the Young." *Wall Street Journal,* May 25, 1983, 1, 21.

"Murdoch's Broadside." *Newsweek,* January 16, 1984, 59–62.

Parkman, Allen M. "The Effect of Television Station Ownership on Local News Ratings." *The Review of Economics and Statistics* LXIV, no. 2 (May 1982): 289–95.

Powers, Ron. *The Newscasters.* New York: St. Martin's Press, 1978.

"Shaking Up the Network." *Time,* August 9, 1982, 50–57.

Sterling, Christopher H., and John N. Kittross. *Stay Tuned, A Concise History of American Broadcasting.* Belmont, Calif.: Wadsworth, 1981.

"Television Broadcasting." *U.S. Industrial Outlook, 1982.* Washington, D.C.: U.S. Government Printing Office, 1982.

Wright, John W. *The American Almanac of Jobs and Salaries.* New York: Avon, 1982.

Part Four

Auxiliaries and Accessories in the Media System

Every industry develops a support system, and the mass communication industry is no exception. In America, Detroit manufactures automobiles, but only with the help of a large number of companies that provide automakers with parts and services—tires, paint, upholstery, engines, transmissions, radios, advertising and publicity. Auto industry auxiliaries operate at every stage of the automaking process, from original parts making to auto delivery to the post-sale making and selling of seat covers, tassels, and the ever-popular fuzzy dice.

In much the same way, the mass media produce and distribute messages for public consumption while auxiliary companies offer support by supplying presses and transmitters, message content, advertising and product information, and other accouterments that make the media system operate. The auxiliaries and accessories of the media system are not considered mass media since they do not produce and distribute messages directly to the audience. Instead, they produce, lease and/or distribute messages to the media, or provide services or technology to the public, that aid media reception.

For years, the press associations have been among the most important of these auxiliaries, providing the media with news around the clock—and from around the world. As a result, they extend the reach of newspapers and broadcast news reporting in much the same way the media extend the reach of their audiences. Media auxiliaries also include syndicates that serve the media system with commentary and entertainment, providing much of the content newspapers and broadcasting stations use daily to entertain their audiences.

Through syndicates, newspapers receive recipes, horoscopes, bridge columns, comics, and political commentary; television gets prime time reruns of sitcoms, adventure mysteries, game shows, and late night movies. Radio formats, as already noted, have been in syndication for some years now.

As noted in chapter 5, as much as 70 percent of the modern American newspaper is advertising. It has been suggested that as much as 60 percent of newspaper news stories originate with public relations agents and agencies. Advertising and public relations are unabashed advocates in the media system, dedicated to the purpose of presenting images of corporate products and good performance through mass communication. Advertising is a paying customer and contributes the largest portion of income to all the ad media (all except motion pictures and book publishing). Public relations, like the press associations, can also extend news media surveillance, providing stories and viewpoints the media may not get otherwise.

An important technological auxiliary in the media system at the present time is the communication satellite, especially the new domestic satellite in orbit to relay messages across North America. We have had the use of international communication satellites since the 1960s, when signals from AT&T's Telstar first began to leap both tall buildings and entire oceans, and bring news from Europe, Vietnam, or China "faster than a speeding bullet." Since the 1970s domestic communication satellites have reduced the cost of sending communication signals across country. They also have changed the structure of our

mass communication system with the ability to link one point in America with another—at low cost—with little chance of interference.

And what of the postsale accessories—the "fuzzy dice" of the system? They include the home video disc and home video tape machine, which are used with the television set. Video tapes and discs greatly increase the consumer's enjoyment of the media system by giving more personal control over the media content he or she watches.

In the next three chapters, we will discuss the auxiliaries and accessories of the media system. Chapter 12 will review the press associations, print and broadcasting syndicates, communication satellites, and conclude with a discussion of the home video tape and disc industry. Chapters 13 and 14 will review the two advocate auxiliaries, advertising and public relations, respectively.

Media research is a rapidly growing, increasingly important auxiliary function in mass communication. It is used by the media, advertisers and public relations counselors alike. Rather than discuss it in this section, however, it will be reviewed in chapter 18, along with public concerns about media effects and performance and some research findings regarding those concerns.

Chapter
12

Press Associations, Syndicates, and Satellites

The modern wire service teletype machine.

The Press Associations

The oldest mass media auxiliary service is the press association. As noted in chapter 2, colonial editors exchanged newspapers to bring news from outside their communities to their readers. The invention of the telegraph in 1844 opened the door to the first news service by wire, and created a name still associated with it today: the wire service. At present, there are five global wire or press services: Reuters, the English press service; Agence France-Presse, the French service; TASS, the Soviet news service; and the Associated Press (AP) and United Press International (UPI), both American services. The United States is the only country at the present time with two major wire services.

There is a sizable number of smaller services in the United States that are sometimes referred to as supplemental news services. The Gannett News Service, owned and operated by the Gannett newspaper group, has a dozen bureaus across the country, from Washington, D.C. to Olympia, Washington. The Copley News Service, owned by the Copley newspaper group, has four news bureaus. Two of the most successful supplemental services are the New York *Times,* and the Washington *Post*-Los Angeles *Times* services. Both now have more than three hundred subscribers and offer a heavy flow of news to their clients by wire machine. Unlike AP and UPI, the supplemental news services tend to provide investigative and in-depth pieces to "supplement" a newspaper's hard news content, rather than continual spot news coverage.

Figure 12.1

Comparison of AP and UPI Statistics

	AP	UPI
Employees	2,600	2,000
Bureaus		
U.S.	123	146
Other	75	224
Members/Subscribers		
Newspapers/Magazines	1,430	1,800
Broadcast	4,000	3,900
Words Per Day	14 million	13 million

A major function of Associated Press and United Press International is to extend the reach of local news—newspaper or broadcast—to state, national and international levels on a continuous daily basis. To do this, the two news agencies maintain staffs of two thousand or more in hundreds of news bureaus in hundreds of countries around the world. The AP and UPI each distribute more than twelve million words a day to five thousand or more subscribers.

Development of U.S. Press Associations

As reported in chapter 3, six New York newspapers formed the first news association in 1849 "to procure foreign news by telegraph from Boston," to share the costs of two news boats to meet incoming ships, and to sell news to papers not members of the association and outside the New York City area. According to historian Edwin Emery, the group established a firm grip on cooperative telegraphic news by 1856 under the name of the New York Associated Press.

As the nation moved westward, and other local and regional press associations sprang up across the country, the management of AP was careful to see that their organization remained in control and distribution of wire service news. By 1866 the completion of the Atlantic cable connected America and London; the AP of New York, as it had controlled news from arriving ships, quickly took control of cabled news from Europe. The New York AP enticed midwestern and southern newspapers to its foreign and domestic news service by granting them exclusive contracts in their areas. It also strengthened its monopolistic control by winning preferential rates with Western Union and by withdrawing service from any newspaper that subscribed to any other press association service.

The Joint Executive Committee

As the midwestern newspapers grew in number and importance, however, they chafed under eastern control and some important aspects of the news service. The New York group often ignored major stories in wire coverage—while covering them competitively for its own respective newspapers. The group also gave preference in news selection to its own morning papers, ignoring the needs of the large evening dailies in the Midwest. There were complaints, too, about autocratic New York control and the association's arbitrary methods of charging for its services.

In 1882 the Western Press Association, a group of midwestern newspapers, and one of the more powerful regional associations subscribing to the AP service, demanded reforms. The New York Associated Press recognized the importance of the midwestern papers by forming a joint executive committee with the Western group to oversee the operation of the two organizations. The joint executive committee had five members. Two were from the Western Press Association, the other three from the New York AP.

The First United Press

While the joint executive committee muffled (but did not end) the conflict of the Western and New York associations, it did little or nothing for the many papers still without a wire service. As competitors of AP newspapers, they still were restricted from access to AP news. Several would-be agencies struggled to serve this growing number of papers, but AP's control of foreign news, and the fact that Western Union would raise rates for AP competitors to protect its major client, hampered their efforts. Still, the market was there in the persons of many unhappy newspaper publishers, leading Arthur Jenkins of the Syracuse, New York, *Herald* to inaugurate a wire service that offered news to any who wished to buy it. In 1882 Jenkins formed a commercial press association with several silent or near-silent partners. It was called United Press (no relation to the twentieth century news service). Phillips also created a subsidiary, the Cable News Company—again no relation to twentieth century news organizations—to collect and sell foreign news to publishers.

Much of the strength of the UP was behind the scenes and in its partners. One UP silent partner was William Laffan, the business manager of the New York *Sun,* who worked for Charles Dana, the chairman of the Western Press/New York AP joint executive committee. The two "enemies" were in business together—as was soon the case for their respective wire services, too. In 1885, just as it appeared the two associations might be headed for stiff competition, the management of United Press and the joint executive committee of the Western Press Association and New York Associated Press agreed to a secret exchange of news. The AP quietly bought UP's foreign Cable News and agreed to supply the UP with news of the East and the nation. Under-the-table stock sales—the sales prices were actually refunded—established the partnership, and it quickly flowered into a lucrative arrangement for the men at the top of the two associations. In the transaction, UP received the great bulk of its news from AP at very low cost. In exchange, the members of the joint executive committee took a percentage of UP's receipts (not profits) as dividends on UP stock they held. In the arrangement, UP also could recruit AP newspaper subscribers as clients by threatening to sell UP service to the newspaper's competition. Of course, AP newspapers that bought United Press service actually were paying twice for the same service. But this, evidently, was of little concern to the joint executive committee or UP management.

Down with Commercial Gain

In 1890 the members of the Western Press Association decided to investigate evidence that UP was siphoning off AP dispatches and that there were irregularities in the dealings of the joint executive committee. They asked Victor Lawson, publisher of the Chicago *Daily News,* to head a committee of three to investigate the situation. From the beginning, Lawson and his committee met strong opposition—even attempted sabotage—but in 1891 they were able to confirm that United Press was virtually in control of the press association's news gathering and that members of the joint executive committee were profiting from the situation through gifts of hundreds of thousands of dollars in UP stock. With Lawson's report, the joint executive committee arrangement between the Western association and the New York AP was doomed. The committee fell, as AP historian Oliver Gramling has put it, to "outright commercial interests."

With the joint committee agreement in shreds, and the New York members of the committee turning their support to United Press, the Western Press Association seemed to be standing alone. It now had to decide whether to join United Press or try to become a national press association in its own right. Lawson saw no hope for a press association operated by those interested only in commercial gain. He was determined to build a new association under the control of those who collected and reported the news—the journalists.

In 1892 he and members of the Western association laid careful plans to move in that direction. They agreed in principle to a ninety-three-year contract with UP, but it was mainly a delaying tactic to prepare announcement of a new Associated Press of Illinois. The new AP was, in reaction to the joint executive committee scandal, a nonprofit cooperative that would not and could not declare dividends. The idea of a cooperative had great appeal to the newspapermen of the day. According to Gramling, when the New York AP was absorbed into the United Press in 1893, the majority of its staff—the "rank and file of the scattered news army which had made it great in its day"—aligned itself with the AP of Illinois rather than the privately owned United Press. A recruiting trip to the big newspapers of the East was just as fruitful, as a list of papers, including Joseph Pulitzer's *World,* joined the cooperative.

Moving quickly and carefully, the new AP named Lawson's colleague and editor, Melville E. Stone, as general manager. Then, with funds volunteered by excited AP members (more than $800,000), Lawson and Stone set out to wage a "holy war" against the monopolistic UP. Stone went abroad in 1893 and found foreign news agencies also receptive to the new cooperative. He returned with ten-year renewable contracts for foreign news. Lawson traveled the East, meeting with publishers of the New York AP group and winning their support for the new AP while also holding southerners and midwesterners within the cooperative.

By then it was clear the UP had been planning all along to do away with the Western association, but now it found itself in a death struggle with an enemy it had sorely underestimated. By the fall of 1895, Lawson had been so effective in stealing UP clients and its funds were so low, that UP was having difficulty maintaining its news service. Stone even uncovered evidence UP was stealing dispatches to serve its clients. He laid a trap, adding a name to one dispatch reporting a revolt in India. He gave the leader's name as Siht El Otspueht. After the story appeared in United Press newspapers, Stone revealed that the phrase, reversed, read: "The UP stole this." The UP had declared bankruptcy and discontinued its service by April, 1897.

Ironically, AP of Illinois also was out of business within three years, a victim not of competition, but of the hasty wording in its own incorporation papers—written when it seemed UP would monopolize wire service news. Following the practice of its predecessors, the new AP group threatened to withdraw its news service from the Chicago *Inter Ocean,* a member newspaper that had decided to subscribe to a second, UP-associated wire service. In retaliation, the newspaper sued and in 1900 won its case before the Supreme Court of Illinois. The courts held the incorporation papers were written so broadly as to make AP of Illinois a public utility required by law to provide its news service to any newspaper wishing it. The *Inter Ocean* applied for reinstatement as an Associated Press member, and sued for losses sustained during its suspension from AP service. Other newspapers, also denied service, got in line to take AP to court.

The Rise of the Modern AP

Lawson and his colleagues were crushed, but their dream of a cooperative press association did not die. New York state had passed a law that allowed the incorporation of cooperative, nonprofit organizations. And so a new Associated Press, the modern AP, was incorporated under New York law in 1900. As a cooperative, its incorporation papers specified that "no person not so elected shall have any right or interest in the corporation or enjoy any of the privileges or benefits thereof." Its members supply each other with news from their individual publication areas and share the cost of the exchange of news and of maintaining a press association staff to operate the service. The cooperative also does not make a profit. The modern AP, as historian Edwin Emery has pointed out, is an agency organized for the benefit of its membership, not the agency.

The new organization still encountered some of the same old wire service problems, though. In 1915 AP ended the practice of withdrawing service from a newspaper that subscribed to a second wire service. An opinion by the U.S. attorney general convinced the press association the practice was monopolistic and should be discarded. In 1928 the association faced up to charges it gave preferential service to morning and large newspapers; as a result, it spread association voting rights more evenly. In 1937, again in answer to charges of large newspaper favoritism, it gave three of its eighteen board directorships to representatives of small papers. The Supreme Court finally ended the press association practice of denying service to those not elected to membership when in 1945 it ruled the practice an unfair restraint of competition. From then on, any newspaper could purchase AP service—even one in competition with an AP member paper.

The United Press Associations

The second press association that survived into modern times was founded by E. W. Scripps in 1907. Scripps, like other publishers of the 1900s, found many of his papers could not buy AP service because they were competitors of AP members. In the 1880s and 1890s the Scripps (now Scripps-Howard) papers were clients of the old United Press. But when that wire service died, Scripps, without a press service, and with only a few correspondents in key cities around the country, decided to join AP. He offered all his chain of papers to Stone and the AP of Illinois. But, true to form, AP agreed to accept some, not all, of the papers, refusing membership to those in competition with AP member papers.

Always the eccentric, Scripps decided to withhold all his papers from AP. The service, he decided, was "too conservative" and "too capitalistic." It was dominated by the big morning papers that used the association to give them "a monopoly of all the important news." It also was possible, he feared, that joining AP could hamper any future competition he might want to undertake against AP papers.

In 1907 he scratched together several regional wire services to form the United Press Associations—the modern United Press. The incorporation papers stated the UP Associations planned to "buy and sell news; to own, lease, manage, buy and sell news agencies . . . to hold stock in associations and corporations for such purposes." And so, while AP was a nonprofit news-gathering cooperative, the UP was founded as a news business.

The new service opened for business with 369 newspaper clients that summer. It benefited greatly from the fact that many of its clients were Scripps' papers. As he himself said, all he had to do to pay UP bills was figure the costs of conducting UP business each month, count the money received from clients, then assess the Scripps newspapers the remaining amount. Owning 51 percent of the company made many things possible.

Roy Howard became general manager of UP in 1908 (and eventually the second name in the Scripps-Howard title). He set about establishing bureaus in major European capitals and found fortune smiling when during World War I the British halted the cabling of German news to subscribers. Argentine newspapers did not want the biased reporting from Havas, the French news agency. And AP, due to its foreign news contracts of 1893, was unable to sell foreign news. (AP did not offer a world service until 1946.) Howard exploited the situation, providing the Argentine papers with the news they wanted and building a string of bureaus and clients in Latin America.

UP survived one unfortunate incident near the end of World War I, when Howard dispatched a report based on a message he had seen in U.S. naval headquarters at Brest: that the war was over and the armistice had been signed at 11 that morning. In New York, the report precipitated wild celebrations—until AP reported the story was false. The war slogged on four more days. Howard had inadvertently provided an anecdote that contributed to UP's lingering reputation for inaccuracy. Still, by 1920 UP had acquired 780 clients, many of them in South America, and was well on its way to becoming a viable competitor to the AP.

Hearst, the INS, and the UPI

In 1909 William Randolph Hearst launched a third major wire service, the International News Service, or INS. INS was an outgrowth of wire facilities Hearst had leased for his own group of newspapers. It concentrated its efforts on establishing bureaus in major news centers and on stories by well-known writers: Quentin Reynolds, Paul Gallico, Damon Runyon, Hollywood columnist Louella Parsons and radio commentator Edwin C. Hill. The strategy won INS many subscribers, and its talented group of reporters produced many major news beats, but INS coverage was not as comprehensive as AP's or UP's. Few newspapers or radio news departments could rely on it as a primary source of national and international news. And so its existence came from a limited market: newspapers and broadcast news departments that wanted a second, or perhaps a third, wire service. INS had 400 newspaper clients in 1918, but only 334 forty years later, in 1958, when it merged with United Press to form United Press International, or UPI.

The merger between UP and INS strengthened the competition between the new UPI and the AP in the 1960s and 1970s. AP held the advantage of more newspaper subscribers into the 1970s, serving some three hundred more papers than UPI. The two services remained close in the number of broadcasting clients. (See figure 12.1.) But in the 1960s UPI began to fall behind and lose money. In the first two years of the 1980s it lost more than $20 million. As journalist Mitchell Stephens has pointed out, one obvious problem was the mortality rate of domestic evening newspapers, once the foundation of the Scripps UP empire. With fewer newspapers to sell to, UPI also found itself in competition with a growing number of supplemental news services entering the marketplace. And AP, the last holdout in the press radio war, had recovered from that old error to become a strong competitor for modern broadcast subscribers. With a reputation for more extensive news coverage, AP cut the advantage UPI had enjoyed in broadcast clients since the 1930s. The E. W. Scripps Company decided to sell UPI in 1978.

There were not many buyers. After more than one attempt to arrange a deal (including an offer to give UPI to National Public Radio), the press service was sold in 1982 to a newly formed company, Media News Corporation of Nashville. Media News pledged to develop an improved news service at UPI and give vigorous competition to the Associated Press.

The Wire Service Operation

Like the mass media, the press associations have the usual administrative, business, promotion, sales, and technical functions to maintain, and do so with specialized departments and roles within their organizations. Administrative offices for AP are in New York. The UPI administrative offices were moved from New York to Nashville in 1983. The news operations of the press association also are similar to that of media news operations, with stories assigned, covered, written, edited, and sent. The press associations do not distribute their news stories directly to the public, of course.

In general, press associations operate in three major areas of news coverage: regional, national, and international. And unlike the media, they do not operate from one central organization but rather from a series of *bureaus* established across the United States and around the world. The bureaus are connected by an assortment of telegraph and telephone wires, microwave relays, undersea cables, shortwave radio, telephones, and communications satellites.

The Wire Service Bureau

The bureau of the modern news service, as researcher Oliver Boyd-Barrett has written, is the essence of the news-agency operation. By maintaining local bureaus around the country—and in foreign countries—the press association is better prepared to survey the local news, recognize local news interests, and understand local news needs. With bureaus in Arkansas, Colorado, New Hampshire, Taiwan, and Tanzania, the press association is able to know what the local news is, know what news local people want, and provide informed coverage of a local crisis when one arises.

Bureaus vary greatly in size, from one to forty or more in regional bureaus, such as AP's London bureau of recent years. A survey of fifteen press association bureaus in the 1970s (both American and major foreign) revealed a total of 364 full-time staff, with 53 percent engaged in news gathering and reporting. The others were ancillary staff—including messengers and technicians. Of the 194 journalists, thirty-four were photographers and five were specialists in sports or political writing. And so the fifteen bureaus in the survey covered the news in their areas with an average of twenty-four staff members, thirteen of which were full-time journalists, two or three photographers, and occasionally a special interest reporter. Most reporters were general assignment.

Rovers, Firefighters, and Stringers

The press bureau may have a "rover" reporter, and, Boyd-Barrett has reported, reporters who are used more or less as "firefighters." Rover reporters usually are senior journalists with established reputations. They have a great deal of freedom to travel about in pursuit of their stories, but they also work closely with the bureau chief in each area they enter. Only a very few press association reporters obtain the status of rover. The total number on the staffs of the five major global wire services probably is about twelve. Firefighters are reporters who are given responsibility for covering a sudden crisis, a sudden news story—a revolution, or the eruption of a volcano. Almost any press association reporter might become a firefighter on a given story.

A common practice among press bureaus is to build a reliable list of stringers to augment the staff's news coverage. Stringer, originally a newspaper term, denotes a reporter paid by the piece, literally for the "string" of stories the bureau decides to use. Beginners, media news reporters and others who want to moonlight on their regular news jobs often string for wire services.

Still another potential source of news coverage for the press associations is the association member or client. The AP, of course, organized as a news cooperative relies on newspaper and news media members to feed stories to the wire. UPI encourages its clients to contribute to the

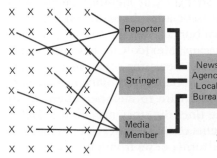
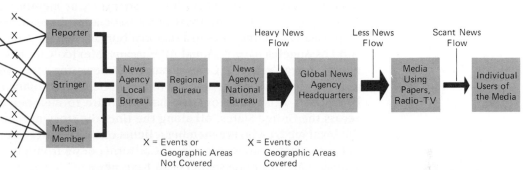

X = Events or Geographic Areas Not Covered

X = Events or Geographic Areas Covered

Figure 12.2 The flow of news through the International News Agency: Events (X's) reported by wire service stringers, as well as by service and media reporters, are fed into local and regional, then national and international bureaus, and finally to the media and audience.

wire too. The news agencies also have exchange agreements with other news organizations which allow them to use their stories. The news agencies from time to time may also buy stories—exclusives—from the various news media, depending on the significance of the story.

The Flow of Press Association News

A story reported by a bureau reporter, a stringer, or client passes through tiers of the wire service network before it reaches national and international distribution. (See figure 12.2.) Area reporters select and write about events and file them in their local bureau. The local bureau chief edits the story and sends it along to the regional bureau, where the chief decides whether or not to use it on the state or regional wire. The story may appear to have national significance as well. If so, the local or regional editor can submit it to the national bureau. And the national news bureau may distribute it with the national and international news sent along the trunk to all parts of the country.

Let us assume there is a story about a large local dam that has developed a large crack, forcing the government to evacuate hundreds of thousands of people from their homes and closing a north-south interstate through the area. Quite likely, both the regional and national bureau chiefs will "move" such a story or some part of it on the regional and the national wires. When the story reaches the national level, it may face another decision. Will it be of interest to clients overseas? Where? Will the cracking dam be of interest in Egypt, the home of the Aswan Dam, for example? If the global agency in New York believes it has interest overseas, the story is sent along the "feeder line" (or by satellite relay) to Africa, Latin America, Asia or the Pacific, and finally to the foreign member/client news media that publish or broadcast it in their own countries. Foreign news finds its way into the United States in much the same fashion. AP and UPI reporters, stringers, or member/clients overseas, report stories to the local press association bureau. Small bureaus then usually feed the story to a regional bureau. Atlanta, Columbus, Ohio, and Los Angeles have regional AP bureaus. Mexico City has been the regional bureau for AP's Central American news for some years. The regional bureau passes the story on to the global agency office in New York. From there it is sent along the national wire to member/client media across the United States. All along the line, the story may be fed back to the local media who are member/clients of the wire service; in that way, California newspapers can report California news from elsewhere in the state and Mexican newspapers can have news of their country and from the Central American region.

Where Speed Is King

Both AP and UPI compete with each other to report news to their member/client media as quickly as possible. Moving a story on the wire first—if only by a matter of seconds—can be an important victory. The press association's dedication to fast reporting and "scoops" also is illustrated by the fact that any bureau chief can put a bulletin on the wire at any time he or she sees fit. The press association bureau chief can sound alarms in more cities, towns and villages than perhaps any person in the world—or at least, sound them to more working news professionals than anyone else. For example, when Marxist Salvador Allende was elected president of Chile, the story was sent from Santiago as a bulletin to New York. From there, it was relayed to other overseas bureaus by feeder line and also sent across the United States on the national trunk to regional and local bureaus. Within a matter of minutes it had been distributed around the world. For more important news, there is the "flash" designation. The first report of the shooting of President Kennedy in 1963 moved on the wire as a flash.

The Press Association Services

A diagram of Associated Press lines inside the United States is given in figure 12.3. The solid lines represent national trunk lines that run across the country. The lighter, broken lines indicate the regional/state offshoots. The lines also reflect the basic news services offered by the press associations: the national/international news service, commonly called the A wire, and the state/regional service, usually referred to as the state wire. The first two services are written and distributed primarily for newspapers. They are written in newspaper style so they fit into newspapers with only minor corrections. The A and state wire news is presented as individual news stories and features or as updates and corrections of individual stories.

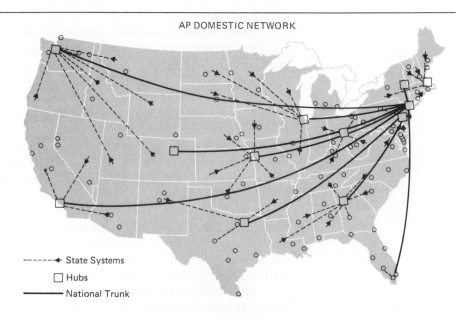

Figure 12.3 The Associated Press communications network in the United States. The "hubs" are regional bureau offices.

AP DOMESTIC NETWORK

-----◄ State Systems
□ Hubs
— National Trunk

The daily news service is divided into morning and evening news cycles to serve morning and evening newspapers. Each cycle is preceded by a "budget" that announces the dozen or so stories that are to be transmitted, a device that helps editors plan the layout of their newspapers. Unlike the mass media, the wire services do not always distribute polished stories. While a wire reporter may work on a story for days, then transmit it to media clients for release, the press association also sends related facts on breaking stories to help client/members flesh out the story before deadline. As time for publication draws near, the wires are constantly updating the stories of the day, bringing new facts to clients where needed, even rewriting the story's lead or opening as events dictate. There is, as an old UPI saying goes, a "deadline every minute" in press association work.

The third major press association news service is the radio, or broadcast wire. The radio wire sends five- and fifteen-minute newscasts rather than individual stories. The newscasts are written in conversational broadcasting style so they can be read over the air with little editing. The radio wire offers both regional (state) and national newscasts throughout the day. Radio style is strikingly different from newspaper style, and not everyone finds changing from one to another an easy task. (David Brinkley is said to have decided to go into broadcast news because he found writing for the radio easier and more interesting.)

There is some crossover in the use of newspaper and radio wire services. Newspapers that present teletext news on cable television channels are finding that broadcast copy scans better than traditional newspaper copy. Some broadcasting stations, on the other hand, aware that the radio wire is a summary of national and state wire stories, subscribe to both services to insure they have the detail they need when they rewrite newscasts for the second, third, or even fourth time throughout the news day. Some large broadcasting operations are quite capable of writing their own newscasts without the radio wire service.

Both AP and UPI also offer around-the-clock audio news services of five-minute newscasts as well as special Washington, farm, business, and stock market reports. They provide an "actuality" service of voice reports and audio interviews for broadcasters who wish to include national news in their local newscasts. For example, an interview of a prominent economic expert in Washington can be recorded off the AP or UPI audio wire and inserted into a local station's newscast in the farm belt.

Both wire services also offer black and white photos delivered by facsimile machine to member/client offices. UPI operates a video news service for television. AP has a color slide service and distributes video tape by mail to its television news department members. Both AP and UPI have special news services for magazine clients.

Generally speaking, the two press associations converted to word processing equipment with the newspaper industry. UPI's new two-way newspaper computer system allows newspaper clients with computer hookups to dial the UPI computer and share stories from an entire morgue (newspaper library of its own clippings) of data. The UPI computer also can drive typesetting equipment so the newspaper can call out the story and have it set in type in the newspaper's own shop, ready for the press the moment the process is completed.

Media News and UPI: Success Story?

Clearly one of the important press association questions of the 1980s concerns the new management at United Press International and its ability to turn the press association around. Can UPI survive? To be specific, can it survive under the management and control of two relatively young media executives who have little background in news reporting and media management?

The two men in charge of UPI's parent company, Media News, are Douglas Ruhe and William Geissler, of Focus Communications, a television company whose principal holding is pay-television station WFBN in Chicago. (Three other partners spent time with Media News in its first year, then departed, amicably professing lack of time to participate or noting differences over management policies.) News professionals were disturbed when they learned Ruhe and Geissler had limited experience in news reporting and management. More disturbing was the knowledge both had been civil rights activists in the 1960s, that Ruhe had been arrested for those activities, and Geissler had actually served time in prison for refusing to be inducted into the service during the Vietnam War. (He now says he would serve if called again.) The fact both men are members of the Baha'i faith added to fears UPI had come under control of two radicals who were likely to turn the press service into a "religious commune, a propaganda organ, or a science fiction workshop," as journalist Mitchell Stephens put it.

A Realistic Approach Indications are, however, that Ruhe and Geissler have taken a highly realistic approach to UPI's problems by cutting costs, increasing services, raising UPI company morale, and attracting new clients. To reduce UPI's $14 million annual Bell System land-line costs, the two partners have pursued a program to convert from wire to satellite distribution, a move that should save $6 million a year. To convert, UPI had to persuade its clients to install reception dishes or antennas, but by summer's end 1983, the 2,000 receive-only antennas were installed. To save money UPI also has moved its national and international news headquarters from expensive New York to less-expensive, yet newsworthy Washington, and relocated its business offices in Nashville, where Media News established its office services. To ease the costs of top-heavy management, forty-five administrative and clerical positions were replaced with thirty news and editorial personnel in 1983. The following year, as money problems continued to plague the press association, management asked wire service guild members to take a sizable pay cut to keep the company afloat. In a three-to-one vote the guild agreed, accepting a cut of top-scale news salaries from $558 to $423 a week, and a three-month cut to lower-scale salaries of $220 to $165 a week. Salaries were scheduled to rise slowly and return to former levels in 1986. Management was subject to the same wage reductions as the employees. With the cutbacks came 200 layoffs of personnel at all levels. In return the company agreed to concessions that management, too, was to get "lean and mean," and all union members became stockholders in UPI. UPI president Luis Nogales estimated that the changes would save a total of $14 million through 1985.

Perhaps the most imaginative financial move UPI has made to date came when it entered into a joint agreement with Prudential and Comsat to develop a nationwide direct broadcasting satellite (DBS) network (see p. 351). If completed, the agreement will give UPI a place in direct satellite broadcasting and a highly economical way of distributing its news to the news media as well as directly to the public. A $25-million investment was required, but Ruhe and Geissler felt UPI would be more attractive to investors as part of a new DBS enterprise than as an older wire service which had been unprofitable for twenty years.

UPI also is working to become more competitive with its press association offerings. The news service now offers news briefs to give updated information faster, a mini-debate column on important issues, Latin success stories to highlight Hispanic-Americans who have made a contribution to their communities, as well as regular reports on regional economic and financial trends. To improve its news coverage, the service has added news bureaus to its system—two dozen or more in the first year of new management.

The Challenge

UPI's greatest challenge may well belong to Ruhe and Geissler personally and may be won or lost in their ability to convince the news establishment that they are competent, dedicated news professionals.

More is at stake, though, than their professional images. As writer Laura Hill has observed, if they fail, we lose UPI and the competitive check the press service provides for AP. And without competition, many feel, the Associated Press likely would not continue as the efficient, fair, accurate, enterprising news-gathering agency it is today. Losing UPI could mean losing the two best press services in the world.

Diversification

UPI's attempts to cut costs and meet the news service competition of the Associated Press are both necessary and commendable. As already noted, however, the company also must diversify its products and services if it is to remain successful. Boyd-Barrett notes press associations have been diversifying since the early days of radio. Having lost their ability to hold newspaper clients under monopolistic control, he has written, they developed clients among the broadcasting media in order to expand. The challenge to the press associations in the next few years may well be the challenge of finding new, nonmedia clients to serve, now that broadcast media growth has begun to stabilize.

What Else to Sell?
Who Else as Client?

Boyd-Barrett has suggested that press association diversification has been and will be of three types: (1) providing services for news media other than newspapers, (2) providing new kinds of services for newspapers, and (3) providing information and news for nonmedia clients. Each may involve the general news service currently offered, or new, specialized information services tailored for media or nonmedia clients. A nonmedia client, for example, might purchase the regular radio wire for distribution to employees over a factory loudspeaker or for special daily business reports collected and edited for the business executives. In the past, nonmedia clients of the press agencies have included financial and commercial institutions; advertising agencies and advertisers; departments or ministries in government; and private clients (including individuals, clubs, and even educational institutions).

**New Technology,
New News Topics**

UPI's plans include a new high-speed wire service to computer companies that will provide clients with instant access to a librarylike videotext system well-stocked with up-to-date collections of UPI news stories. The service is aimed at business customers as well as news organizations; businesses contemplating buying oil in the Middle East, for example, could read up on events in that area before deciding to make a purchase.

If we look at the four major commercial news agencies, AP, UPI, Reuters, and Agence France-Presse, there is good reason to believe business/economic news will be among the first areas chosen for diversification in the future. Reuters' earliest and most important group of clients were merchants. General news was not added to the economic news service until much later, after telegraph rates were lowered to allow more wordy dispatches. AP and Dow Jones set up a joint overseas operation in 1967 to gather and distribute economic news. The combination gave foreign newspapers financial reports backed by the prestige of Dow Jones and the wide distribution and general news service of the AP.

Despite their ability to gather large amounts of information, press agencies have had only moderate success in publishing and selling books to the public. The AP has attempted educational publications and an annual sports almanac. Both AP and UPI have published major news stories compiled into books. For example, UPI published one "instant" book—an in-depth report—about the Watergate scandal. Expansion into publishing would seem to depend upon the press associations' ability to publish books that would not tarnish their reputation for press service objectivity.

**This Press
Association for Hire?**

Through diversification, the spectre of press associations giving special services to government agencies looms nearer and darker than we like to imagine. In 1963 the Senate Foreign Relations Committee found that INS had hired out its reporters. For a fee, INS agreed to have specific questions put to specific sources. The answers were reported on the INS wire. Later, UPI revealed it had a special service bureau that asked questions, in exchange for fees, on behalf of domestic and foreign corporations and publications. The UPI-collected material was not distributed on the UPI wire, and the revenue from it, UPI claimed, amounted to only one-tenth its yearly earnings. (See p. 338.)

As Boyd-Barrett has suggested, the evidence is that diversification is not the panacea for the economic problems of the press association, although it is an important factor in keeping away government regulation. The major news agency that has diversified the least, Agence France-Presse, has paid a high price in credibility by becoming dependent on too many government departments and agencies for income. TASS, the press association with the most readily identifiable political views, is owned and operated by the Soviet government, of course, and pleases only the government, not private clients or the general public. It collects many kinds of information to report to the Soviet government and the Soviet-owned media.

Careers in the Press Associations

Since AP and UPI both are dedicated to rapid coverage of hard news stories on a moment-by-moment basis, in the eyes of news professionals they are one of the best-training grounds in journalism. The press associations usually are good places to job hunt, too. News agency work requires a good variety of journalistic staff—reporters, editors, photographers, motion picture editors, and newscasters—to cover and distribute print, audio, and picture stories. And press agencies usually are able to pay for talent since salaries are set by the standards of the American Newspaper Guild. (See chapter 5.)

The wire service daily routine has given more than one young journalist outstanding training. Those who have gone from wire work to excel in the profession include the New York *Times'* Harrison Salisbury, television anchor and commentator Howard K. Smith, CBS reporter-commentator Eric Sevareid, Helen Thomas, now senior White House correspondent in Washington, as well as two one-time competitors in television: Walter Cronkite and David Brinkley. There are many more. Those listed are all from UP or UPI.

Newspaper Syndication

A media syndicate is an organization that sells publication rights of media messages to media organizations. Syndicates are important message sources for both the print and broadcast media. They offer use of their syndicated materials—exclusive publication or broadcasting rights—to media at a price usually determined by the publication's circulation or the broadcast station's market size.

Ansel N. Kellogg of Baraboo, Wisconsin, introduced the idea of syndication into American journalism following the Civil War. With his partner Andrew J. Aikens, Kellogg inaugurated "ready print" service to give busy publishers features and poetry already printed on one side of a newspaper sheet. The publishers finished the job by printing their own ads and news on the other side. Thus the ready print page gave editors a low-cost, high-quality newspaper they could not have produced on their own.

The principle of syndication is the same today.

For convenience, we can divide modern print media syndication into five basic categories: (1) news, picture and press services, (2) feature, news and picture syndicate services, (3) newspaper comic sections, (4) newspaper magazine sections, and (5) newspaper art services.

Other than the news services already discussed, there is a large number of smaller, more specialized news and information syndicates that offer news and photos to the print media. Some are special interest companies, such as the Alternative Press Syndicate or the Religious News Service. Some offer news photography services—Black Star and Photo Communications Co., Inc., for example. But all supply, often through the mails, hard-or soft-syndicated news of one type or another to media clients across the nation.

Feature syndicates include some of the largest syndicates in the newspaper field. Early feature syndication focused on literary works, the writings of such authors as Jack London, Mark Twain, Henry James, Rudyard Kipling, and Robert Louis Stevenson. In time, the feature columnist became a syndicated staple. Joel Chandler Harris' "Uncle Remus" tales reached the nation through syndication from the Atlanta *Constitution;* Edgar A. Guest of the Detroit *Free Press* gained a national reputation as a poet through syndication; and from Chicago, Finley Peter Dunne's Irish saloonkeeper, "Mr. Dooley," entertained readers with his views of the political world. Today's feature columnists include Art Buchwald, Russell Baker, and Erma Bombeck, each of whom proves the genre is alive and well.

The 1920s brought gossip columnists and political columnists to American journalism and newspaper syndication. Walter Winchell became a star of Hearst's King Features Syndicate, and more serious political commentary was offered by David Lawrence (later of *U.S. News and World Report*). Walter Lippmann and Drew Pearson established the precedent for such modern-day political columnists as William F. Buckley, Jr., Kevin Phillips, Tom Wicker, and Jack Anderson. Anderson, incidentally, worked as a reporter for Drew Pearson on the "Washington Merry Go Round" column, then continued the column after Pearson died in 1969.

Also important to feature syndicates is the editorial cartoon, the newspaper feature that suggests the drawing pen is mightier than the sword. Through the work of such gifted practitioners as Thomas Nast of *Harper's* and the *New York Times,* the editorial cartoon became a part of newspaper repertoire after the Civil War. Attacks by Nast on the Tammany Hall Tweed Gang are still some of America's best political cartoons. Rollin Kirby of Pulitzer's New York *World* and Edmund Duffy of the Baltimore *Sun* were both three-time Pulitzer Prize winners for their work during the first thirty years of this century. Since the end of World War II, the nation has enjoyed the syndicated political barbs of some remarkably talented cartoonists. Among them are Herbert L. Block ("Herblock") of the Washington *Post,* Paul Conrad of the Los Angeles

The syndicated political cartoon and two presidents of the United States: (A) Don Wright on President Reagan; (B) Mike Peters on President Carter. (A) © 1984 Don Wright, *The Miami News,* Tribune Company Syndicate. (B) Reprinted by permission of United Feature Syndicate, Inc.

A

B

Times, Bill Mauldin of the St. Louis *Post-Dispatch,* Jeff MacNelly of the Chicago *Tribune,* and Mike Peters of the Dayton *Daily News.* Peters is only one of several young talented cartoonists now at work.

Almost always overlooked but still the first to be missed in the newspaper are crossword puzzles, bridge columns, and horoscopes. Few editors would dare to go to press more than one time without them.

Comics have been a part of newspapers since Pulitzer's "Yellow Kid" was printed in the 1890s. Hearst's King Features and United Features entered the field before World War I, and both still are important in comic syndication today. The first regular daily comic strip was "Mutt and Jeff" by H. C. "Bud" Fisher. It appeared in the San Francisco *Chronicle* in 1907. Ten years later, Sidney Smith introduced "Andy Gump" for the Chicago *Tribune*-New York *Daily News* syndicate. It was the first continuing comic strip, "The Waltons" of its day. In 1924 the same shop also produced the still popular "Orphan Annie."

Newspaper magazines still are good advertising vehicles for family products, although they have decreased in number in recent years. (See chapter 6.)

Art services, like some features, seem to be invisible, until you have to do without them. Much of the artwork in newspapers and magazines is not original, but drawings, designs, or sketches provided by art services.

Broadcast Syndication

The Radio Music Format

Of all the media syndication available today, radio syndication of music formats seems closest to Ansel Kellogg's ready print service. Music format syndication was one of the major factors in helping FM challenge AM for dominance in radio ratings. A wide range of companies offers a full range of syndicated music formats for radio stations. One syndicate—CnB Studios—advertises format B (beautiful yesteryear), format C (contemporary plus MOR), format N (nostalgic 78s), and format P (potpourri of

Comics, Comic Readers, and Syndication's Number One Cat

Research has indicated readership of comics is down significantly since the advent of television. In the mid-1950s, more than 99 percent of children and 80 percent of all adults read at least something in the Sunday comics. By the early 1980s only 53 percent of adults and 80 percent of children read the Sunday comics. Children still are the heaviest readers of comics, but readership drops off significantly after age seventeen. As a rule, adults view comic reading as second in importance to the main news sections, but college graduates read comics more frequently than other adults.

All in all, the comic strip audience still is sizable and loyal. Eighty percent of comic readers read *all* sections of the Sunday comics, for example. And when Garry Trudeau, creator of "Doonesbury," took a sabbatical from the strip from 1982 to 1984, more than one newspaper attempted to fill the void with reruns of older strips. One newspaper poll found readers more willing to read old "Doonesbury" strips rather than any replacement. Universal Press Syndicate stopped the practice, however, to reduce confusion when Trudeau took up the strip again in 1984.

The trend continues to be toward the "funny" comic. In one study, adults and children asked to evaluate 108 strips put those with light humor in the top ten and placed six dramatic strips in the bottom ten spots. "Peanuts" and "Blondie" tend to be popular with females while males prefer "Beetle Bailey," according to research by the Gene Reilly Group of Connecticut.

The first choice by both sexes in all parts of the country was "Garfield," the grouchy, fat cat that loves lasagna. "Garfield" also has been at the top of more than one newspaper poll. The strip now is seen in fourteen hundred newspapers around the world and has been the subject of television specials as well as some eight books. A paradox is that Garfield's creator, Jim Davis, has given some credit for the success of the popular feline character to his sometimes competitor, television. The television sources for Garfield? They were "Morris the Cat" commercials and Archie Bunker, the chunky bigot in "All in the Family."

© 1983 United Feature Syndicate, Inc.

unusual formats). Like the nineteenth century editor with ready print, all the contemporary radio station manager has had to do is add local news and advertising to the syndicated radio format.

Other than the complete format syndication service, radio also occasionally uses syndicated dramatic series and features. Old, off-network nostalgic series such as "The Lone Ranger" show up from time to time. Newer and shorter syndicated features that fit the disc jockey format also have been in vogue in recent years. The "Simon Q" detective feature gives a short, dramatic description of a crime, with clues, then waits for the audience to call in and solve the problem for a prize.

Television Syndication

Television syndication, on the other hand, is devoted for the most part to individual programs: (1) old film productions, (2) original television programs from independent companies, and (3) off-network, rerun programs. When we recall (from chapter 11) that network programming accounts for only 65 percent of local station program offerings and that local news is the principal production of the local station, it is easy to understand how program syndication is now an $800 million a year business and one of the most significant factors in television programming today.

It always has been important. The first decade of television saw local stations desperate for programs—with old films from Hollywood's lesser studios coming to the rescue. The likes of Hollywood's Hopalong Cassidy and George "Gabby" Hayes rode the television range so often in the 1950s, mothers joked about vacuuming trail dust out of the carpet.

One leading syndicator, Sandy Frank, started his television syndication business in 1964 with one old off-network game show: "You Asked For It." The program was five years old then, but Frank still earned $1 million with it, more than enough to continue his success with such film fare as the original "The Lone Ranger," "Our Gang" comedies (still in syndication today) and, more recently, reruns of Chuck Barris' "$1.98 Beauty Contest" and "The Parent Game."

The Prime Time Access Rule

Television syndication, nevertheless, was on the downswing when the 1970s arrived. The television networks had made very satisfactory arrangements with program packagers in Hollywood, and station program schedules depended on the Hollywood product. In 1972, however, there was a change in program rules. In the now-famous prime time access rule (see chapter 15), the Federal Communications Commission, hoping to diversify the sources of television programming and encourage more local

Jerry Mathers as The Beaver and Tony Dow as the older brother, Wally, of the sitcom "Leave it to Beaver." "Beaver" originated in 1957 and stayed on network television until 1963. As a syndicated program, it still draws audiences that number in the millions.

production, limited networks to three hours of prime time programming. But the local stations, rather than chance expensive and relatively low-quality productions, turned instead to syndicated shows. A large group of producers jumped into the field, reviving old, low-cost formats (such as quiz shows) to fill the time that had suddenly opened up. The hours between 4:00 P.M. and 6:30 P.M. became syndication time for the most part, as did the half hour following 7:30, after the station's newscast.

Syndicated shows—both original and rerun—now thrive on the open time around the local newscast, with the rerun having gained status as counter programming against the competition's newscast. "Three's Company," "Happy Days," "Star Trek," and "Laverne and Shirley" are often winners in the ratings race against the local news.

Under most conditions, reruns do well in the ratings. Such old, black and white fare as "Leave it to Beaver," "The Adventures of Ozzie and Harriet," and "The Andy Griffith Show" still are drawing sizable audiences. For example, "Beaver," first on the air in 1957, ran for six years on CBS and ABC. As a rerun, it still was drawing ratings of 3.5 in the early 1980s, and audiences of three million households.

The Independents

Independent stations and cable television have capitalized on the fact that many in the television audience would rather see off-network reruns and old movies than watch new Hollywood dramatic efforts. San Francisco's KTVU, one of over two hundred independent television stations in the country, is a good example. KTVU has been gaining steadily in local ratings by broadcasting syndicated reruns, winning audiences with "Star Trek," "The Odd Couple," and "Barney Miller," and such older movies as *Casablanca, Born Yesterday,* and *The Maltese Falcon.* With some news, clever promotion, and a lot of syndicated material, independent stations showed a 22 percent gain in local advertising and a 24 percent growth in national advertising in the early 1980s—more than twice that of local network affiliates. Ironically, running even old syndicate programming has helped the image of some independent stations—ones that programmed roller derbies and grunt-and-groan wrestling matches in earlier years. Before they seemed only to attract the type of advertiser who "sold used cars while holding onto the leash of his pet armadillo," as the *Wall Street Journal* has put it. The more sedate atmosphere of off-network reruns has brought the national advertiser back to independent stations in droves.

Cable television is capitalizing on the popularity of reruns, too. Ted Turner, owner and promoter of Superstation WTBS in Atlanta, has argued forcefully that wholesome family programs, such as "Beaver" and "Ozzie and Harriet," are meaningful alternatives to the more recent, bizarre television adventure shows in which a school bus is "attacked by truck drivers wearing bikinis." WTBS and other cable-distributed stations (WGN from Chicago and WOR from New York) depend on syndicated reruns and old movies to hold audiences in fifty states.

Transcending Gender, Age, and Education

But programming reruns is tricky business. Programs that were smash hits on the networks the first time around do not always do well as reruns in the 4:00 to 6:30 P.M. news hour. "Mission: Impossible," "Ironside," and "Marcus Welby, M.D." were unsuccessful in the late afternoon slot, although they all were big network hits. One big disappointment was the "Six Million Dollar Man." Although designed for younger viewers who usually watch during that time period, it struggled and failed. Apparently, the show was a fad for viewers and by the time it was rerun, the fad had passed.

The rule seems to be that to succeed in local syndicated time periods a show's appeal must transcend gender, age, and education. Programs cannot be men's or women's shows, for the young or old, for the highbrow or lowbrow. As writer Earl Gottschalk, Jr., has pointed out, they have to be like singer Willie Nelson and pull all segments of the audience together, closing generation gaps, intellectual gaps, and social gaps.

For years now, the leading money winner of television syndication has been "I Love Lucy," the slapstick sitcom produced by Lucille Ball and Desi Arnez in the early days of black and white television. A new "king" is assuming the throne, however. The Korean War satire "M*A*S*H" first went into syndication in 1979, four years before the show's final network season ended in 1983 with a long, two-and-one-half-hour farewell to prime time. The first round of reruns indicated the show probably would surpass "Lucy" in dollars earned. It won such boffo ratings in New York and Los Angeles that stations there carried episodes three times a day. Even UHF stations found "M*A*S*H" had drawing power. Estimates in 1983 projected the second round of "M*A*S*H" reruns would gross about $125 million—some $50 million of which would go to pay residuals for the actors. (Alan "Hawkeye" Alda will make $25 million on the second round of reruns alone.)

The network series that becomes even a fair candidate for syndication is the exception rather than the rule. The practice of recent years has been for networks to order twenty-four episodes of a new prime time series, which means the show must stay on the air for five seasons in order to acquire the necessary one hundred or more episodes needed to fill the five-day-a-week syndication strip. Only one in forty shows now has a network run that long.

Buck Owens and Roy Clark of "Hee Haw," one of the longest running programs on television.

Some First-Run Champions

All television syndication programs are not reruns. All do not run in the news hours between 4:00 and 8:00 P.M. Highly honored and respected is the syndicated "Donahue" show, with moderator Phil Donahue, and his five-mornings-a-week, in-depth and balanced discussions of social and political issues. Donahue and his audiences have questioned consumer advocates, part-time prostitutes, a father who seduced and carried on an extended affair with his maturing daughter, Vice-President George Bush, Julia Child, and news commentator Paul Harvey.

Dedicated more toward "fun and games"—and making losing weight "fun and games"—is the "Richard Simmons Show." Simmons, a former foodaholic, overcame obesity and established weight-reducing salons before coming onto syndicated television. The show is filled with zany antics, dietetic cooking recipes, weight loss advice, and on-camera exercise with studio audience members who bring their own leotards and join in the show's calisthenics.

One of the longest-running national television shows is the syndicated "Hee Haw." The country variety show first went into production as a CBS replacement for the Smothers Brothers in 1969. Although it climbed to sixth in national ratings in the 1970–71 season, the network decided to cut the show; as a result, it moved from New York to Nashville and to syndication. Its format of blackouts and one-liners has given it the label *corn pone "Laugh In,"* but the show offers more than corn pone to viewers. Along with the regular Nashville crew (Minnie Pearl, Buck Owens, Roy Clark, and Gunilla Hutton, as Nurse Goodbody), there have been such unpone-like guest stars as Ernest Borgnine, Senator Robert Byrd, Sammy Davis, Jr., Senator Howard Baker, and the Reverend Oral Roberts. The mix has been popular. In 1984 the show, syndicated to two hundred stations across the country, completed its sixteenth year on the air, passing such long-running, fourteen-year-old series as "Bonanza" and "The Adventures of Ozzie and Harriet," and equalling such fifteen-year series as "The Jackie Gleason Show" and "The Jack Benny Show." ("Gunsmoke" and NBC's "Tonight" shows have had twenty or more seasons.)

If there is a middle-of-the-road program in original syndication it might be "Entertainment Tonight," a slick, newsy six-day-a-week series produced by Paramount and owned by Paramount Television, Cox Broadcasting, Taft Broadcasting, and TeleRep. "Entertainment Tonight" is a nightly news program about the entertainment industry. Managing editor of the program is James G. Bellows, who resigned as editor of the Los Angeles *Herald Examiner* to take the job. The program's closest syndicated competition is "PM Magazine," a feature news show produced by Westinghouse's Group W and local stations as a cooperative venture in feature reporting.

Communications Satellites

One of the most significant communication innovations since broadcasting is the communication satellite. Following entry into space by the Soviet Union with its Sputnik I satellite in 1957, the United States launched weather, navigational, surveillance and military satellites into earth's orbit to receive and send signals back to earth. To develop the transmission of signals across oceans and around the world—especially television signals—Congress passed the Communications Satellite Act of 1962 and formed Comsat, a privately owned corporation to create a communication satellite system. Worldwide communication required that satellites be placed at three primary positions above the earth's oceans: one above the Atlantic, one above the Indian, and the third above the Pacific. Beginning in 1967 it was possible to send and receive signals to and from any point on the earth's surface by way of the three strategically placed satellites.

In the mid-1970s the launching of domestic satellites into orbit over the United States made possible domestic satellite signal relays—instead of telephone long line relays—from any point in the country to another. Those who moved into satellite transmission (PBS, for example) found that even with the initial cost of sending and receiving hardware, satellite costs proved no higher than those of the old AT&T long lines, and satellite relays were much "cleaner"—lower on noise—than long-line relays. With hardware in place, too, the cost of relays began to drop.

Figure 12.4

Leading Syndicated Shows by Household Ratings

Top 25 Programs, Ranked by Weighted DMA Ratings

1. Family Feud PM	12.3
2. Wheel of Fortune	12.1
3. M*A*S*H	11.2
4. Three's Company	10.2
5. PM Magazine	9.8
6. People's Court	9.1
7. Hee Haw	9.0
8. Entertainment Tonight	8.8
9. The Jeffersons	8.3
10. John F. Kennedy (tie)	7.6
10. Solid Gold (tie)	7.6
12. WKRP in Cincinnati	7.4
13. Dance Fever	7.3
13. Hayden Fry	7.3
15. Taxi	7.0
16. Being with John F. Kennedy	6.8
17. Barney Miller	6.6
18. Little House on the Prairie	6.5
18. Love Boat	6.5
20. Maude	6.4
20. Tic Tac Dough	6.4
22. Fight Back	6.2
23. Alice	6.1
23. Happy Days	6.1
25. Phil Donahue Show	6.0
25. Fame	6.0

Source: Courtesy *Television/Radio Age.*

There is little doubt that the communications satellite will be a very influential force in mass communication for years to come. The satellite itself is a deceptively simple device. Once in orbit it performs its communications functions with transponders (*trans*mitter/re*sponders*) that receive signals from earth stations below, then relay them back to other stations on earth. A transponder can handle only one message at a time, but each satellite has several transponders. The satellite is stationed 22,300 miles out in orbit, rotating around the earth one time every twenty-four hours so that it "hovers" over one spot. Signals to and from the satellite are transmitted under FCC control in gigahertz (GHz), or billions of cycles per second. One problem: the system already is crowded with television network, cable, and syndicated programs.

Earth and	Wold Communications, a leader in leasing transponder time (a "common
Television	carrier") transmits two thousand major league baseball radio broadcasts
Stations	from game sites back to home markets each season. It relays such regular

Wold Communications, a leader in leasing transponder time (a "common carrier") transmits two thousand major league baseball radio broadcasts from game sites back to home markets each season. It relays such regular syndicated programs as "Entertainment Tonight," "The Merv Griffin Show," "Entertainment This Week," "Dance Fever," and "Solid Gold" as well as some sixty hours weekly for ABC, CBS, and NBC news and sports, teleconferences, and business symposia. Wold has forty-five permanent earth stations on the U.S. mainland, another in Hawaii, and two portable/ earth uplink/downlink stations—one on each coast—to transmit anything from sports to sales conferences from any site in the country.

Satellite transmission also has reached local stations. Television station WCTV in Tallahassee, the capitol of Florida, recognized in 1980 that the highly competitive television stations in Miami, Orlando, and Tampa-St. Petersburg had a difficult time covering news of state government. With an uplink/downlink ground station of its own, WCTV could send all the stations in central and southern Florida news feeds from the state capital. What is more, the uplink/downlink also offered an inexpensive way of feeding Florida State and Florida A & M athletic programs to area stations, including the already popular "Bobby Bowden Show," WCTV's Sunday morning recap of Florida State's weekly football game sent to ten stations. At last report, the station was working on plans to schedule rock concerts and business teleconferences with their earth station and get a license as a common carrier so it could lease time on its equipment to other organizations.

Entertainment Pie in the Sky

The satellite relay system, meanwhile, has one interesting flaw. The satellite transponder is efficient and distributive. It distributes signals so efficiently that anyone with the right equipment—a well-aimed antenna dish and a minimum of amplification—can capture the signals and wire them into his or her television set, receiving free what cable companies and cable subscribers pay to receive. The dozen or so satellites in orbit over the United States during the late 1970s and early 1980s beamed seventy channels of the best possible television viewing to the properly equipped domestic satellite pirate.

The satellites offered such fare as

Regis Philbin exercising on the floor, Tip O'Neill live from the floor of the House of Representatives, stock quotations, Spanish soap operas, a twenty-four hour weatherman, the Canadian parliament, private corporate conferences, the local Hamilton, Ontario station, the Armed Forces Network, the Eternal Word Network, the Playboy Network, "Sewing With Nancy," "The Erotic Adventures of Pinocchio," a man planting a garden, and a woman making chicken cordon bleu, to name a few. Want Popeye speaking French and tossing down cans of épinards for strength? You got it, (as the New York *Times* has pointed out) or anything else that is transmitted by satellite over North America—for free.

By the early 1980s an estimated fifty-five thousand Americans paid between $500 and $20,000 for antenna dishes, and cable channel operators were concerned that their expensive pay cable services, still not profitable, were being stolen. Home Box Office considered plans to scramble its signal so only paying cable customers could receive it. As they pondered, some three thousand to four thousand new backyard antenna dishes were going into service every month—mostly in remote areas not served by cable.

The Direct Broadcasting Service

In 1982, the FCC looked beyond the problem of satellite signal pirates to the advantages offered by satellite broadcasting. It authorized a direct broadcasting service (DBS) to establish a completely new pay and commercial television service for public consumption. The direct broadcasting satellite transmitters were to be more powerful than those in existing communications satellites, and able to relay signals directly into homes by way of a rooftop dish antenna (which some say would cost $200, others $400). While many were concerned that DBS would greatly reduce the audiences and the advertising of local television service, the commission believed the overall effect would be to increase television service. DBS was viewed as being especially valuable in serving rural areas where cable and over-the-air penetration is lowest. Following the approval of uplink and downlink frequencies by the regional administrative radio conference (RARC) in 1983, the commission began consideration of nine applications for DBS system construction. The major companies applying included Comsat Satellite Television Corporation, RCA, CBS, and Western Union. The most innovative application came from Hubbard Broadcasting, a company that owns television stations in Minneapolis and Tampa-St. Petersburg and five radio stations across the country. Hubbard's U.S. Satellite Broadcasting Company, Inc. planned a fourth television network by having the one hundred or so independent stations join USSB and form a cooperative news network. Stations would get stock in the network and be paid for carrying network advertising.

Reaction to the new system has remained mixed, however, running the gamut from cynicism to enthusiasm. With the airwaves already crowded, one analyst called DBS a solution to a problem nobody has. There were doubts in financial circles, too, that huge sums should be spent for another pay television system, when the cable and STV were not always making ends meet.

A shock wave hit the budding industry in 1984 when CBS and Western Union both decided to drop out of the DBS race. RCA, dragging its feet on the first round of applications, served notice it would be competitive in the second round. According to *Broadcasting,* CBS had second thoughts on the advisability of committing hundreds of millions of dollars to a DBS pay television operation when there was still doubt about pay television in general. Many agreed with CBS's concern. CBS's proposed DBS partner, Comsat, was spending $15 to $20 million a year on DBS. United Satellite Communications Inc., with a lower-power direct broadcasting satellite that went into operation in November, 1983, was in need of $40 million by mid-1984.

DBS supporters predict it is the television distribution method of the future, and that it will give a highly efficient, high quality service not possible from earth-bound transmitters. Of the nine companies originally nominated by the FCC to launch DBS satellites, only three remained in diligent pursuit of a direct broadcasting satellite launch as this book went to press. They were the Direct Broadcast Satellite Corporation (DBSC), Hubbard Broadcasting's United States Satellite Broadcasting (USSB), and Dominion Video Satellite (DVS). In 1984, *Broadcasting* reported DBSC was seeking funds, and USSB was working for the 1988 satellite launching that would be the foundation for its plans for a fourth network. DVS was continuing with its plans for a 1987 launch, and its subsequent broadcasting of religious and family-oriented programs nationally.

The FCC's plans called for the DBS system to be in operation no later than 1989. Review of the system was to come after use of the first generation of satellites, or about seven years after launching, so any necessary corrections and adjustments could be made.

Home Video Recording
Video Discs

Home video disc players and records were introduced to the American consumer market in the 1970s, allowing the public to play educational and entertainment video discs on their television set. RCA led the field with the introduction of a low-cost, stylus-in-groove player that also was sold by Zenith. Sears and Radio Shack marketed similar players manufactured in Japan by Hitachi and Toshiba. Phillips, the Netherlands electronic firm, introduced a laser video disc machine in 1978. Pioneer Electronics of Japan introduced its Lasermax machine in the early 1980s. The RCA system did not offer the picture and sound quality of the two laser players, but, with lower initial costs, and backed by RCA marketing, promotion, and an extensive library of video discs, it was easily the best seller of the three.

The video disc has several advantages. It gives pictures that are higher in quality than cable or broadcast pictures. Because the video disc is only slightly larger and heavier than an album of recorded music, it is easy to handle and store. RCA's prerecorded video discs were fairly inexpensive ($15 to $35 each).

RCA expected sales of two hundred thousand in 1981 after investing $200 million to bring the machines to the public. To the corporation's dismay they ran half that, with RCA selling sixty-five thousand, and Zenith, Sears, and Radio Shack together selling only forty thousand by 1982. In 1981, meanwhile, video tape machines sales reached 1.4 million. The only consolation RCA had was that laser disc players, much more expensive, were faring even worse in the market than its stylus-type machine.

Foremost among the problems was that the RCA player was a playback-only machine. While owners did have access to an extensive number of prerecorded discs, the machine could not tape television shows and movies off the air, make home video tapes of family's gatherings, or of the kids at play. That RCA had offered the disc player for sale at $499, within $100 of its own video cassette tape machines, may have underscored the shortcoming for the consumer.

Despite the growing competition (and lower prices) of video tape machines, RCA changed its marketing strategy for its disc player and adopted a give-away-the-player-sell-the-disc approach. It lowered the player's price to about $275, and continued to add to its extensive catalogue of prerecorded entertainment, sports, and "best of television" discs. It turned to the industrial market, too, negotiating with Avon products to sell thousands of players and discs for use in Avon's sales training programs. But by 1984, with some home VCR machines selling at $300, dealers found a $200 disc player virtually impossible to sell. RCA announced it would withdraw from player production rather than add to a total loss of $580 million. In the months that followed, CBS also abandoned stylus disc production, citing low demand as the reason. RCA announced it will continue production of video discs until 1987, to serve the half million customers who bought its players.

While the RCA disc player, like Edison's musical cylinders, seems destined to become a novelty to amuse the kids and grandkids, supporters of the high-quality laser disc predict it has a future. RCA's machine had a fixed arm that required the operator to run through the disc's grooves in sequence to find a particular picture or scene. The laser players, in contrast, offer random access to their discs, so that pictures and sound can be called up and displayed by moving the player arm. Random access has several educational, industrial and commercial uses, suggesting laser video disc players may still have a future as training programs and catalogues.

If the video player becomes an important part of the home video market, it may be as an auxiliary to the video tape machine. Victor of Japan (JVC) claims that 80 percent of those who buy video disc players already have a VCR to tape programs from television. As one Pioneer executive has suggested, the people who want to watch movies again and again want to get as close to cinema quality as possible. A laser disc player can produce a television picture with resolution that is 40 percent clearer than the average television set or video tape recorder.

The VCR

Sony introduced the first home video recorder, the Betamax, in 1975. It sold only thirty thousand units that first year, but the machine has grown in popularity, with sales passing the four million mark in 1983. The number of machines has created a sizable home theatre market—and a market for prerecorded video tapes as well. Commercial sources now offer virtually every type of recorded feature for sale or rent—from the Marx Brothers' *Duck Soup* to the classic whodunit *Laura* to the in-flight pornography of *Emmanuelle*. Buying prerecorded video tapes is an expensive hobby. Depending on the content, prerecorded cassette prices of $35, $55 and $80 were not unusual in the first half of the 1980s. Some tape prices were lowered to make tapes more competitive with disc recordings. By the middle 1980s video tape rentals of three dollars, with occasional bargain rentals of a dollar a day were not unusual. The best video tape bargain, however, was to be found at some public libraries, many of which developed large collections of video tapes to circulate the way they circulate books.

Sales trends in prerecorded tapes have produced some surprises. Unexpectedly, some of the worst motion pictures ever made—the worst of the B's—became highly saleable as cassette tapes: poor acting, rotten direction, ridiculous plot, and all. One hot selling tape-movie of the early 1980s was *The Attack of the Killer Tomatoes* (about $50) a tongue-in-cheek account of the invasion of San Diego by gigantic tomatoes. Some sample title song lyrics: "I know I'm going to miss her. . . . A tomato ate my sister." *The Creeping Terror,* another big hit (for $54.95), tells the story of a killer carpet from outer space that eats all the teenagers in Lake Tahoe. History seems likely to give the award for "best seller" of the 1980s to "Jane Fonda's Workout," which remained atop sales charts from 1982 into 1984.

Cassette pornography, like cable television pornography, also has been a saleable commodity. Estimates put the sale of X-rated tapes at 5.5

Pre-recorded pornographic and novelty tapes held high percentages of tape sales until 1983 when the release of such box office successes as *Raiders of the Lost Ark* pushed general interest tapes into leadership.

million cassettes in 1981 and 6.5 million in 1982. Pornography made up about 20 percent of all cassettes sold in 1981 and 1982, but demand for porn cassettes seemed to be leveling off, if not dropping. In 1983 general interest prerecorded tape sales shot up more than 50 percent while X-rated tapes rose only 10 percent, with porn tapes making up only 15 percent of all tapes sold. The rise in sales in general interest films was the result of Hollywood's decision to release on tape some of its box offices smashes; as a result, the sex industry's *Debbie Does Dallas,* the best selling of all porn tapes (about 50,000 cassettes in four years) was put in competition with *Raiders of the Lost Ark,* which sold 500,000 cassettes in less than one month. In 1984, there were about fifty-five companies producing the industry's total of $80 million worth of sex tapes. The tougher competition was expected to reduce the market in sex tapes even further and drive many of the smaller sex tape production companies out of business.

Time Shifting or Piracy?

As already noted, the video cassette recorder's popularity came, to a large extent, from the VCR's ability to record television programs: movies, adventure programs, and sitcoms. The VCR gave the owner the freedom to record programs when there was no time to view them, then play them back for viewing later, a practice known as "time shifting." The machine's ability to record off-the-air was viewed with apprehension by many in Hollywood, however. Hollywood producers and bankers feared the VCR would be used to tape expensive-to-make, copyrighted Hollywood products to show over and over from home theatre libraries ("librarying," as some called it). For Hollywood, the VCR was the harbinger of dwindling movie audiences and great losses in film revenue—of out and out living room piracy. In 1976 Universal and Walt Disney studios filed suit against Sony, charging the distribution and use of the Sony Betamax tape machine violated the copyright act. The case worked its way through the courts as the number of VCRs in operation and the sale of blank video cassettes grew. In 1984 the Supreme Court ruled Sony could not be restrained from distributing its products under the current copyright law, especially since primary home VCR use had been established as time shifting rather than the pirating of television programs. (The VCR decision is discussed more fully in chapter 17.)

As the Supreme Court handed down its opinion, well-financed campaigns already were underway to win—or defeat—new legislation to tax VCR technology. A proposal from the entertainment industry called for compensation of copyright holders through establishment of user fees, or taxes on the sale of VCR machines and blank video tape cassettes. Other plans called for a tax on prerecorded tape rental fees at retail stores. Those against the user fees argued they would hamper VCR sales, raise the prices of VCR's and blank video tapes unnecessarily, and be unfair to the majority who used their video tape machines legally.

Summary

Every industry develops support systems, and media industries are no exception. Wire services, syndicates, and communications satellites service the media with message content or distribution facilities. An important accessory is the home video tape or disc machine.

The news services are among the oldest of the media auxiliaries. The Associated Press evolved as an association that shares the costs of exchanging news, as well as the cost of association operation. UP, INS, and the news services that followed were organized as businesses to sell news to customers. UP and INS merged to become UPI, or United Press International, in 1958. UPI's performance was weakened by the loss of afternoon newspapers during the 1960s and 1970s. In 1982 the news service was sold to Media News of Nashville, Tennessee, a new company formed to buy it.

News services have a deadline every minute. Wire service reporters cover the globe in search of news stories and publish millions of words of news a day for newspapers and broadcasters. Both AP and UPI also offer around-the-clock audio news and photo, cable, and video services as well.

Several other companies—newspapers, for the most part—offer news services. The New York *Times* and the Washington *Post*-Los Angeles *Times* news services offer more in-depth and interpretative stories than AP and UPI. Overseas news services include Reuters (English), Agence France-Presse (French), and TASS (Soviet). TASS is owned by the government and reflects the Communist point of view.

Many newspaper companies offer domestic news services, too.

A media syndicate is an organization that sells content to media companies. Newspaper syndication can be divided into five categories: (1) news and press services, (2) feature services, (3) comic sections, (4) magazines, and (5) arts and mats services.

Radio syndication consists mostly of music formats. Occasionally, stations will broadcast a syndicated dramatic series (from new or old radio recordings).

Television syndication is comprised of original productions, network reruns, and old films. Syndicated television programs got their biggest boost when the FCC passed its prime time access rule in 1962. Many stations turned to syndicated programming to fill the time around the news the networks had vacated. The most successful programs for television syndication cross traditional sex, age, highbrow and lowbrow boundaries to reach the general audience. "M*A*S*H" seems to have that appeal, and promises to become the new king of television reruns, surpassing all-time leader "I Love Lucy."

Despite the profitability of off-network reruns, only one show in forty makes it into reruns—due to production costs and the difficulty of collecting enough episodes (100) for a series.

Communications satellites are one of the most significant communication innovations since the invention of broadcasting. International satellite communication (including international television communication) came of age in 1967 with placement of three satellites. By the mid-1970s domestic satellites also were in place to relay signals from American earth stations to any point in the country. The satellites proved to be a cheaper means of communication than telephone lines—while also providing a higher quality signal.

Several thousand television viewers have built their own backyard receiver earth stations to capture the wealth of television entertainment carried on satellites. Some pay cable channel operators have threatened to scramble their signal to keep their expensive products from these backyard pirates.

The FCC, meanwhile, has inaugurated an experimental plan to establish a direct broadcast satellite (DBS) service so that home television viewers can receive directly from some satellites. The FCC hopes to have DBS operations in service by 1989.

Home video tape recorders were introduced in the 1970s, with Sony's Betamax the first on the market in 1975. Taping off the air, while viewing another program or away from the set, plus the ability to add video cameras for home movies, has made video cassette recorders more popular than video disc players.

Questions for Discussion

1. Take the first section of your daily newspaper and count the total number of news stories in it. How many of the stories are news service stories? If the newspaper did without the wire stories, what would be the basic content and source of the news in the paper? Try to imagine a nation without AP and UPI services.

2. A few years ago, the Soviet news agency TASS did not report the crash of a Soviet Aeroflot airliner. Western reporters took pictures of the crash and even received information from Soviet officials about it. Still, the Soviet media did not report the accident. How do you account for the silence? How is it we are able to know about it?

3. Television prides itself on its massive audiences. Yet in this chapter we noted that Chic Young's "Blondie" comic strip reached as many as eighty billion people. How large is the audience for the average comic strip (or for the most popular)? Do comic strip readers outnumber audiences for such television programs as "Roots"?

4. Will the video disc player become a useless relic of the communications industry? Why? Why not?

References

Astor, David. "Doonesbury Strip Forced Out Again." *Editor & Publisher,* April 30, 1983, 50.
——— . "Comics Readership Down Significantly, Says Report." *Editor & Publisher,* May 7, 1983, 14.
——— . "Garfield: Five Years Old and Still Eating." *Editor & Publisher,* June 4, 1983, 42.
Berger, Arthur Asa. *The Comic-Stripped American.* Baltimore: Penguin Books, 1973.
Boyd-Barrett, Oliver. *The International News Agencies.* Beverly Hills: Sage, 1980.
Buck, Jerry. "Entertainment Tonight," *Columbus Dispatch Teleview,* February 7, 1982, 10.
"CBS Drops out of Running for DBS." *Broadcasting,* July 2, 1984, 38.
"Comsat's STC: Poised for Blastoff into TV's Space Frontier." *Broadcasting,* February 22, 1982, 38–45.
Consoli, John. "UPI 'White Paper' Refutes Rate-Busting Allegations." *Editor & Publisher,* May 7, 1983, 12.
——— . "Judge Us By Our Product, Not By Our Personalities." *Editor & Publisher,* May 21, 1983, 14, 36.
——— . "UPI Gets a Reprieve." *Editor & Publisher,* September 22, 1984, 9.
Davis, Bob. "X-Rated Video Losing Share of Tape Sales." *Wall Street Journal,* January 19, 1984, 31.

Emery, Edwin. *The Press and America.* 3rd ed. Englewood Cliffs, N.J.: Prentice-Hall, 1972.

"Excerpts From Court's Majority and Dissenting Opinions" [on home videotape recorders]. New York *Times,* January 18, 1984, 42.

————. "FCC Opens the Skies to DBS." *Broadcasting,* June 28, 1982, 27–29.

Fuerbringer, Jonathan. "Industry's Jack Valenti Vows to Keep Up Fight." New York *Times,* January 18, 1984, 42.

Geist, William, E. "In Jersey, Dish Antennas for TV Raise Storm." New York *Times,* October 5, 1982, 1, 18.

Gottschalk, Earl C., Jr. "S*M*A*S*H." *Channels,* February/March 1982, 45–48.

————. "TV Station in Oakland Does Fine with Shows Networks Had Before." *Wall Street Journal,* March 4, 1982, 1 et seq.

Gramling, Oliver. *AP—The Story of News.* New York: Farrar and Rinehart, 1940.

Hester, Al. "International News Agencies," in *Mass Communications, A World View,* edited by Alan Wells. Palo Alto: National Press Books, 1974.

Hill, Laura. "The Mystery Mavericks of Troubled UPI." *Washington Journalism Review,* July/August 1983, 18–21.

Hull, Jennifer Bingham. "Subscriber TV Market Seems To Be Fizzling." *Wall Street Journal,* November 23, 1983, 29.

Kierstead, Phillip. "Uplink to Stardom." *Broadcast Communications,* November, 1981, 44–52.

Landro, Laura. "RCA Tries to Combat Its Growing Problems by Returning to Roots." *Wall Street Journal,* March 4, 1982, 1 et seq.

Levy, Stephen. "Living with a Satellite Dish." *Channels,* June/July 1982, 46–49.

McLellan, Dennis. "Harriet Visits Ozzie in Reruns." *Columbus Dispatch Guide,* August 30, 1981, 2.

Medved, Michael and Harry Medved. "I Know I'm Going to Miss Her, A Tomato Ate My Sister." *TV Guide,* July 24, 1982, 36–39.

Morris, Joe Alex. *Deadline Every Minute.* New York: Doubleday, 1957.

Radolf, Andrew. "The Next Move Is Up to UPI Management." *Editor & Publisher,* September 22, 1984, 10.

"RCA's Rivals Still See Life in Video Discs." *Business Week,* April 23, 1984, 88–90.

Rothenberg, Fred. "'Leave It To Beaver,' Still Popular." *Columbus Dispatch,* June 15, 1982, D8.

Stephens, Mitchell. "Can UPI Be Turned Around?" *Columbia Journalism Review,* September/October 1982, 54–58.

Takiff, Jonathan. "RCA Is Reworking Marketing Strategy for Video Discs." *Columbus Dispatch,* April 7, 1982, C10.

"TV's Guru of Gastronomy." *Newsweek,* November 9, 1981, 102–103.

Wesslund, Paul. "Home Satellite Antennas: They Work, But They're Expensive." *Country Living,* December 1981, 18–19.

Chapter
13

Advertising.

While advertising may be one of the most controversial of all mass communications functions, it is by its very nature one of the easiest to identify. Probably the best definition was created by the American Marketing Association (AMA) several years ago:

> Advertising is any paid form of non-personal presentation and promotion of ideas, goods, or services by an identified sponsor.

The definition stresses four points:

Advertising is (1) a *paid form* of communication as opposed to publicity, which also may promote ideas, companies, products, and services in the media, but is *unpaid.* Advertising is (2) nonpersonal, or *public,* and public *mediated* communication (see p. 20) since a face-to-face presentation usually is considered selling. We primarily think of advertising as (3) *selling* consumer goods and services, but in the twentieth century it has been used to effectively sell social ideas as well. Finally, advertising (4) has an *identifiable sponsor.* The propagandist attempts to persuade, as does the advertiser. Both are advocates. But the propagandist may remain anonymous. The advertiser, to bring buyers to his product, may not.

Some Notes on the Development of Advertising

Advertising probably was created when our ancestors first experienced a surplus in goods and services, making trading desirable. We probably will never know when that actually occurred, but we do know the hunting tribes of Europe were trading in fruit, fish, and arrowheads as far back as 15,000 B.C. Drawings on the caves at Lascaux, France, from the same period, also indicate the tribes paid their witch doctors for magic deer-attracting services. Payment for goods or services is the requisite for the beginning of advertising.

Thus, advertising, if not as old as the hills, was probably one of the first things written or painted on them. Around 1200 B.C., the Phoenicians painted commercial messages on stones along trade lanes. The Romans painted signs on the walls of buildings to advertise goods, theatrical performances, gladiatorial exhibitions, and houses for rent. By medieval times the English had improved on the practice by moving the sign from the wall to a hanger over the door—so it could be seen more readily. The signs of those times were designed for illiterate customers. A shoe over the door announced a bootmaker, and the pictured bottle promised drink for those who could, and could not, read the King's English.

The centuries of trading also saw development of important oral traditions in advertising. In the sixth century B.C., ships in port advertised their cargoes by sending criers, or barkers, about the town with signboards strapped over their shoulders. Caravans in the Middle East used a similar practice, sending messengers around to sing out what goods the caravan had brought from afar. The Greeks used the crier to announce a forthcoming auction, and in time English shopkeepers hired barkers to stand in the street and attract passersby into their place of business.

Archaeologists have discovered vessels among prehistoric ruins with the mark of their maker on them. Trademarks were required by English parliament in the thirteenth century to protect the consumer and punish the maker of faulty goods. The marks also helped guide those looking for quality products, and eventually became an asset to the manufacturer, and gave us, in time, the idea of the brand name.

Written advertising has a long history, too. There is in existence a three-thousand-year-old papyrus advertisement offering half a gold coin for the return of a five-foot-two-inch Hittite slave with brown eyes. In the fifteenth century, an unemployed English clergyman placed his name with his qualifications on the door of a church. His success brought emulation, and the handwritten notices gradually broadened in scope to include announcements of items for sale and even requests for the return of a lost pet. They were called *si quis,* a Latin phrase which means "If anybody knows of," or "If anyone wishes." These notices have their modern counterparts in newspaper want ads and the "roommate wanted" signs that crowd campus bulletin boards. The *si quis* became known as "advices" in the seventeenth century, a few years before book publishers also began heading their announcements with the word *advertisements.*

Advertising and Printing

The first printed advertisement was a handbill from the press of William Caxton in 1478. It offered one of his religious books for sale. The first ad in a news pamphlet was printed in Germany in 1525. A doctor offered for sale a rare herb—his own discovery. As newspapers established sizable lists of subscribers, they attracted more ads for goods and services. Colonial printers—Franklin in particular—did much to attract advertising, and Revolutionary newspapers, with their circulations of one thousand to eight thousand, began to realize success as advertising media.

The mercantile newspaper of the late 1700s became the first American paper to be supported by advertising. By the end of the eighteenth century advertising had become critical to the American economy and merchants crammed their ads into the pages of the mercantile press, operating in a seller's market where goods were scarce and demand high. Those who advertised in and read the mercantile papers usually were of the same merchant and political class so there was little conflict over the fact or means of advertising (or that advertising should be truthful).

But with rising industrialization, manufacturers could produce more goods than they could possibly sell in their home region. The better mousetrap theory did not work. People could not and would not beat a path to an unknown product. To sell, manufacturers found they had to reach out with advertising. As the century passed, increased efficiency in manufacturing produced more and more goods. As several advertising scholars have pointed out, to keep production and profits flowing, advertising became less of an announcement of goods for sale and more of an advocate: it attempted to lead the consumer into new tendencies in tastes, and persuade them to buy new and different products associated with those new tastes.

Advertising and the New Mass Newspaper

The first mass newspaper, the Penny Press, became the first mass advertising medium. Publishers quickly found the ads a mixed blessing. They did bring excellent financial support for newspaper operations, but there was a flood of them, many of them scurrilous patent medicine ads, filled, as New York *Herald* publisher James Gordon Bennett said, with "imposture and humbug." The publishers could not satisfy the public outcry to cut the patent medicine ads; the loss in revenue would have been too great—or enough to bring about a price increase that would hurt circulation. And so, they framed an open door policy of accepting the ads while also disavowing and attacking their content. As one publisher put it:

> Our advertising columns are open to the "public, the whole public, and nothing but the public." We admit any advertisement of any thing or any opinion, from any persons who will pay the price, excepting what is forbidden by the laws of the land, or what, in the opinion of all, is offensive to decency and morals. . . .

In essence, the papers gave freedom of the press to their advertising clients, but they did not shy away from making sharp attacks on the patent medicine ads they accepted, often placing the editorial attack directly beside the ad. This open door policy is not unlike newspaper ad policy today.

The success of the penny papers soon brought such a demand for advertising space that Bennett began to fear the flood of ads would compromise the integrity and quality of his *Herald.* So in the 1840s he departmentalized the ads, separating them from the rest of the paper. He also limited them to one column in width, prohibited illustrations and typographical display, and made the advertiser renew the ad copy every day. The policies became the standard for the industry until well after the Civil War, keeping almost all newspaper advertising dull and want-ad-like for years. But they also allowed the papers to process more ads than before so that the major gain for both newspapers and advertisers was more advertising than before—without a loss in space, diversity, or revenue.

As the century moved on, newspaper advertising gradually included pictures and display type, and appeared as full-page spreads. The change first came from the clever advertisers who learned to repeat lines in their one column messages, or use type to make pictures to break the gray, want ad look (see chapter 3). From the mid-1800s, the country began to see, too, the attractive poster art perfected by French artists. Also of influence was the American city directory, which took full-page ads in contrast to the small ones newspapers allowed.

The Magazine Becomes an Advertiser

For most of the nineteenth century, magazine publishers were as wary of advertising as those at newspapers. As long as they were profitable without advertising, most gave advertisers and ad representatives little better than cavalier treatment. Well into the last half of the century, for example, Fletcher Harper of *Harper's* magazine turned down an $18,000 ad contract to advertise the Howe sewing machine because he decided to use the same back page space to advertise one of Harper Brothers own books. And when ad agent George P. Rowell, with some of the best ad agency credentials available (he had published the first *American Newspaper Directory* in 1868 and founded *Printer's Ink,* the advertising trade magazine in 1888), asked to see *Harper's* circulation figures before placing an ad, the firm decided he was a prying busybody and didn't want to do business with anyone who "talked that way."

Much of the fear that advertising would hurt the quality of magazines was put aside when *Century* magazine, a dignified periodical of the 1870s and 1880s accepted advertisements and gave them a certain decorum. By 1890 magazines were beginning to base ad rates on circulation (rather than prestige) and learning to sell their magazines cheaply while still making large profits—if they had the mass circulation to attract the advertising. By 1900, as one statistician discovered, there was more advertising in one issue of *Harper's* than there had been in the preceding twenty-two years combined. By 1910 the monthly magazine contained over 50 percent advertising, and magazines had become America's first national advertising medium.

The Medicine Scandals and the FTC

Near the end of the century, the scurrilous patent medicine ads of the Penny Press, having survived the one-column newspaper ads, appeared, bold and Barnumlike, in more open ad displays. With trumpets and flourishes of promises, they announced the cure for virtually every pain and ill, from nagging backaches to cholera to alcoholism. But in the 1900s some leading magazines, including *Collier's* and the *Ladies Home*

BUFFALO LITHIA SPRING No. 2
NATURE'S GREAT SPECIFIC FOR DYSPEPSIA AND GOUT.

At Eighty years of age bedridden from Dyspepsia and Gout. She was miraculously restored by this Water.

Her case stated by Dr. James Shelton, residing near the Buffalo Springs:
"Dolly Shelton, formerly a family servant, resides a mile from BUFFALO SPRINGS. When about eighty years of age, she was bedridden, a sufferer from ATONIC DYSPEPSIA and RHEUMATIC GOUT. I advised remedies in the case as palliatives merely, not regarding her recovery as among possibilities. While she was in this condition, a Spring was discovered at Buffalo, now known as Spring No. 2. Without suggestion, she at once commenced the use of it, and in a few months (I saw her only at long intervals, not feeling that I could be of service to her), I found, to my great astonishment, that it was proving highly beneficial. There was marked Improvement of the DIGESTION, and also of the GOUTY SYMPTOMS. Under continued use of the water, there was continued improvement until she was able to substitute a diet of *meat* and *vegetables* for bread and milk, boiled rice and corn meal, mush, &c., and there was also entire disappearance of the GOUTY AFFECTION. At the same time there was a gradual increase of flesh and nervous vigor until she could walk, without unusual fatigue, several miles at a time over the surrounding hills. She is now living, and certainly not under ninety-five years of age. She claims to be a hundred; would weigh I suppose, two hundred; is in good general health, and walks without difficulty about her house, yard and garden, having had no return of DYSPEPSIA or GOUT."

February 1, 1889.
For sale by leading druggists everywhere.
            THOMAS F. GOODE, Proprietor,

Testimonials with good credibility and a strong before-and-after theme were invaluable. This gem, high in human interest, characterized both the doctor and the patient.

A patent medicine ad of the late nineteenth century.

Journal, began to open the hidden flaps of the patent medicine tents and expose the ingredients used in the magic elixirs that had "saved" so many. Some proved to be pain killers of great strength, featuring generous portions of alcohol, cocaine, and/or morphine. The formula for one popular remedy, Peruna, was one-half pint of 180 proof alcohol, one and a half pints of water, some herbal flavoring, plus burnt sugar for color. The store cost was one dollar; the homemade version cost eighteen cents. And it was a fairly reliable pain killer.

In 1906 the muckraking magazines and the American Medical Association won their campaign against the medicine makers with passage of the Pure Food and Drug Act, which prohibited misrepresentation (including in the claims of cures), and required that all ingredients be identified on the label—alcohol, morphine, and cocaine included. Congress established the Federal Trade Commission (FTC) in 1914, and eventually gave the commission power to monitor deception in advertising and to regulate it. (See chapter 17.)

The medicine men—and most were men—did make at least one positive contribution. To insure the success of their own products, they became serious students of the advertising process. And those agents who had produced medicine ads had learned to study ad placement, ad appeals, seasonal effects of sales, and the effectiveness of uncounted numbers of attention-getting devices in headlines, ad illustrations, and ornaments. The ad agents and agencies who worked for the patent medicine hucksters received excellent training and education in advertising. Some of the best advertising professionals of the first half of the twentieth century graduated from the patent medicine "school."

Advertising and the Electronic Media

The arrival of radio as a potential mass medium brought a new round of charges that advertising would be offensive on the new medium. Much concern was eased, beginning in 1924, when AT&T's network and flagship station WEAF began commercial broadcasts of high quality. The ads were unoffensive and seemed a small price to pay for the improved programming their revenue provided.

Opponents of advertising on radio called for government support of the new medium—by government ownership, endowment, or tax funds. But talk of the support remained only talk. The 1927 radio act provided no funds, leaving radio (and later television) to support itself through its own devices. And advertising was the only device at hand.

Radio's unreliable, even erratic reception made it less than attractive as an advertising medium in its early years. But as the service grew more stable and NBC and CBS established themselves as networks, radio's potential as a practical, national advertising medium became more evident. It seemed an exceptional opportunity to the still slightly disreputable, medicine-tainted ad agencies. After 1890 the agencies were active in choosing media for client campaigns, preparing ad copy and print layout, and even offering a rudimentary kind of market analysis for clients. At Lord & Thomas, Albert Lasker, who had made a fortune selling Wilson Ear Drums, was among the first to realize radio's national advertising potential. One of his clients, the National Biscuit Company, was formed from several hundred local cracker companies to gain a national trademark and became the first $1 million radio account advertising a trademark. The American Tobacco Company, another Lord & Thomas account, also created a national brand name by concentrating its ad efforts on Lucky Strike cigarettes.

Unlike the newspapers and magazines, the new radio medium had not established its content or its source of revenue. The networks were more open to suggestion. Into this void moved the ad agencies. The stiuation allowed them to get their usual 15 percent commission for placing ads with the networks; they also charged their clients 15 percent of costs for all radio materials, talent, and production expenses. So the agency that produced an entire series of radio programs made a handsome commission off the programs and the ads within them. By producing the radio show they also were assured they had a superior vehicle for their client's product. The networks, meanwhile, welcomed the revenue and the programming so that by 1931 almost all sponsored network programs were developed and produced by ad agencies, and network approval of ad agency program suggestions was a formality.

The relationship continued with the rise of television, until the quiz show scandal rocked television in the 1950s (see chapter 11), forcing the networks to assume responsibility for the production of their programs. As already noted, advertising remains the primary means of support for both radio and television, but the agencies provide no programs, only spot advertisements for the two media.

The Importance of the Advertising Auxiliary

It is sometimes difficult to prove the importance advertising has in our economic and social system with hard scientific data. Advertising's impact is great, but it operates in such a complex field it is difficult to isolate its effects. Still, advertising's importance has been demonstrated in hundreds of cases and during more than one hundred years of history.

Advertising, first of all, makes possible the ongoing operation of most of our mass media. As a rule we put 2 percent of our gross national product into advertising, giving us a national advertising budget of more than $60 billion. The mass media take the lion's share of those expenditures. In 1982, out of a total $67.3 billion in advertising revenue, daily newspapers received 27 percent, or $18.3 billion; television 21.1 percent, or $14.3 billion; radio 6.9 percent, or $4.6 billion; magazines 5.6 percent, or $3.8 billion; farm and business publications 3 percent, or $2 billion. The mass media captured more than 60 percent of the advertising dollar in 1982; outdoor advertising received 1.1 percent and direct mail 15.4 percent, accounting for part of the remaining 36.4 percent.

Advertising is absolutely necessary to the success of all the American mass media. Motion pictures, music recording, and book publishing depend heavily on it to sell their products to the public. But newspapers, magazines, and broadcasting "publish or perish" by the ad revenue they attract. While subscriptions and newsstand sales have become more important to the print media in recent years, advertising still provides 70 to 75 percent of the total income for newspapers. The broadcast media, with no palpable message to sell, rely on advertising for virtually all receipts. And one of their minor sources of revenue also is tied to advertising: the selling of production and recording services for the creation of commercials. If media advertising were to disappear, media costs might quadruple—a newspaper might sell for a dollar instead of twenty-five cents—and commercial broadcasting would disappear until a completely new source of revenue could be found.

Other than the loss of news and entertainment, the disappearance of the mass media would mean a drastic decline in advertising. Proctor and Gamble, General Motors, and General Foods each spend more than $400 million a year (see figure 13.1) to advertise and sell their products, and there are some fifty corporations that spend $125 million or more every year. The figures seem high, perhaps wasteful. But as advertising theoretician Harry Tosdal has observed, it is clearly more efficient for the manufacturer of a product to reach a hundred thousand customers through advertising than for all those would-be customers to try to find the manufacturer of a product they want. Imagine what our major advertisers would have to do to reach the public without the support of the mass media. Could General Foods survive by using a million billboard ads for its food products? Could they hire salespeople to go door to door as Avon does? (Jello calling?) We can imagine what sales problems General Motors, Ford, and Chrysler would have if they were forced to introduce their new models each year with speeches and presentations from the steps of one county courthouse after another.

It takes little to imagine, too, how sales, production, employment, and society would suffer from long-term deprivation of advertising. As ad theoretician Harold Demsetz has suggested, we have become a highly specialized society, with many specializations in both producing and consuming. To lose advertising would be to lose much of the knowledge of invention and specialization—the variety of products and services—

Figure 13.1

Top Fifty Leading Advertisers

Rank	Company	Advertising (in millions)
1	Procter & Gamble	$726.1
2	Sears, Roebuck & Co.	631.2
3	General Motors Corp.	549.0
4	R. J. Reynolds Industries	530.3
5	Philip Morris Inc.	501.7
6	General Foods Corp.	429.1
7	AT&T Co.	373.6
8	K mart Corp.	365.3
9	Nabisco Brands	335.2
10	American Home Products Corp.	325.4
11	Mobil Corp.	320.0
12	Ford Motor Co.	313.5
13	PepsiCo Inc.	305.0
14	Unilever U.S.	304.6
15	Warner-Lambert Co.	294.7
16	Beatrice Foods Co.	271.0
17	Johnson & Johnson	270.0
18	Colgate-Palmolive	268.0
19	McDonald's Corp.	265.5
20	Coca-Cola Co.	255.3
21	General Mills	244.4
22	Anheuser-Busch Cos.	243.4
23	H. J. Heinz Corp.	235.7
24	Batus Inc.	235.0
25	Warner Communications	232.2
26	J. C. Penney Co.	230.0
27	Ralston Purina Co.	220.0
28	Mattel Inc.	217.9
29	U.S. Government	205.5
30	Bristol-Myers Co.	205.0
31	Dart & Kraft	199.2
32	Esmark Inc.	197.8
33	Norton Simon Inc.	191.2
34	Consolidated Foods Corp.	178.0
35	Chrysler Corp.	173.0
36	Pillsbury Co.	170.4
37	Gillette Co.	163.0
38	RCA Corp.	160.1
39	ITT Corp.	159.1
40	General Electric Co.	159.0
41	CBS Inc.	159.0
42	Gulf & Western Industries	155.0
43	Kellogg Co.	154.2
44	Seagram Co. Ltd.	153.0
45	Eastman-Kodak Co.	142.8
46	Sterling Drug	140.2
47	American Cyanamid Co.	133.0
48	Chesebrough-Pond's	131.0
49	Time Inc.	130.1
50	Richardson-Vicks	129.3

Total ad dollars in millions: 1982. Reprinted with permission from the April 18, 1983 issue of *Advertising Age.* Copyright 1983 by Crain Communications, Inc.

Figure 13.2

Top Ten U.S. Advertising Agencies (in 1983)
(Gross Income in Millions)

Rank	Agency	1983	1982
1	Young & Rubicam	274.4	246.7
2	Ted Bates Worldwide	244.4	233.4
3	Ogilvy & Mather	204.1	176.9
4	BBDO International	199.0	155.0
5	J. Walker Thompson Co.	189.9	167.2
6	Foote, Cone & Belding	158.9	129.2
7	Doyle Dane Bernbach	146.0	138.0
8	Leo Burnett Co.	135.0	136.0
9	Grey Advertising	125.1	109.0
10	McCann-Erickson Worldwide	95.4	82.5

Reprinted with permission from the March 28, 1984 issue of *Advertising Age*. Copyright 1984 by Crain Communications, Inc.

we now enjoy as individuals and as a society. Better computers or better tennis racquets or better skis are not sold automatically, they need to be advertised—again, very unlike the proverbial mousetrap.

Modern Advertising Organizations

While the press association centers around the press bureau, modern advertising primarily operates through the independent advertising agency, advertising departments in companies that manufacture and/or sell goods and services, and media advertising departments, including station reps that sell ad time and space to national advertisers. Other important organizations include the Audit Bureau of Circulation, and the Advertising Council, one of the largest advertisers in the world, which coordinates much of the public service, or nonprofit advertising. Figures on the number of professionals in the field vary somewhat. According to *Advertising Age,* there was a total advertising work force of approximately 125,000 advertising professionals in the early 1980s.

The Advertising Agency

The most widely known advertising organization is the independent advertising agency. *Advertising Age,* the industry's newspaper, has estimated there are some six thousand agencies. While many of the important agencies are located in major cities such as New York City, Chicago, and Los Angeles, agencies also are found in cities across the country and range in work force size from one full-time employee to hundreds. Agency and ad account size are measured by billings, or the total amount an agency bills its clients in costs and commissions. About 15 percent of all agencies bill $1 million or less a year while only 2 percent bill $10 million or more a year. The ten leading agencies in U.S. billings are presented in figure 13.2. Throughout the years, ad agencies have incorporated all the

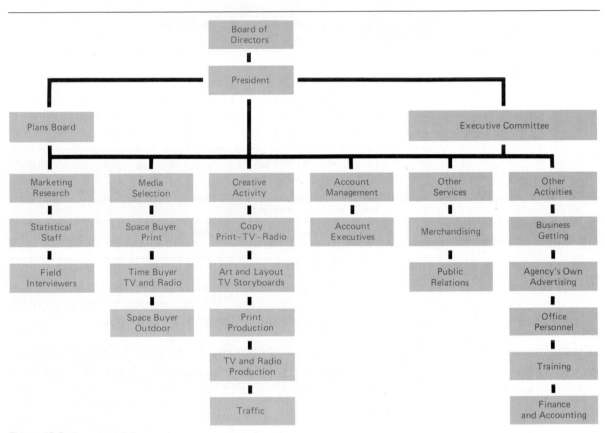

Figure 13.3 A modern, full-service advertising agency.

skills and services of advertising into their operations: copywriting, artwork, layout of print pages, selection of media for placements of advertisements, and research. (See figure 13.3.)

Agency Services

The full-service agency is one that offers a full range of marketing services and counseling. It is usually equipped to offer most of the following services to clients:

1. Research. Marketing is the process of selling goods—from production to transportation to consumer—including advertising. Marketing research considers all problems and situations in the marketing process, for example, size and location of a particular market, the living and buying habits of people within it, or the effectiveness of the product's package. Advertising research concentrates on the effectiveness of ad messages. Full-service agencies perform both marketing and ad research for their clients or refer the work to special research agencies.

2. Sales expertise. The full-service agency may offer counseling for the client's sales methods and forecasting, including the creation of point-of-purchase (in-store) displays.
3. Ad placement. Often overlooked is the importance of ad placement, which must be based on detailed studies of mass media audiences and an understanding of what portion of the audience reads, views, and listens to which media and when.
4. Ad messages. Agencies formulate ad plans and campaigns, create the ad, decide when and how long it will run, and place and verify advertising insertions.
5. Public relations. When needed, an agency gives aid in company public relations.
6. Special services. It provides special associated services to go with advertising, such as the creation of contests and games.
7. Accounting. The agency audits and bills for its advertising services.

Agency Organization

The larger agencies tend to be one of two organizational types: they operate in departments or groups. Figure 13.3 illustrates the organization of a departmental agency. Each department funnels talent to the account. The liaison between the account and the agency is the account executive, whose job it is to see that the client is satisfied and stays with the agency. There are senior account executives and junior account executives. In larger agencies, an account manager oversees the work of the account supervisors, who in turn supervise the account executives—the number depending, of course, on the size of the agency. The departmental system offers depth and variety in executive experience and the ability to bring a great deal of advertising experience to the account. The client, at the same time, may find the account in the hands of a committee of account executives.

The second type of organization, the group agency, leans heavily on one account executive as the go-between with the account. Instead of calling on talent from the various departments of the agency, the account executive is assigned a group of people to work with on the account. The group can include a copywriter, an art director, and a media placement person, or whatever talent is required to develop the advertising, keep clients satisfied, and their products selling. The group is like an agency within an agency but with the backing of the larger organization. The client deals with one account executive, who is responsible for the work, and has a stable group of advertising professionals to work with on the account.

Figure 13.4

Top Ten International Ad Agencies (for 1982)

Figures Shown Here in Millions, are Based On Total Equity Interest in Foreign Shops

Rank	Agency	Gross Income	Billings
1	Dentau	$402.9	$2.9 bill.
2	Young & Rubicam*	376.6	2.5 bill.
3	Ted Bates Worldwide*	356.1	2.4 bill.
4	J. Walter Thompson Co.*	347.1	2.3 bill.
5	Ogilvy & Mather*	315.0	2.2 bill.
6	McCann-Erickson Worldwide	276.1	1.8 bill.
7	BBDO Intl.*	238.3	1.6 bill.
8	Leo Burnett Co.	221.2	1.5 bill.
9	Saatchi & Saatchi Compton Worldwide	186.5	1.3 bill.
10	Foote, Cone & Belding*	178.1	1.2 bill.

*Billings include acquired agencies.
Reprinted with permission from the April 18, 1983 issue of *Advertising Age.* Copyright 1983 by Crain Communications, Inc.

Types of Agencies

Whether the agency is a departmental or group agency all strategy and ads are first presented to the agency's planning board for consideration and approval. (See figure 13.3.) The presentation gives agency management a chance to consider the work; it also gives the account executive an opportunity to make a presentation before the work is shown to the client.

The major portion of the advertising agency business, as popular fiction would suggest, is the consumer agency—the agencies that sell aspirin, antacids, and automobiles. Some agencies specialize in other types of advertising, including industrial, trade, financial and agricultural. Still others specialize in advertising for one or another of the media: newspapers, magazines, radio, or television.

The international trade looks to the international advertising agency to sell products overseas. The true international agency has offices in the United States and abroad. The foreign office can place ads for home agency accounts or export ads for other U.S. agencies. It also can act as an agency in its own right, servicing accounts in countries where it has offices. The ten leading international agencies, by billings, are listed in figure 13.4.

One of the hybrids in ad agencies is the house agency, established by large corporations with the goal of gaining advantages enjoyed by the independent agency. The hope is the corporation will get more personal attention from its house agency than from an independent one, and that the business it attracts from other accounts will cut expenses and qualify it for media rebates the independent agencies receive. The house agency tends to suffer from a lack of versatility and competition. And it does not usually enjoy a long life.

An interesting trend in agencies since the 1960s has been the formation of the creative agency—the boutique, as it has been called. As clients began to demand more creative advertisements, some of the brighter professionals set up their own shops, specializing in copywriting, art, broadcast production, and so on. Advertisers that patronize boutiques turn to other agencies for other services they need, such as placement or research. For a few years, agencies or individuals specializing in placement of ads also had good success in the advertising business.

Getting the Money:
The Agency Business

The agency has several methods of collecting its pay:

1. It obtains money from the media with which it places ads. The agency gives the total media bill to the client, who pays the agency. The media company then accepts 85 percent of the total bill from the agency, leaving the agency a 15 percent commission. The media usually discount about 2 percent for early payment of bills, which the agency credits to the client.
2. Most printing, graphics, and television commercial production work is done by special groups outside the agency. The agency hires these services (the crew to shoot a television commercial for example), pays the bill, then adds a 15 percent commission and bills the account.
3. The client pays for agency expenses, such as travel, entertainment, and expenses incurred as it produces and creates the account's ad campaign.
4. If the account requests special projects or activities not a part of the agency's standard service, the agency does the work, and then bills the account at a per-job price—plus a profit.
5. Agencies sometimes add a specific fee for special projects, especially large and expensive projects. Where the media commission is likely to be small, as in trade or industrial magazines, for example, the agency usually charges a flat fee.
6. The agency usually bills the account for the hours spent on the account by agency personnel.
7. And the account is charged a fee for agency overhead costs and such agency expenses as receptionists, local taxes, housekeeping costs. The agency determines a standard amount and rate for overhead costs, usually a 60 to 80 percent markup.

Figure 13.5

Major Ad Agency Acquisitions
1982 and 1983
(in millions)

Buyer Seller (Revenue*)	Price Paid
Saatchi & Saatchi McCaffrey & McCall ($21)	$15
Interpublic Dailey & Associates ($23)	$22
Lorimar Kenyon & Eckhardt ($65)	$21
Mickelberry Cunningham & Walsh ($37)	$18
Ted Bates William Esty ($67)	Undisclosed
Saatchi & Saatchi Compton ($119)	$57
BBDO Tracy-Locke ($16)	$9
Interpublic Lintas (51% interest) ($66)	$20

*Annual revenue at time of the acquisition.

Reprinted by permission of *The Wall Street Journal,* © Dow Jones & Company, Inc.
1983. All Rights Reserved.

Every financial arrangement varies, according to the services offered by the agency and the needs of the account. Whatever the agreement, one estimate places agency profit at about 3 to 4 percent of net
income after taxes, with larger agencies making somewhat more.

**The Trend in
Acquisitions**

As are other organizations in the media system, ad agencies are experi-
encing a pronounced trend in mergers acquisitions. Within eighteen
months in 1982 and 1983, eight sizable agencies were bought by larger
ones, with one Los Angeles agency selling for $22 million and another
for $57 million. (See figure 13.5.) It seems ad agencies are headed for
dividing into two types of operations: small ones serving local accounts,
and a dozen or so multinational agencies with huge, multinational accounts. The bidding has been hottest in medium-sized agencies with billings of $100 million. While some viewed the trend as healthy and
inevitable, a way for the buyers to add new territory, clients and revenue,
others have been concerned about the conflicts of philosophy and interest resulting from merging agencies. Executives in agencies that have
been sold, often chafe under the new administration. And mergers sometimes bring competing accounts into the same agency—a situation that
makes both clients and ad people edgy.

Independent agencies are listed in the *Standard Directory of Advertising Agencies.*

Ad Departments

Some manufacturers and retail stores depend entirely on the ad agency for their advertising needs; others look to their own advertising department to accomplish what is needed. Many, however, use a combination of in-house ad departments and agency services to sell their products to their publics.

Manufacturers and Large Retail Outlets

The organization of departments of manufacturers and large retail outlets varies somewhat from company to company. Some ad department chiefs report directly to the corporation president, others to the chief of marketing. (If there is an ad department, however, it is usually responsible for both the company's product and institutional advertising—or the ads that sell the company rather than its products.) The Association of National Advertisers has outlined five basic patterns to ad department organization. (See figure 13.6.)

1. By advertising function. In this case, copywriting, production, media, art departments and so forth are set up much the same way as in the departmentalized independent agency. This type of department creates a lot of in-house advertising and meshes well with the outside ad agency often used by the company.
2. By media. Departments are organized around specialists such as those in newspapers, broadcasting, outdoor media. These departments are strongest at supervising and reviewing the work of independent agencies hired by the company and at supporting the marketing and sales departments in the company.
3. By product. Organization is departmentalized by company products, such as clothing, toys, or camping gear so departments may develop and redevelop the advertising of those products.
4. By consumer, the end user. There may be departments for the consumer market, industrial markets, farm or urban market. The target market approach, as it has been called, allows the company to create a base of ad experts who know and can communicate with the people in the company's particular markets.
5. By geography. The ad function is divided geographically with each department responsible for a different part of the country.

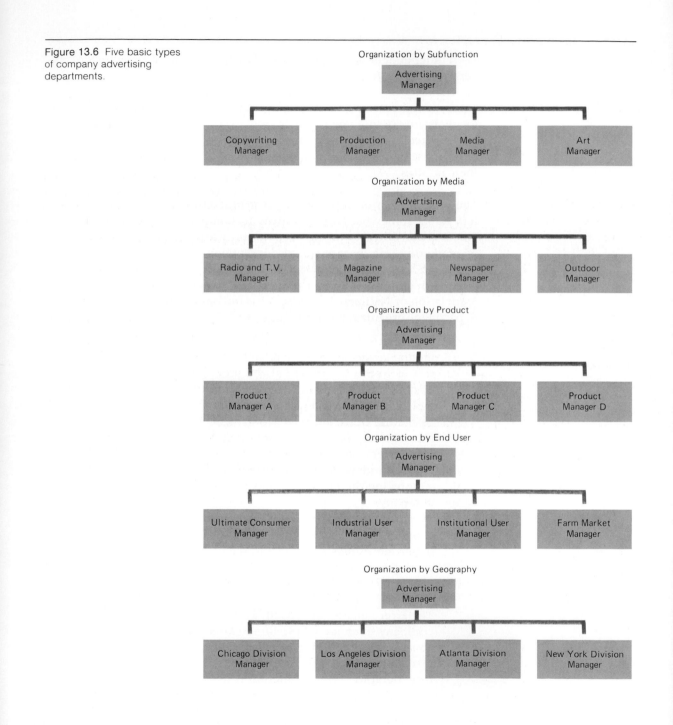

Figure 13.6 Five basic types of company advertising departments.

Organization by Subfunction

Advertising Manager

Copywriting Manager | Production Manager | Media Manager | Art Manager

Organization by Media

Advertising Manager

Radio and T.V. Manager | Magazine Manager | Newspaper Manager | Outdoor Manager

Organization by Product

Advertising Manager

Product Manager A | Product Manager B | Product Manager C | Product Manager D

Organization by End User

Advertising Manager

Ultimate Consumer Manager | Industrial User Manager | Institutional User Manager | Farm Market Manager

Organization by Geography

Advertising Manager

Chicago Division Manager | Los Angeles Division Manager | Atlanta Division Manager | New York Division Manager

Whatever its structure, the ad department has the responsibility for determining the ad budget for the company and for seeing that the advertising plan works well with the company's marketing strategy. Its main advertising goal, of course, is to establish the brand name of the product—to define it for the public—and persuade the public to purchase the product in retail stores.

To achieve this, the national manufacturer often uses the services of an independent agency to develop the product's campaign. Firms with several products may use one agency for each of its products, especially if the products are in competition with each other, or if one is a consumer product and another an industrial product. McDonald's, with its four thousand fast-food outlets, uses one independent ad agency for its advertising and another for sales promotion.

As a rule, the company's ad department recommends themes to the agency for development, then takes the finished ad campaign, and adopts it to its own uses. To cut costs, the department usually handles those parts of the campaign for which there is little or no commission (ad placement in trade publications, etc.). The department probably will work out details of the cooperative advertising in the campaign. The national product manufacturer pays from 50 to 100 percent of costs for local ads that promote its products, with the local store paying any remainder. The local ad displays both the national product and the name and address of the local store selling it, giving the local retailer the advantage of tying his store's name to the national brand name. Cooperative ads also give the national manufacturer a good advertising buy, putting a national product before the public at local advertising rates.

Finally it is the ad department that has the responsibility of verifying and assessing the agency's performance and of making final judgment on the campaign's effectiveness.

Retail Sales

A second group of advertisers, those involved in retail sales, also advertises heavily in the media. Within this huge group are at least three discernible categories of advertisers: (1) the local/national retail advertisers, (2) chain stores, and (3) local businesses and retail stores.

The local/national retail advertisers, such as Sears and Roebuck, K-Mart, and Kroger, have central advertising departments that work with independent agencies; they also have outside specialists to prepare and distribute national material to the national media as well as to their local stores. The national advertising usually contributes to store name brand recognition (Kenmore and Craftsman for Sears, etc.) while advertising distributed locally, like most retail advertising, offers products at competitive prices. Due to their tie-ins with national ad support, and their

Products at competitive prices: the retail sales store ad.

healthy local budgets, the stores in local/national chains have an advantage over local competition.

Chain Stores and Local Merchants

Chain stores, meanwhile, are made from stores that have done well. A successful downtown store expands with a second store in the suburbs, then another, say, in the East or West, and then another in the next city, to form a chain. The Federated Department Stores of the Midwest is a good example. Some chains are formed by merging several stores into a cooperative.

Regional and local chain stores reach their customers through the regional and local media and have little need for national, independent ad agencies. For one thing, the chains usually advertise at local, bulk rates, which are lower than the national rates agencies bill. The chains also need a more rapid ad service than the agencies usually offer. Retail advertising is life in the fast lane and must be prepared within a few weeks. Agencies are geared to produce ads during a period of months. Such a delay in retail advertising could mean Thanksgiving ads at Christmas, or the New Year's white sales at Easter. The national agency lacks local expertise, too. With its in-house ad department, the chain has its own advertising personnel who know the store's customers and merchandise.

Media

Media ad departments make up one of the largest groups of ad departments, since virtually every commercial radio and television station and every newspaper and magazine maintains some in-house ad function to aid and encourage advertisers to use its medium. The principal client of the media ad department is the local business person. (The station rep brings in the national business.) Often the department works with local ad agencies—those hired by local business persons able to afford agency services—to schedule the auto, grocery and appliance ads so important to local advertising.

Local retailing calls for quick advertising service. Newspaper ad departments provide their small retail clients with copywriting, layout and art services while radio and television stations offer broadcast copywriting and commercial production by the station's talent (announcers) and its studio facilities. If the local advertiser has an idea for an ad or commercial, the media department will sketch it out in a matter of days. The idea for the campaign may come from the media ad salesperson or the media department copywriter, since the media advertising department often creates advertising on speculation. While some ad professionals feel ads created on speculation do not do justice to the client, the media department knows that small retailers do not always understand what can and cannot be done with advertising. The aim of the speculative ad is to show possibilities and win a client.

Media Reps and Buying Agents

Two other twentieth century advertising specialists, the media representative, or rep, and the independent media buying agent also are active in local media advertising. The media rep calls on national advertisers on behalf of groups of local media to sell space or time. The rep gives local media direct access to the national advertiser and brings the local media a significant part of their advertising business. The independent media buyer, on the other hand, negotiates with the media for better ad rates from the local media. Neither the media rep nor the media time/space buyer are directly involved in creating ad messages.

Shane . . . Oh, Shane . . .

In this modern world of big manufacturers and full-service ad agencies, there is still room for the small entrepreneur—the lone retail gunslinger as it were—to buck the competition and take a shot at marketing his or her own home-made product. One such story unfolded not many months ago when Jerome Milton Schulman came riding out of the West—in his Lincoln Continental—to market his brand of toothpaste to drugstores in the East.

Schulman—or Jerome Milton, Inc.—a chemist, created the paste in 1981 to soothe sores and pains associated with bleeding gums. (The formula included aloe gel, a folk remedy for minor burns.) Friends with these discomforts liked the toothpaste, and Schulman decided to market it. He hired a company to produce it, and named it *Shane,* the Hebrew word for tooth.

The cost was high, $5.95 for a tube, about three times the cost of other brands. But by promising to advertise and agreeing to take back unsold tubes, he was able to get seven hundred drugstores in the Chicago area to stock Shane. He had no clinical evidence to support his claims for the paste so he filled his one- to two-hundred a week radio ads with testimonials from users.

Shane began selling as rapidly as Crest in Chicago, and Schulman was soon riding East. At last report, he was planning to expand his advertising, and his staff, to continue his "shoot out" with the big toothpaste makers. To his staff he added a second employee, a college student—his granddaughter. Schulman, the lone toothpaste entrepreneur, is more than 70 years old.

The Audit Bureau of Circulation

As advertising began selling on the basis of circulation, some means had to be found to authenticate circulation figures. In 1914 the Audit Bureau of Circulation (ABC) was formed as a nonprofit association supported by publishers, agencies, and advertisers. ABC data gives advertisers detailed information about the circulation of a publication, as well as detailed breakdowns on the publication's distribution to help improve advertising placement. ABC, along with Nielsen and Arbitron ratings in broadcasting and Standard Rate and Data Services (see chapter 11), are the basic audience research organizations.

The Advertising Council

The Advertising Council, Inc., first saw life as the War Advertising Council during World War II. It had so much potential for public service it was continued as the Ad Council "to utilize some of the power of advertising in the interest of all the people; to give by its use an example of advertising as a social force in a nation at peace." Supported by business, the ad industry, advertisers, and the media, it screens about three hundred requests for public service ad campaigns each year. It chooses those which are socially significant, noncommercial, politically nonpartisan, noninfluential legislatively, and national in scope. The ideas approved are given to a volunteer advertising agency that works with an experienced advertiser to guide the campaign. The council's campaigns have focused on education, environmental protection ("Don't be fuelish."), concern for health and safety, and aid to the disadvantaged ("A mind is a terrible thing to waste."). Since World War II, the media have contributed an annual average billing of more than $500 million to carry Ad Council advertisements. The media contributed $654 million in free space and time to council advertising in 1982 alone.

Types of Advertisements

There are three basic categories of advertising: institutional, commercial, and noncommercial.

Institutional

Institutional advertising focuses on the sponsoring institution, to improve its image (and therefore profits), without advertising the company's products. Patronage advertising, attempts to invite patronage by giving reassurances about the company. Westinghouse's "You can be sure if it's Westinghouse," and Ford's "better ideas" are good examples. Public relations (or image) advertising attempts to improve a deteriorating company image. Chrysler President Lee Iacocca's pitches in the early 1980s for the "New Chrysler Corporation" are examples. Institutional public service ads promote the sponsor's image by offering a message of social significance. In the 1920s Metropolitan Life Insurance boldly decided to run a series of public health ads on a then undiscussable unmentionable subject: syphilis. Just a few years ago, *Newsweek* produced a full magazine ad on "Ten Facts Parents Should Know about Marijuana" to help dispel rumors about the weed.

Similar to public service advertising is advocacy advertising, ads giving editorial views by corporations on controversial political and social issues of the day. Often these ads touch on matters that relate to the corporations' public relations effort. (See pp. 485–86.)

Commercial

Commercial advertising usually is divided into at least two categories: consumer advertising and business advertising.

Consumer ads themselves are of two kinds. One includes those primary appeal ads that sell the type of product ("Eat more beef." "Beer belongs.") and that are usually created by a product or trade association. The other kind is comprised of selective ads that sell a particular brand of product ("The Big Mac attack"; "Ponderosa. The biggest little steak house in the U.S.A."; "It's Miller time"; and "From the land of sky blue waters. Hamms."). These ads come from those who make or sell the product.

Business advertising is a general category and includes industrial, trade, professional, and agricultural advertising. Industrial advertising sells goods and services to manufacturers. It sells raw materials such as plastic or metal to toy and cookware makers and asphalt plants to asphalt distributors. As noted in chapter 6, there is an extensive industrial press, and much industrial advertising also finds its way into industrial magazines, catalogues, manuals, and direct mail. Industrial goods and services are expensive, and the buying pattern is more rational, with ads less influential than personal contact.

Trade advertising is aimed at the intermediary salesperson in the sales and distribution process. Trade ads stress product sales records, dealer sales aids, and sales promotions.

Professional advertising is the advertising of goods and services to the professions—lawyers, dentists, physicians. It is designed to open the door to help salespeople persuade the professional customer to adopt products, recommend them to colleagues, or prescribe them to patients.

Agricultural advertising is an important form of business advertising that also is a type of a consumer advertising. Recent advertising stresses farming and agribusiness, with less emphasis on farming as a way of life.

Noncommercial

ALCOHOLISM: A TREATABLE DISEASE CAMPAIGN
MAGAZINE AD NO. AT-1360-82 (7" x 10") (110 Screen)
Volunteer Agency: N.W. Ayer · Volunteer Coordinator: Edward B. Wilce, American Telephone & Telegraph Co.   CM-6-R

Public service advertisements deal with public issues in the public interest.

There are two kinds of noncommercial advertisements: political ads and public service ads. Political advertising has a long history in this country. But use of ad agencies and scientific research to market political candidates the way products are marketed began in 1964; the practice has grown by leaps and bounds since. Some agencies refuse to handle political campaigns, arguing the clients make unsubstantiated claims, are slow in paying, and take time from more worthwhile consumer projects. Supporters of political advertising claim it clarifies political issues and offers the best opportunity for the candidate to put his or her message before the public without interference.

Public service advertising is advertising from noncommercial sources dealing with public issues in the public interest. Media ad departments create thousands of public service ads each year for local charities, school and church functions, and other civic causes. As noted earlier, perhaps the most important single influence in public service advertising is the Advertising Council, which arranged for Smokey the Bear's forest fire prevention ads, the Red Cross' "Sign of a good neighbor" ads, and the "Give to the college of your choice" ads, among others. In recent years, the council, with the help of the N. W. Ayer agency of New York, produced the anti-alcoholism series "I'm living proof you don't have to die for a drink." The ads featured such renowned personalities

Business advertising in the media business.
a. Selling the equipment and services needed by the businesses in the field: the industrial advertisement.
b. Selling the company's success story: the trade ad.
c. Selling the tools of the trade for the individual: the professional ad.

Courtesy Harris Graphics Corporation, Commercial Press Division, Dallas/Fort Worth Airport, TX

A

Courtesy United Press International

B

Courtesy Writers Digest Books, Cincinnati, Ohio

C

and reformed alcoholics as actor Jason Robards, Jr., Los Angeles Dodger pitcher Bob Welch, and James S. Kemper, Jr., of Kemper Reinsurance. Businessman Kemper's ad was created especially for the business press.

Public sector advertising is a rapidly growing field, also. The federal government has become one of the largest advertisers—the twenty-fifth largest—with its public service ads for national parks, national art galleries and museums, and its continuing campaign for recruits for the military. The annual post office campaigns to remind shoppers to mail Christmas packages early and to ask movers to send change-of-address cards are both examples of federal public sector advertising.

Cities and states also have found advertising a useful tool in attracting industry, conventions, tourists, and in improving their image. Much of this nonprofit, public sector advertising would be called institutional advertising if the source were commercial instead of government, since the ads clearly seek patronage from tourists and conventions. One of the more successful public sector campaigns was the now-famous "I love New York" campaign the state launched to bolster its tourist trade. A heart replacing the word *love* in the sentence has since turned up on thousands of T-shirts and bumper stickers, and different parts of the country or other objects of affection have been substituted for *New York*.

Like all other advertising attempts, public sector campaigns can go awry. Columbus, Ohio, engaged the Carl Byior agency to create a slogan and campaign in the early 1980s, then dropped the agency in 1983 when it became dissatisfied with the results. The slogan "Columbus, we're making it great" implied the city was not great before, as one Columbus critic pointed out; yet the city had spent $100,000 exhibiting the ad in 1982. The city gave its account to a Columbus agency in 1983, in hopes of obtaining a more appealing ad theme.

Creating the Mass Media Ad

We usually think of the ad process as beginning with the creation of the ad itself, but it is with the client and the target audience that many ad professionals prefer to start. With the product under study and the market understood, the creative people can begin their work of putting the product before the public and the competition. Ad and marketing research can contribute a great deal to the formulation of the ad message. It can guide the creative function with information about how consumers feel about the product, the relative importance of consumer ideas, uses for the product, and what other products the customer might see as competitors. No doubt research played a large part in the framing of the Ford auto ad "Ford isn't afraid of the dark," which showed a relaxed young mother, with a child in bunny ears, driving through a dark night. Research conducted for Raid showed that housekeepers liked a product that killed insects hiding out of sight. The agency was able to make use of that information in a new slogan: "Kills roaches dead where they hide."

Not all ad ideas come from research, of course. One agency adman overheard a chance remark in a bar that led to the line, "When you're out of Schlitz, you're out of beer."

Some Leading Theories of Advertising

Several distinguishable modern day ad-persuasion theories have helped develop the modern advertising message. Here are a few of the more influential ones.

Unique selling proposition. Many ad professionals agree with Rosser Reeves and the late Ted Bates that ads should center around a Unique Selling Proposition, which tells the consumer, "Buy this product and get this specific benefit." An early Bates ad for Colgate toothpaste read, "Cleans your breath while it cleans your teeth."

The inherent drama in products. Products, Leo Burnett has suggested, have some little dramatic aspect that keep them in the marketplace. Good advertising captures what it is that makes people continue to buy the product. Burnett gave the macho image to Marlboro cigarettes by using western scenes, a horse, and rider. His agency capitalized on the feminist success story to sell Virginia Slims cigarettes with "You've come a long way, baby." Burnett found the drama of Maytag's reliability in the loneliness of the Maytag repairman.

The brand image. David Ogilvy has argued that "it pays to give your brand a first class ticket through life." The founder of Ogilvy & Mather sells sophisticated products by giving them a total personality to decide their position in the market. His Rolls-Royce automobile ads carried the headline, "At 60 miles an hour, the loudest noise in this new Rolls-Royce comes from the electric clock." The setting for the car was luxurious and prestigious, with even the low-key advertising copy suggesting the seriousness of the purchase. Other Ogilvy ads include the now famous Hathaway shirt ad with a distinguished-looking model wearing a black patch over one eye.

Honesty with a twist. William Bernbach of Doyle, Dane and Bernbach (DDB) believes the most important thing in the ad message is to be "fresh, to be original . . . and to be able to compete for attention with the shocking events of the day." DDB tries to turn disadvantages into advantages with total honesty plus a twist. The agency's original campaign for the Volkswagen Beetle carried such headlines as "Think small" and "Got a lot to carry? Get a box—or a VW van." DDB also was startlingly honest in advertising Levy's Rye Bread: "You don't have to be Jewish to love Levy's." The ad included a picture of people of various ethnic backgrounds enjoying the rye bread. The agency's recent ads placed James

Garner and Mariette Hartley together to chat and snipe at each other, family style, about Polaroid cameras.

(Sexual) motivational research. This theory has been drawn from the work of Sigmund Freud and modern psychiatric theory. Dr. Ernst Dichter has gained considerable respect from the industry for the practicality of his findings. His research, for example, has suggested men see a convertible as a mistress, but think of a sedan as a wife. His headline for an ad for the 1978 Pontiac read, "You'll find something new to love every time you drive it."

More startling in theory, at least, is *subliminal advertising,* the idea that goods can be sold by images and ideas received subconsciously by the audience. In the 1950s James Vicary claimed he was able to increase the sales of popcorn and cola in a movie house by flashing visual cues on the screen with such quickness the audience was not aware they were there. More recently, author Wilson Bryan Key has charged that hidden images and messages—genital symbols, breasts, nude couples—are embedded in the graphic art of advertising by artists who create them to help sell products. The Vicary experiment has not been repeated successfully. And laboratory experiments have yet to substantiate a general subliminal advertising effect.

Positioning. Ad executive Jack Trout has said today's marketplace suffers from too much noise—too many products. America has only 5 percent of the world's population, but 57 percent of the advertising;

NO MORE
MR. NICE GUY.

INTRODUCING OMNI GLH. WE'VE TURNED A MILD-MANNERED ECONOMY CAR
INTO ONE OF THE FASTEST PRODUCTION CARS IN AMERICA. Dodge

This little hummer contains the same high-output 2.2 engine we put in our Shelby Charger, yet it weighs even less. So it snuffs performers like VW's GTI and Chevy's Z-28 with a 0-50 time of 5.75 seconds.* And gets back from 50 to 0 in an incredible 2.38 seconds.*

GLH also handles corners. With super-fast 14 to 1 steering, special Shelby suspension and brakes, and oversize 15-inch Eagle GT radials.

Everything about the new Omni GLH is intimidating...except its $7350 price tag** ($1000 less than VW's GTI)†† and a mileage rating an economy car would be proud of.*

All this is covered by the industry's only warranty that protects the engine and powertrain for 5 years or 50,000 miles.° And by an aura that just might make it the world's newest cult car.

You can buy or lease° the GLH at your Dodge dealer. You can even take it out for a test drive. But never, never take it home to meet Mom.

BUCKLE UP FOR SAFETY.

Positioning: establishing an acceptable place for the product in relation to known products already on the market.

overcommunication causes Americans to accept only products and companies they find useful while closing their minds to new or different ones. Thus, knowing the competition is vital to selling in today's market. Rather than compete with established companies and products, it is better to find a new "position." The 7–Up Company, Trout has said, gained a good position in relation to Coke and Pepsi with its "Uncola" campaign, but lost its advantage with "America is turning 7–Up." One of the best ad campaigns in recent years, Trout has indicated, was the one introducing low calorie Lite Beer with the slogan, "Everything you've always wanted in a great beer. And less."

Maurice Mandell has written that all modern advertising revolves around one basic theory of persuasion, the AIDA theory. To persuade, the ad must attract *attention,* create *interest,* stimulate *desire* for the product, and ask for *action.* Careful analysis suggests the major theories of advertising all seem to underscore the AIDA concept, and are more similar to each other than different.

Advertising Media Planning

With the ad campaign prepared, the advertiser/agency must find a way to place the messages before the public. The advertising media represent a collection of advertising vehicles. The agency has to decide which media, or medium, to use, which vehicles (programs, etc.) within the media to use, and how to schedule the ad campaign.

Placement

Placement may be in a magazine, a newspaper, or a combination of media. Hunts Foods found great success advertising on matchbook covers—with recipes on the inside—before it moved its ads into the mass media. David Ogilvy's Hathaway shirt ads found their target audience through the pages of the slick *New Yorker* magazine.

The vehicle within the medium—television, for example—might be a news show, a situation comedy, or a crime show. Deciding on a vehicle means looking for the program—or section or feature of the newspaper—that will carry the ad to the intended audience. Soapmakers seem to have found an excellent vehicle in afternoon melodramas, just as auto tire dealers often prefer the sports pages of the newspaper.

Scheduling involves deciding on the time of year for the ad, the relative effectiveness of print versus broadcast media, and the intensity and pattern of the campaign. Media ad planners have learned it is futile to schedule ads where those of similar products are located. It is more effective to schedule campaigns by looking for the desired audiences in different media or at different times. Several years ago, Shell Oil decided to put all its media ad dollars into newspapers while other oil companies concentrated on other media. The move pushed Shell into the attention of the reading public almost immediately, eventually allowing the company to move into more traditional ad campaign scheduling.

Cost Per Thousand

The medium that succeeds with the advertiser is the one that delivers the target audience at the lowest cost. Advertising agents compare costs of reaching media audiences by estimating the cost of reaching each thousand members. The cost per thousand (cpm) is computed as follows:

$$\text{cost per thousand} = \frac{\text{price of the medium's ad}}{\text{delivered audience in 1,000s.}}$$

A careful advertiser will pay a higher cost per thousand for the target audience rather than jump at bargain rates for larger audiences with customers that do him little good. The ABC-TV program "Happy Days" could deliver fifty-two million family viewers each week in the late 1970s, but only twenty-two million of these viewers were in the 18-to-49-year-age group. Thirty seconds of air time on the program cost $60,000 and, therefore, yielded the following cost per thousand:

$$\frac{\$60,000}{52,000}, \text{ or } \$1.15 \text{ for the general family audience, and}$$

$$\frac{\$60,000}{22,000}, \text{ or } \$2.73 \text{ for the 18 to 49 age group audience.}$$

If the advertiser is selling a family product—say a popcorn popper, or promoting a rerelease of Walt Disney's *Lady and the Tramp*—then the $1.15 cpm is probably a good buy. But the manufacturer looking for a medium with which to reach single working women with sophisticated ads for feminine cosmetics might find the $2.73 cpm for adults—including many men—a false bargain. In contrast, consider the audience buy offered by a women's magazine such as *Mademoiselle*. With its circulation of about 1.3 million, and with an ad cost of $11,280 for a four-color, one-column ad the *Mademoiselle* cpm for one ad is: $\frac{\$11,280}{1,300}$ or $8.68. The higher cpm from the women's magazine is attractive since it gives the ad a better vehicle. The working woman's magazine would be more supportive of women's fashions and cosmetics than would The Fonz in the teenage "Happy Days" comedy.

Success Story: Advertising and the Truth

The final stage of the advertising occurs beyond the control of the advertiser. The consumer accepts or rejects the product or idea offered. One popular notion is that the "happy ending" of advertising comes when the consumer snaps up the product, needed or not, and goes on his or her bamboozled way, a victim of clever lies the advertiser has told for profit. The argument—not quite as overstated—gets its strongest voicing from those who fear the effects of ads on children. As ad researcher Glen Smith has written, they

> . . . usually claim that advertisers create artificial needs among children, which parents are reluctant to gratify, so leading to the creation of additional family "tensions," or they claim advertisers abuse the child's natural credulity and lack of experience.

There is little scientific data to indicate advertising can create artificial needs or abuse anyone's credulity. Human beings are not completely gullible and stupid. And children are not ignorant little sponges. Smith's research has shown children regard television commercials as useful and significant sources of product information, and that the commercials are neither the *only* or the *most important* factor in their decision to buy a product. Good case study material has suggested that with proper parental guidance advertising can become a source of entertainment, social information, and a way to learn the value of money—since the child must choose between advertised products and other needs, wants, and products.

That we all use advertisements as sources of information—especially product information—has been demonstrated by more than one scientific study. An intriguing Cableshop experiment was mounted on cable television in the early 1980s. The J. Walter Thompson agency produced three all-advertisement channels for the fifty-two-channel cable system in Peabody, Massachusetts, along with a fourth channel with a constantly updated schedule of the ads. A telephone was connected to a computer that could interpret coded advertising requests. Thus, viewers not only could watch a continuous string of advertising, they also could tune into ads they wanted to see and even request particular ads on the schedule.

The results were remarkable. About 60 percent of the town's sixty-four hundred households looked in on the three commercial channels by the end of the first six months of the one-year experiment, and 75 percent began to tune in once a week and watch for *half an hour or longer.* J. Walter Thompson has stated that interest in the ads was the result of the Cableshop ads being longer—much longer—and having more information than those broadcast by the television networks. One sponsor, the manager of the Laredo Boot Company, spent five minutes discussing construction, testing, and oil proofing of work boots. All seventeen national sponsors used the talk show format.

The fact that we all look to advertising for information about goods and services may be the key to testing and correcting advertising in the future. Rather than look for the deceitful, lying ad, perhaps, as John Kottman has suggested, we should study how ideas, facts, inferences from advertisements contribute to the decisions we make in the marketplace. Or, do the facts presented in the dramatic Marlboro ads, the honesty-with-a-twist Polaroid commercials, the 7–Up, or Lite Beer ads provide the consumer with enough accurate, factual information to make appropriate buying decisions? If so, perhaps that should be considered advertising's happy ending, and the success story for a responsible advertiser.

Careers in Advertising

Hard economic times and a crowded job market tightened the competition for entry level positions in ad agencies in the first half of the 1980s. Large agencies were forced to cut back their intern and trainee programs. A meticulous mind, typing skills, and high qualifications for being a "gofer" came in handy for most applicants. Unfortunately, many local agencies and advertising departments also suffered from the weak economy. More than one veteran ad person found himself or herself having a long talk with the local agency head, who sadly announced that account money had dried up.

John W. Wright, an advertising practitioner and academic, has suggested four entry level positions for today's up-and-coming advertiser:

1. Creative department, production assistant. Office skills are needed, with a potential to move into print, television, radio, or art production.

2. Creative department, assistant copywriter. Requires proofreading and editing skills, with potential for creative writing career.
3. Marketing sales assistant. Features beginning work with telephone, typing, sales reps, and clients.
4. Marketing media assistant. Job includes buying, planning, and scheduling media.

Agency salaries ranged from about $12,000 a year for billing typists and beginning artists and copywriters in the early 1980s to $300,000 and $400,000 for agency presidents. Account executives' salaries during the same period ranged from $20,000 to $45,000, and account directors were paid $60,000 and up.

A college education is highly recommended. In 1981 the American Academy of Advertising formed a curriculum committee to help develop college programs of study that would reflect the real needs of prospective advertising professionals. The committee since has recommended a college plan that includes courses to enhance the student's knowledge of and skills in general business, entry level advertising positions, and specific advertising areas (copywriting, media planning, creative development, etc.). The committee also recommended general courses in economics, organizational behavior, and social psychology.

Summary

Advertising is paid, nonpersonal communication that advocates the purchase of goods, services, and ideas—while identifying the sponsor.

It probably developed during a prehistoric time when availability of surplus goods introduced the possibilities of trade. Newspapers in the nineteenth century restricted ads to one column widths, to prevent irresponsible advertisers from intruding on the quality of the papers. Magazines also were careful that advertising would not offend. Scurrilous patent medicine ads precipitated the Pure Food and Drug Act of 1906. Eventually there was further control of advertising deception under the Federal Trade Commission, established in 1914. As talk of funding radio with taxes, endowments, or government ownership died, the national radio networks were launched as commercial networks, and advertising agencies became the principal source of radio programs. The relationship lasted until the television quiz show scandals of the 1950s.

Advertising remains important to the economy and society. In recent years it has had a budget of more than $60 billion, with the mass media receiving 60 percent of that money. The mass media would shrink dramatically in size and service without ad revenue, as would business sales, consumer comfort, production, and jobs.

The chief functionaries of advertising are (1) independent ad agencies, (2) company ad departments, (3) media ad departments, (4) the Audit Bureau of Circulation, and (5) the Advertising Council. Full-service agencies offer a broad range of advertising services. Ad departments in manufacturing companies often coordinate their efforts with those of outside agencies. Retail ad departments are less likely to use national agencies since retail needs require a faster and significantly different ad service. Media ad departments usually service small retail clients and work with local agencies who place ads in their own medium. The Audit Bureau of Circulation gives accurate information on circulations and distribution. The Ad Council coordinates national public service ads.

Ad professionals usually recognize three general types of advertising: institutional, commercial, and noncommercial.

Institutional ads sell the company rather than the company products, asking for patronage, correcting a public relations problem, or offering a public service message.

Commercial ads sell products from trade associations or manufacturers. Commercial ads are of two kinds: primary ads that sell generic classes of products, or selective ads that sell brand products from manufacturers. Noncommercial ads include political ads, and public service ads to support charities, prevent forest fires, or combat alcoholism.

Public sector advertising comes from noncommercial sources. The federal government is the twenty-fifth largest advertiser with its military recruiting, postal service, and safety ads. States and cities use advertising to attract tourists and improve their images.

There are several theories on how to create advertising messages. While each is intriguing, they all seem to follow the AIDA theory: attention, interest, desire, action, as suggested by Mandell.

Ad placement is as important as ad creation. The agency must decide which medium or media to use, which programs to use, and how to schedule the campaign. The most important yardstick for measuring media effectiveness is the cost per thousand: the price of time and space bought divided by the audience number in thousands. Media placement and scheduling includes careful study so the target audience is reached.

Despite continued fears, there has been little evidence to indicate that adults and children soak up advertising thoughtlessly. Since advertisers wish to give product information and consumers wish to receive it, the best approach to the study of ad effects may be through the study of inferences, facts and ideas that consumers take from ads. Research should determine if ad information leads to appropriate decisions in the marketplace.

Questions for Discussion

1. It has been suggested that advertising supports the economy, aids production, and services the needs of the consumer. How much do you depend on advertising in your daily life? How many days could you go, buying only products you know about now? Would you like to live that way? What does this say about the continuing argument that advertising creates false needs in consumers?

2. Although many of the prominent advertising theories appear to be similar, how does the *unique selling proposition* differ from Ogilvy's brand image idea? Is the Marlboro man related to positioning? Is there anything sexy about the drama of the Maytag repairman? The Polaroid cameras commercials? Subliminal ads supposedly have unseen messages in them. What would be the persuasive advantage of unseen words or pictures? Can you find an example of U.S.P. in a current ad or commercial?

3. Circulations and prices for ad space are given in *Standard Rate and Data* books in the library. Pick your two favorite magazines. What would be the cpm for a back page ad in each of them? In which magazine would you advertise a soft drink? A pizza mix? A Mercedes automobile? A new type of lawn mower?

4. Consider these ad slogans and jingles:
   "Pepsi Cola hits the spot,"
   "Be a pepper, drink Dr. Pepper,"
   "It's the re-al thing."
   They are from three soft drink ads. Is there "truth" in these ads? Compare that "truth" with the "truth" in the name of your college or university sports teams. Are they truthfully named? If our university sports teams aren't truthfully named should we expect to have truth in advertising?

References

Abrams, Bill, and Dennis Kneale. "Ad Agency Acquisitions Increasing as Firms Seek World-Wide Market." *The Wall Street Journal,* July 11, 1983.

Atwan, Robert. "Newspapers and the Foundations of Modern Advertising." In *The Commercial Connection,* edited by John W. Wright. New York: Delta, 1979.

Bird, Harry Lewis. *This Fascinating Advertising Business.* Indianapolis: Bobbs-Merrill, 1974.

Coe, Barbara J. "Successful Preparation for Advertising Careers: The Highlighting of Important Knowledge and Skill Areas." (Paper presented to the advertising division, Association for Education in Journalism, Ohio University, Athens, July 1982.)

Demsetz, Harold. "Advertising in the Affluent Society." In *Advertising and Society,* edited by Yale Bronzen. New York: New York University Press, 1974.

Dougherty, Philip H. "N. W. Ayer Involved in New Fight." New York *Times,* October 14, 1982, 45.

Fryburger, Vernon, ed. *The New World of Advertising.* Chicago: Crain Books, 1975.

Johnson, Douglas J. *Advertising Today.* Chicago: Science Research Associates, Inc., 1978.

Key, Wilson Bryan. *Subliminal Seduction.* New York: New American Library, 1972.

Kottman, E. John. "Toward an Understanding of Truth in Advertising." *Journalism Quarterly* 47, no. 1 (1970): 81–86.

Mandell, Maurice I. *Advertising.* 2nd ed. Englewood Cliffs, N.J.: Prentice-Hall, 1974.

Morgan, Ted. "New! Improved! Advertising!: A Close-Up Look at a Successful Agency." In *The Commercial Connection,* edited by John W. Wright. New York: Dell Publishing, 1979.

Peterson, Theodore. "Magazine Advertising: Its Growth and Effects." In *The Commercial Connection,* edited by John W. Wright. New York: Dell Publishing, 1979.

"Positioning." *Advertising Age,* July 16, 1979, 1 et seq.

Potter, David. "The Meaning of Commercial Television: The Historical Perspective." In *The Commercial Connection,* edited by John W. Wright. New York: Delta, 1979.

Ray, Micheal. *Advertising Communication Management.* Englewood Cliffs, N.J.: Prentice-Hall, 1982.

Rowsome, Frank, Jr. *They Laughed When I Sat Down.* New York: McGraw-Hill, 1959.

———. *Think Small.* Brattleboro, Vermont: Stephen Greene Press, 1970.

Telsar, Lester G. "Advertising and the Consumer." In *Advertising and Society,* edited by Yale Bronzen. New York: New York University Press, 1974.

Wright, John W. *The American Almanac of Jobs and Salaries.* New York: Avon, 1982.

———, and John E. Martes, eds. *Advertising's Role in Society.* St. Paul: West Publishing, 1974.

———, and Daniel S. Warner. *Advertising.* 2nd ed. New York: McGraw-Hill, 1966.

Chapter
14

The Advocates: Public Relations

Business meets the press: Lee
Iacocca tells Chrysler's story.

A paradox of the mass communication system is that public relations,
the communication profession that has done so much to win appreciation for so many, has not always been able to perform that feat for itself.
To use the language of the day, PR has a public relations problem. As
public relations professional Don Bates has written:

> Frequently, people not in public relations view us as cigar-chomping
> snake oil salesmen. Judging by typical reactions, you would think that
> our forte lies in packaging elephants to look like *Playboy* bunnies, or in
> bribing Russian *refusniks* to support capitalism in exchange for safe
> passage to the United States. . . .

Others have called public relations the "parasite of the press" and its
practitioners "pitch men with Harvard accents and trick polls." A recent
mass communications textbook charged public relations "is dangerous." It continued:

> Publicists do not often lie, but telling half the truth is an integral part
> of their business, and stretching the truth is not uncommon. Moreover,
> they do it in secret.

Managers of Problems and Issues

These stereotypes of public relations, quite obviously, have more to do
with our own fears than with public relations practice. If we wished, we
could condemn most of the newspaper profession for supporting the half
truth that Americans enjoy freedom of the press when in reality the right
to *publish* belongs only to those who own newspapers or magazines.
Broadcasters, too, advertise over-the-air broadcasting as free. But in truth,
the average American household pays about $225 a year for radio and

television—in advertising costs added to the sale price of consumer products. These ad costs, of course, are the unavoidable admission price for free television and radio. As to secrecy, one wonders if public relations is much more secretive than the conferences in which newspaper managers decide what stories will be placed before the public. And can public relations possibly be more secretive than the meetings in which television management discuss the latest ratings of the station or the station's newscasts?

The public relations profession has developed several definitions that give a more accurate indication of what the practice is all about. The British Institute of Public Relations, calls public relations, "the deliberate, planned and sustained effort to establish and maintain mutual understanding between an organization and its publics."

Professor Rex Harlow, with research and the help of scholars and professionals, has synthesized a working definition of public relations by listing its major activities:

> Public relations is a distinctive management function that helps establish and maintain lines of communication, understanding, acceptance and cooperation between an organization and its publics. . . .

This is accomplished by:

1. management of problems and issues,
2. helping management keep informed of and responsive to public opinion,
3. defining and emphasizing the responsibility of management to serve the public interest,
4. helping management stay abreast of and effectively utilize change, serving as an early warning system in anticipating trends, all while
5. using research and sound ethical communication techniques as principal tools.

The purpose of public relations is to work with the publics of an organization—the followers, helpers, employees, customers, stockholders, government, or parts of the mass audience that relate to the organization—to develop a spirit of responsible cooperation while also keeping management advised on trends in company policy that might help, harm, or derail that cooperation. Snake oil hucksters succeeded because they could disappear after the sale. They turned their greasy concoctions into miracles with a sensational pitch that was seldom tried on the same public twice. Public relations works in a long-term relationship. It must be more than a quick sale, fly-by-night profession. It is the part of management that watches over the organization's continuing relations with its publics. And, as Harlow has suggested, its overriding strategy is to "demonstrate a keen sense of social responsibility" to keep the good will of the public alive and growing.

In 1982, for example, Johnson & Johnson, makers of the respected line of household products, had little inclination to trick the public or cover up when police in the Chicago area discovered a link between its product, Extra Strength Tylenol capsules, and several tragic deaths. All the victims had taken capsules which contained cyanide. Johnson & Johnson did not consider what damage the reports were doing to the public image of its Tylenol product. Instead, the company plunged into the business of trying, as Chairman James Burke said, to "end the deaths, [and of] finding the perpetrator and solving the problem." The only course to take was to "demonstrate that we'd taken every single step possible to protect the public."

Within an hour of hearing of the first deaths, the company began testing Tylenol samples in the same production lot as the deadly ones to determine if there had been any contamination at the factory. Although the tests were negative, the company decided to recall the entire lot and inform the Food and Drug Administration of its action. The company also—at great expense—notified 450,000 hospitals, doctors, and distributors, asking that capsules from the lot in question be returned. And it instructed some one hundred company salesmen in Chicago, where the first deaths were reported, to collect all Extra Strength capsules in that area. The company then flew experts from headquarters in New Jersey to Chicago to establish a laboratory where they could investigate the extent of contamination of capsules in that area. It also took all Tylenol television advertisements off the air.

As it became clear the deaths were the result of a deliberate action on the part of a deranged person, Johnson & Johnson offered a $100,000 reward for information leading to the arrest of the person responsible. It also began a thorough check of its personnel files for likely suspects.

Meanwhile, public relations staff was busy answering "every single press inquiry" it received. Press calls had jumped from three to about one hundred a day. (Much of what the public learned about Johnson & Johnson's handling of the situation came from the public relations staff.)

The Tylenol murders gave Johnson & Johnson two serious problems: protection of the public and protection of its own corporate image. The only way to do the latter was to do the former. Attempting to deny responsibility would have been industrial suicide.

The Importance of Public Relations

As the media auxiliary that specializes in communication and media communications services, public relations represents all types of organizations in all parts of the media system—from audience interest groups or social movements, labor or management, to government and financial backers. The media themselves rely on public relations practices to deal with publics they have in the mass communication system. RCA, the parent company of NBC, for example, has a public relations department with forty staff members.

As a Communications Bridge

Public relations serves three important functions in the media system. It is a bridge in communication between the client organization and its publics. It serves as an aid to the media by providing news and information and by helping the media to acquire other content. And it serves as a skilled advocate for the responsible and wrongly accused in the court of public opinion.

Our complex, highly diverse society seems to create conflict by the minute. Work role specializations, for example, give rise to complicated and continuing communication gaps. The almost constant conflicts among owners, managers, and labor are, unfortunately, good examples. (Even in sports, there are problems in employee-management relations, two of which have resulted in extended player strikes in recent years.) In the 1970s, during the first of two oil crises in the country, uncertainty and lack of proper information led many to believe oil company tankers were standing offshore, withholding oil from the market, waiting for the price of gasoline to go up. The charge was untrue. In fact, oil traffic was normal. Besides, it cost $15,000 a day to keep a tanker operating at sea or offshore, and gasoline price increases could not have defrayed that cost. Also, the oil price had been set when the oil was put on board the tanker in the Middle East. There would have been loss, not profit, in holding it from the market. Still, the oil-withholding rumor persisted and was even broadcast as news by more than one of the media. And it was all due to misinformation—a communication gap—and not oil company treachery.

As an Aid to the Media

Public relations fulfills its second role as an aid to the media. As noted earlier, estimates suggest that as much as 50 or 60 percent of the daily newspaper's news originates with public relations practitioners. Public relations professionals write and release newsworthy stories for a range of clients—industrial, political, scientific, academic, social welfare—that the news media could not possibly gather on their own. And it gives invaluable aid in news coverage by providing background, technical details and fact sheets, and arranging interviews and press conferences. For example, companies with public relations practitioners who serve science and health care clients—pharmaceutical firms, medical colleges,

New York City Mayor Edward Koch (center, holding cap high) leads the parade across the Brooklyn Bridge on its one-hundredth anniversary. The celebration and arrangements for media coverage of the celebration were the work of public relations agency Dudley-Anderson-Yutzy (D-A-Y).

and medical trade associations—have the difficult job of translating highly technical company information into easy-to-understand media programs that can educate the public in consumer health or help prevent and treat sports injuries.

In 1983, much of what the nation read and watched as the city of New York celebrated the one hundredth anniversary of the Brooklyn Bridge came as a result of the efforts of Dudley-Anderson-Yutzy, a New York public relations firm. D-A-Y handled the anniversary for the city of New York. It placed some six thousand articles in papers and magazines during the year leading up to the event (some with the "Wanna buy a bridge?" theme). The firm made most of the pictorial media coverage possible by negotiating with New Yorkers for rooftop space for two hundred photographers and by arranging with the Coast Guard to take forty other media people to Governor's Island, a good vantage point for viewing the festivities. What the nation saw on live television was the doing of D-A-Y's staff as well as those of ABC, NBC, or CBS.

As a Defender in the Court of Public Opinion

Public relations also plays a vital role in our public opinion process. As we have become more highly educated as a nation, public opinion has become more important to us. It is, as one observer has put it, the highest court in the land—the court where we judge our government policies,

PR challenge: Dignitaries attending the industrialized nations summit in Williamsburg, Virginia, in May 1983, stroll to lunch as security personnel, the press, and observers (note roped-off area) watch. Left to right: Italian Prime Minister Fanfani, European Communities President Gaston Thorn, Japanese Prime Minister Nakasone, West German Chancellor Kohl, British Prime Minister Thatcher, and President Reagan, followed by French President Mitterrand and Canadian Prime Minister Trudeau. The Williamsburg public relations staff was called on to meet the information needs of two thousand international press members by creating a press center, news coverage pools, and special tours.

our issues, our presidents, and even our products. Unfortunately, it also is a court where the accused is held guilty until proved innocent, and where the news media, by reporting the news, assume the role of prosecutor. Some see one role of public relations as that of defense advocate in the court of public opinion.

A classic example of such a public opinion trial happened just before Thanksgiving in 1959. The Secretary of Health, Education and Welfare, Arthur S. Flemming, announced on Monday, November 9, that the cranberry crop had been contaminated by a weed killer (aminotriazole) which produced cancer in rats in lab tests. Although no proof existed that cranberries produced cancer in humans, he advised the public to use its own discretion.

As a result of Flemming's headlines, grocery shelves were cleared of cranberries in their best-selling season. The vice-president for Ocean Spray, Ambrose Stevens, had been warned and was already in Washington to offer a rebuttal. Under the guidance of the public relations department of Batten, Barton, Durstine & Osborn, the New York ad agency, the counterattack was launched. It included:

1. Public denial of the charges and an affirmation of the purity of the crop;
2. Formation of a panel of seven to answer all press questions about the purity of the cranberry crop;

3. Announcement of a news conference for the following day (one of many throughout the week);

4. On Tuesday, November 10th, an interview on the "Today Show," and an address to the Grocery Manufacturers Association meeting in New York to allow Ocean Spray's Stevens an opportunity to state the industry's case;

5. A telegram sent to Secretary Flemming, asking for "immediate steps" to correct the "incalculable damages" of "your ill-informed and ill-advised press statement;"

6. On Wednesday, November 11th, a telegram to President Eisenhower asking that all cranberry districts be classified as disaster areas, another to Flemming informing him that a $100 million damage suit was being filed against the government;

7. BBD&O public relations staffers continued arranging interviews to stress the "unfair, ill-informed, and ill-advised" theme of the attack and distribution of scientific facts to the food industry;

8. An invitation to the two presidential candidates. Richard Nixon ate four helpings of cranberry sauce. John Kennedy drank a toast with cranberry juice;

9. Work began November 13 between the Department of Health, Education and Welfare and Ocean Spray to find a way out of the crisis;

10. Nine days after the trial began, agreement was reached to test the crop for contamination. With public announcement of the agreement, cranberries were back on the shelves in time for Thanksgiving.

That year, sales fell short of previous years, but public relations had saved the industry from an unwarranted disaster.

Development of Public Relations

Public relations seems to have begun developing in civilizations around the world as soon as there were civilizations. There is in existence from 1800 B.C., for example, a farm bulletin that told Iranian farmers how to sow, irrigate, and harvest crops, and deal with field mice. We know the kings of ancient India kept agents who were spies and who kept in touch with public opinion, championed their king in public, and spread rumors favorable to the government. The kings of England established and maintained the role of Lords Chancellor—Keeper of the King's Conscience—to facilitate communication and give advice on the policies of governing.

Our own public relations profession has developed from the same social and political trends that created our mass communication system—and with the mass media themselves. No doubt advertising had a great influence, but the practice of public relations itself owes much to political propaganda, publicity, and campaigns of press agents, and to the irresponsible public performances of the nineteenth century robber barons of American industry.

Propaganda, Publicity, and Politics

In 1641 Harvard College sent three ministers to England to raise funds. They decided their begging mission would succeed more readily if they had a fund-raising brochure. And so, "New England's First Fruits," written in Massachusetts and printed in London, became the first of billions of public relations pamphlets and brochures. In 1758 King's College—now Columbia University—held its first class commencement—staged by the College Cutlip and Center have suggested, to attract public attention to itself. The event was reported in all New York City newspapers by an identical account provided the publishers—an eighteenth century press release.

The revolt against British authority provided an opportunity for the development of American political propaganda. The popular American image of indignant colonials rising to cast out the arrogant British is more nationalistic fable than history. The majority of the colonial population was apathetic to the patriot cause throughout much of the early Revolutionary period and was eventually roused to the cause by a band of skilled and articulate propagandists. Sam Adams stands out as the master propagandist. One of his achievements was the establishment of the Committees of Correspondence to gather and circulate information throughout the thirteen colonies. By 1774 there were committees in every colony, passing reports and exhortations along to each other, all in the interest of the patriot cause. Adams tried to be "ready for all events" so that he might best make "improvement of them." His version of the "Boston Massacre" turned a confrontation between British soldiers and water-front toughs into a drama of brutality and oppression. He helped stage the Boston Tea Party and then, to discredit Tory versions of the event, made sure the patriot version was in the newspapers first.

The Kitchen Cabinet

More like modern conflict management was the publicity approach of President Andrew Jackson. As a president of the people, Jackson needed popular support to win the presidency and later to get his programs into law. His unofficial "kitchen cabinet" kept him in touch with working class voters and advised him on political strategy.

His wordsmith was slight Amos Kendall, a one-time newspaper editor who has been called the first presidential press secretary. From Kendall's office poured a flood of news releases that stated politically complex ideas in the simple language of frontier people. Kendall's function, also, was to discern what particular publics—farmers or bank presidents—were thinking, and then relay the information to the president. The intention was not to create public opinion but to sense and reflect what people wanted.

The increase in population, the flow of immigrants, and the growth of the press brought the mass media into the political campaigns of the late 1880s and the 1890s. In 1896 the Bryan-McKinley presidential campaign marked the beginning of the modern media campaign, as both Republicans and Democrats flooded the country with pamphlets, news releases, posters, and other publicity materials on a mass scale. The emerging importance of the press in political life is indicated by the fact Theodore Roosevelt was the first president (1901–1909) to provide working space for reporters in the White House. Roosevelt developed astute use of the press. He learned to make pronouncements on Sunday to get more play in Monday's slow-news-day newspapers. He developed the "trial balloon," allowing him to obtain public reaction to an idea before committing himself to it. His sense of story and how to stage news events for maximum attention allowed him to rule the country from the "front pages of the newspapers," as one observer of the day put it.

Press Agents and Robber Barons

The publicist, or press agent, an extension of the age-old barker, appeared in the nineteenth century to sell goods and services along with paid advertising. The legend of Daniel Boone originally was created by publicists to promote western land sales, for example. The premiere press agent of the century was imaginative P. T. Barnum (1810–1891), who gave the country such well-publicized entertainments as tiny "general" Tom Thumb, and Jenny Lind, "The Swedish Nightingale." Due in great part to Barnum's success, press agents had infiltrated most of the business world by the 1890s.

The Public Be Damned

As was noted earlier, business, in the years following the Civil War, was filled with such graft, exploitation, and corruption the public and the press cried out for reform. At first, big businessmen—both ethical and unethical—were silent. The ethical business people saw no need to explain their actions while the unethical ones—robber barons, as some called them—were arrogant to public demands. In 1882 it was arrogance that the public heard when a reporter asked William Vanderbilt about the removal of a popular train from the New York Central schedule. As Cutlip and Center have reported, the answer that reached the paper read, "The public be damned . . . I don't take any stock in this silly nonsense about working for anybody's good but our own because we are not." Vanderbilt later denied the remark, but the behavior of the robber barons gave it currency. (A decade later, Henry Clay Frick coldbloodedly ordered people killed as he crushed the labor union in the Carnegie-Frick Steel plant in Homestead, Pennsylvania.)

Facing public anger, big business turned from ignoring public complaints to whitewashing their irresponsible behavior. To do so, they hired publicity agents. John D. Rockefeller offered public apologies while the muckraking magazines led the hunt for the corrupt in industry. (See chapter 3.) Gradually, however, corporations realized they would have to deal with public hostility directly, and even court public favor, if they were to survive. What can be called the first public relations department was established by George Westinghouse in 1889 to help him get his story to the public. The Association of American Railroads, under threat of heavy regulatory legislation, was an early user of whitewashing publicity and seems to have been the first commercial organization to use the term *public relations* (in 1897). The Publicity Agency, the first independent agency of its kind, was founded in 1900 but died after trying to defeat much-needed railroad legislation.

Ivy Ledbetter Lee

The publicist who led the change from whitewashing to responsible public relations was Ivy Ledbetter Lee. As reported in chapter 3, Lee believed truth and honesty were the best means to win public approval. In 1906, as publicist for anthracite coal operators faced with a strike, he established his open bureau policy, promising newspapers details or verification on any news story "promptly" and "most cheerfully." Rather than cover up or rebut attacks, or become an apologist for his client's views, Lee counseled clients to act to *achieve* the goodwill of the public. He advised the American Tobacco Company to establish a profit-sharing plan for employees. He advised the movie industry to stop using inflated, overblown advertising to attract customers.

He was widely criticized near the end of his career for working with the I. G. Farben Corporation of Nazi Germany. But Lee's ethics with the German company seem to have been at their finest. As Hitler's antics became more insane, Lee counseled Farben to divorce the company from Hitler and his Nazi government, or to change that government, if he wished to have friends in America. Not once did Lee try to whitewash the Hitler atrocities.

Lee has been called the father of modern public relations.

The World Wars and Growth of the Profession

World War I brought a new need to reach the public through the media. When America entered the war, the country was divided. For the Northeast, it was a rich man's war. The West favored isolationism. The Irish had hopes the English would lose. Everyone distrusted the warmongers who were sure to profit from the sale of arms.

CPI Launches a Profession	In 1916 journalist George Creel convinced President Wilson to form the Committee on Public Information (CPI) to apply the latest media techniques to writing and pictorial layout in support of the war effort. Named chairman of the committee, Creel mounted a massive communications effort to emphasize the theme that United States participation in the war was just. Posters, signboards, movies, and print media were pressed into service, as were seventy-five thousand speakers. In 1917 and 1918 the CPI placed more than fifteen thousand stories in newspapers and magazines. By the time the war was over, the CPI had raised the prestige of media persuasion to the status of a profession and provided a unique training ground. What is more, since Creel had decentralized the CPI system and placed publicists in every type of industry in the country, industry heads, directors, and specialists had met publicity workers and learned the value of publicity. The result was a large scale growth of industrial publicity during the years following the war. AT&T, for example, created a program of accurate news releases and direct contacts with editors and the public. Bell executives made speeches to business, civic, and educational groups. The company also encouraged all employees to join community groups and represent the company in club or group discussions. By 1929 almost fifty-three million people had seen Bell films at church, school, or civic meetings.

During this time, large corporations adopted the view that the success of the employee was the employer's success, establishing welfare programs, employee stock plans, and personnel counseling, all to make employees feel like part of the team. By 1925 more than half of all manufacturing corporations had established employee magazines.

Independent Counsels	The period also saw the beginning of the independent public relations firm or counsel. Carl Byior and Edward L. Bernays created their own agencies after leaving the CPI. Representing Libby-Owens-Ford, Byior was the master of the indirect publicity approach. He publicized safety glass to bring larger windows to automobiles. His book on home architecture increased the use of glass in homes. His acumen helped him build one of the largest public relations-advertising agencies in the country. Bernays had worked as a publicist for Enrico Caruso and Richard Bennet's sexy play, *Damaged Goods,* before joining the CPI. He turned to consumer publicity using "leader approval" statements—or endorsements by influential people—to publicize luggage, hair nets, and other products. His book, *Crystallizing Public Opinion,* introduced the concept of public relations counsel in 1923. He was the first to teach public relations at the college level.

The 1920s also saw the foundation of the John W. Hill agency of Cleveland, which later became Hill and Knowlton of Cleveland and New York. During the period, too, the enterprising N. W. Ayer advertising agency became the first to offer public relations to go with their advertising service.

FDR and the OWI

The economic crash and the ensuing Great Depression heightened the need for both government and industry to court public opinion. In government, President Franklin Roosevelt's publicity effort included the now famous fireside chats of radio; by 1936 the president had a staff of almost 150 on the publicity payroll. Roosevelt's promotional efforts—including his uncanny use of the press conference—forced his opposition to escalate its own publicity efforts; in many ways, the Great Depression was a great public debate.

With the attack on Pearl Harbor, the government again accepted the task of promoting the war effort and keeping citizens informed of the war's progress. The effort was directed by respected newsman Elmer Davis, as head of the Office of War Information (OWI). Again, thousands of men and women were trained in public relations skills, and when the war ended, they returned to civilian life where they found growing opportunities to make use of them.

Public Relations Today

It is difficult to determine precisely how many public relations practitioners there are today. The Bureau of Labor Statistics reported a total of 144,000 public relations workers in 1983, but that total, as practitioners are quick to point out, includes all workers in agencies and departments—printers, typists, bookkeepers—as well as the athlete or show business personality who decides to capitalize on his or her celebrity status. A total of between fifty to seventy thousand actual practitioners probably is more accurate.

The public relations practitioner now works within one of two types of operations: (1) the independent counsel or agency, including those in public relations divisions in advertising agencies, and (2) the public relations department within an organization or corporation. According to *O'Dwyer's Directory of Public Relations Firms,* there were thirteen hundred firms and agency departments in the early 1980s. *O'Dwyer's Directory of Corporate Communications* listed twenty-six hundred companies and five hundred trade associations in 1982, 80 percent of which had formal public relations departments (listed under any one of several names, including press relations, institutional advancement, corporate communication, public affairs, public information, and special services).

Figure 14.1

10 Largest U.S. Public Relations Operations, Independent and Ad Agency Affiliated

FOR YEAR ENDED DECEMBER 31, 1983. *DENOTES ADVERTISING AGENCY SUBSIDIARY

	1983 Net Fee Income	Employees as of Oct. 15, 1983	% Change from 1982 Income
1. Burson-Marsteller*[1]	$63,771,000	1335	+ 26.2
2. Hill and Knowlton*	60,807,000	1100	+ 12.3
3. Carl Byoir & Associates*	23,800,000	473	+ 8.7
4. Ruder Finn & Rotman	17,650,000	400	+ 8.3
5. Ogilvy & Mather PR*[2]	13,020,000	235	+ 19.7
6. Manning, Selvage & Lee*	10,758,000	178	+ 27.8
7. Daniel J. Edelman	10,120,397	221	+ 21.2
8. Doremus & Company*	9,680,328	163	+ 16.4
9. Booke Communications Incorporated Group	8,784,328	112	+ 60.8
10. The Rowland Company	8,417,500	131	+ 14.2

1 Does not include Cohn & Wolfe, with net fee income of $2,124,529 in 1983, acquired Jan. 3, 1984.

2 Includes Dudley-Anderson-Yutzy PR, billing $3,449,000 in 1982, acquired May 1, 1983. O&M PR's 1982 fees adjusted to include D-A-Y.

Courtesy J. R. O'Dwyer Co., Inc. 271 Madison Ave., New York, NY 10016.
Copyright 1984 by J. R. O'Dwyer Co. Inc.

The Public Relations Agency

As a rule, the larger the firm's staff, the larger its number of clients. Large agencies with a staff of two hundred or more handle as many as one hundred separate accounts. A list of the leading ten independent public relations firms in the United States, with number of employees and net 1983 income, is presented in figure 14.1. The top fifty independent firms range from four hundred down to fifteen in staff size, but the agency that is operated by a husband and wife team, or the one operated by only one practitioner and a secretary, is not uncommon.

Public Relations and Ad Agencies

A large number of advertising agencies are involved in public relations. For some years ad agencies with public relations departments only provided services to those who also were advertising clients. Some now offer their public relations service to nonadvertising clients (as N. W. Ayer began doing in 1969), but the future of the advertising-public relations tie-in remains tentative. BBD&O dropped its public relations services entirely in 1970 (despite its victory in the cranberry trial.) A list of the ten leading ad agency public relations departments is reported in figure 14.2. Like the national advertising agency, the public relations agency offers a wider variety of skills than the corporate department. Since it draws clients from across the country and often can call on talent in any one

Largest Public Relations Operations Associated with Advertising Agencies

	1983 Net Fee Income	Employees as of Oct. 15, 1983	% Change from 1982 Income
1. Burson-Marsteller	$63,771,000	1335	+26.2
2. Hill and Knowlton	60,807,000	1100	+12.3
3. Carl Byoir & Associates	23,800,000	473	+ 8.7
4. Ogilvy & Mather PR	13,020,000	235	+19.7
5. Manning, Selvage & Lee	10,758,000	178	+27.8
6. Doremus & Company	9,680,328	163	+16.4
7. Ketchum PR	8,411,096	125	+ 8.4
8. Creamer Dickson Basford	5,435,000	94	+ 1.5
9. Bozell & Jacobs PR	4,500,000	70	+ 5.4
10. Ayer Public Relations Services	3,573,000	42	+ 1.9
11. Porter, Novelli and Associates	2,535,300	51	+ 6.6
12. Creswell, Munsell, Fultz & Zirbel	1,135,193	18	+17.6
13. Dorn Public Relations	1,101,524	18	+ 7.0
14. Dailey & Associates, Public Relations	1,050,000	22	+ 7.1
15. Ingalls Associates, PR Department	1,010,347	23	+ 2.8
16. Wood + Cohen	820,100	6	+ 8.9
17. Pringle Dixon Pringle	740,000	19	+27.5
18. Grey & Davis[1]	676,479	18	+23.9
19. McKinney/Public Relations	673,000	14	−30.5
20. AC&R Public Relations	622,782	12	+44.8
21. Earle Palmer Brown Public Relations	—	10	—

1—Includes six months fees of Weintraub & FitzSimons acquired in 1983.
Courtesy J. R. O'Dwyer Co., Inc. 271 Madison Ave., New York, NY 10016.
Copyright 1984 by J. R. O'Dwyer Co. Inc.

Figure 14.2

of its offices, it acquires more variety, depth, and experience, and stands prepared to handle a great range of problems creatively.

Perhaps the most valuable trait of the independent firm is the ability to bring objectivity to an account. The business of the independent firm usually is the large organization or corporate account—large enough to have its own public relations department. Since the firm does not have a long-standing identification with the client company—or the policies that caused the organization's problems—it can offer a more objective perspective.

One of the largest independent counseling agencies is Hill and Knowlton, Inc. With more than one thousand employees this advertising-affiliated public relations firm offers a wide range of counseling services to corporations, institutions, professional associations, and some governments. There are Hill and Knowlton offices in Cleveland (the founding office), Los Angeles, Dallas, Seattle, London, Geneva, Paris, Frankfurt, and Rome, to name a few. Headquarters are in New York. Other than domestic public relations services, Hill and Knowlton offers a localized, international counseling service through its many foreign offices and by maintaining working relationships with other agencies around the world. A corporation could have a public image problem in one country, a government relations problem in a second, and a labor problem in a third—all unrelated—and still find appropriate counsel for all three at Hill and Knowlton.

Agency Services

The services of the public relations agency, like those of the advertising agency, are passed to the client through an account supervisor who works with an account executive, and agency talent, to place print, film, brochures, or tape publicity with the media or before the client's publics. There has been a noticeable trend toward specialization of services in recent years as agencies have identified the services that clients find most useful. O'Dwyer's directory of firms lists specialists in design and graphics work, editorial publicity materials, financial public relations, and press release distribution, and clipping services. Whatever its specialization, a public relations firm most likely will offer all or most of the following services:

1. Writing and editing news releases, newsletters, shareholder reports, book and booklet texts, speeches, television copy, trade and/or magazine articles, technical material, and in-house organizational materials (employee newsletters, etc.);
2. Placement of materials with the media, such as a news release or press conference, and maintaining contact for further placement;
3. Promotion and publicity of special events, news conferences, exhibits, anniversaries, new facilities, contests, telethons, and awards;
4. Speaking arrangements, including finding appropriate platforms for talented speakers in an organization; preparing speeches for the president of a company or college, for example;
5. Institutional advertising to help the public relations program improve the company image. (See chapter 13.)
6. Production of messages including art and layout for brochures, photographic communications, and films;
7. Programming the order in which the program is to be carried out, how messages are to be framed, and what publics are to be reached; the programming agent is a high-level executive;
8. Research examines all aspects of the public relations process. The agency either maintains its own research department or hires needed research specialists.

Finally, there is, as Cutlip and Center have noted, the participation *function*. The independent firm may represent the client in civic, social, cultural, or public affairs activities.

Billing in public relations, unlike billing in advertising, usually begins with a flat fee rather than a commission. Hill and Knowlton charges corporations $5,000 a month, associations $6,000 per month, and bills expenses at cost, with no 15 percent commission. Ruder, Finn & Rotman do not have a minimum, but make a direct charge for professional time plus expenses. And for those prices, editor Jack O'Dwyer, has written, a client can expect to get *daily* contact with his public relations firm and at least four article placements in major national media a year.

The Public Relations Department

If the public relations department can not offer the objectivity, range of experience, and versatility of the public relations firm, it does have advantages. The department staff knows the company and the company knows it. As a member of the organization's staff, it is a member of the team and does not provoke the antagonism the outside agency does when it comes to work. Being inside, the department is more available, and not half a continent away on another line, when trouble breaks. Being in close contact means the department readily can tailor its activities to meet the needs of the parent organization. Finally, the department is economical. It is not appreciably more expensive than any other department—even with the occasional expenditures for birthday cakes or fireworks it demands for special events.

Organization

The administrator of a corporate public relations department usually is given the title of vice-president or director of public relations or company communications. O'Dwyer has reported that one-half of all public relations departments report directly to the corporate chairperson, one-sixth report to a vice-president, and one-sixth report to an advertising or marketing head. In some consumer product companies, public relations may be considered advertising or marketing. As a rule, the more removed the public relations department from the head of the organization, the more likely the department will have a skills function and the less likely it will be involved in problem management and counseling on organizational policy. Researcher Alan W. Jensen has found, for example, that public relations departments in major banks are often in the marketing departments. Their practitioners say their major problems deal with media relations rather than communication policy.

Functions

Members of a public relations department usually are assigned regular job responsibilities, with one person handling the news media, another the house magazine, or employee relations; still another might be responsible for plant tours or the preparation of speeches. If necessary, two or three people may work together on one task—the publication of the company magazine, for example. The assignments, of course, reflect the special needs and interests of the organization. A practitioner for an eye care organization might be given the regular assignment of making presentations to school teachers on testing children for vision problems. Beginners in corporate departments might find themselves doing detail work related to one of the company's many planned events—an anniversary or the announcement of a new product. Academic public relations automatically includes alumni relations; industrial public relations includes labor relations.

A few years ago 250 corporate heads were asked in a survey to indicate the functions of their public relations departments. The answers are as follows:

1. Ninety percent or more wrote news releases, speeches, and engage in policy making.
2. Eighty percent worked on community relations, product publicity, special events, manuals and leaflets, and annual company reports.
3. Seventy percent or more were involved in external publications, customer relations, employee relations, and stockholder relations.
4. Sixty percent or more handled investor relations, employee publications, institutional advertising, trade shows and exhibits.
5. Fifty percent or more worked on still photography, sales promotion, slide film creation, direct mail campaigns, and survey research.
6. Forty-three percent were involved in movie production.
7. Thirty percent were involved in school relations, fund raising, advertising, and labor relations.
8. Twenty percent or more handled company contributions, training programs for lobbyists, and motion picture distribution.

The annual report is one of the most important public relations responsibilities. It presents the company's financial picture and hopes for the future to the stockholders and investing public.

Public affairs matters have become a concern of more than 50 percent of all corporate departments, according to one survey. Public affairs communication improves company participation in civic and political life. One practitioner has argued, for example, that the failure to properly explain affirmative action regulations during the recent years of recession and layoffs has caused much unnecessary discontent among white employees who do not understand the regulations and often see them as reverse discrimination. Usually the public relations department handles such internal communications situations.

O'Dwyer reports that one-third of all corporate organizations retain outside public relations counsel. The outside counsel may serve only as advisor or may both advise and execute the program with or without the company public relations department. The corporation may want the experience, the counselor's up-to-date contacts, or any one of several special services (research, annual report construction, programming, etc.). Or, it may want the entire job done by outside practitioners.

In the cranberry scare, for example, Ocean Spray and the cranberry growers took advantage of BBD&O's New York location and its up-to-date contacts with the national media. On the other hand, when the public relations staff at Williamsburg, Virginia, learned in 1982 that the Summit of Industrialized Nations would meet there in 1983 (bringing President Reagan, various heads of state, Secret Service Agents, and 2,000 members of the international press), Williamsburg public relations department head Albert Louer saw little need for outside counsel. He and his three member staff developed background material on the colonial town, comparing eighteenth century American problems with modern ones in trade, national deficits, and government regulation. They prepared a press kit for reporters and photographers and established a press center at nearby College of William and Mary, with representatives from the Commonwealth of Virginia available to answer news media questions. Louer and his staff also gave one hundred foreign press members a special tour to promote tourism and helped local reporters get extra coverage by sneaking them into coverage pools. Only one outside agency was tapped. A New York firm was hired to place two locally developed video tapes on Williamsburg to television and cable outlets.

Some Types of Public Relations Programs

The purpose of the public relations firm or department is the most significant factor in determining the nature and character of the public relations program. Corporate public relations—as reflected in surveys as well as the Tylenol, Ocean Spray, and Rentokil examples—is the prevalent, but not the only, form. The program is derived from and varies with the needs of the client.

Political

Political public relations has grown with the shift of political campaigns from the control of the political "machine" to the channels of the mass

Doing the Job: Snake Oil and the Cockroach Kids

The experiences of practitioner Peter Bateman, director of public relations for Rentokil, Ltd., an English pesticide company, are typical of department operations. Bateman's press and community relations include spending a great deal of time listening to complaints of accidental poisonings. His press conferences require that he be prepared to give elementary chemistry lessons for "bewildered" news reporters. He always can count on having to reassure members of the conservationist lobby. To keep informed in his field, Bateman spends hours poring over impending legislation containing controls for the pesticide industry and reading up on entomology, mycology, and zoology.

From time to time, he gets a challenging problem. In 1979 Rentokil scientists asked him to help collect a large sample of cockroaches for study. They wanted to learn where certain species were currently living in order to chart changes in the national distribution of the roach population and determine if the roaches had become immune to current pesticides. To meet these demands, a campaign had to be devised to capture cockroaches from all over the country. And the scientists had to know the location where each cockroach was captured. To make matters worse, each cockroach had to be alive, or the research on immunity could not be undertaken.

So Bateman created "Catch A Cockroach Month." With the cooperation of a UNICEF organization, a campaign was launched to encourage the public, especially children, to capture and record the place of capture of each cockroach. For all live cockroaches caught, labeled, and turned into Rentokil offices, the company promised to make donations to UNICEF—with a minimum $10,000 to go to the charity—and to give each child a certificate. Progress reports, charts, films, and reprints supported the effort, as did UNICEF T-shirts, promotional badges, and stickers. The month ended with a final press conference, which included the presentation of a check to UNICEF, and a display of live roaches, pest control methods, and the work of UNICEF. Results: 125 press stories, forty-four broadcasts, and a surprise increase in pest control contracts for the company. Best of all, the UNICEF contribution was used to provide emergency sanitation service for refugee boat people near Malaya, and forty organizations requested information about UNICEF charities.

---

media. To succeed, the contemporary candidate must know his potential voting audience and have extensive knowledge of media practices and skills. Modern political public relations has acquired the methods to discern public sentiment to a high degree of accuracy. (President Carter knew before the voters did that he would not be reelected.) And the profession has the skills and media knowledge to win approval of candidates from the voters. As a result, the demand for public relations services is much greater than the supply. Local political candidates are forced to operate without public relations or hire former newspeople as press agents. More than one gifted candidate has lost an election because he or she lacked public relations counsel. At the same time critics have suggested political public relations gives the voters little more than images of candidates—deceptive images—at the expense of important political issues. Political scientist Stanley Kelley has suggested those who fear political public relations should recognize that it replaced much less desirable nineteenth century machine politics, with its party bosses and block voting. Whatever shortcomings political public relations has, defenders insist, its public opinion research and media skills allow the presentation of significant political issues and debate more efficiently than has been done before.

Government

Government public relations programs primarily are shaped by the need to make successful laws. The methods used by Andrew Jackson and Amos Kendall to test public opinion and put ideas before the public in palatable form are still in use today. And public opinion polls and the network television address have been added to the presidential communication repertoire. The media campaign one California congressman launched to support his needed legislation is reported in chapter 16.

Other than win approval for laws, government also must provide reliable information about how it works if participation in government is to continue. The government must supply clear instructions on where and how to vote, how and when to file income taxes, what benefits are available and where. Civil defense and disaster control precautions are of little use unless the public is aware of them and knows how to use them.

Often overlooked is the need to interpret laws to the public; interpreting public opinion to law enforcement also is important in keeping regulations realistic and acceptable. Some states, for example, have passed laws requiring that toddlers be strapped in car seats while the car is in motion. The public relations job was to explain to doubtful parents why their child was much safer strapped in a seat than riding snugly in its mother's arms. Keeping the police informed in public opinion matters also is essential. In Detroit a few years ago, police department public relations counsel Andrew F. Wilson created a detailed brochure, "Meeting the News Media," to guide Detroit officers in interactions with news reporters. "The power of the police . . . is dependent on public approval," it read, and warned officers that a "no comment" answer can result in a "black eye" in the news; he advised them to give facts as they knew them, without personal opinion, leaving out only the names of witnesses, juvenile suspects, and victims of certain cases (rape, etc.) for their own protection.

Direct contact with the public can be the most important part of a public relations program. Good relations with the public are vital to police department public relations, for example.

Public relations in government has been one of the most openly rejected and also one of the fastest growing public relations fields. Government public relations is reviled as propaganda by the political opposition, industry, and the public. Yet its growth reflects how necessary it has become to modern government operation.

One important form is military public relations. The military services must represent the armed forces to an American public often hostile to military life itself. All three services have extensive information programs administered from the Office of Public Information in the Defense Department. The three programs are divided into internal and external programs, aimed at two kinds of military publics. Internal publics are those with a strong military connection—men and women in the service, reserves, retirees, civilian employees, and their families. External publics include Congress, the news media, business, labor, community organizations, education, and the general public.

The services consider the men and women in the military their best public relations with the public. All three services have attacked the problem of image and made special attempts to put an end to the notion of the service person as a public drunk. All give briefings and reminders to military people of the contribution each makes to the image of the American military at home and abroad. Members of the reserves and the National Guard have stronger civilian ties than regular military personnel. For this reason, the reserves are seen as important channels of communication to and from the public.

Since all military grants and operating funds come from the federal government, each military public information program is weighed in terms of its impact on Congress and the executive branch of government before it is undertaken.

The military pursue orientation programs that keep industry and community leaders informed of the services. All three services have a hometown news bureau to keep local communities informed of the activities of their own service members. There are community relations sections in all information offices that keep in touch with the local community and represent the base at local civic events. And the Army's Golden Knights parachute team, the Navy's Blue Angels, and the Air Force's Thunderbirds flying teams have given astonishing public performances across the country.

Military press relations have a long history of conflict. The military needs security, and the news media need news. When pressed, the military office still is likely to side with security, withholding news from reporters. With the creation of DINFOS, the Defense Information School (which trains information officers), the flow of information has improved. But military information officers, no matter how well trained and capable, still come under the command of senior officers, who often hold an unfavorable public relations attitude and often negate even the best DINFOS training.

Trade and Professional Associations

Trade associations and professional associations have such diverse memberships it is necessary for them to concentrate their efforts where there is substantial member agreement or at least a controlling minority. Trade associations usually consist of groups with a common interest in a product or service—milk, plumbing, beef, pork, electricity. Their public relations programs stress trade information services to the membership and campaigns for public education for the use of their product. Professional associations share an interest or skill: anthropologists, physicians, broadcasters, journalists, attorneys, and public relations practitioners. The professional group's public relations program also stresses professional information services, but it is aimed at enhancing the profession in the public eye, usually by maintaining a strict code of ethics and, perhaps, disciplining those who violate that code.

Labor Unions

Labor union public relations depends on acts which in themselves cause public relations problems. Striking and picketing a company brings negative attention to the union, not the company. By taking political stands and supporting political candidates, labor also alienates those supporting the opposition. Labor's fundamental policy has been to be a good citizen by participating in community life and sponsoring radio network news and commentary programs while also attracting and keeping people who can bargain with management and promote employee participation in the labor movement. By forming union councils for special interest groups, labor has attracted new groups of employees—teachers, government employees, computer technicians—to the union. And over the years, labor has worked hard to educate its membership with pamphlets, magazines, and articles by experts on labor-management relations. The problem still remains that if management refuses to bargain, it is labor that has to strike, and public opinion will accuse labor.

Welfare, Hospital, and Church

One group of organizations—welfare agencies, hospitals, and churches—has similar public relations programs, which share four problems:

1. As nonprofit organizations, they must raise money through a variety of fund-raising drives, activities which almost become an end in themselves.
2. Since funds are low, they depend on volunteer helpers who must be recruited and kept satisfied.

3. They often advance new and controversial concepts, which must be handled judiciously. Organ transplants now are common occurrences but promoting donor participation has been a matter for careful consideration by the responsible agencies.
4. They must reach out to the disadvantaged who often do not have access to the usual channels of communication. "Come and get it" promotions usually do not reach the inner city, but attract the streetwise instead. New channels and methods are needed.

The Public Relations Process

Whatever the organizational need, all types of public relations, Cutlip and Center have proposed, follow a four-step process in exchanging opinions and information and establishing a harmonious relationship between client and public. The process incorporates:

1. Research/listening, or probing the public to determine what problem or problems exist.
2. Planning/decisionmaking, or deciding what can be done about the problem.
3. Communication/action, or explaining and dramatizing the course of action to the public involved.
4. Evaluation, or checking the effectiveness of the program.

The process may follow this pattern, or any one of the steps may be taken as needed. The process applies to complex government and corporate programs, as well as to more simple public relations cases. Note the four stages in the following situation that occurred in Philadelphia a few years ago.

Friends of Peter Maggio, a South Philadelphia cheese plant operator, introduced him to experienced public relations counsel Philip Bucci, also of Philadelphia. Maggio had received "bad press," as he explained, due to his submitting a zoning change request to the city council; he asked the council to allow him to close a little-used city street beside his plant so he could expand his business. When the request got to the council, however, the district attorney had two assistants warn the council that Maggio was an organized crime leader in the state and had been labeled as such by the Pennsylvania crime commission. The two also leaked the story to the press. The zoning change was sent back to committee—for burial.

Public relations counsel Bucci began to research the situation through the newspapers and by talking to police, customers and neighbors in Maggio's neighborhood. He read up on the Mafia and researched

Senate hearings on organized crime. He even wrote FBI director J. Edgar Hoover, asking him to confirm Maggio's criminal connections. Hoover replied by letter that Maggio's FBI files were clean. But Bucci also learned that Mrs. Maggio, a talented artist, had a brother, Angelo Bruno, a known criminal and in prison in New Jersey at that time.

With this information, Bucci made his public relations decisions. Although there were some publicity dangers (Headline: "Snake Oil Salesman Whitewashes Mafia Henchman?"), he would proceed to clarify the situation and defend Maggio and his wife. A public image was at stake. He set up an interview with the Philadelphia *Bulletin*. But rather than publish the letter from J. Edgar Hoover, he gave it instead to the president of the city council, Paul D'Ortona.

The Sunday article carried several columns and pictures of Maggio and his wife. It featured her talent as an artist and Maggio's denial of any connection with organized crime. It also carried Maggio's statement that he believed he was being harassed by government officials because he was the brother-in-law of a known crime leader.

Two days later, a second story appeared in the *Bulletin* to report that Bucci, a "blue chip" public relations man who had worked for the American Legion, the Fraternal Order of Police, and boxing Champ Joe Frazier, had been hired to improve Maggio's image. But the story was generally favorable, noting Bucci's references included J. Edgar Hoover and former Pennsylvania Governor Raymond Shafer (headline: "Famous PR Practitioner Holds Out Hand to Charged Merchant?").

Meanwhile, council president D'Ortona had written the district attorney and asked for a public statement of evidence connecting Maggio with the Mafia. The reply indicated there was no evidence. Maggio's zoning request was revived, passed, and eventually signed into law.

Winning the zoning change was only part of the victory for Bucci and Maggio. Both survived considerable risk to their public reputations, with Maggio escaping what might have been irrevocable damage. As it was, his firm lost many customers and $100,000 that year, the first such financial loss he had known in fifty-five years. No doubt one of the astute decisions of the campaign was the one to give the letter from director Hoover to the city council president rather than to the papers for publication. It helped resolve the case without embarrassing the district attorney and extending the coverage in the media.

Becoming a Professional

Philip Bucci's handling of the Peter Maggio case has been applauded by many as an excellent example of professional public relations behavior—a high compliment from a profession that has been striving for ethical and professional excellence since World War II.

Some Professional Concerns

The importance public relations practitioners give their professional status was indicated by a poll taken of New York public relations personnel in 1954. When asked to indicate the ten greatest needs of public relations for the upcoming year, the practitioners ranked "further development of professional standards and ethical practices" at the top of the list. In fourth place was "official acceptance of public relations as a profession." As several writers have pointed out, attainment of professional status would require the following:

1. consensus on a body of knowledge that forms the foundations of theory and practice of the profession;
2. establishment of a code of ethics with procedures for disciplining those who violate the code;
3. development of a system to determine and certify competence in the field.

Attaining a body of public relations literature, comparable, say, to that held by the medical or legal professions, may prove one of the largest stumbling blocks to professionalism. Definitions are vague. Some would accept "how to" or "techniques" material. Others call for scientific findings from sociology, political science, and public opinion, for instance. Meanwhile, public relations has developed two high-quality journals: *Public Relations Journal* (of the Public Relations Society of America, PRSA), which presents cases, philosophy, and discusses professionalism, and *Public Relations Quarterly,* which publishes in-depth articles, including behavioral research studies.

Ethics and Accreditation

The greatest success of public relations in its drive to professionalism has been its establishment of a code of ethics and a plan to certify members. Both have been accomplished under the leadership of PRSA, first formed with the merger of two smaller organizations in 1948 and then merged with the American Public Relations Association in 1961. PRSA fostered professional public relations education by forming the Public Relations Student Society of America (PRSSA) in 1968.

The first PRSA code of ethics was written in 1951, revised in 1963, and again in 1977. The code calls for responsible, fair, and truthful dealing with clients, the media, and society, and for abandoning unethical clients.

PRSA became the first media association to attempt certification of members in 1965. The program certifies public relations professionals the way many academic institutions examine M.A. or Ph.D. students. Candidates take written and oral exams on the history, theory, and fundamentals of public relations, and the techniques and ethics of the profession. Exams are administered by a three-person team of professionals. Only full-time practitioners with high personal and professional standards, and the respect of their colleagues, may become candidates. By 1983 there were about three thousand accredited members out of a total membership of almost eleven thousand.

If an accredited practitioner is shown to violate the code of ethics, he or she may be removed from membership. But PRSA cannot prevent anyone—accredited or not—from going into practice as he or she sees fit, regardless of PRSA code or accreditation. And any attempt to do so would probably be a violation of the First Amendment to the Constitution.

Those who support accreditation point out it is not the same as medical or legal accreditation, whereby disbarment ends the right to practice. Instead, PRSA accreditation is more like a trademark. The hope is that the accredited public relations practitioner will be recognized as a high-quality performer, and professional status eventually will be attained through outstanding performance—clearly identified.

Careers in Public Relations

As the fastest-growing mass media field, public relations has a wide selection of entry-level positions. The beginning range of pay is great, reflecting the variety of organizations now in need of public relations personnel.

Since almost all public relations personnel are first and foremost news writers, the traditional college entry into the field is journalism. It is the ability to write the news story and to discern what the news media need and like that is still the heart of public relations. The student is well advised to study research methods, especially polls and sampling. The practitioner who does not specialize in research still needs to understand the methods, values, and limitations of surveys.

High on the agenda is the ability to work with people in hectic situations, to handle phone contacts and interviews with the-sometimes-prosecuting print and electronic news media while remaining courteous, creative, and professional. Review the Peter Bateman cockroach story for further insights.

In the early 1980s the median salary for public relations was $35,000, with individual salaries ranging from a low of $10,000 to a high of about $125,000. The high salaries are in corporate and conglomerate public relations departments, where about 42 percent of all practitioners work. Most beginners hired into the field, however, enter with small independent agencies and with welfare, trade association, or educational institution departments. Experience allows a move up in the corporate world.

Summary

Public relations suffers from an image problem. In reality, public relations works to gain cooperation and understanding between an organization and its publics.

It has three major roles in modern society. It builds communication bridges between those who are at odds with each other or who are having difficulty understanding one another. It extends the functions of the mass media by providing news stories the media could not otherwise obtain. And it contributes to the public opinion process, or acts as defense counsel in the court of public opinion, defending with communication expertness those attacked.

Modern public relations has developed from advertising, political propaganda, publicity, and business. Propagandist Sam Adams led revolutionary forces, passing news and information from colony to colony, and staging the Boston Tea Party. Andrew Jackson's popular campaigns and administration depended on close contact with the people and carefully written news releases by the first presidential press secretary, Amos Kendall. The nineteenth century press agents created publicity for all types of commercial enterprises, with P. T. Barnum as the master publicist.

As the mass media became essential to political life in the 1890s, irresponsible business adopted a "damn the public" attitude, bringing great public resentment and government regulations. After failing in attempts to cover up irresponsible practices, corporations turned to courting public favor with responsible practices and public relations methods.

World War I saw an extensive government publicity effort which raised the prestige of mass media publicity and also produced a large number of trained personnel. There was sizable growth in corporate public relations in the 1920s and appreciable growth in political publicity when Franklin Roosevelt was president during the Depression years. World War II brought a massive government publicity effort, which again produced trained personnel for the new profession.

Modern public relations operates from independent agencies and departments. Compared to corporate departments, agencies are more flexible, varied in their abilities, and more objective. The department, on the other hand, has the advantages of being part of the company team, is close at hand when needed, in touch with company needs, and inexpensive.

The purpose of an organization tends to determine the nature of the public relations program. Political, government, military, trade and professional association, and welfare public relations vary considerably for that reason.

Public relations practitioners have strived to become more professional since World War II. The Public Relations Society of America was formed and has created a code of ethics, encouraged professional public relations education and accreditation. Loss of accreditation for a member, however, only can mean loss of PRSA membership, not disbarment from practice. Still, some in the society view accreditation as a trademark of professional quality.

Questions for Discussion

1. Pretend for the moment you are a snake oil publicity person or, if you prefer, a "public be damned" apologist for a robber baron. Your job is to manage the Tylenol case the way the robber barons of the nineteenth century might have done. What strategies would they have used? What would have been the result of each?

2. Proposition: Public relations practitioners should be banned from politics. Support or attack.

3. Was the "Catch a Cockroach Month" campaign an ethical campaign, or did it use little kids in an unethical manner to catch roaches for experiments and commercial gain?

4. Can the PRSA accreditation program build public relations into a responsible profession the equal of the American Medical Association or the American Bar Association? Should a law be written to keep the quacks and snake oil salespeople out of the profession? Why? Why not?

References

America, Richard F. "Public Relations and Affirmative Action." *Public Relations Quarterly,* Summer 1983, 24–28.

Bagdikian, Ben H. "Who Pays for the News?" In *The Commercial Connection,* edited by John W. Wright. New York: Dell Publishing, 1979.

Bateman, Peter. "For 'Public Relations' Substitute 'Public Awareness.' " *Advertising,* 67 (1981): 17–19.

Bloom, Melvyn H. *Public Relations and Presidential Campaigns: A Crisis in Democracy.* New York: Thomas Y. Crowell, 1973.

Canfield, Bertrand R., and H. Frazier Moore. *Public Relations.* Homewood, Ill.: Richard D. Irwin, 1973.

Cooper, Michael. "Planning the Big Media Event." *Public Relations Journal,* July 1983, 12–15.

Cutlip, Scott M., and Allen H. Center. *Effective Public Relations.* 4th ed. Englewood Cliffs, N.J.: Prentice-Hall, 1971.

Doig, Ivan, and Carol Doig. *News A Consumer's Guide.* Englewood Cliffs, N.J.: Prentice-Hall, 1972.

Emery, Edwin. *The Press and America.* Englewood Cliffs, N.J.: Prentice-Hall, 1972.

Garver, Joan Zimmerman. "A Functional Analysis of 272 Public Relations Counseling Firms in the United States." (Unpublished master's thesis, Ohio State University, 1966.)

Harlow, Rex F. "Building a Public Relations Definition." *Public Relations Review* 2, no. 4 (1976): 34–42.

Heibert, Ray Eldon. *Courtier to the Crowd.* Ames: Iowa State University Press, 1966.

Jensen, Alan W. "The Status of Public Relations in Major U.S. Banks." *Public Relations Review,* 9, no. 2 (1983): 54–63.

Kelley, Stanley Jr. *Professional Public Relations and Political Power.* Baltimore: Johns Hopkins Press, 1966.

McLaughlin, Joseph P. "We Are Advocates!" In *Readings in Mass Communication.* 2nd ed. edited by Michael Emery and Ted Curtis Smythe. Dubuque, Iowa: Wm. C. Brown, 1974.

"Meeting the News Media." (Pamphlet published by Detroit Police Department, 1970).

Sandman, Peter, David Rubin, and David B. Sachsman. *Media.* 2nd ed. Englewood Cliffs, N.J.: Prentice-Hall, 1976.

Siefert, Walt. "Our Highest Court: Public Opinion," *Public Relations Journal,* December 1977, 24–25.

Wright, John W. *The American Almanac of Jobs and Salaries.* New York: Avon, 1982.

Part
Five

Freedom and
Control in Mass
Communication

Undoubtedly, one of the most important factors in the development of our mass media has been the desire and willingness of American society to see them develop as free institutions. Americans of all political persuasions take great pride in the fact that the American mass media are free. As political scientist William Kornhauser has pointed out, those of us who are liberals view freedom as being unrestrained by a dictatorial and elitist tyranny, while those of us who are conservatives define it as freedom from the influence of the unquali-fied or disrupting mob. We liberals hold freedom of speech and press to be a right of life, liberty, and the pursuit of happiness. We conservatives look on it as the basis of, the required condition for, growth and achievement. Both sides see the need for some degree of communication control and regulation as necessary for preserving freedom. Liberals argue freedom comes from controlling government and restraining censorship. Conservatives usually insist on restrictions against those who disrupt communication for their own gain or against the unqualified who debase understanding with their sloth, indifference, or lack of comprehension.

Without some controls, freedom of speech, press, and communication would lead to breakdowns and disruptions in communication. Thinking only of ourselves we find the thought of absolute freedom highly appealing. Free! To say whatever we want to say! But the citizen who is absolutely free to say anything, anytime, would soon find himself or herself shouting over the voices of others who also had the absolute right to say anything they wish, anytime. Absolute freedom of speech for all

could mean absolute noise. (We only have to recall the example of radio and the chaos in the airwaves in the 1920s for an instructive example.) At the same time, without some social or political controls on media message content, media managers could distribute whatever insults, defamations inanities, or communication garbage they wished to say, without fear of punishment.

Both the American Left and Right realize freedom of communication must be distributed as equally as possible. To achieve this, there are at least two areas where regulation and control of communication is necessary. First, there is the problem of communication traffic. To be free to communicate we must maintain rules and regulations on how the opportunity to speak is granted—especially in the case of mass communication, wherein so many people wish to contribute to the marketplace of ideas. Without some regulation of communication traffic, messages could hardly travel from senders to receivers. Second, there is the problem of regulation of content. Some messages threaten safety; others can harm, disgust, or defame. Freedom of speech, as one Supreme Court Chief Justice has written, does not include the right to cry "fire!" in a darkened theatre. The right to speak freely does not include the right to slander or defame with gossip and or the poison pen. Few in American society would argue there should be a Constitutional right for anyone to depict pornographic acts on public billboards. Few would argue that the mass media should publish information vital to national security as freely as they broadcast popular music or political editorials.

Every society decides how it will control or direct its communications traffic—and what

information it will allow into its various communications pathways. Scholarship suggests human societies have developed at least four general theories to outline the goals and methods of control of mass communication. They are the (1) authoritarian theory, (2) libertarian theory, (3) social responsibility theory, and (4) Soviet-totalitarian theory.

Our American mass communication system has evolved through and from the first three. The authoritarian philosophies of fifteenth, sixteenth, and seventeenth century England controlled the number of printers, allowing only those loyal to the crown to print, and kept sharp restraints on criticism of king and government. The libertarians, in reaction, rejected government control of media and preferred open criticism of government. Libertarian views are reflected in the

Bill of Rights and the operating philosophies of many nineteenth century American publishers. In this century, the social responsibility theory has developed in reaction to both authoritarian and libertarian theory. Social responsibility fears authoritarian-like government restrictions will return if the media chose to ignore the social responsibilities under freedoms acquired along with their libertarian freedoms. Social responsibility calls for self-regulation of the media, with media management and the media professions themselves keeping the public informed on the significant events of the day and providing mature entertainment for society. In sharp contrast to the libertarian and social responsibility theories is the Soviet-totalitarian theory. It sees control of the media by the capitalistic upper and middle classes as the enemy of freedom for the Soviet working class. The Soviet

system, therefore, places the Soviet media under the control of the Soviet government and the Communist party so it may function in the interest of the working class. Media content is dedicated to "building Communism" and reporting the continued depravity and failure of capitalism to Soviet society.

There are no pure types of mass media systems, of course. And the four media theories discussed here are not the only ones now found around the world. (It is often difficult to place some of the emerging media systems within any one of these four general categories.) But these four theories do make good beginning reference points in discussions of media freedom and control.

The three chapters of this section will discuss freedom and control of mass communication in the United States. Chapter 15 discusses the development of American media

freedoms, including some notes on the content we allow and disallow in our system. Chapter 16 reviews the major "traffic" problems of our media system—clashes and conflicts of media rights with other rights and freedoms—and the principal court decisions that have resulted. Chapter 17 is an overview of media controls now established by the public and the media professions themselves; special attention is given to the social responsibility aspects of media self-regulation.

Chapter
15

Freedom and Mass Communication in America

The United States Supreme
Court.

The Theoretical Background

As reported in chapter 3, the American concept of freedom of the press, and subsequently of all American mass media, has come in large part from the ideology of our libertarian forefathers and their opposition to authoritarian beliefs, especially those of the fifteenth, sixteenth, and seventeenth century English monarchies. Authoritarian philosophers argued the interest of the state was paramount and the true place of the individual was as a member of the state (in unquestioned submission to the will of the monarchy). As Thomas Hobbes argued, to question or divide the power of the monarch was to threaten a return to anarchy and put all at the mercy of families of robber barons who would, as they had years before, despoil the land and population by robbing and living off others. To question sovereign rulers, to restrict their power, or to place them lower in esteem than others, rightfully or wrongly, was sedition— an attempt to overthrow the good and legal government. Personal criticism of the king became seditious libel.

The duty of the printer was to support the monarchy by communicating state policies. To ensure the press would both refrain from seditious acts and distribute the policies of the sovereign, the authoritarian monarchies developed several methods to control the press, which included the following:

1. Censorship of material before it was printed.
2. Licensing of printing rights, giving loyal subjects a profitable monopoly in exchange for their continued loyalty. By the seventeenth century the Stationer's Company, a private concern, was in control of print trade membership in England and could punish infractions of rules.

The punishment of John Stubbes in sixteenth-century England.

3. Prosecution of publishers who distributed undesirable material. While only three printers were executed in England between 1500 and 1800, scores were maimed for minor crimes. In 1579, for example, John Stubbes published a protest against a proposed marriage between Queen Elizabeth and the Duke of Alencon. These seditious libels resulted in Stubbes and two associates being punished by having their right hands cut off.
4. Passage of special taxes to limit newspaper circulation. These taxes have been called "taxes on knowledge."

The reaction against authoritarian philosophy and controls began as early as 1644, when John Milton, the English poet, wrote his famous *Areopagitica* (areo as in *areo-plane* and pagitica as *in page*) as an argument against government censorship and for a "free and open" public encounter between truth and falsehood. The average person can tell right from wrong, truth from error, Milton insisted, and so truth will always win if people have the information and opportunity to judge. This trust in a self-righting process, as it is called, was echoed years later by Thomas Jefferson, who wrote he would prefer to have newspapers without government than government without newspapers—assuming the populace could receive and read the papers.

Rather than value the state above all, the libertarians placed the individual at the center of the universe. For them, people and their God-given rights were more important. The role of government was to make sure the individual had the opportunity to exercise those rights as long as he or she did not interfere with the rights of others.

The First and Fourteenth Amendments

The First Amendment, which protects speech, printing, and the other media, is a clear reflection of libertarian philosophy. It reads in part: "Congress shall make no law . . . abridging the freedom of speech, or of the press. . . ." The First Amendment *does not define* freedom of speech or the press. It establishes its existence and places it beyond the restraining legislative reach of Congress. Following the Civil War, Congress extended control of the First Amendment through the Fourteenth Amendment. Added to the Constitution in 1868, it holds: "No state shall make or enforce any law which shall abridge the privileges or immunities of citizens of the United States." Again, the Fourteenth Amendment does not define the privileges or immunities we know as the First Amendment freedoms of speech or press, but, places them beyond restraints that the states and their legislatures might contrive. The final decision as to what is and is not an abridgement of First Amendment freedoms is left to the federal courts and the final appellate court in Constitution matters—the nine Justices of the Supreme Court. It is important to remember that the Supreme Court is an appellate court. It cannot and does not give offhand interpretations of the Constitution or definitions of Constitutional rights. To define and interpret the First Amendment the nine Justices must have a First Amendment case. And they must wait for the case to work its way through the court system before they can review it.

Prior Restraint

Throughout most of the nineteenth century, it was more or less assumed that the First Amendment protected the rights of the citizen, printer, and publisher to speak and print without previous restraint by government. As a concept, previous restraint denotes the authoritarian practices of censorship, the requirement of a government license to print as well as the very real restraint produced when one knows the publication of a message can result in physical punishment. From colonial days, taxes on newspaper circulation—called taxes on knowledge—also were considered prior restraint.

It was not until 1931, in the case of *Near v Minnesota,* that the Supreme Court had the opportunity to confirm the prior restraint concept. A Minnesota law called for the forced cessation of any "malicious, scandalous and defamatory" publication. In Minneapolis, Jay M. Near and Howard Guilford were publishing a weekly newspaper and crusading against what they saw as the blight on their community: that "Jew-gangsters" controlled racketeering in the city. The Hennepin County attorney finally brought charges against the paper, and the court ordered the publishers to cease publication—once and for all. On appeal the Minnesota Supreme Court agreed, holding that the state had the power to suppress a defamatory and scandalous publication. On further appeal, however, the U.S. Supreme Court held the Minnesota law was a clear violation of the First and Fourteenth amendments, since it punished a newspaper by prior restraint. By making the paper cease publication, the law restrained future editions *before* they were printed.

Since the *Near* case, the court, time and again, has refused to allow any law or government body to censor, suppress, or control the flow of public information. In 1948 in *Saia v New York,* the Supreme Court decided an ordinance that gave the chief of police authority to decide who could use loudspeakers in a public park was unconstitutional since it gave the police uncontrolled discretion to curtail freedom of speech. It would be difficult to imagine a more effective method of previous restraint, the court observed. In *Martin v Struthers, Ohio,* the city of Struthers passed an ordinance that forbid anyone distributing handbills from ringing doorbells or summoning inhabitants of households to the door. One intention was to relieve citizens from having to answer the door for salespeople. When Thelma Martin, a Jehovah's Witness, attempted to distribute her religious pamphlets, she was arrested. The Supreme Court overturned Martin's conviction. She had the right to ring doorbells and offer her messages to individuals, the court ruled, and individuals had the right to accept or reject the messages. The city government could not intervene and preempt these individual rights. (See pp. 437 and 440.)

Film and Prior Restraint

Introduction of the film and broadcast media into American life has brought some modification of our attitude toward licensing. As Pember has reported, the first First Amendment ruling on movies came in 1915 in *Mutual Film Corp. v Industrial Commission of Ohio.* The Supreme Court, viewing the peep show novelties of the day, held they were "business, pure and simple," and, therefore, not protected by the First Amendment. The decision made the licensing of films, exhibition, and film distributors as legal as the licensing of beer and food vendors.

Film did not come under the protection of the First Amendment until 1952. In *Burstyn v Wilson,* the Supreme Court held films could not be subjected to "unbridled censorship." The decision came following the suppression in New York of *The Miracle,* a film by Roberto Rossalini, the gifted Italian filmmaker. It told the story of an ignorant, superstitious peasant woman who did not understand that her seduction by a passing stranger was the cause of her pregnancy. Instead, she concluded it was a miracle, an immaculate conception. Some religious viewers were so offended they asked the state of New York to ban the film as sacrilegious. Reviewing the case, however, the court reversed the

Anna Magnani as the superstitious peasant woman in "The Miracle."

ban. It ruled that "motion pictures are a significant medium for the communication of ideas," and as such could not be subjected to censorship under such undefinable terms as *sacrilegious*. The decision went on to note there is no right to show *every* film of *every* kind at *all* times. It noted films had a greater "capacity for evil," especially among the impressionable young, a fact that could help determine the degree of community control used for film exhibition.

In 1961 the court ruled the act of licensing films for distribution to be constitutional. The city of Chicago required distributors to obtain a license to show a film within the city. But one distributor, the Times Film Corporation, refused to submit its film *Don Juan* for review, arguing the city ordinance was prior restraint. The constitutionality of the licensing, the court held, rested on the *standards* in granting the license—not on the act of licensing itself. In 1974, following several film licensing cases, the court suggested standards. In *Star v Prellar,* it held film review boards that acted promptly (eight days) and assumed the burden of proving a film was obscene were acting constitutionally.

Broadcasting and Prior Restraint

As noted in chapter 4, strict licensing of radio stations was instituted by Congress in 1927 to achieve clear radio reception for the public. The Supreme Court, in 1941, reviewed the constitutionality of the government's regulation of radio in *NBC v FCC*. When the FCC moved to reduce NBC's two network operations to one and reduce the control network stations had in broadcasting programs in their areas, NBC went to court. It charged (1) FCC control was limited to the regulation of *technical* aspects of broadcasting, and (2) the FCC's attempts to regulate both the technical and programming aspects of radio were *prior restraint* and violated First Amendment rights. The court, however, decided in favor of the FCC, ruling that limitations of the broadcast spectrum required regulation to prevent interference. Since the spectrum was limited, the court continued, it was necessary also for the Commission to determine the composition of the radio traffic—the programming—to insure that what was offered over the air was in the public interest.

To the argument that licensing of stations by the government was a violation of prior restraint, the court replied:

> . . . it would follow that every person whose application for a license to operate a station is denied by the Commission is thereby denied his constitutional right to free speech. Unlike other modes of expression, radio inherently is not available to all . . . and that is why . . . it is subject to governmental regulation. The *right of free speech does not include . . . the right to use the facilities of radio without a license.* [emphasis added]

Charges of racial discrimination in programming led to an important court decision to revoke a radio and television license in Jackson, Mississippi, in 1969. Complaints against the licenses of WLBT(TV) began accumulating as of early 1955, with charges the station cut programs discussing race relations and refused to allow opposition to segregationist views on the air. In 1962 the FCC began an investigation of these and other complaints. In 1964, despite evidence of inequalities and a petition from a black group, the Office of Communication of the Church of Christ, the commission gave WLBT one year to change its policies. The Church of Christ group pressed its case with the court of appeals, at that time under Judge Warren Burger (later Chief Justice of the United States). Judge Burger ordered the FCC to hold a license renewal hearing, noting there was no stated willingness by WLBT to change any of its policies. When, after that hearing, the majority of FCC commissioners voted to renew the license, Judge Burger revoked it in 1967 and ordered the FCC to invite any applicants who wished to file for the opening to do so. As Burger wrote in his 1966 decision:

> A newspaper can be operated at the whim or caprice of its owners; a broadcast station cannot. After nearly five decades of operation the broadcast industry does not seem to have grasped the simple fact that *a broadcast license is a public trust subject to termination for breach of duty.* [emphasis added]

The public has the right to receive "social, political, aesthetic, moral, and other ideas and experiences," the court decided, and it is the duty of the radio and television licensee to see to it the public receives it.

Broadcast licensing in America, then, was not established as prior restraint for political control, but as a means of ensuring that programs reach the public through a limited broadcast spectrum. In recent years, even proposals for the deregulation of licensing have reflected this point of view, charging not so much that licensing is politically motivated but rather that it is inefficient and unnecessary. (The trends in broadcast deregulation will be discussed in chapter 16.)

Advertising and Prior Restraint

In 1976 the Supreme Court faced the issue of whether advertising is protected by the First Amendment, and in *Virginia State Board of Pharmacy v Virginia Citizen Consumer Council, Inc.,* the court ruled that it is. A Virginia statute held the practice of advertising drug prices was unprofessional conduct on the part of pharmacists. But a consumer group brought suit to allow pharmacists to advertise prescription drug prices, charging the public suffered as a result of the statute. The group argued that the poor, the sick, and the aged suffered the most because they had greatest need for the drugs but were least able to shop for prices.

Writing the majority decision, Justice Blackmun agreed that professionalism should be maintained among pharmacists, but that the state had not maintained that professionalism "by keeping the public in ignorance" and suppressing the flow of information on prescription prices. The effect of the Virginia statute was to prevent completely the dissemination of commercial messages. Speech "does not lose its First Amendment protection because money is spent to project it," Blackmun wrote. Neither does it lose it if the message involves a solicitation to purchase or contribute. He continued, "Advertising, however tasteless and excessive it sometimes may seem, is nonetheless dissemination of information." And the free flow of commercial information "is indispensible to the proper allocation of resources in a free society." The justice did note that protection of the First Amendment did not free advertising from restrictions and controls regulating time and place of publication, and according to whether or not the ad was false or deceptive. Thus it still is possible to legislate when and where ads might be published. (The question of control of deceptive advertising will be discussed in chapter 17.)

Some Special Situations
Criticizing Public Figures

As reported in chapter 3, the trial of John Peter Zenger in 1735 centered on the charge that Zenger's truthful attacks on Governor Cosby were seditious libel and threatened the governor's authority. Andrew Hamilton, Zenger's attorney, won the case with a successful plea to the jury that falsehood, not truth, created the libel. As American libel law developed in the nineteenth century, truth became a dominant defense in libel suits. One could defame another—hold him or her up to scorn, ridicule, or cause him or her to be shunned—and still avoid punishment by the courts by proving the charges were true, and that the printer had not used the truth maliciously (had not been out to "get" or purposefully embarrass the one defamed). Members of government enjoyed no special privilege in this regard. They, too, were obliged to show the falsehood of the defamation in order to win damages in libel suits. (See p. 49.)

In 1964 the Supreme Court opened even wider the door to comment and criticism of political figures in the *New York Times v Sullivan* case.

During antisegregationist demonstrations in Montgomery, Alabama, a group sympathetic to the demonstrators wrote and paid for an editorial advertisement in the *Times*. The ad, entitled "Heed Their Rising Voices," charged that, among other things, the Montgomery police had engaged in a "wave of terror" through a "lockout" and by encircling students at nonviolent demonstrations. Montgomery Police Commissioner L. B. Sullivan sued the *Times* and won in Alabama courts. An important part of his case was based on the factual errors in the reports about the "wave of terror." The Montgomery police had not acted as the ad–editorial charged. Sullivan won his case, and the Alabama Supreme Court, following traditional libel law, approved the decision and an award of $500,000.

The paid advertisement that precipitated the *Times v Sullivan* libel case.

When the *Times* appealed, however, the U.S. Supreme Court winced. The $500,000 was clearly punitive (only twenty-two copies of the *Times* with the "Rising Voices" editorial had been distributed in Alabama). Such huge damage settlements could hamper political discussion, the court held, and even put modern newspapers out of business. As to factual errors, the court decided they are inevitable and cannot become a warrant for repressing free speech. It concluded that the only way in which a court could award damages to public officials was if the officials proved *actual malice*. That is, the official would have to show in court that the criticism was produced and distributed with *full* knowledge it was false, or with *reckless disregard for its truth*. Discussion of public officials and public issues should be "uninhibited, robust, and wide-open," the court concluded, "and it may well include vehement, caustic, and sometimes unpleasantly sharp attacks on government and public officials."

In the years following the Sullivan case the Supreme Court extended the actual malice test in libel cases to apply to celebrities and public figures—those who step into the public spotlight on their own (actors and sports figures, for example). These additional rulings are discussed in chapter 16.

As a result of the Sullivan case, the public and the media now enjoy more latitude in discussing and criticizing government officials and their performance than ever before in history. Between the trial of John Peter Zenger in 1735 and the reversal of the Sullivan decision in 1964, American law turned 180 degrees to make malice, not truth, the punishable evil and free the media from fear of prosecution for minor errors that have little affect on the truth of political and public messages.

Clear and Present Danger

In 1917 Congress passed an espionage act, and in 1918 it passed a sedition act. The former made it a crime to issue a false report that interfered with the efforts of World War I; the latter made it a crime to interfere with recruiting for the military service. Several political groups, meanwhile, were actively dissenting the war effort. The Socialist Party of America and party secretary Charles Schenck distributed fifteen thousand leaflets, some by mail, to men drafted into the armed service. Schenck called the war a "bloody adventure" which would profit only a few on Wall Street and urged his readers to oppose conscription, join the party, and fight the draft. He was arrested and convicted under the two wartime acts. He appealed the conviction on grounds the two laws violated his freedoms under the First Amendment. The Supreme Court, under Chief Justice Oliver Wendell Holmes, upheld the convictions, however, noting the country was at war and in a time of *clear and present danger.* "The most stringent protection of free speech would not protect a man in falsely shouting fire in a theatre and causing a panic," Holmes wrote.

The clear and present danger test has been one of the most controversial of the twentieth century. It underscores the need for a nation to protect itself in time of war, but it also offers a simple and ready excuse to curtail media freedoms at any time with the logic, "We usually could do this but now—now there is a clear and present danger of. . . ."

Two such incidents occurred in the 1970s.

In 1979 *The Progressive,* an opinion magazine of the Left, announced it would publish an article with information on how to manufacture a hydrogen bomb. The staff refused to submit the article to the Department of Energy for "editing" (censorship) and also to refrain from publishing it. The Department of Justice, fearing it would reveal restricted data that would give the nation's most desperate enemies an atomic bomb, asked the federal courts for a restraining order, pending a hearing, to stop publication of the article. Court rulings eventually extended the prior restraint for a total of seven months, by which time it finally became clear the article only contained information readily available in the scientific community—and on the open shelves of the government library at Los Alamos. The Justice Department dropped the case the day after a Madison, Wisconsin, newspaper, in *The Progressive*'s hometown, published a letter from an H-bomb hobbiest, which contained essentially the same information considered so sensitive in the *Progressive* article. The magazine finally published the article in November, 1979. It was $284,000 in debt from the legal and research costs incurred in its struggle against prior restraint.

In 1974 one of the most important clear and present danger cases to date came when the Nixon administration moved to stop the New York *Times* from publishing the Pentagon Papers, the official government study of the development of American involvement in Vietnam. The first installment appeared in the *Times* on June 13, 1974. On the following day, just as the paper was going to press with the second installment, Attorney General John Mitchell asked the editors to refrain from publishing any "further information of this character" since it would "cause irreparable injury to the defense interests" of the nation. Mitchell claimed the papers had been stolen from top secret files and that publication of them was directly prohibited by current espionage law. The *Times,* however, continued to publish the series, taking the view the papers were of great public interest. The attorney general and the Justice Department filed suit, and on June 15, 1974, for the first time in American history, a judge ordered a newspaper to cease publication of information of an obviously political nature. The court held any temporary harm done the *Times* by the prior restraint would be outweighed by the potential, irreparable harm that might be done the country by continued publication of the papers.

The *Times* honored the court order and waited for a court decision to lift the ban. But on June 18, with the *Times* silenced, the Washington *Post* took up publication of the papers, knowing full well it would probably bring reaction from the Nixon administration. After two installments, it did, and the *Post,* too, was placed under a temporary restraining order not to print the Pentagon Papers.

Even then the American press was not to be stifled. The Boston *Globe,* then the Chicago *Sun-Times,* eight Knight newspapers, and the St. Louis *Post-Dispatch* all published Pentagon Papers material in time.

On June 30, the Supreme Court reviewed the *Times* and *Post* cases, and vacated the stays against the two newspapers. The court's decision, taken from earlier precedent, was straightforward and simple:

> Any system of prior restraints of expression comes to this court bearing a heavy presumption against its constitutional validity . . . the Government thus carries a heavy burden of showing justification for the enforcement of such a restraint.

"All the News That's Fit to Print"

The New York Times

VOL. CXX..No. 41,413   © 1971 The New York Times Company.   NEW YORK, SUNDAY, JUNE 13, 1971   BQLI   50 CENTS

Tricia Nixon Takes Vows In Garden at White House

CITY TO DISCLOSE BUDGETARY TRIMS FOR DEPARTMENTS

Mayor's Aides Make Decision on Final Figures Scheduled to Be Announced Today

By MAURICE CARROLL

Vietnam Archive: Pentagon Study Traces 3 Decades of Growing U. S. Involvement

By NEIL SHEEHAN

U.S. URGES INDIANS AND PAKISTANIS TO USE RESTRAINT

Calls for 'Peaceful Political Accommodation' to End Crisis in East Pakistan

FIRST PUBLIC APPEAL

Statement Is Said to Reflect Fear of Warfare If Flow of Refugees Continues

By TAD SZULC

The first of the Pentagon Papers news stories. Copyright © 1971 by the New York Times Company. Reprinted by permission.

The government had not met that burden, the lower courts had decided, and the Supreme Court agreed. The newspapers returned to the publication of the Pentagon Papers, but with the lingering knowledge that for sixteen days the Nixon administration had been able to restrain the press legally, in the "national interest." That was in spite of the fact that (1) no case could be made, and (2) the rule of clear and present danger *might* have been applied to overrule First Amendment if the case could have been made.

Advocating Violent Overthrow of Government

In 1940 the threat of war again produced another espionage act, the Smith Act, that prohibited advocating the overthrow or destruction of any level of American government by force or violence. Eleven members of the Communist Party were arrested and charged under the act; in their defense, they claimed the Smith Act violated their First Amendment rights. In 1951, in *Dennis v U.S.,* the Supreme Court decided, however, that a conspiracy to overthrow the government by violence and force did not present a clear and present danger of "substantial evil" that the government was not helpless to prevent. It is one thing to discuss, hypothetically, the philosophies and theories concerned with violent overthrow of government, the court held, but quite another to form a conspiracy to advocate and actually engage in the violent destruction of a government that can be changed through orderly, democratic means.

Obscenity and Pornography

One of the most troublesome problems for the Supreme Court has been obscenity and pornography. For the most part, the problem has not been whether obscenity is protected by the First Amendment, but rather just what is and is not obscenity. Without a workable definition, one can never be sure if what is restrained is pornography, art, instruction—or therapy.

Several states limited the sale and distribution of obscene material in the 1820s and 1830s. Congress passed its first obscenity law in 1842. The first American test for obscenity was borrowed from an English case. In *Regina v Hicklin,* 1868, the English courts held that a literary work was to be considered obscene if any part of it tended to *deprave* or *corrupt* anyone susceptible to corruption—a child, for example. The thinking at that time tended to group all erotic material into one category. The Comstock Law of 1873 gave authorities the power to keep all obscene books and other material out of the mails. Even one edition of a scholarly journal on eugenics was suppressed because it carried an advertisement for a scholarly book, *The History of Prostitution.* The attitude carried into the twentieth century. In the 1930s more than one novel of quality was banned from the mails. Hemingway's *For Whom the Bell Tolls* was one of them.

Following World War II, the Supreme Court heard a series of cases that brought about significant changes. In 1946 it held the Postmaster General did not have the right to deny mailing privileges to *Esquire* magazine simply because he thought it vulgar and in poor taste. In 1957 the court shifted away from the Hinklin obscenity test when it questioned whether isolated passages of a book should determine if the whole book is to be suppressed. The same year, in *Roth v United States,* and later in the so-called *Fanny Hill* case of 1966, the Court rejected the Hinklin rule in favor of a new test for obscenity. According to the Roth test, all the following were to apply:

1. The dominant theme of the material taken as a whole must appeal to prurient, or sexually base, interests;
2. The obscenity is patently offensive in that it affronts contemporary community standards in the description or representation of sexual matters;
3. The material is "utterly without redeeming social value."
     All three elements must be present for the material to be labeled obscene. The test did meet with considerable dissention on the court.

The court continued to pursue a workable test for obscenity in *Miller v California* in 1973 and *Hamling v U.S.* in 1974. In *Miller* the court held material qualified as obscene if (1) the average person applying community standards found the work, taken as a whole, appealed to prurient interests, and if (2) the work lacked serious literary, artistic, political, or scientific value. The court did not continue the "utterly without redeeming social value" phrase, but it did ask that state statutes clearly define what "patently offensive" descriptions of sexual conduct were punishable (masturbation, defecation, etc.) and also give notice as to what promotion and sales activities would be prosecuted. These general directives were intended as fair warning to those who wished to comply with the law but might not due to the obscurity of a state statute.

In both *Miller* and *Hamling,* the court stressed the idea of community standards of obscenity rather than national ones. The community standards also were to be determined by the average person, and not by the jurors themselves.

The community standards test has brought criticism from legal scholars and concern from media producers. The former question the practicality of jurors judging community standards of obscenity based on an abstract and unknown average person. Media producers question how it is possible to produce sexual material that meets a variety of divergent standards. Undoubtedly the court will have another opportunity to review the subject and, perhaps, clarify the situation.

Bribes and Taxes on Knowledge

The controls used by authoritarian governments also have included the (1) paying of publishers or buying of newspapers to print the government's story, and (2) taxes on knowledge. As we saw in chapter 2, government support of newspapers to publish party ideology was attempted in the American partisan press period of the early nineteenth century. That experiment was such an abject failure it has not been attempted again.

While we cannot detail all the U.S. government's secret attempts to manipulate the press, we know such attempts have been made. Both the Central Intelligence Agency (CIA) and the FBI came under strong criticism in the 1970s for their secret, public-funded propaganda activities *within* the United States. The FBI, under director J. Edgar Hoover, conducted illegal surveillance and personality smears against such public figures as Martin Luther King, Jr. The CIA conducted massive, illegal intelligence operations against members of the antiwar movement during the Vietnam conflict. In the 1960s it engaged in extensive fabrication of information during the Bay of Pigs invasion.

The Supreme Court confirmed the protection of the Constitution against taxes on knowledge in a Louisiana case in 1936. Under the influence of Governor Huey P. Long, the Louisiana legislature levied a 2 percent gross receipts tax on newspapers with circulations of twenty thousand or more. (Only thirteen Louisiana newspapers had that much circulation at the time; twelve of the thirteen were openly opposed to Long and his political career.) The tax, the court noted, was not designated to support the State of Louisiana but limit the circulation of information to the public. It was a tax on knowledge—the same type tax used by the British and not unlike the one that led to the American Revolution.

Freedom and the Student Press

A seriously underestimated problem in First Amendment protection is the student press. Can student journalists be controlled by school administrators? Can students who are only beginning to learn the ways of society be held responsible for their "immature" editorials and editorial attacks?

Early appellate court cases involving student-school administrator conflicts are surprisingly similar in theme to the conflict between colonial printers and their royal governors. School principals and school boards often have taken the position of being *in loco parentis*—in the position of being the parent—or, as often has been the case, in a position of authority.

In 1870, as John Nichols has reported, one school board suspended a young journalist who wrote two newspaper articles showing insubordination and disrespect for the board, "ridiculed" school board members in a "scandalous" way, tended to weaken the school board's control, and caused students to become insubordinate and disrespectful. A state court held the student's punishment—dismissal from school—was too severe, but failed to consider the First Amendment aspects of the case. A 1904 Massachusetts case developed when a high school student not only used his father's newspaper to publish criticism of his school principal's management abilities, but also invited fellow students to write similar articles for the paper. In a Zenger-like hearing, the student was not allowed to argue the truth of the printed matter but only his responsibility for publication. Again the court ruled on the fairness of the student's treatment while ignoring the First Amendment aspects of the case.

The first decisions considering restraint and punishment in student expression came in the 1960s. Two Mississippi "freedom button" cases held that students did have the rights to First Amendment freedom of expression (to wear political slogan and emblem buttons) as long as the buttons did not disrupt school activities. Banning them, however, was ruled legal and *reasonable* if necessary to prevent disruption and discipline in the school.

Months later, a student press censorship case developed at the University of Alabama, where students wrote an editorial for their school paper on world revolution that angered Alabama state legislature members. Despite pressure, University of Alabama President Frank Rose refused to censor the paper. Rose's liberal stance attracted admiration from others in the state, including Gary Dickey, editor of the Troy State College newspaper. Dickey wrote an editorial for his school paper commending Rose and attacking the Alabama legislature. But Troy State had a rule forbidding editorial attacks on the governor and the legislature, and Dickey's school newspaper advisor instructed him not to publish the editorial. He published his defiance anyway, placing the word *Censored* in the editorial space, and was suspended from the college for insubordination.

Federal district court Judge Frank Johnson reviewed the appeal in 1967 and held Dickey's suspension a clear violation of his First Amendment rights. The rule forbidding criticism of the state government was unreasonable, Johnson held. Dickey had been dismissed for publishing his remarks, not for insubordination. Johnson further ruled that public school administrators cannot censor or punish students for exercising their rights of expression unless there is material and substantial interference with proper discipline in school.

Two years later, the Supreme Court confirmed the material and substantial interference test in *Tinker v Des Moines Independent Community School District*. Several Des Moines students were suspended from high school for wearing arm bands expressing their feelings about the Vietnam war. Evidence indicated the students had been silent and orderly and had not disturbed the activities of any classes. Since school officials had not proved schoolwork had been disrupted or that disruption was even likely, the court held the suspension violated their freedom of expression.

It is important to remember that *Tinker* and *Dickey* hold only for public school expression and newspapers. Private colleges and universities receive few funds, little regulatory support, or policy control from the state. Court decisions have held that private school actions are *not* state actions. And so, since a private school administrator is not a government official, a private university president can control his school's newspaper the way a corporation chairperson controls the company's public relations program, or the way a publisher edits and determines policy for the daily newspaper.

A private university student press conflict that received national attention occurred at Baylor University in the 1979–1980 school year. Baylor, a Baptist-supported institution, was publicly scheduled for a visit by *Playboy* photographers in pursuit of the magazine's "girls of the Southwest Conference" picture feature. In response, President Abner V. McCall called *Playboy* a "pornographic magazine" and promised disciplinary action for any Baylor coed who posed in the nude or seminude. The three editors of the school paper, *The Lariat,* took an impish stance, arguing "to pose or not to pose" was a question for the individual Baylor woman. They reported McCall's opposition under the headline: "Baylor Beauties Better Not Bare It." Further *Lariat* features on the issue brought McCall's opposition. In a meeting with the three editors the president not unwisely instructed them to turn their attention to problems of campus life—the length of ticket lines, the quality of dorm food—and away from *Playboy.* Eventually, the editors returned to the *Lariat* office and wrote a full-page editorial that protested the president's actions and charged he had infringed on their academic freedom. McCall's reply also came in writing. It read, in part:

> Historically and legally, freedom of the press under the First Amendment has always been freedom of the publisher. The publisher of the newspaper has the freedom to establish the policies of the newspaper and determine the editorial stands of the newspaper. This constitutional freedom does not belong to the editors or reporters employed by the publisher.

The student editors soon lost their school newspaper jobs, and two lost scholarships. All three chose to remain at Baylor. But they had no legal recourse other than to accept the decision of their publisher, President McCall. Intrusion by government in the matter would have been a violation of the First Amendment rights of the newspaper's owner, Baylor University.

Some Contrasts in Restraint

In 1940 the Supreme Court gave something of a summary definition of freedom of speech and the press in *Thornhill v Alabama:*

> The freedom of speech and of the press guaranteed by the Constitution embraces at the least the liberty to discuss publicly and truthfully all matters of public concern without previous restraint or fear of subsequent punishment. . . . Freedom of discussion, if it would fulfill its historic function in this nation, must embrace all issues about which information is needed or appropriate to enable the members of society to cope with the exigencies of their period.

That many of the world's presses do not enjoy these basic freedoms sometimes is difficult to believe. Many people still struggle under authoritarian controls—especially those in developing countries ruled by dictators. In recent years Argentina and Egypt have provided examples.

The military junta that ruled Argentina between 1976 and 1983—the one which ordered the invasion of the Malvinas, or Falkland Islands, in 1982—subjected the Argentine press to brutal repression. In April, 1977, the regime arrested and held captive, without formal charges, Jacobo Timerman, publisher of the Argentine newspaper, *La Opinion.* For the first forty days of his imprisonment, Timerman was tortured and interrogated daily. By the early 1980s some sixty journalists had been kidnapped, imprisoned, and tortured for publishing opinions contrary to the junta's interests.

Egypt also has strong controls on its media. In 1980 Egypt passed a constitutional amendment making the media the country's fourth estate. All newspaper people became government employees, all editors and news managers were to be appointed by the government. The purpose was, the government said, to position the press so it might protect Egypt's democracy and not indulge in "slandering opposition to, hatred of, or contempt for the Egyptian political, social and economic systems." The amendment made it a crime to publish misleading news, to repudiate religion, or moral and national values. The major source of news is the government-run news service.

The Soviet System and Media Control

The media philosophy that stands in sharpest contrast to our own is that of the Soviet Union. While most recent American trends have tended to espouse social responsibility and self-regulation of media to avoid government ownership, the Soviet system bases its concept of freedom on government ownership of the media.

The Soviet system has its roots in the writings of Karl Marx and Fredrich Engels, and the rise to power in 1917 of the Bolsheviks in Russia. When they assumed power, the Bolsheviks had the awesome task of taking the Communist truth to multitudes of illiterate peasants living in a country six times the size of the United States. To reach their population and solidify their position at the head of government, the new leaders established a far-flung network of newspapers, magazines, and broadcast media. The specific purpose of the media was to educate the Soviet public to Communism and achieve a strict unity of knowledge among the people by interpreting events and life from the Communist point of view.

The Communist media are filled with "positive" stories about communism: how it is succeeding, how the tiniest details in current events point to the silent, inevitable workings of Marxist theory. The antithesis of these stories are the ones that report the depravity and failure of capitalism and its tyrannical, imperialist threats to Soviet worker's.

The Soviet constitution grants its citizens, in "the interests of the working people," both "freedom of speech" and "freedom of the press."

But since Marxist theory holds that working class truth cannot come from media owned by the middle class, freedom must come *from class control of the press*—or ownership of the media by the worker's Communist government. And since power in the Soviet Union has been in the hands of the party leaders since the 1920s, it is this group that determines the party line and the content of Soviet media.

Since freedom of the press means ownership of the media by the Communist government, control is not by censorship, licensing, taxation, or even threat of punishment. The editors, broadcasters, filmmakers, and book publishers are government employees who are as dedicated and interested in publishing the party line as any other member of the government. In fact, as journalists, they are the ones specifically trained to build communism by relating the current party line to (or squaring it with) Communist ideology and truth—for the education and guidance of the Soviet public.

The World Information Order

Many feel one of the more serious threats to media freedom as we know it has developed in recent years in the United Nations Educational, Scientific, and Cultural Organization (UNESCO). In 1974 the Soviet Union called for a "new world order." Major purposes of the new order were to establish the licensing of international journalists and to support the right of individual governments to control their own mass media. Supporters of the order—mostly emerging and Communist bloc nations—say it is needed to stop the biased news reports of western journalists covering less-developed nations. By licensing only mature or qualified journalists, they say they can ensure realistic reports of their nations' accomplishments. Opponents charge, however, the purpose is to control the flow of world information by licensing journalists who will report only news that is favorable to the licensing nations. In short, both sides charge bias. The proposal is expected to meet strong opposition from western nations in the years ahead. It seems to have been one reason behind the Reagan administration's decision to withdraw from UNESCO by 1985. (As a member, the U.S. contributed 25 percent of UNESCO's total budget.)

Summary

Freedom of speech and the press has traditionally meant freedom from previous or prior restraint: censorship, licensing, fear of punishment, and restrictive taxes. In our system, media freedoms generally are protected under the First and Fourteenth amendments, as interpreted by the Supreme Court.

A long list of cases has verified the First Amendment right to speak and print without prior restraint from government.

Films were held to be under the protection of the First Amendment in 1952, but the court also has ruled that film distribution may be licensed if the licensing board acts expeditiously and bears the burden of proof for charges of obscenity. Broadcasting has been licensed in the interest of ensuring that the public receives the widest possible service in a limited medium. A broadcast license can be recalled for improper performance.

The court has held that public discussion should be open, uninhibited, and robust, and that political figures and public figures must prove actual malice (knowing and reckless disregard for the truth) to win libel actions.

The courts also have held that First Amendment rights may be suppressed in times of "clear and present danger" to the country, but the courts have appeared reluctant to suppress these rights with only casual evidence of danger. Calling for the violent overthrow of the government, however, is punishable, since government can be changed by orderly, democratic means.

The Supreme Court has continued to hold that obscenity is not protected by the First Amendment, but it has had difficulty defining obscenity. Recent tests have held that a work is obscene if (1) the dominant theme appeals to prurient interests, (2) it affronts community standards, and (3) the work lacks serious literary, artistic, political or scientific value. The court has relegated the definition to each community, leaving many media producers confused as to how to create entertainment for such a diverse nation.

Bribes and taxes on knowledge have been used in this country, and in this century, to control the press. Secret manipulation is difficult to uncover. But the Supreme Court has held that taxes on knowledge or taxation designed to curtail circulation, is unconstitutional.

The student press parallels the public press in its freedoms. Public school administrators cannot indulge in previous restraint of editors of school newspapers. The private school president, however, is protected from government restraint in the same way public school students are protected from government action.

The western countries face a challenge from UNESCO, the Soviets, and developing nations in the next few years. The latter want to license international journalists, in hopes of putting international news under government control.

At home, meanwhile, our own traditions seem to grow stronger with development of the social responsibility theory, and the belief that freedom carries the responsibility of good performance and service to society. To be free and responsible is the best way to remain free, media professionals are coming to believe.

Questions for Discussion

1. I do not want to be bothered with anyone who is "pushing" political and religious tracts door-to-door. I put up a sign that reads, "No pamphlets or tracts, please." A county prosecutor calls at my house a week or so later. "We've had a complaint. You must take down your sign. It's unconstitutional!" What do I tell him or her? Why?

2. Recent debate has centered on the need to deregulate broadcasting. Can you make an argument for deregulation? Under what conditions would the change make for a better broadcast service?

3. Many feel the Supreme Court has gone too far in forcing political and public figures to prove actual malice in order to win a libel judgment. It has now been more than twenty years since actual malice became the required condition for "damage" payments. Have political and celebrity libel cases all but disappeared? What cases have you heard of lately that involved a politician or celebrity? What media were involved?

4. Review the section in this chapter on school newspapers. What First Amendment rights do you, as a college student, have in private schools? In public schools? Who in America enjoys the right to print? To broadcast? To make recordings?

References

Barnouw, Erik. *The Image Empire*. New York: Oxford University Press, 1970.

Blanchard, Margaret A. "The Hutchins Commission, the Press and the Responsibility Concept," *Journalism Monographs,* no. 68 (May 1977).

Emery, Edwin. *The Press and America*. Englewood Cliffs, N.J.: Prentice-Hall, 1972.

"The First Amendment on Trial," *Columbia Journalism Review,* September/October 1971, 7–58.

Knappman, Edward W., ed. *Government & the Media in Conflict/1970–74*. New York: Facts on File, Inc., 1974.

Mencher, Melvin. "Where Freedom Stops at the Schoolhouse Gate." *The Quill,* May 1980, 31.

Millecam, Melissa, Juan Ramon Palomo, and Charles Long. "Blowup at Baylor." *The Quill,* May 1980, 23–25.

Nichols, John E. "The Tinker Case and Its Interpretation," *Journalism Monographs,* no. 52, (December 1977).

————. "The Pre-Tinker History of Freedom of Student Press and Speech," *Journalism Quarterly* 56, no. 4 (1979): 727–33.

Pember, Don R. *Mass Media Law*. Dubuque, Iowa: Wm. C. Brown, 1977.

Sanford, Bruce, W. *Synopsis of the Law of Libel and the Right of Privacy*. New York: Newspaper Enterprise Association, Inc. 1977.

Schmidt, Jr., Benno C. *Freedom of the Press vs. Public Access*. New York: Praeger, 1976.

Siebert, Fred S., Theodore Peterson, and Wilbur Schramm. *Four Theories of the Press*. Urbana: University of Illinois Press, 1963.

Timerman, Jacobo. "The Bodies Counted Are Our Own." *Columbia Journalism Review,* May/June 1980, 30–33.

Chapter

16

Rights in Conflict: The Media, The Government, The Citizen

The curious, newspaper reporters, broadcasters, and photographers all crowded into the courtroom for the kidnap-murder trial of Bruno Hauptmann in 1935.

Rights and Conflict

Our First Amendment rights are so important to our way of life it is easy to overlook the fact that they are not the only rights protected by the Constitution and do not always hold the highest priority in competition with other rights. The Constitution has freed the media from prior restraint by the government, but the daily pursuit of freedom by more than two hundred million citizens sets the stage for conflict, even contests of rights—sometimes placing the rights of media, government, and citizen at odds with each other. The news media, for example, have claimed the right to watchdog government, but as the Supreme Court has held, the government clearly has the right and duty to protect itself from those who would use the First Amendment to destroy it. The news media have the right to report matters of public interest, including those involving individuals. But individuals also have rights—rights to their good names, to a fair trial, to be secure in the privacy of their homes, to remain silent, to be left alone. And clearly they are as important as the media's rights to gather and publish news.

The purpose of freedom of speech and press is to enhance freedom, not diminish it. And so when rights come into conflict, maintaining freedom requires careful deliberation to see which freedoms may and may not be exercised in a given situation or at a given moment. A free society can no more abide a tyranny of mass communication (we speak, you listen) than it can abide the tyranny of a self-appointed government (we decide, you agree without exception).

The News Media and Government

The relationships between the news media and the executive and legislative branches of government are complex. The press, throughout the years, has taken the view that the press-government relationship is an adversary relationship. More recently, it has been suggested that the press and government also have a pronounced symbiotic relationship.

The Adversary Relationship

The role of the news media as a government adversary has been discussed by several writers. As former presidential press secretary Jerald ter Horst has written:

> A truly free press does not have an obligation to support government policy. . . . The press need not be hostile, but it must remain an adversary—willing to test, investigate and challenge governmental decisions.

One of the best examples of the adversary or watchdog role of the media was the performance of the Washington *Post* during the Nixon administration's Watergate scandal. Throughout the months of investigation, the *Post* remained willing to test and challenge what was said and done, and then publish documented accounts of the improprieties. Other examples abound from state and local political situations. The news media reported in the late 1970s, for example, that reporters were asking Tennessee Governor Ray Blanton tough questions concerning $17,000 Blanton and his staff had spent on trips outside the state, including $12,000 reportedly paid for limousine service in Washington D.C. The questions evidently struck home. Blanton refused to answer, claiming "the public is tired of the negativism of the news media." He set a policy of refusing to respond to any reporter who did not report the positive side of the news. As a result, the expenditures, the governor's refusal to answer questions about them, and his manner of refusal also became part of the news, as reporters continued to question his official performance.

The Symbiotic Relationship

Other than acting as an adversary to all levels of government, the news media function, as many journalists and political scientists have pointed out, as the fourth branch of government. Much of what the news media do is a necessary, integral part of the governing process. Our popular government could not operate properly without them. They have the important function of keeping the people informed while also acting as messengers to keep the government informed. As journalist Douglas Cater has written, in any hot debate on the floor of Congress, senators or representatives bring the latest news releases to the floor for information and ammunition. The information service given to government can be more subtle, too.

> The reporter serves as one systematic channel of communication between Congress and the Executive which continues to function when others have broken off. Through him the opposition as well as lesser members of the President's own party can bring their queries to the President's ear with some certainty of a response. Conversely, select reporters enjoy an intimacy with the congressional leaders that few members of the White House staff share.

In summary, the relationship between the news media and the government ranges from open conflict to open cooperation. In professional writings and observations journalists seem to talk more of the adversary relationship than their cooperative efforts with government. But more if not most of the interaction between the news media and government—local, state, or federal—is symbiotic, mutually supportive, rather than adversarial. Both the news media and government need to talk to the public. The news media hold their audiences by giving vital and interesting reports of government while the government hopes to win favor with the public with needed laws and popular policies. The press needs news and the government needs publicity. And so, frequently, these sometimes adversaries come to the aid of each other in ways beneficial to themselves and the public.

A good example of the advantages of a symbiotic relationship evolved a few years ago between the offices of California Congressman Fortney "Pete" Stark and the Los Angeles *Times*. Stark had received several letters from constituents concerning a large number of California citizens being held in Mexican jails. The letters complained the Americans were being subjected to torture, extortion, and sexual abuse, and U.S. State Department officials had been unresponsive to requests for aid from the prisoners and their families. To promote an investigation of the case, Stark invited Los Angeles *Times* Washington Bureau Chief Jack Nelson to review the letters and evidence his office had compiled on the situation. The file convinced Nelson that his newspaper should join the investigation. From then on, the offices of the newspaper and congressman shared information. Each gained as the two proceeded with a coordinated investigation.

Eventually, the *Times*'s investigation in Mexico revealed brutalization and systematic extortion of American prisoners. Just as important,

THE MUSES

many of the Americans were in jail from drug arrests made by Mexican officials as a courtesy to U.S. drug officials. The *Times*'s series exposing the situation won public support for the cause, helping Congressman Stark get a congressional hearing, an official fact-finding trip to Mexico, and support from fellow congressmen to resolve the problem. The first American prisoners returned to the United States in 1977, more than two years after the investigation began.

The News Reporter as Government Agent

While reporters might agree cooperation, even symbiotic cooperation, is a necessary part of the news media/government relationship, most would disagree that the news reporter should become an agent for the government—collecting information not for news media publication but for government intelligence files. In the 1970s it became known, however, that a large number of reporters had actually conducted investigations for the government, acting during a period of years on a part-time basis as agents for the Central Intelligence Agency.

The advantages of the news reporters serving as government agents are obvious. Reporters are trained observers who can move inconspicuously in public places. And many reporters consider it an honor to be recruited for such patriotic duty. But thoughtful news people see a conflict in the arrangement. Could the reporter who acts as a government agent hope to approach and gather news from the agency he or she is serving, or after having served it? Since the 1970s many news organizations have adopted formal policies forbidding reporters to work for any government intelligence or law enforcement agency. United Press International, for example, now allows reporters to swap basic information with FBI or CIA people, but insists reporters refuse invitations to join in gathering undercover information.

The Trade Relationship

Journalism professor Walter Gieber has suggested the proper relationship between the news media and government—federal, state or municipal—is a trade relationship. As Gieber has argued, the congressional or the city hall reporter must neither dominate nor become the agent, servant, or toady of government. The news media are not equipped to govern. On the other hand, if they chose to slavishly promote government as publicist or mouthpiece, they default on their responsibility to inform the people and keep the government in check and responsive to the public will. They serve themselves and the public best if they trade accurate reporting of government programs and problems in exchange for access to government operations and government officials—with no government strings attached on what and how things shall be said about them.

Fortunately or unfortunately, even the best of trade relationships have some slack in them—some room for sharp trading and manipulation. Much of the governmental manipulation of the news media is done in the interest of gaining publicity—perhaps personal publicity. Most news media attempts to manipulate government seem aimed at uncovering information—or getting a scoop, to use newspaper jargon.

Some critics argue news media reporters encourage manipulation by being too willing to accept exclusives without double-checking the information. Some seem to take whatever politicians dish out. The Communist witch hunts of the McCarthy era of the 1950s had its share of this type of reporting. During the period much was reported that was not examined—although there is good reason to believe, too, that Senator Joseph McCarthy understood the cycle of news publication well enough to manipulate it for his own ends, to get headlines without making news announcements, and to project himself and his own special kind of anti-Communist agenda into national attention.

Observers today insist television's constant need for pictures makes it highly susceptible to manipulation. Presidents, governors, and mayors all take trips or create special ceremonies and situations to win media coverage. In 1984 President Reagan made a "nonpolitical" trip to China, managed to greet the Pope in Alaska as their paths crossed, then appeared in full command on the beaches of Normandy on the fortieth anniversary of D-Day—all with extensive television coverage. Such extravaganzas are a highly valuable means of enhancing positive political images while revealing absolutely nothing about plans, policies, or government.

There are definite limits to political manipulation of the media. As one observer has pointed out, today's reporters—local and national—are sophisticated and more difficult to fool. They know their turf and politicians find they may hold them off with a clever or inspiring phrase for a while but not for the long run. Sooner or later reporters will demand that government or political figures deal in facts. At the same time, the people who guide political campaigns, the political consultants, also know there are limitations to image making: If there is too much, the candidate loses credibility with the press—and the political consultant loses his or her job.

Secrecy and Sunshine: Reporting Government

The rights to speak, print, and distribute news without prior restraint would be empty without the right to report. To gather the information needed to inform the people, the news media must have access to government officials and access to government offices, deliberations, and records. Government cannot be expected to be subservient to the news media any more than the media can be expected to be the servant of government. But in American society, there has been growing support for the right to report, since both the news media and our democratic government recognize the need for an informed public.

The press interview is now a regular part of American political life. Established by newspaper practice in the nineteenth century, it has become a daily ritual of the television news media. We rarely pass a day without comments from one member of Congress or the president on matters of national interest. Our legislative bodies at the state and federal levels are open to the public by tradition, and now a significant move is under way to televise coverage of government deliberations. The House of Representatives maintains its own television production system. House sessions are now transmitted around the country by cable television. The U.S. Senate had considered but not approved in-house television coverage at last report. Still, the right to report is not as firmly established as other news media freedoms. And the years ahead promise continued conflict over the news media's demands for information from government, and the government's insistence on withholding it for reasons of efficiency, national security, and the national interest.

The epitome of the political interview is the presidential press conference, with its open challenges and exchanges on government policy. The modern presidential press conference format was inaugurated by President Franklin Roosevelt, who scrapped the practice of requiring written questions and told reporters to "let fly" on any and all topics. President Truman moved the conferences from office to auditorium. President Eisenhower's administration saw the arrival of fast, Tri-X film, which facilitated motion picture coverage of the conferences. President Kennedy pioneered live television coverage. President Reagan tried, then abandoned, "Reagan roulette," or random assignment of rights to ask questions. More successful was his attempt to keep reporters seated unless called on—and bring more order and decorum to the conference process. (Outside the press conference situation, but in view of television cameras, President Reagan often would answer reporters' questions on the spot, giving an impression of open, informal news exchanges.)

Few would argue that presidential press conferences are not exciting and often informative—an example of democracy replicated in few parts of the world. Few world leaders are asked to submit themselves and their policies to the open questioning of journalists. At the same time, State Department critics have said the thirty-minute presidential press conferences have a high potential for error, since the president must quickly answer reporters' complicated questions with millions of people watching. For reasons of national security—not to mention the problem of political security—it is unreasonable to expect the president, or any government official, elected or not, to be entirely candid in interviews, especially public, televised ones.

Secrecy and the Public Interest

Few would disagree that in the public interest some types of information must be withheld from publication. In 1979, following the attempt to rescue the Iranian hostages by military action, President Carter refused to discuss some details of the mission. Recognizing the information might endanger friends in Iran, and that some details of the rescue attempt also might make a subsequent attempt more difficult, reporters acceded to the President's decision to withhold details on the matter—for the time being anyway.

But, again, publication of sensitive information also can be in the public interest. In 1961 the New York *Times* uncovered details of the Cuban Bay of Pigs invasion before the operation was under way. Editors of the paper decided not to publish the story, however, since publication could cost lives and endanger the attempt. As it turned out, the invasion was a monumental blunder that cost Cuban lives and was deeply humiliating for the president and the nation. Afterward, the *Times* editors regretted their decision—often and publicly—with promises they would not make the same mistake again. President Kennedy is reported to have said he would have called off the operation if the *Times* had published the story before the invasion began.

Too often, the attempt to withhold information is not warranted. But it is not always clear just when government is withholding information in the public interest and when it is withholding information in its own interests. In recent years a bitter debate over withholding information came with the 1983 American invasion of Grenada. American forces landed on the island the morning of October 25, but without prior warning to American reporters who were *not* allowed to join the invasion force. Reporter-attorney Jack Landau has summarized the government actions of censorship as follows: (1) the press was totally excluded from the island for days, and the military announced it would shoot down any boats attempting to drop reporters on shore; (2) four reporters already on Grenada were detained aboard a naval ship and not allowed to transmit their stories; (3) the military established its own information monopoly using its own photographers and government reporters; (4) the military published stories false in content and with serious omissions; (5) but it also permitted foreign reporters to report for their own media; and (6) its only justification was to protect the reporters' lives (although the press had not sought that protection). If any claim to access has the support of the First Amendment it would seem to be the claim of American news reporters to view the American military in frontline combat.

It still is unclear why the Grenada invasion was accompanied by such heavy and absolute censorship. There is reason to believe that much of the misinformation given press and public at the time was the result of bureaucratic bungling. One chilling explanation is that the military has been studying ways to keep the news media from reporting military operations since the Vietnam war, and that the treatment of the press in Grenada represents the new military posture in press relations. Speculation on the latter came to an end in 1984, however, when the Pentagon and a group of media representatives reported agreement on a new policy to insure coverage of future small military actions. The policy called for the creation of a pool of eleven correspondents and camera people who would be allowed to go onto the battlefield with American troops to report for all the news media. The pool would be composed of representatives from the major television network news organizations (ABC, CBS, NBC, and CNN) and the two major wire services, one news magazine representative, one radio network reporter, and one photographer from an undesignated news medium.

What is certain about secrecy is that what government withholds (and what, therefore, we do not know) may certainly harm us, so that discovering and knowing and publishing it—with or without governmental cooperation—must be a necessary news media preoccupation.

Executive Privilege

From the days of George Washington, American presidents have maintained the doctrine of executive privilege as a rationale for withholding information. Legal scholar William Francois has pointed out the doctrine rests on the argument that the president has the privilege of deciding what information "should or should not be made public" as part of his Constitutional responsibilities of managing foreign affairs and national

The Right to Know, The Need to Know

Wearing surgical masks, one group of people belonging to a social movement demanding the release of secret or withheld information pickets government buildings. The demonstrators are not students, social radicals, or intellectuals, but factory employees, disabled workers, lawyers, environmentalists, police, fire fighters, and union organizers—members of the blue- and white-collar establishment—who picket city halls and state capitol buildings carrying signs that read, "We Need to Know." They are members of a new "Right-to-Know" alliance dedicated to bringing about laws that require businesses to reveal to employees the toxic substances used in making their products.

"For some of us, it's already too late," one fifty-four-year-old worker told the *Wall Street Journal* in 1983. He retired with full disability at age thirty-eight, after twenty years of work in an asbestos factory. While the Bureau of Labor Statistics reported forty-four thousand employees filed for compensation for chemical injuries and illnesses in 1980, it is difficult to know the extent of the problem since some illnesses from toxic exposure are not evident for many years. As one New Jersey attorney pointed out, workers have no way of knowing what precautions to take when working with unlabeled materials.

A New Jersey pipefitter, Charles Morris, has said the large manufacturers already have excellent programs for informing and training employees to deal safely with hazardous substances. "We worry about the little plants and the non-union plants. Why shouldn't everyone be entitled to this information?" The manufacturers who oppose "right-to-know" legislation fear open labeling of chemical ingredients might jeopardize trade secrets. "Competitive companies will be looking with a careful eye to acquire that information," one chemical executive has argued. Other business leaders have hoped for a voluntary, self-regulating code that will reduce problems of dealing with many legal variations introduced in laws by different states. *Journal* reporter Frank Allen also found the chemical industry is not so much interested in withholding information from workers as it is in avoiding an unworkable regulatory burden. "If you require every employer to make these disclosures," as one chemical industry spokesman said, "you're talking about almost everything, right down to powdered cleanser under bathroom sinks."

security. There seems to be little legal basis for the doctrine—only the Constitutional interpretation of the president's role. President Washington and his cabinet established executive privilege in 1792 when enemies in Congress demanded to see all papers concerning a disastrous military expedition to the Northwest. Rather than release all the papers he gave up only those "the public good would permit," Francois has reported, while withholding those "which would injure the public." Washington used the doctrine again in 1796, refusing a request from the

Hazel Staats, Princeton area coordinator for the National Organization for Women, calls for "Right to Know" legislation before a rally in New Jersey in 1983.

The movement has learned much in its pursuit of "right-to-know" laws. By telling state legislators about their eye damage, burns, and blisters from industrial chemicals, these workers have pushed through laws in at least eight states and three cities (Philadelphia, Cincinnati, and Pennsauken, N.J.) and put "right-to-know" bills into the legislative process in twenty other legislatures.

House for papers on the Jay Treaty. The doctrine has been in the presidential repertoire ever since.

Those who distrust executive privilege point to President Nixon's use of it during the Watergate scandal. Nixon attempted to withhold the famous White House tape recordings under executive privilege, arguing the tapes should be kept from publication since they contained confidential conversations between him and his advisors. On hearing the tapes, however, the Supreme Court noted there would be no question of a breach of national security in releasing the tapes. The court then held the President's desire to protect confidentiality with advisors might be in the public interest, but that this protection was not reason enough to withhold the tapes from examination in a criminal trial. There can be no absolute, unqualified executive privilege, Chief Justice Burger ruled in the case. The public has the right to all evidence—including that held by a president—with the exception of sensitive material relating to national security and specifically protected by law.

Executive Orders and Classification

Clearly the most sweeping attempts to keep government information from public view came in the years following World War II. President Truman and then President Eisenhower issued executive orders to classify government documents in the interests of national security. The classifications "top secret," "secret," and "confidential" were placed on documents to restrict their distribution, to protect against, as William Francois has reported, "all hostile or destructive action by covert or overt means, including espionage. . . ." The legality of the executive orders, like that of executive privilege, was questionable from the beginning.

More frustrating was the fact they proved to be highly effective. Much government information—too much of it—was classified and hidden away in the public interest. Researcher-historian Julius Epstein, Stanford University, began attempts in the 1950s to secure the Keelhaul file, the record of a joint British-American operation during World War II. It was still classified and unobtainable in the 1970s, twenty-five years after the war's end. One retiring government documents worker told a House subcommittee in 1971 that less than .005 percent of all documents given government security classification actually warranted them.

The Freedom of Information Act

To combat the misuse of document classification, Congress passed the Freedom of Information Act (FOIA) in 1967. As amended in 1974, the FOIA allows classification of documents to protect national security, trade and financial secrets, and personal medical files; it also allows classification for law enforcement purposes. But it allows the public and news media access to a classified document, if a district court judge rules the document may be released. Thus far, judges have been more likely to grant FOIA petitions than deny them; as a result, many documents that otherwise would have remained hidden have been brought into public view or public knowledge. According to one estimate, the act and the documents it brought to public scrutiny had been the source of at least 250 news stories by the early 1980s.

Some law enforcement agencies have been sharp critics of the FOIA however. Reagan administration Attorney General William French Smith moved to limit the act with complaints from the National Association of Manufacturers, the CIA, and FBI. The business community complained the act gives too much information about American corporate policies and products that can be used by corporate competitors to illegal advantage. The CIA and FBI feared criminals would use the act to discover the identities of informants, and/or frustrate efforts by the CIA or FBI to collect information. There were also complaints that access to documents should be reduced because operating costs—of staff and producing the documents, for example—were too high.

At last report, critics of the FOIA had not been able to bring forth enough hard evidence to change the act, however. At the same time, news stories of national significance continue to come from government documents that report:

1. Evidence that atomic bomb testing in the West produced radiation dangers to Utah residents.
2. Predisaster suspicions of supervisors in the Nuclear Regulatory Commission that the Three Mile Island nuclear plant in Pennsylvania was dangerous.
3. The fact the CIA had confined a foreign political figure to a mental hospital.

Snepp and Government Restrictions

One recent court case suggests the government may curtail some disclosures of information by government employees. In 1980 former CIA agent Frank Snepp III published his book *Decent Interval,* an account of activities of the Central Intelligence Agency during the Vietnam War. As a CIA agent, Snepp had signed a lifetime secrecy oath that he would, after leaving the agency, submit anything he wrote for review before publishing it. He published *Decent Interval* without submitting it for CIA review. The book contained no classified material, but its publication motivated the government to bring Snepp into court.

In a six to three decision, the Supreme Court ruled Snepp violated his CIA secrecy contract and should forfeit all earnings from the book. At the time of the decision, the earnings had mounted to $115,000. The punishment was given, the court said, to deter others who might be tempted to reveal sensitive information. The three justices who dissented in the ruling argued taking the book's profits was not supported by law. They feared, too, the ruling might lead to restrictions on citizens' rights to criticize government.

A large group of citizens soon did lose that right. In 1983 President Reagan signed National Security Directive 84, binding some one hundred thousand former and current federal officials to lifetime censorship regarding governmental affairs and giving the federal government the right to censor—to approve or disapprove—what these officials revealed about the national government. No doubt one purpose of the directive was to tighten security and reduce leaks of government information. The security that was gained should be balanced against an important loss. As journalist Robert Lewis has observed, the directive now in effect "places a powerful restraint on criticism of government by those in the best position to identify wrongs and debate policy."

Sunshine Laws

Federal and state legislatures, meanwhile, have taken giant steps to give the public and the news media much greater access to meetings of government agencies. The federal government enacted the Government in Sunshine Act in 1976, opening meetings of the "alphabet soup" agencies (FCC, NLRB, SEC, TVA, etc.) to the public, including all of their subunits. When these agencies and subagencies meet to conduct official business, they now are automatically open to the public, and, therefore, to the press. The agencies may hold closed meetings, but only if subjects bearing on national defense or subjects similar to the ones protected under the FOIA are on the agenda.

A survey of state sunshine legislation by the Freedom of Information Center at the University of Missouri revealed more than sixty state sunshine meeting and open records laws enacted between 1974 and 1978. They varied greatly in content and specificity. Some were so vague as to allow the withholding of public records in the public interest. Others had trouble defining, exactly, an agency meeting. (Should it include a luncheon meeting at which all members of the agency happen to be present? Is a conference telephone call a meeting?)

Whatever their shortcomings, the state sunshine laws are a step forward against secrecy in government, as is the growing trend toward televising of state legislative meetings. By the early 1980s, forty states had statutes allowing radio and television coverage of legislative sessions. Still dedicated to working in secret, however, are many congressional committees. About 40 percent of all congressional committees conduct public business behind closed doors.

The News Media and the Sixth Amendment

Just as libertarian ideology proposed free and open reporting as the best check against tyrannical government, the news media today maintain reporting of police and court procedures as the best means of guaranteeing a citizen Sixth Amendment rights to a speedy trial before an impartial jury. Beginning as early as the 1930s, however, the judiciary has held a dimmer view of trial coverage. Some judges consider trial reporting more of a threat than a help to the legal process, charging the news media contribute to lynch-mob psychology and a circus atmosphere in court. There has been more than one historical incident to support their view.

On Roman Holidays

One of the most notable incidents occurred in 1963, following the assassination of President Kennedy. The tragic death brought hordes of news reporters to Dallas. Their sheer numbers pressured Dallas police to produce facts and results which reporters, often too eager, relayed as half-completed stories to their anxious audiences. The Warren Commission Report later termed press performance in Dallas "irresponsible" and "lacking in self-discipline." The flood of prejudicial publicity left many attorneys with the grave concern that Lee Harvey Oswald, had he lived, could not have gotten a fair trial anywhere in America. One United Press International story reported, for example, the Dallas police had an airtight case against Lee Harvey Oswald, along with photos of him holding a rifle identified as the one which killed the president. The story quoted a homicide detective as saying the case was "cinched," and noted that Oswald had lost his confidence and appeared frightened after he was shown photos of the rifle. Pressure mounted following the assassination to control pretrial and courtroom news coverage.

In 1966 an important Supreme Court decision reversed the 12-year-old murder conviction of an Ohio osteopath, Dr. Sam Sheppard, on grounds he had not received a fair trial due to prejudicial, pretrial publicity. Sheppard had been arrested and convicted of murdering his wife—in a storm of prejudicial news headlines. The courtroom proceedings were described as having a Roman holiday atmosphere. The trial judge told one reporter—as the trial began—that Sheppard was obviously guilty, then stayed on the bench to try and sentence him. The press table was set up inside the bar so the jury could see materials shown the press, whether they were entered in evidence or not. During one recess, the jury overheard a radio broadcast that reported Sheppard had fathered an illegitimate child by a female in prison in New York.

In granting a new trial, the Supreme Court held the trial judge had not (1) controlled the use of the court by the press, (2) insulated witnesses from prejudicial media reports, (3) controlled the flow of prejudicial information from police and trial attorneys, and (4) warned the news media against writing prejudicial stories or using information not on record in the proceedings.

In 1968 the American Bar Association (ABA), to tighten its stand on pretrial publicity, adopted a report from a committee chaired by Massachusetts Supreme Judicial Court Justice Paul C. Reardon. The Reardon Report gave the following suggestions:

1. proposed that pretrial publicity be limited to vital statistics of the accused and circumstances of the arrest;

Some of the pretrial coverage in the Sam Sheppard case.

2. charged the courts, attorneys, and police to withhold any report of a confession, prior criminal record, or "he's guilty" statements;
3. prohibited news media interviews or pictures without the written consent of the accused; and
4. called for news reporters to be held in contempt of court— jailed and/or fined—if they published any statements not on the court record, taken from a *closed* hearing, or aimed at influencing the trial's outcome.

As it turned out, the ABA was the only organization to formally adopt the Reardon Report, but it did have a pronounced effect. Bar, bench, and press committees in several states accepted its principles—in particular the stands on pretrial publicity and confessions and the use of statements not on the court record (but without the contempt clause).

Meanwhile, the Sheppard case also was having a strong impact on reporting from court. Judges, hoping to avoid reversals of their verdicts, took firm steps to control pretrial news and courtroom news coverage and publication. Between 1966 and 1976 they wrote some 175 restrictive orders limiting news coverage of court proceedings. The news media more and more found themselves under prior restraint—gagged, as they put it—with their First Amendment rights in direct conflict with the Sixth Amendment rights of those on trial.

Gag Orders and the Supreme Court

In the last few years, the Supreme Court has handed down at least three important decisions dealing with the conflict. The first came in 1976, when a Nebraska judge prohibited any news reporting of any testimony or evidence given in a pretrial hearing of a brutal Nebraska murder case— although the hearing was to be open to the public. Since the case dealt with sensational details of the murders of a six-member family in a small town (population 850), the judge feared the material, if discussed in the media, would bias potential jury members. The Nebraska Press Association protested the ruling and brought the matter to the Supreme Court. The high court held the rule was too broad and vague, that restraining the media in this manner gave little assurance that prejudicial publicity would be controlled. The court noted the pretrial hearings remained open to the public, and there was little reason to believe the people in the small town would not discuss the crime—even without media coverage. One could only speculate, the court observed, what rumors would circulate, and how much more damaging they might be to a potential juror than a news report. Change of trial venue, trial postponement, and careful questioning and giving of instructions to the jury were more effective ways of insuring an impartial jury, and a better alternative than prior restraint of the news media, the court insisted.

The Nebraska decision seemed to place gag orders squarely in the category of prior restraint. Within months, however, another decision seemed to signal the end of open trials in the country, while underscoring some real problems inherent in the debate over access to court trials.

In 1979 near Rochester, New York, police began a search for former police officer Wayne Clapp and found his fishing boat riddled with bullet holes. They launched a search for Clapp's body, his pickup truck, and two young men seen with him. Within days police in Michigan spotted the pickup truck and arrested the two men and the wife of one of them.

The body was not found but New York officials charged the men with second-degree murder. At a pretrial hearing scheduled to hear motions on evidence, the defense moved that the hearing be closed to the press and the public. Defense attorneys planned to argue that confessions given by the men and recovery of the victim's revolver were inadmissible evidence. But they were reluctant to do so in open court. The Rochester newspapers—both Gannett group papers—had given coverage to the story that, the defense contended, had been prejudicial to the defendants' case. If the confessions and the revolver were discussed in open court the press could report their existence to the community—including future members of the jury—with the result that inadmissible evidence could come back to convict the defendants. The defense therefore moved the preliminary hearing be closed to protect the defendants' right to a fair trial. The judge, Daniel DePasquale, agreed. The following day a Gannett reporter presented a letter claiming a right to cover the hearing. But the judge again held in that situation the defendants' right to a fair trial outweighed First Amendment rights of the press.

The Gannett newspaper group appealed the ruling, taking the position that open judicial proceedings were in the public interest. In *Gannett v DePasquale* the Supreme Court held that publication of arguments concerning evidence that might be suppressed in the court trial carries special risks of unfairness. Publication of such material could influence public opinion against a defendant, and give potential jurors information wholly inadmissible in the actual trial. The judge should take protective measures to minimize prejudicial pretrial publicity, the court warned. More disturbing to the news media were remarks regarding the right of access to criminal trials. The court wrote, "The Constitution nowhere mentions any right of access to a criminal trial on the part of the public; its guarantee, like the others enumerated, is personal to the accused."

That is, the public and the media have no constitutional right to attend criminal trials, and the guarantee of a public trial is for the benefit of the defendant.

In the controversy that followed, Allan Neuharth, chairman of the Gannett company, charged the Supreme Court had ruled it was a private club that could close courtroom doors and conduct public business as it wished. Chief Justice Burger pointed out in public speeches the court had ruled on the closing of pretrial or preliminary hearings rather than trials. Even on those grounds there was reason for concern. Almost 90 percent of all criminal cases are settled in pretrial hearings—through plea bargaining, dismissal, and so forth. Excluding the press and the public from pretrial hearings means closing 90 percent of the administration of justice in America. (As a case in point, the two accused men did not stand trial for the murder of Wayne Clapp. Through plea bargaining they agreed to plead guilty to lesser offenses among the charges against them.)

Fortunately, *Gannett v DePasquale* did not prove to be the forerunner of a landslide of "no access" rulings. The next year, 1980, the court was asked to rule on the closing of a trial in a Virginia court. The defendant asked that the trial be closed and when the prosecution did not object, the judge agreed. The Supreme Court reversed the ruling, however, in *Richmond Newspapers v Virginia,* giving one of the strongest statements of the rights of news media to report court activities to date.

The "trial courtroom," it held, "is a public place where the people generally—and representatives of the media—have a right to be present." Their presence there, it pointed out, "has been thought to enhance the integrity and quality of what takes place." Judges do not have the "unfettered discretion" to close criminal trials, it insisted, although it noted there are special conditions in which they may be closed. Some conditions for closing the courtroom already are established. Rape trials are usually closed to protect the victim of the crime, for example.

Only time, and the Supreme Court, can tell exactly what other conditions are to be considered dangerous enough to warrant closing a trial. At present, it seems safe to say judges may exclude the public and the news media from closed, pretrial hearings to protect a defendant's rights. And they may exclude them from the trial itself if highly unusual "clear and present danger" circumstances warrant it.

Cameras in the Courtroom

The relationship between the news media and the courts also has included a sharp conflict over the right of the news media to use cameras and broadcasting equipment in the courtroom. The conflict dates back

Development of lighter, smaller television cameras helped overcome years of opposition to the use of cameras and broadcasting equipment in court.

to the sensational Bruno Hauptmann trial of 1935. Hauptmann was accused of kidnapping the child of Charles and Anne Morrow Lindbergh, at a time when Charles Lindbergh, who made the first successful flight over the Atlantic to Europe, was the nation's most loved hero.

The trial attracted worldwide attention, and a circus atmosphere. Tourists took turns snapping pictures of each other sitting on the bench while court was in recess. Hawkers sold wooden ladder souvenirs as mementos of the second-floor kidnapping and subsequent murder of the Lindbergh baby. During the proceedings the jury considered going into vaudeville as a feature act after the trial was over! Inside the courtroom, newsreel cameras, complete with hot lights, and still cameras, complete with smoking flash trays, took pictures of the trial. Microphones for radio coverage, were situated around the courtroom, with one bank of them before the witness box.

Hauptmann was convicted and sentenced to die in the electric chair. Despite the carnival atmosphere, he was unable to win a new trial and was electrocuted by the state of New Jersey. The American Bar Association cast the blame for the travesty on the print and broadcast media. In 1937 the ABA adopted Canon 35 of the association's ethics, charging that photography and broadcasting were "calculated to distract from the essential dignity of the proceedings, degrade the court, and create misconceptions with respect thereto." The canon has undergone several revisions since. Television was included in 1952. The title was changed to Canon 3A(7) in 1972, but the gist remains the same: news photography and broadcasting are not to be allowed in court and in adjacent areas. The federal courts joined most states in these prohibitions with Rule 53 of the Federal Rules of Criminal Procedures in 1946. Only two states, Texas and Colorado, allowed cameras and broadcasting in court as the 1960s began.

In 1965 Billie Sol Estes, a bureaucrat in the Johnson administration, came to trial for swindling hundreds of thousands of dollars by trading on nonexistent fertilizer tanks. Full television coverage of the Texas trial was possible, but due to defense attorney protests, only pretrial sessions and closing remarks were telecast, along with some filming of brief segments for daily newscasts. Estes used the coverage to appeal his conviction, and the Supreme Court gave an important reversal. Witnesses, the jury, even the judge are adversely affected by television coverage, the high court held. Radio and television coverage of a trial inevitably results in bias in a trial. The court did note, however, that advances in technology could result in coverage that would not bias and when that day came the court would have a different case to consider.

Time, improved technology, and an intensive public relations campaign by the National Association of Broadcasters eventually helped bring television back into court. Two distinct court/television plans evolved. In 1976 Alabama allowed coverage as long as all parties in the trial agreed. The next year, Florida decided to allow it if the presiding judge approved. By 1980 ten states had a permanent program, sixteen had experimental programs, and eleven were considering programs for television in court. All were based on the Alabama "parties" or the Florida "judge" approval plans.

The breakthrough in the cameras/courtroom debate came in 1981. The Supreme Court, in a unanimous decision, erased the stand of the Estes case and held that television coverage did *not* automatically violate a defendant's constitutional right to a fair trial—even when the defendant objected to the presence of the cameras. In *Chandler v Florida,* the court noted the appellants, two Miami police officers who were convicted of burglarizing a restaurant, offered "nothing to demonstrate their trial was subtly tainted by broadcast coverage." The court also held that an absolute constitutional ban on broadcast coverage of trials cannot be justified simply because there is danger that, in some cases, prejudicial broadcast accounts of events may impair the ability of jurors to decide the issue of guilt or innocence. The decision gave the states the right to permit television, but it did not apply to the federal courts.

The Court v The News Media

It is a fact of life that judges and attorneys have not always welcomed the news media into their courtrooms, but at the same time, they have not been beyond using news pictures and information in the prosecution of trials. The subpoena, the search warrant, and the judge's power of contempt all have been used to force the press to yield information, film, and even confidential sources for court perusal.

Sheriff's deputies ruffle through files and desk drawers in a warranted search of the newsroom of KCBI-TV in Boise, Idaho, in 1980. While constitutional, such searches can play havoc with news' files and procedures.

The subpoena duces tecum is a court order for an individual to produce documents, pictures, and so on before the court. Following the violent battle between political demonstrators and Chicago police at the Democratic Convention in 1968, and the growing number of public demonstrations related to civil rights and the Vietnam war, police turned more and more to the subpoena duces tecum to obtain television and newspaper pictures of demonstrations as court evidence. In some ways, it was a "free lunch" for law enforcement, who could obtain broadly stated subpoenas to gain access to material reporters had worked long and hard to produce.

The situation peaked in April, 1971, when Vice-President Agnew, the FCC and a House subcommittee, chaired by Congressman Harley Staggers of West Virginia, attacked the CBS documentary, "The Selling of the Pentagon." Staggers issued a House subpoena ordering the network to deliver any and all notes, film, sound tape, scripts, and names and addresses of all persons in the telecast. CBS President Frank Stanton stood firm. He said CBS would comply only with the demand for film copy and transcript. He said no part of the press should be forced to produce unpublished material—that the First Amendment does not depend on whether the government believed the media were right or wrong in their news judgments. The House disavowed the Staggers order in July, ending that threat. But the flood of subpoenas did not subside.

The search warrant had its most notable use against the media in a student newspaper case in 1971. Some sixty people had staged a demonstration over the dismissal of a hospital employee, eventually barricading themselves in a hospital corridor and attracting 175 police to the scene. Police and rioters were injured. Twenty-three were arrested. All of this was reported, with pictures, by the Stanford *Daily*. On April 12, four officers with a search warrant entered the offices of the newspaper and searched for evidence, including pictures. They found nothing. The *Daily*, as a policy, destroyed all outtakes. It filed suit anyway. It asked the courts if third parties, such as a newspaper or television news department, guilty of no crime, should not receive consideration under the Fourth Amendment, which guarantees freedom from "unreasonable searches and seizures." The Supreme Court, however, held the courts could not refuse to issue search warrants for evidence simply because the owner or possessor of the place to be searched was not suspected of any criminal involvement in the case. The Fourth Amendment to the Constitution grants the people (and the news media) the right to be secure against unreasonable searches and seizures. But search warrants are issued for probable cause, or reasonable belief that the items sought in relation to a criminal act may be there. In short, if a judge thought there was reason to believe evidence was in a newsroom, the judge could issue a search warrant and the newsroom could be searched legally.

In 1980, however, in one of his last acts in office, President Carter signed The Privacy Protection Act requiring federal, state, and local law officials to obtain subpoenas rather than search warrants when seeking evidence from writers, editors, and others involved in news-gathering activities. A subpoena forces the law officer to name specific items of evidence which are to be produced by the news organization. Thus the news organization, rather than the police, searches its files for the subpoenaed materials and saves the trouble and havoc of a search. Critics of the Privacy Act argue it contains too many loopholes and will allow the ready return of the search warrant on grounds a journalist or writer is "involved" in a crime, or on grounds delay will "threaten the interests of justice." On these grounds, the act allows law enforcement officials to request search warrants rather than subpoenas.

The contempt of court power is given so a judge can maintain order around and within the court. A judge can impose an immediate sentence of as much as six months in jail for contempt actions within the courtroom. Other contempt actions can be prosecuted through regular legal procedures—with charges, hearings, and trials. Journalists have been held in contempt and sentenced to jail and fines usually on grounds of refusing to reveal confidential sources. For example, in the 1950s New York columnist Marie Torre was brought into a libel case by Judy Garland. Torre had quoted an unnamed CBS executive in reporting remarks about the singer and refused to identify the executive for the court, on grounds the First Amendment gave her the right to keep her source confidential. She was held in contempt of court and sentenced to ten days in jail. The Supreme Court would not review the decision.

In 1966 Annette Buchanan wrote a story about the use of marijuana for the University of Oregon newspaper, the *Daily Emerald*. She interviewed seven Oregon students, promising to keep their names confidential. When she refused to reveal her sources to a grand jury, she was held in contempt and fined $300. The Supreme Court refused to review the case.

In 1982 reporter Paul Corsetti of the Boston *Herald-American* refused to reveal to the court confidential sources for his story involving a murder case. He was held in contempt and sentenced to ninety days in jail. But his sentence was commuted by the governor of Massachusetts.

In 1984 Richard Hargraves, editorial writer with the *St. Louis Globe-Democrat,* was ordered to jail until he revealed his sources for material used in an editorial he wrote in 1980 while with the Belleville, Illinois, *News-Democrat*. The Supreme Court denied without comment a motion to stay the lower court order.

Shield Laws

One relatively successful line of defense against contempt of court charges has been the state shield law. Shield laws grant bona fide newspeople the right to remain silent when asked to reveal confidential sources in court. The Ohio shield law, for example, reads that anyone "engaged in the work of, or connected with, or employed by" broadcasting stations or newspapers or press associations in "gathering, procuring, compiling, editing, disseminating, or publishing news" cannot be required to disclose a source of information to any court or jury or any state official or agency.

The majority of states have shield laws now, but their protection is limited. The laws often are vague, and they vary considerably in what they protect. The first, passed in Maryland in 1896, granted only limited privileges not to testify in court. Some modern ones do not protect reporters from revealing confidential sources in libel suits. The U.S. Court of Appeals, in a California case in 1975, waived the protection of the California shield law in the famous Charles Manson murder case. The court held that protection of confidential sources was not as important as the trial court's need to insure a fair trial in the notorious case. As a result, reporter William Farr could not refuse to answer demands for names of confidential sources without facing contempt of court charges.

There is no federal shield law and, therefore, no protection of confidential sources for journalists in federal courts. It does not seem likely there will be protection in the near future. A few years ago, Representative Phillip Crane of Illinois tried to put a shield law bill through Congress, but journalists were wary. They believed that a federal shield law could create more problems than it eliminated. Also, once involved in the process of creating one media law, the Congress could feel free to pass other, restrictive legislation. Journalistic support for the federal shield law disappeared, and the idea itself fell from sight.

Special First Amendment Privileges?

From the view of the news media, the greatest limitation of shield laws is that they are not nearly broad enough in their protection. Journalists have long held the view that the First Amendment protects them from revealing their confidential sources as well as from revealing any notes or other information they gather in their work. Under the First Amendment, journalists have argued they have special privileges that must be maintained if the news-gathering process is not to be inhibited.

In the early 1970s the Supreme Court dealt a massive blow to this point of view in a case developed in three states from the work of three reporters.

In 1970 New York *Times* reporter Earl Caldwell was ordered to appear before a federal grand jury with tapes and notes he had collected in reporting the Black Panther movement. The *Times* and Caldwell argued his relationship with the Panthers would be ruptured if he produced the materials or testified in secret session with the grand jury. To force Caldwell to do so would be a violation of his First Amendment rights, they insisted.

Meanwhile, Paul Branzburg of the Louisville *Courier-Journal* was publishing two stories on drug use in Kentucky. In the first story, he wrote about two persons in Jefferson County, Kentucky, who synthesized hashish from marijuana. Called before a grand jury and asked to identify the pair, Branzburg refused, claiming protection under the Kentucky shield law and the First Amendment. The appellate court ruled that if the shield law did protect him from naming confidential sources, Branzburg could not refuse to testify on what he had seen or the names of people he had seen. Regarding the second drug story, Branzburg was called to identify the lawbreakers he had seen while gathering information for the story. Like Caldwell, Branzburg argued he could not go behind the closed doors of the grand jury without losing his effectiveness as a reporter.

In 1970 Paul Pappas of WTEV in Providence, Rhode Island, was covering civil rights disturbances also involving Black Panthers. On the promise of confidentiality he was allowed inside Black Panther headquarters in New Bedford, Massachusetts. But later Pappas also was called to testify before the grand jury in Bristol County. He refused to report anything he had seen inside Panther headquarters, claiming protection of the First Amendment.

In 1972 the Supreme Court reviewed the three cases as one: *Branzburg v Hayes, et al.; In the Matter of Paul Pappas,* and *U.S. v Caldwell.* It ruled the Constitution does not grant special privileges to journalists, and that First Amendment rights are not abridged when newspeople are required to appear and testify before state and federal courts and grand juries. The journalist is not exempt from the normal duties of all citizens, the court held. If Congress wishes to create special privileges for reporters, the court concluded, it may do so through legislation.

The decision in the Branzburg cases has not stopped journalists from refusing to testify in courts or before grand juries. The profession has continued to insist that court demands for reporter testimony is an intrusion into the First Amendment rights of the news media.

In 1976 reporter Myron Farber published stories in the New York *Times* on mysterious deaths at Riverdell Hospital in Oradell, New Jersey. During the trial of the physician implicated in the deaths, the judge ordered Farber to produce his notes on the stories. When Farber refused, the judge ordered him jailed and levied a fine to accrue daily until he produced the notes. Farber was in jail forty days and the fine mounted to $285,000 before both Farber and the *Times* decided to comply with the judge's demands. Any presumed First Amendment argument of a right to withhold information from the court was weakened by the disclosure that Farber had earlier submitted the notes to Doubleday and Warner Communications in anticipation of publishing a book on the hospital murders. (Thus, journalist Farber's book editor had seen more of the notes than Farber first was willing to hand over to the judge.)

But the commitment of the journalistic profession to freedom of the press is apparent from the fact that the *Times* was willing to pay more than a quarter of a million dollars before it decided to give the reporter's notes to the court. Journalistic dedication to the principle is so strong that each year as many as a dozen journalists are held in contempt of court, placed in jeopardy of imprisonment, and fined for refusing to divulge to judges or grand juries what they believe to be privileged information.

The Media and the Citizen

Conflicts between media and citizen most often occur over questions of (1) libel, (2) privacy, and (3) media access, a growing belief citizens have a right to use the media to express views and reach media audiences.

Libel and the Citizen

To oversimplify, libel is media-delivered defamation, a publicly distributed message that (1) identifies a citizen or group of citizens, and (2) associates them with acts or qualities that (3) causes others to avoid, hold in contempt, hate, shame, or ridicule them. Libel law also provides awards for actual damages resulting from defamation. Just a few years ago, for example, radio station WZZP in Cleveland was ordered to pay a local man $30,000 because the FM station named him "Turkey of the Year." The award was a jest, and the station assumed the winner of the call-in contest would take it as a good-natured ribbing. He did not, however. The notoriety he gained forced him to resign his job as a cosmetics buyer, and he had a difficult time getting other employment in the cosmetics field. Unable to establish the truth of its assertion that the buyer was a social "turkey," the station paid, with the damages.

Public Officials and Public Figures

For more than one hundred years, truth was the primary libel defense for the media. As noted in chapter 15, the Supreme Court made significant changes in libel in the 1960s, beginning with the *Times v Sullivan* case in 1964. In that case, the court established that proving actual malice was the only way a public official might win a libel suit from the media. Proving actual malice meant proving the statement was a lie or had been printed with reckless disregard for whether or not it was false.

In 1966 a federal court included public figures along with public officials as having to prove actual malice to win libel judgments. The court held the *St. Louis Globe-Democrat* should not be held liable for an error made when it asserted that Nobel prize winner chemist Linus Pauling had been convicted of contempt of Congress. While the charge the newspaper made was false, the court noted chemist Pauling became a public figure by knowingly projecting himself into a public controversy in order to influence the outcome of the issues. As a public figure, he would have to prove more than the falsity of the *Globe-Democrat's* error to win his libel case. He would have to prove the newspaper did it maliciously (lied), either knowing the information was false or by showing reckless disregard for whether or not it was false.

Due Care in Reporting

Two cases from the Southeast contributed to establishing the public figure concept, while also expanding on the importance of reporting methods as a factor in libel law. In the 1960s, as Francois has noted, *The Saturday Evening Post,* struggling to compete with television, had reviewed sophisticated muckraking to attract readers. In one article, "The Story of a College Football Fix," the magazine charged that University of Georgia Athletic Director Wally Butts and Alabama's legendary coach Paul "Bear" Bryant had colluded to fix an Alabama-Georgia football game. The story was thin; the evidence thinner. Both men filed lawsuits. Butts won a judgment in Georgia courts, making it possible for Bryant to drop his case and settle out of court. The *Post's* appeal brought the case, *Curtis Publishing Co. v Butts,* to the Supreme Court in 1967. The court held Butts was a public figure (meaning he would have to prove actual malice to win his libel case), but it also held the article in question readily could have been checked since it was not "hot" news. The *Post's* decision not to check it showed reckless disregard for the truth and an extreme departure from responsible reporting standards. And so, Butts won.

A case decided at the same time was *Associated Press v Walker.* It developed when retired Army general Edwin Walker, known for his conservative political views, sued the Associated Press for news reports that said he led rebellious students against U.S. marshalls in desegregationist riots at the University of Mississippi. In truth, Walker had not, and he

Retired General Edwin Walker with U.S. marshals at Oxford, Mississippi, in 1962. Erroneously accused in Associated Press reports of leading illegal attacks against U.S. marshals during desegregation events at the University of Mississippi, Walker won a libel judgement in lower courts, but the Supreme Court reversed the ruling, holding that the news reports showed due care in reporting, and the errors were not malicious or made with reckless disregard for the truth.

won a libel judgment. The AP appealed, however, and the Supreme Court held that Walker was a public figure—he had projected himself into the controversial situation at Oxford. The court could find no evidence of actual malice on the part of the AP. In reporting the rapidly breaking (hot) news of the situation, the court noted, the AP had not departed from reasonable reporting standards. The AP's errors were honest—not malicious—mistakes.

Thus the decision in the cases allowed Butts to retain his libel judgment but Walker to lose his—on the same grounds: good reporting or lack of it.

Private Citizen or Public Figure?

The Supreme Court made the concept of public figures more complex in the 1970s. In 1971 the court ruled in *Rosenblum v Metromedia* that the actual malice defense could extend to issues of public importance. It held that if a matter was of general interest to the public, any private individual who was defamed in its discussion would have to prove malice to win a libel suit. Thus, an error made by a news reporter who defamed someone speaking out on an issue of public interest (dumping chemicals, civil rights, or the use of atomic energy, for example) would be protected if it was an honest error.

The court held in *Gertz v Welch* that there were two types of public figures. While some individuals were public figures for all purposes and contexts; others were public figures in only a limited range of issues. *American Opinion,* a publication of the John Birch Society, accused

Elmer Gertz, prominent Chicago attorney, author, and activist, of being a Communist, having a criminal record, and being involved in the frame-up of a police officer. Gertz sued for libel, and the Supreme Court ruled the attorney was not a public figure in all contexts. He had projected himself into a particular controversy (civil liberties issues), but the defamation in question was made in an area—his law practice—in which Gertz was not a public figure, only a private citizen. The court concluded the states "may define . . . the appropriate standard of liability for a publisher or broadcaster of defamatory falsehood injurious to a private individual." This meant private citizens could still turn to the common law and proof of error, falsehood, and so forth to win awards plus damages for being defamed.

Ever Larger Libel Awards

There is good reason to believe the Supreme Court's introduction of "public official" and "public figure" into libel law reduced the number of libel judgments won against newspapers. An examination of cases involving businesspeople following the Gertz decision found seven of thirteen plaintiffs were held to be public rather than private citizens. Four of the six private citizens won their case. All the plaintiffs held to be public figures lost.

Still the number of libel suits and the size of libel judgments have been increasing in recent years. Large libel awards seem to beget large headlines which apparently beget larger libel awards—and so on. Popular comedienne Carol Burnett, for example, won a $1.6 million libel judgment from the *National Enquirer* in 1981 after the *Enquirer* published a story that portrayed her as being drunk in a public restaurant. The *Enquirer* later retracted the story, admitting in court it was false. Following the trial the comedienne's appealing personality and the public's distaste for the *Enquirer*'s style of journalism made it easy to ignore the fact that the award was excessive, especially since the comedienne could prove no damages—that the libel had harmed her career, for example. The judge later reduced the amount of the award. But the *Burnett v Enquirer* case underscores a problem faced by many media organizations in a libel suit: the suit is often brought by individuals sympathetic to members of the jury while the media organization may appear to be large, cold, and unscrupulous with an endless supply of revenue.

In the early 1980s the Washington *Post* lost a libel case with a large jury award. In 1979 the *Post* began an investigation into what appeared to be irregularities in Mobil Oil. In two articles the *Post* charged Mobil President William Tavoulareas "set up" his son Peter in a shipping firm and arranged illegal, sweetheart contracts for the firm with Mobil, using money and influence to the detriment of Mobil shareholders. Both men brought a libel suit against the *Post* in 1982, charging reckless disregard for the truth and asking for damages. The jury awarded them a judgment of more than $2 million. Under close scrutiny in court the *Post's* evidence of the "set up" was not conclusive, charges of illegal actions were tenuous or unfounded, and the effect of the entire affair on Mobil shareholders was far from clear.

The *Post* appealed, and in 1983 the appellate court overturned the jury's award of $2 million. The court found there was insufficient evidence that Tavoulareas had been injured to that extent. Journalist C. T. Hanson reported the judge found the *Post's* stories were "far short of being models of fair, unbiased, investigative journalism," but there was no proof of lies and reckless disregard for the truth.

As the *Post* case suggests, and as media attorneys have discovered, appeals courts often have been more sympathetic to media defendants than juries. A study of libel decisions from 1980 to 1983 revealed the average award in eighty libel and privacy cases was $2.2 million—more than enough to put a deep hole in even a large news medium's budget. But 80 percent of the awards in cases appealed were thrown out or sharply reduced. The situation and a 1984 decision by the Supreme Court—in *Bose v Consumer Reports*—gave the media reason to cheer. In 1970 *Consumer Reports,* in reviewing loudspeakers for use in high-fidelity sets, wrote that the sound from the Bose speakers "tended to wander about the room." The jury in the district court trial held the *Consumer Reports* article was written in actual malice and awarded Bose $210,905. But the appeals court refused to support the award and the actual malice charge, and so Bose appealed to the Supreme Court, charging the appeals court could not set aside the original, factual finding. The high court, however, ruled that appeals court judges should take care to analyze the facts in libel cases, even though that duty had traditionally been handled by juries and trial judges. The court's duty is not limited to elaborating on constitutional principles, the court held, it also must review the evidence to make certain those principles are constitutionally applied. The call for appeals courts to give close scrutiny to facts led media attorneys to call *Bose v Consumer Reports* the media's greatest Supreme Court victory in many years.

In 1984, another libel suit with a potentially large jury award went on trial. In 1982 CBS News broadcast a news documentary, "The Uncounted Enemy: A Vietnam Deception." It charged that the U.S. military bureaucracy made a concerted effort to suppress and alter reports of enemy troop strength during the Vietnam War in the belief gloomy news would contradict the military's argument the war was being won. When he could not get a public apology and forty-five minutes of air time to reply to the program (CBS offered fifteen minutes), retired General William Westmoreland sued for $120 million. At this writing we can anticipate that, should the general win his case with CBS, the network quite likely will appeal the decision.

The threat of libel suits and large libel judgments, if diminished, has not passed. Court decisions have been of considerable aid in helping reduce the threat. But one serious (if less obvious) effect of libel suits may be taking its toll on news media performance. Continued high libel judgments may not be making the news media more careful, as juries seem to hope, but more timid in reporting significant issues.

Privacy

Privacy as a legal concept grew from the yellow journalism idea that newspapers could invite themselves into the lives of the rich, the famous, and the infamous. In 1890 Samuel Warren and Louis Brandeis wrote a law review article arguing for "the right to enjoy life—the right to be left alone. . . ." Legal scholars still debate whether the right to privacy exists in law, or as a reflection of other aspects of law. Four types of privacy have been established:

1. Intrusion on one's seclusion or private affairs. In 1971 *Life* magazine reporters, pretending to be patients, entered an herb doctor's home and secretly took photos and voice recordings of the home and owner. The "doctor" won $1,000 in damages for the intrusion.
2. Public disclosure of embarrassing facts. A prostitute, charged with murder, won an acquittal and repented of her former life. She married and became an accepted member of society until a motion picture, *The Red Kimono*, revived her past, embarrassing her. California courts awarded damages.
3. Publicity placing one in a false light. A Utah television news report included film of a man who, as it happened, was arrested and taken from his home in the nude. His suit won $15,000 from the station after the Utah Supreme Court ruled the news media do not have the privilege of making news reports with obviously embarrassing facts or with reckless disregard for embarrassing aspects in a story.
4. Appropriation of one's name or likeness for another's advantage. A long series of cases have held the use of someone's name or the use of his or her picture in an advertisement, without permission, is an invasion of privacy. In 1963, however, New York courts held the man who killed Russian mystic Rasputin could not win damages from CBS just

because the network used his name in a dramatization of the event since the program, although produced for commercial sponsorship, had news, educational, and historical value.

Copyright: The Right to Messages

Copyright grants the holder control over reproduction and distribution of a message. The modern copyright law was signed in 1976 by President Ford and covers literary and media works, sculpture, motion pictures, books, and sound recordings. The law protects the specific content of a work, not the ideas, procedures, processes or principles involved in it. A photographer, for example, can copyright a picture, but the copyright covers the exact composition of a specific picture. The general idea and makeup cannot be copyrighted. For example, the famous World War II picture of American Marines raising a flag on Iwo Jima in 1945, if copyrighted, could not be legally reproduced with actors in closely similar poses. The copyright, at the same time, would not prevent others from using combat pictures of other flag raisings or prevent pictures of flag raisings in general—on Memorial Day or July Fourth. Under the new law, and since January 1, 1978, the copyrighted work is protected for life plus fifty years. To promote science, art, and education, the law allows for fair use of the work without payment of royalties. Traditionally, fair use has meant:

1. limited noncommercial or educational use;
2. use of only limited amounts of the work;
3. use where the commercial value is not decreased appreciably;
4. use in the public interest.

The nature of the copyrighted work also is considered in judging fair use. Fair use, of course, is what makes possible limited photocopying of books and articles for college classwork, the performance of copyrighted plays in classrooms or for on-campus educational television, without payment of royalties to the copyright holder.

The courts never have allowed a news event to be copyrighted. A newspaper, television news department, or wire service can copyright its version of the story, but if another news organization covers the same event, it may report its version without having to pay royalties. The common practice today is for news organizations to use limited amounts of the copyrighted story and give credit to the copyright holder if the story is used without further investigation. News media and agencies, as a rule, do not sue each other for copyright infringement, but use copyright mainly to gain credit for their enterprise in news investigation.

The courts have held that the public interest outweighs copyright in some cases. For example, Time, Inc. purchased the famous Zupruder eight-millimeter home movie film taken as the assassin's shots killed President Kennedy in Dallas in 1963. In time, a book was published that included sketches from the copyrighted film. Time sued, charging its film copyright had been violated. The court held, however, the public interest in the president's death was great and should be served. It allowed the book to be published, sketches included.

Entertainment features have been given tight copyright protection, however. The court has, for example, held that video taping a circus "human cannonball" and showing the tape on television greatly reduced the economic value of the act. In 1982 a federal judge in Los Angeles issued an injunction against the distribution of a feature film entitled *Great White,* the story of a monstrous shark that terrorizes a town on the Atlantic seaboard. The judge held that *Great White* not only borrowed from the plot of Universal's *Jaws,* it also captured the "total concept and feel" of the earlier film. The Italian-made *Great White* was showing in some three hundred theatres at the time of the injunction.

One of the most troublesome areas of copyright law has centered around cable television. Over-the-air stations argued for years that cable operators were pirates who capitalized on the signals of broadcasters without paying their share for them. The new copyright law brought some equity to the situation. Cable operators now have the right to pick up and distribute signals without negotiating with the signal copyright holders. They pay copyright fees based on size of their gross revenues and number of out-of-town television signals they import. Fees go to a copyright tribunal that then pays the copyright holders appropriate shares of the revenue; fees can change as FCC changes its cable regulations.

In cases of actual pirating, the court has the power to destroy or stop the manufacture and distribution of pirated works and award damages from $250 to $50,000 to the copyright holders.

What may prove to be the most important copyright case in this century began in the 1970s with the introduction of the Sony Betamax video cassette recorder (VCR). Sony promoted the invention as a recorder for home use, but in Hollywood, where box office returns are life's blood, the machine looked more like a home video vampire whose primary function was to siphon off studio revenues.

In 1976 MCA, parent company of Universal Studios Inc., and the Walt Disney studio brought suit against Sony, its advertising agency, some of its retailers, and one Betamax owner. MCA charged the video cassette tape machine was used to record commercially sponsored studio productions off-the-air and that the practice was in an infringement of copyright. Universal and Disney asked for money damages, an equitable accounting of profits from Sony, and an injunction halting the manufacture and marketing of the machines. The two studios did not seek compensation from the already large number of home VCR owners, probably because it would have been impractical, as well as poor public relations, to do so.

In the first trial, the Ninth Federal District court held taping television programs did not diminish the value of the programs and therefore was fair use of the copyrighted material. The studios appealed and in 1981 won a reversal; Sony then appealed to the Supreme Court. The complexity of the case was indicated when the Supreme Court, after hearing the arguments in 1982, did not render a decision as expected in 1983 but called instead for further arguments.

The court's decision finally came in 1984. It relied to a large extent on studies made by both Sony and the studios on how owners used their home video recorders. The results indicated the average owner's primary use of the machine was for "time-shifting," or recording television programs to be played back at the viewer's convenience. Time-shifting, the court held, did not diminish the audience but enlarged it; and it did not diminish the value of the programs. It was fair use, not copyright infringement.

In regard to the studio demands that Sony and its distributors be held liable for copyright infringements made by home video cassette recorder owners, the court observed that there was no precedent for such an action. Sony's only contact with users was at the time of purchase, and copyright law does not recognize "vicarious liability." (Holding Sony liable for the owner's actions would be like holding the Ford Motor Company liable for the money stolen by someone who used a Mercury in a bank robbery.) Patent law, the court continued, allows the courts to hold a company responsible if it sells a machine to encourage patent violations or does so knowing the user intends to violate the law. But, again, copyright law has no such contributory precedent. At the same time, patent law would allow the courts to halt distribution of an invention if its use can be shown to infringe on, or be the same as that of a machine already patented. But if the invention has significant, unobjectionable, noninfringing uses there is no precedent for halting its use or distribution. The home video tape recorder, in the court's view, did not infringe upon another invention's use, or have objectionable uses, and therefore, could not be suppressed or withheld under patent law.

In summary, the time-shifting use of the video cassette recorders is fair use and not objectionable. There was no precedent in copyright law for vicarious liability, under which Sony and the VCR could be held accountable even if the machine's owners did infringe on copyright. And even current patent law would not allow halting distribution of the VCRs. The decision was a clean sweep for Sony and home video taping.

Following the decision, many in the motion picture industry remained convinced home video taping was a significant drain on movie studio revenue. What if, Disney attorney Peter Nolan asked, *"The Wizard of Oz* were taped by everyone who watched it? Who would want to see it next year on television?"* Copyright protection, he insisted, is the only rule insuring a studio's fair return on its work.

As the decision in *Sony v Universal and Disney* pointed out, Congress, not the courts, has the "constitutional authority and the institutional ability to accommodate fully" the competing interests of those affected by the new technology. At present, it seems likely new copyright legislation and/or legislation to tax the sale of blank video cassettes will soon be debated in Congress.

The Right to Reply

A growing source of conflict for the mass media is the insistence of individuals and corporations on the right of access to mass communication. Traditionally, the legal right to print belongs to the person, organization, or corporation that owns the printing press. By law, freedom of mass communication belongs to the one whose name is on the building. It is the individual's right to edit a publication as he or she sees fit—and no one else's. If a person denies someone access to his or her newspaper, magazine, or film studio, is that person violating another's freedom of the press? A growing number of media critics think so.

Washington attorney Jerome Barron has led the movement to win media access for the average citizen. It is no longer possible for most of us to establish our own medium of communication to send our thoughts to the American people, he points out. The cost of creating a newspaper, motion picture, or sound recording prohibits the average citizen from entering the field. Also, what about the citizen who only has one message to distribute to the people? Should he or she be required to create an entire communication organization—buy presses or broadcasting technology—just to present that one view?

The Red Lion Case

The idea of right of media access received some support from the Supreme Court decision in the *Red Lion Broadcasting v FCC decision* in 1969. WGCB, a radio station in Pennsylvania, broadcast a fifteen-minute talk by Reverend Billy James Hargis, who attacked Fred J. Cook and his book, *Goldwater: Extremist on the Right.* He charged among other things that Cook worked for a Communist-affiliated publication. Cook contacted WGCB, demanding free air time to reply to charges made by Hargis, but the station refused to grant the time. The FCC and the courts, however, held Cook did have the right to reply to the attack. FCC rules called for a station to send notification of an attack—tapes, transcripts, or summaries—and offer air time to reply. As legal scholar Don Pember has reported, the Supreme Court ruled the licensee has no "constitutional right to monopolize a radio frequency to the exclusion of his fellow citizens." The court noted the First Amendment does not prevent the government from requiring a licensee to "present those views and voices which are representative of his community and which would otherwise, by necessity, be barred from the air waves." Thus in Red Lion, the personal attack rules and the FCC's Fairness Doctrine, its principal policy for regulating broadcasting content, were held constitutional.

The Tornillo Case

The court has failed to recognize the existence of a similar situation in newspaper editorial attacks, however. In 1972 the Miami *Herald* attacked political candidate, Pat Tornillo, Jr., in an editorial. At that time, Florida law gave Florida citizens the right to demand and receive space in a newspaper to reply to attacks. When Tornillo requested space, however, the newspaper refused. Attorney Jerome Barron pleaded Tornillo's case before the Supreme Court, arguing the First Amendment did not intend to restrict press freedom to the monopolistic control of a few, privileged newspaper owners. A right to reply, requiring publishers to give access to their publications, he argued, would enhance freedom of the press, extending discussion of public issues to those that could not enjoy it. The court held otherwise. Faced with the penalties and problems that a right of access statute could bring, the court ruled that many publishers might decide the safe course was to avoid controversy. Chief Justice Burger concluded:

> The choice of material to go into a newspaper, and the decisions made as to limitations on the size of the paper, and content, and treatment of public issues and public officials—whether fair or unfair—constitutes the exercise of *editorial control and judgment*. It has yet to be demonstrated how governmental regulation of this crucial process can be exercised consistent with First Amendment guarantees of a free press. . . . [emphasis added]

Advertorials

In contrast to the right-to-reply idea is the argument for right of original access made by corporations who insist they should have a right to buy media time and space to present original editorials, or "advertorials." The idea of the advertorial gained dignity and support in 1963 in the *Times v Sullivan* case in which the Supreme Court supported the paid

editorial as a channel of expression for the public. Several large corporations since have argued they have the right to contribute to public opinion and also the right to buy air time to deliver their views on social and political matters.

Newspapers, having been confirmed in their right to control their editorial decisions in *Tornillo v Miami* Herald, have not been troubled by a right to buy issue. Paradoxically, they have been free to reject advertorials but usually have accepted them if they were within the papers' usual ad policy guidelines. On the other hand, supporters of the right to buy air time have argued that FCC regulation and especially Fairness Doctrine rules oblige broadcasters to sell time to anyone wishing to discuss matters of public significance. Advocates argued the FCC should force broadcasters to accept advertorials if they would not accept them willingly. Broadcasters have resisted such an interpretation of federal rules and regulations and more often than not refused to accept advertorials.

Two of the corporations most interested in expressing their views were Mobil Oil and Kaiser Aluminum & Chemical. Mobil had broadcast its views by paying for time on NBC in 1974—although ABC and CBS both had rejected the same advertorial. Mobil wanted to ask the public for opinions about drilling for oil under the continental shelf, and offered to pay for any Fairness Doctrine time required for opposing viewpoints. Kaiser's ads asked viewers to write to their representatives in Congress concerning the energy crisis and free enterprise. When refused network time, the corporation printed and distributed its own brochure, arguing forcefully for its right to say what it wanted to say to the public:

> Only by being exposed to a diversity of views will the American public have the ability to choose an ultimate course of action in its own, and therefore, the nation's best interests. If television is not responsive to this need for fairness and balance and does not provide access itself, then regulators and legislators may make the decision for it. . . . That is not the way this issue should be resolved.

The battle of advertorials was fought throughout the 1970s in public debate and the courts. In 1973, in *CBS v Democratic National Committee,* the Supreme Court ruled broadcasters could refuse to sell advertising time to citizens or groups who wished to speak out on public issues. The court held that while broadcasters were obliged, by regulatory law, to present issues of importance, broadcasters were given wide leeway in fulfilling that obligation. The ruling confirmed the broadcasters' position that the decision to sell time for political editorials should remain under the control of the broadcast licensee, the group responsible for keeping broadcasting's public service function intact and paramount.

The next year, 1974, saw the court give some support to the corporations. In *First National Bank v Bellotti* the Supreme Cout held that corporations do have the right to be heard in the marketplace on important issues. Speech otherwise protected by the First Amendment, the court decided, does not lose that protection because it comes from a business corporation, confirming the position several corporations had been advocating for years.

Both Mobil and Kaiser, although denied advertorial time on network television, have produced newspaper and magazine advertisements, radio programs and mailing pieces to send their editorial messages to the American public. And both have printed and distributed well-made pamphlets to discuss their conflicts with the television networks. The flow may have helped the corporations advertise their views, but it also has underscored another concern of the networks. If given the right to buy network television time, corporations, with their vast ad buying power, could flood the airways with enough political editorials to bias or even control public opinion.

At present, the conflict is at a stalemate, with the networks advocating their right to refuse to sell television time to potentially manipulative political propagandists, and corporations insisting on their right to contribute to a wider range of public discussion through television advertorials.

Summary

First Amendment freedoms are not the most important ones in every situation. They often are in conflict with other rights granted by the Constitution. For example, the news media have the right to gather significant information, but they do not have the right to force citizens to speak if they wish to remain silent. The news media must have access to government information and affairs, but they cannot control government or override its right to protect itself and refuse access and information in the national or public interest. The news media test (watchdog) and cooperate with government in adversary and symbiotic relationships, respectively. Ideally the two operate in an ongoing trade relationship where the press gives government publicity for its programs in exchange for news of interest to the public.

The right to access won sweeping victories in the 1970s with passage of many "sunshine laws" to hold government executive board and committee meetings in public. While the president still can claim executive privilege to withhold information from publication, the Freedom of Information Act allows citizens to petition for the release of classified documents. About 60 percent of all congressional committees now conduct public business in public sessions. As of 1976 all federal executive agencies (FCC, FTC, NLRB, etc.) were open to the public for business meetings.

Fears that press actions and adverse publicity may violate rights of a defendant to a fair trial have caused courts to halt press coverage of judicial proceedings and close pretrial hearings. While the Supreme Court has held that sweeping gag orders are unconstitutional, it also has held the public and the press have the right to attend trials except where clear and present danger suggest they be closed. The courts have shown deep concern with the presence of cameras and broadcasting equipment in the courtroom. The American Bar Associaton, in Canon 35 of its code of ethics, restricted both from the courts after the 1935 circuslike trial of Bruno Hauptmann, charged with and convicted of kidnapping the Lindbergh baby. In the 1960s the Supreme Court held the presence of television cameras in court during that trial automatically biased the proceedings. But improvement in technology led the court to rule states could allow television in court if they wished.

News media demands for access to judicial proceedings are paralleled by court insistence the press should give confidential sources and information as evidence in trials. The subpoena and the search warrant, as well as the court's power of contempt, have been the principal weapons used to extract information from reporters. A large number of news personnel have gone to jail rather than reveal their confidential sources. The news media fear their sources would be silenced if names were revealed in court. Many states have shield laws to protect news professionals from revealing sources. Search warrants have been obtained to search news media offices for information wanted by police and the courts. Such searches disrupt the offices and files of the news medium. In 1980 President Carter signed the Privacy Protection Act which limits the use of search warrants and instead encourages arbitration and subpoena.

The citizen and the media conflict in three principal areas: libel, privacy, and citizen access to media audiences. The media may be sued for defaming a citizen, but they may discuss public figures and public issues in an "open, robust and uninhibited" manner, defending error with evidence of good reporting methods and absence of malice or reckless disregard for the truth. The right of privacy protects citizens from media intrusion in their private life—including the use of one's name or likeness in an advertisement.

The courts have ruled the citizen has a right to reply to personal attacks on radio and television stations, but that no such right exists for attacks made by newspapers. Several corporations have argued for a right to buy television network time for commercials that advocate political and social points (rather than sell goods or services). While many corporations have published their paid editorials, or advertorials, in the print media, the networks have refused to carry them, fearing wealthy corporations could put enough advertorials on the air to bias or dominate public opinion.

Questions for Discussion

1. There is reason to believe the news media may cooperate more with government than they watchdog it. Review the accounts of how the news media cooperate with government officials. What are the dangers? Are there real benefits? Why do newspeople insist they are adversaries of government?

2. One of the thorniest problems we face today is the conflict over the reporter's right to withhold his or her confidential resources as a news professional, and the court's demands that all information must be given the courts, since the reporter is, after all, a citizen. Journalists fear they will lose their confidential sources if they give them up. At the same time the courts seem to say they cannot find out what is going on, through law enforcement procedures, without the help of reporters. Are these two assumptions correct? Which has the weaker argument? What shield law protection does your state offer?

3. Is there still good reason to believe that the presence of television cameras and coverage will obstruct justice and encourage bias for or against the defendant? How could we predict? What is the law on this matter in your state?

4. Journalists have feared that attempts to pass a federal shield law would inaugurate a long line of legislation that might rob the press of much of its hard-won freedoms. What do you think is the likelihood of this happening? What kind of legislation might be passed that could survive a First Amendment test and still harm press liberty?

References

Allen, Frank. "Battle Over 'Right to Know' Laws." *Wall Street Journal,* January 4, 1983, 27.

Cater, Douglas. *The Fourth Branch of Government.* New York: Random House, 1959.

Czerniejewski, Halina J. "Your Newsroom May Be Searched." *The Quill,* July/August, 1978, 21–28.

Devol, Kenneth S., ed. *Mass Media and the Supreme Court.* 3rd ed., New York: Hastings House, 1982.

Drechsel, Robert E., and Deborah Moon. "The Public/Private Figure Status of Corporate and Executive Libel Plaintiffs after Gertz." (Paper delivered to the annual convention of the Association for Education in Journalism, Athens, Ohio, July, 1982.)

Edwards, Verne E., Jr. "Some Legal Pitfalls." In *Mass News,* edited by David J. Leroy and Christopher H. Sterling. Englewood Cliffs, N.J.: Prentice-Hall, 1973.

Fitzgerald, Mark. "Manipulating the Press." *Editor & Publisher,* May 12, 1984, 9 et seq.

"Forced Disclosure of Confidential Notes." *Columbia Journalism Review,* November/December, 1978, 48–49.

Francois, William E. *Mass Media Law and Regulation.* Columbus, Ohio: Grid, 1978.

Franklin, Marc A. *The First Amendment and the Fourth Estate.* Mineola, N.Y.: Foundation Press, 1977.

"Ganging Up Against Gannett Decision." *Broadcasting,* August 17, 1979, 21.

Gloede, Bill. "The Courts and the Press: 'Things Could Get Worse.' " *Editor & Publisher,* November 26, 1983, 10–11.

Greenhouse, Linda. "High Court Decides States Can Permit Television of Trials." *New York Times,* January 27, 1981, 1.

Hanson, C. T. "What Went Wrong at the Washington *Post?" Columbia Journalism Review,* January/February 1983, 31–41.

"High Court Rules Defendant Rights Supersede Those of Press, Public." *Broadcasting,* July 9, 1979, 46.

"The Home Video Decision: The Legal and Political Thrust." *New York Times,* January 18, 1984, 42.

Kelly, Margie. *Public Records and Public Meetings.* Freedom of Information Center Report no. 397, School of Journalism, University of Missouri, Columbia, December 1978.

Landau, Jack. "Excluding the Press from the Grenada Invasions; A Violation of the Public's Constitutional Rights." *Editor & Publisher,* December 10, 1983, 10–11, et seq.

Miller, Susan Heilmann. "Reporters and Congressmen: Living in Symbiosis." *Journalism Monographs,* no. 53, January 1978.

"No to Advertorials." *Newsweek,* July 2, 1979, 57.

O'Reilly, James T. *"Government in Sunshine."* Freedom of Information Center Report no. 366, School of Journalism, University of Missouri, at Columbia, January, 1977.

Overbeck, Wayne. "Unmuzzling America's Corporations." (Paper delivered to the annual convention of the Association for Education in Journalism, Michigan State University, East Lansing, August, 1981.)

Pember, Don R. *Mass Media Law.* Dubuque, Iowa: Wm. C. Brown Publishers, 1977.

Radolf, Andrew. "News Organizations Protest Grenada Restrictions." *Editor & Publisher,* November 5, 1983, 14–15.

Roper, James E. "Supreme Court Rules on Libel." *Editor & Publisher,* May 5, 1984, 15.

Shenon, Phillip. "A Ruling Backs Mrs. Onassis on Ad." *New York Times,* January 13, 1984, B1, B3.

Stein, M. L. *When Presidents Meet the Press.* New York: Julian Messner, 1969.

"Supreme Court Says Snepp Violated CIA Contracts." *Publisher's Weekly,* March 7, 1980, 12.

"TV in Court." *The News Media and the Law,* December, 1977, 23.

"UPI Restates Spy Policy." *Editor & Publisher,* May 3, 1980, 18.

Chapter
17

Regulation and Self-Regulation of the Media

The Social Responsibility Theory

Authoritarian philosophy stressed the need to protect and serve the state. Libertarian philosophy argued for freedom from oppressive state controls in the interests of truth, liberty, and the pursuit of happiness. The twentieth century has seen the rise of yet another view of media performance: the social responsibility theory that argues the media are not only free from prior restraint by government, they also are free to serve society with information and entertainment that contribute to the public good. As media analysts Fred Siebert, Theodore Peterson, and Wilbur Shramm have observed, social responsibility theory rejects the libertarian view that a mass communication medium is a private enterprise owing nothing whatever to the public, which grants it no franchise. It is therefore affected with no public interest. It is emphatically the property of the owner, who is selling a manufactured product at his own risk. . . .

A Free and Responsible Press

Media freedoms carry obligations, social responsibility philosophy argues. The privileged position of the media under the First Amendment is a franchise granted in the public interest. Too often, responsibility theory argues, media management has evaded its social responsibilities and sought profits and influence by distracting rather than informing and entertaining. Publishers and media professionals alike, reacting to the excesses of the press (yellow journalism, for example), made early contributions to the theory. In 1904 Joseph Pulitzer wrote:

> Nothing less than the highest ideals, the most scrupulous anxiety to do right, the most accurate knowledge of the problems it has to meet, and a sincere sense of moral responsibility will save journalism from a subservience to business interest, seeking selfish ends, antagonistic to public welfare.

Professionals in the field contributed professional codes of media ethics, with the earliest, the Canons of Journalism, adopted by the American Society of Newspaper Editors in 1923. The greatest portion of social responsibility theory came from the work of an academic committee, the Commission on Freedom of the Press. In 1942 Henry R. Luce, founder of the *Time* magazine empire (see chapter 6), saw the need to restate the importance of freedom of the press in America and examine press failures and press performance. To explore the problem, he gave $200,000 to his former Yale classmate, Robert Hutchins, president of the University of Chicago. Hutchins collected an outstanding group of thirteen scholars to make the study. Their report, entitled a "Free and Responsible Press," was issued in 1947. It concluded:

1. that freedom of the mass media was endangered in America, due in part to the irresponsible practices of some media managers and their failure to recognize the needs of the American public;

2. that the media had the responsibility of providing a "truthful, comprehensive, and intelligent account of the day's events in a meaningful context";

3. that the media had the responsibility of providing a forum for the exchange of ideas—of becoming a "common carrier" of public expression, if necessary, to carry out a wide variety of views;

4. that the media should project a representative picture of society, avoiding stereotypes and explaining the values and goals of society as much as possible. The commission called on the press to report more of the successes of American life and fewer "night-club murders, race riots, strike violence, and quarrels among public officials."

Toward Self-Regulation

The commission warned that if the media continued to act irresponsibly and failed to serve the people, the government would step in and force them to do so. Only strict, responsible, self-policing operations could prevent a return to governmental control. The choice offered by social responsibility advocates is either media responsibility by government control or self-control, by government regulation or self-regulation.

Today when we speak of media regulation we usually speak of regulation designed to ensure responsible performance. Ironically, American government regulation has been one of the major contributors to social responsibility theory. Government agency regulation, unlike the controls of the authoritarian governments of England, has had little to do with prior restraint, torture, and taxation, but with assuring responsible performance from media and media auxiliaries. Irresponsible misrepresentation of medicines, cosmetics, and food items brought the advertising industry to the government with a plea for aid in controlling the problem in the early 1900s. Irresponsible use of the airways produced a similar appeal from radio broadcasters in the 1920s.

As reported in chapter 2, the public and organized special interest groups within the public also have been important factors in pressing for socially responsible performances from media. Groups representing

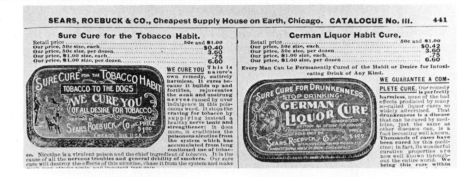

the interests of children, women, gun hobbyists, or political groups (people who know how to present problems to elected officials in the Congress) have had a profound effect on media operation and message content.

Commission Regulation: The FTC

Near the end of the nineteenth century, it was obvious to responsible professionals in the advertising business that much of the nation's advertising was not only shoddy but outright deceptive. To put it bluntly, it lied, boldly and outrageously. Patent medicine sellers led the parade of those making fraudulent claims for cures of rheumatism, diabetes, cancer—with money back guarantees! One ad lauded Antidipso, a miracle cure for alcoholism, and praised a fictitious Mrs. George Fuller as a "heroine of the home" for putting Antidipso into her husband's tea and coffee, curing him of his addiction to booze. In the early 1900s muckraking exposés of the soothing syrups offered to children were shown to contain laudanum, or morphine; others proved to be 40 percent alcohol.

At the same time, responsible advertisers and ad agencies gave public support to the idea that truthful advertising could sell good merchandise. As advertising organizations moved to police the problem with ethical codes, *Printers Ink,* a leading industry magazine, published a model state law requiring the penalization of anyone who published false and misleading ads.

The Federal Trade Act

In 1914, with ad industry support, Congress passed the Federal Trade Act, establishing the Federal Trade Commission (FTC) to curb overly monopolistic trends in American business. In 1922 Supreme Court interpretations of the act made it clear the FTC had the power to control advertising. The Wheeler-Lea amendment to the act in 1938 gave the FTC the power to bring suit against an advertiser who ignored FTC rulings and also to bring an injunction to stop advertising that might be injurious to public health. Important amendments to FTC powers have come since

World War II. In 1975 Congress gave the commission rule-making authority to define and specify regulations for attacking deceptive advertising. Under the law, the FTC gained the power to investigate and prosecute any person or company engaged in, or about to engage in, what seemed to be false, deceptive, or unfair advertising. The FTC was also given the right to order advertisers to cease and desist publishing a particular ad and order them to produce corrective advertising to clarify past errors. In one classic case in the mid 1970s, Listerine was ordered to include the following statement in its $10 million advertising campaign:

> Contrary to prior advertising, Listerine will not prevent colds or sore throats or lessen their severity.

The law requires that advertising not be misleading in a "material respect." Material consequences of using the product advertised must not be disregarded in the product's promotion. (If the pill soothes your headache but also makes you sleepy that second fact must be made clear, too.)

Deceptive Advertising

Defining *deceptive advertising* has been the difficult work of the commission over the years. The law specifically states that advertising oleomargarine as a dairy product is deceptive. But the commission has resorted to policy statements and its growing body of case material for a general definition. For example:

1. The commission and the Supreme Court have held that using mashed potatoes for ice cream in television commercials is not necessarily deception. (Hot lights melt the cream but not potatoes.) On the other hand, shaving lathered sandpaper to promote shaving cream was held to be deceptive, since the lather could not make the sandpaper soft enough during the time period shown.
2. The commission ordered Hudson Pharmaceutical to drop ads for childrens' vitamins since they used a hero figure, Spider Man, to promote sales. Hudson consented.
3. The commission established the policy that ad testimonials by celebrities must be made on a "personal basis." In 1978 singers Pat and Debbie Boone were sued by a customer who claimed Acne Statin, a mail-order cream product the Boones endorsed, had given her blisters and permanent scars. In interrogatories returned to federal court, the Boones admitted they had not used the product they endorsed.

Gale Sayers tried them all.

And the former Chicago Bears football star chose The Lean Machine—for four very important reasons.

"First," says Sayers, "The Lean Machine is easy to use. I can fit under the pressing bar and into the other workout positions with ease. Some of the others I tried seemed designed for kids.

"Second, I can adjust the machine and change routines easily and quickly. That means I don't waste a lot of workout time fussing with the equipment.

"Third, The Lean Machine lets you work out all the muscle groups and that includes a full set of leg exercises. With my football knees, leg extensions and curls are very important to me.

"And finally," says Sayers, "It's priced fairly. For what you get, it's clearly the best value in home exercise equipment."

For a handsome brochure that tells all, call toll-free **1-800-621-1203**. (In Illinois it's **1-800-942-2835**.) Also available at Abercrombie & Fitch.

THE *LEAN MACHINE.*™
Inertia Dynamics Corp., 7245 S. Harl, Tempe, AZ 85283

A testimonial ad—made on a "personal basis."

4. Deception by implication, or unintentional deception, also violates FTC rules. Recently, several traveler's check companies complained American Express ads were unfair. The ads dramatized (with a cast that included actor Karl Malden) the plight of people far from home whose traveler's checks were lost or stolen. The ads concluded that travelers could get refunds if they had American Express traveler's checks. There was an implication that the money paid for all other lost traveler's checks was not refunded, when in fact other companies do give refunds. American Express reworked the ads to dramatize the relief of travelers who lost American Express checks and discovered they could get a refund. No mention was made of competitors.

FTC pressure was in large part responsible for a court decision removing restraints on advertising by professional people. Since 1977 and the *Bates v State Bar of Arizona* case, lawyers have been free—as a First Amendment right—to advertise their routine legal services to the public. In 1979 the commission issued two orders barring the American Dental Association and the American Medical Association from interfering with truthful advertising by dentists and doctors.

In the late 1970s *Time* magazine charged the commission with trying to become the advertising "nanny" of the nation when it stopped Vida Blue, a major-league baseball player, from advertising milk on the grounds that blacks sometimes have trouble digesting it. A year later, the commission wondered if it should allow ads suggesting consumption of energy without also requiring the ads to include reminders of energy conservation. Should an ad for a hair dryer, for example, remind people that their hair will dry naturally in a few minutes without using a dryer? Such proposals, and ad industry reaction to some FTC policies, led Congress to curtail FTC power in 1980 by requiring the commission to submit its regulations to the Senate and House for approval.

Deregulation of Advertising

The trend toward reducing FTC power—deregulation—continued under the Reagan administration and FTC Commissioner James C. Miller III. Miller mounted a public campaign to further reduce FTC power, arguing, among other things, that overzealous commissioners had had a "chilling effect" on ad creativity. Miller took the position that advertisers should be free to continue false advertising so long as it was clear the ads did not bring "substantial economic injury" to consumers.

Industry reactions to Miller's suggestions were positive, with many industry spokespeople supporting the deregulation program. Still, an editorial in *Advertising Age,* the industry newspaper, warned the commissioner to "go slow." The "industry which pioneered in supporting 'truth in advertising' since the turn of the century is not going to be easily sold on new statutory language that makes cheating less risky," it argued.

Still, by 1983 *The Wall Street Journal* was reporting that critics were finding the FTC's pursuit of advertising violations less than vigorous. One charge was that the agency was all but ignoring national advertising in terms of bringing ad complaints. At the same time, the agency's decisions were easing requirements that advertisers produce two clinical studies to back up claims in their ads. It ruled in one case, for example, that AHC Pharmacal Inc. could claim its acne medication was effective against pimply skin, since one Food and Drug Administration study could be used to support the claim. The ruling reversed a 1980 decision, which ordered AHC to substantiate its ad with two clinical studies.

Commission Regulation: The FCC

As noted in chapter 4, Congress found it necessary to regulate radio and, consequently, television, beginning in 1927 with the Federal Radio Act and then with the Federal Communications Act of 1934. Today's commission still operates under the Communications Act and its six hundred sections, as revised. The act defines the Federal Communications Commission, empowers it to regulate radio (the term is used now to include television), and create policies to implement regulation. The commission has the power to grant a broadcast license, ask the licensee to justify a program policy, or recall licenses in its role as protector of the public airways. Section 326 of the act specifically forbids the commission from interfering in free speech in broadcasting. So the commission has no power to censor, only to regulate in the public interest.

Equal Time

At the heart of station regulation is the equal time concept in Section 315 of the Communications Act. Equal time requires every station to give or sell political advertising time to all political candidates on an equal basis—and at the station's lowest rate. Newscasts, spot news reports, and news documentaries are excluded from the equal time requirement. Thus news reporters are free to cover political campaigns without drawing a rash of equal time demands from politicians who do not make the news on a given day.

A major problem of Section 315 is that splinter party candidates can demand equal time. Section 315 was held in abeyance in the presidential and vice-presidential campaigns of 1960 so that major party candidates John F. Kennedy and Richard Nixon could engage in their so-called great debates. All presidential candidates from all other parties collected a total of only .02 of all votes cast that year. But each of them—Prohibitionist, Socialist, etc.—could have demanded and won equal network time, had

The first Reagan-Mondale presidential debate of 1984. Political debates can qualify as news events, and broadcasting them can be classified as spot news coverage; as a result, splinter-party candidates cannot demand equal time under Section 315 of the 1934 Communication Act, the equal time rule.

equal times rules been enforced. In 1975 the FCC solved the dilemma by ruling that political debates arranged and produced outside a station's facilities by an outside agency were to be considered spot news. Thus, the Carter-Ford debates of 1976, and the Reagan-Anderson and Carter-Reagan debates of 1980, were broadcast by the networks as news events created by the League of Women Voters. The FCC since has allowed in-house political programs to qualify as news.

Stations do not have a choice about carrying political campaign ads. FCC rulings require them to give reasonable access (30– and 60–second spots) to candidates. Section 315 specifically warns there is no "power of censorship" over the ads. In 1972 an Atlanta station requested advice on what should be done with political spots for a senatorial candidate who was using the public airways to insist "you cannot have law and order and niggers too." The commission advised the station to censor the ad only if there was a clear and present danger of racial rioting. In 1980 Citizen's Party Candidate Barry Commoner took advantage of the no censorship clause in Section 315 and began his political ads with an earthy word usually used to denote baloney and steer manure. His point was that major political parties were giving the public little more than "bull———"; the ads won him national attention. Station managers had to run the ads, and then answer complaints about the barnyard epithet. (Even Ann Landers was asked at least once to explain how such cattle calls could be made over regulated radio.)

The courts have absolved broadcasters of any responsibility for libel contained in political ads. Otherwise, they would be at the mercy of any quack who decided to run for office and had enough money to buy thirty seconds of uncensored, unedited radio time.

The Fairness Doctrine

The most important of all FCC policies and regulations is the Fairness Doctrine, which the commission developed in the years following World War II. The concept of fairness in broadcasting was derived from the equal time concept, but fairness applies to programming in general, while equal time and Section 315 apply only to political candidates. The Fairness Doctrine developed from the 1941 attempt by the Mayflower Company of Boston to win the radio license held by WAAB. Mayflower complained WAAB had broadcast a number of editorials that reflected the views of WAAB's management on various issues and political candidates. Truly free radio, the commission held, "cannot be used to advocate the causes of the licensee . . . the broadcast cannot be an advocate." The commission returned WAAB's license, but only because the station had stopped its newspaper-like editorializing.

In 1949 the commission expanded on the Mayflower decision by noting the station had a duty not only to present the views of station management but also to "encourage and implement the broadcast of all sides of controversial public issues over their facilities," and to give a "balanced presentation of . . . opposing viewpoints." These tenets are the foundation of the Fairness Doctrine and policies created in the years that followed.

Historically, the commission has given stations wide latitude in meeting their Fairness Doctrine obligations. Using reasonable judgment to obtain balance and fairness in the presentation of significant issues has been the FCC's rule in approving station licenses. No absolute standard would have been workable, at any rate, since it has seldom been clear what the sides of a controversial issue are, and just how a balanced viewpoint of opposing views might be presented.

Should, for example, entertainment be regulated under the doctrine? Many dramatic programs stress social and political ideas, suggesting time should be given for opposing ideas. The commission, after discussing one program, did not extend Fairness Doctrine regulation to entertainment.

Should commercials be regulated under the doctrine? In 1966 New York Attorney John F. Banzhaf III asked WCBS-TV in New York for free time to present messages opposed to tobacco smoking. CBS refused on grounds it had reported the negative aspects of smoking in news and special reports. When Banzhaf appealed to the FCC, the commission decided cigarette smoking was an "issue of public importance," and it required stations to inform the audience of the harmful effects of cigarettes. Anticigarette ads became a part of television, until cigarette ads themselves were banned from the air by a federal law signed in 1971. In 1970, and again in 1974, the commission held the Fairness Doctrine had applied to one product, and one product only. The decision on cigarette advertising did not become a precedent.

The converse of the counter-commercial is the advertorial discussed in chapter 16. The commission has held that paid-for editorial spots are subject to fairness provisions. Therefore, if NBC sells time to, say, the Widget Corporation of America, who uses the time to make a strong argument for not drilling oil in the American west, NBC must be prepared to sell time to Drill Bits of North America, Inc., who may want to see more drilling in that part of the country.

Should the Fairness Doctrine apply to broadcast journalism? In 1971 CBS editors rearranged answers recorded on film so it appeared they came from questions different from the ones asked. The edited interviews were for the documentary "The Selling of the Pentagon," an investigation of military propaganda in America. In looking at the editing problem, the FCC found no evidence of deliberate distortion and would not intervene in the matter. In 1972 another complaint charged that NBC's documentary, "Pensions: the Broken Promise," was one-sided and unfair. The FCC ordered NBC to give equal time to advocates of private retirement plans, although the documentary had received a Peabody Award for excellence. In an appeal, however, NBC won a reversal. A full, three-person appeals court held the FCC had pushed too far and had no right to make NBC's programming decisions. More often than not, the commission has preferred a policy of deferring journalistic decisions to stations. Yet, in 1976 it ordered WHAR, a Clarksburg, West Virginia, AM station, to broadcast an eleven-minute tape advocating anti-strip-mining legislation on grounds WHAR had not produced its own programs on the subject. WHAR complied without appeal, probably because its license renewal was due. The WHAR case took on considerable significance since the commission pointed out the Fairness Doctrine was the most important requirement for operating in the public interest, the primary goal of the American broadcaster.

Other Areas of FCC Regulation

The commission has found it necessary to restrict programs in some areas. The U.S. Criminal Code calls for fines and imprisonment of persons using "obscene, indecent, or profane" language. In the 1970s "topless radio" call-in shows gained sudden popularity. Across the country, over one hundred shows broadcast frank sexual discussions between anonymous telephone callers and a moderator who often directed the program with a smirk and a snicker. The commission, fearing restrictive legislation, moved against one especially unseemly program on WGLD-FM, in Oak Park, Illinois. The station paid a $2,000 fine; when a citizens' group appealed, the court of appeals upheld the FCC action.

The commission also won its "dirty words" case against Pacifica station WBAI-FM in New York City in 1978. WBAI-FM played George Carlin's nonprurient "Seven Dirty Words You Never Say on Television" record in the middle of the afternoon. The courts ruled in *FCC v Pacifica* that such material was "patently offensive" and "indecent," especially at the time of day it was played.

One of the most controversial of all FCC policies has been the so-called prime time access rule, first stated in 1970 with the goal of creating more local and more diverse programming. The prime time access rule limited television stations to three hours of network programming between 7 P.M. and 11 P.M. each evening. The rule proved to be something less than a success. Instead of producing their own shows, local stations quickly turned to inexpensive syndicated material to fill the open hour, retrieving formats of the 1960s; such game shows as "To Tell the Truth" reappeared, then were replaced by such shows as "Family Feud" and "Wheel of Fortune."

Deregulation of Broadcasting

Improved, stable broadcasting equipment, the high cost of renewing a license every three years, and frustration over irritating content regulations that seemed to contribute little to the public interest or station profit brought an increasing number of calls for deregulation of broadcasting beginning in the 1970s. California Congressman Lionel Van-Deerlin led one attempt to restructure the 1934 Communications Act, but the proposal attracted many supporters and died under a landslide of conflicting interests.

In 1981 the FCC voted six to one to deregulate radio and asked Congress to repeal Section 315 and the license renewal process, so radio would be open to marketplace forces and stations could find their own audiences and better serve the public. When Congress did not act, the FCC relaxed some regulations on its own, allowing more freedom in advertising and presentation of public affairs programs and public service announcements. It also reduced the amount of paperwork required of stations (annual and financial reports, etc.) and dropped the cumbersome ascertainment procedure that required stations to determine the interests of the community it served. (Studies indicated ascertainment did not result in better service.) The changes were challenged by two civic-minded groups: the Office of Communication of the United Church of Christ (see p. 511) and the National Black Media Coalition, both of which feared the renovations would usher in a new era of irresponsible programming by radio management. Still, almost all the changes were approved by the court of appeals in Washington, D.C., in 1983.

The same year, the commission followed up the piecemeal approach to deregulation of radio by presenting proposals to Congress to broaden radio's deregulation and begin deregulation of television. Resistance was stiff. Some legislators were reticent to relinquish control of potentially high profit public resources without retaining some means of keeping the new owners accountable. Another legislative view supported the creation of a rule requiring licensees to pay a fee for their spectrum space, with returns going to public broadcasting.

The FCC proposals, as chairman Mark Fowler told reporter Merrill Brown, have the overriding goal of making sure government is "not to be involved in program content regulation in any form whatsoever." For Fowler, equal time provisions and the Fairness Doctrine constitute censorship, forcing local broadcasters to ignore good programs and use those which satisfy a bureaucratic notion of fairness. As *Broadcasting* magazine reported, those supporting deregulation argue fairness will result automatically from "quantification," or from the fact there now are large numbers of stations to serve the public. There are five or six broadcasting stations for every newspaper in the country, Fowler pointed out, yet newspapers are not subjected to fairness controls.

Even with all the talk of deregulation, there has been, at last report, no proposal to dissolve the Federal Communications Commission. Under deregulation proposals, the commission would still be around to regulate the broadcasting frequencies and handle extraordinary cases, such as divestment of broadcast and cable monopolies in small communities.

Some reaction to suggestions of deregulation has been strong. AP reporter Norman Black reported strong reactions from leaders of two consumer interest groups. Samuel A. Simon, executive director of the Telecommunications Research and Action Center, told Black that FCC chairman Fowler's plans were a "real and present danger to our democratic form of government." Peggy Charren, founder and president of Action for Children's Television (see pp. 510–11), charged "broadcasters have proven time and time again they will do as little as possible for the public and as much as possible for the bottom line. . . . Does [Fowler] really think that's enough to handle the elderly, the black, the Hispanic and the various child audiences?"

The Senate began hearings on the Fairness Doctrine in 1984. At last report, it still was unclear just how much control of broadcasting content and licensing Congress was willing to relinquish.

Responsibility and Regulation: Some Problems

The recent trends toward FTC and FCC deregulation may seem a sudden reversal of the thinking of many years, but careful investigation indicates even the best regulation presents problems. Government regulation is supposed to be evenhanded and in the best interest of all parties concerned. That it cannot be and that it cannot work to the mutual satisfaction of the public, the government, and the regulated bodies—the media themselves—becomes all too clear in time. An overriding problem is that government has limited knowledge of the industry it regulates. Changes in administrative personnel contribute to uneven application of rules and regulations. Enforcement of rules too often is uneven. All of which leads to the conclusion that the most well-founded, well-intentioned government agency can be bungling and insensitive—stupid to those at the mercy of it.

Consider the record of the FCC, as reviewed by author Stuart DeLuca:

1. In 1940 alone it both opened and closed FM broadcasting; then after World War II changed the broadcasting frequency, leaving broadcasters and thousands of consumers with worthless FM radio equipment.
2. In 1956 the FCC created four classes of CB radios, although one class was requested. It restricted class D to a type of transmission that guaranteed poor reception. Yet class D became the one class to be used by the public.
3. In 1968 it restricted cable television signals, stopping its development. In 1972 regulation of cable became so severe it was almost locked out of metropolitan areas. Free market competition was given to cable in 1979, but from a Supreme Court decision not FCC policy.
4. Since the 1970s the FCC has ignored licensing Dick Tracy two-way wrist radios because of concern for what they would do to mobile telephones (owned by AT&T).
5. At present the FCC has waffled on adoption of the CBS HDTV system, which will bring dramatically sharper, larger, and clearer television pictures to the home viewer (see chapter 19).

Self-Regulation

To protect themselves from inept governmental intervention, media professionals regulate themselves with written policies, boards, and codes. Media codes attempt to set standards and ideals for mass media content and for self-regulation of competition between media units. The codes also uphold ideals of professional performance consistent with public morals and ethics.

Media Codes

The standards and ideals in the Canons of Journalism of the American Society of Newspaper Editors, for example, say the function of the newspaper is to communicate to the "human race;" it demands of journalists "the widest range of intelligence, or knowledge, and of experience, as well as natural and trained powers of observation and reasoning." Any journalist who uses his or her powers for any unworthy purposes, the code of ethics continues, is "faithless to a high trust."

The Code of Ethics of Sigma Delta Chi, the professional journalism society, and the Public Relations Society of America describe the duty of their groups as serving the truth. Members of the Radio and Television News Directors Association (RTNDA) promise to "govern their personal lives . . . in a manner that will protect them from conflict of interest" in their work. Each of the journalistic codes places informing the public and maintaining public welfare high in its ethical system. Each of the codes—journalistic or otherwise—sets a high standard of ideals, with the radio code regarding radio as a "living symbol of democracy"; advertisers call for ads to comply with principles of "fair competition," and deal "fairly with clients or employers, past and present, with fellow practitioners and the general public."

The ethics and morals of the media professions also are spelled out in detail. The RTNDA code eschews undue, bombastic broadcast news promotional gimmicks and pointedly calls for dignified behavior of broadcast news reporters in the courtroom—including the use of "unobtrusive and silent" equipment for trial coverage. No broadcast news reporter is to endanger the fair trial of any defendant. The National Association of Broadcasters (NAB) codes prohibit ads by astrologers and mind readers and for lotteries and hard liquor. Both deal extensively with the subject of broadcasting's responsibilities to children. The American Society of Newspaper Editors (ASNE) code charges newspaperpeople should refrain from supplying readers with incentives for "base conduct, such as are to be found in details of crime and vice. . . ."

Upholding the Codes

Upholding the codes and performance of the media and media professions means maintaining review or regulatory boards to weigh complaints against codes and performances. In broadcasting, for example, the Radio Code Board and the Television Code Review Board have the power to suspend or revoke the use of the NAB seal of approval for any station held in violation of broadcasting codes. One of the strongest review boards is the Code Authority of the Comics Magazine Association of America. It reviews all comic book material prior to publication and can order changes in art or text. An appeal board hears any complaint about code authority actions.

**Project Censored:
The Underreported
News**

Among the groups of professionals and media-associated experts who monitor and critique news media performance is Project Censored, a national research project that annually identifies significant stories "underreported" by the news media. The project's director is Carl Jensen of Sonoma State University, California; its panel of jurors has included Dr. Donna Allen, publisher of *Media Report to Women,* Ben Bagdikian, noted journalist and media researcher, Hodding Carter, chief correspondent for PBS's "Inside Story," and Noam Chomsky, professor of linguistics and philosophy, Massachusetts Institute of Technology. Since 1975 Project Censored has researched and published a list of the significant underreported news stories of the year—with the suggestion the news media have erred in not giving the stories more attention. In 1983 the project's ten top underreported stories were as follows:

1. Israeli arms to Central America. According to CIA, estimates Israel is the fifth largest exporter of arms in the world and the largest supplier of arms to Latin America and Sub-Saharan Africa. Thousands of Latin Americans receive their police training in Israel.
2. U.S. never dropped out of the arms race. Defense Secretary Caspar Weinberger announced we never dropped out of the arms race and still lead in many critical areas.
3. U.S. ignored U.S.S.R. nuclear freeze proposal. On October 5, 1983, the Soviet minister of foreign affairs made sweeping proposals for freezing nuclear weapons that were ignored by the Reagan administration and the press.
4. America's agricultural disaster. Reagan's Payment in Kind farm subsidy program was one of the worst agricultural disasters in U.S. history— and largely ignored by the news media.
5. KAL 007 and the U.S./U.S.S.R. spy war. Sources reported KAL planes regularly overflew Soviet air space on intelligence missions, and the U.S. could have interceded in the attack that killed 269 people.
6. Peter Fox and Central America. A conservative city editor of a Billings, Montana, newspaper visited Central America and then resigned his commission in the National Guard in protest of what he saw.
7. Media neglect South Africa politics. While media coverage of Lech Walesa and Poland's Solidarity Movement is high, the news media

The advertising industry maintains the National Advertising Division (NAD) of the Council of Better Business Bureaus to investigate cases; the National Advertising Review Board (NARB) hears appeals and gives judgment on deceptive advertising practices. In its first five years of existence, the NARB handled two hundred complaints a year—more than the FTC did during the same period. It gained respect with early decisions that showed its intention to be more than window dressing. In 1972 ignore Nelson Mandela, South Africa's National Congress, and their fight against racist apartheid in South Africa.

8. Nuclear navy accidents. An unpublicized list documents 126 accidents of nuclear powered naval vessels, including thirty-seven involving nuclear reactors and thirteen discharges of radioactive material into U.S. waters.

9. DNA—key to biological warfare? Biological warfare researchers at the Department of Defense are applying recombinant DNA (splicing) technologies to military use. Its peace time use still is highly questioned.

10. The DOD taxpayer swindle. The Department of Defense "cost plus" contracting system allows overruns and open-ended price tag systems. It reduces national military strength while encouraging contractors to overcharge for weapons and services.

Editor & Publisher, the leading magazine of the newspaper industry, published the list of leading underreported stories along with the Associated Press's estimation of the top ten stories the same year:

1. Marines massacred in Beirut
2. Soviets down KAL airliner
3. U.S. invades Grenada
4. The American economy
5. Missiles deployed in Europe
6. European nuclear projects
7. Lech Walesa/Nobel Peace Prize
8. Menachem Begin resigns
9. Weather
10. James Watt resigns.

Project Censored does not suggest its underreported stories are the most important of the year, only that they are highly significant and not as thoroughly reported as they should have been. (Director Jensen invites anyone who wishes to nominate an underreported story to send him a copy at Sonoma State University, Rohnert Park, CA 94928.)

the NARB reviewed a complaint that a Kal Kan dog food advertisement made "false disparagement and unsubstantiated claims" directed at a competitor; it won an agreement from Kal Kan to remove the ads from distribution.

The news media have been the least interested in forming boards of self-regulation, due, no doubt, to the journalistic tradition that news reporting should be free from any regulation. In 1947 The Commission on Freedom of the Press, reviewing the responsibilities of the news media, suggested the establishment of a national press council to review press performance and require offenders to print corrections of errors. The idea gained a toehold in 1963 when Barry Bingham, president of the Louisville *Courier-Journal,* established a local press council to serve as a forum between his newspapers and the community. Three years later, as an experiment, the Mellet Fund for Freedom established several local councils, with trained observers to judge how well they might work. The results were encouraging. Observers found (1) the press councils gave news executives valuable feedback, making them more aware of the need for responsible performance; (2) they acted as an avenue to the public, providing an opportunity to explain paper policies to the public; and (3) they enhanced the esteem of the paper in the public eye.

The success of the Minnesota Press Council, established in 1971, and a contribution by the Twentieth Century Fund helped create the National News Council (NNC) in 1973. Although no longer in existence, it was the most ambitious news council attempted in this country to date. It published occasional "white papers" dealing with the ethical problems of the media. For more than ten years its most widely recognized function was to review complaints concerning media performance and publish its decisions and judgments for the edification of the public and media professionals.

In its ten year history the NNC rejected 80 percent of the complaints submitted to it and made decisions against the media in only eighty-two of 242 cases investigated.

Council president (and former president of CBS News) Richard Salant, cited lack of news media interest and cooperation and lack of financial support as the two principal reasons for the council's death. Many publishers seemed to distrust the idea of the council, again exhibiting the newspaper industry's traditional, libertarian reluctance to have any outside body, even one that could not impose sanctions, looking over its shoulder. For some there was the fear that the norms suggested by NNC white papers and in council decisions would become rules the courts would impose on the news media.

The death of the council in 1984 left the public and the profession with only a few sources dedicated to news media criticism. Among them were the magazines *Channels,* the *Columbia Journalism Review,* and the *Washington Journalism Review.* These seem to see press criticism as a paramount goal of their publication. Unfortunately, the one television program dedicated to news media criticism, PBS's commendable "Inside Story," left the air in 1984 due to a lack of funding. At last report, plans were underway to revive the program, however.

At last report, thirty-two newspapers had their own full-time ombudsmen to respond to reader complaints and help correct the situation where warranted. A *Washington Journalism Review* survey suggests the key to the success of such a program is keeping the ombudsman independent of management. Research indicates all thirty-two of those active in the profession write columns for their respective papers discussing public complaints. Those inside the paper who are involved see the copy before publication, but no one is allowed to make other than grammatical changes in it before it is printed. Ombudsman Art Nauman of the Sacramento *Bee* says he no longer parties or drinks with the *Bee* staff because he may have to cross swords with one or more of them later on. There is no doubt the job is a difficult one. Ruth Wilson, working for the Milwaukee *Journal,* says the job should have a tenure of only two or three years since people in it tend to go stale rapidly.

Social Control: Audiences and Interest Groups

Nicholas Johnson, former FCC commissioner, author, columnist, and head of the National Citizen's Communication Lobby (NCCL).

While it may seem difficult to believe, an audience also can have a "regulatory" effect on the system. Simply with a telephone request for a recording, one person, anywhere, late at night can affect the program of almost any disc jockey. The newspaper editor who receives no letters to the editor will soon become an anxious person indeed. One of the problems of the media, in fact, is that management is more likely to pay attention to mail or telephone calls than to the scientific survey research at its disposal.

Former FCC commissioner Nicholas Johnson has suggested anyone can bring about change in the mass media with the proper approach. First, he has written, there must be a basis for change—a well-defined case. Then citizens need to find the legal rule for the change. Finally, they must have a workable solution. An organization can help, of course. But an organization alone is not even one important step in the three-step process. Attorney John Banzhaf III, for example, succeeded alone in his attempt to get antismoking commercials on the air (see chapter 16). In contrast, in 1980, the Reverend Robert G. Grant and the American Christian Cause (ACC) flooded the FCC with fourteen thousand cards and letters complaining about a proposed ABC-TV program entitled "Adam & Ives," which was to feature two leading homosexual characters. The write-in campaign was a complete waste. First of all, the FCC, under Section 326 of the 1948 Communications Act, is not allowed to censor program plans, and so there was no legal way to stop the program. Second, the ACC's complaint had no factual basis. There was no "Adam & Ives" program to stop. ABC-TV had considered one similar program idea three years earlier but had dropped it. There was not, nor had there ever been, an "Adam & Ives" program. The result of the ACC write-in campaign was that the FCC was left with a large pile of letters to dump—and an unexpected government expense.

Media pressure and interest groups constitute, nevertheless, an effective component in our mass communication system. A variety of interested groups press their cases effectively to the media, media regulators, and government. Some attack from the Left; others from the Right. Some fear the media will lead the nation astray with smut and sex. Others charge media are sexist, liberal, or too violent. Some have charged they are childish; others say they have nothing proper for children.

Citizen Groups

Among the more prominent interest groups in recent years have been:

The Rev. Jerry Falwell, critic of media programming and leader of the Moral Majority movement.

1. ACT, or Action for Children's Television, with headquarters in Boston. ACT is dedicated to television reforms in the interest of children. It pressed for reduction of television violence and won revisions in the National Association of Broadcaster's television code, increasing the amount of educational children's programming on the air. It also helped reduce the advertising of sugar-laden products and has recently called on the FTC to issue a guide for toy manufacturers to reduce the unfair and deceptive nature of toy commercials aimed at children.

2. AIM, or Accuracy in Media. Formed in 1969, AIM is an ultraright watchdog of the news media. Established to promote accuracy and fairness in reporting, it also seeks corrections in response to well-founded complaints. AIM often attacks reporting that smears police or government officials.

3. CBT or Coalition for Better Television. Led by the Reverend Donald Wildmon of Tupelo, Mississippi, it has called for a return to moral values in television, charging on one occasion that Christian characters and culture are excluded from many programs, and that when they are included they are scorned and ridiculed. He and the CBT attacked the syndicated "Phil Donahue Show" as filled with sex, especially abnormal sex. Wildmon once called for a boycott of sponsors of objectionable programs, but the idea was abandoned at the last minute.

4. NOW or National Organization of Women. The group is not only interested in changing sexist media content but in changing sexist attitudes and prejudices in society itself. To further its cause, it petitioned the FCC regarding transfer of broadcast licenses, then dropped the petitions when the concessions were won from station management.

5. The Office of Communication, United Church of Christ. It has had a far reaching impact on broadcasting through only one of its many cases: The WLBT case. It has stressed local community coverage and access to media, and sponsored petitions to the FCC regarding the moral obligations and the quality of broadcasting.

Jawboning

Peggy Charren of Action for Children's Television.

Reed Irvine of Accuracy in Media (AIM).

When pressure from the audience or interest group becomes great enough to suggest legislative or rule-making action, the government or the regulatory body, and the media professions involved, often turn to jawboning. This practice represents an attempt to talk out a compromise or solution to correct an unpopular media practice without government legislation or regulation. The original Motion Picture Production Code was created under such conditions in 1930.

Another good example occurred in 1974 as the result of pressure brought by Action for Children's Television. ACT wanted to reduce the advertising in children's programs and remove sex and violence from programs shown during the early evening when children are viewing. In May 1974 then FCC chairman Richard Wiley, in a speech in Atlanta, announced he would meet with network vice-presidents to seek a limit to children's program ad time. The National Association of Broadcasters gave a quick response. On June 15 it announced it would limit ad time in children's programs to nine and one-half minutes per hour. In the fall, Wiley announced the FCC found the change acceptable and a commission rule would not be necessary.

The question of violence and obscenity in evening programs proved more of a problem. In October Wiley announced he would call a meeting with the three network vice-presidents for programming to discuss scheduling programs with violence and sex no earlier than 9 P.M. E.S.T. and having the networks give prior warnings about the content of questionable programs shown before 9 P.M. At the meeting Wiley suggested the possibility that scheduling of programs with violence and sex might be included in a station's license renewal form if some rescheduling could not be made. The idea was not popular with the vice-presidents, who knew the move would bring strong reactions from their affiliates. Wiley noted, at the same time, that independent and public broadcasting stations would have to be a party to any agreement to keep unwanted program content out of the early evening hours.

Other conferences followed in early December, with CBS proposing that the Television Review Board be contacted to discuss a code change that would set aside the first hour of prime time for family viewing (the family hour, as it now is called). CBS board chairman William S.

Paley supported the idea. And a CBS team, one of whose members was on the NAB code board, flew to San Antonio to present the idea to Wayne Kearl, chairman of the NAB television code review board. CBS presented a letter proposing the code dedicate the first prime time hour to family viewing, have audiences forewarned of any special material presented in family hour programs that might require parental guidance, and give prior warning in other hours of material that might be disturbing to adults.

Kearl received the proposal by noting citizens in his own community were upset, and he promised to call a code board hearing in January 1975. In February the code board adopted the proposal, adding that programs shown between 7 P.M. and 9 P.M. should not be "inappropriate for viewing by a general family audience. . . ." The family hour was born.

Author Geoffry Cowen has written that on February 19, chairman Wiley sent a report to Congress describing his meetings with the networks, the NAB action, and his intention to gain similar self-regulatory concessions from independent and public television licensees. The results indicated to Wiley that "the broadcasting industry is prepared to regulate itself in a fashion that will obviate any need for government regulation in this sensitive area.

Problems of Self-Regulation

Self-regulation is not without its problems. To work, it must be able to mobilize the significant parties in the profession and maintain a high degree of commitment to the professional program and professional code. The establishment of the family hour by the NAB television code board came as a result of much effort, especially by CBS.

The mobilization of significant members of the profession reflects the complaint that self-regulation is not objective—that it favors the "insiders." (Recall that the FCC dealt with independent stations and public television separately in the family hour code revision.)

Self-regulation can be better than government regulation since it comes from those who understand the needs and problems of the profession concerned. But it, too, has a chilling effect on creativity. From the beginning, those involved in the discussions of the family hour recognized the change was a threat to mature television programs such as "All in the Family" and "Maude." Producer Norman Lear was asked to "tone down" Archie Bunker as a result of the NAB code change. CBS editors had problems with "M*A*S*H" episodes that dealt with venereal disease, adultery, and a bombardier who developed a personality problem: Corporal Jesus H. Christ. Legally speaking, this was not censorship but *editing*. But family hour editing for taste and morality became such a problem that one group of television writers and producers, including

Norman Lear's Tandem/TAT company, filed suit in federal district court charging the networks, the NAB, and the FCC with violating their First Amendment rights. In November 1976 the court held that FCC pressure on the networks had indeed been too great (when the FCC had threatened to ask about sex and violence programs in station license renewal forms). After the Supreme Court refused to review the decision, the case drifted into limbo; in 1980 the appeals court ordered it returned to the FCC for review and consideration. Whatever the final outcome, there was little reason to believe the FCC, the NAB, or the three major networks were eager to discard the family-viewing concept. The next step toward controlling sex and violence in television would be legislation. The parties to the family hour agreement wanted no new legislation with new, unintended restrictions, and new problems to be solved.

Summary

Conflicts, abuses, and practical necessity have forced some regulation of the media. Regulation has not been in the political interest of a regime or a party in power; it was intended to increase efficiency and insure that the public enjoys the media service. On occasion, the media themselves have asked government to bring abuses under control.

In the early 1900s there was so much deception in advertising—especially by patent medicine makers—many responsible professionals joined the truth-in-advertising movement and asked the government for controls. The result was the Federal Trade Act and the Federal Trade Commission. Under amendments to the act, the FTC now can investigate and/or prosecute any person or company engaged in false, deceptive, or unfair advertising. It also can order an offender to publish advertisements to correct the errors or deceptions of earlier ads.

Industry reaction to some FTC proposals led the Congress to curtail its power in 1980, and the idea of deregulating the advertising industry continued during the Reagan administration. Some industry spokespersons believe removing the FTC's ability to stop deceptive ads would give the industry a more creative atmosphere. Others fear it might bring a return to the troubles of the early 1900s. Meanwhile, the Supreme Court has held that truthful commercial messages fall under the protection of the First Amendment and may not be suppressed without compelling public interest.

The Federal Communications Commission, like the FTC, was formed largely at the request of the industry it now regulates. It operates under the 1934 Communications Act, which gives it rule-making power to regulate broadcasting. Section 315 requires stations to give or sell equal time to political candidates.

The Fairness Doctrine evolved from the equal time idea and is the keystone of FCC regulation. Station managers are expected to encourage and implement the broadcasting of all sides of controversial public issues. The FCC has allowed only one application of the doctrine to commercials (cigarette smoking), none to entertainment programs, and a few to news documentaries. The Fairness Doctrine remains the FCC's most important requirement for operating "in the public interest." One controversial policy, the prime time access rule restricting the use of network programs during prime time, was undertaken to diversify television program sources, but it was not successful.

The media professions have put their own standards and ethics into professional codes. Most of the media professions also have review boards or councils.

Individuals and groups have a profound effect on media operations and offerings. When pressure from groups becomes great enough to suggest legislation or rule making, government and media professionals can make the change without legislation. The amount of ad time in children's television programs and the family hour concept were instigated through an NAB code change rather than through the FCC.

Self-regulation requires mobilization of significant numbers of professionals. Like outside regulation, it can have a chilling effect on creativity. Several mature television programs were submitted to frustrating censorship/editing after the family hour was established.

Most media, and most American government leaders, remain wary of new government regulation and legislation of the media. Once legislation is started it cannot always be stopped. And even carefully worded laws and rules can create needless new restrictions.

Questions for Discussion

1. The American Medical Association and the American Bar Association fought FTC attempts to win the right to advertise for medical doctors and lawyers. Why would the AMA and the ABA object to this, and who has gained or suffered as a result of the right to advertise? Why?

2. We seem to have come to a strange turn of events in the history of the mass media. There are now more radio and television stations than daily newspapers. Should we now regulate newspapers in the "public interest, convenience, and necessity" due to their limited accessibility? If so, what should newspapers be required to do that they do not do?

3. It has been charged by at least one special interest group that radio and television managers always operate by the bottom line and will not take the trouble to provide responsible broadcast service without government regulation. Is there merit to this argument? Is there evidence that it is flawed? What hard evidence is there that such is not the case?

4. Which is better, regulation by government or self-regulation? What might be the results of each type of regulation?

References

"ACT Wants Guidelines for Toy Advertising." *Broadcasting,* July 12, 1982, 49.

"Ad Industry Votes to Cut FTC's Power." *Broadcasting,* April 16, 1982, 72–73.

"Are Child Ads Unfair?" *Business Week,* June 20, 1977, 27.

"Back on the Warpath Against Deceptive Ads." *Business Week,* April 19, 1976, 148.

Black, Norman. "FCC Proposal Angers Citizens." *Columbus-Dispatch,* October 16, 1982, D10.

Brown, Merrill. "New FCC Chief Talks about 'Unregulating,' the Communications Industry." *Washington Journalism Review,* January/February 1982, 33–40.

"Commoner Radio Ad Draws Complaints, But No Action." *Broadcasting,* October 20, 1980, 36.

Cowan, Geoffrey. *See No Evil.* New York: Simon and Schuster, 1978.

DeLuca, Stuart M. "FCC: The Quibbler." *The Christian Science Monitor,* March 23, 1982, 22.

Foster, Eugene S. *Understanding Broadcasting.* Reading, Mass.: Addison-Wesley, 1978.

"The FTC's Ad Rules Anger Industry." *Time,* November 1, 1976, 30.

"FTC's Children's Inquiry Delayed." *Broadcasting,* October 13, 1980, 66.

"Inside the FCC." *Television/Radio Age,* December 13, 1982, 127–28.

Johnson, Nicholas. *How To Talk Back To Your Television Set.* Boston: Little, Brown, 1970.

Kahn, Frank J., ed. *Documents of American Broadcasting.* 3rd ed., Englewood Cliffs, N.J.: Prentice-Hall, 1978.

"NAB Wins Big in the House . . . Maybe." *Broadcasting,* May 23, 1983, 31–33.

"National News Council at a Crossroad." *Editor & Publisher,* December 3, 1983, 13 et seq.

"National News Council Report." *Columbia Journalism Review,* January/February 1981, 76–86.

"NNC Folding." *Washington Journalism Review,* May 1984, 11–12.

"The Ombudsman's Story." *Washington Journalism Review,* May 1984, 12.

"Open Season on FTC." *Time,* December 3, 1979, 84.

Overbeck, Wayne. "Unmuzzling Americas' Corporations: Corporate Speech and the First Amendment." Paper presented to the Association for Education in Journalism Convention at Michigan State University, East Lansing, August 1981.

Phelan, John M. *Disenchantment: Meaning and Morality in Media.* New York: Hastings House, 1980.

Rivers, William L., William B. Blankenburg, Kenneth Starck, and Earl Reeves. *Backtalk: Press Councils in America.* New York: Harper & Row, 1972.

Saddler, Jeanne. "FTC Easing Rules Requiring Firms to Support Ad Claims." *The Wall Street Journal,* July 21, 1983, 25.

"Senate Pressure." *Advertising Age,* March 19, 1982, 6.

Siebert, Fred S., Theodore Peterson, and Wilbur Schramm. *Four Theories of the Press.* Urbana: University of Illinois, 1956.

Turner, E. S. *The Shocking History of Advertising.* New York: E. P. Dutton, 1953.

"Underreported Stories." *Editor & Publisher,* June 16, 1984, 14–15.

"Why Industry Wants Miller to Slow Down." *Advertising Age,* March 19, 1982, 16.

Part Six

Public Concern and Mass Communication: Our Hopes and Fears

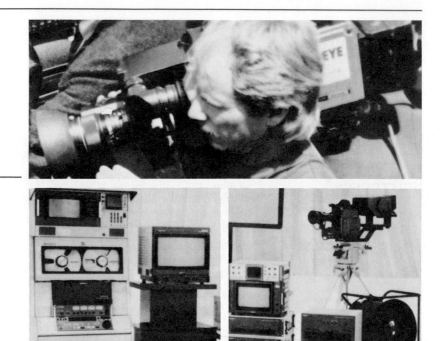

Since the mass media first appeared in Western civilization some five hundred years ago, they have precipitated an amazing body of comments, predictions, and expressions about what they may or may not be doing for us. In an early study of perspectives on the media, sociologist Leo Lowenthal identified two themes of media criticism. One was the view that the media had positive potential for socialization of the individual, the other was a deep concern for the inner fate of those subjected to media messages.

In detailed research a few years ago, Robert Davis reported each media invention, from the phonograph on, was greeted by a wide discussion of its faults and merits. Supporters tended to view the medium as an unprecedented opportunity to improve the lot of the average person—to enlighten the young and bring democracy to art, among other things. Movie producer D. W. Griffith argued, for example, the motion picture would widen the entertainment horizons of the "parched American deserts of small towns and villages." Motion picture inventor Thomas Edison predicted films

would improve the social condition of the average citizen, and "brighten the lives of the masses." Publisher E. W. Scripps held the newspaper was the classroom of the working class.

Davis found, on the other hand, that detractors of the media feared the new devices would contribute more to moral and artistic laxity than moral and cultural growth. The famous bandmaster, John Phillip Sousa, for example, made public attacks on the Berliner disc recording, charging it could not record (like Edison's cylinder record) and would turn a potential army of

musicians into a passive audience of music listeners. Still others decried media content as banal, a threat to morality, health, or the nation's political system. *Commonweal* magazine argued in 1932 that the majority of Hollywood films were "illiterate . . . when not emotionally or morally primitive." More recently, we have tended to view television as both "the greatest classroom in the world" and the instrument that produces aggressive and lazy children.

Psychologist Sylvan Tomkins has suggested that any conflict and debate that evolves from our personal values tends to reflect ideas that recur in the perennial debate between Left and Right ideologies. Since our hopes and fears about media reflect personal values, it follows that many of the ideas expressed in the media debate reflect Left-Right ideologies, too. The idea of the media as educator of the people is a hope of the Left, for example, while the notion that media entertainment is a purveyor of immoral behavior seems to be a fear of the Right.

Whatever its source and makeup, the debate over the values and dangers of the mass media continues as it has for centuries. One new, relevant factor is contributing to the debate, however. Since the 1930s scientific research has been introduced into media affairs. It continues to produce more reliable knowledge about the media than we have known before. To often factless arguments on media marvels and ills we now can add verifiable knowledge of how the media actually perform—and how they compare to our subjective impressions of them.

In this final section we review major hopes and fears about the media. Chapter 18 reviews fears about media effects and news media performance, along with some

scientific findings regarding these fears. Chapter 19 offers a hopeful projection of mass communication in the years ahead, with particular attention paid to the trend toward specialization, the emergence of the "electronic cottage," and the rapidly developing computer-oriented world information network.

References

Davis, Robert Edward. "Response to Innovation: A Study of Popular Argument about Mass Media." Ph.D. diss., University of Iowa, 1965.

Kornhauser, William. *The Politics of Mass Society.* Glencoe, Ill.: The Free Press, 1959.

Lowenthal, Leo. "Historical Perspectives of Popular Culture." In *Mass Culture,* edited by Bernard Rosenberg and David Manning White. Glencoe Ill.: The Free Press, 1957.

Tomkins, Sylvan. "Left and Right, A Basic Dimension of Ideology and Personality." In *The Study of Lives,* edited by Robert W. White. London: Prentice-Hall International, 1963.

Chapter

18

The Media, Public Concern, and Mass Communication Research

Public Concern and the Media

The growth of mass communication and our growing dependence on it has not come without the creation of a considerable degree of uneasiness and concern. Even in the early days of printing, philosophers and religious leaders raised questions as to what the new invention might do to individuals and society and how well it would serve them. In the late 1800s there was concern about excesses of the press. Later, there was greater concern about the effects of the more emotional media propaganda campaigns of World War I. The use of the media for political propaganda between the two World Wars—especially that of the Hitler and Mussolini governments in Germany and Italy—raised even greater alarms. As a result many people urged social scientists to study, with systematic research methods, the power of the media to persuade and manipulate the masses. As twentieth century audiences grew large, then huge, media managers found they also were in dire need of reliable information about their vast, unseen audiences. To keep and attract audiences for advertisers, they needed research that could tell them who was reading, who was listening, and who was watching.

Unfortunately, the gathering of information is not always the same as the gathering of reliable information. As philosopher Charles Pierce has observed, there are four basic ways of knowing about any subject.

One of the oldest is knowing by *tenacity,* or supporting a belief as true because it always has been true. In earlier chapters, we have discussed knowing by *authority,* or holding information to be true because the monarch, the leader, or an expert says it is true. Or, we can accept as true what appears to be true, by *reason,* or a priori, because it seems true on the face of things. However, mass communication has proved to be so complex and difficult to understand that *scientific inquiry* has been our most reliable means of accumulating reliable knowledge about the media. Through scientific inquiry, we are best able to test what tenacity, authority, and a priori reasoning would have us believe to be true about media processes and their effects in the real world.

Scientific Research and Mass Communication

Mass communication is human communication and human behavior, so mass communication science is communication science, one of several types of behavioral sciences. The first goal of mass communications scientist is to produce findings that are reliable—that will stand up under repeated investigations. The ones that do then may qualify as valid, or accurate, in describing and predicting human processes, operations, and behaviors involved in media affairs. But to be valid a hypothesis must first be reliable.

Mass communication science is both a quantitative and an interdisciplinary science. Like the other behavioral sciences, it tests its hypotheses and inferences against mathematical models (the laws of probability). It also uses the quantitative tools of descriptive statistics (percentages, averages, medians, etc.) and inferential statistics (Are these groups alike? What part of this group of numbers is doing most of the work?) to deal with the overwhelming numbers of people and large amounts of data such a complicated discipline requires. And since its immediate academic roots are in the other behavioral sciences of psychology, sociology, and political science, it is interdisciplinary; it continues to borrow (and contribute) hypotheses, theories, and knowledge from (and to) those associated disciplines. Clearly its greatest significance is its focus on human activity in and around the mass media—on broadcast program choices, media message content, response to media messages, news selection and production, and changes in society—to gain reliable knowledge about mass communications processes and effects.

There are three basic types of mass communications research: surveys and field studies, experiments, and content analysis.

Survey and Field Research

Surveys usually are study groups of people or audiences in the mass communications system: audience surveys or public opinion surveys. Media researchers, for example, have made surveys of the attitudes of religious public relations personnel toward their profession, women's page editors of newspapers and the problems they face in their work, and changes in television news departments as reflected in their news-gathering equipment.

In a classic field study some years ago, media researchers Kurt Lang and Gladys Lang used three groups of observers to study what impact television coverage had on the perceptions of people viewing civic ceremonies—including a parade. They placed one group of observers in front of television sets to watch a local parade, another in the field (at curbside) to view the parade without television coverage, and a third in a position to watch the parade both ways. Following the parade and subsequent ceremonies, the descriptions of the three groups were collated to ascertain how the television version differed from the firsthand viewing.

The results indicated the television version of the events evoked significantly different reactions than did viewing the real life events. Television viewers had extended contact with the ceremonies and central attractions, while gaining supportive information from the announcer's comments. Real-life viewers saw the passing parade for only a few moments. From their viewpoint on the sidewalk it was not nearly the highly emotional event it was for the television viewers.

Surveys of audiences, such as opinion polls and rating surveys, usually are conducted through telephone, mail, or personal interviews with respondents selected as a part of the survey sample. Since sampling was discussed in chapter 11, only a brief review of the concept is necessary here.

Sampling is a way to save time and money in studying a large population of people, events, or items. Rather than study all the people in the total population, a representative sample is drawn so studying and describing the sample is equivalent to studying and describing the population. A properly drawn sample of one thousand to twelve hundred can accurately portray a population of millions—and with only a slight amount of error. It does not matter whether the population is the national voting population, a national television audience, or fourteen- to sixteen-year-old school students. A properly drawn sample can describe any population accurately. Media researchers have sampled news stories, political cartoons, and motion pictures to describe trends, campaign symbols, and types of movies, respectively.

To be representative, samples are either drawn at random so that all people in the population have an equal chance of getting into the sample, or sample individuals are selected purposely so that proportions of individuals are represented in the sample the way they exist in the population (the proper percentage of men, women, children, or members of ethnic groups, for example).

Experiments

Experiments are conducted in the laboratory and in the field. Laboratory experiments give greater control of a media situation than field experiments, but the laboratory environment also may be so unnatural that the findings are not valid in the real world. Experimental work explores relationships in behavior by arranging or manipulating events, then testing or observing the results. The *independent* variable is manipulated to see what effect it may have on the *dependent* variable. (In the statement, "If clouds, then rain," *clouds* are the independent variable, and *rain* is the dependent variable.) A much studied dependent variable in media experiments is violent behavior. Researchers have often posed media messages as the independent variable, testing to see if the messages influence (encourage or confirm, etc.) aggressive behavior in audience members—frequently children. In a frequently cited laboratory study of the effects of violence on children, three researchers, Albert Bandura, Dorothea Ross, and Sheila Ross, introduced two independent variables: frustration and violence. Since earlier research findings suggested that adopting aggressive actions from the media was facilitated by audience member frustration, the research team introduced the independent variable—frustration—into the experiment. The experimenters frustrated each child, mildly, by giving the child a toy, then taking it away. The child then was exposed to one of three violent treatments. There was a film of a person beating an inflated punching doll, a cartoon film of a character beating the doll, and a real person beating it. Each treatment included acts of hitting, punching, hammering and sitting on the doll, accompanied by calls of "kick him," "throw him in the air," and so forth.

After the children were exposed to the violence, they were placed in an observation room containing one of the inflated dolls and other toys. The measurement of the dependent variable—the children's aggression—came from judges who did not know the purpose of the experiment. They observed and recorded the number of aggressive acts the children made toward the doll. For comparison, the judges also recorded the playroom acts of a control group of children. The results indicated that film displays of aggression heighten and shape (determine the kind of) aggression in children. Among other things, the research team found

The Bandura, Ross, and Ross experiment: sitting on, tossing, hitting, striking the Bobo doll after watching filmed models doing the same.

all three experimental groups more aggressive than the control group. Boys tended to exhibit more hitting and gunplay than girls, who were more inclined to sit on the doll without punching it.

About the same time, media researchers were interested in understanding how person-to-person information campaigns might compare in effectiveness with media information campaigns. Researchers designed a field experiment to investigate the situation. A person-to-person health information campaign was conducted in one city; a media health information campaign in another; no information was given in the third city. Tests of samples taken before and after the two health campaigns revealed that the person-to-person campaign resulted in more direct action (more calling doctors, etc.) than the mass media campaign. But people exposed to the media information campaign proved more knowledgeable about the health topic when the campaign was completed.

Content Analysis

Content analysis was developed during the years before World War II, when students of political propaganda found they needed an objective, systematic, and quantitative method to study international propaganda—especially that coming from Nazi Germany. The technique allows researchers to obtain a systematic count of content categories or themes in the message and gain a more-than-intuitive idea of what the message does and does not contain. Some of the more interesting content analyses in recent years have been performed by professors George Gerbner and Larry Gross of the University of Pennsylvania. Their studies of situations and characters in dramatic television programs suggest these action/adventure worlds are seldom accurate reflections of the world about us. In television drama they have found, for example, one-fifth of the people work in law enforcement. More than half are involved in some violence, and at least one-tenth are associated with killing others. In the real world, Gerbner and Gross note, only one percent of the population is active in law enforcement, and most violent deaths are not murders but the result of automobile or industrial accidents.

Content analysis, although useful, cannot tell what effects the message may have on the audience. Content categories are the researcher's inventions, and may or may not be relevant to the attending audience.

Mass communications researchers have used all the methods of behavioral science to examine the process and effects of mass communication, and have been at the forefront of behavioral science research methods and statistical tools.

Two Types of Mass Communication Research

Mass communications research can be divided into two distinct types: (1) theoretical research, performed for the most part by academic researchers, and (2) institutional, or commercial research, usually performed by media organizations, advertising, public relations, and commercial research agencies. Both focus on sender, message, and receiver in the communications process, and on interactions of all three.

Theoretical or Academic Research

Theoretical, or academic research, has pursued in various ways the study of the process and effects of the mass media. *Gatekeeper research* studies media individuals whose decisions open and close news gates and control the flow of information through the organization to the public. For example, studies of the wire service editor—one of many gatekeepers—indicate he or she is more concerned with deadline pressure and getting news stories into the paper than in the social value of the wire stories. Other studies suggest the gatekeeper's decisions are affected by his or her position within the organization. The gatekeepers who make the first decisions about news seem to work in broader categories ("If we can get a picture of it, hold on to it.") than those closer to actual publication or broadcasting of the story ("Leave in the part where he's being shot, but take out the part where the guy is on the ground.").

The media organization also has been the subject of media research. Warren Breed found, for example, that much of the cohesion of the newspaper comes from the staff's dedication to collecting and publishing the news—in the public interest. Breed's survey found news professionals rationalize a great deal, including highly biased publishing policies, by putting the importance of reporting the news above all else. The media organizations, cultural businesses that they are, have a great deal of potential for internal conflict. Fred Friendly's book *Due to Circumstances Beyond Our Control* was one of the first to deal with the conflicts between business and public affairs interests in network television. Unfortunately, much of our knowledge about organizational conflict still is at the anecdotal, or a priori stage.

News, information, and product diffusion research has studied the diffusion of air conditioners, medical drugs, and news. The two-step flow theory of media effects of the 1940s and 1950s was an early, if incomplete, model of information diffusion. Diffusion research has made us aware again that word-of-mouth advertising still is highly important in determining the diffusion of a product. People still discuss products and ideas with friends and neighbors, over the back fence, so to speak. Research following the assassination of President Kennedy found about half of the American people first learned of the president's death by word of mouth rather than from the news media.

Uses and gratifications research turns from the question, "What do the media do *to* people?" to "What do audiences *do with* media?" The emphasis is on understanding the motivations of the audiences, and the uses audiences make of mass media content. Classic radio research studied radio audiences to discover what uses and gratifications they found in radio soap opera content. The research found that the audiences looked to the programs not only for relaxation (escape) but also for emotional release and for *advice on how to conduct important aspects of their daily lives!*

Effects of mass media message studies are among the oldest media studies. Many have attempted to determine if media violence tends to make or encourage an audience to be violent. A sizable body of effects research also has investigated the impact of media messages on attitudes of readers and listeners. Professor Carl Hovland of Yale University did much to advance experimental research in communication through carefully controlled communication studies to explore the effects of messages, senders, and receivers. In one often cited experiment near the end of World War II, Hovland, Arthur Lumsdaine and Fred Sheffield gave a message that strongly argued one side of a viewpoint to one group, and a second message that included two sides of the issue to a second group.

Careful measurement of the effects of the two messages indicated the message that included points from both sides was more effective on better educated audiences and with audiences initially opposed to the view. The "two sided" message also gave less informed participants information about the opposing viewpoint they did not have before.

Agenda-setting research explores the tenet that the media do not tell us what to think but do tell us what to think *about*. "Audiences not only learn about public issues and other matters through the media," researchers Max McCombs and Donald Shaw have written, "they also learn how much importance to attach to an issue or topic from the emphasis placed on it by the mass media."

Readership and audience studies are performed by theoretical and commercial researchers alike, although with somewhat different goals. Theoretical research has explored "information-seeking behavior" in media audiences as well as such topics as whether being a "heavy media user" is desirable or undesirable in terms of personal and social behavior.

Commercial or Institutional Research

Commercial or institutional research examines questions important to the cultural business of mass communication. The broadcast media and the movie industry also have engaged in several types of audience studies. But their research was more intended to discover important message factors—what broadcast and movie audiences wanted in the way of heroes, villains, and plots in popular drama, for example. Newspaper and magazine readership studies usually seek to understand what parts of the audience read what parts of the publication. They, like advertisers, want to know what aspects of print, design, and layout of a publication attract and hold a reader.

Readership studies, along with many ad agencies, now have gone beyond the research of demographic descriptions of an audience (age, sex, income, social status) and have ventured into life-style research to understand audience attitudes and living styles that affect the use of the mass media. For example, the radio station that finds its audience moving away from its format now looks for the attitudes and changes in life-style that caused the shift. Has the audience grown older and disinterested in the music format? Are the disc jockeys' chatter and style compatible with audience interests? Recent newspaper research indicates readers develop well-defined times and habits for reading their newspapers; readers of the morning paper read while they eat breakfast, but evening readers listen to music in the family living room. Just as important: Altering the newspaper's content does not necessarily attract new readers. Research indicates the newspaper habit must be incorporated into life-styles before the age of eighteen, or it never will become part of the daily routine.

One type of life-style research, psychographics, focuses closely on attitudes: likes and dislikes of audience members. A detailed study by one advertising agency recently asked more than three thousand consumers what they were doing with their life, how often they saw an X-rated movie, if they ever wore a wig, how often they took a nap, if they jogged, and if they bought common stock. After rating the questions, the consumers were divided into groups (a Q-factor analysis). The results yielded ten types of American consumers, five male types and five female types. One type, named Candace, is a chic suburbanite. She is well educated, probably married to a professional man, a prime mover in community and club affairs who thinks soap operas are a complete waste of time. Needham, Harper & Steers, the ad agency that undertook the research, found the ten types very useful in advertising and selling products. Only four of the ten consumer types buy liquor, for example, and so liquor advertising can be most successful if pitched to the psychographics—the likes and dislikes—of those four. And Candace? No liquor for her. She buys yogurt and cottage cheese to eat on the run as she pursues her hectic life-style.

In contrast to life-style research, marketing research, as already reported in chapter 13, studies not only consumers and their life-styles but the entire range of marketing problems that arise into working out marketing strategy for a particular product or service.

Institutional or commercial mass media research has not contributed to theoretical knowledge of mass communication for at least two reasons. First, commercial research is undertaken to gain scientific solutions to specific commercial problems and does not generalize well to other situations. Second, most commercial research is tied to commercial products or services, and therefore is guarded as carefully as a trade secret by the corporation that paid for it.

It has been the academic research community that has pursued the questions of media effects and explored the concerns of media performance raised by the public.

The Effects of Mass Communication

The most persistent concern about the media and mass communication has been the one raised over media effects. Since the early days of mass communication there has been concern over the impact of the media on both the inner life of the individual and society itself. Beginning with World War I and government war propaganda, an image gradually evolved of the media as all powerful, as capable of persuading the public to do just about anything.

"The Invasion from Mars," the day after.

The *a priori* evidence seemed great. Historians, looking to individual cases from the past, pointed to the biting cartoons of Thomas Nast and their successful attack on Boss Tweed. The charge that William Randolph Hearst had single-handedly produced the Spanish-American War seemed more than plausible in the still-flickering light of yellow journalism.

The idea of an all powerful press lived on into the 1920s and 1930s, and was expanded to include radio when it arrived on the scene. A radio program in 1938, a "Halloween prank," as its producers called it, seemed to validate the concern. On October 30, Orson Welles's "Mercury Theatre" presented an adaptation by Welles and colleague John Houseman of H. G. Wells's *War of the Worlds*. The clever script utilized the radio news conventions of the day, giving reports from the scene with "live" interviews of important "officials." Even today the recording seems authentic for the first few minutes as it presents a nearly convincing report of a Martian invasion of the United States. Unfortunately, the program proved all too real in 1938. Hundreds of thousands of listeners mistook the fictitious reports for news reports and dashed into the streets to make their escape before the aliens flooded across the country from their landing sites in New Jersey.

If the invasion from Mars seemed to again prove the media are all powerful, it also provided a springboard for another look at media effects. Many social scientists had begun collecting evidence suggesting media effects were limited rather than all powerful. After studying the events surrounding the Welles Halloween prank and interviewing many of those who had heard the program, Hadley Cantril of Princeton pointed out that those who panicked had been "highly suggestible" people, at least during the time period of Wells's drama. Following a careful survey of those involved in the panic, Cantril noted that many were very religious people who believed God willed and controlled the destinies of individuals and were prepared to see the invasion from Mars as an act of God. For others, Cantril found, the war in Europe also had helped create a suggestible state of fear, or enough to bring about the panic. On the other hand, most people did not panic. They checked to see if the broadcast was real and found it was a play. They retained their critical faculties throughout the dramatic situation.

Limited Effects

Two years after the "War of the Worlds" panic, a scientific study of voter behavior in Erie County, New York, again discredited the all-powerful theory of mass communication. Paul Lazarsfeld and his colleagues from Columbia University found few direct political propaganda effects from the media-reported campaign. Voters, the research indicated, had been more widely influenced by face-to-face communication with friends than by political news and advertising in the mass media. Through selective perceptions individuals chose media messages that were agreeable to their existing point of view rather than listening to both sides of the political debate. Media effects, the researchers concluded, filtered through the individual's social groups—through respected friends or opinion leaders in a two-step flow of information and opinion. The media did not change attitudes, they reinforced those that already existed. Reinforcement was the principal effect of the mass media, not direct attitude change or psychological conversation.

Still, the media were not considered impotent, limited effects theorists warned. The media could confer status on individuals and organizations, for example. Anyone who appears regularly in the media automatically gains in public stature. (Ask Johnny Carson or Joan Collins.) The media can enforce social norms by exposing deviations from them (as Richard Nixon found out). The media also can act as social narcotics by absorbing time that might otherwise be used in social action. There is the danger, too, limited effects theory warned, that the superficial knowledge given by the media might pass for in-depth knowledge and convince media audiences they were better informed than they were.

Uses and Gratifications Research

Much of the research that contributed to the limited effects theory also contributed to uses and gratification research. Uses and gratifications studies ask the question, "What do people do with the mass media?" rather than the one asked by media effects: "What do media do to people?" Some of the findings of the uses and gratifications research on radio soap opera audiences were reported earlier.

An early contribution to uses and gratifications newspaper research came with Bernard Berelson's "What Missing the Newspaper Means," a study he undertook during a New York City newspaper strike. The findings were something of a surprise. Berelson found elderly newspaper readers missed the obituaries. The obituary column was a tie to their friends, a means of keeping up with those who were alive or had died. The research also indicated the paper was used primarily to keep in touch with the world rather than in touch with any one particular news story. Newspaper readers were not swept along by headlines or by sensational murder stories, as some had suspected. Instead the readers took active part in using the newspaper for their own needs and gratifications.

As Wilbur Schramm and William Porter have pointed out, limited effects theory and uses and gratifications research did not end the idea of direct media effects, but they did greatly encourage the idea that media audiences are not passive receivers but very active—even obstinate—in refusing to be overwhelmed by media.

The Adoption Process

Within a few years, the idea of the active receiver also found support in the work of sociologists attempting to understand how people decided to adopt new products and ideas. Sociologists in Iowa studied farmers who adopted high-yield hybrid corn for planting. Others followed the attempts of government officials to convince farm area mothers to can their own food rather than buy it. Still others studied physicians as they adopted new medical drugs. In general, the mass media seemed to play their most influential role at the initial stages of the adoption process. The media most likely are among the first to tell the potential adopter what products and ideas are available for use. Then other types of communication become more important.

One recent model describes the stages of the adoption procedure as follows:

1. Need assessment: the potential adopter assesses his or her priorities, needs, and resources.
2. Knowledge: *a search is made for information on new practices, products, and ideas* that might serve recognized needs.
3. Consideration: discussion, *advice,* investigation using the experience of others, a trial, then a choice is made of available ideas or products.
4. Trial: the new idea or product is used.
   Quite obviously, the mass media are the most likely to be a part of what is described in stages two and three (*indicated by italics*).

The media may supply *information* during those two stages, but note that *discussion* is not a mass communication function—especially the kind of two-way discussion needed in stage three. (The needs expressed in stage three, however, seem to reflect the interest cable television viewers have shown for the extended commercial experiments discussed in chapter 13.)

Limited effects theory and uses and gratifications research, and adoption stages of the adoption/diffusion models all tend to stress the importance of the individual and his or her use of ideas and products rather than the power of the media to distribute ideas. They underscore, too, the importance of face-to-face communication (discussion), personal influence (expert personal advice), and personal trial and decision in spreading ideas and products. Adoption/diffusion research, like the earlier two-step flow of media effects, helped put "people back in mass communication," to use an often-quoted phrase.

Weak Effects Models

In the 1950s and 1960s, as communication scientists applied scientific methods to the study of the mass media, they tended to expand the themes and limited effects models as well as uses and gratifications and innovation/diffusion research. Rather than ask questions concerning effects, they looked instead to media choice, motivation, media content and predispositions for attitude change. The experimental studies performed were highly refined, with carefully selected message content, carefully chosen experimental treatments, and a limited number of experimental subjects (usually college people). Too often the research was, if methodologically admirable, unlike media situations in the real world. More often than not, they were one-shot, unconnected studies with little or no attempt by researchers to study repeated exposure to media messages, in the way day-by-day living exposes all of us to media content.

The result was research that concluded the media were not central to changing thoughts and actions but peripheral in their effect at best. From this large number of studies, it was all too easy to assume the mass media had minimal effect—or no media effect at all.

The Media, Learning, and the Real World

In the early 1970s, the belief in a weak mass communications media was challenged as several researchers began to point out that much of the research that supported generalizations about mass media effects, while methodologically superior, was far from adequate. As Don Pember has reported, communication researcher Elisabeth Noelle-Neumann suggested a more powerful media concept when she pointed out "the decisive factors of mass media are not brought to bear in the traditional laboratory design experiment." And some media researchers suddenly realized they were contradicting themselves.

On the one hand, they proclaimed the wonders of mass communication and its ability to spread information, ideas, and improve the lives of, say, Third World nations and countries in poverty. On the other hand, however, they argued vehemently that the media had minimal effect—that people received few ideas from the media, that violence in media drama seldom gave violent notions to the audience, that the media hardly could spread political sentiment, or produce any one of several profound changes in the society. Research on effects had failed to take into account three important factors:

1. Ubiquity of the mass media. The media dominate the information environment. In modern society, it is difficult for an individual to avoid coming in contact with at least one form of media each day.

2. Cumulation of messages. Messages add up. Reruns and other repetitions reinforce the impact of the media message.
3. Consonance of journalists. News from separate sources still tends to be about the same. Even with many media, there are only a few distinct voices in the marketplace.

Through selective perception, Noelle-Neumann has pointed out, individuals see much the same content, day after day, in the modern media. Her content analysis and analyses of opinion polls suggest the effects of the media tend to increase in direct relation to the degree selective perception is made more difficult. In other words, the more similar the messages we have to choose from, the less likely we will make distinctive choices, and the more likely we will take the same ideas, opinions, and concepts from the various media.

As Schramm and Porter have suggested, we can gain an idea of the effects media have by asking ourselves where we acquired some of our own personal knowledge. For example, where did you learn what you know about Margaret Thatcher? Muammar Qaddafi? The Delorean automobile and its namesake? What the earth looks like from space? A Soviet fighter attack on a Korean commercial airline flight? What you know about Poland? Central America? Who is the mayor of the town you live in? Has there been a serious crime in town this week? Answers to such questions make it difficult to deny the mass media have positive, informational, and attitudinal effects on us. They give us clues for liking and disliking objects and people around us. (What is your attitude, for example, toward Margaret Thatcher? Muammar Qaddafi? Do you like or dislike either of them?) We watch television to relax, for example, but media entertainment programs present many possibilities for learning—about social interaction, the way men and women interact, what clothes are worn, who is important, what society thinks about minorities, marriage, government, what is just and moral, and what is not.

Media learning is not evitably good social learning, of course. A recent study of two hundred 1978–80 prime time television programs by The Media Institute revealed the potential for a great deal of inaccurate learning about business executives. Sixty-six percent of all executives portrayed were foolish, greedy, or evil. A content analysis of two hundred episodes revealed that more than half of all corporate leaders portrayed committed illegal acts—from fraud to murder—while 45 percent of all business acts depicted were illegal. The same study revealed that a great deal of the hard work portrayed was ridiculed as "workaholism."

The National Institute of Mental Health Report on Television Effects

In 1972 the Surgeon General's Advisory Committee on Television and Behavior, noting the lack of reliable information on the relationship between television viewing and the psychological growth and development of children, asked for studies to be funded by the federal government. By 1979 the government had collected twenty-five hundred research projects, and a new body of knowledge that made up 90 percent of all research ever attempted on the subject. The National Institute of Mental Health (NIMH) analyzed and assessed the results, then in 1982 published its two volume report, *Television and Behavior: Ten Years of Scientific Progress and Implications for the Eighties*. Rather than focus tightly on the question of television and violence, the NIMH report looked into other television effects as well. Among the conclusions:

1. Television violence was found to be associated with serious real life violence in teenage boys. Heavy viewing of television, especially of violence, is associated with unwarranted aggressive behavior in preschool and school-age children. These and many other studies led to the conclusion that the evidence "seems overwhelming that televised violence and aggression are positively correlated in children." One of the most significant findings, the report noted, is that heavy viewers of television also exhibit more "fear, mistrust, and apprehension" than light viewers.

2. Television presentations of socially desirable behavior have positive effects. In one reported study, children who watched an altruistic "Lassie" program scored much higher in an altruistic "save the puppy" game than children who watched another program. "The clear and simple message derived from the research on prosocial behavior," the report concluded, "is that children learn from watching television. . . . If they look at violent or aggressive programs, they tend to become more aggressive. . . . But if they look at prosocial programs, they will more likely become more generous, friendly, and self-controlled."

3. Television viewing has been thought to have a negative impact on education and learning. One study indicates heavy viewing leads to heavier reading over a period of years, but the heavy viewers begin to read materials similar to the material they watch on television—love, family, and true stories about Hollywood stars. Light viewers chose science fiction, mysteries, and nonfiction, on the other hand. The results of the research investigating the relationships among heavy television viewing, desire to achieve in school, and life aspirations are more complicated. The report concluded, "The primary finding in all this research is that not only the intensity but the direction of television's consequences for education—both achievement and aspiration—depend on many factors which may mediate, condition, enhance, diminish, or reverse the associations." There is, it seems, no direct effect from television in these matters, and personal, social and family influences on education and learning still are undetermined.

Studies of media content suggest media messages also may teach some troublesome lessons—original and reinforcing lessons—about women, blacks, and Chicanos, among others. Of course, we must not confuse media content and content analysis with media effects. Audience members view the media with selective attention, but view media *content* with selective perception, as suggested in chapter 1. Some aspects of the message may not even be seen or read.

Nevertheless, a recurring finding in the content analysis of fictional television is that there are more men than women, that men are usually portrayed as heroes while women are helpless. In a recent study, researchers Bradley S. Greenberg and Laura Henderson found 72 percent of the characters were males, 28 percent were females. An examination of the activities of dramatic characters in programs from the 1975–76 and 1976–77 television seasons revealed females were much more likely to engage in entertaining others, in preparing and serving food, and performing indoor housework. Male characters, on the other hand, were more likely to participate in sports, drive automobiles, use firearms, conduct business on the telephone, and drink and smoke. Such findings suggest such programs should be examined more closely to determine if they produce sex role stereotyping among members of the audience.

That women may not be getting important social information in the news has been suggested by a recent survey of content in prominent newspapers. In a study of ten major newspapers in 1984, researchers Virginia Allan, Catherine East, and Dorothy Jurney concluded the newspapers' emphasis on controversy, confrontation, and sensation does not help the reader understand many of the forces at work in the changing world. The researchers studied coverage of six important women's issues in such influential papers as the New York *Times,* the Los Angeles *Times,* the Miami *Herald,* the St. Louis *Post-Dispatch,* and the Cincinnati *Enquirer.* They found that the reporting of one women's conference emphasized emotional issues—abortion, ERA, and sexual preference—but ignored positive strides made at the conference; the newspapers also ignored, or often did not treat thoroughly, other women's issues, including the problem of pay equity with men and federal enforcement of Title IX (the laws prohibiting discrimination in education). The researchers called for several changes, including publication of more human interest news, as opposed to fast-breaking news; more attention to the impact of court decisions and other changes on the lives of readers; more sensitivity by editors and reporters to issues that are important to readers; and more time for on-the-job study to help gatekeepers stay abreast of developing issues and become specialists in the fields they are reporting.

There is reason to believe Hispanic-Americans are misrepresented and underreported in the media. In the past, television and the movies often portrayed Hispanics as sadistic bandits who robbed and killed everyone who crossed their path. A humorous variation on the stereotype was the Frito Bandito, a cartoon bandit who touted Frito Lay Potato Chips between shots from his six-gun. A second, recurring stereotype seems to be the downtrodden Hispanic peasant, amiable, but bumbling and lazy. Greenberg and Pilar Baptista-Fernandez have suggested Chicanos or Hispanic-Americans are the new minority on television. Of 3,549 fictional characters found in a three-year (1975–1977) study of television, only 53, or fewer than 1.5 percent, could be called Hispanic. The characters found were mostly males, dark complected, with heavy accents. They were gregarious and pleasant, with strong family ties. Half worked hard; the other half were lazy with little education, menial jobs, and little concern for their futures. Although the situation is changing, the dramatic productions of the media seem to ignore Hispanic-Americans, or cast them in unfavorable roles, as they once did blacks.

Also ignored in television drama, evidence has suggested, are the elderly. Content analysis of programs from three consecutive television seasons in the late 1970s indicated characters 65 years old and over made up only 3 percent or about one hundred of the 3,500 characters analyzed during the study. The world of television fiction, on the other hand, was overpopulated with 20- to 49-year-olds, with teenagers seeming to be the only age group on the increase. The analysis also indicated the elderly, like blacks, were more likely to appear in situation comedies. There were few female characters in the age group—a potential misrepresentation of reality.

Cedric Clark has suggested that the mass media have treated minority groups in four phases: nonrecognition, ridicule, regulatory roles, and egalitarian roles. The phases are overlapping to a good degree. After being neither seen nor heard, minority members become visible by being cast as objects of ridicule—lazy and ignorant buffoons. With the achievement of regulatory roles (the black cop, for example), the minority moves over to the right side of society, ready to assume other roles of respect, status, and responsibility—the physician and the soldier, for example. Playing the villain also has been a step up to egalitarian status for minority characters.

If in some ways blacks have won egalitarian status in media dramatizations, a recent study of eighty-one television episodes indicates there still were differences between white and black characters. The blacks were younger, leaner, funnier, and flashier. They were also poorer, jobless, or in jobs below the top echelons. The study also delineated a new trend. Nearly half of the black characters were cast in situation comedies. One-third of the whites had roles in crime shows, one-fifth in action-adventure programs, and one-fifth in situation comedies. And so, although a majority of shows had some blacks, the trend clearly was toward serious programs that featured a single black in a predominantly white program, or a concentration of four or more blacks on a program. Forty-one percent of all blacks were on shows without any white characters, and the characters they portrayed were comical ones. That television blacks talk to blacks and television whites talk to whites more than both groups talk to each other has been a disquieting finding, to say the least.

There still are complaints from the black community that the news is racist. In Detroit in 1983 one civic-minded committee became concerned about the quality of news reporting involving the city's black mayor, Coleman Young, and his administration. The committee established a research team—Professors Lee Becker, Thomas Schwartz, and Sharon West—to examine the coverage in detail and interview officials, news sources, and reporters involved in the stories. The team concluded that the news stories in question did not reveal gross errors or distortions in the facts. Their report suggested much of the conflict was more the result of misunderstanding than racial prejudice on either side. The researchers found that the mayor assumed the news media would go away or lose interest when he refused to hold press conferences or answer questions. To the media, however, his decision not to give information seemed more like stonewalling. If there were a racial bias in the conflict, the team concluded, it was the result of the news system, not the reporters themselves. News is what is exceptional or unique. Being a black mayor in a predominately white society is exceptional. Detroit's mayor Young, as one attorney pointed out to the research team, "is the first black mayor in the history of Detroit. The coverage is unique because he's so unique."

In the same vein, critics of the coverage of the Democratic presidential primaries in 1984 noticed the news media treated candidate Jesse Jackson more as the first black man running for president than as a Democratic candidate with views and policies. In 1983, however, Jackson's success in winning freedom for a captured American flyer had already brought a change in the coverage given him by the news media, which began to treat him as a statesman and potential world leader. The situation illustrated not only one type of racial bias in the news but also the impact television has had on politics and political processes. In the eyes of the press, Jackson's political image as a candidate with little general appeal changed virtually overnight; public opinion quickly followed suit. The power of television to produce what appears to be instant images has led political scientists to observe that it is possible to "package" a political candidate so as to get an incompetent or a tyrant elected to office. Democrats make the argument in relation to Richard Nixon, Republicans in relation to Jimmy Carter. Both men made adroit use of television to overcome political handicaps and win the presidency.

Do the media teach violence and crime? At this writing we seem to be moving closer to the position that they do—although the evidence is far from conclusive (see the box, p. 534). The question is a complicated one.

In 1974 NBC-TV broadcast the movie *Born Innocent,* dramatizing the rape in prison of a young woman by women inmates using a mop handle. Four days later, two young girls, playing on a beach near San Francisco, were raped with a beer bottle by a fifteen-year-old boy and three teenaged girls; they told police they got the idea from a television show they had seen a few nights earlier.

In 1984 NBC presented "The Burning Bed," a dramatization of a real-life story about a woman who, after years of brutal abuse, poured gasoline on and set fire to her husband's bed as he slept. She was not convicted for the deed. In a "copycat" burning incident, one man set fire to his estranged wife. Over 90 percent of her body was burned and she died days later. The man told police "The Burning Bed" had inspired him to "scare" his wife. Another man who had viewed the film beat his wife senseless, saying he wanted to get her before she got him.

While these tragic, brutal crimes seem to be open-and-shut cases of violent media effects, media researchers would quickly point out that only a limited number of violent incidents followed the showing of such films. More than one psychiatrist has argued that normal people do not react violently to films of this type. It is important to ask, therefore, what intervening variables kept most members of the audience from attempting to copy the dramatized rape or burning crimes, and what learning and behavior encouraged the perpetrators? Finally, even with the growing evidence of a positive relationship between media violence and violent behavior, it is important to recognize that the effects of violence are not simple and require much more study. Some of those viewing the violence in "The Burning Bed" seem to have been enlightened about the battered-wife problem. *Newsweek* reported that following the program, battered-wife centers across the country were flooded with calls for help—many from men seeking counseling.

Agenda Setting

One major attempt to understand the effects and functions of mass media public affairs and news content comes from the agenda-setting hypothesis. Agenda setting suggests the media, especially the news media, do not tell the public what to think so much as what to think about. By providing news and public affairs content, the media establish the agenda for public discussion. Agenda research has attempted to test this hypothesis by comparing media news agendas with those held by the public. Other agenda research indicates the media vary from time to time in their agenda-setting capabilities. Newspapers, for example, seem more efficient as agenda setters in the early stages of presidential campaigns, but television takes command and sets the agenda as election day approaches. Agenda-setting research must answer several important questions in the future. As researchers Chaim H. Eyal, James P. Winter, and William F. DeGeorge have indicated, time is a problem for agenda research because the amount of time necessary to bring issues to the public's attention varies so widely. "An oil embargo may suddenly thrust the issue of energy shortage and conservation onto public agendas . . . whereas it may take years for the honesty in government issues to become prominent in public awareness."

Also awaiting detailed examination is the role that entertainment media play in agenda setting. In research reported in 1982 researchers Bradley S. Greenberg, Kimberly Neuendorf, Nancy Buerkel-Rothfuss and Laura Henderson found that television soap operas had significant agenda-setting effects on viewers. They concluded that viewers considered the problems dramatized in the soaps (marriage, divorce, health, etc.) to be the severe problems facing the country today. Just how soap operas and other entertainment media impact on questions of political and social significance is unclear. As Greenberg and his colleagues have suggested, the process may be a complicated one, since each soap opera may be dramatizing different agendas for its audience.

McLuhan and Effects

Perhaps the most unusual suggestions of media effects came from the late Marshall McLuhan, a Canadian scholar who popularized the phrase, "the medium is the message." Roughly translated, McLuhan's theory suggests the various media form our perceptions and therefore affect knowledge. To use the telephone or television is to be affected by them. And the knowledge we get from television is not anything like the knowledge we get from print—newspapers, books, and so on. Since McLuhan's ideas suggest the media determine our modes of thinking, he can be classified as a technological determinist. Despite the fact his early works were provocative, his ideas have not been systematically and scientifically tested. Perhaps in time they will.

Public Concerns and the News Media

Public concerns about the entertainment media have centered on the effects of media violence, the ability of entertainment programs to steal time from work or achievement, and the fear media teach audiences to indulge themselves in unhealthy escapes from reality. Public concerns about the news media, on the other hand, have centered more on news performance rather than on the effects of news reading and watching. They have asked not what the news is doing to us but if the news is accurate, significant, and worth acting on. The public's trust of the news media seems to rise and fall, but the same questions are debated constantly.

Are the News Media Accurate?

An example of the concern for accuracy was precipitated by the assassination attempt on President Reagan on March 30, 1981; television viewers watched in frustration as harried television news professionals broadcast error after error in reporting the event. John Hinckley, the suspected assassin, was first thirty years old—then younger. The President was not hurt, then he was in a hospital—then undergoing open heart surgery—when he was not. Perhaps the most senseless error came with the report presidential press secretary James Brady died from bullet wounds when, in fact, he had not.

Research on the accuracy of news stories dates back to the 1930s. The research completed to date, some forty or more studies, is far from definitive but it does indicate that between 40 and 60 percent of all newspaper stories contain at least one error. One study indicates newspaper sports and society stories have the fewest errors (77 and 90 percent accurate). Still other research suggests that by far the most newspaper errors fall into a gray area of interpretation, or as Professor William Tillinghast has written, "the subjective errors of omission, misquotes, headline distortions, underemphasis and overemphasis."

One major contributor of error in news is the news source itself. During the Three Mile Island atomic plant breakdown, the Boston *Herald American* published pictures of clocks, showing different times, to indicate the many shifts and changes made during the day in the government's news releases. The Associated Press rewrote its lead for that news

The challenge of reporting: Moments after this picture was taken, President Reagan and others were shot in an assassination attempt. In the chaos that followed, reporters had to work long and hard to learn what had happened. Even with hindsight, it is difficult to know from which point the shots came, who in the picture was wounded, how badly, and in what manner.

story twenty-eight times one afternoon just to keep abreast of the government's "facts." In many instances, the news media are dependent on a news source that simply will not or cannot be accurate. Many of the errors reported by television news following the attempt on President Reagan's life, for example, came from government sources—the White House press staff, which was in turmoil without its wounded leader, James Brady. The report of Brady's death, meanwhile, came from a known and trusted government source, according to CBS reporter Phil Jones, who broadcast the story. An undeniable reporter's error came from NBC's Chris Wallace, however, who misunderstood (through semantic noise?) the phrase "open chest surgery" and reported "open heart" as the type of surgery the president was undergoing at the time.

To ascertain error in newspaper news reporting, researchers usually ask the people who were in the stories, or the sources of news, to judge whether the published stories are accurate or erroneous. In judging news error, then, it is important to consider the judgment of the news sources themselves. Tillinghast has reported that the sources in news stories are no more likely to find errors in stories written by young reporters than in those written by older professionals. But at the same time,

Who Was That Unmasked Man?

One intriguing charge made against the news media has come from Robert King, a professor of English literature, who has pointed out political journalism often becomes "hero" journalism. King has caught more than one journalist in the act of treating political figures melodramatically, the way the old radio programs treated the Lone Ranger.

"Where's the masked man?" one radio show character would ask after the villain was vanquished and things had quieted down. "Why he's gone," would come the reply, as a hearty "Hi yo" cry to the mighty Silver came floating back, and the William Tell theme came "up and over."

In much the same heroic "he's gone" theme, King has pointed out, *Newsweek* described Richard Nixon's departure from Washington following political disgrace and his resignation:

> He spoke with thickening voice of his past and his future— 'Only if you have been in the deepest valley can you ever know how magnificent it is to be on the highest mountain.'
>
> And then he was gone, walking down a red carpet on the south lawn to his helicopter Army One.

As King noted, Washington *Post* reporters Robert Woodward and Carl Bernstein in *The Final Days,* also reported the departure with a quote and a heroic ending:

> "And so, we leave with high hopes, in good spirits and with deep humility, and with very much gratefulness in our hearts. . . ."
> And he was gone.

The theme is not reserved for Richard Nixon. King has noted that *Time,* describing the appearance of Senator Edward Kennedy on the platform with President Carter at the 1980 Democratic National Convention, wrote:

> Finally, Senator Kennedy appeared, striding tight-lipped through the joyous crush to shake the President's hand and wave solemnly at the throng. . . . After barely three minutes Kennedy tried to leave; the roar of the crowd . . . brought him back for one last, brief pose with the President. And then he was gone, plunging into the night. . . .

King has suggested the Lone Ranger hero formula is a "false sentimentality that the harsher reality does not allow." Journalists should not conspire with "image builders in Washington," King has argued, "and help them work their dubious trade."

news sources in one study found fewer errors in stories if the sources had considerable contact with the reporters before the story was written. Some of the problems of inaccuracies may be due, then, to the news source's perception of what reporters can or may do when they write the story. Evidently, if the person in the news, the source, perceives the reporter as hasty or careless, then the source is more likely to find errors in the story than if the reporter gave a professional, calm, and collected impression.

There is much to learn about errors in news reporting. As of yet, there seems to be no study comparing the ability of news professionals with the ability of other professionals—in law or medicine, for example—to receive and write information without error. In such a test, could the average citizen do as well as the average news professional in taking accurate notes of a simple telephone conversation? It seems unlikely.

Meanwhile, a 1978 study by Joseph Scalon concluded that news reporting in six major crisis events produced twenty-three specific and verifiable errors—independent of news source judgment—but that the news stories on the whole did give accurate reports of the events. Reporting, it seems, does not have to be errorless to be accurate.

Are the News Media Gullible?

In 1981 the three major television networks reported that hit teams, formed by Libyan leader Muammar Qaddafi to assassinate President Reagan and other high officials, had been sent into the United States. The announcement shook the nation. The so-called Libyan plot never was confirmed, however. Was the story a real news story—with substance? Did some enemy leak it, just to make the U.S. and the American news media look foolish? Or did the gullible media simply swallow a false tale?

Many critics would opt for the gullible explanation. Nobel prize winning economist Milton Friedman might be one. In 1982 U.S. Food and Drug Administration (FDA) officials announced the arrival in this country of beta blocker drugs that could sustain heart attack patients by pacing their heart beats. The FDA called the arrival a great breakthrough, and the news media echoed the sentiment. But Friedman called the self-congratulatory publicity highly misleading. Beta blockers had been successful for years in other countries, he noted, and it was the FDA's bureaucratic delay that had kept them out of the country while thousands of Americans died early deaths, unnecessarily. That the FDA finally had allowed beta blockers in could hardly be called a breakthrough, he argued. He also thought the press should have investigated before passing on the FDA's self-serving version of the story. In his *Newsweek* column, Friedman concluded:

> The news media frequently find it easier to rewrite press releases than to engage in . . . investigative reporting . . . [and often] serve as unpaid press agents for government agencies rather than as the public's eyes and ears.

In the early 1980s many in the New York City news media left themselves open for even more damning charges of gullibility. Joseph Skaggs, of the School of Visual Arts in New York, concocted a hoax with the help of friends and students. They staged a false press conference featuring "entomologist" Dr. Josef Gregor, who supposedly had discovered a superstrain of cockroaches from which he learned to manufacture pills to cure allergies and other ailments—including the common cold. With manufactured press releases, pictures of cockroaches, a cockroach birthday cake, and invitations to the news media, Skaggs and associates attracted every major news organization in New York to their press conference. His performance as Dr. Gregor and his demonstration of the cockroach pills (actually vitamins) were so convincing many reporters missed some "obvious" references to a short story by Kafka, and the bogus press conference became news. UPI put the story on the wire and into some one hundred newspapers. Television and radio stations also ran the story.

The question of how and why news professionals choose the news they publish has been addressed by a considerable body of gatekeeper research, which focuses on the decisions and behavior of reporters and editors within the news organization. One consistent finding from gatekeeper studies is that deadline and competitive pressure is the overriding concern of the news gatekeeper. When the gatekeeper errs, it usually is due to that pressure. Only a moment's reflection is needed to see how deadline pressure could affect the decision to report the hit team, beta blocker, and cockroach cold pill stories.

It is important to recall, too, that even seasoned news personnel usually only have limited knowledge of technical fields—biology, chemistry, engineering, medicine—or the fine arts. (See chapter 14 for a public relations view of this problem.) The effects of beta blockers and Skaggs's references to Kafka's *The Metamorphosis,* while obvious in hindsight and to those educated in literature, were lost on reporters more comfortable with press law, crime coverage, interviewing, and city politics. And, too, one must ask how the news media, even network television news reporters, could have checked the story of the Libyan hit team? By calling Qaddafi? With the choice to run it or ignore it, should they have ignored it?

There is good reason to believe, as Friedman has suggested, that journalists, for these and other reasons, too often do rely on experts. The Dr. Gregors and the usually authoritative agencies such as the Federal Drug Administration do seem a safe "hook" on which to hang a good story. There has been more than one research study to suggest the news media do not step out and survey the environment in technical fields but waits instead for the official governmental release before publishing the news.

"It's not a bad idea to remind journalists where their flaws are," media observer Ben Bagdikian told the *Chronicle of Higher Education* following the Dr. Gregor hoax. If the hoax "reveals" that the press "got fooled I suspect it might do some good." Fortunately, checking and re-checking remains an important part of the journalistic profession and an ongoing part of journalism education. The challenge for the news media is to improve its methods of investigation, especially in areas where journalists have little expertise.

Are the News Media Biased?

"How much," one Massachusetts reader asked an editor in that state, "does the Kennedy family pay the American press for continuous publicity?" If the media had not made constant references (in jokes and news) to former President Gerald Ford as bumbling and inept, critics have argued, he might have served a second term as president. Other than political bias, the news media, especially newspapers, also have been accused of several other types of bias—being a tool of the establishment, against big business, against organized labor, or being the voice of the masses. It has been suggested for some time that news editors and publishers are conservative while the news reporters are liberal. (The former are business executives while the latter are working men and women.)

There is no doubt that the news media are, *in some ways at least,* biased. It is the function of media research to discover and understand how biased they are, in what manner, and why.

Sociologist Warren Breed has provided a research basis for the understanding of news organization bias. From intensive interviews with some 120 news reporters, Breed discovered that newspapers have a socialization process that teaches reporters the norms of the paper he or she works for. Reporters are never told to slant news copy, but they learn their newspaper's policies by osmosis. The reporter fashions his or her own stories after those seen in the paper. The editing of stories gives clear clues as to what is and is not expected, as do instructions for covering stories. A lukewarm reception to a story covering a union strike but an emergency call to rush to cover the signing of a contract that will bring a new industrial firm to town conveys much about policy or bias. Those who learn and adhere to the paper's policies are rewarded and promoted; those who do not remain in the lower ranks or move on. And it all, as Breed has noted, is handled in a *democratic* way, with most policy differences settled by debate and suggestion rather than direct order from superiors.

Breed has concluded that while the problem of bias does exist, and that it contravenes journalistic norms, organizational bias usually offsets only policy stories, not all news stories. Just what stories might be affected by newspaper policy, and what news bias might be published or broadcast as a result, and how general or specific is the resulting bias remain important subjects for mass communication research.

Are the News Media Callous and Arrogant?

In 1981 reporters covering the departure from the Reagan administration of national security advisor Richard Allen dangled from trees to peer into Allen's bedroom window to snap pictures. A large crowd of reporters encamped on Allen's lawn, and even thrust microphones in front of his six-year-old daughter.

The same year, the Associated Press reported hundreds of journalists from around the world suddenly appeared in Atlanta to cover the mysterious slayings of more than twenty black children. Reporters were everywhere, scribbling notes at every corner, interviewing on the sidewalks with television cameras. A flock of reporters and nine television cameras covered the funeral of one of the young murder victims. When it was determined a total of twenty-eight children had been victims of the Atlanta murderer, the police debated arresting and charging Wayne Williams. They watched and followed him day and night for two and a half weeks. The national and international press watched and followed, too.

Many felt one of the greatest tragedies of the entire Iranian hostage crisis was the pressure put on hostage relatives by reporters continually pressing for interviews. Many of the relatives felt they were grilled for answers—even by polite reporters.

There is much to learn about the thundering herd of reporters who suddenly appear to cover the big story. Does the big news break create reporter behavior like that of shoppers at a bargain sale? Like that of fortune seekers at a gold rush?

The news organization itself again may give a clue. In 1977 a team of three media researchers spent fourteen weeks observing the operations of a large metropolitan television newsroom. Charles Bantz, Suzanne McCorkle, and Robert Baade concluded the television news department can resemble a news factory more than a creative enterprise. Tasks are divided along a news production line, with reporters being sent out to bring in chunks of news that are turned over to editors. The editors edit and polish the chunks, then pass them along to those who assemble more news chunks into the newscast. A result of the news assembly line

The Objective, the Callous, the Human Thing To Do

One of the continuing problems for the news profession is knowing when the journalist, including the photographer, should step out of the role of observer and recorder and into the role of participant and helper. The problem arose again in 1983 when an unemployed roofer called a television station in Anniston, Alabama, and threatened to set himself on fire to protest the nation's dismal unemployment problem, and the fact he also was out of work. News director Phil Cox of WMHA-TV notified the police of the four phone calls, then finally sent a camera crew to the scene—the town square in Jacksonville, south of Anniston—to help police locate and apprehend the man.

The Jacksonville police patrolled the square for forty-five minutes, but found no one fitting the roofer's description. They returned to headquarters before the two-person camera crew and the roofer arrived. The roofer asked the two newsmen if they wanted to "see someone burn," then stooped, soaked his jeans with lighter fluid, and lit them with a match. The camera crew recorded the spreading of the lighter fluid and the strike of the match, and photographed the flames as they creeped up the roofer's pant leg, then exploded into a fireball. Then the man panicked and ran. The camera crew, shocked that the police had not arrived, helped subdue the flames. The roofer suffered second- and third-degree burns over more than half of his body, but was in fair condition following hospitalization and, in time, recovered from the burns.

WHMA-TV cameraman Ronald Simmons told *Newsweek,* "My job is to record events as they happen. I thought, 'The police are going to arrive. I'm going to have video of them subduing this guy.' " From his point of view he seems to have been playing an ethical role, informing the people of a significant event without interfering in police procedures.

Local citizens and professional journalists alike criticized the WHMA-TV camera crew for letting the situation get out of hand. More than one news organization reported its policy for dealing with such calls was to refuse to send a camera crew and to notify police. Other news professionals, and police, quickly asked if the WHMA-TV's cameras should have been turned on and if the camera crew should not have, at least, dropped their equipment and subdued the roofer when he began spreading lighter fluid over his jeans.

The situation again underscored the problem journalists sometimes have knowing when they should report events and when they should try to prevent them. Being objective can mean being callous and indifferent, while becoming involved can mean being biased and/or manipulating events.

---

is it discourages personal involvement in stories, the researchers decided. The factory stresses productivity, not distinctive work. "Doing one's assignment and doing it on time" and "getting the news" are the important values.

A major concern has been that news reporters are callous and unthinking. In covering the funeral of young David Kennedy (son of the late Senator Robert Kennedy) who was found dead in a Florida motel in 1984, camera reporters pressed close behind the casket and behind David's brother Joe as he and funeral attendants placed the casket in the hearse. Note the cameras in the foreground, at the right.

Reporters in Atlanta helped police search for bodies. At times, those covering the Iranian hostage relatives acted as members of the family, babysitting and helping out with chores. Reporters are human. But more research is needed to understand just how and when getting the news can transform them into a thundering herd.

Do the News Media Make Up News?

The belief persists that many news stories are concocted or grossly exaggerated. The first successful newspaper in America, John Campbell's Boston *News-Letter,* carried a fictitious story of a maiden captured by Indians at a spring. As it turned out, the young lady had stayed too long with her boyfriend and created the story to excuse her tardy return.

One of the most successful concoctions appeared in the New York *Sun* in the 1830s. A *Sun* writer, Richard Adams Locke, convinced a large number of readers and editors of other papers that a new telescope revealed there were batlike creatures living on the moon. In 1972 the San Francisco *Examiner* printed a five-part series by an experienced reporter before the paper learned the China stories all had been written in Hong Kong. The notable fictitious story of recent years came in 1981, when the Washington *Post* returned a Pulitzer Prize awarded for reporter Janet Cooke for her reports of ''Jimmy's World,'' a completely fabricated story of an eight-year-old heroin addict.

Do journalists make up stories? Unfortunately, some do, sometimes. But the problem is not a news media exclusive. Consider the following examples from medical research:

John Long, a researcher working under a $750,000 federal grant at Massachusetts General Hospital, for seven years forged data in studies of a cell line of Hodgkin's disease. The research subsequently was proved absolutely worthless.

Yale University researcher Vijay Soman plagerized a paper and fabricated data to win a total of $100,000 for his 1980 research alone. Soman's papers reporting the falsified research were recalled.

At Boston University, Marc Straus was awarded $1 million in several cancer research grants for work that was shown to carry repeated falsifications. He resigned under fire.

There also are countless cases of people who have engaged in medical practice without a license or degree.

The news hoax, like these medical hoaxes, seems to be a problem more of personality than of the individual's profession. As Washington *Post* editor Benjamin Bradlee told *Newsweek* following the "Jimmy's World" story, "You cannot make a rule that is going to . . . save you from a pathological liar." (The *Post* did, nevertheless, attempt to improve communication with newer and younger staff members and to communicate the paper's ideals and responsibilities with them through brown bag lunches and other means.)

Following the "Jimmy's World" hoax, the Washington *Post* and the news media found themselves in a position similar to that of Johnson & Johnson after the infamous Tylenol cyanide murders. The *Post* and the press had not intended to harm the public, but their products and names were tainted. The trust they hoped to build and hold onto was in grave jeopardy. As respected editor Norman Isaacs of the National News Council told *Time* magazine, the Pulitzer Prize hoax was a "punch to the solar plexis" of journalism. Immediately following disclosure of the hoax, a *Newsweek* poll revealed 33 percent of Americans believed news reporters "often make things up," while only 5 percent were willing to say they believed "almost all" of what they heard and read in the news media (see figure 18.1). When we realize that communication effects research consistently finds that the image of the communicator is an important factor in delivering the news and influencing attitudes, we know how important it is for the news media to be credible.

Questions of news media accuracy, gullibility, bias, arrogance, and reliability all challenge media credibility, and make the job of the news reporter and news editor all the more difficult. They also point to the most important problems of successful news media operation: the need for continuing responsible performance to win the respect of the reading, listening, and viewing public day after day after day.

Figure 18.1

A Newsweek Poll: How the News Media Rate
For this NEWSWEEK Poll, The Gallup Organization conducted 760 telephone interviews between April 22 and 23. The margin of error is plus or minus 4 percentage points. Percentages may not add up to 100 because "don't know" responses have been eliminated.

How would you rate the honesty and ethical standards of people in these different fields?

	High	Average	Low
Clergy	71%	22%	4%
Physicians	58	35	6
Police	52	37	9
Journalists	38	44	13
Business executives	31	49	15
Congressmen	16	44	34
Advertising executives	12	45	33

How much of what you hear and read in the news media can you believe?

Almost all 5%   Most 33%   Only some 52%   Very little 9%

Do you think the Janet Cooke hoax was an isolated incident or do reporters often make things up?*

Isolated incident   58%   Often make things up   33%

How good a job do different media do in providing accurate, unbiased news accounts?

	Excellent/Good	Fair/Poor
Network television	71%	29%
Local television	69	31
News magazines	66	34
Daily newspapers	57	43
Personality/Show-business publications	21	79

Should reporters always reveal their sources or should they be allowed to keep them confidential if that is the only way they can get a story?

Always reveal   13%   Sometimes keep confidential   83%

*Asked only of the 70 percent of the NEWSWEEK sample who said they had heard about the Janet Cooke hoax.
Chart: Rebecca Pritt, Robert George. Copyright 1981 by *Newsweek*, Inc. All rights reserved. Reprinted by permission.

Careers in Mass Communication Research

Mass communications research generally requires a background in research training. Also required is competency in survey, experimental, and content analysis research, with knowledge and skills associated with the most sophisticated statistical methods and computer-supported research.

Those who plan to enter commercial research probably will find college studies in business and marketing research to their advantage while theoretical researchers will want to lean more toward psychology, sociology, social psychology, and public opinion. While commercial researchers—including those who wish to enter research with a daily newspaper—might decide to conclude their training at the bachelor's or master's level; theoretical researchers will find the Ph.D. degree much more important.

Both commercial and theoretical research show great career promise for the future. Large newspapers now maintain their own research staff for political polls, market studies, and readership research. Broadcasting stations, usually not as well-situated financially as newspapers, turn to research agencies or individuals for audience information and acceptance of their programming. There also is a significant group of large, but independent industrial agencies and corporations that operate on a nonprofit basis, servicing government and industry with research services.

Advertising agencies, and advertising departments of large companies, offer good research career opportunities. Ad agency research salaries ranged from $14,000 to $35,000 a year in the early 1980s. And some well-qualified graduates (with a master's degree, perhaps) have entered the field at higher than minimum salary. Research-trained media graduates usually attract a higher salary than their colleagues who are trained in media or media management skills. And there always seems to be more demand for them—since the supply usually is limited.

The publish or perish admonition for academic positions signals the importance of research in university and college education. In general, beginning academic teach/research salaries are comparable to those for researchers in ad agencies. But again, basic requirements include a Ph.D.

Summary

Mass communications research is behavioral science research that attempts to produce reliable and valid predictions about media operations and media associated behavior. Since it tests its hypotheses against mathematical—statistical—models, it is a quantitative science. Since it draws from psychology, sociology, and political science, it is considered an interdisciplinary science.

There are four basic types of mass communication research methods:

1. Survey and field studies that investigate audiences and/or situations related to the media.
2. Experiments in the laboratory or the field that manipulate variables for study.
3. Content analysis that allows objective, systematic, and quantitative measurement of media content.

There are two distinct types of mass communication research: theoretical and institutional or commercial. Theoretical research focuses on the process and effects of media communication while commercial media research tends to investigate audiences and ways to produce messages that attract audiences.

Theoreticians have investigated the gatekeeper, or decision maker, in the media organization, especially the news organization. Media organizations also have been an important object of scientific research, as have news, information, and product diffusion. Uses and gratifications research raises the question of what people do with media rather than what media do to people. Effects research has included the investigation of the impact of violence on the audience. Agenda-setting research holds that the media more or less establish the topics of interest for society. Readership studies are performed by theoretical and commercial researchers alike to understand who in the audience reads what in a publication, and what nonreaders are like, and why.

Commercial researchers are more active in life-style research, which attempts to understand how individual life-styles (time of reading or viewing, musical tastes, etc.) affect media habits. Psychographics, a type of life-style research, focuses closely on attitudes and behavior—to understand preferences for products and media content and better understand how to market products to various types of individuals.

Marketing research studies consumers and the entire range of problems that arise as a marketing strategy is developed for a product.

The public's most persistent concern about the mass media is media effects, or what the media do to the people. The fears of propaganda effectiveness during the two World Wars enhanced the idea of a powerful press. The 1938 "War of the Worlds" broadcast by CBS contributed to the theory. Social scientists, however, began to question the all-powerful theory; instead of it, they created a limited effects theory, which held that if the media could confer status and enforce social norms, their basic effect was reinforcement.

Research in the 1960s and 1970s seemed to confirm the limited effects model. In the 1970s, however, several researchers began to challenge the idea of a weak mass media as an overgeneralization. As Elisabeth Noelle-Neumann has pointed out, most media studies did not take into account the ubiquity of the mass media, the accumulation of messages that occurs in the real world, and the consonance of news reports. Investigations continue on the effects of violence on audiences, and the problems of agenda setting.

Questions concerning news media performance have included the following:

1. Are the news media accurate?
2. Are the news media gullible?
3. Are the news media biased?
4. Are the news media callous and arrogant?
5. Do the media make up news?

Questions for Discussion

1. The a priori nature of the examples given in the discussion of the news media can be challenged. How would scientific investigation attack the charges made by Milton Friedman? By Joseph Skaggs? What would it take to prove that the news media as a rule do not investigate stories properly?

2. The Bandura, Ross, and Ross study is a good example of the methodologically refined work done on media effects since World War II. Judging from Elisabeth Noelle-Neumann's criticism, what seems to be wrong with this research?

3. What would it take for America to have another "invasion from Mars?"

4. The test of knowledge gained from the media probably could be charged with being biased. (See pp. 532–33.) Can you list twenty names, not using your personal friends, who can be said to be important, and whom you did not hear about from the media?

References

Backstrom, Charles H., and Gerald D. Hursh. *Survey Research.* Evanston: Northwestern University Press, 1963.

Bandura, Albert, Dorothea Ross, and Sheila Ross. "Imitation of Film-Mediated Aggressive Models." *Journal of Abnormal and Social Psychology* 66, no. 1 (1963): 3–11.

Bantz, Charles R., Suzanne McCorkle, and Robert C. Baade. "The News Factory." In *Mass Communication Review Yearbook* 2, edited by G. Cleveland Wilhoit and Harold de Bock. Beverly Hills: Sage Publications, 1980.

Becker, Lee B., Thomas A. Schwartz, and Sharon C. West. "A Report on Media Coverage of Magnum and Vista." Paper for the Move Detroit Forward Committee, January 1984.

Breed, Warren. "Social Control in the News Room." *Social Forces* 33 (1955): 326–35.

Budd, Richard W., Robert K. Thorp, and Lewis Donohew. *Content Analysis of Communications.* New York: Macmillan, 1967.

"The Camera's Cold Eye." *Newsweek,* March 21, 1983, 53.

Cantril, Hadley. "The Invasion from Mars." In *The Process and Effects of Mass Communication,* edited by Wilbur Schramm. Urbana: The University of Illinois Press, 1954.

"Covering Three Mile Island." *Newsweek,* April 16, 1979, 93.

Cowan, Geoffrey. *See No Evil.* New York: Simon and Schuster, 1978.

Dennis, Everette E. *The Media Society.* Dubuque, Iowa: Wm. C. Brown Publishers, 1978.

"Did the Media 'Get' Allen?" *Newsweek,* January 18, 1982, 93.

Dolman, Joe. "Atlanta Child Murders Pose Classic Challenge to Editorial Judgment." *The Quill,* November 1981, 24–26.

"A Fraud in the Pulitzers." *Time,* April 27, 1981, 52.

Friedman, Milton. "Investigative Reporting?" *Newsweek,* January 11, 1982, 56.

Gerbner, George, and Larry P. Gross. "Living with Television: The Violence Profile." *Journal of Communication* 26, no. 2 (Spring 1976): 172–99.

Gieber, Walter. "News Is What Newspapermen Make It." In *People, Society, and Mass Communication,* edited by Lewis Anthony Dexter and David Manning White. Glencoe, Ill.: The Free Press, 1964.

Greenberg, Bradley S. *Life on Television.* Norwood: Ablex, 1980.

———, and E. B. Parker. *The Kennedy Assassination and the American Public: Social Communication in Crisis.* Stanford, Calif.: Stanford University Press, 1965.

———, Kimberly Neuendorf, Nancy Buerkel-Rothfuss, and Laura Henderson. "The Soaps: What's On and Who Cares?" *Journal of Broadcasting* 26, no. 2 (Spring 1982):519–35.

Guzda, M. K. "A Need to Reevaluate." *Editor & Publisher,* June 30, 1984, 15.

Haskins, Jack B. *How to Evaluate Mass Communications.* New York: Advertising Research Foundation, 1968.

Hovland, Carl I., Arthur A. Lumsdaine, and Fred D. Sheffield. "The Effect of Presenting 'One Side' versus 'Both Sides'." In *The Process and Effects of Mass Communication,* edited by Wilbur Schramm. Urbana: University of Illinois Press, 1954.

Kerlinger, Fred N. *Foundations of Behavioral Research.* New York: Holt, Rinehart and Winston, 1964.

King, Robert L. " 'And then he was gone . . . ' " *Columbia Journalism Review,* January/February 1981, 51.

Lang, Kurt, and Gladys Lang. "The Unique Perspective of Television: A Pilot Study." *American Sociological Review* 18, no. 1 (1953): 3–12.

Lowenthal, Leo. "Historical Perspectives of Popular Culture." In *Mass Culture,* edited by Bernard Rosenberg and David Manning White. Glencoe, Ill.: The Free Press, 1957.

McCombs, Maxwell, and Donald L. Shaw. "A Report on Agenda-Setting Research." Paper presented to Association for Education in Journalism, Theory and Methodology Division, San Diego, Calif. August 18–21, 1974.

McDonald, Kim. "A 'Superstrain' of Cockroaches Hoodwinks News Organizations." *The Chronicle of Higher Education,* October 21, 1981, 9.

Mott, Frank. *American Journalism.* New York: Macmillan, 1962.

Poindexter, Paula M. "Daily Newspaper Non-Readers: Why They Don't Read." *Journalism Quarterly* 56, no. 4 (1979): 764–70.

Schramm, Wilbur, and William E. Porter. *Men, Women, Messages, and Media.* 2nd ed., New York: Harper and Row, 1982.

"A Searching of Conscience." *Newsweek,* May 4, 1981, 50–53.

Singletary, Michael. "Accuracy in News Reporting, A Review of the Research." *ANPA News Research Report No. 25,* January 25, 1980.

"The Story of a Lifetime." *Newsweek,* February 2, 1981, 76–77.

"Teddy and the Press." *Newsweek,* October 8, 1979, 86.

Tillinghast, William A. "Newspaper Error: Causes, Source Perception and Reporter Response." Paper presented to the Newspaper Division, Association for Education in Journalism Annual Convention, East Lansing, Mich., August, 1981.

"TV Entertainment Study Draws Media Attention." *Business and the Media,* Spring 1981, 4–5.

Weaver, David H., and Richard G. Gray. "Journalism and Mass Communication Research in the United States." In *Mass Communication Review Yearbook 1,* edited by G. Cleveland Wilhoit and Harold de Bock. Beverly Hills: Sage Publications, 1980.

Weisman, John. "Why American TV Is so Vulnerable to Foreign Propaganda." *TV Guide,* June 12, 1982, 4–16.

White, David Manning. "The Gatekeeper: A Case Study in the Selection of News." *Journalism Quarterly* 27, no. 4 (1950):383–390.

Wright, John W. *The American Almanac of Jobs and Salaries.* New York: Avon, 1982.

Chapter
19

The Mass Media, Society, and the Future

Observers believe that the communication revolution is just beginning. The homes of tomorrow will have access to even greater amounts of entertainment and information, with much better control of it.

Toward Even More Diversification

The system is in place. We have used it for years. But we cannot sit back, relax, and enjoy it. Like the proverbial river, the mass media system is changing—even as we talk about it. As discussed earlier, the major change is a shift in emphasis from a system dedicated to distributing mass messages through mass communication media to diversification of messages and services. Already newspapers, magazines, radio, and cable television send messages to special interest groups and individuals. With this shift another, more basic, change is happening. There are exciting changes in communication technology, and more people are finding more uses for individual media (telephones, recorders, personal computers) alongside the mass media.

Experts predict the home of the future not only will get more information, but more information to the individual's liking. Also through developing technology, audiences will have greater opportunity to control what messages are received. In medieval Europe the town crier informed the population of important news. Wandering minstrels walked by with musical entertainment. And the audience had little control over their coming and going. The mass media multiplied the voices of the criers and minstrels, and, to be overly simplistic, made important messages more available to society as a whole. But the evolving media system promises to free individuals from being followers of the criers and singers to become controllers of their works. The modern media revolution promises to put a hundred, a thousand different town criers and minstrels into audience homes. And the recitation or performance of any of them cannot begin until the individual gives the order—pushes the button—to raise the electronic curtain. Some of the trends supporting this change have been discussed but are worth mentioning again.

Cable television, with all its problems, still has the capability of delivering programs through one hundred channels and has great potential for becoming, like the modern magazine, a premier servant of the special interest audience. While recent economic conditions have forced the cable industry into a more conservative stance, an inexpensive method for measuring specialized channel audiences and more realistic terms from city governments for franchises could produce considerable growth in cable in the late 1980s.

Low-power television (LPTV) promises to give the viewer the electronic equivalent of a neighborhood or small-town newspaper. If advertising support develops for the new, low-power stations, viewers may have access not only to discussion of neighborhood news and issues, but to school and neighborhood sporting events as well (Little League, etc).

Direct broadcasting satellites (DBS), as noted in chapter 12, were authorized by the FCC to provide another new television programming service for home viewers. As this book went to press DBS was struggling to find its niche within the communication system. It was faced with the problems of creating programming to compete with network television, cable, and video cassette movies. The high costs ($300 million) of establishing a nationwide DBS service also slowed growth in the mid-1980s. In 1984, with the one DBS company in business—United Satellite Communications, Inc.—having trouble raising capital, RCA dropped its plans for a high-power DBS system in favor of a smaller, lower-powered one that could be used for other kinds of satellite operation if home entertainment possibilities faded.

HDTV, or high definition for television, is a long-needed renovation of the current television picture. The addition of color has been the only major improvement in the 525 line picture of the 1950s. The existing picture system is extremely coarse (especially for reading textual material) and gives poor definition in televised night scenes. It also is so narrow that it can show little more than twenty yards of a football field, for example. Movie producers must reduce their 35mm films by 8 percent in width to show them on television.

High definition television, which has much sharper picture definition and a better perspective (note the size and shape of the screen in the center), will bring better television to viewers in the future.

NHK Research Laboratories in Japan, in association with CBS, has developed a high-definition system that utilizes 1,125 lines in the picture, a five to three picture ratio (as opposed to the current four to three), and a scanning system that improves picture definition as much as five times. The new, crisper, panoramic HDTV pictures may not be available for some time, however. CBS was unable to persuade the FCC to include the system in the new DBS broadcasting specifications; also, converting to HDTV would mean scrapping all existing television technology, including all sets in use.

Optical fiber transmission of signals is developing rapidly. Fine strands of glass fiber—very inexpensive to manufacture—are able to carry more signals with much less channel noise and signal leakage than the traditional copper wires. One optical glass fiber can carry the equivalent of 672 telephone conversations, and cables of twelve fibers have been found reliable in Bell company experiments. One expert estimates that the use of fiber optics will not only reduce the already low error factor in computers, but also allow new computers to operate ten times faster than the ones now in use. It is predicted that fiber optics will increase our capacity to transmit information from point to point so rapidly that by the year 2000 it will be possible to send and receive the thirty volumes of the *Encyclopaedia Britannica* in one-tenth of a second. Adding optical fiber to cable television will increase greatly the variety and quality of available messages.

Several innovations seem likely to change the course of home entertainment, much the way the phonograph, and then radio, did in the first half of the century.

Video tape and video discs, as noted in chapter 12, have greatly improved the viewer's control over what he or she views. While the video disc and disc player are fading from the home market, the future of the video cassette recorder seems bright indeed. Predictions are that the boom in VCR sales will continue and that the VCR's ability to "time shift" television programs for later viewing, to present movies more recent than those on cable, and to play video music tapes as well as "how to" exercise and information tapes will put the machine in one-third of all households by 1987.

Television stereo sound should prove a welcome addition to the VCR. Following authorization by the FCC in 1984, some manufacturers promised sets with four speaker systems with their next model change.

Microbooks, or books engraved on microchips and sold for about twenty cents, are a technical possibility. Viewed through television set terminals, or projected on the ceiling by those who wish to read in bed, the microbook could revolutionize book reading and distribution.

Video games already have come under fire as a health hazard, and, in some cases, for carrying lewd content. Other than the many arcade games around the country, home computer game programs offer everything from "Star Wars" to golf, football, backgammon, and auto racing. But as one advertising executive has put it, we have hardly scratched the surface in creating games. The possibility that computerized games can become national pastimes is very real. However, there is no reason to believe they will replace existing athletic games.

Teletext is the use of television technology to transmit graphics and textual (reading) material to television screens in homes and offices. It was first used in the news and weather channels of cable. At present there are about seventy teletext newspaper channels on cable television across the country. Teletext can present two hundred pages of information and may be transmitted to home screens by over-the-air television stations as well. The low-cost teletext signal is sent "piggyback" with the regular color signal and is received by those with special decoders. It is, therefore, a low-cost, second source of advertising revenue for the local television station. Experiments have provided a variety of information for receivers: stock market reports, listings of air fares, and sports scores. The National Captioning Institute offered the first nationwide teletext service when it began close captioning of ABC-TV news for the hearing impaired. (See figure 19.1.)

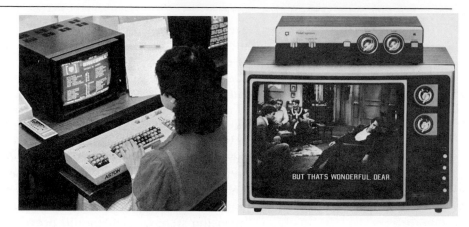

Figure 19.1 (*Left*) A teletext operator preparing sports information for distribution. (*Right*) One use of teletext for home viewers, closed caption television for the deaf.

BUT THATS WONDERFUL, DEAR.

Videotext is a communication medium that operates through a telephone network to connect television terminals to graphics and other information in a central computer. Videotext is a two-way system, with those at home typing instructions onto a keyboard to call up data in a central computer, and/or using the computer in a dozen or more other ways. AT&T and CBS, in cooperation with eighty national advertisers and sixteen New York ad agencies, launched an experimental videotext system in New Jersey in the early 1980s. The Knight-Ridder newspaper chain inaugerated a full-blown videotext system, Viewdata in Miami, Florida, in 1982. Viewdata offers seventy-five thousand pages of advertising, news, restaurant menus, and movie reviews—with such computer services as telebanking, teleshopping, computer games and quizzes for a monthly subscription price of fifteen to forty dollars, or about the same price as a subscription to cable television.

The electronic computer, whether in a central location serving a network of subscribers or in the home, is predicted to be at the forefront in the communications revolution. The electronic computer established itself as a miracle of information and calculations in the 1960s and 1970s. The low-cost microcomputer—which utilizes engraved microchips as processors—entered the consumer market so rapidly in the early 1980s that the 150 or so brands available had trouble finding shelf space in computer stores. About two million had been sold by 1983. Entrepreneur H. Ross Perot estimates there will be nine million in American homes by 1990, and that computer programs for youngsters will be so common they will be sold in toy stores.

The Electronic Cottage

The list of information services possible with the home computer is even more impressive. Again, using either a home computer attached to outside data banks by a telephone line, or with a terminal connected to a centralized computer also connected to other data banks, families have ready access to:

1. specialized directories that help find business associates, old classmates, tennis or chess partners, or dates;
2. goods and services directories, including ready reference to *Consumers Union* tests of merchandise, current grocery or clothing sales, repair services, and Yellow Pages references;
3. catalogue shopping services, including want ads with picture demonstrations of goods and services, ordering, delivery, and payment of goods (the Sears, Roebuck catalogue has been on memory disc for many months now);
4. calendars of local events, with lists of local museum shows, July Fourth fireworks, and club meetings, for example;
5. organizational news and information indexes, with notes on church, social, and civic groups, and means of contacting them;
6. public information connections, with specific information on where and how to make changes, apply for benefits, get redress—all without having to telephone government offices;
7. general information services, allowing at-home search of library stacks, the display of a book on video screen, and the return of it without going to the library (computerized card catalogues and checkout of books have been used in many libraries for ten years).

Detailed print media news services have been possible almost from the beginning of the revolution. The Columbus, Ohio, *Dispatch* was the first daily newspaper to offer a home information news service through computer. Many papers have followed suit. As noted in chapter 12, UPI has formulated a computer news service for business personnel. Computer news is stored for recall by topic—a great timesaver for the reader who does not want to scan the paper.

An ABC-TV computer art logo.

A wealth of other services already are available, too, including such specialized information as real estate listings, transportation schedules, and, in time, electronic mail, or the ability to send a letter from one home computer to another.

The home computer also can be a great entertainment and recreation tool. Connected to the stereo, the radio, the television set, and the video tape machine, it can tune media in or out, make tapes, and entertain on demand. With the addition of outside networks and data banks, it is possible for one home computer operator to play in a computer game network, in a team game or "against the house," with the central computer being "the house." With simulation tapes or programs, the individual operator can fly a plane or play the great golf courses without worrying about the weather.

At the same time, the hobbyist can choose one of thirty graphics/animation systems currently on the market; all allow a computer to animate figures and make movies much the same way the Walt Disney film *TRON* was produced.

Added to all these potential services are existing media: newspapers, magazines, cable television with commercial as well as low-power and DBS signals, AM and FM radio, digital stereo, and home video discs and video tape recordings. It promises to be a rich, heady mix.

But can it all come true? Researchers Herbert S. Dordick, Helen G. Bradley, and Burt Nanus believe it not only can but probably will come true. They see a new world of information coming into existence, based in time on interconnected private, national and, international computer networks and data banks. While they feel forecasts of growth are overly optimistic, they realize there already is a network computer marketplace emerging. Its growth will depend on the cost and type of computer technology offered the public in the next few years, as well as its acceptance.

As Leo Bogart, general manager of the National Advertising Bureau, has observed, so much of what happens depends on existing social conditions. The new communications technology, he has written, must "carve out a place for itself by better serving a society whose needs and interests are not going to be fundamentally different than we know today."

The Media, Society, and Tomorrow

Some of our present needs are reflected in statistics, Bogart has suggested. For example, today only 7 percent of all U.S. homes have a "traditional" family, with a father, nonworking mother, and two children. People marry later; divorce rates have doubled since 1970. And families no longer sit and talk together the way they did before World War II. "The impersonal communication of the media," Bogart has suggested, "substitutes to a degree, for the close, interpersonal family communication of the past." There also is a growing discrepancy between the household exposure to television and the individual's exposure to it. Media are becoming more individualized.

Several other factors also may contribute to the individualization trends in media content, Bogart has written. Minorities and women continue to demand fair representation of their viewpoints. As a population, we also are growing older, forcing the youth culture into more specialized channels. Our level of education is rising, which usually signals a turn toward more special interest messages. Entertainment, news, and advertising media will need to pay attention to new, special interest trends, with advertisers having the difficult problem of finding a way to measure smaller, splinter audiences.

Two important social trends seem likely to encourage adoption of the electronic cottage. Americans continue to move to the suburbs, and American women continue to return to the work place. More than 70 percent of all women between the ages of eighteen and sixty-four will be in the work force by 1990. Both trends could stimulate the growth of the electronic cottage since commuters and working women (including working women who commute) will find a greater need for computerized banking, information services, home security services, and teleshopping. Adopting telecommunication services, though, depends on whether these two groups view teleshopping as depersonalizing, whether they trust financial institutions to deliver funds as requested (or the Sears and Roebuck computer to send long underwear rather than bathroom curtains). Once trusted, however, the home computer might well be the boon its producers promise, especially for those with not enough time to do everything.

It seems likely, as Bogart has suggested, the years ahead will bring a continuing demand for information of a special, individualized nature, with audiences much more active in pursuing the information they want and using the media where they find it. The newer, specialized media probably will not make existing mass media obsolete, however. People still will want to participate in the popular mainstream of mass entertainment, or so research would suggest. Since we are not likely to have more leisure time, it also is unlikely the newer media will take up more of the individual's time. The amount of time spent with the media will probably be about the same as now, but with television networks losing some viewers. Existing mass media, however, will not just disappear.

The newer media are not likely to replace print media either. Most authorities agree that newspapers and magazines have strong appeals as packages of information, with a readability that excels the cathode ray tube with its item-by-item computerized readout. There also is very good

Will We Accept Life in the Wired Nation?

Those who predict the rise of the new information network—with banking, shopping, and information services at home—are among the first to warn some adjustments will have to be made in current habits if people are to adopt themselves to the "wired" society. John Warwick, director of marketing for Times Mirror Company's videotex system is optimistic about videotext information going into the home, but skeptical about home shopping. "To say that technology is going to make dinosaurs of retail stores is a little silly," he has said. Others question the ability of the computer to sell many types of goods effectively—using only the words and still pictures of current computer graphics—even color graphics. "You can't sell a dress that looks like it is made of Lego blocks," one executive commented. Name brand products that sell locally through competitive pricing would seem a likely candidate for home computer merchandising. And there is some speculation that home banking will be accepted sooner than home shopping, since browsing and socializing are less a part of banking activities, and since bankers have more to gain and less to lose by promoting it. One prediction holds that shopping at home will see a major breakthrough when manufacturers realize they can cut out intermediaries (stores, wholesalers, etc.) and sell directly to the home. When that happens, the market will be only a step away from production on demand, with orders tapped out on the home terminal directing an industrial robot in the factory to produce a customized version of a product. But to succeed, "on demand" selling will require enough people who understand computers well enough to tap out commands. And the home computer may well be the biggest stumbling block to the realization of the information network. Computers are very precise and they can be difficult for the uninitiated. (There is more than one horror story—more than one true horror story—about the sad but wiser operator who pushed the wrong button and lost hours, even weeks, of work "to the electricity.") After three years of struggling with his computer, one Massachusetts engineer told the *Wall Street Journal* the ads that make computer work seem easy are hype. Engineer Don Baine spent $15,000 on Apple II hardware and software to run his business before he realized he should have hired a bookkeeper and saved himself the long struggle to make his machine work.

At the same time, there are success stories. Iowa hog farmer Barry Trindle isn't a hog farmer anymore. His Apple II home computer showed him the animals were bringing him less than $1,000 a year. "I was working for the pleasure of the company of the hogs," he said. He dropped his hog production and turned his attention to corn and soybeans, using his Apple II to analyze how he manages his 405 acres of land.

reason to believe that advertisers will continue to want mass coverage of local and mass market audiences at a low cost. Their support should keep the existing mass media in operation for some time to come.

The media themselves also have needs and interests that are contributing to the coming changes. Newspapers led the media and other industries in using the computer for word processing and typesetting. There is a growing trend among television news departments to use computers and videotext services to improve background information for complicated business, economic, and environmental stories. It is now possible for the television news director to call up and feed information to reporters in the field, who then can quickly incorporate it into their stories. For the first time, too, the computer has given the television news department the possibility of its own news morgue (files of back-story data). Such uses probably will encourage the building of more data networks.

Computer graphics/animation programs, meanwhile, have been a boon to local and network television production departments and local television advertising departments. Computer art adds a dynamic dimension to a sports or news show; it also can give a local television advertiser "action art" equal to that of national network artists.

One serious problem haunts the new media revolution. The daily newspaper has already been affected by the problem. Newspapers must find a way to serve both the deprived ghettos and well-to-do suburbs. Bogart has written:

> Social disorganization in America's ghettos, as measured by family disintegration, illegitimacy, crime and drug use is unmatched anywhere in the world. How will the bright new possibilities of advanced telecommunication jibe with the unemployment, dependency, incapacity, despair and rage of the black underclass?

As journalist Michael Pollan has observed, the child in Grosse Pointe, Michigan, whose parents can afford an Apple II microcomputer, already is a child of the "information society"; the child whose parents cannot afford a typewriter is information poor. What is worse, the parents of the child in Grosse Pointe, having settled their own information problems with their private computer and information services, are not as likely to be concerned about the old information system built years ago to serve all of society: the public library. With federal funds disappearing, and some of the most influential people in the community no longer in need of its services, with vendors selling information to computer networks, can the public library survive and compete as a full source of informa-

Shopping: interesting social activity or social drudgery? The decision should greatly affect the growth of information networks and the acceptance of shopping by computer.

tion for the poor? The library either might have to operate with a restricted budget or charge for its services in order to offer quality information. Either way, it would contribute to an information gap that could be a great disservice to society. The major governmental policy problem of the 1990s is likely to be the inequity in computer information services between those who can afford them and those who cannot.

The new telecommunications media may well change some fundamental aspects of our mass communication system and our society. Sociologist Richard Maisel has pointed out:

> We must . . . abandon the outmoded view of the individual as simply the recipient of standardized messages emanating from the mass media, whose only recourse in self-expression is the primitive sound of his own voice in direct face-to-face interaction. Rather, we must begin to think of, and study, the individual in our society as a *communicator having access to a very powerful set of media tools* and as a recipient of a wide range of equally enriched communications directed to him by others. [Emphasis added.]

The challenge of the future may be that we not allow the new media technology, even without malice, to subvert our democratic society. We must continue to encourage the media to develop their technology and other capabilities to reach all individuals in our society. But we also must find ways of assuring that individuals of all walks of life gain access to the newer media technology and information systems. Both our unity and our knowledge depend on it. And the ongoing success of our democracy depends on our unity and knowledge.

Summary

The media and our mass media system now are at one of the most revolutionary periods of their history. Cable television, low-power television, direct broadcasting satellites, high definition television, and optical fiber transmission will bring a wide range of new messages to the public in the immediate future, while video tape and disc machines, microbooks engraved on microchips, video games played on cable channels or computers, teletext, videotext, and the electronic computer will allow greater individual control of message consumption and use.

The new communications media are predicted to combine with the personal and videotext computer to create an electronic cottage, with telebanking, home security services, specialized information services, consumer information, and teleshopping. The services may be especially attractive to those with little time to spare. Experts believe the electronic cottage and the computer information network will become a reality in the near future, but the new media must carve out a place for themselves by serving the needs and interests of the society we now know. The current family structure will enhance the move toward more individualized media content. Family members now look to media interaction as a substitute for interpersonal family communication. Minorities and women continue to call for representation of their special viewpoints. The level of education continues to rise, encouraging an increase in special interest messages.

Still, it is not likely that the mass media as we know them will disappear. Time spent with the communications media should remain about the same, with any time spent with newer media taken from existing media. The mass media likely will lose influence, but people still will use them to keep in touch with the rest of society. Their readability and their attractiveness as a package, along with their established advertising support, should keep the joint media in operation for some time to come.

The challenge of the future may well be to find a way for the poor and the rich to have equal access to the computer network and electronic cottage. Otherwise, the new communications technology could produce an information gap that could be a great disservice to the society.

Whatever the problems, we no longer can think of the individual as the recipient of standardized media messages, but as a communicator with access to a very powerful set of media tools, and a wide range of enriching messages transmitted by others.

Questions for Discussion

1. Describe the electronic cottage you might build for yourself. Which of the new media would you reject? Which would you insist on having? Would you want an extensive set of games, for example, or would you prefer to spend your money for special information? What do you think the general public will support in the way of newer media?

2. What will it take, do you believe, to bring HDTV into general use? Can you conceive of a way CBS will be able to convince the FCC, and the public, to make the change to the new system?

3. Review the discussion on the adoption of innovations in chapter 18. How do they jibe with the ideas concerning the growth of the information networks in this chapter? Where might you fit into the process?

4. It is suggested that we face the strong possibility the newer media will create an information gap. Do you believe this will be a real problem? Why?

References

Bogart, Leo. "Media and a Changing America." *Advertising Age,* March 29, 1982, M52–M55.

Bylinski, Gene. "Fiber Optics Finally See the Light of Day." *Fortune,* March 24, 1980. 110 et seq.

"Cracked Dishes." *Newsweek,* July 23, 1984, 58–59.

Deken, Joseph. *The Electronic Cottage.* New York: William Morrow, 1982.

Dordick, Herbert S., Helen G. Bradley, and Burt Nanus. *The Emerging Network Marketplace.* Norwood, N.J.: Ablex, 1981.

Maisel, Richard. "The Decline of Mass Media." *The Public Opinion Quarterly* 37, no. 2 (Summer 1973): 159–70.

Merrell, Ron. "Computer Art: Ads and L.O. Are Just the Beginning." *Broadcast Communications,* October 1982, 58–61.

Pollan, Michael. "The Electric Library." *Channels,* June/July 1982, 30–31.

Powell, Jim. "Fiber Optics: At the Threshold of a Communications Revolution." *Science Digest,* January 1977, 28–35.

Roizen, Joe. "HDTV Is Still in a Holding Pattern." *Broadcast Communications,* October 1982, 62–66.

"To Each His Own Computer." *Newsweek,* February 22, 1982, 50–56.

"The Video Revolution." *Newsweek,* August 6, 1984, 50 et seq.

Weiss, Merrill, and Ronald Lorentzen. "How Teletext Can Deliver More Service and Profits." *Broadcast Communications,* August 1982, 54–60.

Credits

Index